Research Developments in Computer Vision and Image Processing:

Methodologies and Applications

Rajeev Srivastava
Indian Institute of Technology (BHU), India

S. K. Singh
Indian Institute of Technology (BHU), India

K. K. Shukla
Indian Institute of Technology (BHU), India

A volume in the Advances in
Computational Intelligence and Robotics
(ACIR) Book Series

An Imprint of IGI Global

Managing Director:	Lindsay Johnston
Production Manager:	Jennifer Yoder
Publishing Systems Analyst:	Adrienne Freeland
Development Editor:	Allyson Gard
Acquisitions Editor:	Kayla Wolfe
Typesetter:	Christina Barkanic
Cover Design:	Jason Mull

Published in the United States of America by
Information Science Reference (an imprint of IGI Global)
701 E. Chocolate Avenue
Hershey PA 17033
Tel: 717-533-8845
Fax: 717-533-8661
E-mail: cust@igi-global.com
Web site: http://www.igi-global.com

Library of Congress Cataloging-in-Publication Data

Library of Congress Cataloging-in-Publication Data

Research developments in computer vision and image processing : methodologies and applications / Rajeev Srivastava, S.K. Singh and K.K. Shukla, editors.
    pages cm
  Includes bibliographical references and index.
  Summary: "This book brings together various research methodologies and trends in emerging areas of application of computer vision and image processing for those interested in the research developments of this rapidly growing field"-- Provided by publisher.
  ISBN 978-1-4666-4558-5 (hardcover) -- ISBN 978-1-4666-4559-2 (ebook) -- ISBN 978-1-4666-4560-8 (print & perpetual access) 1. Computer vision. 2. Image processing. I. Srivastava, Rajeev, 1974- editor of compilation. II. Singh, S. K., editor of compilation. III. Shukla, K. K., 1958- editor of compilation.
  TA1634.R47 2013
  006.6--dc23
                                2013020694

This book is published in the IGI Global book series Advances in Computational Intelligence and Robotics (ISSN: 2327-0411; eISSN: 2327-042X)

British Cataloguing in Publication Data
A Cataloguing in Publication record for this book is available from the British Library.

Advances in Computational Intelligence and Robotics (ACIR) Book Series

ISSN: 2327-0411
EISSN: 2327-042X

Mission

While intelligence is traditionally a term applied to humans and human cognition, technology has progressed in such a way to allow for the development of intelligent systems able to simulate many human traits. With this new era of simulated and artificial intelligence, much research is needed in order to continue to advance the field and also to evaluate the ethical and societal concerns of the existence of artificial life and machine learning.

The **Advances in Computational Intelligence and Robotics (ACIR) Book Series** encourages scholarly discourse on all topics pertaining to evolutionary computing, artificial life, computational intelligence, machine learning, and robotics. ACIR presents the latest research being conducted on diverse topics in intelligence technologies with the goal of advancing knowledge and applications in this rapidly evolving field.

Coverage

- Adaptive & Complex Systems
- Agent Technologies
- Artificial Intelligence
- Cognitive Informatics
- Computational Intelligence
- Natural Language Processing
- Neural Networks
- Pattern Recognition
- Robotics
- Synthetic Emotions

IGI Global is currently accepting manuscripts for publication within this series. To submit a proposal for a volume in this series, please contact our Acquisition Editors at Acquisitions@igi-global.com or visit: http://www.igi-global.com/publish/.

Titles in this Series

For a list of additional titles in this series, please visit: www.igi-global.com

Exploring Innovative and Successful Applications of Soft Computing
Antonio D. Masegosa (Universidad de Grenada, Spain) Pablo J. Villacorta (Universidad de Grenada, Spain) Carlos Cruz-Corona (Universidad de Granada, Spain) M.S. Garcia-Cascales (University of Cartagena, Columbia) María T. Lamata () and José L. Verdegay (Universidad de Granada, Spain)
Information Science Reference • copyright 2014 • 291pp • H/C (ISBN: 9781466647855) • US $190.00 (our price)

Research Developments in Computer Vision and Image Processing Methodologies and Applications
Rajeev Srivastava (Indian Institute of Technology (BHU), India) S. K. Singh (Indian Institute of Technology (BHU), India) and K. K. Shukla (Indian Institute of Technology (BHU), India)
Information Science Reference • copyright 2014 • 388pp • H/C (ISBN: 9781466645585) • US $195.00 (our price)

Handbook of Research on Novel Soft Computing Intelligent Algorithms Theory and Practical Applications
Pandian M. Vasant (Petronas University of Technology)
Information Science Reference • copyright 2014 • 1004pp • H/C (ISBN: 9781466644502) • US $495.00 (our price)

Intelligent Technologies and Techniques for Pervasive Computing
Kostas Kolomvatsos (University of Athens, Greece) Christos Anagnostopoulos (Ionian University, Greece) and Stathes Hadjiefthymiades (University of Athens, Greece)
Information Science Reference • copyright 2013 • 351pp • H/C (ISBN: 9781466640382) • US $195.00 (our price)

Mobile Ad Hoc Robots and Wireless Robotic Systems Design and Implementation
Raul Aquino Santos (University of Colima, Mexico) Omar Lengerke (Universidad Autónoma de Bucaramanga, Colombia) and Arthur Edwards-Block (University of Colima, Mexico)
Information Science Reference • copyright 2013 • 347pp • H/C (ISBN: 9781466626584) • US $190.00 (our price)

Intelligent Planning for Mobile Robotics Algorithmic Approaches
Ritu Tiwari (ABV – Indian Institute of Information, India) Anupam Shukla (ABV – Indian Institute of Information, India) and Rahul Kala (School of Systems Engineering, University of Reading, UK)
Information Science Reference • copyright 2013 • 320pp • H/C (ISBN: 9781466620742) • US $195.00 (our price)

Simultaneous Localization and Mapping for Mobile Robots Introduction and Methods
Juan-Antonio Fernández-Madrigal (Universidad de Málaga, Spain) and José Luis Blanco Claraco (Universidad de Málaga, Spain)
Information Science Reference • copyright 2013 • 497pp • H/C (ISBN: 9781466621046) • US $195.00 (our price)

www.igi-global.com

701 E. Chocolate Ave., Hershey, PA 17033
Order online at www.igi-global.com or call 717-533-8845 x100
To place a standing order for titles released in this series, contact: cust@igi-global.com
Mon-Fri 8:00 am - 5:00 pm (est) or fax 24 hours a day 717-533-8661

Table of Contents

Section 1
Image Representation and Reconstruction

Section 2
Medical Applications

Detailed Table of Contents

Section 1
Image Representation and Reconstruction

In this chapter, the authors propose a Super-Resolution (SR) method using a vector quantization codebook and filter dictionary. In the process of SR, we use the idea of compressive sensing to represent a sparsely sampled signal under the assumption that a combination of a small number of codewords can represent an image patch. A low-resolution image is obtained from an original high-resolution image, degraded by blurring and down-sampling. The authors propose a resolution enhancement using an alternative l1 norm minimization to overcome the convexity of l0 norm and the sparsity of l1 norm at the same time, where an iterative reweighted l1 norm minimization is used for optimization. After the reconstruction stage, because the optimization is implemented on image patch basis, an additional deblurring or denoising step is used to globally enhance the image quality. Experiment results show that the proposed SR method provides highly efficient results.

This chapter presents the 3D sparse and dense reconstruction approaches using multiple views stereo. The basic properties of the projective geometry and the camera models are introduced to understand the preliminaries about the subject. Methods for point correspondences among images are discussed for multi-view reconstruction. An introduction to Microsoft Kinect, which captures 3D information in real time, and methods to enhance the Kinect point cloud using vision framework has been discussed.

This chapter discusses the fundamental concepts of wavelet transforms and its applications to image processing and computer vision. The inherent properties of wavelets which makes it useful in image denoising, edge detection, image compression, compressed sensing, and illumination normalization have been discussed.

Chapter 4

Computational modeling of neuro-psychological phenomenon has potential to enrich many computer vision tasks. This chapter provides a survey for computational models of visual attention showing the latest research developments in this field. It also discusses various aspects related to computational modeling of attention such as choice of features and evaluation of these models.

Chapter 5

This chapter presents a brief review of image restoration methods. The latest developments in this field and the performance metrics of evaluation have been discussed. The concept behind the metric selection for the assessment and evaluation has been introduced along with the need for shifting the dependence of the research community towards the newly proposed metrics than the old ones.

In this chapter, the authors provide an overview of state-of-the-art image enhancement and restoration techniques for underwater images. Underwater imaging is one of the challenging tasks in the field of image processing and computer vision. Usually, underwater images suffer from non-uniform lighting, low contrast, diminished color, and blurring due to attenuation and scattering of light in the underwater environment. It is necessary to preprocess these images before applying computer vision techniques. Over the last few decades, many researchers have developed various image enhancement and restoration algorithms for enhancing the quality of images captured in underwater environments. The authors introduce a brief survey on image enhancement and restoration algorithms for underwater images. At the end of the chapter, we present an overview of our approach, which is well accepted by the image processing community to enhance the quality of underwater images. Our technique consists of filtering techniques such as homomorphic filtering, wavelet-based image denoising, bilateral filtering, and contrast equalization, which are applied sequentially. The proposed method increases better image visualization of objects which are captured in underwater environment compared to other existing methods.

The automatic inspection of quality in fruits is becoming of paramount importance in order to decrease production costs and increase quality standards. Computer vision techniques are used in fruit industry for fruit grading, sorting, and defect detection. In this chapter, we review recent approaches for automatic inspection of quality in fruits using computer vision techniques. Particularly, we focus on the review of advances in computer vision techniques for automatic inspection of quality of apples based on surface defects. Finally, we present our approach to estimate the defects on the surface of an apple using grow-cut and multi-threshold based segmentation technique. The experimental results show that our method effectively estimates the defects on the surface of apples significantly more effectively than color based segmentation technique.

Section 2
Medical Applications

In this chapter, an overview of recent developments in image analysis and understanding techniques for automated detection of breast cancer from digital mammograms is presented. The various steps in the design of an automated system (i.e. Computer Aided Detection [CADe] and Computer Aided Diagnostics (CADx)] include preparation of image database for classification, image pre-processing, mammogram image enhancement and restoration, segmentation of Region Of Interest (ROI) for cancer detection, feature extraction of selected ROIs, feature evaluation and selection, and classification of selected mammogram images in to benign, malignant, and normal. In this chapter, a detailed overview of the various methods developed in recent years for each stage required in the design of an automated system for breast cancer detection is discussed. Further, the design, implementation and performance analysis of a CAD tool is also presented. The various types of features extracted for classification purpose in the proposed tool include histogram features, texture features, geometric features, wavelet features, and Gabor features. The proposed CAD tool uses fuzzy c-means segmentation algorithm, the feature selection algorithm based on the concepts of genetic algorithm which uses mutual information as a fitness function, and linear support vector machine as a classifier.

Chapter 9

De-Noising, Clustering, Classification, and Representation of Microarray Data for Disease
Diagnostics 149

Nitin Baharadwaj, Netaji Subhas Institute of Technology, India

Sheena Wadhwa, Netaji Subhas Institute of Technology, India

Pragya Goel, Netaji Subhas Institute of Technology, India

Isha Sethi, Netaji Subhas Institute of Technology, India

Chanpreet Singh Arora, Netaji Subhas Institute of Technology, India

Aviral Goel, Netaji Subhas Institute of Technology, India

Sonika Bhatnagar, Netaji Subhas Institute of Technology, India

Harish Parthasarathy, Netaji Subhas Institute of Technology, India

A microarray works by exploiting the ability of a given mRNA molecule to bind specifically to the DNA template from which it originated under specific high stringency conditions. After this, the amount of mRNA bound to each DNA site on the array is determined, which represents the expression level of each gene. Qualification of the mRNA (probe) bound to each DNA spot (target) can help us to determine which genes are active or responsible for the current state of the cell. The probe target hybridization is usually detected and quantified using dyes/flurophore/chemiluminescence labels. The microarray data gives a single snapshot of the gene activity profile of a cell at any given time. Microarray data helps to elucidate the various genes involved in the disease and may also be used for diagnosis /prognosis. In spite of its huge potential, microarray data interpretation and use is limited by its error prone nature, the sheer size of the data and the subjectivity of the analysis. Initially, we describe the use of several techniques to develop a pre-processing methodology for denoising microarray data using signal process techniques. The noise free data thus obtained is more suitable for classification of the data as well as for mining useful information from the data. Discrete Fourier Transform (DFT) and Autocorrelation were explored for denoising the data. We also used microarray data to develop the use of microarray data as diagnostic tool in cancer using One Dimensional Fourier Transform followed by simple Euclidean Distance Calculations and Two Dimensional MUltiple SIgnal Classification (MUSIC). To improve the accuracy of the diagnostic tool, Volterra series were used to model the nonlinear behavior of the data. Thus, our efforts at denoising, representation, and classification of microarray data with signal processing techniques show that appreciable results could be attained even with the most basic techniques. To develop a method to search for a gene signature, we used a combination of PCA and density based clustering for inferring the gene signature of Parkinson's disease. Using this technique in conjunction with gene ontology data, it was possible to obtain a signature comprising of 21 genes, which were then validated by their involvement in known Parkinson's disease pathways. The methodology described can be further developed to yield future biomarkers for early Parkinson's disease diagnosis, as well as for drug development.

Chapter 10

Detection of Cancer from Microscopic Biopsy Images Using Image Processing Tools 175

Rajesh Kumar, Indian Institute of Technology, Banaras Hindu University, India

Rajeev Srivastava, Indian Institute of Technology, Banaras Hindu University, India

Presently, most cancer diagnosis is based on human visual examination of images in a qualitative manner. Human visual grading for microscopic biopsy images is very time-consuming, subjective, and inconsistent due to inter-and intra-observer variations. A more quantitative and reproducible approach for analyzing biopsy images is highly desired. In biopsy images, the characteristics of nuclei are the key to estimate the degree of malignancy. The microscopic biopsy images always suffer from the problem of impurities, undesirable elements, and uneven exposure. Thus, there is a need of an automatic cancer diagnosis system based on microscopic biopsy images using image-processing tools. Therefore, the cancer and its type will be detected in a very early stage for complete treatment and cure. This system helps pathologists to improve the accuracy and efficiency in detection of malignancy and to minimize the inter observer variation. In addition, the method may help physicians to analyze the image cell by using classification and clustering algorithms by staining characteristics of the cells. The various image-processing steps involved for cancer detection from biopsy images include acquisition, enhancement, segmentation, feature extraction, image representation, classification, and decision-making. With the help of image, processing tools the sizes of cells, nuclei, and cytoplasm as well as the mean distance between two nearest neighboring nuclei are estimated by the system.

With the advent of telemedicine, Digital Rights Management of medical images has become a critical issue pertaining to security and privacy preservation in the medical industry. The technology of telemedicine makes patient diagnosis possible for physicians located at a remote site. This technology involves electronic transmission of medical images over the internet, thus raising the need for ensuring security and privacy of such information. Digital watermarking is a widely used technique for the authentication and protection of multimedia data such as images and video against various security and privacy threats. But such digital rights management practices as watermarking often lead to considerable distortion or information loss of the medical images. The medical images being highly sensitive and legally valuable assets of the medical industry, such information loss are often not tolerable. Most importantly, such information loss may lead to incorrect patient diagnosis or reduced accuracy of disease detection. In this chapter we investigate the impact of digital watermarking, and its effect on the accuracy of disease diagnosis, specifically diagnosis of malarial infection caused by Plasmodium vivax parasite. We have used a computer–aided, automatic diagnostic model for our work in this chapter. Our experimental results show that although general (lossy) digital watermarking reduces the diagnostic accuracy, it can be improved with the use of reversible (lossless) watermarking. In fact, the adverse effect(s) of watermarking on the diagnostic accuracy can be completely mitigated through the use of reversible watermarking.

The proposed chapter describes the need of data security and content protection in the modern health care system. A digital watermarking technique is used as a strong and secure tool to achieve ultimate security. In this chapter the authors discuss some existing watermarking techniques and also describe some new types of data hiding techniques using biomedical watermarking techniques in both spatial and frequency domain which would help keep the authenticity and secure the contents of the hidden biomedical information for accurate tele-diagnosis. These techniques use multiple copies of the same information that is to be hidden in the cover image. The bandwidth requirement is greater, but reconstruction of hidden information is more accurate at the time of recovery even under several unintentional attacks. Some new types of embedding and recovery processes have also been employed for better results and success of the different proposed schemes. The Modified Bit Replacement (MBR) embedding process and the Bit Majority Algorithm (BMA) technique for recovery of the hidden information are the newer approaches that are also described here.

Chapter 13

Tushar Kanti Bera, Indian Institute of Science, India
J. Nagaraju, Indian Institute of Science, India

Looking into the human body is very essential not only for studying the anatomy and physiology, but also for diagnosing a disease or illness. Doctors always try to visualize an organ or body part in order to study its physiological and anatomical status for understanding and/or treating its illness. This necessity introduced the diagnostic tool called medical imaging. The era of medical imaging started in 1895, when Roentgen discovered the magical powerful invisible rays called X-rays. Gradually the medical imaging introduced X-Ray CT, Gamma Camera, PET, SPECT, MRI, USG. Recently medical imaging field is enriched with comparatively newer tomographic imaging modalities like Electrical Impedance Tomography (EIT), Diffuse Optical Tomography (DOT), Optical Coherence Tomography (OCT), and Photoacaustic Tomography (PAT). The EIT has been extensively researched in different fields of science and engineering due to its several advantages. This chapter will present a brief review on the available medical imaging modalities and focus on the need of an alternating method. EIT will be discussed with its physical and mathematical aspects, potentials, and challenges.

Chapter 14

Shailendra Tiwari, Indian Institute of Technology, India
Rajeev Srivastava, Indian Institute of Technology, India

Image reconstruction from projection is the field that lays the foundation for Medical Imaging or Medical Image Processing. The rapid and proceeding progress in medical image reconstruction, and the related developments in analysis methods and computer-aided diagnosis, has promoted medical imaging into one of the most important sub-fields in scientific imaging. Computer technology has enabled tomographic and three-dimensional reconstruction of images, illustrating both anatomical features and physiological functioning, free from overlying structures.In this chapter, the authors share their opinions on the research and development in the field of Medical Image Reconstruction Techniques, Computed Tomography (CT), challenges and the impact of future technology developments in CT, Computed Tomography Metrology in industrial research & development, technology, and clinical performance of different CT-scanner generations used for cardiac imaging, such as Electron Beam CT (EBCT), single-slice CT, and Multi-Detector row CT (MDCT) with 4, 16, and 64 simultaneously acquired slices. The authors identify the limitations of current CT-scanners, indicate potential of improvement and discuss alternative system concepts such as CT with area detectors and Dual Source CT (DSCT), recent technology with a focus on generation and detection of X-rays, as well as image reconstruction are discussed. Furthermore, the chapter includes aspects of applications, dose exposure in computed tomography, and a brief overview on special CT developments. Since this chapter gives a review of the major accomplishments and future directions in this field, with emphasis on developments over the past 50 years, the interested reader is referred to recent literature on computed tomography including a detailed discussion of CT technology in the references section.

Vijay Kumar, JCDM College of Engineering, India
Jitender Kumar Chhabra, National Institute of Technology, India
Dinesh Kumar, GJUS&T, India

Image segmentation plays an important role in medical imaging applications. In this chapter, an automatic MRI brain image segmentation framework using gravitational search based clustering technique has been proposed. This framework consists of two stage segmentation procedure. First, non-brain tissues are removed from the brain tissues using modified skull-stripping algorithm. Thereafter, the automatic gravitational search based clustering technique is used to extract the brain tissues from the skull stripped image. The proposed algorithm has been applied on four simulated T1-weighted MRI brain images. Experimental results reveal that proposed algorithm outperforms the existing techniques in terms of the structure similarity measure.

P. Geetha, Anna University Chennai, India

Today digital imaging is widely used in every application around us like Internet, High Definition TeleVision (HDTV), satellite communications, fax transmission, and digital storage of movies and more, because it provide superior resolution and quality. Recently, medical imaging has begun to take advantage of digital technology, opening the way for advanced medical imaging and teleradiology. However, medical imaging requires storing, communicating and manipulating large amounts of digital data. Applying image compression reduces the storage requirements, network traffic, and therefore improves efficiency. This chapter provides the need for medical image compression; different approaches to image compression, emerging wavelet based lossy-lossless compression techniques, how the existing recent compression techniques work and also comparison of results. After completing this chapter, the reader should have an idea of how to increase the compression ratio and at the same time maintain the PSNR level compared to the existing techniques, desirable features of standard compression techniques such as embeddedness and progressive transmission, how these are very useful and much needed in the interactive teleradiology, telemedicine and telebrowsing applications.

Nilanjan Dey, JIS College of Engineering, India
Bijurika Nandi, CIEM, Tollygunge, India
Anamitra Bardhan Roy, JIS College of Engineering, India
Debalina Biswas, JIS College of Engineering, India
Achintya Das, Kalyani Government Engineering College, India
Sheli Sinha Chaudhuri, Jadavpur University, India

Blood cell smears contain huge amounts of information about the state of human health. This chapter proposes a Fuzzy c-means segmentation based method for the evaluation of blood cells of humans by counting the presence of Red Blood Cells (RBCs) and recognizing White Blood Cell (WBC) types using Harris corner detection. Until now hematologists gave major priority to WBCs and spent most of the time studying their features to reveal various characteristics of numerous diseases. Firstly, this method detects and counts the RBCs present in the human blood sample. Secondly, it assesses the detected WBCs to minutely scrutinize its type. It is a promising strategy for the diagnosis of diseases. It is a very tedious task for pathologists to identify and treat diseases by manually detecting, counting, and segmenting RBCs and WBCs. Simultaneously the analysis of the size, shape, and texture of every WBC and its elements is a very cumbersome process that makes this system vulnerable to inaccuracy and generates trouble. Hence, this system delivers a precise methodology to extract all relevant information for medical diagnosis with high germaneness maintaining pertinence. This present work proposes an algorithm for the detection of RBCs comparing the results between expert ophthalmologists' hand-drawn ground-truths and the RBCs detected image as an output. Accuracy is used to evaluate overall performance. It is found that this work detects RBCs successfully with accuracy of 82.37%.

Preface

Image processing is a rapidly growing field that deals with the manipulation of an image for the purpose of either extracting information from the image or producing an alternative representation of the image. Image analysis includes modelling and analysis of the original image itself (i.e. from image space analysis to different methods to represent the image). The various tools of image analysis include spectral analysis, wavelets, statistics, level-sets, and Partial Differential Equations (PDEs). On the other hand, image processing is to modify the original image to improve the quality or extract information from the given image, for example, image restoration, compression, segmentation, shape, and texture analysis. There are two dual fields that are directly connected to image processing in contemporary computer science. These are computer vision, which is related to the construction of the 3D world from the observed 2D images, and computer graphics, which pursues the opposite direction in designing suitable 2D scene images to simulate our 3D world. Image processing can be considered the crucial middle way connecting the vision and graphics fields. This book incorporates the contents related to the latest research trends in emerging core areas and applications of computer vision and image processing.

The book will serve as a research reference book in the area of computer vision and image processing that provides useful cutting edge research information to the students, researchers, scientists, engineers, and other related professionals in the said area. This book provides the latest research trends and concepts to develop new methodologies and applications in the areas of image representation and reconstruction and medical applications.

The image representation and reconstruction section of the book contains recent research developments in the field of general image processing and computer vision. The various topics include various important topics such as image representation, 3D reconstruction, wavelet-based image processing, a survey on computational model of visual attention, a review on image restoration, image enhancement and restoration techniques for underwater images, and computer vision-based techniques for surface defect detection in apples.

The Medical Application section reports various important research developments in the field of medical image processing and its applications. The various important topics in this section include design and development of a Computer-Aided Diagnostics (CAD) tools for breast cancer detection from digital mammograms, cancer detection from microscopic biopsy images, cancer/disease detection from microarray gene expression data, digital watermarking techniques in telemedicine, blood cell analysis, research developments in the field of medical image reconstruction, and electrical impedance tomography.

SCHOLARLY VALUE, POTENTIAL CONTRIBUTION/IMPACT, AND PURPOSE

At present most of the books available in the field of image processing and computer vision are tuned to a very specific limited research field. This book intends to serve the purpose of a large audience working in related or allied areas including students, researchers, professors, practicing engineers, application developers, radiologists, etc. Also, this book will be helpful for new as well as experienced researchers to familiarise themselves with the new research areas and their possible applications in the field of image processing and computer vision. This book incorporates the methodologies to develop algorithms for related problems and new research trends. In addition, this book also incorporates chapters related to new challenging application areas of image processing and computer vision. Emphasis has been given to develop each and every chapter incorporating a latest literature review, methods and models, implementation, experimental results, performance analysis, conclusion, future work, and latest relevant references.

POTENTIAL USES/INTENDED AUDIENCE

- Interdisciplinary engineering students at final year UG level, PG level, and doctoral research students.
- Faculty members/trainers/professors.
- Research scientists.
- Medical professionals and radiologists.
- Practicing engineers and software application developers.

ORGANIZATION OF THE BOOK

This edited book titled *Recent Advances in Computer Vision and Image Processing: Methodologies and Applications* provides an overview, recent research developments in the field of computer vision and image processing, and related applications. This book contains 17 chapters divided into two sections, namely Section 1: Image Representation and Reconstruction and Section 2: Medical Applications. Section 1 contains 7 chapters from Chapter 1 to Chapter 7, and Section 2 contains 10 chapters from Chapter 8 to Chapter 17.

Section 1: Image Representation and Reconstruction

Chapter 1: Image Representation Using a Sparsely Sampled Codebook for Super-Resolution

This chapter presents a Super-Resolution (SR) method using a vector quantization codebook and filter dictionary wherein the idea of compressive sensing is used to represent a sparsely sampled signal under the assumption that a combination of a small number of code words can represent an image patch. A method for resolution enhancement has been proposed using an alternative l_1 norm minimization, where an iterative reweighted l_1 norm minimization is used for optimization followed by an additional de-blurring step to globally enhance the image quality. Results obtained show the efficacy of the proposed scheme.

Chapter 2: 3D Reconstruction Using Multiple View Stereo and a Brief Introduction to Kinect

This chapter presents the 3D sparse and dense reconstruction approaches using multiple view stereo. The basic properties of the projective geometry and the camera models are introduced to understand the preliminaries about the subject. Methods for point correspondences among images are discussed for multi-view reconstruction. An introduction to Microsoft Kinect, which captures 3D information in real time, and methods to enhance the Kinect point cloud using vision framework are discussed.

Chapter 3: An Introduction to Wavelet-Based Image Processing and Its Applications

This chapter discusses the fundamental concepts of wavelet transforms and its applications to image processing and computer vision. The inherent properties of wavelets that make it useful in image denoising, edge detection, image compression, compressed sensing, and illumination normalization are discussed.

Chapter 4: Computational Models of Visual Attention – A Survey

Computational modeling of neuro-psychological phenomenon has potential to enrich many computer vision tasks. This chapter provides a survey for computational models of visual attention showing the latest research developments in this field. It also discusses various aspects related to computational modeling of attention such as choice of features and evaluation of these models.

Chapter 5: A Brief Review on Recent Trends in Image Restoration

This chapter presents a brief review of image restoration methods. The latest developments in this field and the performance metrics of evaluation are discussed. The concept behind the metric selection for the assessment and evaluation is introduced along with the need for shifting the dependence of the research community towards the newly proposed metrics.

Chapter 6: Image Enhancement and Restoration Methods for Underwater Images

Underwater imaging is one of the challenging tasks in the field of image processing and computer vision. This chapter provides an overview of state-of-the-art image enhancement and restoration techniques for underwater images. Further, a method for the restoration and enhancement of underwater images is proposed. Results show that the proposed method increases better image visualization of objects captured in an underwater environment.

Chapter 7: Computer Vision-Based Techniques for Surface Defect Detection of Apples

In this chapter, review of the recent computer vision-based techniques for automatic inspection of quality of the fruits and in particular automatic inspection of quality of apples based on surface defects is presented. Further, a method using grow-cut and multi-threshold-based segmentation technique is proposed to estimate the defects on the surface of an apple. The obtained results show the efficacy of the proposed method.

Section 2: Medical Applications

Chapter 8: Image Analysis and Understanding Techniques for Breast Cancer Detection from Digital Mammograms

This chapter discusses the steps involved in the design and development of a CAD tool for early breast cancer detection from mammograms. Detailed overviews of the various methods developed in recent years for each of the design stages for the CAD tool are provided. Further, the design of a new CAD tool using fuzzy c-means segmentation, hybrid features, genetic algorithm-based feature selection method, and support vector machine-based classification are proposed. Results obtained show the efficacy of the proposed methodology.

Chapter 9: Denoising, Clustering, Classification, and Representation of Microarray Data for Disease Diagnostics

The microarray data gives a single snapshot of the gene activity profile of a cell at any given time, which is typically used to compare the relative abundance of specific disease causing genes in different pathogenic conditions. Microarray data helps to elucidate the various genes involved in the disease and may also be used for diagnosis/prognosis. In spite of its huge potential, microarray data interpretation and use is limited by its error-prone nature, the sheer size of the data, and the subjectivity of the analysis. This chapter describes the use of established methodologies algorithms for eliminating error, classification, clustering, differential data analysis, and representation of microarray data.

Chapter 10: Detection of Cancer from Microscopic Biopsy Images Using Image Processing Tools

This chapter discusses the methodologies for the design and development of an automatic cancer diagnosis system based on microscopic biopsy images using image-processing tools. The proposed tool can be used to detect the cancer and its type in its early stage for complete treatment and cure. This system may help pathologists to improve the accuracy and efficiency to detect malignancy and to minimize the inter-observer variation. In addition, the tool may help us to analyze the image cell by using classification and clustering algorithms by staining characteristics of the cells.

Chapter 11: Digital Image Watermarking – Impact on Medical Imaging Applications in Telemedicine

The technology of telemedicine makes patient diagnosis possible for physicians located at a remote site. This technology involves electronic transmission of medical images over the Internet, thus raising the need for ensuring security and privacy of such information. Digital watermarking is a widely used technique for the authentication and protection of multimedia data. This chapter investigates the impact of digital watermarking and its effect on the accuracy of disease diagnosis, specifically diagnosis of malarial infection caused by *Plasmodium vivax* parasite. A computer-aided automatic diagnostic model is proposed. The experimental results show that although general (lossy) digital watermarking reduces the diagnostic accuracy, it can be improved with the use of *reversible* (lossless) watermarking. In fact, the adverse effect(s) of watermarking on the diagnostic accuracy can be completely mitigated through the use of reversible watermarking.

Chapter 12: Biomedical Watermarking – An Emerging and Secure Tool for Data Security and Better Tele-Diagnosis in Modern Health Care System

This chapter describes the need of data security and content protection in modern health care systems. A review of existing watermarking techniques is presented. Some new types of data hiding techniques using biomedical watermarking techniques in both spatial and frequency domain, which would help keep the authenticity and secure the contents of the hidden biomedical information for accurate tele-diagnosis, are discussed. These techniques use multiple copies of the same information that is to be hidden in the cover image. Some new types of embedding and recovery processes are also employed for better results and success of the different proposed schemes. The Modified Bit Replacement (MBR) embedding process and the Bit Majority Algorithm (BMA) technique for recovery of the hidden information are the newer approaches which are also described here.

Chapter 13: Electrical Impedance Tomography (EIT) – A Harmless Medical Imaging Modality

This chapter presents a brief review on the available medical imaging modalities and focuses on the need of an alternating method. Further, the concepts of Electrical Impedance Tomography (EIT)-based medical imaging, which is a harmless medical imaging modality is discussed with its physical and mathematical aspects, potentials, and challenges.

Chapter 14: Research and Developments in Medical Image Reconstruction Methods and Its Applications

This chapter presents the review and opinions of the authors on the research and developments in the field of medical image reconstruction techniques, Computed Tomography (CT), challenges, and the impact of future technology developments in CT, computed tomography metrology in industrial research and development, technology and clinical performance of different CT-scanner generations used for cardiac imaging, such as Electron Beam CT (EBCT), single-slice CT, and Multi-Detector row CT (MDCT) with 4, 16, and 64 simultaneously acquired slices. The limitations of current CT-scanners are identified, potential for improvements are indicated, and alternative system concepts such as CT with area detectors and Dual Source CT (DSCT), recent technology with a focus on generation and detection of x-rays, as well as image reconstruction are discussed. Furthermore, the chapter includes aspects of applications, dose exposure in computed tomography, and a brief overview on special CT developments.

Chapter 15: Automatic MRI Brain Image Segmentation Using Gravitational Search-Based Clustering Technique

In this chapter, an automatic MRI brain image segmentation framework using gravitational search-based clustering technique is proposed. The proposed framework consists of a two stage segmentation procedure. First, non-brain tissues are removed from the brain tissues using a modified skull-stripping algorithm. In the second step, the automatic gravitational search-based clustering technique is used to extract the brain tissues from the skull stripped image. The proposed algorithm is applied on four simulated T1-weighted MRI brain images. Experimental results reveal that the proposed algorithm outperforms the existing techniques in terms of the structure similarity measure.

Chapter 16: Survey of Medical Image Compression Techniques and Comparative Analysis

This chapter presents a survey of medical image compression techniques and discusses the need for medical image compression, different approaches to image compression, and wavelet-based lossy-lossless compression techniques. The comparative analyses of some existing recent image compression techniques are also presented.

Chapter 17: Analysis of Blood Cell Smears Using Stationary Wavelet Transform and Harris Corner Detection

Blood cell smears contain a lot of information about the state of human health. This chapter proposes a fuzzy c-means segmentation-based method for the evaluation of blood cells of humans by counting the presence of Red Blood Cells (RBCs) and recognizing White Blood Cell (WBC) types using Harris corner detection. An algorithm for the detection of RBCs is proposed, and the results obtained from the proposed automated system are compared with manual results of expert ophthalmologists' hand-drawn ground-truths. The proposed system detects RBCs successfully with accuracy of 82.37%.

Rajeev Srivastava
Indian Institute of Technology (BHU), India

Sanjay Kumar Singh
Indian Institute of Technology (BHU), India

Kaushal Kumar Shukla
Indian Institute of Technology (BHU), India

Acknowledgment

First and foremost, we would like to express our sincere and profound gratitude to our institute (Indian Institute of Technology, Banaras Hindu University, Varanasi, India) administration and Head of Department of Computer Engineering, IIT (BHU), Varanasi for providing all concerned facilities and help to complete this book.

We are very much thankful to all the authors who had submitted their manuscript for consideration and publication and to our editorial advisory board members and reviewers for guiding us during the whole book development process and providing the critical reviews to enhance the quality of the book.

We mention our special thanks to the Director of Intellectual Properties and Contract, IGI Global, USA Ms. Jan Travers who considered our proposal and provided us a reputed international platform for publishing our work. We are thankful to Kayla Wolfe (Editorial Assistant, Acquisitions, Editorial Content Department, IGI Global) to whom we interacted with at our initial stage of proposal submission and she provided all the help required. We mention our special thanks to Miss Allyson Gard (Editorial Assistant, Development Division-Editorial Content Department, IGI Global) who helped us during our final submission stage of the book. We also extend our special thanks to ex-IGI Global official Ms. Monica Speca (Editorial Assistant, Development Division-Editorial Content Department, IGI Global) who helped us at every stage of the development process of the book during the whole period, prior to Ms. Allyson Gard, through her prompt reply, suggestions, and extending all the help required.

We are thankful to our friends and colleagues at IIT (BHU) for their support, encouragement a fruitful discussions at various stages to enhance the quality of the book.

We are thankful to our family members who co-operated with us during the whole book development process.

Editor (Rajeev Srivastava) mentions his special thanks to his mother, wife (Deepti Srivastava), daughters (Dishita and Suhani) and brother for their encouragement, help, support and dedication, which has helped him in great sense to complete this book.

We extend our sincere thanks to our Ph.D. research scholars of the institute Mr. Subodh Srivastava, Mr. Shailendra Tiwari, Mr. Rajesh Kumar, and Mr. Alok Kumar Singh for helping us at various stages.

Last but not least, I would like to thank almighty God and everybody who has directly or indirectly helped us in completing this important book.

Rajeev Srivastava
Indian Institute of Technology (BHU), India

Sanjay Kumar Singh
Indian Institute of Technology (BHU), India

Kaushal Kumar Shukla
Indian Institute of Technology (BHU), India

Section 1
Image Representation and Reconstruction

Chapter 1
Image Representation Using a Sparsely Sampled Codebook for Super-Resolution

Hwa-Young Kim
Sogang University, Korea

Rae-Hong Park
Sogang University, Korea

Ji-Eun Lee
Sogang University, Korea

ABSTRACT

In this chapter, the authors propose a Super-Resolution (SR) method using a vector quantization codebook and filter dictionary. In the process of SR, we use the idea of compressive sensing to represent a sparsely sampled signal under the assumption that a combination of a small number of codewords can represent an image patch. A low-resolution image is obtained from an original high-resolution image, degraded by blurring and down-sampling. The authors propose a resolution enhancement using an alternative l_1 norm minimization to overcome the convexity of l_0 norm and the sparsity of l_1 norm at the same time, where an iterative reweighted l_1 norm minimization is used for optimization. After the reconstruction stage, because the optimization is implemented on image patch basis, an additional deblurring or denoising step is used to globally enhance the image quality. Experiment results show that the proposed SR method provides highly efficient results.

INTRODUCTION

Super-resolution (SR) has been studied for several decades and a large number of SR algorithms have been proposed (Wang & Wang, 2009; Sroubek et al., 2011; Ma et al., 2012; Blunt, 2011). SR is an inverse problem, in which an original image is recovered using a single or multiple Low-Resolution (LR) images. Reconstruction is based on an image generation model that relates a High-Resolution (HR) image to a single or multiple LR images. Most conventional approaches to generating an SR image using multiple LR images require several LR images of the same scene, typically registered with sub-pixel accuracy.

DOI: 10.4018/978-1-4666-4558-5.ch001

There are two main processes on SR using multiple images: registration and reconstruction. Registration estimates motion of LR images with respect to the reference image. After motion estimation, the reconstruction step such as optimization, adaptive filtering, and example based method gives the HR image.

Most of SR methods use optimization to find the best HR image from initial images because the given LR images cannot offer much information for reconstruction of the exact HR image. Many conventional optimization methods define a cost function for reconstruction from distorted LR images. In l_2 norm minimization with Gaussian distribution error assumption, the reconstructed HR image is an average of the contributions from all LR images, in which the Gaussian distribution error assumption is applied to LR input images with global motion. l_1 norm with Laplacian distribution error assumption is good for local motion because of robustness against outliers. However, it uses the median over the measured data, so failure occurs in occlusion cases. To consider both distortion assumptions in a video SR method, Omer and Tanaka (2008) proposed a general cost function that consists of weighted l_1- and l_2-norms considering the SR error model, where weights are generated from the registration error with a penalty to inaccurately registered parts.

Qiao et al. (2005) proposed a SR method using Bayesian maximum a posteriori (MAP) to reconstruct a HR image and Vector Quantization (VQ) to implement blur identification. Example based SR methods, which store patch vectors from a number of training images, search for the most similar patch vector from LR image patch vectors. These methods store feature vectors (gradients) of the patch vector or LR and HR patch vector pairs (Chang et al., 2004; Yang et al., 2008).

Compressive Sensing (CS) is a new approach to recovery of a sparsely sampled signal by reducing the number of samples from bases or dictionary. CS assumes the signal could be described by combination of bases. Thus, though the recovery process is an ill-posed problem, optimization using norm minimization can give good result (Yang et al., 2009, 2012). In image processing fields, the discrete Fourier transform, Discrete Wavelet Transform (DWT), and curvelet can be used for construction of bases. To recover a sparsely sampled signal, l_0 and l_1 norm minimizations are presented (Candes & Romberg, 2004, 2005). Also projection on convex set (Tang et al., 2011) and efficient projection (Nhat & Vo, 2008) are used for optimization.

Recently, SR methods using CS are proposed. Since an image is two-dimensional (2-D), it is difficult to describe an image as a sparsely sampled signal on the spatial domain. Instead of the spatial domain, Duarte et al. (2008) applied a hidden Markov tree model to the DWT to use spatial data of an image and to estimate DWT coefficients. Yang et al. (2008) and Mairal et al. (2008) constructed a dictionary so that a linear combination of dictionary represents an image, where CS searches for the combination of dictionary elements.

In this chapter, it is assumed that an image can be represented using a small number of codewords that are selected from a VQ codebook. Thus, an iterative reweighted l_1 (IRWL1) norm minimization is used to find a suitable combination of code-words.

BACKGROUND

Let $\mathbf{x} \in \Re^N$ be a signal in an N-dimensional space and $\Psi = [\Psi_1, \Psi_2, ..., \Psi_N]$ be a basis matrix in $\Re^N$. We say that x is K-sparse if it can be expressed as a linear combination of K vectors from Ψ, that is, $\mathbf{x} = \Psi\theta$ with K($<<$N) nonzero elements of θ.

Consider a signal x that is K-sparse in Ψ. Consider also an M*N measurement matrix Φ, M$<<$N, where the rows of Φ are incoherent with the columns of Ψ. Compute the measurement vector $\mathbf{y} = \Phi\mathbf{x}$ and note that $\mathbf{y} \in \Re^M$ with M<<N. The problem is ill-posed with the number of independent equations fewer than that of unknowns, usually having an infinite number of solutions. Thus, it is obviously impossible to identify that the candidate solution is indeed the correct one without some additional information.

Sparse Signal Recovery

Under the sparsity assumption, the signal $\mathbf{x} \in \Re^N$, which we want to recover and has a Ψ-coefficient vector $\hat{\theta}$ in the appropriate basis, can be recovered by solving the optimization problem:

$$\hat{\theta} = \arg\min_{n} \|\theta\|_0 \quad \text{such that} \quad \mathbf{y} = \Phi\mathbf{x} = \Phi\Psi\theta \quad (1)$$

where $\|\theta\|_0 = |\{n : \theta_n \neq 0\}|$. This is a common approach that simply seeks the simplest explanation fitting the data. In fact, this approach can recover a sparse solution even in the case of M<<N. Since the optimization problem is non-convex and generally impossible to solve, the solution would not be useful for the SR algorithm.

A common alternative is to consider the convex problem using l_1 norm:

$$\hat{\theta} = \arg\min_{\theta} \|\theta\|_1 \quad \text{such that} \quad \mathbf{y} = \Phi\mathbf{x} = \Phi\Psi\theta$$
(2)

where $\|\theta\|_1 = \sum_{n=1} |\theta_n|$. Unlike (1), l_1 norm minimization is convex so we can recast (2) as a linear program. Typically, the reconstruction result of sparse signals using l_1 norm minimization is exact. So, in most of the conventional CS methods, it is convinced that l_1 norm minimization is suitable for sparse signal recovery (Boyd & Vandenberghe, 2004).

IRWL1 Norm Minimization Problem

In this chapter, we consider the optimization for both sparsity and convexity. To avoid non-convexity of l_0 norm and to reduce the dependency of l_1 norm on the magnitude of the solution, we choose an IRWL1 norm minimization.

IRWL1 norm minimization problem (Candes et al., 2008), expressed as:

$$\hat{\theta}^{(1)} = \arg\min_{\theta} \|W^{(1)}\theta\|_1 \quad \text{such that} \quad \mathbf{y} = \Phi\mathbf{x} = \Phi\Psi\theta$$
(3)

Uses a weighting matrix W that has weights on the diagonal and zeros elsewhere, where the superscript (l) denotes the lth iteration. The magnitudes of the nth diagonal weights are updated as:

$$W_{n,n}^{(l)} = \frac{1}{\left|\hat{\theta}_n^{(l-1)}\right| + \varepsilon}$$

where ε is a small value to avoid dividing by zero. If the original vector θ is K-sparse, then (3) can find the correct solution using these weights.

PROPOSED SR METHOD

Conventional SR Method

SR reconstruction method with a single LR image recovers a HR image of the same scene. The observed LR image Y is blurred (by atmosphere, sensor, and object/camera motion), down-sampled, and degraded by noise (such as white Gaussian noise) from a HR image X. Then, a LR image Y can be modeled as:

$$Y = DHX + e \qquad (4)$$

where D, H, and e represent a down-sampling matrix, blur matrix, and additive noise vector, respectively.

To find a HR image from a single LR image, given information for reconstruction is not sufficient, noting that SR is an ill-posed problem (Borman & Stevenson, 1998). For underdetermined cases, there exist an infinite number of solutions that satisfy (4). Thus, a large number of SR methods choose a minimization error algorithm between the observed LR image Y and reconstructed HR image $\hat{X}$, as expressed as:

$$\hat{X} = \arg \min_X \left\| Y - DHX \right\| . \qquad (5)$$

If there are many LR versions of the same HR image, we can recover a HR image closer to the original one using multiple candidate data than using a single image with only one candidate. Therefore, we consider motion effect to compute difference between LR images and can write LR images as:

$$Y_p = D_p H_p T_p X + e \qquad (6)$$

where T_p denotes motion effect on the pth LR image, $1 \le p \le P$. Then, we rewrite (5) to obtain $\hat{X}$ as:

$$\hat{X} = \arg \min_X \sum_{p=1}^{P} \left\| Y_p - D_p H_p T_p X \right\| . \qquad (7)$$

Proposed SR Method Using Multiple Codebooks and Filter Dictionary

Park et al. (Park et al., 2003) showed an observation model relating LR images to HR images. The model shows process of obtaining a LR image from a HR image. We assume that the additive noise is reduced in the minimization procedure and that the degradation level by blur is known a priori. Then, the LR image acquisition model is given by

$$Y = D(H(X)) \qquad (8)$$

Where H(.) and D(.) are blurring and down-sampling operators, respectively. Thus, we can reconstruct X if inverse operators exist. However, the data acquired is underdetermined, so we cannot reconstruct the HR image exactly.

Figure 1 shows graphically the steps involved in the proposed SR method. First, we decompose a LR image Y into a number of patches by a moving window. Then, IRWL1 norm minimization is performed on each LR image patch to reconstruct a HR patch using a codebook.

Let $\tilde{y}$ be an M*1 vector of M_1*M_2 LR image patch and $\tilde{x}$ be an N*1 vector of N_1*N_2 HR image patch, where M= M_1*M_2 and N= N_1*N_2 with a scale factor L ($N=LM$). We subtract the mean intensity value of a patch, so that reconstruction considers only texture components rather than absolute intensity. Thus, the mean subtracted or zero-mean HR and LR image patch vectors x and y, which are to be reconstructed, are given by $y = \tilde{y} - \mu_y$ and $x = \tilde{x} - \mu_x$, respectively, where μ_x and μ_y are means of $\tilde{x}$ and $\tilde{y}$, respectively. The relation between the two vectors is written as

$$y = DHx \qquad (9)$$

Figure 1. Block diagram of the proposed method using IRWL1 norm minimization

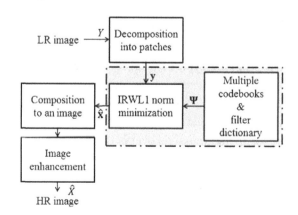

Where D is a down-sampling matrix and H is a degradation operator that blurs a HR image. Additive noise is not considered here.

To represent $\mathbf{x}$ as a sparse signal, we construct a VQ codebook $\Psi = \left[\mathbf{c}_1, \mathbf{c}_2, \ldots, \mathbf{c}_J \right]$ as dictionary of $\mathbf{x}$, which has J codewords ($\mathbf{c}_j$, $1 \leq j \leq J$). In designing a codebook, we train images that have various features, which can be divided into 32 edge types, to obtain essential edge components in $N_1 * N_2$ image patch. The zero-mean codewords are obtained by subtracting the local mean value from the HR or LR patch images. So we can express $\mathbf{x}$ as

$$\mathbf{x} = \Psi\theta \tag{10}$$

By sparsely selected codewords using Ψ-coefficient vector θ that has a few nonzero elements. We use a codebook Ψ for high frequency description of an image. Figure 2(a) shows the relation between a HR image patch vector $\mathbf{x}$ and LR image patch vector $\mathbf{y}$, and Figure 2(b) shows that $\mathbf{x}$ can be represented using sparsely selected codewords using Ψ and θ. Therefore, $\mathbf{y}$ can be described by the coefficient vector instead of $\mathbf{x}$. Thus, (9) can be rewritten as

$$\mathbf{y} = DH\mathbf{x} = DH\Psi\theta. \tag{11}$$

Figure 2(c) shows that it is appropriate to represent the zero-mean LR image patch vector $\mathbf{y}$ using the codebook Ψ with the coefficient vector θ. So using IRWL1 norm minimization (3), we reconstruct θ as

$$\hat{\theta}^{(l)} = \arg\min_{\theta} \left\| W^{(l)}\theta \right\|_1 \quad \text{such that} \quad \mathbf{y} = DH\Psi\theta \tag{12}$$

where $\hat{\theta}^{(l)}$ is the reconstructed Ψ-coefficient vector at the lth iteration. Then, the reconstructed zero-mean HR image patch vector $\hat{\mathbf{x}}$ is obtained by multiplication with the codebook matrix Ψ as

Figure 2. Vector-matrix representation of the relation between $\mathbf{x}$ and $\mathbf{y}$ using θ (a) Relation between a HR image patch vector $\mathbf{x}$ and LR image patch vector $\mathbf{y}$, (b) $\mathbf{x}$ can be represented by θ as sparsely selected codewords, (c) $\mathbf{y}$ can be made using $\mathbf{x}$ in (b), (d) Overall vector-matrix representation

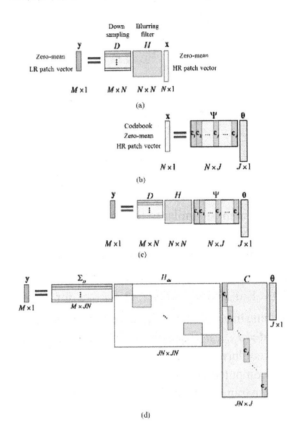

$$\hat{\mathbf{x}} = \Psi\hat{\theta}^{(l)}. \tag{13}$$

It is noted that the aspect of the blurring matrix between the original codeword and blurred codeword one is different for each codeword. As shown in Figure 3, each selected codeword can be blurred by its own blurring matrix. So, codeword $\tilde{\mathbf{c}}_i$ is generated for the LR image as blurred and down-sampled version of a HR image. In the proposed method, the blurring matrix $H_{dic,j}$ is defined for each codeword to find the codeword that is much closer to the original patch vector in the optimization process.

Figure 3. Selected codeword **x** *can be blurred by its own blurring matrix*

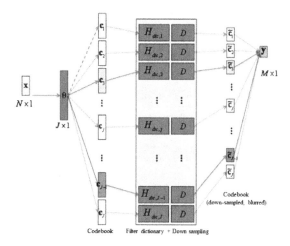

If **x** is most similar to the jth codeword, then the $N*N$ jth blurring matrix $H_{dic,j}$ is formed by $N*N$ auto-correlation matrix $R_j = E[x_j x_j^T]$ and $N*N$ cross-correlation matrix $N*N$ $P_j = E[d_1 x_j\, d_2 x_j .... d_N x_j]$, $1 \leq j \leq J$ for entire training images, where $E[.]$ represents expectation and $\mathbf{d}=[d_1,...,d_N]^T$ denotes the $N*1$ desired vector that is blurred version of **x**. These matrices are pre-computed with the whole set of training images in training stage. Finally, the blurring matrix is given by

$$H_{dic,j} = \left[R_j^{-1} P_j^T \right]^T . \qquad (14)$$

To obtain matrix H_{dic} in Figure 2(d), we put each blurring matrix $H_{dic,j}$ for the jth codeword along the diagonal as

$$H_{dic} = \begin{bmatrix} H_{dic,1} & & & 0_{N\times N} & 0_{N\times N} \\ & \ddots & & & 0_{N\times N} \\ & & H_{dic,j} & & \\ 0_{N\times N} & & & \ddots & \\ 0_{N\times N} & 0_{N\times N} & & & H_{dic,J} \end{bmatrix} \qquad (15)$$

As in Figure 2(d), the codeword matrix C is represented with each codeword c_j on diagonal, which is applied to blurring matrix $H_{dic,j}$ as

$$C = \begin{bmatrix} c_1 & & & 0_{N\times 1} \\ & c_2 & & \\ & & \ddots & \\ 0_{N\times 1} & & & c_J \end{bmatrix} \qquad (16)$$

Thus, a sum the diagonal of $H_{dic,j} C$ is the same as $H\Psi$. Also, Σ_D denotes $D\Sigma$, where D represents a down-sampling matrix and Σ is the $N\times JN$ matrix as expressed as $\Sigma=[I \cdots I]$ using the identity matrix I to convert $JN\times JN$ matrix into $N\times 1$ vector. Therefore, we can represent (11) as

$$y = DH\Psi n = \Sigma_D H_{dic} C\theta \qquad (17)$$

where the identity matrix I converts the size of $H_{dic}C$ to $N\times N$ as $H\Psi$ and makes $\Sigma_D H_{dic}$ equal to DH, so Figure 2(d) is equivalent to Figure 2(c). Thus, reconstruction step uses the same Ψ-coefficient θ. In short, Figure 2(d) shows that if each codeword c_j is blurred by its own blur matrix $H_{dic,j}$ θ could be computed more accurately using the characterized blur matrix rather than using the average blur matrix.

Consequently, we can get the Ψ-coefficient with given LR image patch vector **y** using (12) as:

$$\hat{\theta}^{(1)} = \arg\min_\theta \left\| W^{(1)}\theta \right\|_1 \text{ such that } y = \Sigma_D H_{dic} C\theta \qquad (18)$$

$$W_{n,n}^{(1)} = \frac{1}{\left| \hat{\theta}_n^{(1-1)} \right| + \varepsilon} .$$

Then, the reconstructed HR image patch vector can be computed by $\hat{x} = \Psi\hat{\theta}^{(1)}$.

Figure 4 describes typical stages of the proposed reconstruction method. A LR input image

Figure 4. Stages of the proposed reconstruction method

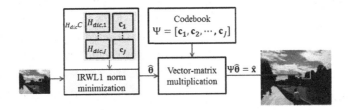

patch vector is only for IRWL1 norm minimization and the reconstructed HR patch vector is obtained by multiplication with codebook Ψ.

Codebook Design for Efficient Reconstruction

The quality of the reconstructed SR image using codebook depends on the size of the codebook. During the reconstruction stage, each mean-subtracted patch vector from a LR image should be compared with codewords in the codebook. To reduce the number of redundant codewords and to include essential codewords, we use multiple codebooks based on the local image structure (Nakagaki & Katsaggelos, 2003).

In training stage, using entire zero-mean patch vectors of training images, we implement Linde, Buzo, and Gray (LBG) algorithm to acquire T representative codewords (Nakagaki & Katsaggelos, 2003). We set T to 32 by taking into account eight edge directions, two edge amplitudes (strong/weak edges), and two edge frequencies (high/low). Then, each representative vector is compared with entire patch vectors and the closest codeword is selected. So we obtain multiple codebooks of a total of 32 types. The number of each codebook type is computed as:

$$M'_t = M_{total} \times \frac{M_t}{\sum_{t=0}^{T-1} M_t} \qquad (19)$$

Where M_{total} is the specified total number of codewords. M_t denotes the number of mean-subtracted patch vectors of training images that are considered as type t ($1 \leq t \leq T$). For each codebook type t, M'_t codewords are designed using the LBG algorithm. Therefore, we can find more similar codeword in view of the direction, amplitude, and frequency.

Extension to SR with Multiple Images

The proposed method could make a SR image efficiently when multiple LR images are used. After motion estimation and warping on the high-resolution grid (Park et al., 2003), we can fill more image information than when we use a single input image. If pixels from multiple LR frames exist at the same location as on the HR grid, we take an average of these pixel values. So, if every LR image $\mathbf{y}_p$ is observed with different motion (T_p), blurring (H_p), and down-sampling (D_p) of all P LR images as:

$$y_p = D_p H_p T_p x, (1 \leq p \leq P) \qquad (20)$$

We convert $\mathbf{y}$ that represents all of data of $\mathbf{y}_p$ in HR grid. With this concept, the pixel values of LR images on the HR grid, $\mathbf{x}$ is down-sampled non-uniformly to $\mathbf{y}$ with higher sampling rate than M/N in (11). That is, the higher sampling can reduce the number of cases to find $\boldsymbol{\theta}$. Thus, it is expected that we can acquire better result image with more initial data. Also, for optimization, computation time could be reduced when the HR grid is filled with more data.

EXPERIMENTAL RESULTS AND DISCUSSIONS

In our experiments, several training images are used for codebook generation. Various orientation components exist in each image of training images. Some of images are provided by Kodak.

The proposed method can be divided two stages; learning stage and optimization stage. We use the same condition in view of the scale factor between HR image and LR image.

Comparison of SR Performance According to the Number of Codewords

In this section, we compare the performance of the proposed method according to the number of codewords. It is assumed that in the proposed method the image can be represented with a few codewords. Figure 5 shows reconstructed results of which resolution is higher than that of the original image by a factor of two. Figure 5(a) shows the 300×300 original image whereas Figure 5(b) shows the 150×150 LR image of Figure 5(a) subsampled by a factor of two. Figures 5(c), 5(d), and 5(e) are the reconstructed images reconstructed with one codeword, two codewords, and three codewords, respectively. Figure 5(f) is the result of bicubic interpolation.

Table 1 shows comparison of results in terms of the peak signal to noise ratio (PSNR) and computation time. Although the reconstructed result with three codewords shows the best result, the quality is a little different from that of the reconstructed image using two codewords. For moderate image quality, there is no need to use many codewords. It is seen that the result with

Figure 5. Experimental results by changing the number of codewords (a) original image (Girl, 300×300), (b) LR image (150×150), (c) reconstructed image with a single codeword, (d) reconstructed image with two codewords, (e) reconstructed image with three codewords, (f) result of bicubic interpolation

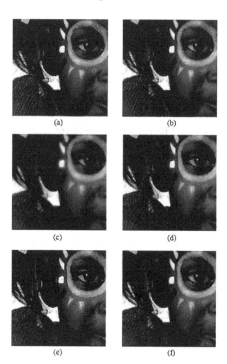

more than two codewords shows higher PSNR than bicubic interpolation method. However, the proposed method has a disadvantage that it takes longer time than bicubic interpolation.

Experimental Results with Various Test Images

In this section, we demonstrate the performance of the proposed algorithm with the test images that have various features. Bicubic interpolation method and example-based method (Chang et al., 2004) are compared for performance evaluation, in which the same training images are used for the proposed method.

Table 1. Comparison of reconstructed images in terms of the PSNR according to the number of codewords

PSNR (dB) time (s)	One codeword	Two codewords	Three codewords	Bicubic interpolation
"Girl"	27. 69 229.63	29.18 659.20	29.43 1451.48	27.79 1.05
"Building"	19.48 607.21	20.89 819.52	21.16 1420.38	20.29 0.2

Figure 6 shows the reconstructed image of which resolution is higher than that of the original image by a factor of two. Figures 6(a) and 6(b) show a 240×240 original image and a 120×120 LR image subsampled by a factor of two, respectively. Figure 6(c) shows the comparison of results of three methods in terms of the PSNR. Reconstructed results of Chang et al's method (2004) and the proposed method are sharper than that of bicubic interpolation. Also, the proposed method has the highest PSNR among the three methods compared. Figure 6(d) shows the abso-

Figure 6. Experimental results (a) original image (Book, 240×240), (b) LR image (120×120), (c) reconstructed images (left: bicubic interpolation, middle: Chang et al.'s method, right: proposed method), (d) absolute difference images of (a) and (c), (e) enlarged results of (d)

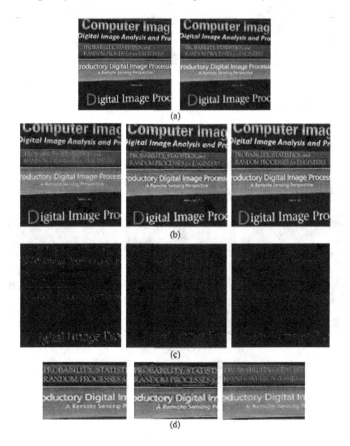

lute difference image between the original and reconstructed images. Figure 6(e) shows enlarged parts of the reconstructed images. The proposed method shows good performance in edge regions.

Figures 7 and 8 show the reconstructed images of which resolution is higher than that of the original image by a factor of three and four, respectively. As shown in Figure 6, results of the proposed method shows the best performance among the methods compared. Figures 7(a) and 7(b) show a 300×300 original image and a 100×100 LR image subsampled by a factor of three, respectively. Figures 8(a) and 8(b) show a 480×720 original image and a 120×180 LR image subsampled by a factor of four, respectively. Figures 7(c) and 8(c) show the comparison of results of three methods in terms of the PSNR. Figures 7(d) and 8(d) show the absolute difference image between the original and reconstructed images. In Figure 7(e), result of the proposed method is clearer than that of Chang et al.'s method (2004). Also, Figure 8(e) shows good performance in edge regions and gives smooth representation.

Table 2 shows the PSNR of each method. The example-based method (Chang et al., 2004) shows sharp results, however, when the value of intensity is large or small, overshoot occurs. Because of the sharpening, bicubic method shows better

Figure 7. Experimental results (a) original image (Lighthouse, 300×300), (b) LR image (100×100), (c) reconstructed images (left: bicubic interpolation, middle: Chang et al's method, right: proposed method), (d) absolute difference images of (a) and (c), (e) enlarged results of (d)

Figure 8. Experimental results (a) original image (Red hat, 480×720), (b) LR image (120×180), (c) reconstructed images (left: bicubic interpolation, middle: Chang et al.'s method, right: proposed method), (d) enlarged images of (c)

Table 2. Comparison of reconstructed images in terms of the PSNR

PSNR(dB)	"Book"	"Lighthouse"	"Red hat"
Bicubic interpolation	20.39	25.64	29.56
Chang *et al.*'s [13]	19.22	23.83	29.39
Proposed method	22.71	25.89	30.55

performance than example-based method. The proposed method shows the best performance among the methods considered in terms of the PSNR.

CONCLUSION

We propose a method that converts a single LR image to a HR image, in which the proposed method uses a signal that is sparsely sampled from CS. It is assumed that an image can be represented with a codeword or combination of a few codewords, where IRWL1 minimization is used with the CS concept to select proper VQ codewords. Experimental results demonstrate that the proposed method shows better performance than existing methods, in terms of the PSNR, however, with a higher computational load. Future research will focus on the reduction of the computation time and on the image quality enhancement by using neighboring regions.

REFERENCES

Blunt, S. D. (2011). The reiterative superresolution (RISR) algorithm. *IEEE Transactions on Aerospace and Electronic Systems, 47*(1), 332–346. doi:10.1109/TAES.2011.5705679.

Borman, S., & Stevenson, R. L. (1998). Super-resolution from image sequences-A review. In *Proceedings of Midwest Symposium on Circuits and Systems* (374-378). Washington, DC: IEEE Press.

Boyd, S., & Vandeberghe, L. (2004). *Convex optimization*. New York: Cambridge University Press.

Candes, E. J., & Romberg, J. K. (2004). Practical signal recovery from random projections. In *Proceedings of SPIE Conference on Wavelet Application in Signal and Image Processing XI, 5914*. Bellingham, WA: SPIE Press.

Candes, E. J., & Romberg, J. K. (2005). *L1-magic: Recovery of sparse signals via convex programming*. Retrieved from http://users.ece.gatech.edu/~justin/l1magic/downloads/l1magic.pdf.

Candes, E. J., Wakin, M. B., & Boyd, S. P. (2008). Enhancing sparsity by reweighted l1 minimization. *The Journal of Fourier. Analysis and Applications, 14*(5), 877–905.

Chang, H., Yeung, D., & Xiong, Y. (2004). Super-resolution through neighbor embedding. In *Proceedings of IEEE Conference on Computer Vision and Pattern Recognition (CVPR 2004)* (I-275-I-282). Washington, DC: IEEE Press.

Duarte, M. F., Wakin, M. B., & Baraniuk, R. G. (2008). Wavelet-domain compressive signal reconstruction using a hidden Markov tree model. In *Proceedings of International Conference on Acoustics, Speech, and Signal Processing* (5137-5140). Washington, DC: IEEE Press.

Ma, J., Chang, C. C.-W., & Cangers, F. (2012). An operational superresolution approach for multi-temporal and multi-angle remotely sensed imagery. *IEEE Journal of Selected Topics in Applied Earth Observations and Remote Sensing, 5*(1), 110–124. doi:10.1109/JSTARS.2011.2182505.

Mairal, J., Elad, M., & Sapiro, G. (2008). Sparse representation for color image restoration. *IEEE Transactions on Image Processing, 17*(1), 53–69. doi:10.1109/TIP.2007.911828 PMID:18229804.

Nakagaki, R., & Katsaggelos, A. K. (2003). A VQ-based blind image restoration algorithm. *IEEE Transactions on Image Processing, 12*(9), 1044–1053. doi:10.1109/TIP.2003.816007 PMID:18237976.

Nhat, V. D. M., & Vo, D. (2008). Efficient projection for compressed sensing. In *Proceedings of International Conference on Computer and Information Science* (322-327). Washington, DC: IEEE Press.

Omer, O. A., & Tanaka, T. (2008). Joint blur identification and high-resolution image estimation based on weighted mixed-norm with outlier rejection. In *Proceedings of IEEE International Conference on Acoustics, Speech, and Signal Processing* (1305-1308). Washington, DC: IEEE Press.

Park, S. C., Park, M. K., & Kang, M. G. (2003). Super-resolution image reconstruction: A technical overview. *IEEE Signal Processing Magazine*, *20*(3), 21–36. doi:10.1109/MSP.2003.1203207.

Qiao, J., Liu, J., & Sun, G. (2005). A VQ-based blind superresolution algorithm. In *Proceedings of the 2005 International Conference on Advances in Intelligent Computing* (320-329). Berlin: Springer.

Sroubek, F., Kamenicky, J., & Milanfar, P. (2011). Superfast superresolution. In *Proceedings of 2011 18th IEEE International Conference on Image Processing (ICIP)* (1153-1156). Washington, DC: IEEE Press.

Tang, Z., Deng, M., Xiao, C., & Yu, J. (2011). Projection onto convex sets super-resolution image reconstruction based on wavelet bi-cubic interpolation. In *Proceedings of 2011 International Conference on Electronic and Mechanical Engineering and Information Technology* (351-354). Washington, DC: IEEE Press.

Wang, Z., & Wang, W. (2009). Fast and adaptive method for SAR superresolution imaging based on point scattering model and optimal basis selection. *IEEE Transactions on Image Processing*, *18*(7), 1477–1486. doi:10.1109/TIP.2009.2017327 PMID:19473944.

Yang, J., Wang, Z., Lin, Z., Cohen, S., & Huang, T. (2012). Coupled dictionary training for image super-resolution. *IEEE Transactions on Image Processing*, *21*(8), 3467–3478. doi:10.1109/TIP.2012.2192127.

Yang, J., Wright, J., Ma, Y., & Huang, T. (2008). Image super-resolution as sparse representation of raw image patches. In *Proceedings of IEEE Conference on Computer Vision and Pattern Recognition, 2008* (1-8). Washington, DC: IEEE Press.

Yap, K.-H., He, Y., Tian, Y., & Chau, L.-P. (2009). A nonlinear L1-norm approach for joint image registration and super-resolution. *IEEE Signal Processing Letters*, *16*(11), 981–984. doi:10.1109/LSP.2009.2028106.

ADDITIONAL REFERENCES

Baraniuk, R. G. (2007). Compressive sensing. *IEEE Signal Processing Magazine*, *24*(4), 118–121. doi:10.1109/MSP.2007.4286571.

Ben-Ezra, M., Zouchen, L., Wilburn, B., & Zhang, W. (2011). Penrose pixels for super-resolution. *IEEE Transactions on Pattern Analysis and Machine Intelligence*, *33*(7), 1370–1383. doi:10.1109/TPAMI.2010.213 PMID:21135446.

Chen, W., Xu, X., Wen, S., & Cao, Z. (2011). Super-resolution direction finding with far-separated subarrays using virtual array elements. *IET Radar. Sonar & Navigation*, *5*(8), 824–834. doi:10.1049/iet-rsn.2010.0289.

Donoho, D. (2006). Compressed sensing. *IEEE Transactions on Information Theory*, *52*(4), 1289–1306. doi:10.1109/TIT.2006.871582.

Farsiu, S., Robinson, M. D., Elad, M., & Milanfar, P. (2004). Fast and robust multi frame super resolution. *IEEE Transactions on Image Processing*, *13*(10), 1327–1344. doi:10.1109/TIP.2004.834669 PMID:15462143.

Heng, S., Ying, W., & Jie, Z. (2012). Super-resolution without dense flow. *IEEE Transactions on Image Processing*, *21*(4), 1782–1795. doi:10.1109/TIP.2011.2173204 PMID:22027381.

Katasaggelos, A. K., Molina, R., Mateos, J., & Bovik, A. C. (2007). *Superresolution of images and video*. San Rafael, CA: Morgan & Claypool Publishers.

Kulkarni, N., Nagesh, P., Gowda, R., & Li, B. (2012). Understanding compressive sensing and sparse representation based super-resolution. *IEEE Transactions on Circuits and Systems for Video Technology*, *22*(5), 778–789. doi:10.1109/TCSVT.2011.2180773.

Ni, K. S., & Nguyen, T. Q. (2007). Image superresolution using support vector regression. *IEEE Transactions on Image Processing*, *16*(6), 1596–1610. doi:10.1109/TIP.2007.896644 PMID:17547137.

Pickup, L. C., Capel, D. P., Roberts, S. J., & Zisserman, A. (2007). Bayesian methods for image super-resolution. *The Computer Journal*, *52*(1), 101–113. doi:10.1093/comjnl/bxm091.

Pickup, L. C., Capel, D. P., Roberts, S. J., & Zisserman, A. (2007). Overcoming registration uncertainty in image superresolution: Maximize or marginalize? *EURASIP Journal on Advances in Signal Processing*, 2007.

Sroubek, F., Cristobal, G., & Flusser, J. (2007). A unified approach to superresolution and multichannel blind deconvolution. *IEEE Transactions on Image Processing*, *16*(9), 2322–2332. doi:10.1109/TIP.2007.903256 PMID:17784605.

Wang, Q., & Shi, G. (2008). Super-resolution imager via compressive sensing. In *Proceedings of 2010 IEEE 10th International Conference on Signal Processing* (956-959). Washington, DC: IEEE Press.

Yang, H., Gao, J., & Wu, Z. (2008). Blur identification and image superresolution reconstruction using and approach similar to variable projection. *IEEE Signal Processing Letters*, *15*, 289–292. doi:10.1109/LSP.2007.911743.

KEY TERMS AND DEFINITIONS

Codebook: In vector quantization, codebook means a list of reconstruction levels. Linde, Buzo, and Gray (LBG) algorithm.

Compressive Sensing (CS): CS suggests a technique to reduce unnecessary computation for reconstruction of a signal. According to the theory, it can represent a signal with a small number of linear measurements.

Iterative Reweighted l1 (IRWL1) Norm Minimization: IRWL1 norm minimization is a method to minimize l1 norm. It solves an objective function by an iterative method.

Linde, Buzo, and Gray (LBG) Algorithm: LBG algorithm is a kind of vector quantization algorithm that is similar to k-means clustering.

Projection onto Convex Sets (POCS): POCS finds the solution from given convex sets with iterative projection.

Super-Resolution (SR): SR method enhances the resolution of an image. Using this method, a single or multiple low-resolution images are converted to a high-resolution image.

Vector Quantization (VQ): VQ finds the closest centroid of a codebook. VQ reduces the memory and the computation cost. Sometimes, quantization error occurs, however, can be reduced by using a larger making the codebook.

Chapter 2
3D Reconstruction Using Multiple View Stereo and a Brief Introduction to Kinect

Brojeshwar Bhowmick

IIT Delhi and Innovation Lab, Tata Consultancy Services, India

ABSTRACT

This chapter deals with the methodology of 3D reconstruction, both sparse and dense. The basic properties of the projective geometry and the camera models are introduced to understand the preliminaries about the subject. A more detail can be found in the book (Hartley & Zisserman, 2000). The sparse reconstruction deals with reconstructing 3D points for few image points. There are gaps in the reconstructed 3D points. Dense reconstruction tries to fill up gaps and make the density of the reconstruction higher. Estimation of correspondences is an integral part of multiview reconstruction and the author will discuss the point correspondences among images here. Finally the author will introduce the Microsoft Kinect, a divice which directly capture 3D information in realtime, and will show how to enhance the Kinect point cloud using vision framework.

INTRODUCTION

3D reconstruction from multiple images is an active area of research for past two decades and has come up with enormous stable algorithms in state of the art. In this chapter we mainly deal with basic geometry involved in establishing relations between images and will define camera models. The image formation and relation among images are established in projective geometric framework. A 3D point could be obtained from two or more 2D points in projective space or in Euclidean space depending on the camera models. If the cameras are calibrated in Euclidian spaces, the reconstruc-

tion (getting 3D point) obeys Euclidean geometry laws else the camera model and 3D structure are in projective space. Each of these concepts will be dealt in detail in the following sections. Then, we will focus on the methodologies for point correspondence across image set, which is an important aspect in reconstruction. Once these correspondences are found out we will discuss the method of obtaining the 3D points through triangulation. Then we will present a generalized framework called Bundle Adjustment which generates the camera and 3D structure simultaneously. We will also be dealing with different methods of dense reconstruction using the sparse reconstruc-

DOI: 10.4018/978-1-4666-4558-5.ch002

tion as initial input. The dense reconstruction takes care of the overall geometry in finer scale. This will complete the basic overview on reconstruction from images. With the latest release of Kinect device by Microsoft, there is a scope of vision based work using this device. One of the problems with the Kinect is that it provides the point cloud in VGA resolution. There is a scope of enhancing the resolution of the Kinect using two or more high definition cameras, which will be discussed further.

FUNDAMENTALS OF PROJECTIVE GEOMETRY AND PROJECTIVE CAMERA MODELS

Why Projective Geometry?

Image formation is a perspective transformation from 3D world scene to 2D plane and most of the Euclidean geometric property is lost due to this transformation. One of the most familiar properties is that parallel lines which never meet, or some fancy way of saying they meets at infinity in Euclidean space, doesn't hold true after perspective transformation in image as shown in Figure 1. This figure shows two parallel rail lines meet at a point called vanishing point. This phenomenon distinguishes projective geometry from Euclidean geometry. The notion of distance and parallelism is destroyed in projective transformation. When the notion of distance is removed from Euclidean geometry keeping only parallelism, the structure becomes affine. Further, removing the preservation of parallelism property gives rise to projective structure. A more comprehensive detail can be found in (Hartley & Zisserman, 2000).

Perspective Viewing

Figure 1(a) shows the perspective phenomenon, where parallel lines meet at a point called the vanishing point. In perspective drawing an im-

age point is formed at the intersection of the ray emanating from the object through the camera center, with the image plane as shown in Figure 1(b). This also shows that the spacing between the world points are not in sync with the spacing in between the image points. Although Figure 1(b) shows the construction of image under perspective projection, it is difficult to get a similar construction for the image of an image. Figure 1(c) shows that the line S is being imaged through optical center O_S in line s, and this line s is again projected through O_σ. But there is no optical center which is the intersection of the lines joining points of S and σ. A more sophisticated method is required to explain this, and that general method is called projective transformation (Mundy & Zisserman, 1992). A chain of perspective transformations may not be perspective projections but always projective transformation and any projective transformations can be decomposed into two or more perspective transformations (Mundy & Zisserman, 1992).

Properties of Projective Plane

In Euclidean plane, distances are well defined and also parallel lines meet at infinity. If we remove the notion of distance and only preserve the parallelism, then the structure formed, is called affine plane. Here, rectangle can be transformed into arbitrary parallelogram keeping lines parallel. Further, if we remove the notion of parallel lines then the structure is called projective structure, where any two lines meet at a point. In such cases all parallel lines also meet at some point which we call the ideal point. So, in an affine plane, if we introduce these ideal points and consider them as a part of the geometric structure, we get projective plane. In a projective plane following two properties hold,

- **Property 1:** Two distinct points produce a unique line.

Figure 1. (a) Parallel lines meet at vanishing point, (b) construction of image point in perspective draw-ing and vanishing point (image courtesy: geometric invariance in computer vision by Zisserman and Mundy), (c) sequence of two or more perspective projections (image courtesy: geometric invariance in computer vision by Zisserman and Mundy), (d) projective model (image courtesy: geometric invariance in computer vision by Zisserman and Mundy)

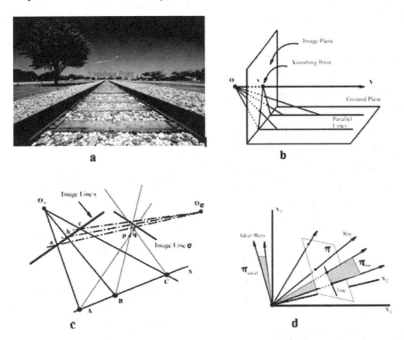

- **Property 2:** Two distinct lines produce a unique point (note, this is not in the case of an affine plane when two lines are parallel).

These two properties make lines and point similar entities and we can interchange lines as points or points as lines. So, in projective plane lines and points are dual of each other. Let us summarize the properties that are invariant under different transformation.

- **Euclidean:** Length, area, collinearity,
- **Affine:** Parallelism, ratio of area, ratio of length,
- **Projective:** Collinearity, crossratio (ratio of ratio of length) (Mundy & Zisserman, 1992).

In projective model, a projective point is de-scribed as a ray in $\Re^3$ as shown in Figure 1(d). There is an origin from which all rays emanate. Let an arbitrary plane π be constructed in $\Re^3$. This plane does not pass through the origin. The rays which intersect the plane correspond to a point in affine plane (Mundy & Zisserman, 1992). Rays parallel to the plane π are called ideal points. The set of rays parallel to the plane π form an ideal line. Since π is arbitrary there is no differ-ence among the ray whether they are affine or ideal, which perfectly describe the projective properties. Also note that the two properties prop1 and prop2 are also satisfied. Two rays define a unique plane and two planes define a unique ray.

Homogenous Coordinate

As discussed earlier, a point in projective plane is represented by 3 Dimensional Cartesian coordinate $(x_1, x_2, x_3)^t$, which is a ray through origin. As it is a ray, only the direction is important and so $(x_1, x_2, x_3)^t$ and $(\lambda x_1, \lambda x_2, \lambda x_3)^t$ are equivalent. The coordinate $(0, 0, 0)$ has no meaning as the length of ray becomes zero. A relation with Cartesian coordinates (x, y) is established by constructing a special plane perpendicular to x^3-axis and at a unit distance from origin along x^3 (Mundy & Zisserman, 1992). The intersection of the ray with this plane is $(x, y, 1)$, where (x, y) is the standard Cartesian coordinate. As mentioned earlier ray parallel to the plane is ideal point, so in this case $x^3 = 0$, and an ideal point is represented as $(x, y, 0)$. Note that these ideal points lies in a line which is called line at infinity or ideal line which has the form $(0, 0, 1)$, because the dot-product $(x, y, 0) (0, 0, 1) = 0$.

Euclidean, Affine, and Projective Transform Matrices

In the previous section we discussed about the invariance properties that are applicable in Euclidean, Affine and Projective transformations. Here we will discuss about the matrix form of these transformation.

- **Euclidean:** As Euclidean geometry preserve length, angle, area, it is a rigid transformation of the form:

$$\begin{pmatrix} x' \\ y' \\ 1 \end{pmatrix} = \begin{pmatrix} s\cos\theta & -s\sin\theta & t_x \\ s\sin\theta & s\cos\theta & t_y \\ 0 & 0 & 1 \end{pmatrix} \begin{pmatrix} x \\ y \\ 1 \end{pmatrix} \tag{1}$$

s represents isotropic scaling and t_x, t_y are the translation. When this s is involved this transformation is also called similarity transformation.

- **Affine:** This only preserves parallelism, ratio of length and ratio of areas and the transformation is of the form:

$$\begin{pmatrix} x' \\ y' \\ 1 \end{pmatrix} = \begin{pmatrix} a_{11} & a_{12} & t_x \\ a_{21} & a_{22} & t_y \\ 0 & 0 & 1 \end{pmatrix} \begin{pmatrix} x \\ y \\ 1 \end{pmatrix} \tag{2}$$

This matrix preserves parallelism as ideal point $(x, y, 0)$ map to another ideal point. So, parallel lines still meet at infinity. For details about preservation of other property please refer to (Hartley & Zisserman, 2000).

- **Projective:** Here parallelism is not preserved. An ideal point may map to any other point.

$$\begin{pmatrix} x' \\ y' \\ 1 \end{pmatrix} = \begin{pmatrix} a_{11} & a_{12} & t_x \\ a_{21} & a_{22} & t_y \\ a_{31} & a_{32} & a_{33} \end{pmatrix} \begin{pmatrix} x \\ y \\ 1 \end{pmatrix} \tag{3}$$

It is easy to see that an ideal point can become an ordinary projective point. Note that, a_{33} might also be zero. A projective transformation can be computed from 4 point correspondences. As projective transformation is more general form of affine and Euclidean transform we can decompose this projective transform into similarity, affine and projective components.

$$H = H_S H_A H_P = \begin{bmatrix} s^R & t \\ 0^T & 1 \end{bmatrix} \begin{bmatrix} A & 0 \\ 0^T & 1 \end{bmatrix} \begin{bmatrix} I & 0 \\ a_3^T & a_{33} \end{bmatrix} \tag{4}$$

where, A is a upper triangular matrix.

Metric (Euclidean/Similarity) Correction from Projective Image

It has been discussed that images are formed by perspective transformation, in a more general sense, by projective transformation. This transformation neither preserves parallelism nor length. So measurement is not possible in this structure. Lets discuss how to rectify image so that we can have parallel lines as parallel and can have measurements of length, angle, and so forth.

Affine Rectification

Let's make projective to affine correction, where parallel lines become parallel. Figure 2(a) shows an image where it is evident that parallel lines are converging to a vanishing point. As discussed, this vanishing point should be a point at infinity in Euclidean or affine structure. But as image formation is a projective phenomenon, ideal points are not distinguished from other points. In Figure 2(a), V1 and V2 are two vanishing points for different parallel lines. The line joining two vanishing points is called the vanishing line. Again as this

is a projective structure, vanishing line is not a special entity and is treated same as other set of lines. Now, if we can send this vanishing line to infinity by some transformation, then we can get the structure where vanishing points and lines are at infinity, i.e. recover the affine structure and get parallel lines. Let us briefly examine certain properties of point, line and transformation first. If, two lines l_1 and l_2 in homogeneous coordinates are intersected at point p, then $p = l_1 \times l_2$. This is a cross product. This is because, p is in both l_1 and l_2, it satisfies the condition $l_1^T p = l_2^T p = 0$, which is equivalent to $l_1 \cdot (l_1 \times l_2) = l_2 \cdot (l_1 \times l_2) = 0$. Similar arguments hold for calculating the line joining two points. Again if a point x lies on line l_1, and is transformed to x' lies on line l_2 through projective transformation H, i.e., if,

$$x' = Hx \tag{5}$$

Then

$$l_2 = H^{-T} l_1 \tag{6}$$

Figure 2. (a) Under projective transformation parallel lines meet at vanishing point and the line connecting vanishing point is vanishing line. (b) Projective corrected and parallel lines are parallel. (c) Metric corrected and angles between lines become 90 degree. Here measurement is possible. (d) point correspondence: The arrow shows a corresponding pixel between two images.

a

b

c

d

since, $l_2^T x' = l_1^T H^{-1} H x = 0$.

Now, given different set of collinear parallel points we can compute the vanishing point as shown in Figure 2(a) using the cross product. Also the vanishing lines are computed using two or more vanishing points. Let (l_1, l_2, l_3) be the homogeneous representation of the vanishing line. Then the projective *point* transformation which will push this vanishing line to infinity is given by:

$$H = H_A \begin{bmatrix} 1 & 0 & 0 \\ 0 & 1 & 0 \\ l_1 & l_2 & l_3 \end{bmatrix} \qquad (7)$$

where H_A is any affine transformation. Note, H is a point transformation and corresponding line transformation is H^T as discussed in the previous paragraph. It is easy to see $H^T (l_1, l_2, l_3)^T = (0, 0, 1)$.

Figure 2(b) shows the output of the correction and it is clear that the parallel lines have now become parallel.

But still the angles are not correct; i.e. the angle between the two lines in Figure 2(b) is actually 90 degree, which is not the case after the transformation. Now to achieve this, we need metric correction.

Metric Rectification

Metric rectification needs some concepts of conics and their transformations. In homogeneous coordinate system, the equation of a conic is

$$ax_1^2 + bx_1 x_2 + cx_2^2 + dx_1 x_3 + ex_2 x_3 + fx_3^2 = 0 \qquad (8)$$

For inhomogeneous representation, substitute $x = x_1/x_3$ and $y = x_2/x_3$. It can be written in matrix form:

$$x^T C x = x^T \begin{bmatrix} a & b/2 & d/2 \\ b/2 & c & e/2 \\ d/2 & e/2 & f \end{bmatrix} x = 0 \qquad (9)$$

The conic has 5 degrees of freedom and five points are needed to define this conic. For details about this please refer to (Hartley & Zisserman, 2000). The conic just described is a point conic consisting of point x. The dual conic is a conic consisting of lines. For the dual conic C* and line l we have $l^T C^* l = 0$, for a non-singular symmetric matrix $C^* = C^{-1}$. For proof see (Hartley & Zisserman, 2000). Similar to line transform as Equation 6 if, $x' = H x$, then, $x^T C x = x'^T (H^{-1})^T C H^{-1} x' = x' H^{-T} C H^{-1} x'$. Under point transformation H, C transforms to:

$$C' = H^{-T} C H^{-1} \qquad (10)$$

$$C^{*'} = H C^* H^T \qquad (11)$$

Conic can be degenerate (not full rank). Degenerate point conic includes two lines and a repeated line, $C = lm^T + ml^T$. Similarly degenerate line conic (dual) include 2 point and a repeated point, T

$$C^* = xy^T + yx^T \qquad (12)$$

Now, let us take the case of circles. Two circles intersect in two points. But algebraically two second order curves intersection should result in four solutions. Then where does the other two points of intersection of circle lies? The other two points are imaginary points. The homogeneous equation of circle is:

$$(x - aw)^2 + (y - bw)^2 = r^2 w^2 \qquad (13)$$

It is evident that $(x, y, w)^T = (1, \pm i, 0)^T$, lie on this circle. Note that the last coordinate is zero, i.e it is a point at infinity and are called circular points, and lie on line at infinity. These circular point satisfies two real equation $x^2 + y^2 = 0$; $w = 0$. Similarly in 3D two spheres intersect in a circle which is not a fourth-degree curve. All spheres intersect the plane at infinity in a curve with equation $X^2 + Y^2 + Z^2 = 0$; $T = 0$. This is a second degree curve lying in plane at infinity and is known as the absolute conic. We can have Euclidean geometry from projective geometry if we single out line at line at infinity and circular point lying on this line. The properties of circular points are they are invariant under Euclidean transformation. Let $I = (1, i, 0)$ and, $J = (1, -, 0)$ then:

$$I' = \begin{bmatrix} s\cos\theta & -s\sin\theta & t_z \\ s\sin\theta & s\cos\theta & t_y \\ 0 & 0 & 1 \end{bmatrix} \begin{pmatrix} 1 \\ i \\ 0 \end{pmatrix} = s\exp(-i\theta) \begin{pmatrix} 1 \\ i \\ 0 \end{pmatrix} = I \quad (14)$$

So, the circular points are fixed under the projective transformation H if and only if H is similarity. We can also have a conic dual to circular point. Similar to Equation 12 this dual conic is represented as $C^*_\infty = IJ^T + JI^T$.

$$C^*_\infty = \begin{pmatrix} 1 & i & 0 \end{pmatrix}^T \begin{pmatrix} 1 & -i & 0 \end{pmatrix} +$$
$$\begin{pmatrix} 1 & -i & 0 \end{pmatrix}^T \begin{pmatrix} 1 & i & 0 \end{pmatrix} = \begin{bmatrix} 1 & 0 & 0 \\ 0 & 1 & 0 \\ 0 & 0 & 1 \end{bmatrix} \quad (15)$$

As in Equation 14, it can be shown the dual conic C^*_∞ is fixed under projective transformation H if and only if H is similarity transform, like,

$$C^{*'}_\infty = H_S C^*_\infty H_S^T = C^*_\infty \quad (16)$$

After rectification upto affine, let us return to the metric rectifications in Figure 2(b). Suppose we obtain $C^{*'}_\infty$ from image, and then by singular value decomposition (SVD) we obtain

$$C^{*'}_\infty = U \begin{bmatrix} 1 & 0 & 0 \\ 0 & 1 & 0 \\ 0 & 0 & 1 \end{bmatrix} U^T \quad (17)$$

Then by Equation 11, we get the point transform corresponding to the similarity rectification is $H = U$. Now it remains to compute $C^{*'}_\infty$. Note that from metric space C^*_∞ is transformed to $C^{*'}_\infty$, as metric x is transformed through projective transform (Equation 4) to x' in image. Our job is to find x from this image coordinate x' in metric/similarity correction. Let's examine how the C changes under C^*_∞ transformation using Equation 4. From Equation 11 and Equation 4 we get,

$$C^{*'}_\infty = \left(H_P H_A H_S \right) C^*_\infty \left(H_P H_A H_S \right)^T \quad (18)$$

$$= H_P H_A C^*_\infty H_A^T H_P^T \quad using\ Equation\ (16) \quad (19)$$

$$= \begin{bmatrix} AA^T & AA^T\mathrm{a} \\ \mathrm{a}^T AA^T & \mathrm{a}^T AA^T\mathrm{a} \end{bmatrix} \quad using\ Equation\ (4) \quad (20)$$

Here since we had already done the affine correction in Figure 2(b), the term due to projective contribution $\mathrm{a} = 0$. So, $C^{*'}_\infty$ becomes,

$$C^{*'}_\infty = \begin{bmatrix} AA^T & 0 \\ 0^T & 0 \end{bmatrix} \quad using\ Equation\ (4) \quad (21)$$

Now we know the form of $C^{*'}_\infty$. One last step is to find out how this can be computed from image. In Euclidean geometry for line $l = (l_1, l_2, l_3)$ and $m = (m_1, m_2, m_3)$ with normals parallel to l_1, l_2 and m_1, $m2$, the angle between them is (Hartley & Zisserman, 2000, June).

$$\cos\theta = \frac{l^T}{\sqrt{\left(l_1^2 + l_2^2\right)\left(m_1^2 + m_2^2\right)}}$$

and similarly an analogous expression which in invariant to projective transformation is

$$\cos\theta = \frac{l^T C_\infty^* m}{\sqrt{\left(l^T C_\infty^* l\right)\left(m^T C_\infty^* m\right)}}$$

If the angle between the line l and m is 90 degree then $l^T C_\infty^* m = 0$ and being projective invariant $l^T C_\infty^{*'} m = 0$. The expression of $C_\infty^{*'}$ is given by Equation 21 which has 3 unknowns after expansion. Two orthogonal lines pair, one is shown in Figure 2(b), need to be provided. When we solve for A in Equation 21 using the constraint $l^T C_\infty^{*'} m = 0$ we get the estimate of $C_\infty^{*'}$. After decomposition of $C_\infty^{*'}$ using Equation 17 we got the rectification point transform H as U and the resultant image is shown in Figure 2(c) where it is clear that the angle between lines becomes 90 degree. We can now have the measurement upto similarity. For a more detailed analysis on direct metric correction from projective structure please refer to (Hartley & Zisserman, 2000, June).

Homography

Homography is a projective mapping from one projective plane to another. Given a set of points x in P^2 (projective 2 space) and their corresponding set of points x' in P^2, we need to compute a projective transformation that transfer x to x'. Figure 2(d) shows an example of correspondence between two pixels in between two images. Considering two images as plane in P^2 and having a set of points (pixels) correspondence $x_i \leftrightarrow x'_i$ we wish to find a 3 × 3 projective transformation matrix H, *homography*, such that $x'_i = Hx_i$. A thorough detail of methods to compute H is described in

(Hartley & Zisserman, 2000, June). We are describing one of the methods called Direct Linear Transform (DLT).

Direct Linear Transform (DLT)

The equation $x'_i = Hx_i$ includes homogeneous vectors, and thus x'_i and Hx_i are not equal in magnitude, but they have same direction. So, this can be written as vector cross product $x'_i \times Hx_i = 0$. If i-th row of H is denoted by h^{iT} then

$$Hx_i = \begin{pmatrix} h^{1T} x_i \\ h^{2T} x_i \\ h^{4T} x_i \end{pmatrix}$$

As x'_i is a homogeneous entity it can be written as, say, $(x'_i,\ y'i,\ w'_i)$ and then cross product is given by as in (Hartley & Zisserman, 2000),

$$x'_i \times Hx_i = \begin{pmatrix} y'_i h^{3T} x_i - w'_i h^{2T} x_i \\ w'_i h^{1T} x_i - x'_i h^{3T} x_i \\ x'_i h^{2T} x_i - y'_i h^{1T} x_i \end{pmatrix} \tag{22}$$

Separating out the variables h_i and further simplifying, this can be written in the form of a linear equation. This equation is of the form Ah=0, where A is 3 × 9 matrix and h is a 9-vector made up of the entries in 3 × 3 matrix H. The solution can be obtained through SVD (Hartley & Zisserman, 2000).

Pinhole Camera Model

A physical camera can be modeled mathematically using a pin-hole model as shown in Figure 3(a). The point X of object is in camera coordinate system. The origin of this coordinate system is the optical center where all rays from object coincide. The intersection of these rays with the image plane creates the image point. In this way the image of X is created. Using standard trigonometry we can obtain the following relations between the object point(X, Y, Z) and image projection(x,y) $x = \dfrac{fX}{Z}$ and $y = \dfrac{fY}{Z}$. These are non-linear equations. If we analyze these equations using homogeneous coordinate system we can get a linear form.

$$
\begin{pmatrix} fX \\ fY \\ Z \end{pmatrix} = \begin{pmatrix} f & 0 & 0 & 0 \\ 0 & f & 0 & 0 \\ 0 & 0 & 1 & 0 \end{pmatrix} \begin{pmatrix} X \\ Y \\ Z \\ 1 \end{pmatrix} \tag{23}
$$

The above is the homogenous representation of $\dfrac{fX}{Z}$ and $\dfrac{fY}{Z}$, which is the image coordinate (x, y) after perspective transform. The center of projection is called camera center. The line joining camera center and perpendicular to the image plane is called principle axis/ray and the point in image plane where this ray intersects is called principle point. The plane through the camera center and parallel to the image plane is called principle plane.

Internal Calibration

The matrix in the Equation 23 is known the basic internal calibration matrix of a camera. Note that all parameters are in Euclidean coordinate system. But our image has its own coordinate system where (0, 0) (i.e. origin starts from the left-top of the matrix). So, if principle point has coordinate (c_x, c_y) instead of (0, 0) then the pinhole model equation becomes $x = \dfrac{fX}{Z} + c_x$ and $y = \dfrac{fY}{Z} + c_y$ and the matrix in Equation 23 becomes

$$
\begin{pmatrix} fX + Zc_x \\ fY + Zc_y \\ Z \end{pmatrix} = \begin{pmatrix} f & 0 & c_x & 0 \\ 0 & f & c_y & 0 \\ 0 & 0 & 1 & 0 \end{pmatrix} \begin{pmatrix} X \\ Y \\ Z \\ 1 \end{pmatrix} \tag{24}
$$

The matrix:

$$
K = \begin{pmatrix} f & 0 & c_x \\ 0 & f & c_y \\ 0 & 0 & 1 \end{pmatrix}
$$

is known internal calibration matrix. Here reader should note that object (X, Y, Z) is located in a coordinate system where the camera is at the origin. More about this topic can be found in (Hartley & Zisserman, 2000, June).

External Calibration

In Figure 3 the coordinate system of the object is in the camera coordinate system and the image coordinate x and object coordinate X is related by Equation 24. But if the object is in different Euclidean coordinate system (called world coordinate), then a rigid transformation is required between world coordinate system and camera coordinate system to establish the relation between object and projected coordinate. Figure 3(b) shows this configuration.

Let C' be the inhomogeneous camera position w.r.t some world coordinate system. If X' is the object inhomogeneous coordinate and X'_{cam} is the coordinate of the same object in camera coordinate system, then,

$$
X'_{cam} = R\left(X' - C' \right)
$$

Figure 3. (a) Pin-hole camera model, (b) world coordinate to camera coordinate transformation, (c) scale space is shown in left. The consecutive Gaussian images are subtracted to produce difference of Gaussian on the right (image courtesy of Lowe, 2004). (d) The keypoint descriptor is calculated by crating histogram over the magnitude and orientation of sample points weighted by a Gaussian window, indicated by overlaid circle (image courtesy of Lowe, 2004), (e) example of SIFT correspondences in stereo images.

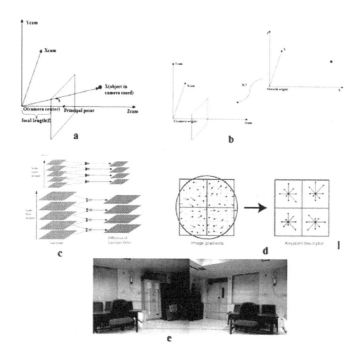

In homogenous coordinate this rigid transformation becomes,

$$X_{cam} = \begin{pmatrix} R & -RC' \\ 0 & 1 \end{pmatrix} \begin{pmatrix} X \\ Y \\ Z \\ 1 \end{pmatrix} \qquad (25)$$

After transforming the object coordinate using 25 we obtain a configuration where 24 can be applied. After applying 24 on $X_{cam,}$

$$x = K[R \mid -RC']X$$

If we denote $t = -RC'$, then the camera matrix becomes,

$$P = K[R \mid t] \qquad (26)$$

Note, that camera matrix P is a 3×4 matrix. Here K has 3 degrees of freedom (f, c_x, c_y) R and C' also have 3 degrees of freedom. Here x is the projected image coordinates (Euclidean) and X is in world coordinate system. Reader must note that until now all derivation has been done using a coordinate system which is Euclidean. So, an image is also considered as a plane in this Euclidean coordinate system. Also in Equation 23 we consider the scale of x and y is same. But in practical CCD cameras this is not true. The number of pixel per unit distance is not same in both directions. Let p_x and p_y be the number of pixels in x and y directions respectively, then, from Equation 24, K becomes:

$$K = \begin{pmatrix} f_x & 0 & U_0 \\ 0 & f_y & V_0 \\ 0 & 0 & 1 \end{pmatrix} \quad (27)$$

where $f_x = f_{px}, f_y = f_{py}, U_0 = c_x p_x$ and $V_0 = c_y p_y$. Moreover, camera CCD can contain skew, i.e. the CCD x-axis and y-axis may not have proper 90 degree between them. In that case a skew parameter s is introduced in K and it becomes

$$K = \begin{pmatrix} f_x & s & U_0 \\ 0 & f_y & V_0 \\ 0 & 0 & 1 \end{pmatrix} \quad (28)$$

If for a particular camera we know this K then we say that we have an Euclidean calibration of that camera. The significance of K is it provides us the ray through an image pixel x through in Euclidean coordinate system.

$$\lambda d = K^{-1} x \quad (29)$$

λ is the scale factor which cannot be determined from single point x. In other words, x = K [I|0] λd, i.e. we can get a ray through the image point x in Euclidean coordinate but we don't know the exact 3D location of x along the ray.

Properties of Camera Matrix

- If P is the camera matrix and C is the homogenous camera center then, $PC = 0$, i.e. C is the null vector of P.
- The column vector p_1, p_2 and p_3 of P are the vanishing point of world coordinate X, Y and Z respectively.

For example X axis has direction $(1, 0, 0, 0)^T$ and its imaged through P is:

$$p_1 = \begin{pmatrix} p_1 & p_2 & p_3 & p_4 \end{pmatrix} \begin{pmatrix} 1 \\ 0 \\ 0 \\ 0 \end{pmatrix}$$

- The column vector p_4 of P is the image of world origin.
- The first two rows of P are the planes defined by the camera center and the line x=0; camera center line y=0.

For example if p^{1T} is the first row of camera matrix P and X is the point on this plane p^1, then $p^{1T}X=0$. If we see the corresponding projection phenomena through P then it becomes $PX = (0, y, w)$ which are the points on Y - axis.

- The third row p^3 is the principle plane. Argument is similar to the above. In this case the projection through P satisfying $p^{3T}X = 0$ is the line of infinity $(x, y, 0)$ in image.
- The principal axis is the first 3 components of the last row of P, i.e. $(p_{31}, p_{32}, p_{33}, 0)$. As the last row is the principal plane, the first 3 vector of this plane is the normal direction.

Computation of Calibration Parameters

There are a lot of methods available for calibrating a camera. Comprehensive details can be found in book (Hartley & Zisserman, 2000). The most commonly used method is given by Zhang as described in (Zhang, 2000). For calibration one has to find out about the world coordinate system. In Zhang's method a checker board is used for calibration. Each corner of the checker board is considered as a world point and all the corners are identified sequentially starting from (0, 0). As the checker board is a plane we can have only (X, Y) coordinates of the corner points.

Coordinate Z is taken as 0 in all case. However, using the orthogonality among X, Y and Z we can find out the Z axis once we compute the X and Y. We need a number of images in different pose of the checkerboard to formulate the system of equation to solve. Writing Equation 25 in another way,

$$s \begin{pmatrix} x \\ y \\ 1 \end{pmatrix} = K \begin{pmatrix} r_1 & r_2 & r_3 & t \end{pmatrix} \begin{pmatrix} X \\ Y \\ 0 \\ 1 \end{pmatrix} \quad (30)$$

which simplifies to:

$$s \begin{pmatrix} x \\ y \\ 1 \end{pmatrix} = K \begin{pmatrix} r_1 & r_2 & t \end{pmatrix} \begin{pmatrix} X \\ Y \\ 1 \end{pmatrix} \quad (31)$$

This is a homography between object plane and image plane. A homography between two planes can be estimated by method described in (Hartley & Zisserman, 2000, June). Let $H = [h_1, h_2, h_3]$ be the homography. Then:

$$\begin{bmatrix} h1, h2, h3 \end{bmatrix} = \lambda K \begin{bmatrix} r_1 & r_2 & t \end{bmatrix}$$

As r_1 and r_2 are orthogonal we have,

$$h_1^T K^{-T} K^{-1} h_2 = 0$$

$$h_1^T K^{-T} K^{-1} h_1 = h_2^T K^{-T} K^{-1} h_2$$

This numerically solves for K and the coordinate is Euclidean. For further numerical derivation please go through (Zhang, 2000, November). The rotation and translation matrix is different for different checkerboard positions as origin of the world coordinate is taken in the checkerboard itself. A more generalized calibration process called the Bundle Adjustment will be described in later section.

Point Correspondence and Epipolar Geometry

Figure 2(d) shows the point correspondences between two images. Here our aim is to describe methodology for this correspondence establishment among points on images automatically. To achieve this we need to find out some key points in image which are scale and orientation invariant (i.e. changing the scale [resize] or orientation does not alter the property of key point).

Scale Invariant Feature Transform (SIFT)

David Lowe (2004) proposes a methodology to find key points in image which are scale invariant. The method consists of four major steps:

Scale-Space Extrema Detection

The scale space of an image $I(x, y)$ is defined as a function, $L(x, y, \sigma)$

$$L(x, y, \sigma) = G(x, y, \sigma) * I(x, y)$$

where,

$$G(x, y, \sigma) = \frac{e^{\left(x^2 + y^2\right)} / / 2\sigma^2}{2\pi\sigma^2}$$

To detect stable keypoint locations in scale-space Lowe propose difference of Gaussian $D(x, y, \sigma)$, which is computed from the difference of nearby scales separated by a constant k.

$$D\left(x,y,\sigma\right)=\begin{pmatrix} G\left(x,y,k\sigma\right)- \\ G\left(x,y,\sigma\right) \end{pmatrix}* I\left(x,y\right) \qquad (32)$$

$$= L\left(x,y,k\sigma\right)- L\left(x,y,\sigma\right) \qquad (33)$$

Local maxima and minima is then computed from $D(x, y, \sigma)$. Each sample of $D(x, y, \sigma)$ is compared to its 8 neighbors and 9 neighbors in scale above and below. The sample is selected as a keypoint candidate if it is larger or smaller than all of these neighbors. Figure 3(c) depicts this idea.

Keypoint Localization

Once the keypoint candidates are found they are fitted in a 3D quadratic function to the local sample points to the interpolated maximum. Using Taylor expansion of $D(x, y, \sigma)$.

$$D\left(x\right)= D +\frac{\partial D^{T}}{\partial x}x +\frac{1}{2}x^{T}\frac{\partial^{2} D}{\partial x^{2}}x \qquad (34)$$

The extremum x can be found by taking derivative of this function and setting it to zero, giving,

$$\hat{x} =-\frac{\partial^{2} D^{-1}}{\partial x^{2}}\frac{\partial D}{\partial x} \qquad (35)$$

An extrema $\hat{x}$ is selected if $|D(\mathrm{x})|\geq 0.03$.

Rejecting keypoints using above criteria is not sufficient. A poor peak in DOG will also have large principal curvature across edge but small in perpendicular direction. The principal direction can be computed using 2×2 Hessian matrix H, computed at the location and scale of keypoint

$$H =\begin{pmatrix} D_{xx} & D_{xy} \\ D_{yx} & D_{yy} \end{pmatrix} \qquad (36)$$

To check the ratio of principal curvatures is below threshold we need to check the ratio $\dfrac{Tr\left(H\right)^{2}}{Det\left(H\right)}$

Orientation Assignment

The scale of the selected keypoint is used to get Gaussian smoothed image L, and gradient magnitude and orientation is computed using

$$m\left(x,y\right)= \sqrt{\begin{aligned} &\left(L\left(x+1,y\right)- L\left(x-1,y\right)\right)^{2} \\ &+\left(L\left(x,y+1\right)- L\left(x,y-1\right)\right)^{2} \end{aligned}} \qquad (37)$$

$$\theta\left(x,y\right)= \tan^{-1}\left(\frac{\begin{pmatrix} L\left(x+1,y\right)- \\ L\left(x-1,y\right) \end{pmatrix}}{\begin{pmatrix} L\left(x,y+1\right)- \\ L\left(x,y-1\right) \end{pmatrix}}\right) \qquad (38)$$

for a particular scale σ. An orientation histogram is formed from gradient orientation within a region around keypoint. Peaks in the histogram correspond to the dominant direction of the local gradients. The highest peak is detected and any other local peak which is 80% of highest peak is also used to create a key point with that orientation. So, for a location with multiple peaks of similar magnitude, there will be multiple keypoints at same location, with same scale but different orientations.

Local Descriptor

The construction descriptor for keypoint is shown in Figure 3(d). An orientation histogram is created over 4×4 region. The Figure 2 shows eight directions for each orientation histograms, with the length of each arrow being the entry in the histogram bins. So 4×4 array of histogram with 8 bins each creates a 128 dimensional feature vector for each keypoint. For more details please refer to the original work (Lowe, 2004). For correspondence establishment we compute SIFT in between two images and find keypoints on both of them. Then a nearest neighbor approach can be applied for correspondence establishment among the 128 dimensional vectors. Figure 3(e) shows the result of the correspondence among stereo images. There are plenty of other method of finding correspondences like ASIFT (Mikolajczyk & Schmid, 2004), DAISY (Guo, Mu, Zeng, & Wang, 2010) etc. which have their own specialties. Readers are encouraged to read the original papers.

Epipolar Geometry

Epipolar geometry is a projective geometry between two views. It is independent of the scene and only depends upon camera parameters. Most of the details of this section has been taken from book (Hartley & Zisserman, 2000). Reader should follow (Hartley & Zisserman, 2000) for greater details. Figure 4(a) shows different geometric entities which are defined below.

Epipole

Epipole is the point of intersection of the line joining the camera centers (base line) with the image plane. Figure 4 shows the epipole E_L and E_R which are formed by the intersections of the line joining O_L and O_R with image plane.

Epipolar Plane

Epipolar plane is the plane containing the base line. Figure 4(a) shows points P_R and P_L are corresponding points which intersect to a scene point P and these 3 points along with camera center lies in a plane called epipolar plane.

Epipolar Line

This is the intersection of the epipolar plane with image plane. In Figure 4(a) line $E_R P_R$ and $E_L P_L$ are epipolar lines. It can be understood as the line in the second view of the ray back-projected from

Figure 4. (a) Epipolar plane, epipole and epiline, (b) fundamental matrix relates a point x in one image to a epipolar line l in other image (image courtesy: (Hartley & Zisserman, 2000, June)), (c) the set of images used for bundle adjustment, (d) the 3D point cloud obtained from bundle adjustment

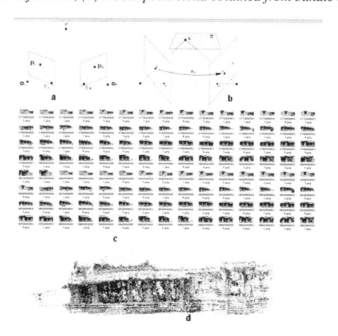

a point in first view and vice-versa. This epipolar line always passes through epipoles. For example $E_R P_R$ is the projection of $O_L P$. Any point in the ray $O_L P$ lies in the epiline $E_R P_R$. So, if we take a point x in an image, its corresponding point in other image must lie on the epiline, which makes correspondence search for that point along a line, instead of whole image.

Fundamental Matrix

Figure 4(b) shows point x and x' are correspondent and x' lies on the epipolar line l'. Also epipole e' is on the line l' and so, l' = e' × x'. Now, consider a plane π not passing through the camera center. The ray through x meets the plane π at X and then projected in x' in second image. This is a transfer of point x and can be related by a homography H_π (Hartley & Zisserman, 2000), i.e. x' = H_πx. So, l' = e' × x' = e' × H_π x = $[e']_x H_{pi} x$ = Fx. We define $F = [e']_x H_{pi}$ as fundamental matrix. Here,

$$[e']_x = \begin{pmatrix} 0 & -e'_3 & e'_2 \\ e'_3 & 0 & -e'_1 \\ -e'_2 & e'_1 & 0 \end{pmatrix}, e' = e_1', e_2', e_3'.$$

Note that till now we have only used the information that there are some points which are correspondent in two or more images. All geometric entities are in projective domain.

Properties of Fundamental Matrix

- If F is the fundamental matrix for a camera pair (P_1, P_2) then, F^T is the fundamental matrix for the pair (P_2, P_1).
- If for a point x in first image the epipolar line l' in second image relates by l' = Fx, then for reverse, l = F^Tx'.
- The epipole lies in epipolar line l' = Fx. So, $e'^T l' = e'^T F x = (e'^T F) x = 0$, which implies, $e'^T F = 0$.

- If P_1 and P_2 are two camera matrices pair, then for any point x in first camera the ray is defined by X $(\lambda) = P_1^+ x \, \lambda \, C$. P_1^+ is the pseudo inverse of 3×4 matrix P_1, such that $P_1 P_1^+ = I$. Two points on this ray X (λ), $P_1^+ X$ (when $\lambda = 0$) and C (when $\lambda = \infty$) projects on another camera P_2 in locations $P_2 P_1^+ x$ and $P_2 C$ respectively. Now the epipolar line passing these two points in second image can be expressed as l' = $(P_2 C) \times (P_2 P_1^+ x)$. Now, $P^2 C = e$, by definition. So, l' = $[e']_x (P_2 P_1^+) x = F x$ and

$$F = [e']_x \left(P_2 P_1^+ \right)$$

- If H is a 4×4 projective transformation matrix then the fundamental matrix F corresponding to camera pair (P_1, P_2) and $(P_1 H, P_2 H)$ are same. Readers are encouraged to prove it.
- The above property can be used to derive the canonical form of the camera matrix where the first camera is *always* [I|0]. This is always possible because we can find out some H which makes $P_1 H$ = [I|0] keeping fundamental matrix F same.
- The *projective* camera matrices corresponding to a fundamental matrix F may be chosen as:

$$P_1 = \begin{bmatrix} I & |0 \end{bmatrix} \tag{39}$$

$$P_2 = \begin{bmatrix} [e']_x & F & |e' \end{bmatrix} \tag{40}$$

For proof see (Hartley & Zisserman, 2000).

The fundamental matrix can be computed in a similar way as homography computation. The details about this computation can be found in (Hartley & Zisserman, 2000).

Essential Matrix

In the previous section we have talked on how to determine camera matrix using point correspondences between a pair of images. The camera matrix, estimated using fundamental matrix, is in projective domain and the reconstruction of the scene 3D point is not Euclidean. But if we have only internal calibration K as additional information we can estimate the 3×4 camera matrix which is Euclidean. The only parameter of camera we need to estimate while K and fundamental F between stereo pair is known is external calibration [R|t] as discussed in section 2.3. As we know the internal calibration matrix K, we can calculate

$x = K^{-1}x$ for an image point x. This $\hat{x}$ is point expressed in Euclidean coordinate corresponding to point x, if K is Euclidean. The camera matrix P is then expressed as $P_1 = [I|0]$ and $P_2 = [R|t]$ for stereo image as the effect of K is removed by applying K^{-1}. If x and x' are correspondent point in stereo image and F is the fundamental matrix between the image pair then we can express:

$$x'^T F x = 0$$

$$\left(K'^{-1} x' \right)^T F K^{-1} x = 0$$

$$x'^T K'^{-T} F K^{-1} x = 0$$

$$x'^T E x = 0$$

where, $E = K'^{-T} F K^{-1}$ is known as *Essential matrix*, and is expressed as $[t]_x R$, which only relates to rotation and translation of camera w.r.t world coordinate system. To estimate the cameras as $P_1 = [I|0]$ and $P_2 = [R|t]$, E needs to be factorized. But as discussed in (Hartley & Zisserman, 2000), the factorisation of essential matrix yields four combinations of camera matrix. E is factorized

using SVD as $E = U$ diag(1, 1,0)V^T. If the first camera of the stereo is $P_1 = [I|0]$, then the second camera can be one of the following four;

$$P_2 = \left[UWV^T \mid u_3 \right] or \left[UWV^T \mid -u_3 \right]$$
$$or \left[UW^T V^T \mid u_3 \right] or \left[UW^T V^T \mid -u_3 \right]$$

where $W = \begin{pmatrix} 0 & -1 & 0 \\ 1 & 0 & 0 \\ 0 & 0 & 1 \end{pmatrix}$

Given these four choice of the rotation and translation of the second camera, one of them is chosen as a valid one if for image points the depth of the scene points is in front of both cameras. To find out this let's assume x = w(x, y, 1)^T = PX, where P = [M |p$_4$] and X = (X, 1). M is the first 3×3 matrix of camera matrix P. then w=P^{3T}X = P^{3T}(X - C), as $PC = 0$ for camera center $\hat{C} = (C, 1)$. So, w=m^{3T} $(X - C)$, where m^3 is the principal ray direction as discussed in pin hole camera model. So, w is the dot product of the ray from the camera center with the principal ray. As, principal ray is in front of the camera this dot product can tell us whether the ray from the derived camera matrix id front of the camera or not. The depth of the X=(X, Y, Z, T) using camera P can be estimated by,

$$depth\left(x, P \right) = \frac{sign \ (\det M) w}{T m^3}$$

For the camera coordinate system described previously, if det $(M) > 0$, then depth of the point should be positive. The summary of calibrating stereo pair from images is

- Calibrate the internal calibration of both the cameras using Zhang (2000, November) technique or any other technique available.

- Find out correspondence between images using any approaches discussed earlier.
- Compute fundamental matrix using these correspondences.
- Compute essential matrix using fundamental matrix and internal calibration.
- Estimate the rotation and translation from essential matrix using the decomposition and depth testing (called chierality [Hartley, 1998]).

This procedure will give us the K and $[R|T]$ for camera pairs using images.

3D POINT ESTIMATION

Triangulation

In previous sections we have seen how to calibrate a stereo pair. After calibration, the remaining thing is to estimate the 3D location of a scene point. Triangulation is a well known technique to achieve this. A 3D point X satisfies $P_1X = x$ and $P_2X = x'$ for camera pairs P_1 and P_2 and corresponding points x and x'. We can write PX × x = 0. This cross product yields:

$$x\left(p^{3T}x\right) - \left(p^{1T}x\right) = 0$$

$$y\left(p^{3T}x\right) - \left(p^{2T}x\right) = 0$$

$$x\left(p^{2T}x\right) - y\left(p^{1T}x\right) = 0$$

where, p^{iT} is the ith row of P_1. Similar equation can be formed using P_2 and then stacked up all equations to solve simultaneously. This is of the form AX=0, and can be solved using SVD (Hartley & Zisserman, 2000).

One of the examples of application of this method is to find distance of pedestrian from car. A stereo camera is mounted in car. The cameras are pre calibrated both internally and externally.

The humans are identified in video and corresponding pixels are found out on humans in both the cameras. Then using the techniques described here one can find out the distance of the pedestrian from the car.

Bundle Adjustment

The more generic way to estimate cameras as well as the 3D structure from set of images is bundle adjustment, Bill Triggs (2000). Bundle Adjustment is a non-linear optimisation which minimises the following objective function:

$$min_{c_j, b_i} \sum_{i=1}^{n} \sum_{j=1}^{m} Vis_{ij} \, D\left(Proj\left(c_j, b_i\right) x_{ij}\right) \qquad (41)$$

where, Vis_{ij} is the visibility of the ith 3D point in the jth camera, *Proj* is the function which projects a 3D point b_i onto camera c_j, x_{ij} is the actual projection of the ith point onto the jth camera and D is the Euclidean distance. Noah Snavely (2006) distributes software of sparse bundle adjustment using a SBA package by Lourakis (2009). The optimisation is done through Levenberg-Marquardt technique.

The key steps of the reconstruction procedure are:

- Find out correspondences among image set.
- Pick up correspondences that satisfy epipolar geometry.
- Pick two images with maximum correspondences.
- Initialize focal length as well as Z of all corresponding pixels with some value and calculate X and Y according to pinhole camera model.
- Optimize the Equation 41 to get the cameras and 3D points. Repeat the following for all remaining cameras.
- Next find out the cameras which have considerable overlap with the estimated cameras.

- Initialize the new camera parameters using DLT method from the 3D to 2D correspondences in overlapped region.
- Initialize the 3D point using triangulation method.
- Optimize all cameras and 3D points using Equation 41.

Figure 3(d) shows a typical example of bundle adjustment where, 120 images are used to reconstruct 3D point cloud and their point cloud. Sameer Agarwal et.al (2009) used this technique for reconstructing scenes in large scale internet collections of images.

Dense 3D Reconstruction

Till now we have discussed the reconstruction from point correspondence which are sparse (i.e we can estimate the 3D location from certain amount of pixels). Dense reconstruction tries to reconstruct the scene with much more 3D points. Sparse reconstruction plays an important role for providing camera parameters and the scene location in 3D. The maximum and minimum along X, Y and Z are recorded from sparse reconstruction. The whole bounding volume is now discretised into smaller units called voxels. Voxel is the unit in a discretized 3D scene, like pixel is a unit in image. The smaller the voxel, finer the resolution of the scene. Now a scene consists of finite number of voxels which are displayed after processing. The voxel which are not part of the scene are not displayed. Figure 5 shows an example of a voxel space. A voxel V is projected through camera matrices into all images in locations $v1$, $v2$, $v3$ and $v4$. If a voxel is on the surface it is displayed (rendered) otherwise it is made off for rendering. The role of the dense reconstruction is to find out which voxels needs to be displayed (ON) and which needs not to be displayed (OFF) and also making continuous surface in 3D. Before we go into the techniques we need to define a couple of things.

Photoconsistency

This is a constraint which needs to be satisfied making voxels on or off. If a voxel is on the scene surface it will project in all its visible images into corresponding location which should have "similar color" under the assumption of constant illumination and Lambertian reflectance. This constraint is called photoconsistency. In Figure 5(a) voxel V is photoconsistent that project into $v1,v2,v3,v4$ which are corresponding location in image 1,2 3 and 4.

Visual Hull

The object is being reconstructed is segmented in images and they are called silhouette images. After calibrating the cameras this silhouette are back-projected to a generalised cone in 3D containing the actual object. Figure 5(b) shows the cones generated by back projected rays from cameras. The intersection of two or more cones is called visual hull as shown in Figure 5(c).

Now we will discuss some of the techniques in brief for dense reconstruction. Readers are encouraged to read the original papers of them.

Space Carving

Space Carving introduced by Seitz et.al. (2000), is a technique for dense reconstruction using plane sweep. Photoconsistent shapes are the key ingredients of space carving. From (Kutulakos & Seitz 2000) let's define photo hull first. Let V be an arbitrary subset in $\mathfrak{R}^3\mathfrak{R}^3$. If $V*$ is the union of all photoconsistent shapes in V then $V*$ is called photo hull. Space carving iteratively removes portion of a volume like in Figure 7 until it converges to photo hull. The most efficient algorithm for space carving is multiplane sweep (Kutulakos & Seitz 2000).Let's discuss the plane sweep algorithm

Figure 5. (a) A cube is a voxel and set of cubes is voxel space. A voxel V, if it is on the surface of the 3D object should project in all its visible images in corresponding location, (b) the cone formed by the back-projected ray from the images, (c) shows the intersection of these cones called visual hull(images are taken from Wikipedia), (d) - (e) the original images and (f), and (g) shows the output of the dense reconstruction using space carving

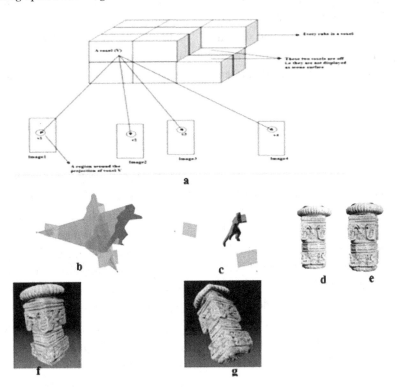

- Initialise a bounding volume V and a plane π for plane sweep.
- Intersect the plane with the current form of V.
- For each voxel v on π, let $c_1, c_2, c_3...c_k$ be the cameras above π where v project to a unmarked pixel. Determine the photoconsistency of v and if it is inconsistent, remove v from V and update $V = V - v$, otherwise mark the pixel where v projects.
- Move π downward one voxel width and repeat step 2 until pi traverses all voxels.

To ensure the consideration of all cameras the plane sweep is performed in all six (increasing and decreasing X, Y and Z) direction in multi sweep algorithm.

Step 1: Apply plane sweep in six principle direction and update V accordingly.

Step 2: For all voxels whose consistency was evaluated in more than one sweep, determine their photoconsistency using cameras $c_1, c_2, c_3...c_k$, which participated in consistency check in some plane sweep earlier. If the voxel v is inconsistent carve it out and set $V = V - v$.

Step 3: If no voxels are removed in step 1 and 2 set $V^* = V$ and stop, otherwise repeat step 1.

Figure 5(d), 5(e) shows the images used for reconstruction and Figure 5(f) and 5(g) show the output reconstruction. The result clearly shows that the reconstruction is quiet dense.

Volumetric Graph Cut

George et.al (2007) proposes a technique for dense reconstruction using graph cut. They construct a graph whose nodes consists of all voxels of size $h \times h \times h$ with two additional nodes called source and sink. The nodes are connected with a 6-neighborhood grid. If two voxels centered at x_i and x_j are neighbors then the edge weight between two nodes is:

$$w_{ij} = \frac{4\pi h^2}{3}\rho\left(\left(x_i + x_j\right) / /2\right)$$

where ρ is a photoconsistency function described in (Vogiatzis, Esteban, Torr, & Cipolla 2007). Each voxels are projected into the visual hull and the camera visibility is determined from the projected point in visual hull. The edge between source and voxel node is weighted as $w_b = \lambda h^3$. Now set of inner and outer voxels are identified using silhouette cue and all outer voxels that are part of bounding box are connected with sink with infinite cost. Figure 6(a) shows a typical graph structure.

PMVS

Furukawa et.al (2010) proposes a patch based technique for surface reconstruction. Features are detected using DOG and Harris operators. These features are matched using epipolar geometry and a patch in 3D is created with its center $c(p)$, normal $n(p)$ and $R(p)$ where $c(p)$ is calculated by triangulation of the corresponding pixels and

$$n(p) = c\left(p\right)\vec{O}(I_i) / \left|c\left(p\right)\vec{O}(I_i)\right|, \quad R(p)=I_i.$$

The reference image is used to calculate photo consistency i.e. correlation among the window centered at candidate point. The $c\,(p)$ always lies along the ray of image $R\,(p)$. Both $c\,(p)$ and $n\,(p)$ are optimised for maximizing photoconsistency. This patch still produces sparse reconstruction. To make it further dense patch expansion procedure is applied where neighboring image cells are used to construct a new patch with new normal, patch center. The visibility of the patch in different images are also computed using threshold. If the photoconsistency is under some threshold while

Figure 6. (a) Graph structure of volumetric graph cut method (b),(c),(d) shows the original images, (e) shows the output of the dense reconstruction using volumetric graph cut, (f),(g) the dense reconstruction using PMVS The original images are same as of Figure 5(d) and 5(e)

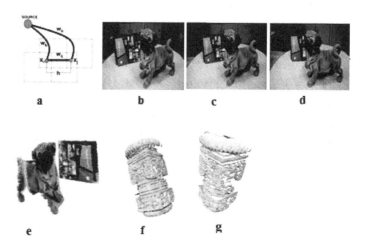

computing with camera C with reference camera then C is in the visible set of cameras for that patch. During the selection of the neighboring patch occlusion and depth test is carried on to avoid noises. Figures 6(f) and 6(g) shows the dense reconstruction obtained through this procedure on the original images of Figures 5(d) and 5(e).

Microsoft Kinect

We have discussed about 3D reconstruction from multiple images both sparse and dense. Microsoft recently released a device Kinect which captures 3D scene at 30fps. It has a RGB camera and IR camera as shown in Figure 7(a). Figure 7(b) and 7(c) shows the point cloud as well as the RGB image from Kinect. The resolution of RGB and IR is 640 × 480, i.e. VGA.

Resolution Enhancement Using Kinect and HD Cameras

The resolution of Kinect is 640 × 480 i.e. VGA. If the resolution can be made higher it can be rendered well and also can be made free of noise. Suvam et.al (2012) proposes a methodology for enhancing the resolution of Kinect. They use additional HD cameras along with Kinect. The HD cameras and Kinect are registered using epipolar geometry i.e. fundamental matrix and essential matrix. Kinect point clouds are transferred using the rotation and translation matrix (external calibration) to one of the HD cameras. After transformation the point cloud contains holes as the resolution is higher. They frame the problem of resolution enhancement of the Kinect point cloud using Markov Random Field (MRF) based techniques. Here, the problem is converted to a voxel labeling problem,

Figure 7. (a) The device Kinect by Microsoft, (b) the point cloud from Kinect, (c) RGB image from Kinect, (d) the graph structure (image courtesy Y. Boykov and V. Kolmogorov, "An experimental comparison of min-cut/max-flow algorithms for energy minimization in vision,"), (e) a RGB image from Kinect, and (f) is the corresponding low resolution transferred image, (g) is the high resolution point cloud

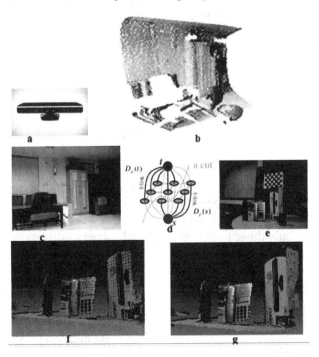

where if a voxel is the part of the surface under consideration then it is labeled as "ON" else if it belongs to non-surface, it is labeled as "OFF".

The voxel labeling problem can be represented as one of the energy minimization function of the form

$$E\left(L\right) = \sum_{p \in \mathcal{P}} D_p\left(L_p\right) + \sum_{(p,q) \in \mathcal{N}} V_{p,q}(L_p, L_q) \qquad (42)$$

where $\wp$ is the set of voxels to be labeled, $L = \{L_p | \in \wp\}$ is a 0-1 labeling of the voxel p, $D_p(.)$ is data term measuring the consistency of the label assignment with the available data, N defines a neighbourhood system for the voxel space and each $V_{p,q}(.)$ is a smoothness term that measures the consistency of labeling at neighbouring voxels. The above energy minimization problem is represented in graphical form; we get an n-terminal graph. Each voxel is represented as a node in the graph and each node is connected to the other nodes by two possible links, the t-links and the n-links. Each of the voxels is connected to both source and sink nodes by t-links with edge weights defined according to the data term of the energy function. In addition, the voxel nodes are also connected to each other with n-links, with edge strengths defined according to the neighbourhood interaction or smoothness term. A typical graph is shown in Figure 7(d). The data term is photoconsistency and the smoothness term is taken as the distance from the approximate smooth surface fitted locally on the point cloud. A minimum cut through this graph gives us a minimum energy of the configuration, provided the edge weights are specified according to the energy function. After the cut, the graph forms two disjoint connected graphs such that only those nodes remain connected to the source node that remains "ON" and the remaining nodes are connected to sink. Figure 7(e) shows the image, Figure 7(f) is low resolution point cloud and Figure 7(g) is the resultant high resolution point cloud.

FUTURE RESEARCH

We have discussed basic geometric framework and camera models. We also discussed both sparse and dense reconstruction. The dense reconstruction technology can be improved to make it more automatic and making robust to occlusion. Although PMVS deals with occlusion, still there is a scope of having a continuous framework, rather than discrete, to deal with dense reconstruction more efficiently. The methodology described is for static scenes. The reconstruction of dynamic scene will be of great challenge and can be of future research. Although there are papers and some state of the art available, but still it is a very good future work which could be carried on. The dynamic reconstruction and motion capture can also be done using Kinect.

ACKNOWLEDGMENT

I would like to thank Miss. Soumali Roychowdhury for her continuous inspiration and helping me in completing this chapter. I would also like to thank Mr. Suvam Patra, IIT Delhi for technical correction and Mr. Kinshuk Sarabhai and Mr. Phanindra Angara for result generation in different section.

REFERENCES

Agarwal, S., Snavely, N., Simon, I., Seitz, S. M., & Szeliski, R. (2009). Building rome in a day. In *Proceedings of International Conference on Computer Vision.* Kyoto, Japan: IEEE Press.

Furukawa Y. & Ponce J. (2010). Accurate, dense, and robust multiview stereopsis. *IEEE Transactions on Pattern Analysis & Machine Intelligence, 32*(8). doi:1362-1376 2010.

Guo, Y., Mu, Z., Zeng, H., & Wang, K. (2010). Fast rotation-invariant DAISY descriptor for image keypoint matching. ISM, 183-190.

Hartley, R., & Zisserman, A. (2000). *Multiview geometry in computer vision*. Cambridge, UK: Cambridge University Press.

Hartley, R. I. (1998). Chierality. *International Journal of Computer Vision, 26*(1), 4161. doi:10.1023/A:1007984508483.

Kutulakos, K. N., & Seitz, S. M. (2000). A theory of shape by space carving. *International Journal of Computer Vision, 38*(3), 199–218. doi:10.1023/A:1008191222954.

Lourakis, M. I. A., & Argyros, A. A. (2009). SBA: A software package for generic sparse bundle adjustment. *ACM Transactions on Mathematical Software, 36*(1). doi:10.1145/1486525.1486527.

Lowe, D. G. (2004). Distinctive image features from scale-invariant keypoints. *International Journal of Computer Vision, 60*(2), 91–110. doi:10.1023/B:VISI.0000029664.99615.94.

Maybank, S. (1992). *Theory of reconstruction from image motion*. Berlin: Springer-Verlag.

Mikolajczyk, K., & Schmid, C. (2004). Scale and affine invariant interest point detectors. *International Journal of Computer Vision, 60*(1), 63–86. doi:10.1023/B:VISI.0000027790.02288.f2.

Mundy, J. L., & Zisserman, A. (Eds.). (1992). *Geometric invariance in computer vision*. Cambridge, MA: The MIT Press.

Patra, S., Bhowmick, B., Banerjee, S., & Kalra P. (2012). High resolution point cloud generation from kinect and HD cameras using graph cut. *VISAPP,* (2), 311-316.

Snavely, N., Seitz, S., & Szeliski, R. (2006). Photo tourism: Exploring photo collections in 3D. In Proceedings of SIGGRAPH. *New York: ACM Press.*

Triggs, B., McLauchlan, P., Hartley, R. I., & Fitzgibbon, A. (2000). Bundle adjustment a modern synthesis. Vision Algorithms: Theory and Practice. *Lecture Notes in Computer Science, 1883,* 298–372. doi:10.1007/3-540-44480-7_21.

Vogiatzis, G., Esteban, C. H., Torr, P. H. S., & Cipolla, R. (2007). Multiview stereo via volumetric graph-cuts and occlusion robust photo-consistency. *IEEE Transactions on Pattern Analysis and Machine Intelligence, 29*(12), 2241–2246. doi:10.1109/TPAMI.2007.70712 PMID:17934232.

Zhang, Z. (2000). An exible new technique for camera calibration. *IEEE Transactions on Pattern Analysis and Machine Intelligence, 22*(11), 1330–1334. doi:10.1109/34.888718.

Chapter 3
An Introduction to Wavelet-Based Image Processing and its Applications

Mahesh Kumar H. Kolekar
Indian Institute of Technology, India

G. Lloyds Raja
Indian Institute of Technology, India

Somnath Sengupta
Indian Institute of Technology, India

ABSTRACT

This chapter gives a brief introduction of wavelets and multi-resolution analysis. Wavelets overcome the limitations of Discrete Cosine Transform and hence found its application in JPEG 2000. In wavelet transform, the scaling functions provide approximations or low-pass filtering of the signal and the wavelet functions add the details at multiple resolutions or perform high-pass filtering of the signal. Applying Discrete Wavelet Transform to an image decomposes it into LL, LH, HL, and HH subbands. The low frequency LL band carries most of the significant information in the image. Wavlet transform allows us to analyse the local properties of a signal or image by shifting and scaling operations. The inherent properties of wavelets makes it useful in image denoising, edge detection, image compression, compressed sensing and illumination normalization. The wavelet coefficients at various levels of decomposition follows a parent-child relationship.

INTRODUCTION TO WAVELETS AND MULTI-RESOLUTION ANALYSIS

In the family of transforms, Discrete Cosine Transform (DCT) is the most popular choice for image compression because of several advantages. However, DCT has performance limitations such as blocking artifacts at very low bit rates. In recent years, a new transformation technique has emerged as popular alternative to sinusoidal transforms at very low bit rates. Unlike DCT and Discrete Fourier Transform (DFT), which use sinusoidal waves as basis functions, wavelet transform use small waves of varying frequency and of limited extent, known as wavelets as basis. The wavelets can be scaled and shifted to analyze the spatial

DOI: 10.4018/978-1-4666-4558-5.ch003

frequency contents of an image at different resolutions and positions. A wavelet can therefore perform analysis of an image at multiple resolutions, making it an effective tool in multi-resolution analysis of images.

Furthermore, wavelet analysis performs what is known as space-frequency localization so that at any specified location in space, one can obtain its details in terms of frequency. It is like placing a magnifying glass above a photograph to explore the details around a specific location. The magnifying glass can be moved up or down to vary the extent of magnification, that is, the level of details and it can be slowly panned over the other locations of the photograph to extract those details. A classical sinusoidal transform does not allow such space-frequency localizations. If we consider the spatial array of pixels, it does not provide any spatial frequency information. On the other hand, the transformed array of coefficients contains spatial frequency information, but it does not give us any idea about the locations in the image where such spatial frequencies appear. The space-frequency localization capability of wavelets makes multi-resolution image analysis, representation and coding more efficient (Gonzalez, 2011; Haidekker, 2011).

MultiResolution Analysis (MRA) deals with analyzing the signal at different frequencies with different resolutions as follows: Good time resolution and poor frequency resolution at high frequencies, Good frequency resolution and poor time resolution at low frequencies. MRA is more suitable for short duration of higher frequency; and longer duration of lower frequency components. It is our common observation that the level of details within an image varies from location to location. Some locations contain significant details, where we require finer resolution for analysis and there are other locations, where a coarser resolution representation suffices. A multi-resolution representation of an image gives us a complete idea about the extent of the details existing at different locations from which we

can choose our requirements of desired details. Multi-resolution representation facilitates efficient compression by exploiting the redundancies across the resolutions. Wavelet transform is one of the popular, but not the only approach for multi-resolution image analysis. One can use any of the signal processing approaches to sub-band coding such as Quadrature Mirror Filters (QMF) in MRA (Gonzalez, 2011), (Haidekker, 2011). The main objective of this chapter is to make the reader aware of the basic aspects of wavelets and the current trends in wavelet based research. Wavelet transform has many applications in image processing, out of which few applications are discussed in this chapter to give the reader a feel of wavelet. In the case of Haar wavelet transform (Radomir and Bogdon, 2003), the scaling and wavelet basis functions are nothing but the rows of the N x N Haar transformation matrices.

Wavelet Basis Function

Wavelets are generated from a mother wavelet function $\varphi\left(x\right)$ by shifting it (by a value 'l') and scaling (by a value 's') as follows:

$$\varphi_{s,l}\left(x\right) = \frac{1}{\sqrt{s}}\varphi\left(\frac{x-l}{s}\right) \tag{1}$$

The different wavelet families make different trade-offs between how compactly the basis functions are localized in space and how smooth they are. We will discuss Daubechies wavelet and Haar Wavelet.

Daubechies Wavelet ·

Daubechies (Marc, Michel, Pierre, & Daubechies, 1992) is a family of popular wavelet filters having four or more coefficients. Coefficients of the low pass filter $h_0(n)$ for the four-coefficient Daubechies filter are as follows:

$$h(n) = \frac{1}{8}\left[\begin{array}{l}\left(1+\sqrt{3}\right),\left(3+\sqrt{3}\right),\\ \left(3-\sqrt{3}\right),\left(1-\sqrt{3}\right)\end{array}\right] \qquad (2)$$

DWT generates a set of basis functions or vectors. The basis functions consist of wavelet functions and scaling functions. Space spanned by 2^j basis vectors at level 'j' can be spanned by two sets of basis vectors φ and $\varnothing$ at level 'j-1'. Here φ and $\varnothing$ are wavelet and scaling functions respectively.

Haar Wavelet

Haar wavelet is one of the widely used wavelet basis function. It consists of a sequence of rescaled 'square-shaped' functions which together form a wavelet family or basis.

$$\varphi_{j,i}(x) = \begin{cases} +1\, when\, 0 \leq x \leq 1/2 \\ -1\, when\, \dfrac{1}{2} < x \leq 1 \\ \quad 0\ otherwise \end{cases} \qquad (3)$$

$$\varnothing(x) = \begin{cases} 1,\, when\ 0 \leq x \leq 1 \\ \quad 0,\ otherwise \end{cases}$$

Shifting and scaling operations are performed on the basis functions as follows:

$$\varphi_{j,i}(x) = 2^{\frac{j}{2}}\varphi(2^j x - i),\ \text{j=0,1......, i=0,}$$
$$\ldots\ldots 2^{j-1}$$

$$\phi_{j,i}(x) = 2^{\frac{j}{2}}\phi(2^j x - i),\ \text{j=0,1......, i=0,}$$
$$\ldots\ldots 2^{j-1} \qquad (4)$$

Different wavelets can be formed by binary dilation (scaling) and dyadic translation (shifting). Coefficients corresponding to $\varphi_{j,i}$ are averages

or sum coefficients. Coefficients corresponding to $\phi_{j,i}$ are differences or detail coefficients. $\varphi_{j,i}$ and $\phi_{j,i}$ together form the basis vectors. Only $\varphi_{0,0}$ is needed since others are expressed in terms of ϕ_i. When size of vector is $n=2^j$, 'j' levels of basis vectors are needed. There are $2^{j-1} + 2^{j-2} + ... + 2^0 = 2^j - 1$ basis vectors corresponding to detail coefficients and '1' basis vector corresponding to sum coefficient at 0th level. The rows of the transformation matrix 'H' is nothing but these basis vectors. The transformed vector can be written as

V'=V.H

Here V is the data vector which is usually a row vector. Composition of the matrices corresponding to all the data vectors gives the final transformed matrix. The Haar matrix is real and orthogonal. Therefore $H = H^*$ and $H^{-1} = H^T$, i.e., $H^T H = I$. An un-normalized 8-point Haar matrix H_8 is shown below:

$$H[m,n] = \begin{bmatrix} 1 & 1 & 1 & 1 & 1 & 1 & 1 & 1 \\ 1 & 1 & 1 & 1 & -1 & -1 & -1 & -1 \\ 1 & 1 & -1 & -1 & 0 & 0 & 0 & 0 \\ 0 & 0 & 0 & 0 & 1 & 1 & -1 & -1 \\ 1 & -1 & 0 & 0 & 0 & 0 & 0 & 0 \\ 0 & 0 & 1 & -1 & 0 & 0 & 0 & 0 \\ 0 & 0 & 0 & 0 & 1 & -1 & 0 & 0 \\ 0 & 0 & 0 & 0 & 0 & 0 & 1 & -1 \end{bmatrix} \qquad (5)$$

Normalized Haar transform matrix for sizes *N=2* is given below:

$$Hr_2 = \frac{1}{\sqrt{2}}\begin{bmatrix} 1 & 1 \\ 1 & -1 \end{bmatrix} \qquad (6)$$

For example: $h_\phi(n) = \left\{\dfrac{1}{\sqrt{2}}, \dfrac{1}{\sqrt{2}}\right\}$ denotes the FIR version of Haar scaling. It averages the adjacent pixels, which is similar to low-pass filtering in discrete space. $h_\varphi(n) = \left\{\dfrac{1}{\sqrt{2}}, \dfrac{-1}{\sqrt{2}}\right\}$ denotes the FIR version of Haar wavelet. It subtracts the adjacent pixels, which is similar to high-pass filtering in discrete space. Sections 5 and 5.1 illustrate the effect of these Haar filters on the image.

One Dimensional Discrete Wavelet Transform

DWT has gained widespread acceptance in signal processing and image compression. Because of their inherent multi-resolution nature, wavelet-coding schemes are especially suitable for applications where scalability and tolerable degradation are important. Joint Photographers Expert Group (JPEG) has released its new image coding standard JPEG-2000 which is based on DWT (Gonzalez, 2011; Haidekker, 2011).

Forward 1-D DWT

The wavelet series expansion of a sequence of numbers (samples) of a continuous function $S(t)$, the resulting coefficients are called discrete wavelet transform. 1-D DWT of a signal $S(n)$ can be computed as follows:

$$W_\varnothing(jo,k) = \frac{1}{\sqrt{M}}\sum_{n=0}^{M-1}S(n)\varnothing_{j0,k}(n), \qquad (7)$$

$$W\varphi(j,k) = \frac{1}{\sqrt{M}}\sum_{\substack{n=0 \\ j \geq j_0}}^{M-1}S(n)\varphi_{j,k}(n) \qquad (8)$$

Equation (7) represents the approximation coefficients and (8) represents the detail coefficients. 'M' refers to the number of samples. Here $\varnothing$ denotes the scaling function and φ denotes the wavelet basis functions.

Inverse 1-D DWT

The original signal $S(n)$ can be reconstructed from the wavelet coefficients as follows:

$$\begin{aligned}S(n) &= \frac{1}{\sqrt{N}}\sum_k W_\varnothing(jo,k)\varnothing_{j0,k},(n) \\ &+ \frac{1}{\sqrt{M}}\sum_{j=j0}^{\infty}\sum_k W\varphi(j,k)\varphi_{j,k}(n)\end{aligned} \qquad (9)$$

$\varnothing_{j0,k}$ and $\varphi_{j,k}$ are the transformation kernels corresponding to low-pass filter and high –pass filter respectively.

Two Dimensional Discrete Wavelet Transform (2D-DWT)

The DWT provides a compact representation of a signal's frequency components with strong spatial support. DWT decomposes a signal into frequency subbands at different scales from which it can be perfectly reconstructed. 2D-signals such as images can be decomposed using many wavelet decomposition filters in many different ways. The simplest approach for 2D implementation of DWT is to perform 1D DWT row-wise to obtain an intermediate image and then to perform the same 1D DWT column wise on the intermediate image to get the final result as shown in Figure 1. This is possible because the two-dimensional scaling functions can be expressed as separable.

For an image $S(m,n)$, 'm' and 'n' refers to the row and column indices respectively. The 2D filters can be realized by cascaded form of LPF and HPF and are separable in nature. The following filters are used in 2-D DWT:

- $\varnothing(m,n) \rightarrow$ Low pass filtered along rows and columns of the image
- $\varphi^H(m,n) \rightarrow$ High pass filtered along rows and low pass filtered along columns
- $\varphi^v(m,n) \rightarrow$ Low pass filtered along rows and high pass filtered along columns

Figure 1. Row-column computation of 2-D DWT

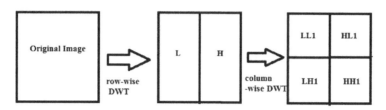

- $\varphi^D(m,n) \rightarrow$ High pass filtering along rows and columns

Every filter decimates the image by a factor '2'. So in total $\varnothing$, φ^H, φ^V and φ^D decimates the image by a factor of '4'. We only study the Haar wavelet filter and the pyramid decomposition method. *H, V* and *D* corresponds to high pass filtering along horizontal, vertical and diagonal of Figure 2 respectively.

Applying $h_\varphi(-m)$ or $h_\phi(-m)$ results in *N* samples in each case. Since their bandwidth is half individually, only *N/2* samples will be required in each case. So the result is down sampled by a factor '2' to get *N/2* samples. From Figure 2, it is observed that we have arrived at scale '*j*' starting from scale '*j+1*'. At scale '*j*', therefore the image has effectively lost the resolution by a factor '2' along both horizontal and vertical directions. Every subband contains *N/4th* of the total samples. It is therefore possible to have a perfect reconstruction of the original 2-D signal (image) by a reverse process of synthesis filtering which is just the mirror of Figure 2. In this case, the synthesis filter banks along the rows and columns will be associated with an up-sampling by a factor of two so that the reconstructed image can be shown at the original resolution. If the filters used doesn't induce any truncation, the original image can be recovered perfectly (Gonzalez, 2011; Haidekker, 2011).

Figure 2. Level-1 wavelet decomposition

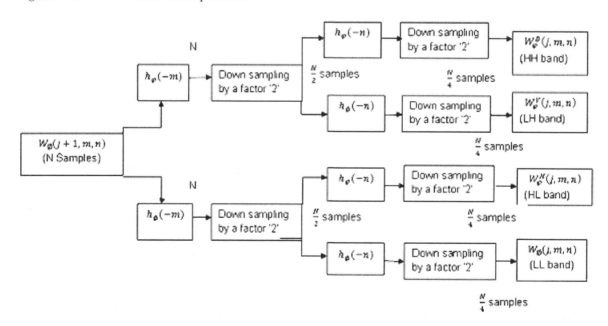

Forward 2-D DWT

For an image $S(m,n)$ having size NxN, the forward transform is defined in Box 1.

Inverse 2-D DWT

The original image can be recovered from the wavelet coefficients as shown in Box 2.

If the filters that are used does not introduce any truncation then the original image can be exactly reconstructed. The symbols used in equations (10), (11), and (12) are already explained in section 4. Section 4 also describes how Haar wavelets work when they are applied on an image. The distribution of the LL-subband approximates that of the original image but all non-LL subbands have a Laplacian distribution as. This remains valid at all decomposition levels (Haidekker, 2011).

The Haar Wavelet Transform (HWT)

The Haar wavelet is discontinuous and resembles a step function. For a function f, the HWT is defined as: (Gonzalez, 2011)

$$f \rightarrow \left(a^L \mid d^L \right)$$

$$a^L = \left(a_1, a_2, a_3 \ldots a_{N/2} \right)$$

$$d^L = \left(d_1, d_2, d_3 \ldots d_{N/2} \right) \tag{13}$$

where L is the decomposition level, a is the approximation subband and d is the detail subband.

$$a_m = \frac{f_{2m} + f_{2m-1}}{\sqrt{2}} \text{ for } m = 1, 2, \ldots, N/2$$

$$d_m = \frac{f_{2m} - f_{2m-1}}{\sqrt{2}} \text{ for } m = 1, 2, \ldots, N/2 \tag{14}$$

For example, if $f=\{f_1, f_2, f_3, f_4, f_5, f_6, f_7, f_8\}$ is a time-signal of length 8, then the HWT decomposes f into an approximation subband containing the Low frequencies and a detail subband containing the high frequencies:

Box 1.

$$W_{\varnothing}\left(jo, k1, k2\right) = \frac{1}{\sqrt{N^2}} \sum_{m=0}^{M-1} \sum_{n=0}^{N-1} S\left(m,n\right) \varnothing_{j0,k1,k2}\left(m,n\right) \tag{10}$$

$$W_{\varphi}\left(j, k1, k2\right) = \frac{1}{\sqrt{N^2}} \sum_{m=0}^{M-1} \sum_{n=0}^{N-1} S\left(m,n\right) \varphi^i_{j,k1,k2}\left(m,n\right), i \in \{H, V, D\} \tag{11}$$

Box 2.

$$S\left(m,n\right) = \frac{1}{\sqrt{N^2}} \left\{ \sum_{k1} \sum_{k2} W_{\varnothing}\left(jo, k1, k2\right) \varnothing_{j0,k1,k2}\left(m,n\right) + \sum_{i} \sum_{j=jo}^{\infty} \sum_{k1} \sum_{k2} W^i_{\varphi}\left(j, k1, k2\right) \varphi^i_{j,k1,k2}(m,n) \right\}$$
$$i \in \{H, V, D\} \tag{12}$$

$$\text{Low} = a = \left\{ f_2 + f_1, f_4 + f_3, f_6 + f_5, f_8 + f_7 \right\} \mid \sqrt{2}$$
(15)

$$\text{High} = d = \left\{ f_2 - f_1, f_4 - f_3, f_6 - f_5, f_8 - f_7 \right\} \mid \sqrt{2}$$
(16)

To apply HWT on images, we first apply a one level Haar wavelet to each row and then to each column of the resulting "image" of the first operation. The resulted image is decomposed into four subbands: LL, HL, LH, and HH subbands. (L=Low, H=High). The LL-subband contains an approximation of the original image while the other subbands contain the missing details. The LL-subband output from any stage can be decomposed further.

Figure 3 shows an image decomposed with level-3 HWT. Wavelet transformed images can be perfectly reconstructed using the four subbands using the inverse wavelet transform. The inverse of the Haar wavelet transform is computed in the reverse order as follows:

$$f = \left[\frac{a_1 - d_1}{\sqrt{2}}, \frac{a_1 + d_1}{\sqrt{2}}, \ldots \ldots \frac{a_{N/2} - d_{N/2}}{\sqrt{2}}, \frac{a_{N/2} + d_{N/2}}{\sqrt{2}} \right]$$
(17)

To apply IHWT on images, we first apply a one level inverse Haar wavelet to each column and then to each row of the resulting image of the first operation.

Haar Example

Example 1: For *f=(2,2,4,6,-2,-2,-2,0)* find the first averaged signal A^1 and the first detail signal D^1.

Solution: The trend a^1 and fluctuation d^1 satisfy

$$a^1 = \left(2\sqrt{2}, 5\sqrt{2}, -2\sqrt{2}, -\sqrt{2} \right)$$

$$d^1 = \left(0, -\sqrt{2}, 0, -\sqrt{2} \right)$$

Hence

A^1=(2,2,5,5,-2,-2,-1,-1)

D^1=(0,0,-1,1,0,0,-1,1)

This can be verified as follows:

Figure 3. Haar wavelet transformed image (a) original image (b) level-1 decomposition (c) level-2 decomposition (d) level-3 decomposition

$A^1 + D^1 = f$

Example 2: For *f=(2,2,4,6,-2,-2,-2,0)* find the second averaged signal A^2 and the second detail signal D^2.

Solution: We found in the previous example that $a^1 = \left(2\sqrt{2},\ 5\sqrt{2},\ -2\sqrt{2}, -\sqrt{2}\right)$.

The second trend is then
$$a^2 = (7,-3)$$
and the second fluctuation is $d^2 = \left(-7,-1\right)$.

Therefore,

$$A^2 = \left(\frac{7}{2},\frac{7}{2},\frac{7}{2},\frac{7}{2},\frac{-3}{2},\frac{-3}{2},\frac{-3}{2},\frac{-3}{2}\right)$$

$$D^2 = \left(\frac{-3}{2},\frac{-3}{2},\frac{3}{2},\frac{3}{2},\frac{-1}{2},\frac{-1}{2},\frac{1}{2},\frac{1}{2}\right)$$

This can be verified as $A^2+D^2=A^1$.

Parent-Child Relationship of Wavelet Transform

In a hierarchical subband system, every coefficient at a given scale can be related to a set of coefficients at the next finer scale of similar orientation. Only, the highest frequency subbands are exceptions, since there is no existence of finer scale beyond these. The coefficient at the coarser scale is called the parent and the coefficients at the next finer scale in similar orientation and same spatial location are the children. For a given parent, the set of all coefficients at all finer scales in similar orientation and spatial locations are called descendants. Similarly, for a given child, the set of coefficients at all coarser scales of similar orientation and same spatial location are called ancestors, (Gonzalez, 2011).

Consider an 8x8 image. The first level of decomposition results in 4 subbands of 4x4 pixels each. For any pixel in a given subband, we have corresponding pixels in the other subbands. In Figure 4(a), it is observed that one pixel in HL_3 subband corresponds to 4 pixels in the HL_2 subband. Similarly each pixel in HL_2 subband corresponds to 16 pixels in HL_1 subband. LL_3 is related to HH_3, HL_3 and LH_3. This follows a tree structure. In Figure 4(b), LLn has three descendants HLn, LHn and HHn while HLn has 4 descendants in HLn-1.

Applications of Wavelet Transform

Wavelet transforms are used in a wide range of image applications. These include Image and video compression, Feature detection and recognition, Image denoising, Face recognition. Most applications benefit from the statistical properties of the non-LL subbands (The Laplacian distribution of the wavelet coefficients in these subbands). Wavelet-based image processing approach has the following steps:

1. Compute the 2D-DWT of an image
2. Alter the transform coefficients (i.e. subbands)
3. Compute the inverse transform

Wavelet-Based Edge Detection

Figure 5(a) shows a gray image and its wavelet transform for one-level of decomposition. Note the horizontal edges of the original image are present in the HL subband of the upper-right quadrant of Figure 5(b). The vertical edges of the image can be similarly identified in the LH subband of the lower-left quadrant. To combine this information into a single edge image, we simply zero the LL subband of the transform, compute the inverse transform, and take the absolute value (Avijit,

Figure 4. (a) Parent-child dependencies of sub bands (b) tree structure of wavelet subbands

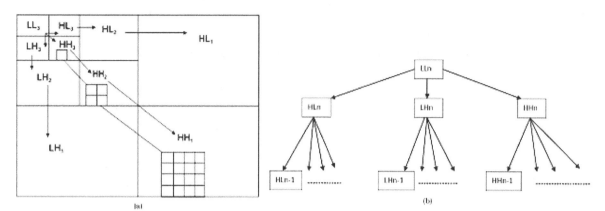

Nilanjan, Santanu, & Intrajit, 2009). Figure 5(d) shows the modified transform and resulting edge image.

Wavelet-Based Image Denoising

The general wavelet-based algorithm for denoising the image is shown in Algorithm 1.

After performing two-level decomposition of a noisy image, we threshold all the non-LL sub-bands at both decomposition levels by 85. Then we perform the inverse wavelet transform on the LL-subband and the modified non-LL subbands to obtain the de-noised image shown in Figure 6(a) in which noise reduction and slightly blurred

edges are visible (Maurits & Dirk, 1997). The loss of edge detail can be reduced by zeroing the non-LL subbands at the first decomposition level and only the HH-subband at the second level. Then we apply the inverse transform to obtain the de-noised image in Figure 6(b).

Applications of Wavelet in Compressed Sensing

Traditional Shannon's sampling theorem states that to reconstruct an image effectively from its samples, we need to sample the image at the Nyquist rate. Such a high number of samples may not be needed for all the image processing

Algorithm 1. Image denoising

```
Input: Noisy Image, type of wavelet basis function
Output: De-noised Image
1. Load Noisy Image I_noise
2. Compute:  [I_LL, I_HL, I_LH, I_HH ]= dwt2(I_noise (m,n), 'wavelet basis') // computing 2-D DWT
3. Threshold every pixel in  I_HL, I_LH and I_HH              //threshold non-LL subbands
                              If Ii(m,n)>τ                          // τ is
the threshold

                                      Ii(m,n)=0

                    end
4.  Compute inverse wavelet transform
R_LL = exp (log S_LL - log L_LL)
```

Figure 5. Wavelet-based edge detection (a) original image (b) level-1 decomposition (c) transform modified by zeroing the LL subband (d) edge image

(a)　　　　　　(b)　　　　　　(c)　　　　　　(d)

applications such as Magnetic Resonance Imaging (MRI). These applications needs a sampling function that samples the image by collecting low number of samples (i.e. far less than the Nyquist rate). The main objective of the CS concept is to reduce the necessary number of measurements for image reconstruction. A Sampling pattern which has both computational efficiency and less memory requirement is shown in Figure 7(b). Variable Density sampling pattern (Zhongmin and Gonzalo, 2010) contains only exponential terms. Assuming the size of the image as M ×N, the probability that the (m, n)th coefficient is sampled is given by:

Figure 6. (a) De-noised image obtained by thresholding all non-LL subbands (b) denoised image generated by zeroing the non-LL subbands

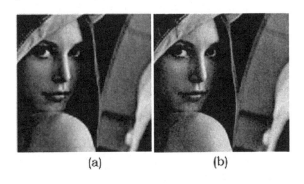

(a)　　　　　　　　(b)

$$P_F(m,n) = \exp\left[-\frac{\left(\sqrt{\left(\frac{m}{M}\right)^2 + \left(\frac{n}{N}\right)^2}\right)^{a_F}}{\sigma_F^2}\right] \quad (18)$$

where $-M/2 \leq m < M/2$ and $-N/2 \leq n < N/2$. a_F is a parameter characterizing the decay of the sampling probability. σ_F is a parameter tuned to obtain the desired number of samples. Note that $a_F, \sigma_F > 0$ and $0 < P_F(m, n) < 1$. Here $P_F(m, n)$ is the probability function. This sampling pattern was derived based on the assumption that most of the information in the image lies in the low frequency subband. So it collects more low frequency samples and comparatively very less high frequency samples.

The qualitative comparison of the boat image reconstructed using different sampling schemes is given in Figure 7 (c)-(g). It can be observed than the reconstructed image using wavelet-based scheme looks far better than the blurred and noisy images obtained using the other techniques like Scrambled Block Hadamard Ensemble (SBHE), Log-spiral sampling pattern, Radial sampling pattern, Model-guided Adaptive Recovery for Compressive Sensing (MARX). It is also observed that the reconstructed image in Figure 7(c) has almost all the vital information present in the original image shown in Figure 7(a) in spite of compressive sampling in the wavelet domain.

As shown in Table 1, it is evident that MARX took 19600 samples to yield a low PSNR of around 35dB. But the wavelet based variable density sampling yields PSNR around 42dB with only 17160 samples. This shows that the reconstructed image using wavelet-based scheme is of good quality. The scan time in MRI can be reduced using wavelet based sampling method. MRI image can be effectively reconstructed from the frequency domain information collected by this sampling pattern. The algorithm for compressive sampling using wavelets (Lloyds & Kolekar, 2012) is as follows:

Variable density sampling pattern is designed based on the prior knowledge about the inherent statistical distributions that natural images exhibit in the sparse wavelet domain. The sampling scheme works well for wide range of images including medical images. Moreover the sampling pattern is designed such that it doesnot have any image dependent parameter. MRI device is known for its long scanning time. Compressive sensing can speed-up the data acquisition process in MRI. Figure 7(d),(e),(f) and (g) gives a set of reconstructed images using various sampling approaches. It can be observed that the image reconstructed using wavelet based variable density sampling scheme looks visually impressive compared to that of other methods.

DWT Based Still Image Compression System

It may be noted from the results of DWT applied over the images that mostly the LL subband at the highest level of decomposition has significant

Algorithm 2. Compressed Sensing

```
Input: Original Image
Output: Reconstructed image from less number of wavelet coefficients.
1. Load the input image I of size MxN.
2. Compute DWT of input image to transform it to frequency domain
[I_LL, I_HL, I_LH, I_HH]= dwt2(I, 'haar')
3. For every pixel in I_LL(m,n)
Compute:    P_F (m, n) using equation (180)    with σ_F =0.501 and a_F = 3.5
If (P_F (m, n)=1)
                        S(m,n)=1   // Sampling pattern
Else
S(m,n)=0
4. Compute   I_CS(m,n)= I_LL(m,n) .* S(m,n).  // Sampling the image in frequency domain
5. Compute the IDWT using I_CS(m,n), I_HL, I_LH and I_HH. This results in reconstructed
image I_rec.
I_rec=idwt2 (I_LL, I_HL, I_LH, I_HH, 'haar')
6. Apply min-TV algorithm(Emmanuel, Justin and Terrance, 2006) or any denoising algo-
rithm to the image I_rec to eliminate the noise.
7. Compute peak signal to noise ratio of input and output images to test the perfor-
mance of the algorithm.
```

Figure 7. (a) Original image (b) variable density sampling pattern with $\sigma_F =0.501$ and $a_F = 3.5$. (c),(d),(e),(f),(g) reconstructed image using wavelet based variable density Gaussian sampling, scrambled block Hadamard ensemble, log-spiral sampling pattern, radial sampling pattern, model-guided adaptive recovery for compressive sensing respectively

Table 1. Comparison of the wavelet based compressed sensing with the existing techniques

		Wavelet Based Variable Density Gaussian Sampling Function	MARX	Radial	Log-Spiral	SBHE
No. of Samples		17160	19600	20000	20000	20000
PSNR in dB	Baboon	42.67	35.60	26.30	24.12	22.45
	Lena	42.45	36.00	29.04	28.55	26.13
	Boats	42.76	34.75	25.89	25.62	22.70

information content and all other subbands have less significant content. This is expected, since all natural images are rich in low frequency information content, as compared to the high-frequency content and the results demonstrate excellent energy compaction properties of DWT. This property can be very effectively utilized to achieve image compression (Zhigang and Yuan, 2008). Figure 8(a) shows the block diagram of an image compression and coding system based on DWT. The DWT coefficients are suitably quantized and the quantized coefficients are grouped within the subband or across the subbands, depending upon

the coding scheme employed. The grouping basically exploits the self-similarity of DWT across different subbands. The quantization and subband coefficient grouping are integrated in some of the coding schemes. Finally, the quantized and grouped DWT coefficients are encoded through a variable length coder, before generating the encoded bitstream. Figure 8(b) shows the block diagram of the decoder, which does the reversal of the encoder operations to reconstruct the image. Exact reconstruction is never possible, since the quantization is employed. However, it has been observed that at very low bit-rate, DWT shows better reconstruction results as compared to block-based DCT at comparable bit-rate and does not suffer from blocking artifacts as in DCT.

Wavelet Based Retinex Method for Illumination Normalization

Retinex theory mainly compensate for the images affected by illumination (Lloyds & Kolekar, 2012; Shan Du, 2005; Ming and Xingbo, 2010). Based on Retinex image formation model:

$$S(x,y) = R(x, y) * L(x, y) \qquad (19)$$

An image is pixel-by-pixel product of the ambient illumination and the scene reflectance. As the ambient illumination is independent of object itself, only the scene reflectance reflects the inhesion characteristic of object itself. Illumination is a kind of low-frequency image information which is slow changing, and reflectance contains the most high-frequency detailed image information. The Retinex theory deal with the problem of separating the two quantities: first estimating the illumination and then obtaining the reflectance by division. From the mathematical point of view based on logarithmic domain, complex multiplication can be converted to a simple addition operation. So the first step taken by most Retinex Algorithms is the

conversion of the given image into Logarithmic domain as shown below:

$$\log S = \log R + \log L \qquad (20)$$

First, the image is subjected to wavelet decomposition. Second, the horizontal and vertical low-frequency component LL obtained by wavelet transform is processed by Retinex algorithm. And then an enhanced image is obtained by computing inverse wavelet transform of the subbands. Only LL band is subjected to Gaussian low-pass filtering in order to overcome the limitation of traditional Retinex Algorithm that some high-frequency components are lost by filtering. Figure 9 displays the results for some images from the well-known extended Yale-B database. The results are given only for worst-case images. The wavelet based algorithm for illumination normalization is shown in Algorithm 3.

CONCLUSION

Wavelet has widespread applications in the field of image processing. Using a wavelet transform, the wavelet compression methods are adequate for representing transients such as percussion sounds in audio, or high-frequency components in two-dimensional images (for example: an image of

Figure 8. DWT –based (a) image compression system (b) image decoding system

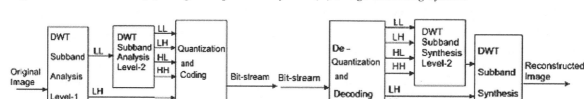

Figure 9. Illumination normalization performed on extended Yale-B database, row-1: input images captured under harsh illumination conditions, row-2: LL bands subjected to Gaussian filtering, row-3: illumination normalized images.

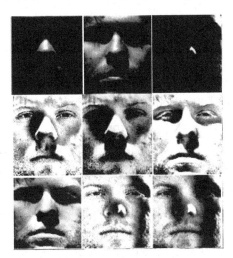

Algorithm 3. Illumination normalization

```
Input: Image captured under harsh illumi-
nation conditions
Output: Illumination normalized image
1. Load the input image I_un
2. Compute:  [I_LL, I_HL, I_LH, I_HH ]= dwt2 (I_un
(m,n), 'wavelet basis') // computing 2-D
DWT
3.  I_GLL = Gaussian_Filtering (I_LL) // LL
subband is subjected to gaussian low-pass
filtering
4.  log R_GLL = log S_LL - log L_LL // loga-
rithm of the reflectance component of I_GLL
is computed
5.  R_GLL = exp (log S_LL - log L_LL)
// reflectance component is computed
6.  The illumination normalized image can
be computed as
I_n=idwt2 (R_GLL, I_HL, I_LH, I_HH, 'wavelet ba-
sis')                      // illumina-
tion normalised image
```

stars on a night sky). This means that the transient elements of a data signal can be represented by a smaller amount of information compared to other transforms. Wavelet compression is not good for all kinds of data. Smooth, periodic signals are better compressed by other methods, particularly traditional harmonic compression by Fourier transforms. Some of the exciting applications of wavelets like image denoising, edge detection, compressed sensing and illumination normalization are also addressed in this chapter.

Future Scope for Wavelet-Based Research

Wavelet techniques have not been thoroughly worked out in applications such as practical data analysis of discretely sampled time-series data. Such applications offer exciting avenues for exploration. Wavelets can also be applied in the other fields like astronomy, acoustics, nuclear engineering, sub-band coding, neurophysiology, music, magnetic resonance imaging, speech discrimination, optics, fractals, turbulence, earthquake-prediction, radar, human vision.

REFERENCES

Antonini, Barlaud, Mathieu, & Daubechies. (1992). Image coding using wavelet transform. *IEEE Transactions on Image Processing*, *1*(2), 205–220. doi:10.1109/83.136597 PMID:18296155.

Candes, Romberg, & Tao. (2006). Stable signal recovery from incomplete and inaccurate measurements. *Communications on Pure and Applied Mathematics*, *59*(8), 1207–1223. doi:10.1002/cpa.20124.

Du. (2005). Wavelet-based illumination normalization for face recognition. In *Proceedings of IEEE International Conference on Image Processing* (954-957). Washington, DC: IEEE Press.

Gao & Zheng. (2008). Quality constrained compression using DWT-based image quality metric. *IEEE Transactions on Circuits and Systems for Video Technology, 18*(7), 910–922. doi:10.1109/TCSVT.2008.920744.

Gonzalez. (2011). *Digital image processing* (3rd Ed.). Upper Saddle River, NJ: Pearson publication.

Haidekker. (2011). *Advanced biomedical image analysis*. Hoboken, NJ: John Wiley and Sons.

Hao & Sun. (2010). A modified retinex algorithm based on wavelet transformation. In *Proceedings of International Conference on Multimedia and Information Technology* (306-309). New York: ACM Press.

Malfait & Roose. (1997). Wavelet-based image denoising using a markov random field a priori model. *IEEE Transactions on Image Processing, 6*(4), 549–565. doi:10.1109/83.563320 PMID:18282948.

Raja & Kolekar. (2012a). Wavelet transform based fluctuating density gaussian sampling algorithm for efficient image reconstruction. In *Proceedings of International Conference on Sensor Signal Processing for Defense*. Washington, DC: IEEE Press.

Raja & Kolekar. (2012b). Illumination normalization for image restoration using modified retinex algorithm. In *Proceedings of Annual IEEE India Conference* (941-946). Washington, DC: IEEE Press.

Stankovi, R. S., & Falkowski, B. J. (2003). The haar wavelet transform: Its status and achievements. *Elsevier Journal on Computers and Electrical Engineering, 29*, 25–44. doi:10.1016/S0045-7906(01)00011-8.

Stankovi & Falkowski. (2003). *The haar wavelet transform: Its status and achievements*. Elsevier Journal.

Sur, P. Chakraborty, & Saha. (2009). A new wavelet based edge detection technique for iris imagery. *IEEE International Advance Computing Conference* (120-124). Washington, DC: IEEE Press.

Wang & Arce. (2010). Variable density compressed image sampling. *IEEE Transactions on Image Processing, 19*(1), 264–270. doi:10.1109/TIP.2009.2032889 PMID:19775971.

KEY TERMS AND DEFINITIONS

Compressed Sensing: Performing sub-Nyquist sampling in the frequency domain of the image.

Illumination Normalization: It is a image processing technique used to make the imaging system insensitive to dramatic change of illumination conditions and robust against large static cast shadows.

Multi-Resolution Analysis: A scaling function is used to create a series of approximations of a function or image, each differing by a factor of 2 in resolution from its nearest neighboring approximations.

Sampling Pattern: It is a sampling function used to select or reject the frequency domain details for image reconstruction.

Scaling Function $\varnothing$(t): Scaling function filters the lowest level of the transform and ensures all the spectrum is covered.

Subbands: Computing wavelet transform to an image results in four subbands (or sub-images) whose resolution is reduced by a factor 2 compared to the original image.

Wavelet Function ϕ(t): Wavelet function behaves like a band-pass filter and scaling the image for each level.

Wavelets: Small waves of varying frequency and limited duration.

Chapter 4
Computational Models of Visual Attention:
A Survey

Rajarshi Pal
Institute for Development and Research in Banking Technology, India

ABSTRACT

Even the enormous processing capacity of the human brain is not enough to handle all the visual sensory information that falls upon the retina. Still human beings can efficiently respond to the external stimuli. Selective attention plays an important role here. It helps to select only the pertinent portions of the scene being viewed for further processing at the deeper brain. Computational modeling of this neuro-psychological phenomenon has the potential to enrich many computer vision tasks. Enormous amounts of research involving psychovisual experiments and computational models of attention have been and are being carried out all within the past few decades. This article compiles a good volume of these research efforts. It also discusses various aspects related to computational modeling of attention–such as, choice of features, evaluation of these models, and so forth.

INTRODUCTION

What is Visual Attention?

We, the human beings, are amazingly efficient in real-time interaction with the dynamic environment surrounding us. We, constantly, gather information about our surroundings through five senses. After analyzing or interpreting the information, the brain decides the course of action, but do we process all the incoming sensory information at the deeper levels of the brain? Let this question be put in a slightly different manner. All the time, our senses are actively sensing the outside world. All of that sensory information is routed towards the brain though nerves. But does all this information reach the deeper level of the brain where recognition and decision making takes place? For example, we cannot effectively listen to the important discussion on a television channel while we simultaneously carry out the conversation with a friend over the telephone. So, there is a limit to the number of things the brain can process simultaneously.

The human brain intelligently filters out the majority of incoming sensory information before it can reach the deeper levels of the brain. This phenomenon is known as attention. Attention helps

DOI: 10.4018/978-1-4666-4558-5.ch004

us to attend only a selective subset of sensory information. In the pretext of the subject matter of this article, we limit the discussion only to visual attention. Even, only a few selected portions of the visual stimuli sensed in the retina of the eye are able to draw our attention.

Why is a Computational Model Required?

Like humans, computer vision tasks also face the challenge of dealing with huge amount of input (Tsotsos, 1990). The attention mechanism of human vision has influenced computer vision researchers to restrict the computation in certain areas of input. As a result, modeling visual attention draws significant research effort within the past few decades. It gathers theories from psychology, neurobiology of human visual system, and other related topics. Psycho-visual experiments have provided some theoretical reasoning for saliency of a location or an object. Computer vision researchers try to fit various types of models on acquired salient data on the basis of these psycho-visual experiments.

Selective attention to relevant salient locations in a scene has various advantages. It reduces the computational burden by decreasing the amount of data to be processed. Moreover, suppression of irrelevant information ensures influence of only the relevant locations of the scene in the outcome of the system.

Applications of Visual Attention Models in Computer Vision

Computational modeling of visual attention enriches many application areas of image processing and computer vision. In these applications, scene contents get discriminative treatment based on their relative saliency. Some of these applications are listed here:

- Autonomous road following guided by artificial vision system is demonstrated in (Baluja & Pomerleau, 1997). This artificial vision system is capable of finding task-related salient locations in a scene.
- Artificial vision system having attention mechanism helps a human robot to easily interact with its surrounding (Stasse et al, 2000).
- Identified salient landmarks are used for robot localization and mapping as demonstrated in (Bur et al, 2006).
- An attention model is successfully applied to target detection tasks reported in (Gao et al, 2009; Itti & Koch, 1999b).
- Finding out salient regions is useful in image retrieval (Jing et al, 2002).
- Visual attention model has been applied to video shot matching in (Li & Lee, 2007). Shot matching is an essential step for video indexing and retrieval.
- Visual saliency model has been used in image segmentation (Ouerhani & Hugli, 2003a).
- Object tracking in dynamic scenes is also facilitated by attention model (Ouerhani & Hugli, 2003b).
- Computer graphics based applications needs rendering of salient locations in a scene with more details (Chalmers et al, 2003; Sundstedt et al, 2005). Some of these applications are graphics based story telling, playing a game, advertising a product, and so on.
- In image and video compression (Bradley & Stentiford, 2003; Itti, 2004), more bits are allocated to salient areas to retain the perceptual quality of the compressed version.
- Attention model is also used to display images for devices with various screen sizes to enhance viewing pleasure (Liu et al, 2003; Pal et al, 2012a). Methods of thumbnail

view generation (Suh et al, 2003) can also be included in this category of application.

- Attention also helps in perceptual grouping of spatially distributed patterns (Aziz & Mertsching, 2007).
- New avenues of intelligent photography are coming up with cameras having saliency estimator (Pal et al 2008; Vazquez & Steinfeld, 2011).

NEURAL PATHWAY

Human vision efficiently deals with huge amount of information. It is attributed to selection of salient stimuli for processing at higher level of brain. It rejects other stimuli. This section presents a few known facts related to neurological pathway of visual saliency computation in brain and subsequent attentional shift.

A retina is composed of light-sensitive cells at the inner surface of human eye. The scene being viewed falls upon the retina. At first, retina reduces the amount of incoming information as photoreceptors process the electromagnetic wave in the range of optical frequency, i.e., termed as visible light. The central part of this retina is called fovea. Photo-receptive cells are abundant in this portion compared to peripheral parts of it. As a result, the retinal image is sampled at high spatial resolution in the fovea. The image is relatively coarsely sampled towards periphery of it. Therefore, portions of the scene that fall upon fovea become prominent. Due to this biological structure of the retina, visual attention guides eye movements such that the fovea can contain the salient parts of a scene. The part of the scene imaged onto the fovea can then be processed in more details. But relatively small size of fovea ensures that selected information is much less compared to the total amount that falls upon the retina. This gives birth to the phenomenon of selective visual attention.

After the photoreceptors in the retina, retinal ganglion cells appear in the neural pathway. These cells are insensitive to uniformity in the scene. Spatial organization of the retinal receptive fields is responsible for this property (Hartline, 1938). These receptive fields form a center-surround organization. The circular center portion is surrounded by an annular region. These two regions provide an opposite response for the same stimulation. This promotes contrast in feature around a region and suppresses uniformity. Various psychovisual experiments demonstrate how a location or object gets attracted when it is remarkably different from its surroundings. Therefore, these observations conform to the center-surround structure found in neural pathway.

Neural signal then passes through Lateral Geniculate Nucleus (LGN) to primary visual cortex. Primary visual cortex is also known as V1 region or striate cortex. The visual information is processed within visual cortex while it passes through V1, V2, V3, V4 regions. Computation in these regions produces a saliency map of the scene being viewed. Moreover, in task-specific attentional shifts, feedback from higher cortical areas guides computation of saliency (Wolfe, 1994). Influence of cortex to LGN cells via top-down feedback is also argued in (Grossberg, 1976a, 1976b). These feedback pathways ensure the presence of top-down attention. Finally, it reaches to Infero Temporal (IT) cortex. This IT region (the highest visual area in the hierarchy of ventral visual stream) is crucial for object recognition (Bruce et al, 1981; Ungerleider & Haxby, 1994).

Saliency map is also active in posterior parietal cortex (Gottlieb et al, 1998). This portion of brain is responsible in producing planned movements. It uses the generated saliency map and subsequent knowledge obtained in infero temporal cortex to produce attentional shifts.

PSYCHO-VISUAL THEORIES/ EXPERIMENTS AS FOUNDATIONS FOR VISUAL ATTENTION MODELS

Analytic vs. Synthetic Theories of Visual Perception

Attention has an important role in perceiving the scene being viewed. Several experiments (ORegan et al, 1999; Simons & Levin, 1997) demonstrate that significant changes in scene are not perceived under natural viewing conditions. But observers can notice these changes once attention is directed to them. These change blindness experiments support the fact that only some selected portions of the scene reach higher level of brain for further processing.

Two broad categories of theories further clarify how attention helps in detailed perception of the scene. According to the analytic theory (Monahan & Lockhead, 1977), objects in the scene and their relationships are recognized at an early stage of visual perception. At later stage, if necessary, these objects are analyzed to identify their various features (color, brightness, orientation, shape, size, movement, etc.).

On the contrary, feature integration theory of attention (Treisman & Gelade, 1980), assumes that visual scene is separately encoded using various features and at the early-stage of neural information processing. These features are registered in parallel across the visual field. While attention is paid to a particular location in the scene, the features of the location are combined to provide a perception of the object present there. Majority of the computational models are based on this feature integration theory of attention.

Spotlight theory of attention (LaBerge, 1983; Posner, 1980) is akin to the feature integration theory (Treisman & Gelade, 1980) in the context that attention sequentially highlights locations to attend. The spotlight theory also suggests that the attention shifts smoothly from one location to a next attended location. Contradictory to this smooth shift of attention, several researchers have argued for abrupt shift of attention (Remington and Pierce, 1984; Sperling & Weichselgartne, 1995). Later, experiments reported in (Shioiri et al, 1999) indicate that smooth shifting of attention is noticed while observers are tracking a moving object. But abrupt shift of attention occurs when attention is directed to the location with new information.

Bottom-Up and Top-Down Theories of Attention

Feature-integration theory suggests early registration of visual stimuli (encoded using several features) and competition among them to capture attention. There are two types of attentional mechanism: bottom-up and top-down which determine what part of the scene draws our attention. Bottom-up attention involuntarily guides our vision to salient portions in a scene (Itti & Koch, 2001). It is purely stimulus driven. It models attractiveness of scene components at early stage of vision in the absence of semantic or context dependent knowledge about the scene being viewed. It is primarily driven by the unusualness in stimulus (in terms of one or more features) with respect to surroundings of a location or an object. In other words, this component of attention guides our vision towards distinguishable items in a scene.

On the other hand, top-down component of attention is driven by the demand of the task to be performed (Pelz & Canosa, 2001; Yarbus, 1967). This type of attention is controlled by semantic, context-dependent, or task-specific knowledge. For example, the importance of top-down control is demonstrated in (Shinoda et al., 2001) for detecting traffic signs in a driving simulator. Goal of the task of finding these traffic signs and learnt possibilities about the environment combine to spot the traffic signs. It is concluded that bottom-up attention has limited role during this task. Moreover, ignorance of objects those are irrelevant to perform a desired task, is highlighted in (Cater et al., 2002). In this experiment, subjects were asked to count number of pencils in a sequence of mugs presented in an animation clip. These subjects could not report significant changes in the quality of the scene in other unattended parts. These are strong evidence in support of task-driven attentional focus.

Basically, attention is guided by the combination of both of bottom-up and top-down control strategies in normal viewing circumstances. At first glance, stimulus driven bottom-up attention guides our vision. Interpretation of contents of attended locations and semantic relationship among these, then, influences the next fixation locations. As reported in (Yarbus, 1967), the consistency of attended locations among various observers decreases with time. This is explained in (Parkhurst et al., 2002) using attentional focus as a combination of bottom-up and top-down mechanisms. Involuntarily controlled bottom-up attention plays a role in early vision. Therefore, attended locations of various observers are consistent during this phase. With passage of time, recognition of attended scene contents biases observers to a varying degree. Effect of involvement of this top-down component may vary over various observers. It leads to the reported inconsistency. In short, in normal viewing conditions, the bottom-up attention guides vision within the first few hundreds of milliseconds of viewing a scene, with time the influence of bottom-up attention decreases and enhanced interpretation of the scene increases the role of top-down, task-dependent influences. But this balance of roles between bottom-up and top-down components of attention may change at the abrupt onset of a new stimulus.

Role of Abrupt Onset

Role of abrupt onset on visual attention has been studied at large. Abrupt onset of certain stimuli in the visual field invokes the bottom-up component of attention. It can be concluded from the experiments in (Jonides & Yantis, 1988) that abrupt onset of a stimulus better captures attention as compared to the differences in stimulus in terms of color and luminance. But comparatively recent analysis in (Franconeri et al., 2005) concludes that the new stimulus does not capture attention unless they cause a strong change in one or more features.

Moreover, capability of drawing attention by the abrupt onset of a stimulus is also dependent on the task at hand. As demonstrated in (Yantis & Jonides, 1984) using visual search experiments, abrupt onset of the search target captures attention quickly as compared to onset of a distracting element.

Apart from abrupt onset of a new object and luminance contrast change, translating and looming stimuli also capture attention as demonstrated by the experiments reported in (Franconeri & Simons, 2003). But this phenomenon is not observed for all dynamic scenes. For example, receding stimuli does not capture attention. They have also concluded that stimuli related to behaviorally urgent events are more likely to receive attention.

Features That Capture Attention

A study involving human observers suggests that they prefer to look at highly informative portions of images (Mackworth & Morandi, 1967). In this analysis, a subjective measure of informativeness is used. Studies also indicate that attention is drawn towards image portions having highly surprising content (Loftus & Mackworth, 1978), high spatial contrast of intensity (Parkhurst & Niebur, 2003; Reinagel & Zador, 1999), or high spatial frequency (Mannan et al., 1997). Role of several features, like, color intensity, orientation, size, motion (Wolfe and Horowitz, 2004) has been undoubtedly established through various studies. Work in (Privitera & Stark, 2000) shows that a linear combination of a collection of image processing operators (e.g., Laplacian of Gaussian, entropy in a local window) matches well with attended locations recorded from human observers.

Influence of semantic content on gaze fixation positions are also experimentally studied in (Cerf et al., 2008). The studied image set contains faces, texts and cell phones as high-level objects. It is observed that participated volunteers fixate on a face in 80% of cases within first two fixation locations. With text and cell phones, this statistics comes around 65% and 8%, respectively. Though estimated count of fixations on cell phones is low, this study indicates that incorporation of some high-level semantic contents (face and text) with low-level features results in better prediction of attended locations.

Perceiving Changes in Scene: Coherence Theory of Attention and Change Blindness

In an attempt to explain how changes in a scene are perceived, (Klein et al., 1992) suggest that any change in the scene introduces motion, which attracts our attention. But it is noticed that we cannot always perceive the changes in a scene. This phenomenon is known as change blindness. The coherence theory of attention (Rensink, 2000) explains why only certain changes in a scene are noticed. According to this theory, proto-objects are formed in parallel across the visual field at the pre-attentive stage. A proto-object has limited coherence in space and time. It disappears when a new stimulus appears on the same location. A small number of proto-objects capture attention at a time. When attended, these proto-objects are interpreted as objects having larger coherence over space and time. These objects and their relationships are recognized. Because of this temporal continuity, any new stimulus in the attended locations is perceived as a change in the object and easily comes into notice. After focused attention is released, the objects lose its coherence and dissolves back into constituent proto-objects. Therefore, according to coherence theory, a change in the scene can be noticed only if it is given focused attention.

Space-Based vs. Object-Based Visual Attention

There also exists a dispute on whether visual attention is space-based or object-based. Supporters of space-based theory (LaBerge, 1983; Posner, 1980) suggest that visual field is represented by purely spatial representation of visual features. Visual attention is directed to a particular location in the visual field. On the contrary, the supporters of object-based theory (Driver & Baylis, 1989; Duncan, 1984) suggest that the visual scene is preattentively segmented in accordance with perceptual grouping principles. Attention is directed to candidate objects (or perceptual groups).

It is suggested in (Vecera & Farah, 1994) that both theories prevail depending on the type of task. Experiments in (Egly et al., 1994; Soto & Blanco, 2004) also provide evidence that computation in visual attention system may be location-based, object-based, or both.

BOTTOM-UP MODELS FOR VISUAL ATTENTION

Koch-Ullman Framework of Selective Visual Attention

On the basis of feature-integration theory (Treisman & Gelade, 1980) and bottom-up mechanism of attention as discussed in the previous section, a fundamental framework has been provided in (Koch & Ullman, 1985) to select the portions of a scene that draws attention. According to this framework, a set of features are extracted in parallel. Locations of the scene that differ from their surrounding are singled out to generate conspicuity maps for each of these features. These maps are, then, combined to generate one single saliency map encoding the relative saliency of the locations of in the visual scene. A Winner-Take-All (WTA) mechanism selects the most salient location from the saliency map. Attention is paid to the location to bind the features to understand the objects present there. The WTA mechanism then selects the next most salient location, and so on. The shift to the subsequent location may be biased by the proximity and feature similarity.

A schematic diagram of this framework is given in Figure 1. Existing bottom-up attention models follow this framework. Bottom-up attention models are discussed under following few categories. Of these, lot of models compute saliency on the basis of measuring difference with respect to surrounding of a computational unit (pixel or region). Some models are computationally pixel-based, whereas some other need segmentation as a preliminary step and differences are computed considering segments as the units of computation. Among other categories, graph based modeling has become a recent trend. Learning based, information theory based, and other models are also available in literature.

Difference with Surrounding

Center-surround difference, which measures feature difference of a location with its surroundings, is suggested to capture saliency (Koch & Ullman, 1985). Following this guidance, the model in (Itti

et al., 1998) depends on center-surround difference of various low-level features, such as color, intensity and orientation. These features are represented at multiple scales using Gaussian pyramid. Center-surround difference is implemented as the difference of feature values represented in finer and coarser scale. The static part of the attention model for videos (Rapantzikos et al., 2004) also follows this form of center-surround computation.

In this context, Difference-of-oriented-Gaussian (DoG) operator is applied at multiple scales (Milanese et al., 1994) to encode saliency. This operator is defined by the difference of two Gaussians of different sizes. The simplified expression is given as:

$$DoG(\theta) = b_1 \Phi_1(x,y,\theta) - b_2 \Phi_2(x,y,\theta) \qquad (1)$$

where function $\Phi_1(x, y, \theta)$ and $\Phi_2(x, y, \theta)$ are 2D Gaussians oriented at angle θ. The constants b_1 and b_2 normalize the sum of the coefficients of each Gaussian component to 1. The general expression of the 2D Gaussian oriented at angle θ is as follows:

$$\Phi_i(x,y,\theta) = A e^{-\left(a(x-\mu_x)^2 + 2b(x-\mu_x)(y-\mu_y) + c(y-\mu_y)^2\right)} \qquad (2)$$

where

$$a = \frac{cos^2\theta}{2\sigma_x^2} + \frac{sin^2\theta}{2\sigma_y^2} \qquad (3)$$

$$b = -\frac{sin\,2\theta}{4\sigma_x^2} + \frac{sin\,2\theta}{4\sigma_y^2} \qquad (4)$$

$$c = \frac{sin^2\theta}{2\sigma_x^2} + \frac{cos^2\theta}{2\sigma_y^2} \qquad (5)$$

Figure 1. Framework of saliency computation

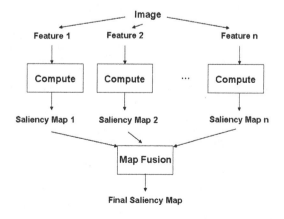

60

(μ_x, μ_y) is the center and σ_x, σ_y are the x and y spreads of the Gaussian.

Feature difference between a region and its surrounding models saliency in (Luo & Singhal, 2000). It is a region based model where prior segmentation is carried out. Various schemes are experimentally studied for determining the regions to be considered as 'surrounding'. Better results are reported by considering regions within a relatively large window as 'surrounding'. Another region based feature contrast computation is applied to estimate saliency in (Backer et al., 2001). Contrast c_i of a region i is defined as difference in mean feature values with surrounding regions using the following expression:

$$c_i = \frac{1}{u_i} \sum_{j \in R_i} b_{ij} d_{f_{ij}} \qquad (6)$$

where u_i is circumference of the region i. R_i is the set of surrounding regions of i sharing a common boundary of length b_{ij} with region j. $d_{f_{ij}}$ denotes the Euclidean distance between the mean feature values of regions i and j.

In (Wu et al., 2009), contrast is determined as sum of thresholded feature difference with neighboring pixels. A suitable threshold is estimated for each pixel using Just Noticeable Difference (JND) model. Difference in features with neighboring pixels is also reported to capture saliency in (Ma & Zhang, 2003).

On the contrary to capturing the difference between a pixel and its surrounding, the model in (Vikram et al., 2011) captures attention considering the differences of a pixel with a set of randomly selected pixels.

Computation Using Graph

In (Harel et al., 2006), shift of gaze is modeled as a random walk on a directed graph constructed from feature map representation of the image. Each pixel in the image is represented by a node in the graph. There is a pair of edges between each pair of nodes. Weight of such an edge is proportional to feature distance of the concerned nodes, when spatial distance is constant. It is also proportional to positional proximity when feature distance is same. A Markov chain is obtained from such a graph to represent gaze transitional probabilities between any pair of pixels. Equilibrium distribution on this Markov chain gives saliency of each node.

Another graph based approach is proposed in (Gopalakrishnan et al., 2009). Similar to (Harel et al., 2006), each pixel is represented by a node. Edge-weight is kept proportional to feature difference of concerned pixels. Two Markov chains are constructed from feature representations of the image. The first one uses a complete graph. The second Markov chain is constructed from a k-regular graph to capture local compactness of pixels. Equilibrium distributions on these Markov chains are computed. The most salient pixel is selected as the one which is globally attractive but falls on a compact object. Few background pixels are also identified through certain random walk based approach. Then, salient regions are identified using the most salient pixel as well as the background pixels as seed points.

Unlike equilibrium distribution based computation in above two models, the graph-based model in (Pal et al., 2010) demonstrates how a simple estimation of degree of each node provides the saliency map. According to this model, each feature map is partitioned into non-overlapping blocks of homogeneous pixels using quad-tree decomposition technique. Then a complete graph is constructed for the feature map. Each node in the graph corresponds to one block. The weight of an edge between any pair of nodes is proportional to the feature distance, which is modulated by positional proximity, between the concerned blocks. Then the complete graph is binarized by retaining the edges having weights greater than a threshold. The edges with lesser weights are discarded. Then degree of each node in the binarized graph provides us the saliency of pixels of the concerned block.

Measure of Information

Shannon's self-information measure has been applied in (Bruce, 2005) in the context of determining saliency. The basic assumption, here, is that the information conveyed by a feature is inversely proportional to the likelihood of observing the feature in the image. This paper outlines the procedure to compute the likelihood of observing a set of features in the image. This work has been extended in (Bruce & Tsotsos, 2009) to provide an information theoretic perspective for computing attention. Similar work can also be found in (Qiu et al., 2007).

Learning

In a learning based approach (Kienzle et al, 2006) to model visual saliency, Fixated salient locations are recorded a priori from human interaction. A 13-by-13 square patch of pixels around each pixel (at fixated location or at any other random location) constitutes the feature vector. Then, Support Vector Machine (SVM) is trained to differentiate between the fixated salient points and non-salient points.

In (Liu et al., 2007), saliency is determined in terms of multi-scale contrast, center-surround histogram, and color spatial distribution. A Conditional Random Field (CRF) is also learnt to effectively combine these features to detect saliency.

Spatio-Temporal Approaches

In this section, models which can handle spatio-temporal characteristics of a video are mentioned in brief. Model proposed in (Rapantzikos et al., 2004) is just spatio-temporal extension of the static attention model in (Itti et al., 1998). Preliminary processing involves splitting the video into constituent shots. Then, each shot is processed separately to construct a spatio-temporal saliency map, which is 3D equivalent of 2D saliency maps obtained for images. Computation involves center-surround differences implemented in a way, which

can be called as direct spatio-temporal extension of the computation depicted in (Itti et al., 1998).

It is assumed in (Guironnet et al., 2005) that movements of objects cause saliency. Therefore, along with static component derived from individual frames, the dynamic component of it estimates movement of objects. At first, camera motion is estimated. Then, a frame is subtracted from camera motion compensated next frame to generate displaced frame difference. This measure corresponds to changes due to displacement of objects.

Dynamic component of (Zhai & Shah, 2006) corresponds motion contrast to saliency. Planar motions between frames are estimated by applying RANSAC algorithm on point correspondences in the frames. Spanning areas of motion segments are also incorporated in motion contrast computation to compensate the non-uniformity of spatial distribution of interest-points.

In an information-theoretic model (Qiu et al., 2007), spatio-temporal uniqueness is computed using the joint spatial and temporal conditional probability distributions of the spatio-temporal event.

Another notable approach in (Li & Lee, 2007) computes motion attention using the rank deficiency of gray-scale gradient tensors. Some other models of spatio-temporal category include (Chen et al., 2008; Longfei et al., 2008).

Other Approaches

Saliency is computed in (Gesu et al., 1997) using discrete moment transform and discrete symmetry transform. It is assumed that both of contrast in intensity and symmetrical shape of object have a role in saliency. Discrete moment transform measures local contrast moments around each pixel. It is sensitive to variation of intensities in a locality. Discrete symmetry transform estimates symmetry of an object. Two different approaches are proposed in (Gesu et al, 1997). They vary in how the two transforms pair with each-other. 1.)

In an approach, the above mentioned transforms are applied parallelly on the input image. Their results are combined later. 2.) In another approach, discrete symmetry transform is applied on the area selected by discrete moment transform.

In (Hou & Zhang, 2007), log-spectrum of an image is obtained by taking logarithm of the amplitude of Fourier transform of the image. A spectral residual based estimation produces the saliency map by eliminating redundancy in the image.

Edge detection based saliency computation method is described in (Rosin, 2009). In the simplest form, an edge map is obtained using Sobel operator. Dense regions in the edge map correspond to salient locations. Use of multi-scale edge detection or Difference-of-Gaussians (DoG) over multiple scales further improves the performance.

A rule-based approach for detecting attention regions at the object level is proposed in (Yu & Wong, 2007), which uses a real-time clustering algorithm. At first, the image is segmented by the real-time clustering algorithm. It is followed by a noise removal step. For each region, a rule-based combination of feature contrast and geometric property of the region determines its potential to be a background. A set of hierarchical attention regions is then obtained based on a proposed confidence factor.

In (Sun & Fisher, 2003), salient regions are selected in a hierarchical fashion. At first, saliency is computed in a coarser scale. Then, only the salient regions as specified at previous scale compete to grab attention using computation at a finer scale.

Bottom-Up Attention for Omni-Directional Images

The attention models, discussed so far, are based on Euclidian geometry. Therefore, these methods can only be applied on conventional images (Euclidean in nature). Due to increased deployment of omni-directional sensors in various applications, a new paradigm has been opened up in visual attention modeling. Images captured by omnidirectional sensors suffer distortions. Specific mappings, such as, log polar mapping cannot remove these distortions. Euclidean mapping cannot represent omnidirectional views homogeneously. Therefore, spherical geometry based attention model has been proposed in (Bogdanova et al, 2008) for omni-directional images.

TOP-DOWN MODELS OF VISUAL ATTENTION

Top-down control of attention is modeled by prioritizing certain features depending on requirement of a task. A few of these approaches are discussed here in brief.

An attention model is proposed in (Tagare et al., 2001) which is more suitable for visual search using top-down attention mechanism. As the features of target objects are known, top-down attention plays an important role here. The basic assumption made by this work is that an object is constituted of several parts and each part is characterized by a set of features. This model finds out parts of objects which have a higher likelihood of becoming a target object by comparing features of the object part and the target feature.

In (Milanese et al., 1994), recognition of familiar objects using Distributed Associative Memory (DAM) provides the cue for the top-down model.

The output of the DAM, i.e., the top-down attention map is integrated with several other bottom-up attention map (derived from various features) using a relaxation based map combination strategy.

Selective tuning model (Tsotsos et al., 1995) proposes to selectively tune parts of the computation by a top-down hierarchy of winner-take-all processes embedded within a pyramidal processing architecture. Inhibition of unwanted locations is achieved by suppressing feature values different from those of the target features. A game theoretic approach based on this model is proposed in (Ramstrom & Christensen, 2002). Concepts from game theory are applied for distributed control of attention.

A feature-gate based model is used in (Driscoll et al., 1998) to find out task-specific targets. Feature gate is described as pyramidal artificial neural network. At each level of the featuregate, several networks exist for various feature channels. This model combines both bottom-up and top-down components of attention. Like bottom-up attention, it enhances locations having unique feature values with respect to their neighbors. Top-down component decreases saliency of a location in the presence of target-like objects in its neighborhood.

In (Choi et al., 2004), attention is modeled as integration of bottom-up saliency and Adaptive Resonance Theory (ART) network. ART network is a neural network model that is used to find patterns in input data. Supervised classification of salient and non-salient areas helps to train an ART network about characteristics of unwanted areas. Bottom-up saliency is computed using center-surround operations acting upon various features. A trained ART network is used to identify important areas among those specified by the bottom-up component.

In (Begum et al., 2006), a dynamically constructed Gaussian adapted resonance theory is employed to learn the features for attended locations. Then it guides attention to desired locations when performing desired task.

To incorporate the top-down bias in computing saliency, the model in (Peters & Itti, 2007) proposes to learn relation between gaze patterns and low-level signatures computed from features to represent image gist (Siagian & Itti, 2007). For a new scene, linear least-square best fit mechanism is employed to search for a suitable gist and corresponding gaze pattern is followed.

When the task is to search for objects with given features, a dissimilarity based top-down model is proposed in (Jing et al., 2009). At first, salient maps are constructed using a bottom-up model for each of the considered features. Manhattan distance is estimated between the task map and each of the generated bottom-up saliency maps. Each map is then boosted by a weight multiplier which is inversely proportional to its estimated distance.

In (Navalpakkam & Itti, 2006), top-down bias is controlled by the ratio of saliency of a target and that of distractors. Features that maximize this signal-to-noise ratio are chosen for search related tasks.

OTHER IMPOTANT ASPECTS OF VISUAL ATTENTION MODELS

Features Considered

In the computation of saliency map, relevant features must be used to improve performance of a model and to reduce its computational burden. Usage of various features can be observed through out the saliency literature. Intensity and color are commonly used by the models (e.g., [Heinen & Engel, 2009; Ho et al., 2003; Itti et al., 1998; Li et al., 2003; Rapantzikos et al., 2004; Sun & Fisher, 2003; Zhao & Cai, 2007]). Opponent-process theory of vision, proposed by Ewald Hering, plays a major role in color and luminance perception of human vision (Hurvich & Jameson, 1957). This theory suggests that there are three opponent channels: red/green, blue/yellow, and black/white. According to this theory, these opponent colors in a pair never appear together, such as reddish-green or yellowish-blue, etc. Most of the existing saliency models abide by this theory though they vary in using color space. RGB color space is used in (Choi et al., 2004; Itti et al., 1998; Rapantzikos et al., 2004). Two double-opponent color channels (reg-green and blue-yellow) (Hurvich & Jameson, 1957) are constructed from RGB representation (Choi et al., 2004; Itti et al., 1998). Some other methods use color spaces that directly follow the opponent process theory. CIELUV, CIELAB and YCbCr are three such color spaces. Computations in models (Li et al., 2003; Ma & Zhang, 2003) are carried out in CIELUV space. YCbCr color space is used in (Ho et al., 2003). The model in (Yu & Wong, 2007) uses CIELAB space. Experiments in (Ngau et al., 2009) also suggest for CIELAB color space as against HSV, RGB and YCbCr spaces.

Saturation of a color also significantly effects saliency as shown in (Luo & Singhal, 2000). The model in (Aziz & Mertsching, 2008) assumes that saturated colors of warm color objects are attractive to human. The red color has been observed to strongly attract our attention (Osberger & Maeder, 1998). In (Pal et al., 2012c) further investigation is carried out to inquire the role of warm colors in attracting attention of observers. In this context, statistical analysis of hue and saturation of salient and non-salient locations is carried out in the HSV color space. It is observed that distributions of chromatic features (hue and saturation) are different for warm colors that draw attention and those which do not. The likelihood of drawing attention by a warm color is found to be determined by both of its hue and saturation component. This dependency is not related to the absolute hue and saturation of a concerned pixel, but is relative to these components of other warm color pixels present in the image. In most images, warm colors with hue closer to red attract our vision. Moreover, warm colors having higher saturation are more likely to guide attention.

Orientation is another notable feature used in several models (Aziz & Mertsching, 2008; Harel et al., 2006; Heinen & Engel, 2009; Itti et al., 1998; Li et al., 2003; Pal et al., 2010; Rapantzikos et al., 2004; Sun & Fisher, 2003; Zhao & Cai, 2007). Other features include edge (Choi et al., 2004), symmetry (Aziz & Mertsching, 2008; Choi et al., 2004), intensity contrast (Chen & Leou, 2008; Harel et al., 2006; Osberger & Maeder, 1998; Zhao & Cai, 2007), color contrast (Chen & Leou, 2008), size (Aziz & Mertsching, 2008; Osberger & Maeder, 1998), shape (Osberger & Maeder, 1998), eccentricity (Aziz & Mertsching, 2008), foreground/background nature of an object (Osberger & Maeder, 1998), and depth of objects in a scene (Ouerhani & Hugli, 2000).

Table 1 summarizes combination of features used in some of these models. Models with same combination of features are grouped together in one row of this table. It is to be noted that a few models (Harel et al., 2006; Osberger & Maeder, 1998; Pal et al., 2010) have not used color in computation. This is because they have been proposed for monochrome images.

As discussed above, most of the models use predetermined features for computation. But there are few approaches to select features based on the characteristics of features or saliency maps. For example, importance of a feature in determining saliency is indicated by composite saliency indicator as proposed in (Hu et al., 2004). This indicator is estimated based on spatial compactness and saliency density of the saliency map derived from a feature. For search related tasks, the model in (Navalpakkam and Itti, 2006) selects features based on the criteria of maximizing signal-to-noise ratio.

Fusion of Saliency Maps from Multiple Features

As indicated by the basic framework in Figure 1, saliency computations across feature channels are independent of each other. Then, these saliency maps are combined to identify a set of salient

Table 1. Combination of features used in attention models

Model	Features
(Heinen and Engel, 2009; Itti et al, 1998; Li et al, 2003; Sun and Fisher, 2003)	Color, intensity, orientation
(Ouerhani and Hugli, 2000)	Color, depth
(Ho et al, 2003; Ma and Zhang, 2003; Rapantzikos et al, 2004)	Color, intensity
(Choi et al, 2004)	Color, intensity, edge, symmetry
(Pal et al, 2010)	Intensity, orientation
(Harel et al, 2006)	Intensity, orientation, intensity contrast
(Zhao and Cai, 2007)	Color, intensity, orientation, intensity contrast
(Aziz and Mertsching, 2008)	Color, orientation, size, symmetry, eccentricity
(Chen and Leou, 2008)	Color contrast, intensity contrast
(Osberger and Maeder, 1998)	Intensity contrast, size, shape, foreground/background

locations that attract vision. Some of these map combination strategies are briefly stated here.

In (Itti & Koch, 1999a), four different combination strategies are experimentally studied. These are termed as: 1.) simple normalized summation, i.e., simple summation after scaling to a fixed dynamic range, 2.) linear combination with learned weights, i.e., linear combination with weights learned by supervised additive trainning, 3.) global non-linear normalization followed by summation, i.e., nonlinear combination that boosts feature maps with few isolated peaks of value and suppresses feature maps with uniform value, and 4.) local non-linear competition between salient locations using Difference-of-oriented-Gaussians (DoG). According to reported experiments, the global non-linear normalization based strategy performs well. It is also computationally efficient. According to this strategy, all the saliency maps are, at first, represented in the same dynamic range. These maps are then scaled by $(m_{max} - m_{avg})^2$, where m_{max} and m_{avg} are the maximum and average of all local maxima, respectively, of concerned maps. The used multiplicative weight indicates how the most salient location differs from others. Several saliency models (Itti et al., 1998; Ouerhani & Hugli, 2000; Rapantzikos et al., 2004; Pal et al., 2010) adopt this strategy. The saliency model in

(Ho et al., 2003) uses slight variation of this fusion strategy. Instead of estimating average over all local maxima, pixels with larger value than a threshold are considered and their mean value is used.

Some other notable approaches include linear combination of saliency maps (Chen & Leou, 2008) and independent component analysis based strategy (Choi et al., 2004).

EVALUATION OF VISUAL ATTENTION MODELS

Subjective judgments from several volunteers have been reported in (Chen & Leou, 2008; Ma & Zhang, 2003; Zhao & Cai, 2007) to establish saliency models. Volunteers were instructed to give a score within a predecided range or a rank to each of the compared models.

Objective evaluation of saliency models requires comparison of their outcomes with those of human visual system. This section discusses available procedures to record groundtruth salient contents in a scene according to human observers. Metrics used for comparison of outcomes of human and artificial computational systems are also stated.

Acquisition of Groundtruth Data

Eye-tracking devices record gaze fixation locations of human observers. These systems, in general, consist of a headset with a pair of infrared cameras, which track the observer's eyes. Another camera, termed as head camera, is also present to monitor the screen position. It is used to compensate for any head movements of the observer. Once the observer sits in front of a display and observes the presented stimulus, pair of infrared cameras provides the position of his pupils. Combining the pupil and head positions, the device computes the fixation points. A 2D Gaussian patch around each fixation location models groundtruth salient locations (Meur et al., 2004; Ouerhani et al., 2004). Usage of eye-trackers is also reported in many other literature (Harel et al., 2006; Kienzle et al., 2006; Meur et al., 2006; Peters & Itti, 2007; Reinagel & Zador, 1999; Renninger et al., 2005; Tatler et al., 2005).

As stated in (Liu et al., 2007), volunteers were asked to draw rectangles encompassing the most salient object according to her opinion. Hand-labeled data is also taken for evaluation of the model in (Hou & Zhang, 2007; Rosin, 2009). But enough viewing time while hand-labeling groundtruth introduces the effect of having the knowledge of objects and their semantic relationships.

(Pal et al., 2009) mentions a hand-eye coordination based alternative to collect the groundtruth data. Images are presented to observers for a very short duration. They are instructed to mark the center point of each location that seems to be salient to them. Then the collected set of points for all participating volunteers is clustered and the groundtruth data is represented by a circular disk around each cluster center. Later, this circular representation of groundtruth data is improved using image segmentation and subsequent region based analysis (Pal et al., 2012b). This later representation of groundtruth data reflects the shape and size of underlying objects.

Evaluation Metric

Average Discrimination Ratio (ADR) is defined in (Hu et al., 2005) to measure distinctiveness of groundtruth salient location from non-salient locations in terms of model generated saliency values. ADR is expressed as

$$ADR = \frac{\sum_{(i,j)\in A} M(i,j)/|A|}{\sum_{(i,j)\in A} M(i,j)/|A| + \sum_{(i,j)\in B} M(i,j)/|B|} \tag{7}$$

where A and B represent the set of salient and non-salient pixels indicated by groundtruth data, respectively. Saliency map is defined as a 2D function $M(x, y) \rightarrow R$, where coordinates x and y are discrete quantities. Moreover, the value of the function at any coordinate is any real value in the set of real numbers R.

Normalized Saliency (NS) is defined in (Pang et al., 2008; Peters & Itti, 2007) as average saliency value at salient locations when the map has been normalized to have zero mean with unit standard deviation. If μ_M and σ_M be the mean and standard deviation of the saliency map M, then NS is mathematically defined as

$$NS = \frac{1}{\sigma_M |A|} \sum_{(i,j)\in A} (M(i,j) - \mu_M) \tag{8}$$

Kullback-Leibler Distance (KLD) measures dissimilarity of two probability distributions. Assuming both of groundtruth and model generated saliency map as probability distribution functions, KLD estimates dissimilarity between them (Meur et al., 2004, 2006). Mathematical expression is given here:

$$KLD(p|h) = \sum_x p(x) log\left(\frac{p(x)}{h(x)}\right) \tag{9}$$

where *p(x)* and *h(x)* are probability distribution functions of model predicted saliency map and groundtruth data, respectively.

Correlation Coefficient (CC) between groundtruth *G* and computed saliency map *M* is used to evaluate the saliency model (Meur et al., 2006; Ouerhani et al., 2004). The correlation coefficient of them is estimated as

$$CC = \frac{cov(G,M)}{\sigma_G \sigma_M} \tag{10}$$

where *cov( )* returns the covariance of its arguments. σ_G and σ_M denote the standard deviations of the groundtruth and the saliency map, respectively.

Precision and recall are also used to determine correctness of saliency model (Gopalakrishnan et al., 2009; Liu et al., 2007). Precision is the fraction of correctly identified salient pixels among all pixels those have been predicted as salient by the model. Recall is the fraction of correctly identified salient pixels among all ideally salient pixels as specified by the groundtruth.

FUTURE RESEARCH DIRECTIONS

Decades of research has established few facts about visual attention phenomenon. But, the mechanism is not fully understood yet. Analysis of human-specified groundtruth data may reveal new facts. Moreover, challenge lies on how the psychovisual findings are incorporated into computational models. New way of computation may be found to emulate visual attention better than existing models.

Choice of appropriate features is also crucial to obtain desired performance. Most of the existing models use a predetermined set of features. But, image-dependent feature selection can appropriately tune these models. Few works have been carried out in this direction, such as (Hu et al., 2004; Navalpakkam & Itti, 2006). These works

select a feature that satisfies some predefined criteria concerning the characteristic of the feature or the saliency map derived from that feature. But statistics of individual low-level features or derived saliency maps hardly captures true potential of selecting an optimal set of features.

Humans are adept of fast recognition of objects or labeling an object with the semantic associated with it. Deficits of existing computational models sometimes suggest that significant performance benefits cannot be achieved by ignoring the semantics of objects under view. A recent study (Cerf et al., 2008) has shown that faces and texts attract our gaze. Exhaustive studies are needed to observe whether some other semantic concepts capture our attention.

It is to be studied how psychological state (for e.g., motivation, emotion) affect visual attention. Influence of other sensory information (e.g., auditory) on visual attention is needed to be explored. Both the visual and auditory information must be processed to develop a good surveillance system.

CONCLUSION

This article is a compilation of works on visual attention modeling. It also reports various psychovisual observations as basis of these models. Thus, by putting a huge chunk of reference materials under one umbrella, this article will help present and future researchers a lot. Achievements being put together, limitations and potential research avenues have come into focus.

REFERENCES

Aziz, M. Z., & Mertsching, B. (2007). An attentional approach for perceptual grouping of spatially distributed patterns. In *Proceedings of 29th DAGM Conference on Pattern Recognition* (345–354). Berlin: Springer.

Aziz, M. Z., & Mertsching, B. (2008). Fast and robust generation of feature maps for region-based visual attention. *IEEE Transactions on Image Processing*, *17*(5), 633–644. doi:10.1109/TIP.2008.919365 PMID:18390370.

Backer, G., Mertsching, B., & Bollmann, M. (2001). Data- and model-driven gaze control for an active-vision system. *IEEE Transactions on Pattern Analysis and Machine Intelligence*, *23*, 1415–1429. doi:10.1109/34.977565.

Baluja, S., & Pomerleau, D. (1997). Dynamic relevance: Vision-based focus of attention using artificial neural networks. *Artificial Intelligence*, *97*, 381–395. doi:10.1016/S0004-3702(97)00065-9.

Begum, M., Mann, G. K. I., & Gosine, R. G. (2006). A biologically inspired bayesian model of visual attention for humanoid robots. In *Proceedings of 6th IEEE-RAS International Conference on Humanoid Robots* (587–592). Washington, DC: IEEE Press.

Bogdanova, I., Bur, A., & Hugli, H. (2008). Visual attention on the sphere. *IEEE Transactions on Image Processing*, *17*(11), 2000–2014. doi:10.1109/TIP.2008.2003415 PMID:18854253.

Bradley, A. P., & Stentiford, W. M. (2003). Visual attention for region of interest coding in jpeg 2000. *Journal of Visual Communication and Image Representation*, *14*(3), 232–250. doi:10.1016/S1047-3203(03)00037-3.

Bruce, C., Desimone, R., & Gross, C. (1981). Visual properties of neurons in a polysensory area in the superior temporal sulcus of the macaque. *Journal of Neurophysiology*, *46*, 369–384. PMID:6267219.

Bruce, N. D. B. (2005). Features that draw visual attention: an information theoretic perspective. *Neurocomputing*, *65-66*, 125–133. doi:10.1016/j.neucom.2004.10.065.

Bruce, N. D. B., & Tsotsos, J. K. (2009). Saliency, attention, and visual search: An information theoretic approach. *Journal of Vision (Charlottesville, Va.)*, *9*(3), 1–24. doi:10.1167/9.3.5 PMID:19757944.

Bur, A., Tapus, A., Ouerhani, N., Siegwart, R., & Hugli, H. (2006). Robot navigation by panoramic vision and attention guided fetaures. In *Proceedings of 18th International Conference on Pattern Recognition* (695–698). Washington, DC: IEEE Press.

Cater, K., Chalmers, A., & Ledda, P. (2002). Selective quality rendering by exploiting human inattentional blindness: Looking but not seeing. In *Proceedings of the ACM symposium on Virtual Reality Software and Technology* (17–24). New York: ACM Press.

Cerf, M., Frady, E. P., & Koch, C. (2008). Using semantic content as cues for better scanpath prediction. In *Proceedings of Symposium on Eye tracking Research & Applications* (143–146). New York: ACM Press.

Chalmers, A., Cater, K., & Maflioli, D. (2003). Visual attention models for producing high fidelity graphics efficiently. In *Proceedings of 19th Spring Conference on Computer Graphics* (39–46). New York: ACM Press.

Chen, D.-Y., Tyan, H.-R., Hsiao, D.-Y., Shih, S.-W., & Liao, H.-Y. M. (2008). Dynamic visual saliency modeling based on spatiotemporal analysis. In *Proceedings of IEEE International Conference on Multimedia and Expo* (1085-1088). Washington, DC: IEEE Press.

Chen, H.-Y., & Leou, J.-J. (2008). A new visual attention model using texture and object features. In *Proceedings of IEEE 8th International Conference on Computer and Information Technology Workshops* (374–378). Washington, DC: IEEE Press.

Choi, S.-B., Ban, S.-W., & Lee, M. (2004). Biologically motivated visual attention system using bottom-up saliency map and top-down inhibition. *Neural Information Processing-Letters and Reviews, 2*.

Driscoll, J. A., Peters, R. A., II, & Cave, K. R. (1998). A visual attention network for a humanoid robot, In *Proceedings of IEEE/RSJ International Conference on Intelligent Robots and Systems* (1968–1974). Washington, DC: IEEE Press.

Driver, J. S., & Baylis, G. C. (1989). Movement of visual attention: The spotlight metaphor breaks down. *Journal of Experimental Psychology. Human Perception and Performance, 15*, 448–456. doi:10.1037/0096-1523.15.3.448 PMID:2527954.

Duncan, J. (1984). Selective attention and the organization of visual information. *Journal of Experimental Psychology. General, 113*, 501–517. doi:10.1037/0096-3445.113.4.501 PMID:6240521.

Egly, R., Driver, J., & Rafal, R. D. (1994). Shifting visual attention between objects and locations: Evidence from normal and parietal lesion subjects. *Journal of Experimental Psychology. General, 123*(2), 161–177. doi:10.1037/0096-3445.123.2.161 PMID:8014611.

Franconeri, S. L., Hollingworth, A., & Simons, D. J. (2005). Do new objects capture attention? *Psychological Science, 16*(4), 275–281. doi:10.1111/j.0956-7976.2005.01528.x PMID:15828974.

Franconeri, S. L., & Simons, D. J. (2003). Moving and looming stimuli capture attention. *Perception & Psychophysics, 65*(7), 999–1010. doi:10.3758/BF03194829 PMID:14674628.

Gao, K., Lin, S., Zhang, Y., Tang, S., & Zhang, D. (2009). Logo detection based on spatio-spectral saliency and partial spatial context. In *Proceedings of IEEE International Conference on Multimedia and Expo* (322–329). Washington, DC: IEEE Press.

Gesu, V. D., Valenti, C., & Strinati, L. (1997). Local operators to detect regions of interest. *Pattern Recognition Letters, 18*, 1077–1081. doi:10.1016/S0167-8655(97)00084-6.

Gopalakrishnan, V., Hu, Y., & Rajan, D. (2009). Random walks on graphs to model saliency in images. In *Proceedings of IEEE Computer Society Conference on Computer Vision and Pattern Recognition* (1698–1705).

Gottlieb, J. P., Kusunoki, M., & Goldberg, M. E. (1998). The representation of visual salience in monkey parietal cortex. *Nature, 391*, 481–484. doi:10.1038/35135 PMID:9461214.

Grossberg, S. (1976a). Adaptive pattern classification and universal recoding. I. Parallel development and coding of neural feature detectors. *Biological Cybernetics, 23*, 121–134. doi:10.1007/BF00344744 PMID:974165.

Grossberg, S. (1976b). Adaptive pattern classification and universal recoding. ii. feedback, expectation, olfaction, and illusions. *Biological Cybernetics, 23*, 187–202. PMID:963125.

Guironnet, M., Guyader, N., Pellerin, D., & Ladret, P. (2005). Spatio-temporal attention model for video content analysis. In *Proceedings of IEEE International Conference on Image Processing* (1156-1159). Washington, DC: IEEE Press.

Harel, J., Koch, C., & Perona, P. (2006). Graph-based visual saliency. *Advances in Neural Information Processing Systems*, 19.

Hartline, H. K. (1938). The response of single optic nerve fibers of the vertebrate eye to illumination of the retina. *The American Journal of Physiology, 121*, 400–415.

Heinen, M. R., & Engel, P. M. (2009). Evaluation of visual attention models under 2D similarity transformations. In *Proceedings of ACM Symposium on Applied Computing* (1156–1160). New York: ACM Press.

Ho, C.-C., Cheng, W.-H., Pan, T.-J., & Wu, J.-L. (2003). A user-attention based focus detection framework and its applications. In *Proceedings of the Joint Conference of the 4th International Conference on Information, Communications, and Signal Processing, and the 4th Pacific Rim Conference on Multimedia* (1315–1319). Washington, DC: IEEE Press.

Hou, X., & Zhang, L. (2007). Saliency detection: A spectral residual approach. In *Proceedings of IEEE Conference on Computer Vision and Pattern Recognition* (1–8). Washington, DC: IEEE Press.

Hu, Y., Rajan, D., & Chia, L. T. (2005). Adaptive local context suppression of multiple cues for salient visual attention detection. In *Proceedings of IEEE International Conference on Multimedia and Expo* (346-349). Washington, DC: IEEE Press.

Hu, Y., Xie, X., Ma, W.-Y., Chia, L.-T., & Rajan, D. (2004). Salient region detection using weighted feature maps based on the human visual attention model. In *Proceedings of Pacific-Rim Conference on Multimedia* (993–1000). Washington, DC: IEEE Press.

Hurvich, L. M., & Jameson, D. (1957). An opponent-process theory of color vision. *Psychological Review*, *64*, 384–404. doi:10.1037/h0041403 PMID:13505974.

Itti, L. (2004). Automatic foveation for video compression using a neurobiological model of visual attention. *IEEE Transactions on Image Processing*, *13*, 1304–1318. doi:10.1109/TIP.2004.834657 PMID:15462141.

Itti, L., & Koch, C. (1999a). A comparison of feature combination strategies for saliency based visual attention systems. In *Proceedings of SPIE Human Vision and Electronic Imaging* (473-482). Bellingham, WA: SPIE Press.

Itti, L., & Koch, C. (1999b). Target detection using saliency-based attention. In *Proceedings of RTO/SCI-12 Workshop on Search and Target Acquisition (NATO Unclassified)* (3.1–3.10). Washington, DC: NATO.

Itti, L., & Koch, C. (2001). Computational modeling of visual attention. *Nature Reviews. Neuroscience*, *2*, 194–203. doi:10.1038/35058500 PMID:11256080.

Itti, L., Koch, C., & Niebur, E. (1998). A model of saliency-based visual attention for rapid scene analysis. *IEEE Transactions on Pattern Analysis and Machine Intelligence*, *20*(11), 1254–1259. doi:10.1109/34.730558.

Jing, F., Li, M., Zhang, H.-J., & Zhang, B. (2002). An effective region-based image retrieval framework. In *Proceedings of ACM Multimedia*. New York: ACM Press.

Jing, Z., Li, Z., Jingjing, G., & Zhixing, L. (2009). A study of top-down visual attention model based on similarity distance. In *Proceedings of 2nd International Congress on Image and Signal Processing* (1–5). Berlin: Springer.

Jonides, J., & Yantis, S. (1988). Uniqueness of abrupt visual onset in capturing attention. *Perception & Psychophysics*, *43*(4), 346–354. doi:10.3758/BF03208805 PMID:3362663.

Kienzle, W., Wichmann, F. A., Scholkopf, B., & Franz, M. O. (2006). A non-parametric approach to bottom-up visual saliency. *Advances in Neural Information Processing Systems*, 19.

Klein, R., Kingstone, A., & Pontefract, A. (1992). Orienting of visual attention, In K. Rayner (Ed.), Eye Movements and Visual Cognition: Scene Perception and Reading (46-65). New York: Springer.

Koch, C., & Ullman, S. (1985). Shifts in selective visual attention: towards the underlying neural circuitry. *Human Neurobiology*, *4*, 219–227. PMID:3836989.

LaBerge, D. (1983). Spatial extent of attention to letters and words. *Journal of Experimental Psychology. Human Perception and Performance*, *9*, 371–379. doi:10.1037/0096-1523.9.3.371 PMID:6223977.

Li, S., & Lee, M.-C. (2007). An efficient spatio-temporal attention model and its application to shot matching. *IEEE Transactions on Circuits and Systems for Video Technology*, *17*(10), 1383–1387. doi:10.1109/TCSVT.2007.903798.

Li, Y., Ma, Y.-F., & Zhang, H.-J. (2003). Salient region detection and tracking in video. In *Proceedings of International Conference on Multimedia and Expo* (269–272). Washington, DC: IEEE Press.

Liu, H., Xie, X., Ma, W.-Y., & Zhang, H.-J. (2003). Automatic browsing of large pictures on mobile devices. In *Proceedings of ACM International Conference on Multimedia* (148–150). New York: ACM Press.

Liu, T., Sun, J., Zheng, N. N., Tang, X., & Shum, H. Y. (2007). Learning to detect a salient object. In *Proceedings of the Conference on Computer Vision and Pattern Recognition* (1-8). Washington, DC: IEEE Press.

Loftus, G. R., & Mackworth, N. H. (1978). Cognitive determinants of fixation location during picture viewing. *Journal of Experimental Psychology. Human Perception and Performance*, *4*, 565–572. doi:10.1037/0096-1523.4.4.565 PMID:722248.

Longfei, Z., Yuanda, C., Gangyi, D., & Yong, W. (2008). A computable visual attention model for video skimming. In *Proceedings of Tenth IEEE Symposium on Multimedia* (667-672). Washington, DC: IEEE Press.

Luo, J., & Singhal, A. (2000). On measuring low-level saliency in photographic images. In *Proceedings of IEEE Conference on Computer Vision and Pattern Recognition* (84–89). Washington, DC: IEEE Press.

Ma, Y.-F., & Zhang, H.-J. (2003). Contrast-based image attention analysis by using fuzzy growing. In *Proceedings of 11th ACM International Conference on Multimedia* (374–381). New York: ACM Press.

Mackworth, N. H., & Morandi, A. J. (1967). The gaze selects informative details within pictures. *Perception & Psychophysics*, *2*, 547–552. doi:10.3758/BF03210264.

Mannan, S. K., Ruddock, K. H., & Wooding, D. S. (1997). Fixation patterns made during brief examination of two-dimensional images. *Perception*, *26*, 1059–1072. doi:10.1068/p261059 PMID:9509164.

Meur, O. L., Callet, P. L., Barba, D., & Thoreau, D. (2004). Performance assessment of a visual attention system entirely based on a human vision modeling. In *Proceedings of International Conference on Image Processing* (2327–2330). Washington, DC: IEEE Press.

Meur, O. L., Callet, P. L., Barba, D., & Thoreau, D. (2006). A coherent computational approach to model bottom-up visual attention. *IEEE Transactions on Pattern Analysis and Machine Intelligence*, *28*(5). PMID:16640265.

Milanese, R., Wechsler, H., Gil, S., Bost, J., & Pun, T. (1994). Integration of bottom-up and top-down cues for visual attention using nonlinear relaxation. In *Proceedings of IEEE Computer Society Conference on Computer Vision and Pattern Recognition* (781-785). Washington, DC: IEEE Press.

Monahan, J. S., & Lockhead, G. R. (1977). Identification of integral stimuli. *Journal of Experimental Psychology. General*, *106*, 94–110. doi:10.1037/0096-3445.106.1.94.

Navalpakkam, V., & Itti, L. (2006). Optimal cue selection strategy. *Advances in Neural Information Processing Systems*, *19*, 987–994.

Ngau, C. W. H., Ang, L.-M., & Seng, K. P. (2009). Comparison of colour spaces for visual saliency. In *Proceedings of International Conference on Intelligent Human-Machine Systems and Cybernetics* (278–281). Washington, DC: IEEE Press.

ORegan, J. K., Rensink, R. A., & Clark, J. J. (1999). Change-blindness as a result of mudsplashes. *Nature*, 398.

Osberger, W., & Maeder, A. J. (1998). Automatic identification of perceptually important regions in an image. In *Proceedings of 14th International Conference on Pattern Recognition* (701-704).

Ouerhani, N., & Hugli, H. (2000). Computing visual attention from scene depth. In *Proceedings of 15th International Conference on Pattern Recognition* (375-378). Washington, DC: IEEE Press.

Ouerhani, N., & Hugli, H. (2003a) Maps: Multiscale attention-based presegmentation of color images. In *Proceedings of 4th International Conference on Scale-Space Theories in Computer Vision* (537–549). Washington, DC: IEEE Press.

Ouerhani, N., & Hugli, H. (2003b). A model of dynamic visual attention for object tracking in natural image sequences. *Computational Methods in Neural Modeling. Lecture Notes in Computer Science, 2686*, 702–709. doi:10.1007/3-540-44868-3_89.

Ouerhani, N., von Wartburg, R., Hugli, H., & Muri, R. (2004). Empirical validation of saliency based model of visual attention. *Electronics Letters on Computer Vision and Image Analysis, 3*, 13–24.

Pal, R., Mitra, P., & Mukherjee, J. (2012a). Image retargeting using controlled shrinkage. In *Proceedings of 8th Indian Conference on Computer Vision, Graphics, and Image Processing*. Bangalore, India: ICVGIP Press.

Pal, R., Mitra, P., & Mukhopadhyay, J. (2008). Icam: Maximizes viewers' attention on intended objects. In *Proceedings of Pacific-Rim Conference on Multimedia* (821-824). Washington, DC: IEEE Press.

Pal, R., Mitra, P., & Mukhopadhyay, J. (2012b). Generation of groundtruth data for visual saliency experiments using image segmentation. In *Proceedings of IEEE Congress on Image and Signal Processing*. Washington, DC: IEEE Press.

Pal, R., Mukherjee, A., Mitra, P., & Mukherjee, J. (2010). Modelling visual saliency using degree centrality. *IET Computer Vision, 4*(3), 218–229. doi:10.1049/iet-cvi.2009.0067.

Pal, R., Mukherjee, J., & Mitra, P. (2009). An approach for preparing groundtruth data and evaluating visual saliency models. In *Proceedings of International Conference on Pattern Recognition and Machine Inteligence* (279-284). London: Academic Press.

Pal, R., Mukherjee, J., & Mitra, P. (2012c). How do warm colors affect visual attention? In *Proceedings of 8th Indian Conference on Computer Vision, Graphics, and Image Processing*. Bangalore, India: ICVGIP Press.

Pang, D., Kimura, A., Takeuchi, T., Yamato, J., & Kashino, K. (2008). A stochastic model of selective visual attention with a dynamic bayesian network. In *Proceedings of IEEE International Conference on Multimedia and Expo* (1073–1076). Washington, DC: IEEE Press.

Parkhurst, D., Law, K., & Niebur, E. (2002). Modeling the role of salience in the allocation of overt visual attention. *Vision Research, 42*(1), 107–123. doi:10.1016/S0042-6989(01)00250-4 PMID:11804636.

Parkhurst, D. J., & Niebur, E. (2003). Scene content selected by active vision. *Spatial Vision, 16*, 125–154. doi:10.1163/15685680360511645 PMID:12696858.

Pelz, J. B., & Canosa, R. (2001). Oculomotor behavior and perceptual strategies in complex tasks. *Vision Research, 41*, 3587–3596. doi:10.1016/S0042-6989(01)00245-0 PMID:11718797.

Peters, R. J., & Itti, L. (2007). Beyond bottom-up: incorporating task-dependent influences into a computational model of spatial attention. In *Proceedings of IEEE Conference on Computer Vision and Pattern Recognition* (1-8). Washington, DC: IEEE Press.

Posner, M. I. (1980). Orienting of attention. *The Quarterly Journal of Experimental Psychology*, *32*, 3–25. doi:10.1080/00335558008248231 PMID:7367577.

Privitera, C. M., & Stark, L. W. (2000). Algorithms for defining visual regions-of-interest: Comparison with eye fixations. [Washington, DC: IEEE Press.]. *IEEE Transactions on Pattern Analysis and Machine Intelligence*, *22*, 970–982. doi:10.1109/34.877520.

Qiu, G., Gu, X., Chen, Z., Chen, Q., & Wang, C. (2007). An information theoretic model on spatiotemporal visual saliency. In *Proceedings of IEEE International Conference on Multimedia and Expo* (1806-1809). Washington, DC: IEEE Press.

Ramstrom, O. & Christensen, H. I. (2002). Visual attention using game theory. *Biologically Motivated Computer Vision, 462–471.*

Rapantzikos, K., Tsapatsoulis, N., & Avrithis, Y. (2004). Spatiotemporal visual attention architecture for video analysis. In *Proceedings of IEEE 6th Workshop on Multimedia Signal Processing* (83-86). Washington, DC: IEEE Press.

Reinagel, P., & Zador, A. M. (1999). Natural scene statistics at the center of gaze. *Network (Bristol, England)*, *10*(4), 341–350. doi:10.1088/0954-898X/10/4/304 PMID:10695763.

Remington, R., & Pierce, L. (1984). Moving attention: Evidence for time-invariant shifts of visual selective attention. *Perception & Psychophysics*, *35*, 393–399. doi:10.3758/BF03206344 PMID:6739275.

Renninger, L. W., Coughlan, J., Verghese, P., & Malik, J. (2005). An information maximization model of eye movements. *Advances in Neural Information Processing Systems*, *17*, 1121–1128. PMID:16175670.

Rensink, R. A. (2000). The dynamic representation of scenes. *Visual Cognition*, *7*(1-3), 17–42. doi:10.1080/135062800394667.

Rosin, P. L. (2009). A simple method for detecting salient regions. *Pattern Recognition*, *42*(11), 2363–2371. doi:10.1016/j.patcog.2009.04.021.

Shinoda, H., Hayhoe, M. M., & Shrivastava, A. (2001). What controls attention in natural environments? *Vision Research*, *41*, 3535–3545. doi:10.1016/S0042-6989(01)00199-7 PMID:11718793.

Shioiri, S., Inoue, T., Matsumura, K., & Yaguchi, H. (1999). Movement of visual attention. In *Proceedings of IEEE International Conference on Systems, Man, and Cybernetics* (5–9). Washington, DC: IEEE Press.

Siagian, C., & Itti, L. (2007). Rapid biologically-inspired scene classification using features shared with visual attention. *IEEE Transactions on Pattern Analysis and Machine Intelligence*, *29*, 300–312. doi:10.1109/TPAMI.2007.40 PMID:17170482.

Simons, D. J. & Levin, D. T. (1997). Failure to detect changes to attended objects. *Investigative Opthalmology and Visual Science, 38.*

Soto, D., & Blanco, M. J. (2004). Spatial attention and object-based attention: a comparison with a single task. *Vision Research*, *44*, 69–81. doi:10.1016/j.visres.2003.08.013 PMID:14599572.

Sperling, G., & Weichselgartne, E. (1995). Episodic theory of the dynamics of spatial attention. *Psychological Review*, *102*, 503–532. doi:10.1037/0033-295X.102.3.503.

Stasse, O., Kuniyoshi, Y., & Cheng, G. (2000). Development of a biologically inspired real-time visual attention system. In *Proceedings of the 1st IEEE International Workshop on Biologically Motivated Computer Vision* (150-159). Washington, DC: IEEE Press.

Suh, B., Ling, H., Bederson, B. B., & Jacob, D. W. (2003). Automatic thumbnail cropping and its effectiveness. In *Proceedings of 16th Annual ACM Symposium on User Interface Software and Technology* (95-104). New York: ACM Press.

Sun, Y., & Fisher, R. (2003). Object-based visual attention for computer vision. *Artificial Intelligence*, *146*, 77–123. doi:10.1016/S0004-3702(02)00399-5.

Sundstedt, V., Debattista, K., Longhurst, P., Chalmers, A., & Troscianko, T. (2005). Visual attention for efficient high-fidelity graphics. In *Proceedings of 21st Spring Conference on Computer Graphics* (169–175). New York: ACM Press.

Tagare, H. D., Toyama, K., & Wang, J. G. (2001). A maximum-likelihood strategy for directing attention during visual search. *IEEE Transactions on Pattern Analysis and Machine Intelligence*, *23*(5), 490–500. doi:10.1109/34.922707.

Tatler, B. W., Baddeley, R. J., & Gilchrist, I. D. (2005). Visual correlates of fixation selection: Effects of scale and time. *Vision Research*, *45*, 643–659. doi:10.1016/j.visres.2004.09.017 PMID:15621181.

Treisman, A. M., & Gelade, G. (1980). A feature integration theory of attention. *Cognitive Psychology*, *12*(1), 97–136. doi:10.1016/0010-0285(80)90005-5 PMID:7351125.

Tsotsos, J. K. (1990). Analyzing vision at the complexity level. *The Behavioral and Brain Sciences*, *13*, 423–469. doi:10.1017/S0140525X00079577.

Tsotsos, J. K., Culhane, S. M., Wai, W. Y. K., Lai, Y., Davis, N., & Nuflo, F. (1995). Modeling visual attention via selective tuning. *Artificial Intelligence*, *78*(1-2), 507–547. doi:10.1016/0004-3702(95)00025-9.

Ungerleider, L., & Haxby, J. (1994). 'What' and 'where' in the human brain. *Current Opinion in Neurobiology*, *4*, 157–165. doi:10.1016/0959-4388(94)90066-3 PMID:8038571.

Vazquez, M., & Steinfeld, A. (2011). An assisted photography method for street scenes. In *Proceedings of IEEE Workshop on Applications of Computer Vision* (89-94). Washington, DC: IEEE Press.

Vecera, S., & Farah, M. (1994). Does visual attention select object or locations? *Journal of Experimental Psychology. Human Perception and Performance*, *23*, 1–14.

Vikram, T. N., Tscherepanow, M., & Wrede, B. (2011). A random center-surround bottom-up visual attention model useful for salient region detection. In *Proceedings of IEEE Workshop on Applications of Computer Vision* (166-173). Washington, DC: IEEE Press.

Wolfe, J. M. (1994). Guided search 2.0: A revised model of visual search. *Psychonomic Bulletin & Review*, *1*, 202–238. doi:10.3758/BF03200774.

Wolfe, J. M., & Horowitz, T. S. (2004). What attributes guide the deployment of visual attention and how do they do it? *Nature Reviews. Neuroscience*, *5*(6), 495–501. doi:10.1038/nrn1411 PMID:15152199.

Wu, C.-Y., Leou, J.-J., & Chen, H.-Y. (2009). Visual attention region determination using low-level features. In *Proceedings of IEEE International Symposium on Circuits and Systems* (3178–3181). Washington, DC: IEEE Press.

Yantis, S., & Jonides, J. (1984). Abrupt visual onsets and selective attention: evidence from visual search. *Journal of Experimental Psychology. Human Perception and Performance, 10*, 601–621. doi:10.1037/0096-1523.10.5.601 PMID:6238122.

Yarbus, A. L. (1967). *Eye movements and vision.* New York: Plenum Press.

Yu, Z., & Wong, H.-S. (2007). A rule based technique for extraction of visual attention regions based on real time clustering. *IEEE Transactions on Multimedia, 9*(4), 766–784. doi:10.1109/TMM.2007.893351.

Zhai, Y., & Shah, M. (2006). Visual attention detection in video sequences using spatiotemporal cues. In *Proceedings of the 14th Annual ACM International Conference on Multimedia* (815-824). New York: ACM Press.

Zhao, Z.-C., & Cai, A.-N. (2007). Selective extraction of visual saliency objects in images and videos. In Proceedings of 3rd International Intelligent Information Hiding and Multimedia Signal Processing (198-201). Washington, DC: IEEE Press.

KEY TERMS AND DEFINITIONS

Bottom-Up Attention: In the absence of prior knowledge about the scene being viewed, our gaze is attracted towards salient objects (or locations), of the scene. The saliency, here, is computed in terms of low-level visual features like color, intensity, orientation, size, motion, etc.

Top-Down Attention: Sometimes context-specific, task-driven or semantic guided knowledge about the scene guides our vision. This component of attention is known as top-down attention.

Visual Attention: Visual attention is the mechanism of primate brain to pay attention only to selected set of visual stimuli at a particular time. This selective attention capability reduces the processing burden of our brain so that can efficiently interact with the surrounding.

Visual Saliency: Saliency of an object (or a location) of scene specifies the propensity of the object (or the location) to capture our attention.

Chapter 5
A Brief Review on Recent Trends in Image Restoration

Saurav Prakash
National Institute of Technology, India

ABSTRACT

This chapter gives the opportunity to get an idea of recent trends in image denoising and restoration. It relates to the present research scenario in the field of image restoration. As much as possible the newest break-through regarding the methods of denoising as well as the performance metrics of evaluation has been dealt. The assessments done by the researchers have been included first so as to know how much analysis they propose to be done with respect to the application point of view of the denoising methods. The concept behind the metric selection for the assessment and evaluation has been introduced along with the need for shifting the dependence of the research community towards the newly proposed metrics than the old ones. The new trends in image denoising have been referred duly so that the readers can directly refer to the main algorithms and techniques from the papers proposed by their authors.

INTRODUCTION

The chapter starts with an introduction of the various performance metrics used by researchers and tries to find the suitability of a particular metric for a particular application. The various concepts behind the origin of these metrics have been introduced so that the reader would have an idea empirically choosing a particular metric. The main concern is towards the visual fidelity metrics. Then, the reader is acquainted with the notion and dependence of researchers in using the old metrics of evaluations in their research works. The more dependence on mathematically convenient metrics is pointed out and the reasons to shift towards more visually appreciable quality based metrics have been mentioned. A brief introduction of each such metric has been presented and the applicability of them has been discussed.

After that the recently proposed image denoising algorithms have been dealt, one by one referring to each of the methods in brief. Of course, not all methods can be included so only those methods which are most viable to the research community have been discussed. The readers are encouraged to go through the referred papers of the mentioned researchers for a detailed description of these algorithms.

DOI: 10.4018/978-1-4666-4558-5.ch005

BACKGROUND

Right from the notion of random nature of noises came in existence, image denoising and restoration have been a very important area of research. Researchers have been trying to analyse the noise type and understand its model so that by knowing how noising in image occurs, they can reverse the process to get the denoised image. Different types of noises identified till now are gaussian noise, heavy trailed noise, salt and pepper (impulse) noise, quantization and uniform noise, photon counting noise, photographic grain noise, speckle noise, rayleigh noise, erlang (gamma) noise, exponential noise, and so forth (Bovik, 2009). Researchers have been trying to introduce or modify the denoising algorithms for respective noise wise denoising till late 90s, but now a search for more specific application wise as well as more robust and versatile denoising algorithms is in trend, also as the development continues, more qualitative and vision dependent assessment techniques for the efficiency and quality analysis are in recent trends. A brief review of these new trends in the denoising as well as metrics of evaluation of last decade follows.

CHOICE OF THE PERFORMANCE METRICS

The choice of the visual fidelity metric for a particular case varies from the test algorithm, the complexity of calculation and subjective judgments made by humans' perceptions. The Performance metrics have a literature of their own, According to (Chandler & Hemami, 2007) fundamentally, the metric of evaluation has been developed either on bottom-up properties of vision or by relying on how our visual system responds to a distorted image. These metric of evaluations can be divided as:

1. **Mathematically Convenient Metrics:** These take in to account the intensity of distortions; for example: Mean-Squared Error (MSE), Signal to Noise Ratio (SNR), Peak Signal-to-Noise Ratio (PSNR), Root Mean-Squared Error (RMSE), and so forth.

2. **Metrics Based on Near-Threshold Psychophysics:** These take in to account a frequency-decomposition algorithm, which uses the contrast detection thresholds along with the elevations in the thresholds due to masking effects imposed by images. For example, weighted MSE or activity based measures (Teo & Heeger, 1994; Lai & Kuo, 1997; Winkler, 1999).

3. **Metrics Based on Overarching Principles:** Overreaching principles could be structural or information extraction. The basic principle is that if structural content (such as object boundaries or regions of high entropy etc.) most closely matches that of the original image, the image could be considered a high quality image. (Wang, Bovik, Sheikh, & Simoncelli, 2004; Sheikh, Bovik, & Veciana, 2005; Zhai, Zhang, Yang, & Xu, 2005; Shnayderman, Gusev, & Eskicioglu, 2006).

Mathematically convenient metrics have been quite in use for a long time and are the choice of many researchers for comparison and evaluation of their algorithms. (Boracchi & Foi, 2011) took in to account the Root Mean Squared Error (RMSE) for a comparison between rescaled and original image which can be computed as:

$$RMSE\left(\overset{\frown}{y}, y\right) = 255\sqrt{\frac{1}{\#X}\sum_{x \in X}(\frac{1}{\kappa\lambda}\overset{\frown}{y}\left(x\right) - y(x))^2} \quad (1)$$

where, y is the rescaled image and y is the original image, κ and λ are the varying parameters.

They also considered the time (Boracchi & Foi, 2011) as a criteria for observing how the restoration performance varies with the exposure time. They performed the minimization of RMSE through Nelder-Mead algorithm (Lagarias, Reeds, Wright, & Wright, 1998; Nelder & Mead, 1965).

Most of the contemporary researchers prefer the use of only one such mathematically convenient metrics, rather than depending on more qualitative conscience dependent metrics. For instance, (Gupta & Gupta, n.d.; Margos, 2004; Abadi & Nikbakht, 2011) relied only on PSNR (2), while an average of PSNR was used by (Yüksel, 2006) for his Edge Preserving hybrid neuro-fuzzy Filter.

Rajeesh, Moni, Palanikumar, and Gopalakrishnan (n.d.), Devcic and Loncaric (n.d.), Pizurica, Philips, Lemahieu, and Acheroy (2003), Gilboa, Sochen, and Zeevi (2004), and Portilla, Strela, Wainwright, and Simoncelli (2003) used only SNR for their algorithm performance analysis.

In his research paper, Salmeri and Lojacono (n.d.) proposed the use of RME (Robust Median Estimator) for noise estimation for adaptive denoising, which is based on median rather than mean. Whereas, Chen and Liu (2000), preferred the use of RMSE (1) for assessments of their mixed Kalman filter. On the other hand, Gezici, Yilmaz, Gerek, Enis, and Etin (2001), Rosas-Orea, Hernandez-Diaz, Alarcon-Aquino, and Guerrero-Ojeda (2005), and Pappas and Pitas (2000) used MSE (square of RMSE) as the only metric of evaluation.

Few researchers however, to test the robustness of their denoising algorithms prefer to effort a bit more by using combination of metrics of evaluation.

For example, Nabil (2009), used SNR and PSNR for his proposed algorithm for SAR image filtering, (Wan Mahani Hafizah; Eko Supriyanto, 2011) used MSE and PSNR for assessment based measurements for comparative evaluations. Schulte, De Witte, and. Kerre (2007), employed a combination of PSNR and MSE as evaluation metric for their recently proposed fuzzy filter, whereas Faraji and MacLean (2006) depended on MSE, MAE, and SNR for CCD noise removal algorithms.

Many surveys have been done in the past on the denoising methods used by researchers in recent years, but a much needed survey is on the method used for analysing the algorithms by the researchers. Mostly the surveys which have been done recently have also used quantitative and mathematically convenient metrics of comparison and evaluation rather than stressing more on the activity or structural based metrics.

But a few have introduced the use of quality based metrics such as visual quality analysis, for instance, was done by Motwani, Gadiya, and Motwani (n.d.), for reviewing some significant work in the area of image denoising.

The authors used Peak Signal-to-Noise Ratio (PSNR), Signal-to-Noise Ratio (SNR) for quantitative assessments and analysis, as well as qualitative visual quality analysis of the restored images by various algorithms. They presented a comparison of the efficiency of the algorithms based on these mathematically convenient metrics of evaluations (see Box 1).

Box 1.

Where,

$$PSNR = 20 \log_{10}[255 / \sqrt{\frac{1}{m \times n} \sum_{i=1}^{m} \sum_{j=1}^{n} [I'(i,j) - I(i,j)]^2}] \tag{2}$$

and,

$$SNR = 10 \log 10 \left[\frac{\sum_{i=1}^{m} \sum_{j=1}^{n} I^2(i,j)}{\sum_{i=1}^{m} \sum_{j=1}^{n} [I'(i,j) - I(i,j)]^2} \right] = \frac{P_{signal}}{P_{noise}} \tag{3}$$

where, I is the original image without noise, and I' is the filtered image, where power, P is estimated by calculating the variance. (It should be noted that it is important to use high value of variance to test the performance of the algorithm when the noise is comparable to the signal strength).

Achim and Bezerianos (2003) used both qualitative and quantitative aspects for evaluation and comparison of their proposed WIN-SAR algorithm. They employed MSE for quantitative comparisons with other state-of-the-art speckle filtering methods.

$$MSE = \frac{1}{m \times n} \sum_{i=1}^{m} \sum_{j=1}^{n} [I'(i,j) - I(i,j)]^2 \tag{4}$$

Apart from MSE, they also relied on the standard deviation to the mean ratio, which is a measure of the speckle noise, given by:

$$\frac{S}{M} or \frac{SD}{M} \tag{5}$$

For qualitative performance evaluation, a new correlation measure, proposed by (F. Sattar, L. Floreby, G. Salomonsson, and B. Lövström, 1997) was employed, given as,

$$\beta = \frac{\mathbb{T}(\Delta S - \overline{\Delta S}, \widehat{\Delta S} - \overline{\widehat{\Delta S}})}{\sqrt{\mathbb{T}(\Delta S - \overline{\Delta S}, \Delta S - \overline{\Delta S}) . \mathbb{T}(\widehat{\Delta S} - \overline{\widehat{\Delta S}}, \widehat{\Delta S} - \overline{\widehat{\Delta S}})}} \tag{6}$$

where, ΔS and $\widehat{\Delta S}$ are the high pass-filtered versions of S and $\overline{S}$, respectively, obtained with a 3 3-pixel standard approximation of the Laplacian operator, the over-line operator represents the mean value, and

$$\mathbb{T}(S_1, S_2) = \sum_{i=1}^{K} S_{1_i} . S_{2_i} \tag{7}$$

For testing the quantitative smoothing performance and the edge preservation ability of SAR image denoising algorithms, qualitatively (Markus Robertus de Leeuw; Luis Marcelo Tavares de Carvalho, 2009) while comparing adaptive speckle filters in case of SAR imaging used:

Normalized mean (NM), to examine the ability to preserve the mean in the image:

$$NM = \frac{M_{filtered}}{M_{original}} \tag{8}$$

where, $M_{filtered}$ and $M_{original}$ are the mean of the region of interest in filtered and original image, respectively.

Standard deviation to mean (STM), to determine the ability to reduce speckle noise as explained in Equation (5).

Edge Index (EI), to examine the ability to preserve detailed edge information:

$$EI = \frac{\sum P_f(i,j) - P_f(i-1,j+1)}{\sum P_o(i,j) - P_o(i-1,j+1)} \quad (9)$$

where, $P_f(i,j)$ and $P_o(i,j)$ are the filtered and the original pixel values, respectively, of the edges of the four selected land cover segments, with row number i and column number j. And, $P_f(i-1,j+1)$ and $P_o(i-1,j+1)$ are neighbouring pixel values of the edges.

Sarode and Deshmukh (2011), used SNR, PSNR, MSE, RMSE, and MAE as the mathematical criteria of evaluation and comparison of the algorithms used in case of Rician noise, while evaluating the performances of the denoising algorithms in Magnetic Resonance Imaging. For qualitative assessments, they relied on histogram comparison of the noisy and the denoised images.

In another attempt to evaluate the performance of various filters, and their mutual comparison for removing speckle in medical ultrasound images, Vanithamani and Umamaheswari (2010), used mathematically convenient metrics such as SNR, RMSE, PSNR. They also considered other structural similarity indexes for qualitative assessments, such as:

IMGQ (Z.Wang, A.Bovik, 2002) - The universal Quality Index:

$$QI = \frac{\sigma_{xy}}{\sigma_x \sigma_y} \frac{2\overline{y}\overline{x}}{(\overline{y})^2 + (\overline{x})^2} \frac{2\sigma_y \sigma_x}{\sigma_x^2 + \sigma_y^2} \quad (10)$$

where, $\overline{y}$ and $\overline{x}$ represent mean and σ_y, σ_x the standard deviation of original and the despeckled images, σ_{xy} represents the covariance between the original and despeckled image.

SSIM (Wang, Bovik, Sheik & Simoncelli, 2004)-The Structural Similarity Index (see Box 2).

EPF: (Sattar, Floreby, Salomonsson, & Lovstorm, 1997)-Edge Preservation Factor: which compares the edge preservation ability of a filter, given by:

$$EPF = \frac{\sum(\Delta x - \overline{\Delta x})(\Delta y - \overline{\Delta y})}{\sqrt{\sum(\Delta x - \overline{\Delta x})^2 \sum(\Delta y - \overline{\Delta y})^2}} \quad (12)$$

where Δx and Δy are the high pass filtered version of the images x and y, obtained from with a 3x3 pixel standard approximation of the Laplacian operator.

Babu and Alamelu (2009), used the popular PSNR along with a Compression Ratio estimator (CR) for their proposed algorithm for medical image compression.

Few metrics have been proposed but are used which are based on near-threshold psychophysics, such as contrast sensitivity defined as the inverse of the physical contrast of the target when the target is at the threshold of visual detection, it is measured in terms of a Contrast Sensitivity Function (CSF). Visual fidelity metrics which operate based on near-threshold psychophysics are very effective at determining whether or not the distortions are visible and, therefore, whether or not the original and distorted images are visually distinguishable (Chandler & Hemami, 2007).

The most widely used metric based on Over-arching Principles is the Structural SIMilarity

Box 2.

$$SSIM = \frac{(2\overline{xy} + 2.55)(\sigma_{xy} + 7.65)}{((\overline{y})^2 + (\overline{x})^2 + 255)(\sigma_x^2 + \sigma_y^2 + 7.65)} \quad (11)$$

(SSIM) metric of (Wang et al., 2004). The SSIM metric employs a modified measure of spatial correlation between the pixels of the original and distorted images to quantify the extent to which the image's structure has been distorted. Recently Sheikh et al. (2004) proposed an information-theoretic approach to quantifying visual fidelity by means of an Information Fidelity Criterion (IFC). The IFC metric models images as realizations of a mixture of marginal Gaussian densities chosen for wavelet subband coefficients, and visual fidelity is quantified based on the mutual information between the coefficients of the original and distorted images. Also, recently Sheikh et al (2004), proposed an extension of the IFC metric, which begins to incorporate properties of vision, known as Visual Information Fidelity (VIF).

Based on the psychophysical results presented in the paper, Chandler and Hemami (2007), proposed an entirely new metric called the VSNR (Visual SNR) metric which estimates visual fidelity via two stages:

In the first stage, contrast detection thresholds are computed, if the distortions are below the threshold of detection, the distorted image is deemed to be of perfect visual fidelity, and then the algorithm terminates. If the distortions are suprathreshold, a second stage is applied which estimates visual fidelity based on a measure of perceived contrast and a measure of the extent to which the distortions disrupt global precedence.

Thus one can see the gradual shift of towards more visually efficient metric of evaluation of some researchers but, it has not been entirely welcomed. Still, researchers depend on the mathematically intensive metrics of evaluation. This can be because of changes of visual perception and assessments from person to person.

But the recently proposed metrics which are not totally independent of the mathematical computations and takes in to account the visual quality assessments of vision are expected to break the dependence of the researcher on the old and popular metrics of evaluation because (Chandler et al., 2007):

1. These performs competitively well with other visual fidelity metrics,
2. Are efficient both in terms of computational complexity and in terms of memory requirements, and
3. Are based on physical luminances and visual angle and can therefore accommodate different viewing conditions.

IMAGE DENOISING APPROACHES IN THE DECADE

Adaptive Filter Algorithms

Image Denoising with Two-Dimensional Adaptive Filter Algorithms

Several research works have been done in image denoising community, which involved adaptive filter in one dimension and two dimensions. The robustness of 2-D adaptive filters and their applicability to different types of images and applications have interested many researchers in the last two decades.

Abadi and Nikbakht (2011), recently extended the previous works on 1-D adaptive filter algorithms adoption to 2-D structure and established the novel 2-D adaptive filters. These algorithms try to use adaptive noise cancellation technique for denoising.

The problems with the conventional adaptive filters are that there exists a trade-off between low maladjustment and high convergence speed. Another problem is the computational complexity of conventional 2D-NLMS (Normalized least mean squares) and 2D-APA (Affine projection algorithms) algorithms .To overcome this, the authors proposed the use of the concept of Set-Membership (SM) filtering. In this method, by defining an upper bound on the estimation error, the number of adaptation of filter coefficients can be reduced. To reduce the computational complexity of conventional 2D-NLMS and 2D-APA algorithms, the Selective partial update approach was extended.

By using the 1-D variable step-size APA and variable step size NLMS algorithms in 2-D space, they proposed the 2D variable step-size normalized least mean squares (2D-VSS NLMS), the 2D-VSS affine projection algorithms (2D-VSS-APA), the 2D set-membership NLMS (2D-SM-NLMS), the 2D-SM-APA, the 2D selective partial update NLMS (2D SPU-NLMS), and the 2D-SPU-APA filter algorithms.

As per the simulation results, these novel adaptive filters have good ability for elimination of noise in digital images and have low computational complexity accordingly, have close performance to classical 2D adaptive filters.

Image Denoising in Wavelet Domain

Recently, there has been considerable interest in using the wavelet transform as a powerful tool for recovering images from noisy data. The main reason for the choice of multi-scale bases of decompositions is that the statistics of many natural signals, when decomposed in such bases, are significantly simplified and are easy to handle.

Nabil (2009), proposed the use of sub-band adaptive threshold with Translation Invariant (TI) algorithm (Coifman & Donoha, 1995) for additive noise model in case of SAR images. For the SAR image domain, he applied logarithmic transformations on the image and then applied DWT (Discrete Wavelength Transform) to the image, after the inverse DWT, the processed image is exponentially transformed to reverse the logarithmic operation. He applied Daubechies D_1, D_2, D_3, D_4 filter pairs for the wavelet transformations (This is due to the fact the smoothness of the Daubechies wavelet increases as the order the filter increases).

The basic method involves:

1. Calculate the discrete wavelet transform of the image.

2. Threshold the wavelet coefficients. (Threshold may be universal or sub-band adaptive)

Compute the inverse wavelet transforms to get the denoised estimate $\hat{f}$.

The PSNR comparison with other proposed methods in the wavelength domain such as Multilevel soft-threshold based method (Khare & Tiwary, 2005), Universal threshold based denoising and Visushrink shows that this method based on generalized Gaussian distribution modelling of sub-band coefficients is more computationally efficient and apart from denoising the image also succeeds in preserving the sharp features in the original image.

Achim & Bezerianos (2003), proposed a similar method for dealing with the SAR image's noise. They also used logarithmic and DWT based transformations like Nabil (2009), but after that, a statistically dependent MAP processor which relied on heavy-tailed alpha-stable models was used for speckle reduction and signal detail preservation. A flowchart of the used algorithm is shown in Figure 1.

By employing $\beta(4)$, $MSE(5)$ and $\dfrac{S}{M}$ (6) metrics of evaluation it was shown clearly that their WIN-SAR processor exhibits a better performance in speckle noise reduction than Lee, soft-thresholding or GMAP filters.

Gezici, Yilmaz, Gerek, Enis, and Etin (2001), proposed the use space varying filter-banks instead of fixed wavelets to process an image. Their denoising algorithm was based on adaptive wavelet transform, in which the filter coefficients are updated according to a Least Mean Square (LMS) type algorithm.

This work was also aimed at finding the best wavelet basis for decomposing the entire data as done by Tewfik, Sinha, and Jorgensen (1992) and Coifman and Wickerhauser (1992), but unlike others, the authors used varying filters instead of fixed one.

Figure 1. Flowchart of MAP processor based algorithm for restoration in wavelet domain

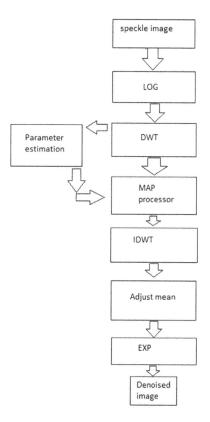

This statistical model differs from the previously proposed models in a number of ways.

1. This model is based on a complete tight frame that is free from aliasing, and that includes basis functions that are selective for oblique orientations, unlike previous models previous models which have been based on either separable orthogonal wavelets, or redundant versions of such wavelets.

2. This model explicitly incorporates the covariance between neighbouring coefficients (for both signal and noise), as opposed to considering only marginal responses or local variance.

3. Also, this model included a neighbour from the same orientation and spatial location at a coarser scale (a parent), as opposed to considering only spatial neighbours within each sub-band.

4. The authors used vectorial form of the LLS solution (Bell & Sejnowski, 1997), thus, taking full advantage of the information provided by the covariance modelling of signal and noise.

5. This model captures correlations induced by the over complete representation as well as correlations inherent in the underlying image.

These all new approaches result in a substantial improvement in the quality of the denoised images, along with keeping the computational cost reasonably low.

Kim and Ra (2005) proposed a more efficient algorithm for ultrasound speckle noise. In ultrasound images, the speckle energy is comparable to the signal energy in a wide range of frequency bands. So it is not easy to discriminate speckle from the signal.

This new approach involves directional filtering and noise reducing procedures from the coarse to fine resolution images that are obtained from the wavelet-transformed data.

The basic method was to pass the corrupted image through a pyramid like structure in which the low-pass filtered version of the image is subtracted from the original, and in this way the high frequency component is obtained. The high frequency component is decomposed by a filterbank and the resulting sub-images are thresholded.

In other words denoising is performed on high frequency component instead of the corrupted image. After it is denoised, it is added to the low-pass filtered image to obtain the restored image. The authors concluded that apart from giving better statistical evaluation results than fixed filter-banks, this approach of collectively mixing the filters adaptively, restore images with much better visually robust results.

Portilla, Strela, Wainwright, and Simoncelli (2003), introduced a new denoising approach based on local Gaussian scale mixture model.

Firstly, discrimination is required between speckle noises from signal. To achieve this, the image is decomposed in wavelet domain. Then, the structural information is obtained from the decomposed image by performing the eigen-analysis at each resolution scale. After that, based on the structural information, directional filtering and speckle reduction procedures are applied to the multi-resolution image adaptively.

The comparison was done with two robust algorithms used in ultrasound domain.

One is based on Nonlinear anisotropic Diffusion filtering (NCD) given by Abd-Elmoniem, Youssef, and Kadah (2002), and the other on Wavelet Shrinkage and Contrast Enhancement (WSCE), given by Zong, Laine, and Geiser (1998).

The experimental results showed that this new algorithm considerably improves the image quality without generating any noticeable artefact, and also provides better performance compared with the existing schemes.

The recent trend in wavelet based denoising has shifted to produce more real time or versatile adaptive algorithms so that they could be used directly for application purposes.

In real time image denoising one often faces uncertainty about the presence of a given "feature of interest" in a noisy observation. To account for this, Pizurica, Philips, Lemahieu, and Acheroy (2003) proposed a new, versatile, robust, interactive and efficient wavelet domain based denoising technique, which is applicable to various types of image noise.

The best thing about their algorithm is that a single parameter can be used to balance the preservation of (expert-dependent) relevant details against the degree of noise reduction; also, it does not rely on the exact prior knowledge of the noise distribution.

The authors employed a preliminary detection of the wavelet coefficients that represent the features of interest in order to estimate the conditional probability distribution of the coefficients along with the local spatial activity indicator.

This algorithm performs a soft modification of the coefficients adapted to the image context. The adjustable parameter is used in the classification step to tune the noise suppression.

The proposed method is adaptive and is of low-complexity, both in its implementation and execution time. It can adapt itself to unknown noise distributions and to the local spatial image context. For these reasons, it can be widely used in the medical imaging domain. The authors analysed this algorithm and by tuning the parameter, in case of MRI images as well as ultrasound images and they concluded that this algorithm was more efficient and robust than the existing medical domain filers like homomorphic and wiener filter.

Demanet and Ying (2007) introduced the so-called wave atoms, that can be seen as a variant of 2D Wavelet packets and obey the parabolic scaling of curvelets:

$$wavelength = (diameter)^2 \qquad (13)$$

Wave atoms have the ability to adapt to arbitrary local directions of a pattern, and to sparsely represent anisotropic patterns aligned with the axes. In comparison to curvelets, wave atoms not only capture the coherence of the pattern along the oscillations, but also the pattern across the oscillations. A more detailed description can be found in (Demanet & Ying, 2007).

Rajeesh, Moni, Palanikumar, and Gopalakrishnan (n.d.), proposed a novel scheme for de-noising of Magnetic Resonance Images using wave atom shrinkage, which can be formulated as a hard threshold function given as:

$$f_h(x) = \begin{cases} x - \dfrac{\sigma^2}{x}, & |x| \ge \sigma \\ 0, & |x| < \sigma \end{cases} \qquad (14)$$

Here, σ is the standard deviation, estimated by histogram based techniques.

The performance of the proposed method with wavelet shrinkage and curvelet shrinkage was evaluated with simulated images and real images which proved, that this new denoising algorithm gives better SNR compared to wavelet and curvelet shrinkages along with the preservation of edges

Total Variation Minimization

In the last decade, Total Variation minimization has become a popular and valuable technique for the restoration of noisy and blurred images. Based on minimizing the Total Variation of the image subject to a noise constraint; Rudin, Osher, and Fatemi (1992) proposed an algorithm, which had been one of the most popular image restoration methods.

Landi (2007), proposed a bit different approach to Total Variation-based image restoration. Briefly, the idea was to replace the original problem of modelling an image restoration problem as a linear system, with a constrained Total Variation minimization problem whose solution is close to an exact solution.

The linear system can be modelled as:

$$y = KX + e \qquad (15)$$

where, y is the observed blurred and noisy image, x is the desired true image, e is a Gaussian white noise and K is a known linear operator.

In particular, an iterative Lagrange method is applied and its iterations are early terminated according to the discrepancy principle before much noise occurs in the approximation. The Lagrange multiplier, which is automatically determined during the Lagrange iteration, acts as a regularization parameter measuring the fidelity to the data y. This image restoration technique is known as Truncated Lagrange (TL) method. The results of the numerical analysis showed that the proposed method is computationally efficient and is effective in solving both image denoising and

image de-blurring problems than the standard total Variation approaches.

Osher, Sol´e, and Vese (2003) proposed a new denoising model which combines the total variation minimization approach given by Rudin, Osher, and Fatemi (1992) with a norm for oscillatory functions proposed by Meyer (2002) involving the H^{-1} norm. The comparison metrics such as RMSE and PSNR shows that this new model performs much better on textured images than existing methods based on total variation minimization approach for such images.

PDE Based Denoising

Srivastava, Gupta, and Parthasarathy (2011) used the three popular diffusion-based PDEs such as anisotropic diffusion-based PDE (Perona & Malik, 1990), non-linear complex diffusion-based PDE (Gilboa et al., 2004), and fourth-order PDE (You & Kaveh, 2000), which were proposed for additive noises were used by logarithmical treatment of the speckle noises and then applying those for ultrasound characteristic multiplicative speckle noise.

Their paper also proposed a new adaptive function for calculating the edge threshold parameter so that the edge threshold value can be empirically calculated and analysed for efficiency. This adaptive function eliminates the need for manual fixing and fine-tuning the diffusion coefficients according to an image. Thus provides a more robust method for digital implementations.

The authors exhaustively compared the efficiency of their proposed scheme with other popular speckle reduction techniques, such as SRAD filter (Yu & Acton, 2002), Lee filter (Lee, 1981, 1983), Frost filter (Frost et al., 1982), and Kuan filter (Lopes et al., 1990). The comprehensive examination concluded that the modified adaptive non-linear complex diffusion-based scheme outperforms all other schemes and is a best choice for speckle reduction from ultrasound images, and can be extended for other multiplicative noises based application domain.

(Ji-Ying Wu, 2006) proposed recently a hybrid model involving different coefficient function with different edge preserving property. The basic idea is to use Total Variation (TV)-PDE and enlarge it to second order, based on Markov random field, this way more information can be obtained. Also, the author concluded that these new TV-Markov model based hybrid filters employs less staircasing and much better denoising effect and edge preservation efficiency.

The TV minimization (Total Variation Minimization) is a PDE that often involves staircasing and an excessive dissipation during the noise removal.

For this reason, Joo and Kim (2003), proposed an Enhanced TV Minimization (ETVM) based approach which uses anti-staircasing in the proposed method which involves algebraic scaling, non-convex minimization, and ODOP (Operator-Driven Optimal Parameter).

The algebraic scaling has been numerically verified to outperform to the variable-p approach. This scaling not only prevents staircasing effectively but also preserves a certain degree of convexity and concavity of the image contents. Although a non-convex minimization does not guarantee the existence of the minimizer, it has performed well for anti-diffusion with a great extent of satisfaction, so to prevent non-necessary diffusion of TVM; the authors used non-convex minimization along with ODOP. The basic idea of Operator-Driven Optimal Parameter (ODOP) is to let the constraint parameter grow wherever an excessive dissipation occurs.

The proposed ETVM was exhaustively tested for effectiveness and robustness in the removal of Gaussian noise; it performed satisfactorily for the edge-preserving noise removal.

The new shift of the image processing community is to apply computer vision and AI along with DIP principles for image denoising and enhancement, so that robust and more interactive methods can be developed, which are application independent and versatile. In PDE based methods

also, these trend interested Fazli (2010) to present a new heuristic based approach for image denoising based on Partial Differential Equations (PDE) using Artificial Intelligence (AI) techniques. In the paper, the author proposed to use a Particle Swarm Optimization (PSO), which is a swarm intelligence technique, inspired by social behaviour of bird flocking or fish schooling for Complex PDE parameter tuning by minimizing the Structural SIMilarity (SSIM) measure. The proposed method was confirmed by the author to be highly effective in denoising as per the simulation results obtained for the standard images.

Inspired by the work of Tasdizen, Whitaker, Burchard, and Osher (2003), Ballaster, Bertalmio, Caselles, Sapiro, and Verdera (2000), and Vese and Osher (2002); Lysaker, Osher, and Tai (2004) proposed a new variational approach to overcome the popular problem of staircasing in case of TV-norm filter.

Basically, to overcome the problem of staircasing, researchers use higher order PDEs. But in the paper, the authors proposed to solve two second-order nonlinear PDEs sequentially by a two-step method for computational efficiency because if the two equations are combined together, one would need to solve one higher order nonlinear PDE. The steps can be summarised as:

1. The normal vectors of the level set curves of the noise image are smoothen using a TV-norm filter (i.e. firstly the normal is denoised for the level sets of the image intensity function).
2. After the normal vectors are smoothed and an image that fits the normal vectors is taken as the recovered image for the corrupted observation.

With this approach, geometric information of the level contours is incorporated in the image processing model. Numerical analysis done by the authors showed that this method holds three important qualities:

1. It is superior in recovering sharp edges of an image.
2. It enhances the recovery of smooth sub-surfaces contained in the image.
3. It is easy to control the amount of smoothing with our method.

Other Methods

Devcic and Loncaric (n.d.), proposed a new Non-linear image noise filtering algorithm based on block SVD processing. Block processing reduces The SVD computations. The proposed algorithm is based on eliminating changes that resulted from additive white Gaussian noise in the image (singular values and singular vectors).

The additive noise increases the Singular values, this increase is proportional to noise variance. Value that is proportional to noise variance is estimated using few last singular values.

The Basic idea is to at First, Dividing the noised image is into square blocks of size $b \times b$. For each block the singular value decomposition is performed. In the consequent step, the average sum of the last singular values is calculated over all image blocks, and consequently, the calculated SVD of image blocks can be used for filtering. Through application to different domain, the authors concluded that this new SVD block processing is computationally efficient and can be applied to coloured and image dependent noise with satisfactory restoration results.

Schulte, De Witte, & Kerre (2007), proposed a new fuzzy filter for additive noise reduction for digital colour images. The main advantages of this filter are its denoising capability and the reconstruction capability of the destroyed colour component in the image.

Any Fuzzy image processing has three main stages:

1. Image Fuzzification.
2. Modification of Membership Values.
3. Image Defuzzification.

The general idea of all fuzzy filters is the same: To average a pixel using other pixel values from its neighbourhood, but simultaneously take into account the important image structures such as edges and colour component distances, which should not be destroyed by the filter.

Fuzzy filters are able to outperform rank-order techniques (such as the median based filters) for impulse noises but till now its use is limited to grayscale images, also current fuzzy techniques do not produce convincing results for additive noise. In their paper, the authors extended the capability of the fuzzy filters to the colour image domain and for gaussian distributions. The authors illustrated that the proposed method outperforms most of the other fuzzy filters and achieves a comparable noise reduction performance to the much more complex wavelet based methods. Another proposal was that if this method would be combined with the wavelet-based methods, one can achieve best performance in terms of numerically as well as visually dependent metrics.

CONCLUSION

The last decade saw a shift of Image denoising research work towards devising more computationally efficient, robust, and versatile filters which can be used for real time systems as well. Much progress was seen in PDE domain, wavelet domain, adaptive filtering domain, total variation minimization based filtering domain, fuzzy logic implementation, hybrid filter modelling etc. The various filters were proposed for one domain and later on are being tested for other domain so that the same algorithm can be efficiently used for other application domain. Researchers are now using a hybrid approach for denoising by combining the wavelet transforms and other intermediate models. Last decade also saw the introduction of more visual fidelity based metrics of assessments. This domain of performance metric evaluation has also seen new models which are not only dependent on the much used mathematically convenient metrics but also speaks for visual quality measurements. The schemes discussed in this chapter justify the robustness and applicability of these new metrics to image denoising, enhancements and related domain effectively.

DIRECTIONS FOR FUTURE RESEARCH

The shift of research work is more towards real time image processing and denoising and it is deemed to be a promising area of research in image denoising domain. Making the previously proposed domain more robust, versatile and computationally as well as space efficient application wise, is a major challenge for the researchers. For accounting for different types of noises, using single filter model is interesting researchers all over the world. Hybrid filters employing different filters for step by step or simultaneous noise reduction and mixed filters are being used and more works are being done in this domain day by day.

The researchers are shifting towards more visual quality based metrics for their algorithms analysis so as to account for the qualitative analysis of the algorithms, these qualitative metrics are still promising field of research and more metrics are being predicted to be proposed in the near future.

REFERENCES

Abadi & Nikbakht. (2011). Image denoising with two-dimensional adaptive filter algorithms. *Iranian Journal of Electrical & Electronic Engineering, 7*(2).

Abd-Elmoniem, Youssef, & Kadah. (2002). Real-time speckle reduction and coherence enhancement in ultrasound imaging via nonlinear anisotropic diffusion. *IEEE Transactions on Bio-Medical Engineering, 49*(9), 997–1014. doi:10.1109/TBME.2002.1028423 PMID:12214889.

Achim & Bezerianos. (2003). SAR image denoising via bayesian wavelet shrinkage based on heavy-tailed modelling. *IEEE Transactions on Geoscience and Remote Sensing, 41*(8).

Babu & Alamelu. (2009). Wavelet based medical image compression using ROI EZW. *International Journal of Recent Trends in Engineering, 1*(3).

Ballaster, C., & Sapiro, V. (2000). Filling-in by joint interpolation of vector fields and gray levels. *IEEE Transactions on Image Processing, 9*, 1200–1211. PMID:18262958.

Bell & Sejnowski. (1997). The "independent components" of natural scenes are edge filters. *Vision Research, 37*(23), 3327–3338. doi:10.1016/S0042-6989(97)00121-1 PMID:9425547.

Boracchi & Foi. (2011). Uniform motion blur in poissonian noise: Blur/noise trade-off. *IEEE Transactions on Image Processing, 20*(2).

Bovik. (2009). *The essential guide to image processing.* Amsterdam: Elsevier Inc.

Chandler & Hemami. (2007). VSNR: A wavelet-based visual signal-to-noise; ratio for natural images. *IEEE Transactions on Image Processing, 16*(9).

Chen & Liu. (2000). Mixed kalman filter. *Journal of the Royal Statistical Society. Series B. Methodological, 62*(3), 493–508. doi:10.1111/1467-9868.00246.

Coifman & Donoha. (1995). *Translation-invariant de-noising. Wavelets and Statistics*. Berlin: Springer-Verlag.

Coifman & Wickerhauser. (1992). Entropy-based algorithms for best basis selection. *IEEE Transactions on Information Theory, 38*(2), 713–718. doi:10.1109/18.119732.

De Leeuw & de Carvalho. (2009). Performance evaluation of several adaptive speckle filters for SAR imaging. In *Proceedings of Anais XIV Simpósio Brasileiro de Sensoriamento Remoto (7299-7305)*. Natal, Brasil: INPE.

Demanet & Ying. (2007). Wave atoms and sparsity of oscillatory patterns. *Applied and Computational Harmonic Analysis, 23*(3), 368–387. doi:10.1016/j.acha.2007.03.003.

Devcic & Loncaric. (n.d.). *Non-linear image noise filtering algorithm based on SVD block processing*. Washington, DC: IEEE Press.

Faraji & MacLean. (2006). CCD noise removal in digital images. *IEEE Transactions on Image Processing, 15*(9).

Fazli, S. (2010). Complex PDE image denoising based on particle swarm optimization. In *Proceedings of 2010 International Congress Ultra-Modern Telecommunications and Control Systems and Workshops* (364–370). Washington, DC: IEEE Press.

Gezici, Yilmaz, Gerek, Enis, & Etin. (2001). *Image denoising using adaptive subband decomposition*. Washington, DC: IEEE Press.

Gilboa, Sochen, & Zeevi. (2004). Image enhancement and denoising by complex diffusion. *IEEE Transactions on Pattern Analysis and Machine Intelligence, 26*(8). doi:10.1109/TPAMI.2004.47 PMID:15641732.

Gupta & Gupta. (n.d.). *Wavelet domain image enhancement using local regularity*. Pilani, India. BITS Pilani..

Hafizah & Supriyanto. (2011). Comparative evaluation of ultrasound kidney image enhancement techniques. *International Journal of Computers and Applications, 21*(7).

Joo & Kim. (2003). *PDE-based image restoration, I: Anti-staircasing and anti-diffusion. Technical Report #2003-07*. Lexington, KY: University of Kentucky.

Khare & Tiwary. (2005). Soft-thresholding for denoising of medical images, A multiresolution approach. *International Journal of Wavelets, Multresolution, and Information Processing, 3*(4), 477–496. doi:10.1142/S021969130500097X.

Kim & Ra. (2005). Improvement of ultrasound image based on wavelet transform: Speckle reduction and edge enhancement in medical imaging, image processing. *Processing of SPIE, 5747*.

Lagarias, Reeds, Wright, & Wright. (1998). Convergence properties of the nelder-mead simplex method in low dimensions. *SIAM Journal on Optimization, 9*(1), 112–147. doi:10.1137/S1052623496303470.

Lai & Kuo. (1997). Image quality measurement using the haar wavelet. In *Proceedings of SPIE: Wavelet Applications in Signal and Image Processing V*. Bellingham, WA: SPIE Press.

Landi. (2007). A truncated lagrange method for total variation-based image restoration. *Journal of Mathematical Imaging and Vision, 28*, 113–123.

Lysaker, Osher, & Tai. (2004). Noise removal using smoothed normals and surface fitting. *IEEE Transactions on Image Processing, 13*(10). doi:10.1109/TIP.2004.834662 PMID:15462144.

Margos. (2004). Morphological filtering for image enhancement and feature detection. *Image and Video Processing Handbook (*2nd edition). Amsterdam: Academic Press.

Meyer. (2002). Oscillating patterns in image processing and nonlinear evolution equations. *University Lecture Series 22*. Providence, RI: AMS.

Milindkumar & Deshmukh. (2011). Performance evaluation of noise reduction algorithm in magnetic resonance images. *International Journal of Computer Science Issues*, *8*(2).

Motwani, Gadiya, & Motwani. (n.d.). Survey of image denoising techniques. *International Arab Journal of e-Technology, 2*(1).

Nabil. (2009). SAR image filtering in wavelet domain by subband depended shrink. *International Journal of Open Problems of Computational Mathematics, 2*(1).

Nelder & Mead. (1965). A simplex method for function minimization. *The Computer Journal, 7*, 308–313. doi:10.1093/comjnl/7.4.308.

Osher, Sole, & Vese. (2003). Multiscale model simulation. *Society for Industrial and Applied Mathematics, 1*(3), 349–370.

Pappas & Pitas. (2000). Digital colour restoration of old painting. *IEEE Transactions on Image Processing, 9*(2).

Pizurica, Philips, Lemahieu, & Acheroy. (2003). A versatile wavelet domain noise filtration technique for medical imaging. *IEEE Transactions on Medical Imaging, 22*(3), 323–331. doi:10.1109/TMI.2003.809588 PMID:12760550.

Portilla, Strela, Wainwright, & Simoncell. (2003). Image denoising using scale mixtures of gaussians in the wavelet domain. *IEEE Transactions on Image Processing, 12*(11). doi:10.1109/TIP.2003.818640 PMID:18244692.

Rajeesh, Moni, Palanikumar, & Gopalakrishnan. (n.d.). Noise reduction in magnetic resonance images using wave atom shrinkage. *International Journal of Image Processing, 4*(2).

Rosas-Orea, H.-D. Alarcon-Aquino, & Guerrero-Ojeda. (2005). A comparative simulation study of wavelet based denoising algorithms. In *Proceedings of IEEE CONIELECOMP*. Washington DC, IEEE Press.

Rudin, L. I., Osher, S., & Fatemi, E. (1992). Nonlinear total variation based noise removal algorithms. *Physica D. Nonlinear Phenomena, 60*, 259–268. doi:10.1016/0167-2789(92)90242-F.

Salmeri & Lojacono. (n.d.). Noise estimation in mammographic images for adaptive denoising. *TELESAL project.* Retrieved from http://www.kell.it/telesal_en.htm.

Schulte, De Witte, & Kerre. (2007). A fuzzy noise reduction method for colour images. *IEEE Transactions on Image Processing, 16*(5). doi:10.1109/TIP.2007.891807 PMID:17491470.

Sheikh, Bovik, & de Veciana. (2005). An information fidelity criterion for image quality assessment using natural scene statistics. *IEEE Transactions on Image Processing, 14*(12), 2117–2128. doi:10.1109/TIP.2005.859389 PMID:16370464.

Shnayderman, Gusev, & Eskicioglu. (2006). A SVD-based grayscale image quality measure for local and global assessment. *IEEE Transactions on Image Processing, 15*(2), 422–429. doi:10.1109/TIP.2005.860605 PMID:16479812.

Srivastava, Gupta, & Parthasarathy. (2011). An adaptive non-linear PDE-based speckle reduction technique for ultrasound images. *International Journal of Biomedical Engineering and Technology, 6*(3). doi:10.1504/IJBET.2011.041468.

Tasdizen, Whitaker, Burchard, & Osher. (2003). Geometric surface processing via normal maps. *ACM Transactions on Graphics, 22*(4), 1012–1033. doi:10.1145/944020.944024.

Teo & Heeger. (1994). Perceptual image distortion. *Proceedings of the Society for Photo-Instrumentation Engineers, 2179,* 127–141. doi:10.1117/12.172664.

Tewfik, Sinha, & Jorgensen. (1992). On the optimal choice of a wavelet for signal representation. *IEEE Transactions on Information Theory, 38*(2), 747–765. doi:10.1109/18.119734.

Vanithamani & Umamaheswari. (2010). Performance analysis of filters for speckle reduction in medical ultrasound images. *International Journal of Computers and Applications, 12*(6).

Vese & Osher. (2002). Numerical methods for p-harmonic flows and applications to image processing. *SIAM Journal on Numerical Analysis, 40*(6), 2085–2104. doi:10.1137/S0036142901396715.

Wang, Bovik, Sheikh, & Simoncelli. (2004). Image quality assessment: From error visibility to structural similarity. *IEEE Transactions on Image Processing, 13*(4), 600–612. doi:10.1109/TIP.2003.819861 PMID:15376593.

Wang & Bovik. (2002). A universal quality index. *IEEE Signal Processing Letters, 9*(3), 81–84. doi:10.1109/97.995823.

Winkler. (1999). Visual quality assessment using a contrast gain control model. In *Proceedings of IEEE Signal Processing Society Workshop on Multimedia Signal Processing* (527–532). Washington, DC: IEEE Press.

Wu. (2006). A new hybrid PDE denoising model based on markov random field. In *Proceedings of First International Conference on Innovative Computing Information and Control* (338–341). Washington, DC: IEEE Press.

Yüksel. (2006). A hybrid neuro-fuzzy filter for edge preserving restoration of images corrupted by impulse noise. *IEEE Transactions on Image Processing, 15*(4).

Zhai, Z. Yang, & Xu. (2005). Image quality assessment metrics based on multi-scale edge presentation. In *Proceedings of IEEE Workshop on Signal Processing Systems Design and Implementation* (331–336). Washington, DC: IEEE Press.

Zong, Laine, & Geiser. (1998). Speckle reduction and contrast enhancement of echocardiogram via multiscale nonlinear processing. *IEEE Transactions on Medical Imaging, 17.*

KEY TERMS AND DEFINITIONS

Edge Index (EI): Which is used for indexing the preservation of detailed edge information.

Edge Preservation Factor (EPF): Which is a comparative factor for edge preservation ability.

Fuzzy Image Processing: A method which involves firstly fuzzification of image and then modification of the values concluded by defuzzification.

Mean-Squared Error (MSE): A quantifier to estimate the difference between values implied by an estimator and the true value.

Restoration: It is one of the steps in image processing tasks that aims at removing or reducing the noise from images to improve its visual quality.

Signal to Noise Ratio (SNR): Which compares the level of a desired signal to the level of noise.

Staircasing: It is an effect of creation of flat regions in the image separated by artefact boundaries.

Total Variation Minimization: An approach of minimizing the total Variation of the image subject to a noise constraint.

Visual Signal to Noise Ratio (VSNR): A newly proposed visually dependent qualitative assessment metric.

Chapter 6
Image Enhancement and Restoration Methods for Underwater Images

C. J. Prabhakar
Kuvempu University, India

P. U. Praveen Kumar
Kuvempu University, India

ABSTRACT

In this chapter, the authors provide an overview of state-of-the-art image enhancement and restoration techniques for underwater images. Underwater imaging is one of the challenging tasks in the field of image processing and computer vision. Usually, underwater images suffer from non-uniform lighting, low contrast, diminished color, and blurring due to attenuation and scattering of light in the underwater environment. It is necessary to preprocess these images before applying computer vision techniques. Over the last few decades, many researchers have developed various image enhancement and restoration algorithms for enhancing the quality of images captured in underwater environments. The authors introduce a brief survey on image enhancement and restoration algorithms for underwater images. At the end of the chapter, we present an overview of our approach, which is well accepted by the image processing community to enhance the quality of underwater images. Our technique consists of filtering techniques such as homomorphic filtering, wavelet-based image denoising, bilateral filtering, and contrast equalization, which are applied sequentially. The proposed method increases better image visualization of objects which are captured in underwater environment compared to other existing methods.

INTRODUCTION

Underwater images are essentially characterized by their poor visibility because light is exponentially attenuated as it travels in the water, and the scenes result poorly contrasted and hazy. Light attenuation limits the visibility distance at about twenty meters in clear water and five meters or less in turbid water. The light attenuation process is caused by absorption (which removes light energy) and scattering (which changes the direction of the light path). The absorption and scattering processes of the light in water influence the overall performance of underwater imaging systems.

DOI: 10.4018/978-1-4666-4558-5.ch006

Forward scattering (randomly deviated light on its way from an object to the camera) generally leads to blurring of the image features. On the other hand, backward scattering (the fraction of the light reflected by the water towards the camera before it actually reaches the objects in the scene) generally limits the contrast of the images, generating a characteristic veil that superimposes itself on the image and hides the scene.

Absorption and scattering effects are not only due to the water itself but also to other components such as dissolved organic matter or small observable floating particles. The presence of the floating particles known as "marine snow" (highly variable in kind of and concentration) increase absorption and scattering effects. The visibility range can be increased with artificial lighting but these sources not only suffer from the difficulties described before (scattering and absorption), but in addition tend to illuminate the scene in a non uniform fashion, producing a bright spot in the center of the image with a poorly illuminated area surrounding it. Finally, as the amount of light is reduced when go deeper; colors drop off one by one depending on their wavelengths.

The most commonly used imaging systems for underwater environment are optical imaging system, SONARs and LIDARs. Optical imaging is cost effective compared to SONARs and LIDARs, but there are some limitations of using the optical imaging system as it provides a limited range of visibility compared to SONARs and LIDARs. The range is visibility of optical imaging for clear water is up to 20 meters, and in turbid water, it is less than 5 meters. And the captured underwater images suffer from non-uniform lighting, low contrast, blurring, and diminished colors due to propagation properties of light in underwater environment. These images cannot be directly employed for applying computer vision and pattern recognition techniques. There has been a great effort from the last few years to improve the quality of underwater images and many methods have been derived to fulfill the task. The processing of underwater images can be addressed from two different points of view: as an image restoration technique or as an image enhancement method. The image restoration aims to recover a degraded image using a model of the degradation and of the original image formation; it is essentially an inverse problem. These methods are rigorous, but they require many model parameters (like attenuation and diffusion coefficients that characterize the water turbidity).

Some of the image restoration methods have been proposed in the literature based on the physical model that describes the light propagation in water. These approaches consider behavior of light propagation and its interaction with the water medium. The constructed physical model is used to estimate this model's parameters in order to minimize the effects on image formation and to correct image intensity distribution. The literature survey reveals that popular image enhancement techniques have been proposed for enhancement of degraded underwater images and for color correction of the image. Image enhancement technique uses qualitative subjective criteria to produce a more visually pleasing image, and they do not rely on any physical model for the image formation. These kinds of approaches are usually simpler and faster than deconvolution methods.

In the last few years, different methods for image quality assessment have been proposed. Peak Signal to Noise Ratio (PSNR) and Mean Squared Error (MSE) are the most widely used objective image quality/distortion metrics. In the last decades, however, a great effort has been made to develop new objective image quality assessment methods which incorporate perceptual quality measures by considering human visual system characteristics.

APPLICATIONS

Underwater imaging is widely used in the field of scientific research and technology. Computer vision methods are being used in this mode of imaging for various applications, such as mine detection, inspection of underwater power and telecommunications cables, pipelines, nuclear reactors, shipwrecks (Negahdaripour & Firooz-fam, 2006) and columns of offshore platforms. Underwater computer vision is commercially used to help swimming pool life guards. As in conventional computer vision, algorithms are sought for navigation and control of submerged robots. In addition, underwater imaging is used for research in marine biology, archaeology and mapping.

In water, inspection is an essential task for general maintenance and damage assessment of underwater structures (Hogue et al., 2007). For example, inspection of ship hulls is necessary as part of periodic maintenance operations. This has become extremely critical with the threat that ships entering ports and harbors for commerce may serve as carriers of nuclear weapons, explosives, deadly chemicals and other hazardous materials, with mass destruction in highly populated cities, national landmarks, and other drastic damages at the nation scale as potentially target activities. To combat this threat, deployment of existing technologies and the development of new ones are sought to implement search and detection systems that can provide no less than 100% success rate. Unlike regular hull maintenance that may be carried out by trained divers, inspection and search for hazardous and (or) deadly materials have to be done with submersible robotics platforms to avoid risk of human lives. In general, it is expected that the deployment of such vehicles, when highly automated, can provide a more effective and efficient solution.

Inspection of naval mine (underwater mine) is a self-contained explosive device placed in water to destroy ships or submarines. Unlike depth charges, mines are deposited and left to wait until they are triggered by the approach of or contact with an enemy ship. Naval mines can be used offensively, to hamper enemy ships or lock them into a harbor; or defensively, to protect friendly ships and create "safe" zones. Inspect the growth

of coral reefs. Coral reefs are underwater structures made from calcium carbonate secreted by corals. Corals are colonies of tiny living animals found in marine waters containing few nutrients. Most coral reefs are built from stony corals, and are formed by polyps that live together in groups. The polyps secrete a hard carbonate exoskeleton which provides support and protection for the body of each polyp. Reefs grow best in warm, shallow, clear, sunny and agitated waters.

The aquatic environment provides a range of recreational activities. Potential applications in the entertainment industry of 3D reconstruction technology include the reconstruction of underwater scenes for documenting recreational scuba diving expeditions. Many diver's videotape their dives using traditional consumer-grade video recording equipment. Automatic 3D reconstruction of the dive could add impact to the experience by increasing the dimensionality of the recording without increasing task-loading on the diver.

RELATED WORK

Over the last few decades, a large number of researchers have contributed their work for enhancing the quality of underwater images for various general-purpose applications. They address image processing problem in two different points of view (Schettini & Corchs, 2010): as an image restoration technique and as an image enhancement technique. 1.) The image restoration technique aims to recover a degraded image using a model of the degradation and of the original image formation; it is essentially an inverse problem. These methods are rigorous, but they require many model parameters (like attenuation and scattering coefficients that characterize the water turbidity). Another important parameter required is the depth estimation of a given object in the scene. 2.) Image enhancement technique uses qualitative subjective criteria to produce a more visually pleasing image, and they do not rely on any physical model for the image formation. These kinds of approaches are usually simpler and faster than deconvolution methods.

Underwater Physical Model-Based Techniques

Light interacts with the water medium through two processes: attenuation and scattering. Attenuation is the loss of power as light travels in the medium, and it depends on the index of refraction of the medium. Scattering refers to any deflection from a straight-line propagation path. In underwater environment, deflections can be due to particles of size comparable to the wavelengths of traveling light (diffraction) or to particulate matter with refraction index different from that of the water (refraction). McGlamery (1979) laid out the theoretical foundations of the optical image formation model while Jaffe (1990) extended the model and applied it to design different subsea image acquisition systems. Modeling of underwater imaging has also been carried out by Monte Carlo techniques (Funk et al., 1972).

According to Jaffe-McGlamery model, the underwater image can be represented as the linear superposition of three components (Figure 1). An underwater image experiment consists of tracing the progression of light from a light source to a camera. The light received by the camera is composed by three components: 1.) the direct component E_d (light reflected directly by the object that has not been scattered in the water), 2.) the forward-scattered component E_f (light reflected directly by the object that has been scattered at a small angle) and 3.) the backscattered component E_b (light reflected by objects not on the target scene but that enters the camera, due to floating particles). Therefore, the total irradiance E_T reads:

$$E_T = E_d + E_f + E_b \tag{1}$$

Figure 1. The three components of underwater optical imaging: direct component (straight line), forward component (dashed line) and backward scatter component (dash-dot line)

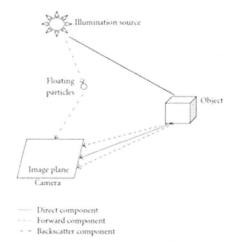

Underwater Image Restoration Techniques

Image restoration aims at recovering the original image f(x,y) from the observed image g(x,y) using explicit knowledge about the degradation function h(x,y) (also called Point Spread Function [PSF]) and the noise characteristics n(x,y).

$$g(x,y) = f(x,y)*h(x,y) + n(x,y) \tag{2}$$

where * denotes convolution. The degradation function h(x,y) includes the system response from the imaging system itself and the effects of the medium. In the frequency domain, we have:

$$G(u,v) = F(u,v)H(u,v) + N(u,v) \tag{3}$$

where (u,v) are spatial frequencies and *G*, *F*, *H* and *N* are Fourier transforms of *g*, *f*, *h* and *n* respectively. The system response function *H* in the frequency domain is referred as the Optical Transfer Function (OTF) and its magnitude is refereed as Modulation Transfer Function (MTF). Usually, the system response is expressed as a direct product of the optical system itself and the medium:

$$H(u, v) = H_{system}^{optical}(u, v) \; H_{medium}(u, v) \qquad (4)$$

The better the knowledge we have about the degradation function, the better are the results of the restoration. However, in practical cases, there is insufficient knowledge about the degradation and it must be estimated and modeled. The source degradation in underwater imaging includes turbidity, floating particles and the optical properties of light propagation in water. Therefore, underwater optical properties have to be incorporated into the PSF and MTF.

Hou et al (2007) incorporated the underwater optical properties to the traditional image restoration approach. They assume that blurring is caused by strong scattering due to water and its constituents which include various sized particles. To address this issue, they incorporated measured in-water optical properties to the point spread function in the spatial domain and the modulation transfer function in frequency domain. The authors modeled H_{medium} for circular symmetrical response systems (2-dimensional space) as an exponential function

$$H_{medium}(\phi, r) = \exp\{-D(\phi) \; r\} \qquad (5)$$

The exponent $D(\phi)$ is the decay transfer function obtained by Wells for the seawater within the small angle approximation

$$D(\phi) = c - \frac{b(1 - \exp\{-2\pi\theta_0\phi\})}{2\pi\theta_0\phi}, \qquad (6)$$

where θ_0 is the mean square angle, b and c are the total scattering and attenuation coefficients, respectively.

Trucco and Olmos (2006) presented a self-tuning restoration filter based on a simplified version of the Jaffe-McGlamery image formation model. Two assumptions are made in order to design the restoration filter. The first one assumes uniform illumination (direct sunlight in shallow waters) and the second one is consider only the forward scatter component E_f of the image model as the major degradation source, ignoring back scattering E_b and the direct component E_d. Liu et al (2001), measured the PSF and MTF of seawater in the laboratory by means of the image transmission theory and used Wiener filters to restore the blurred underwater images. The degradation function H(u,v) is measured in a water tank. An experiment is constructed with a slit image and a light source. In a first step, one dimensional light intensity distribution of the slit images at different water path lengths is obtained. The one dimensional PSF of seawater can be obtained by the deconvolution operation. Then, according to the property of the circular symmetry of the PSF of seawater, the 2-dimensional PSF can be calculated by mathematical method. In a similar way, MTFs are derived. These measured functions are used for blurred image restoration. The standard wiener deconvolution process is applied. The transfer function W(u,v) reads:

$$W(u, v) = \frac{H^*(u, v)}{|H(u, v)|^2 + S_n / S_f}, \qquad (7)$$

where S_n and S_f are the power spectrum of noise and original image, respectively, and $H^*(u, v)$ is the conjugate matrix of $H(u, v)$. Noise is regarded as white noise, and S_n is a constant that can be estimated from the blurred images with noise while S_f is estimated as:

$$S_f(u,v) = \frac{S_g(u,v) - S_n(u,v)}{|H(u,v)|^2}, \qquad (8)$$

where S_g is the power spectrum of the blurred image. Then, the spectrum of the restored image is:

$$F(u,v) = G(u,v) \frac{H^*(u,v)}{|H(u,v)|^2 + S_n/S_f} \qquad (9)$$

Underwater Image Enhancement Techniques

Image enhancement methods make total abstraction of the image formation process, and no a priori knowledge of the environment is needed (i.e. these methods do not use attenuation and scattering coefficients). They are usually simpler and faster than the image restoration techniques. Bazeille et al (2006), proposed an algorithm to preprocess underwater images. It reduces underwater perturbations and improves image quality. It is composed of several successive independent processing steps which correct non-uniform illumination (homomorphic filtering), suppress noise (wavelet denoising), enhance edges (anisotropic filtering) and adjust colors (equalizing RGB channels to suppress predominant color). The algorithm is automatic and requires no parameter adjustment. Arnold-Bos et al (2005), presented a complete preprocessing framework for underwater images. They investigated the possibility of addressing the whole range of noises present in underwater images by using a combination of deconvolution and enhancement methods. First, a contrast equalization system is proposed to reject backscattering, attenuation, and lighting inequalities. If $I(i,j)$ is the original image and $I_{LP}(i,j)$ its low-pass version, a contrast-equalized version of I is $I_{eq} = I/I_{LP}$. Contrast equalization is followed by histogram clipping and expansion of the

image range. The method relevant because backscattering is a slowly varying spatial function. Backscattering is considered as the first noise addressed in the algorithm but contrast equalization also corrects the effect of the exponential light attenuation with distance. Remaining noises corresponding to sensor noise, floating particles and miscellaneous quantification errors are suppressed using a generic self-tuning wavelet-based algorithm.

Chambah et al. (2004) proposed a color correction method based on Automatic Color Equalization (ACE) model, an unsupervised color equalization algorithm developed by Rizzi et al. (2003). ACE is a perceptual approach inspired by some adaptation mechanisms of the human vision system, in particular lightness constancy and color constancy. ACE was applied on videos taken in aquatic environment that present a strong and non-uniform color cast due to the depth of the water and the artificial illumination. Images were taken from the tanks of an aquarium. Inner parameters of the ACE algorithm were properly tuned to meet the requirements of image and histogram shape naturalness and to deal with these kinds of aquatic images. Iqbal et al. (2007) presented an underwater image enhancement method using an integrated color model. They proposed an approach based on slide stretching: first, contrast stretching of RGB algorithm is used to equalize the color contrast in the images. Second, saturation and intensity stretching of HSI is applied to increase the true color and solve the problem of lighting. The blue color component in the image is controlled by the saturation and intensity to create the range from pale blue to deep blue. The contrast ratio is therefore controlled by decreasing or increasing its value. Rafael Garcia et al. (2002) proposed an approach to solve lighting problems in underwater imaging. The approach proposed is slightly modified to adapt them to the peculiarities of the underwater environment. The author carried out a sequence of steps to solve lighting problems, illumination-reflectance model, local histogram equalization, homomorphic filtering, and subtraction of the illumination field by polynomial adjustment.

EVALUATION CRITERIA

Over the last few years, many different methods for image quality assessment have been proposed and analyzed with the goal of developing a quality metric that correlates with perceived quality measurements. Peak Signal to Noise Ratio (PSNR) and Mean Squared Error (MSE) are the most widely used objective image quality/distortion metrics. However, in the last decades, a great effort has been made to develop new objective image quality methods, which incorporate perceptual quality measures by considering human visual system characteristics. The objective image quality metrics are classified into three groups: full reference (there exists an original image with which the distorted image is to be compared), no-reference or "blind" quality assessment and reduced–reference quality assessment (the reference image is only partially available, in the form of a set of extracted features).

Currently, there is no underwater database is available to compare and evaluate the results quantitatively. Many of the authors use subjective visual quality measurements to evaluate the performance of their methods. Beside visual comparison, How and Weidemann (2007) proposed an objective image quality assessment measure for the scattering-blurred typical underwater images. The authors measure the image quality by its sharpness using the gradient or slope of edges. They use wavelet transforms to remove the effect of scattering when locating edges and further apply the transformed results in restraining the perceptual metric. Images are first decomposed by a wavelet transform to remove random and medium noise. Sharpness of the edges is determined by linear regression, obtaining the slope angle

between grayscale values of edge pixels versus location. The overall sharpness of the image is the average of measured grayscale angles weighted by the ratio of the power of the high-frequency components of the image to the total power of the image (WGSA metric). The metric has been used in their automated image restoration program, and the results demonstrate consistency for different optical conditions and attenuation ranges.

OUR APPROACH

In this section, we present an overview of our approach, which is well accepted by image processing community to enhance the quality of underwater images (Prabhakar & Praveen Kumar, 2011). Generally, enhancement of an image is addressed in two different points of view: as an image restoration technique and as an image enhancement technique. The restoration method requires many model parameters to employ deconvolution technique on degraded underwater images. Since, it is very difficult to estimate physical model parameters of underwater; we employed image enhancement method, which doesn't require these parameters. Our approach comprises of filtering techniques such as homomorphic filtering, wavelet-based image denoising, bilateral filtering and contrast equalization, which are applied sequentially. To correct non-uniform illumination of light, we apply homomorphic filtering, which simultaneously normalizes the brightness across an image and increases contrast. After correcting non-uniform illumination, wavelet–based denoising using modified bayes-shrink is employed to remove Gaussian noise present in the underwater image. For the denoised image, bilateral filter is applied, which smoothes the image and improves edge detection capability. Finally, contrast stretching is employed, which stretches the range of intensity values and evenly distributes color values across the image.

Homomorphic Filtering

Homomorphic filtering is used to correct non-uniform illumination and to enhance contrasts in the image. It's a frequency filtering, preferred to others' techniques because it corrects non-uniform lighting and sharpens the image features at the same time. We consider that image is a function of the product of the illumination and the reflectance as shown below.

$$f(x, y) = i(x, y) \times r(x, y), \tag{10}$$

where $f(x, y)$ is the image sensed by the camera, $i(x, y)$ the illumination multiplicative factor, and r(x,y) the reflectance function. If we take into account this model, we assume that the illumination factor changes slowly through the view field; therefore it represents low frequencies in the Fourier transform of the image. On the contrary reflectance is associated with high frequency components. By multiplying these components by a high-pass filter we can then suppress the low frequencies i.e., the non-uniform illumination in the image. The algorithm can be decomposed as follows:

Separation of the illumination and reflectance components by taking the logarithm of the image. The logarithm converts the multiplicative into an additive one.

$$g(x, y) = \ln(f(x, y)) = \ln(i(x, y) \times r(x, y))$$

$$g(x, y) = \ln(i(x, y)) + \ln(r(x, y)). \tag{11}$$

Computation of the Fourier transform of the log-image

$$G(w_x, w_y) = I(w_x, w_y) + R(w_x, w_y). \tag{12}$$

High-pass filtering is applied to the Fourier transform decreases the contribution of low fre-quencies (illumination) and also amplifies the contribution of mid and high frequencies (reflectance), sharpening the image features of the objects in the image:

$$S(w_x, w_y) = H(w_x, w_y) \times I(w_x, w_y) + H(w_x, w_y) \times R(w_x, w_y), \tag{13}$$

With

$$H(w_x, w_y) = (r_H - r_L) \times \left(1 - \exp\left(\frac{w_x^2 + w_y^2}{2\delta_w^2}\right)\right) + r_L \tag{14}$$

where, $r_H = 2.5$ and $r_L = 0.5$ are the maximum and minimum coefficients values and δ_w a factor which controls the cut-off frequency. These parameters are selected empirically. Computations of the inverse Fourier transform to come back in the spatial domain and then taking the exponent to obtain the filtered image.

Wavelet Denoising

Thresholding is a simple non-linear technique, which operates on one wavelet coefficient at a time. In its most basic form, each coefficient is thresholded by comparing against threshold, if the coefficient is smaller than threshold, set to zero; otherwise it is kept or modified. Replacing the small noisy coefficients by zero and inverse wavelet transform on the result may lead to reconstruction with the essential signal characteristics and with the less noise. A simple denoising algorithm that uses the wavelet transform consist of the following three steps, (1) calculate the wavelet transform of the noisy signal, (2) Modify the noisy detail wavelet coefficients according to some rule and (3) compute the inverse transform using the modified coefficients.

Let us consider a signal $\{f_{ij}, i, j = 1, ..., N\}$, where N is some integer power of 2. It has been corrupted by additive noise and one observes

$$g_{ij} = f_{ij} + \varepsilon_{ij}, \qquad i, j = 1, ..., N \qquad (15)$$

where ε_{ij} are independent and identically distributed (iid) zero mean white Gaussian noise with standard deviation σ i.e. $N(0, \sigma^2)$ and independent of f_{ij}. From the noisy signal g_{ij} we want to find an approximation $\hat{f}_{ij}$. The goal is to remove the noise, or denoise $g(i, j)$, and to obtain an estimate $\hat{f}_{ij}$ and f_{ij} which minimizes the mean squared error (MSE),

$$MSE(\hat{f}) = \frac{1}{N^2} \sum_{i,j=1}^{N} (\hat{f}_{ij} - f_{ij})^2 \qquad (16)$$

Let $g = \{g_{ij}\}_{i,j}$, $f = \{f_{ij}\}_{i,j}$, and $\varepsilon = \{\varepsilon_{ij}\}_{i,j}$; that is, the boldfaced letters will denote the matrix representation of the signals under consideration. Let $D = w_g$, $C = w_f$ and $Z = w_\varepsilon$ denote the matrix of wavelet coefficients g, f, ε respectively, where, w is the two-dimensional dyadic orthogonal wavelet transform operator. It is convenient to label the subbands of the wavelet transform as shown in Figure 2. The subbands, HH_k, HL_k, LH_k are called the details, where $k = 1, ..., J$ is the scale, with J being the largest (or coarsest) scale in the decomposition and a subband at scale k has size $N / 2^k \times N / 2^k$. The subband LL_J is the low resolution residual and is typically chosen large enough such that $N / 2^J \leq N$, $N / 2^J > 1$. The wavelet based denoising method filters each coefficient g_{ij} from the detail subbands with a threshold function to obtain $\hat{f}_{ij}$. The denoised estimate is then $\hat{g} = w^{-1}\hat{f}$, where w^{-1} is the inverse wavelet transform.

Figure 2. Subbands of 2D orthogonal wavelet transform

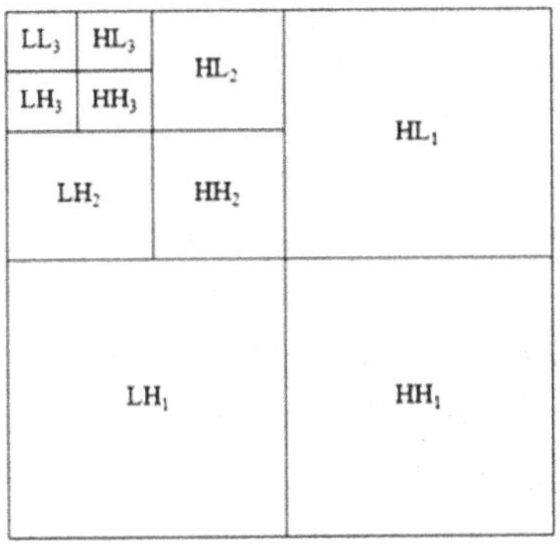

Wavelet transform of noisy signal should be taken first and then thresholding function is applied on it. Finally the output should be undergone inverse wavelet transformation to obtain the estimate $\hat{f}$. There are two thresholding functions frequently used, i.e. a hard threshold and soft threshold. The hard-thresholding function keeps the input if it is larger than the threshold; otherwise, it is set to zero. It is described as:

$$\eta_1(w) = wI(|w| > T), \qquad (17)$$

where w is a wavelet coefficient, T is the threshold and I(x) is a function the result is one when x is true and zero vice versa. The soft-thresholding function (also called the shrinkage function) takes the argument and shrinks it toward zero by the threshold. It is described as:

$$\eta_2(w) = (w - \text{sgn}(w)T)I(|w| > T), \qquad (18)$$

where sgn(x) is the sign of x. The soft-thresholding rule is chosen over hard-thresholding, the soft-thresholding method yields more visually pleasant images over hard-thresholding (Donoho, 1995). The BayesShrink function (Chang et al., 2000) has been attracting recently as an algorithm for setting different thresholds for every subband. Here subbands are frequently bands that differ from each other in level and direction. The BayesShrink function is effective for images including Gaussian noise. The observation model is expressed as follows: Y=X+V.

Here Y is the wavelet transform of the degraded image, X is the wavelet transform of the original image, and V denotes the wavelet transform of the noise components following the Gaussian distribution $N(0, \sigma^2)$. Here, since X and V are mutually independent, the variances σ_y^2, σ_x^2 and σ_v^2 of y,x and v are given by:

$$\sigma_y^2 = \sigma_x^2 + \sigma_v^2. \tag{19}$$

Let us present a method for deriving of the noise: It has been shown that the noise standard deviation σ_v can be accurately estimated from the first decomposition level diagonal subband HH_1 by the robust and accurate median estimator.

$$\hat{\sigma}_v^2 = \frac{\text{median}(|HH_1|)}{0.6745}. \tag{20}$$

The variance of the degraded image can be estimated as

$$\hat{\sigma}_y^2 = \frac{1}{M} \sum_{m=1}^{M} A_m^2, \tag{21}$$

where A_m are the coefficients of wavelet in every scale M is the total number of coefficient of wavelet. The threshold value T can be calculated using

$$T_{MBS} = \frac{\beta \hat{\sigma}_v^2}{\hat{\sigma}_x}, \tag{22}$$

where $\beta = \sqrt{\dfrac{\log M}{2 \times j}}$, M is the total of coefficients of wavelet, j is the wavelet decomposition level present in the subband coefficients under scru-

tiny and $\hat{\sigma}_x = \sqrt{\max(\hat{\sigma}_y^2 - \hat{\sigma}_v^2)}$. Note that in the case where $\hat{\sigma}_v^2 \geq \hat{\sigma}_y^2, \hat{\sigma}_x^2$ is taken to be zero, i.e. $T_{MBS} \to \infty$. Alternatively, in practice one may choose $T_{MBS} = \max|A_m|$, and all coefficients are set to zero.

In summary, the Modified BayesShrink thresholding technique performs soft thresholding with adaptive data driven subband and level dependent near optimal threshold given by:

$$T_{MBS} = \begin{cases} \dfrac{\beta \hat{\sigma}_v^2}{\hat{\sigma}_x}, & \text{if } \hat{\sigma}_v^2 < \hat{\sigma}_y^2 \\ \max|A_m|, & \text{otherwise} \end{cases} \tag{23}$$

Bilateral Filtering

Bilateral filtering smooths images while preserving edges, by means of a nonlinear combination of nearby image values (Tomasi et al., 1998). The idea underlying bilateral filtering is to do in the range of an image what traditional filters do in its domain. Two pixels can be close to one another, that is, occupy nearby spatial location, or they can be similar to one another, that is, have nearby values, possibly in a perceptually meaningful fashion. Closeness refers to vicinity in the domain, similarity to vicinity in the range. Traditional filtering is a domain filtering, and enforces closeness by weighing pixel values with coefficients that fall off with distance. The range filtering, this averages image values with weights that decay with dissimilarity. Range filters are nonlinear because their weights depend on image intensity or color. Computationally, they are no more complex than standard non-separable filters. The combination of both domain and range filtering is termed as bilateral filtering. A low-pass domain filter to an image $f(x)$ produces an output image defined as follows:

$$h(x) = k_d^{-1}(x) \int_{-\infty}^{\infty} \int_{-\infty}^{\infty} f(\xi) \ c(\xi, x) \ d\xi, \qquad (24)$$

where $c(\xi, x)$ measures the geometric closeness between the neighborhood center x and a nearby point ξ. The bold font for f and h emphasizes the fact that both input and output images may be multiband. If low-pass filtering is to preserve the dc component of low-pass signals we obtain

$$k_d(x) = \int_{-\infty}^{\infty} \int_{-\infty}^{\infty} c(\xi, x) \ d\xi, \qquad (25)$$

If the filter is shift-invariant, $c(\xi, x)$ is only a function of the vector difference $\xi - x$, and k_d is constant.

Range filtering is similarly defined:

$$h(x) = k_r^{-1}(x) \int_{-\infty}^{\infty} \int_{-\infty}^{\infty} f(\xi) s(f(\xi), f(x)) d\xi. \qquad (26)$$

Except that now $s(f(\xi), f(x))$ measures the photometric similarity between the pixel at the neighborhood center x and that of a nearby point ξ. Thus, the similarity function s operates in the range of the image function f, while the closeness function c operates in the domain of f. The normalization constant in Eq. (26) is replaced by

$$k_r(x) = \int_{-\infty}^{\infty} \int_{-\infty}^{\infty} s(f(\xi), f(x)) \ d\xi. \qquad (27)$$

Contrary to what occurs with the closeness function c, the normalization for the similarity function s depends on the image f. The similarity function s is unbiased if it depends only on the difference $f(\xi) - f(x)$. The combined domain and range filtering will be denoted as bilateral filtering, which enforces both geometric and photometric locality. Combined filtering can be described as follows:

$$h(x) = k^{-1}(x) \int_{-\infty}^{\infty} \int_{-\infty}^{\infty} f(\xi) c(\xi, x) s(f(\xi), f(x)) d\xi. \qquad (28)$$

With the normalization

$$k(x) = \int_{-\infty}^{\infty} \int_{-\infty}^{\infty} c(\xi, x) s(f(\xi), f(x)) d\xi. \qquad (29)$$

Contrast Stretching and Color Correction

Contrast stretching often called normalization is a simple image enhancement technique that attempts to improve the contrast in an image by 'stretching' the range of intensity values. The full range of pixel values that the image concerned is given by Equation (30). Color correction is performed by equalizing each color means. In underwater image colors are rarely balanced correctly, this processing step suppresses prominent blue or green color without taking into account absorption phenomena.

$$I_{i,j} = \begin{cases} \dfrac{I_{i,j} - \min_I}{\max_I - \min_I} & \text{if } 0 < I_{i,j} < 1 \\ 0 & \text{if } 0 < I_{i,j} \\ 1 & \text{if } 1 < I_{i,j} \end{cases} \qquad (30)$$

where $\min_I$ and $\max_I$ are the minimum and maximum intensity values in the image.

EXPERIMENTAL RESULTS

We have conducted experiments to evaluate proposed image enhancement technique on degraded underwater images with unknown turbidity characteristics. The scene includes several objects, which are kept at distance of [1m, 2m], near the corner of the water body. The images are captured using Canon D10 water proof camera at a depth of 5 feet from the surface level of water (Figure 3). The captured images are diminished due to propagation properties of the light in an underwater environment. These images are suffered from non-uniform illumination of light, low contrast, blurring and typical noise levels for underwater conditions. The image enhancement technique comprises of homomorphic filtering to correct non-uniform illumination of light, wavelet denoising to remove additive Gaussian noise present in underwater images, bilateral filtering to smooth underwater image and contrast stretching to normalize the RGB values. The experimentation is carried out in two stages. In the first stage, we have conducted various experiments on captured images and estimated optimal wavelet filter bank and optimal wavelet shrinkage function. Similarly, in the second stage, we estimated optimal parameters for bilateral filter. Finally, we conducted the experiments using estimated optimal parameters, optimal filter bank and optimal wavelet shrinkage function for evaluating the proposed technique.

The procedure involved in the first stage is as follows: after applying the homomorphic filter for correction of illumination and reflectance components, wavelet denoising is used to remove the Gaussian noise, which is common in the underwater environment. In wavelet denoising, filter bank plays an important role for the best result of denoising. We performed an evaluation of four wavelet filter banks such as Haar, db4, Sym4 and Coif4 for decomposing the image

prior to applying shrinkage function. The Table 1 shows the PSNRs obtained using four filter banks such as Haar, db4, Sym4 and Coif4 for each underwater image. The Coif4 filter bank yields optimal PSNR for all the underwater images. After finding the Coif4 filter bank is the best for underwater images, we identify suitable wavelet shrinkage function by comparing and evaluating various wavelet shrinkage functions based on PSNR. We have considered BayesShrink (Chang et al., 2000), VisuShrink (Donoho & Johnstone, 1994), Adaptive Subband Thresholding (Sudha et al., 2007), NormalShrink (Kaur et al., 2002), and Modified BayesShrink (Prabhakar & Praveen Kumar, 2010) for comparison purpose. The Table 2 presents comparison results of various wavelet shrinkage functions. The experimental result shows that the Modified BayesShrink function achieves highest PSNR compared to other shrinkage functions. Hence, the wavelet based denoising technique with Modified BayesShrink function is suitable for removing the additive noise present in the underwater images. The Modified Bayes-Shrink performs denoising that is consistent with the human visual system that is less sensitive to the presence of noise in a vicinity of image features.

In the second stage, we applied bilateral filter on denoised image for edge preserving smoothing that is non-iterative and simple. The bilateral filtering is performed in CIE Lab color space is the natural type of filtering for color images. To find the optimal parameter for bilateral filter, the bilateral filtering is applied to denoised images

Figure 3. Captured underwater Images

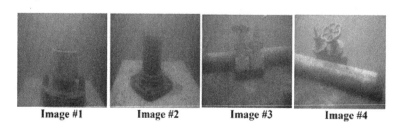

Image #1   Image #2   Image #3   Image #4

Table 1. PSNR values obtained for different wavelet filter families

Image #	Filter Bank	MSE	PSNR (dB)
Image #1	Haar	0.0242	64.2905
	Db4	0.0050	71.1837
	Sym4	0.0059	70.4499
	Coif4	**0.0043**	**71.7861**
Image #2	Haar	0.0540	60.8066
	Db4	0.0144	66.5616
	Sym4	0.0161	66.0607
	Coif4	**0.0128**	**67.0677**
Image #3	Haar	0.1909	55.3232
	Db4	0.2131	54.8456
	Sym4	0.1217	57.2787
	Coif4	**0.1154**	**57.5078**
Image #4	Haar	0.0744	59.4173
	Db4	0.1129	57.6021
	Sym4	0.0643	60.0509
	Coif4	**0.0594**	**60.3960**

by varying the parameters σ_d and σ_r. The interval of parameter values considered, for σ_d is 1-10 pixel values and for σ_r is 10-200 intensity values. The experimental results show that the parameter values $\sigma_d = 1$ and $\sigma_r = 10$ smooth the image compared to other parameter values. Hence, $\sigma_d = 1$ and $\sigma_r = 10$ are the optimal parameters for bilateral filter.

Finally, we carried out various experiments on captured underwater images to evaluate our technique. We identified Coif4 filter bank and Modified BayesShrinkage function for wavelet denoising yields best results on degraded underwater images. Similarly, we identified that $\sigma_d = 1$ and $\sigma_r = 10$ for bilateral filter. Figure 4 shows the results obtained from our approach. We used the same setup to evaluate the technique qualitatively as well as quantitatively. In order to evaluate qualitatively, the edge detection is applied on both original and preprocessed images, shown in Figure 5. The edge detection results of the preprocessed images demonstrate an efficiency of our approach. For quantitative evaluation, the gradient magnitude histogram for original and preprocessed images are estimated and shown in Figure 6. These histograms show that gradient values are larger after preprocessing compared to gradient values obtained on original images.

Our approach was implemented and tested in MATLAB environment. The experiments were carried out on an Intel Pentium Core i5 processor of speed 3.30 GHz and 4 GB of RAM. Our approach spends less computation time compared to Bazeille et al. (2006). From Figure 7, it is observed that our approach yields better visualization compared to preprocessing approach proposed by Bazeille et al. (2006).

FUTURE DIRECTIONS

Since, our work is carried out for still images; it can be further extended to video images for development of real-time image processing ap-

Table 2. Comparison of different wavelet shrinkage functions

Image #	Modified BayesShrink	BayesShrink	NormalShrink	Adaptive Subband Thresholding	VisuShrink
Image #1	**66.2116**	66.2008	65.9764	65.0434	50.6137
Image #2	**63.1458**	63.1301	62.8485	61.6751	48.3258
Image #3	**54.8456**	54.7995	54.0704	52.1615	41.7070
Image #4	**57.6021**	57.5921	57.4179	56.6197	44.7697

Figure 4. First column: original image, second column: after homomorphic filtering, third column: after wavelet denoising, fourth column: after bilateral filtering, last column: after contrast equalization

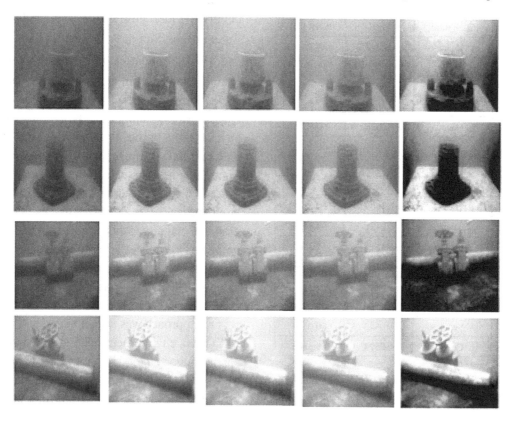

Figure 5. Edge detection results on four images; First row: edge detection results on original images, Second row: edge detection results on preprocessed images

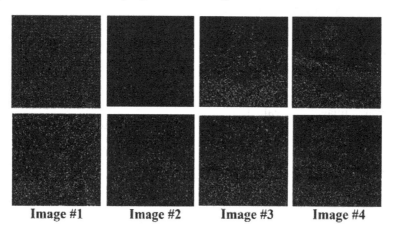

Image #1　　Image #2　　Image #3　　Image #4

Figure 6. Gradient magnitude histogram of the four images; Red line: the gradient magnitude histogram of the original image, Green line: the gradient magnitude histogram of the preprocessed image

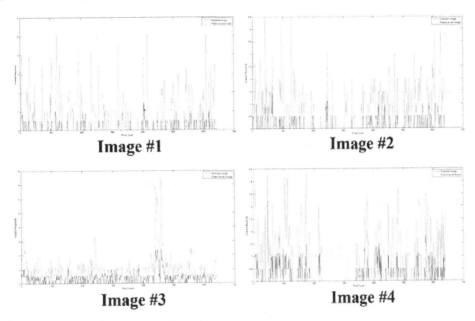

Figure 7. comparison of image enhancement algorithms (a) Our approach (b) Bazeille et al. (2006) approach

plications to navigate ROVs. Instead of using only optical camera, optical camera with polarizer can be used for imaging, which helps in reducing degradation effects usually occur in underwater environment. The literature survey reveals that for contrast enhancement and image denoising, curvelets-based methods seems to give very good results. Therefore, curvelets-based methods can be adopted for contrast enhancement and denoising of underwater images. To restore the underwater images, the deconvolution methods such as Wiener and Inverse filtering can be employed, which gives good results but generally requires a priori knowledge on the environment.

CONCLUSION

In this chapter, we discuss an overview of recent image enhancement and restoration techniques for underwater images. We introduce our approach to enhance the quality of degraded underwater images using well known image preprocessing techniques. Our image enhancement approach consists of combination of different individual filtering techniques such as homomorphic filtering, wavelet-based image denoising, bilateral filtering, and contrast stretching. These individual steps are sequentially applied on the degraded underwater images to obtain visually enhanced image. We evaluated the efficacy of our approach qualitatively using edge detection and gradient magnitude histograms. From experimental results, it is observed that after image enhancement using our approach, better edges are obtained, and the histogram shows that gradient values are larger after enhancement compared to gradient values obtained on original images. The visual evaluation of results of our approach with the results of other existing popular preprocessing approaches shows that our approach yields visually better results. Since, there is no standard benchmark database

is available for underwater images, our approach cannot be compared quantitatively with other existing algorithms based on MSE and PSNR. The development of underwater image database could be one of the future research lines from which the underwater community would certainly benefit.

REFERENCES

Arnold-Bos, A., Malasset, J.-P., & Kervern, G. (2005). Towards a model-free denoising of underwater optical images. In *Proceedings of the IEEE Europe Oceans Conference, 1,* 527-532. Brest, France: IEEE Press.

Arnold-Bos, A., Malkasse, J. P., & Kerven, G. (2005). A pre-processing framework for automatic underwater images denoising. In *Proceedings of the European Conference on Propagation and Systems.* Brest, France: IEEE Press.

Bazeille, S., Quidu, I., Jaulin, L., & Malkasse, J. P. (2006). Automatic underwater image preprocessing. In *Proceedings of the Caracterisation du Milieu Marin (CMM'06).* Brest, France: IEEE Press.

Chambah, M., Semani, D., Renouf, A., Courtellement, P., & Rizzi, A. (2004). Underwater color constancy: Enhancement of automatic live fish recognition. In Proceedings of SPIE (157-168). San Jose, CA: SPIE Press.

Chang, S. G., Yu, B., & Martin Vetterli, M. (2000). Adaptive wavelet thresholding for image denoising and compression. *IEEE Transactions on Image Processing, 9*(9), 1532–1546. doi:10.1109/83.862633 PMID:18262991.

Donoho, D. L. (1995). De-noising by soft-thresholding. *IEEE Transactions on Information Theory, 41*(3), 613–626. doi:10.1109/18.382009.

Donoho, D. L., & Johnstone, I. M. (1994). Ideal spatial adaptation via wavelet shrinkage. *Biometrika*, *81*(3), 425–455. doi:10.1093/biomet/81.3.425.

Funk, C., Bryant, S., & Heckman, P. (1972). Handbook of underwater imaging system design. *Techical Report TR303*. San Diego, CA: Naval Undersea Center

Garcia, R., Nicosevici, T., & Cufi, X. (2002). On the way to solve lighting problems in underwater imaging. In *Proceedings of the IEEE Oceans Conference* (263-266). Washington, DC: IEEE Press.

Hogue, A., German, A., & Jenkin, M. (2007). Underwater environment reconstruction using stereo and inertial data. *IEEE International Conference on Systems, Man and Cybernetics* (2372–2377). Washington, DC: IEEE Press.

Hou, W., Gray, D. J., Weidemann, A. D., Fournier, G. R., & Forand, J. L. (2007). Automated underwater image restoration and retrieval of related optical properties. In *Proceedings of the IEEE International Geoscience and Remote Sensing Symposium* (1889–1892).

Hou, W., & Weidemann, A. D. (2007). Objectively assessing underwater image quality for the purpose of automated restoration. In *Proceedings of SPIE Visual Information Processing XVI*. Orlando, FL: SPIE Press.

Iqbal, K., Abdul Salam, R., Osman, A., & Zawawi Talib, A. (2007). Underwater image enhancement using an integrated color model. *International Journal of Computer Science*, *34*(2).

Jaffe, J. S. (1990). Computer modeling and the design of optical underwater imaging systems. *IEEE Journal of Oceanic Engineering*, *15*(2), 221–231. doi:10.1109/48.50695.

Kaur, L., Gupta, S., & Chauhan, R. C. (2002). Image denoising using wavelet thresholding. In *Proceedings of Indian Conference on Computer Vision, Graphics, and Image Processing*. Ahmedabad, India: ICVGIP Press.

Liu, Z., Yu, Y., Zhang, K., & Huang, H. (2001). Underwater image transmission and blurred image restoration. *Optical Engineering (Redondo Beach, Calif.)*, *40*(6), 1125–1131. doi:10.1117/1.1364500.

McGlamery, B. (1980). A computer model for underwater camera systems. [Bellingham, WA: SPIE Press.]. *Proceedings of SPIE Ocean Optics*, *VI*, 221–231. doi:10.1117/12.958279.

Negahdaripour, S., & Firoozfam, P. (2006). An ROV stereovision system for ship-hull inspection. *IEEE Journal of Oceanic Engineering*, *31*(3), 551–564. doi:10.1109/JOE.2005.851391.

Prabhakar, C. J., & Praveen Kumar, P. U. (2010). Underwater image denoising using adaptive wavelet subband thresholding. In *Proceedings of IEEE International Conference on Signal and Image Processing* (322-327). Washington, DC: IEEE Press.

Prabhakar, C. J., & Praveen Kumar, P. U. (2011). An image based technique for enhancement of underwater images. *International Journal of Machine Intelligence*, *3*(4), 217–224.

Rizzi, A., Gatta, C., & Marini, D. (2003). A new algorithm for unsupervised global and local color correction. *Pattern Recognition Letters*, *24*, 1663–1677. doi:10.1016/S0167-8655(02)00323-9.

Schettini, R., & Corchs, S. (2010). Underwater image processing: State of the art of restoration and image enhancement methods. *EURASIP Journal on Advances in Signal Processing*, 2010.

Sudha, S., Suresh, G. R., & Sunkanesh, R. (2007). Wavelet based image denoising using adaptive subband thresholding. *International Journal of Soft Computing*, *2*, 628–632.

Tomasi, C., & Manduchi, R. (1998). Bilateral filtering for gray and color images. In *Proceedings of the Sixth IEEE International Conference on Computer Vision* (839-846). Washington, DC: IEEE Press.

Trucco, E., & Olmos, A. (2006). Self-tuning underwater image restoration. *IEEE Journal of Oceanic Engineering*, *31*(2), 511–519. doi:10.1109/JOE.2004.836395.

ADDITIONAL READING

Elyasi, I., & Zarmehi, S. (2009). Elimination noise by adaptive wavelet threshold. World Academy of Science, Engineering, and Technology, 462-466.

Fan, F., Yang, K., Xia, M., Li, W., Fu, B., & Zhang, W. (2010). Underwater image restoration by means of blind deconvolution approach. *Frontiers of Optoelectronics in China*, *3*(2), 169–178. doi:10.1007/s12200-010-0012-1.

Hou, W., Gray, D. J., Weidemann, A. D., & Arnone, R. A. (2008). Comparison and validation of point spread models for imaging in natural waters. *Optics Express*, *16*(13), 9958–9965. doi:10.1364/OE.16.009958 PMID:18575566.

Hou, W., Weidemann, A. D., Gray, D. J., & Fournier, G. R. (2007). Imagery-derived modulation transfer function and its applications for underwater imaging. *In Proceedings of SPIE Applications of Digital Image Processing*. San Diego, CA: SPIE Press.

Jaffe, J., Moore, K., McLean, J., & Strand, M. (2001). Underwater optical imaging: Status and prospects. *Oceanography (Washington, D.C.)*, *14*, 66–76. doi:10.5670/oceanog.2001.24.

Kovesi, P. (1999). Phase preserving denoising of images. In *Proceedings of the Australian Pattern Recognition Society Conference*. Washington, DC: IEEE Press.

Senthilkumar, R. (2005). Performance improvement in the bivariate models by using modified marginal variance of noisy observations for image denoising applications. *World Academy of Science, Engineering, and Technology*, *11*, 103–107.

Torres-Mendez, L. A., & Dudek, G. (2005). Color correction of underwater images for aquatic robot inspection. In *Proceedings of the 5th International Workshop on Energy Minimization Methods in Computer Vision and Pattern Recognition (EMM-CVPR '05)*. Berlin: Springer.

Zhishen, L., Tianfu, D., & Gang, W. (2003). ROV based underwater blurred image restoration. *Journal of the Ocean University of Qingdao*, *2*(1), 85–88.

KEY TERMS AND DEFINITIONS

Absorption: The physical process in which light rays interacting with particles in suspension in the medium is converted into other forms of energy is called absorption. As a result, the intensity of a point in the image will decay as the distance between the scene and the camera increases.

Deconvoluation: Deconvoluation permits recovery of the target scene from a single or set of blurred images in the presence of a poorly determined or unknown point spread function (PSF).

Image Denoising: Denoising refers to the recovery of a digital image that has been contaminated by additive white Gaussian noise (AWGN).

Image Restoration: Restoration attempts to reconstruct or recover an image that has been degraded, by using a prior knowledge of the degradation phenomenon.

Scattering: Scattering is caused by the change in direction of a ray of light after colliding with a particle in suspension. For small angular changes in direction the effect is called forward scattering, whereas for larger angles up to 180 degrees, which effectively causes the ray to bounce back at the camera, it is called backscattering.

Chapter 7
Computer Vision Based Technique for Surface Defect Detection of Apples

C. J. Prabhakar
Kuvempu University, India

S. H. Mohana
Kuvempu University, India

ABSTRACT

The automatic inspection of quality in fruits is becoming of paramount importance in order to decrease production costs and increase quality standards. Computer vision techniques are used in fruit industry for fruit grading, sorting, and defect detection. In this chapter, we review recent approaches for automatic inspection of quality in fruits using computer vision techniques. Particularly, we focus on the review of advances in computer vision techniques for automatic inspection of quality of apples based on surface defects. Finally, we present our approach to estimate the defects on the surface of an apple using grow-cut and multi-threshold based segmentation technique. The experimental results show that our method effectively estimates the defects on the surface of apples significantly more effectively than color based segmentation technique.

INTRODUCTION

The appearance of fresh agricultural products is a primary criterion in making purchasing decisions. In this context, the appearance of unities of products is evaluated by considering some characteristics contribute to the overall appearance, which is globally evaluated either in a metric or a subjective manner. This is an important quality indicator throughout the commercial-utilization chain, from the production, to the storage, the

marketing and finally down to the consumer. In order to develop an automated system for food quality evaluation, image processing techniques are often combined with mechanical and instrumental devices to replace human manipulative effort in the performance of a given process. Quality inspection is very important to deliver high-quality products to the customers. For fruit grading, there are many factors that farmers use for measuring the fruit quality. These factors can be classified into two groups the external quality factors and the internal quality factors (Bennedsen,

DOI: 10.4018/978-1-4666-4558-5.ch007

2005). The external quality factors can be defined and extracted from the visual appearance of the fruit. Commonly used factors are size, shape, color, gloss, surface defects and decay, and texture (fruit surface patterns). The internal quality factors can be defined by the fruit smell like aroma, taste, flavor, sweetness and sourness, and fruit nutritive value like vitamins, minerals, nutrients and carbohydrates, and other elements like dry matter content, total soluble solids content, sugar content, and juice acidity. There are some quality factors like firmness, crispness, and toughness that can be defined by touching the fruit and may be considered external or internal factors.

In many industries, at present, grading is performed primarily by visual inspection for a particular quality attribute. Humans are easily able to perform intensive tasks like harvesting and pruning using basically the optical sensory mechanism. Traditionally done by hand, fruit sorting and grading is a very labour-intensive aspect of the fruit processing industry. Labour shortages and a lack of overall consistency in the process resulted in a search for automated solutions (Li, 2002). Visual quality grading remains one of the most difficult processes to automate in fruit and vegetable processing as well as in other areas of the food-processing industry. The use of image processing for grading is being applied to many products, including oranges, potatoes, apples, carrots, green peppers, tomatoes and peaches. Current guidance research includes harvesting oranges, tomatoes, mushrooms, apples, melons and cucumbers. See Figure 1. The guidance research also focuses its attention on navigating robot vehicles

Figure 1. Defected fruits (a) orange (b) tomato (c) strawberry

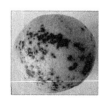

using machine vision strategies or other simple sensors in order to obtain autonomous mobile capabilities. Increased demands for objectivity, consistency and efficiency have necessitated the introduction of computer vision techniques. Recently, computer vision employing image processing techniques has been developed rapidly, which can quantitatively characterize properties of fruits. The performances of grading systems depend on the quality factors that are used in their design. Computer vision techniques offer flexibility in application and can be reasonable substitutes for the human visual decision-making process. Computer vision techniques for fruits are proving to be an objective investigation tool. Grading and sorting of fruits using machine vision in conjunction with pattern recognition techniques offers many advantages over the conventional, optical or mechanical sorting devices. The automatic inspection of quality in the fruits is becoming of paramount importance in order to decrease production costs and increase quality standards.

There are efforts to build general fruit sorting and classification systems, but most of the systems are dedicated systems like the system that can sort tomatoes, apples. A. Herrero-Langreo et al. (2012) have developed the machine-vision system to check the fresh peach and confirm the peach maturity by comparing the peach color to the standard hue of different maturity. The image analysis system (Nimesh S et.al., 1993) was developed to evaluate the color of the stone fruit. Miller (1995) took into account the mean fruit color and a measure of the dispersion (normalized mean squared differences) of the color, plus a shape parameter to grade citrus fruits according to their external quality. The author compared three different classifiers and had the best results with Bayesian–Gaussian techniques, with between 69 and 86% of the fruit correctly graded into two classes (accepted or rejected).

The pistachio nuts grading system (Ghazanfari et.al., 1996) was designed using a neural network and machine-vision system. The apple image data collecting system (Kazuhiro, 1997) was developed to sort the apple into five grades by using two neural network models. The stable model invariant to change in lighting conditions with 12 maturity classes (Edan et.al., 1997) was provided based on the weighted color parameter. The strawberry grading system (Masatera et.al., 1997) was graded according to the shape and size by using image processing. The strawberry orientation and shape determination (Bato et.al., 1999) was implemented by using image processing. Cao et.al. (1997), designed a strawberry grading system driven by vacuums pump, the strawberry was pushed into different gradation by vacuum vat. Research on analysis of hue distribution features by artificial neural network in apple gradation has been completed by (He et al., 1998). Picus and Peleg (1998) presented dynamic dates grading method. A cucumber gradation judgment system based on image processing and neural network technology was developed for long shape fruit (Wang et al., 1999). The system can sort different fruit type after training with sample patterns of different objects. The fruit neural network grading system of (Feng, 2002) provides two ways to inspect the image edge quickly, using the distribution of the hue in fruit surface to grade on-line. The tomato grading system (Laykin et al., 2002), separates oriental tomato into different grades with the information on the values of size; color, shape and surface defection that were acquired by using image analysis and mode identify technology. The tomato classification (Laykin et al., 2002) using image processing algorithms was conducted.

APPLE GRADING SYSTEM

India has an annual apple production of over 2,900 tons every year. After apples are harvested, they are transported to the packing plant to be tested for various quality attributes that determine their price and destination. Apple consumers continuously demand better quality apples. The external appearance is one of the most important factors in pricing the apples. The criterion for evaluating an apple's external appearance includes uniform red color distribution on the surface, a visually appetizing appearance, and a good shape. Usually the color grading of apples is judged by the empirical sense of grading by a worker's eyes. However, it is very difficult to distinguish an individual color grades from similarly colored apples.

Numerous studies have been conducted in order to perform non-destructive measurements of the quality parameters of fresh apples. Characterization of apple features includes the presence of defects, the size, the shape and the color. See Figure 2. To make the work faster and to reduce the human error, it is necessary to grade the fruits by an automated process. The study of apples using computer vision has attracted much interest and can reflect the progress of computer vision technology for fruit inspection. Computer vision based quality grading of apple fruits is a hard but necessary task for increasing the speed of grading as well as eliminating the human error in the process. An automated defect inspection system would significantly enhance the fresh fruit packing process. The research community of computer vision has been contributing a lot to develop apple grading system.

Early studies on apples external quality grading used global parameters. The apple grading system developed by (Yang, 1996) used the structural light image and general image to get sufficient information, and extracted information of characteristics that were used as input value for a Back-Propagation neural network to grade the

Figure 2. Surface defected apples; defection due to (a) Injury (b) & (c) fungus infection

apples. Nakano (1997) used neural networks (two-layer perceptron, five hidden neurons) to sort San-Fuji apples into five color and quality classes. Guedalia (1997) compared two methods to summarize the data resulting from the segmentation and then graded the apples into four classes (on a large set of 1100 fruits). The key point was that the fruits were graded using a reference population which was not constant, but which was a subset (a cluster) from the whole population. During the grading process, the characteristics of the last n fruits were included in a first in, first out heap, which was used to determine the correct sub-set. The error rate dropped from between 65% and 33% for a fixed population to 26% for the dynamic grading. Leemans et al. (1998), used a supervised method to grade the blobs resulting from the image segmentation. Large (above 11mm^2) and small blobs were treated differently. In a first step, for the former the over-segmentation was separated from the other blobs. An automated apple grading system by colour was built by Li et al. (2000). A method of using HIS colour system and neural network technology for apple colour inspection was developed. According to the surface defection by using the black and white image processing, the detection of apple defection was conducted (Li et al., 2007). In this system, the apple grading was completed according to the size and surface defection.

SURFACE DEFECT DETECTION OF APPLES

Apple fruit is susceptible to numerous kinds of injuries that affect its quality. External injuries, specifically, appear on the surface of fruit and directly affect consumers' perception. Thus, their detection is essential for the fresh fruit market. There are different types of defects, which present on the surface of an apple. The defects which may have occurred during harvesting, transportation, rotten (i.e. damaged by decay, bitter pit, fungi attack, scar tissue, frost damages, bruises,

insect attack and scab). Apples with rot, injury, disease, serious bruising, and other defects must be removed to prevent cross-contamination and reduce subsequent processing cost. Tissue from apples was analyzed to determine the defects mechanism at different maturity levels. Bruising is the most important cause of rejection of apples at warehouses. Bruising may be caused by one or more types of loading during harvesting, transportation, sorting, packing and storage. The ability to detect bruises depends on bruise visibility in the fruit, which in turn depends on bruise size and color.

RELATED WORK

In this section, we present brief survey on techniques for detecting defects on the surface of apples. The researchers have adopted image processing and computer vision based techniques to perform detection of surface defects of apples. Li et al., (2002) proposed an approach to detect the defect on the surface of an apple. Initially, the apples are passed through the conveyor belt and captured color images. Background removal is done by image subtraction. For this, local adaptive threshold segmentation is employed to detect the defect. Xiao-bo et al. (2010), proposed an approach for defect detection using three color camera systems. A computer controlled system using three color cameras is placed on the line. Then the apples are placed on rollers rotating while moving, and each camera will capture three images from each apple. In total nine images are obtained for each apple allowing the total surface to be scanned. Then, the apple images are segmented from the black background by multi-threshold methods. The defects, including the stem-ends and calyxes, called Regions Of Interest (ROIs), are segmented and counted in each of the nine images. Since, a calyx and stem-end cannot appear at the same image, an apple is defective if any one of the nine images has two or more ROIs.

Arlimatti (2012) introduced an apple classification system of one variety of apple fruit using the nearest neighbor classifier. The system encompasses pre-processing, dividing the image into windows, features collection, window elimination and classification or decision making step. It discriminates stem end / calyx from defected skin which are natural parts of the apple fruit. Statistical features are extracted from each window, and then the fruit is classified by supervised nearest neighbour classifier. Stem end and calyx part of the apple is considered as a defect in initial processing. After that these class apple features are fed to the classifier to classify whether apple is defected or whether it contains stem end/calyx. Yang (1994) detects the surface features in apple images. By introducing the concept of topographic representation for these images, the detection of the patch-like features is treated as one of catchment basin detection in apple grey-level landscapes. A flooding algorithm is adopted and modified to detect the catchment basins, (i.e. the features). After the flooding process, the catchment basins become lakes for which geometric parameters such as area and perimeter can easily be extracted. The author compared the proposed approach with the existing background subtraction method to show the advantages of the new approach.

Bennedsen et al. (2005), used an experimental machine vision system to identify surface defects on apples, including bruises. Images were captured through two optical filters at 740 and 950 nm, respectively. In the ensuing gray scale images, defects appeared as dark areas, however, so did shadows and parts of the stem/calyx area. A novel approach is proposed to locate the defects and eliminate other dark areas. The method is based on rotating the apples in front of the camera while multiple images are acquired. Dark areas, which are found at the same position, relative to the apple, during the rotation, represent defects, while other dark areas, which change shape and/or position from one frame to the next, are not classified as defects. Throop et al. (2005), developed an auto-mated inspection station to grade apples, which include a conveyor for apple orientation, optics and camera to capture identical images at three predetermined wavebands, a lighting system that illuminates the apple's surface diffusely and image processing algorithms to segment surface defects on apples in real time. Zhiqing Wen et al. (1999), designed a near-infrared machine-vision system for automating apple defect inspection. Fast blob extraction from fruit images was performed by using an adaptive spherical transformation. A binary decision-tree-structured rule base was established using blob feature extraction and analysis. Both off-line and on-line test was conducted to show effectiveness. From the results they demonstrated that the rule-based system was effective for apple defect detection.

OUR APPROACH FOR SURFACE DEFECT DETECTION OF APPLES

In this section, we present our approach to estimate the defects on surface of an apple using grow-cut and multi-threshold based segmentation technique. See Figure 3. Defect detection on the surface of an apple is really a challenging task due to non-uniform distribution of light on the surface of apples which causes specular reflections,

Figure 3. Flowchart of our approach

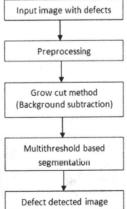

which itself visualizes as a defect. Therefore, we employ median filter for smoothing the images and removing the reflectance components for better defect detection. For background subtraction we use grow-cut approach (Vezhnevets et al., 2005), it removes background and gives fruit part separately. We partition fruit part image into defected part and non defected part using multi-threshold based segmentation.

IMAGE PRE-PROCESSING

Images captured by CCD camera, ultrasound, MRI, and CT are subject to various types of noises. These noises may degrade the quality of an image and subsequently it cannot provide correct information for subsequent image processing. In order to improve the quality of an image, operations need to be performed on it to remove or decrease degradations suffered by the image during its acquisition. The purpose of preprocessing is an improvement of the image data, which suppresses unwilling distortions or enhances some image features that are important for further processing and creates a more suitable image than the original for a specific application. The captured images are suffering from illumination variations, due to specular reflection. Figure 4 shows apple images with specular reflection, the reflected parts become full white and also the shadows, these are the main challenges in defect detection and we overcome these types of challenges by detecting effectively defects on the apple surface.

We employ median filtering to normalize the uneven distribution of light and to suppress noise.

Figure 4. Apple images with specular reflection

Median filtering is similar to using an averaging filter, in that each output pixel is set to an average of the pixel values in the neighborhood of the corresponding input pixel. In this filtering, the value of an output pixel is determined by the median of the neighborhood pixels, rather than the mean. The median is much less sensitive than the mean to extreme values (called outliers). Median filtering is therefore better able to remove these outliers without reducing the sharpness of the image. The median filter technique allowed the edges to be preserved while filtering out the peak noise. For this reason, the median filter is often used before applying defect detection technique to preserve the main apple defect as much as possible.

DEFECT SEGMENTATION

In order to extract apple part from the image, removal of background from the input image is essential step. This can be done using background subtraction method. If we separate background from the image, the remaining part gives our RoI (i.e., apple fruit part). This step helps us to differentiate which is fruit part and which is background part. For background subtraction we used grow-cut approach (Vezhnevets et al., 2005), it removes background and gives fruit part separately. Grow-cut Segmentation is a competitive region growing algorithm using cellular automata. The algorithm works by using a set of user input seed points for foreground and background. For N-class segmentation, the algorithm requires a set of seed points corresponding the N classes and a seed point for a don't care class. The algorithm executes as follows:

- Using the "user input seed points", the algorithm automatically computes a region of interest that en compass the seed points.
- Next, the algorithm iteratively tries to label all the pixels in the image using the label

of pixels in the user seeded portions of the image.

- The algorithm converges when all the pixels in the ROI are labeled, and no pixel can change its label any more.
- Individual pixels are labeled by computing a weighted similarity metric of a pixel with all its neighbors, where the weights correspond to the neighboring pixel's strength. The neighbor that results in the largest weight greater than the given pixel's strength confers its label to the given pixel.

Region growing approach examines neighbouring pixels of initial "seed points" and determines whether the pixel neighbours should be added to the region. The process is iterated on, in the same manner as general data clustering algorithms. In this approach, user have to give the foreground seed points and background seed points, based on these seed points it grows from the given seed points, after iteration process is finally reaches or grows to the end of the neighbour point having changes compared to the seed point it stops growing. Region growing methods can correctly separate the regions that have the same properties we define. The concept is simple. We only need a small number of seed points to represent the property we want, and then grow the region. We can determine the seed points and the criteria we want to make. We can choose the multiple criteria at the same time. It performs well with respect to noise.

Thresholding is a simple but effective tool to isolate objects of interest. Thresholding selection techniques can be classified into two categories: bi-level and multi-level. In bi-level thresholding, one limit value is chosen to segment an image into two classes: one represents the object and the other represents the background. When an image is composed of several distinct objects, multiple threshold values have to be selected for proper segmentation. This is called multilevel threshold-

ing. A variety of thresholding approaches have been proposed for image segmentation, including conventional methods and intelligent techniques.

After extracting the apple fruit part from the image, we partition an apple fruit image into defected part and non defected part using multi-threshold segmentation. In multi-threshold segmentation, the images were segmented several times at different threshold levels. The resulting binary images were added to form a so called multi layer image. This in turn was then subjected to threshold segmentation. This segmentation aimed at identifying the darkest areas in the original image. The resulting, binary image was referred to as a marker image. The final step consists in constructing a binary image, based on the marker image and the multi-layer image. With the position of the defects identified, a simple thresholding routine (i.e. a gradient segmentation is employed to determine the area of these defects).

EXPERIMENTAL RESULTS

In order to evaluate the efficiency of the proposed method for apple surface defects estimation, the experiments are carried out using captured RGB apple images. See Figure 5 and Figure 6. The proposed method was evaluated using a pink lady apples and Ginger Gold apples. The apples had varying degrees of surface defects and were selected to represent the majority of situations encountered in practical implementations. The experimental results of proposed defect detection method is compared and evaluated visually with hill-climbing (Papadias, 2000) and color based segmentation technique (Ozden et.al., 2007). See Figure 7. Figure 5 shows the test images of apples used for experimentation purpose.

In order to extract apple part from the image, we used grow-cut approach; it removes background and gives fruit part separately. Figure 6 shows the result of grow-cut method for background removal of test images shown in Figure 5.

Figure 5. The test images of apples

Figure 6. Background subtraction of test images shown in Figure 5

Figure 7. First row: test images of apples; second row: result of defect detection of proposed method; third row: result of Hill-climbed method and fourth row: result of color based segmentation method

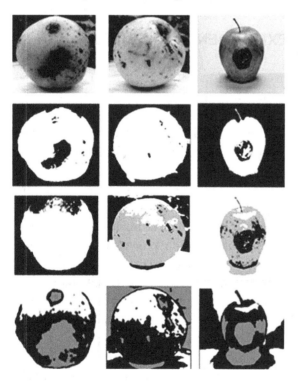

FUTURE DIRECTIONS

In our approach, we used supervised techniques such as grow-cut method for finding region of interest and multi-threshold based segmentation for the detection of defects on the surface of an apple. The future directions for research can be to build unsupervised techniques for background subtraction and segmentation.

CONCLUSION

In this chapter, we presented brief survey on recent approaches for automatic inspection of quality in fruits, specifically, quality of apples based on surface defects using computer vision techniques. We introduced our approach to estimate the defects on surface of an apple using grow-cut and multi-threshold based segmentation technique. We employed median filter for smoothing the images and removing the reflectance components for better defect detection. We used grow-cut approach for background subtraction and to separate fruit part. We partition fruit part image into defected part and non defected part using multi-threshold based segmentation. The experimental results are compared visually with hill-climbed and color based segmentation technique. It is observed that the our method effectively estimate the defects on surface of apples compared hill-climbed and color based segmentation technique. Our approach has the advantage of being able to inspect defects on the surface of the apple, shows how many defects are present in the apple. Proposed approach does not effectively work on apple image with high specular reflection and apple fruits occluded with other objects or apples, which is the objective of further research.

REFERENCES

Arlimatti. (2012). Window based method for automatic classification of apple fruit. *International Journal of Engineering Research and Applications, 2*(4), 1010-1013.

Bato, P. M. M., Nagata, Q., Cao, B. P., Shrestha, R., & Nakashima. (1999). Strawberry sorting using machine vision. *ASAE Paper No. 993162*. St. Joseph, MI: ASAE.

Bennedsen, B. S., Peterson, D. L., & Tabb, A. (2005). Identifying defects in images of rotating apples. [Amsterdam: Elesevier.]. *Computers and Electronics in Agriculture*, 92–102. doi:10.1016/j.compag.2005.01.003.

Cao, Q., Lu, T., & Masatera, N. (1997). Development of the strawberry sorting robot. *Journal of Shanghai Jiaotong University, 7*(7), 881–884.

Dimitris, P. (2000). Hill climbing algorithms for content-based retrieval of similar configurations. In *Proceedings of the ACM Conference on Information Retrieval*. Athens, Greece: ACM Press.

Edan, Y., Pastermak, H., Shmulevich, I., Rachmani, D., Guedalia, D., Grinberg, A., & Fallik, E. (1997). Colour and firmness classification of tomatoes. *Journal of Food Science, 62*(4), 793–796. doi:10.1111/j.1365-2621.1997.tb15457.x.

Feng, B. (2002). *Study on the method of computer vision information processing and fruit gradation and detection technology*. Beijing: China Agricultural University.

Ghazanfari, A. J., & Irudayaraj, K. A. (1996). Grading pistachio nuts using a neural network approach. *Transactions of the ASAE. American Society of Agricultural Engineers, 39*(6), 2319–2324.

He, D. (1998). *Color classification of fresh fruits by neural network*. Shanxi, China: Xibei Agricultural University.

Herrero-Langreo. (2012). Combination of optical and non-destructive mechanical techniques for the measurement of maturity in peach. *Journal of Food Engineering, 108*, 150–157. doi:10.1016/j.jfoodeng.2011.07.004.

Kazuhiro, N. (1997). Application of neural networks to the color grading of apples. *Computers and Electronics in Agriculture, 18*(2–3), 105–116.

Laykin, S., Alchanatis, V., & Fallik, E., & Edany. (2002). Image processing algorithms for tomatoes classification. *Transactions of the American Society of Agricultural Engineers, 45*(3), 851–858.

Li, C., & Heinemann, P. H. (2007). ANN-integrated electronic nose and znose system for apple quality evaluation. *Transactions of the ASABE, 50*(6), 2285–2294.

Li, Q., Wang, M., & Gu, W. (2002). Computer vision based system for apple surface defect detection. Computers and Electronics in Agriculture (215-223). Amsterdam: Elsevier.

Li, Q., Zhang, M., & Wang, M. (2000). Real-time apple colour grading based on genetic neural network. *Journal of Image and Graphics, 5A*(9), 779–784.

Masatera, N., & Osamu, K. (1997). Studies on automatic sorting system for strawberry. *Journal of Japanese Society of Agricultural Machinery, 59*(1), 43–48.

Mustafa, O., & Ediz, P. (2007). A color image segmentation approach for content-based image retrieval. *Pattern Recognition, 40*, 1318–1325. doi:10.1016/j.patcog.2006.08.013.

Nimesh, S., Delwiche, M. J., & Scott Johnson, R. (1993). Image analysis methods for realtime color grading of stone fruit. *Computers and Electronics in Agriculture, 9*(1), 71–84. doi:10.1016/0168-1699(93)90030-5.

Throop, J. A., Aneshansley, D. J., Anger, W. C., & Peterson, D. L. (2005). Quality evaluation of apples based on surface defects—an inspection station design. *International Journal Postharvest Biology and Technology*, *36*, 281–290. doi:10.1016/j.postharvbio.2005.01.004.

Vezhnevets & Konouchine. (2005). Grow-cut-Interactive multi-label N-D image segmentation. In *Proceedings of International Conference on Computer Graphics and Vision* (150–156). Berlin: Springer.

Wang, H., Cao, Q., Liu, W., & Masteru, N. (1999). Neural network based on computer grader judgement. *Transactions of the Chinese Society for Agricultural Machinery*, *30*(6), 83–87.

Xiao-bo, Jie-wen, Yanxiao, & Holmes. (2010). In-line detection of apple defects using three color cameras system. *Journal of Computers and Electronics in Agriculture*, *70*, 129–134. doi:10.1016/j.compag.2009.09.014.

Xu, J. (1997). *Study on parallel processing for computer vision information in fruit gradation*. Beijing: China Agricultural University.

Yang, Q. (1994). An approach to apple surface feature detection by machine vision. *Computers and Electronics in Agriculture*, *11*(2-3), 249–263. doi:10.1016/0168-1699(94)90012-4.

Yang, Q. S. (1996). Apple stem and calyx identification with machine vision system. *Journal of Agricultural Engineering Research*, *63*(3), 9–236. doi:10.1006/jaer.1996.0024.

Zhiqing, W., & Yang, T. (1999). Building a rule-based machine-vision system for defect inspection on apple sorting and packing lines. *Expert Systems with Applications*, *16*, 307–313. doi:10.1016/S0957-4174(98)00079-7.

ADDITIONAL READING

El Masry, G., Wang, N., & Vigneault, C. (2009). Detecting chilling injury in red delicious apple using hyperspectral imaging and neural networks. *Postharvest Biology and Technology*, *52*(1), 1–8. doi:10.1016/j.postharvbio.2008.11.008.

Mehl, P. M., Chen, Y. R., Kim, M. S., & Chen, D. E. (2004). Development of hyperspectral imaging technique for the detection of apple surface defects and contaminations. *Journal of Food Engineering*, *61*, 67–81. doi:10.1016/S0260-8774(03)00188-2.

Mendoza, F., & Aguilera, J. M. (2004). Application of image analysis for classification of ripening bananas. *Journal of Food Science*, *69*, 471–477. doi:10.1111/j.1365-2621.2004.tb09932.x.

Nimesh, S., Delwiche, M. J., & Johnson, R. (1993). Image analysis methods for realtime color grading of stone fruit. *Computers and Electronics in Agriculture*, *9*(1), 71–84. doi:10.1016/0168-1699(93)90030-5.

Wen, Z., & Tao, Y. (1999). Building a rule-based machine-vision system for defect inspection on apple sorting and packing lines. *Expert Systems with Applications*, *16*, 307–313. doi:10.1016/S0957-4174(98)00079-7.

Xiao-bo, Z., Jie-wen, Z., Yanxiao, L., & Holmes, M. (2010). In-line detection of apple defects using three color cameras system. *Computers and Electronics in Agriculture*, *70*(1), 129–134. doi:10.1016/j.compag.2009.09.014.

KEY TERMS AND DEFINITIONS

Apple Grading: Apples are graded into different categories based on different features, such as spherical shape, color and defects present on the surface.

Classification: Classification is the problem of identifying to which of a set of categories (subpopulations), a new observation belongs, based on a training set of data containing observations (or instances) whose category membership is known.

Computer Vision: Computer vision is a field that aims to simulate the effect of human vision using methods such as acquiring, processing, analyzing, and understanding images and, in general, high-dimensional data from the real world in order to produce numerical or symbolic information.

Grow Cut: It works based on seed points given by the user; from the seed point, pixel grows until it becomes to slightly differ in intensity or threshold value than its neighbor pixel. When the seed point slightly differs from neighbor pixel, it stops growing, so it separates different regions based on the user defined seed points.

Multi-Threshold Segmentation: The image is segmented several times at different threshold levels. The resulting binary images were added to form a so called multi layer image. This in turn is then subjected to threshold segmentation. The resulting binary image is referred to as a marker image. The final step consists in constructing a binary image, based on the marker image and the multi-layer image.

Surface Defect Detection: Surface defects is an external feature; if the surface has more defects, then it will be graded into to lower grade, it also gives information to customer, whether the apple is good for purchase or not.

Section 2
Medical Applications

Chapter 8
Image Analysis and Understanding Techniques for Breast Cancer Detection from Digital Mammograms

Subodh Srivastava
Indian Institute of Technology (BHU), India

Neeraj Sharma
Indian Institute of Technology (BHU), India

S.K. Singh
Indian Institute of Technology (BHU), India

ABSTRACT

In this chapter, an overview of recent developments in image analysis and understanding techniques for automated detection of breast cancer from digital mammograms is presented. The various steps in the design of an automated system (i.e. Computer Aided Detection [CADe] and Computer Aided Diagnostics (CADx)] include preparation of image database for classification, image pre-processing, mammogram image enhancement and restoration, segmentation of Region Of Interest (ROI) for cancer detection, feature extraction of selected ROIs, feature evaluation and selection, and classification of selected mammogram images in to benign, malignant, and normal. In this chapter, a detailed overview of the various methods developed in recent years for each stage required in the design of an automated system for breast cancer detection is discussed. Further, the design, implementation and performance analysis of a CAD tool is also presented. The various types of features extracted for classification purpose in the proposed tool include histogram features, texture features, geometric features, wavelet features, and Gabor features. The proposed CAD tool uses fuzzy c-means segmentation algorithm, the feature selection algorithm based on the concepts of genetic algorithm which uses mutual information as a fitness function, and linear support vector machine as a classifier.

DOI: 10.4018/978-1-4666-4558-5.ch008

INTRODUCTION

Cancer is a group of diseases that cause cells in the body to change and grow out of control. Most types of cancer cells eventually form a lump or masses called a tumor, and are named after the part of the body where the tumor originates. Breast cancer begins in breast tissue, which is made up of glands for milk production, called lobules, and the ducts that connect lobules to the nipple. The remainder of the breast is made up of fatty, connective, and lymphatic tissue. Breast cancer is a leading cause of cancer deaths among women. For women in US and other developed countries, it is the most frequently diagnosed cancer. About 2,100 new cases of breast cancer and 800 deaths are registered each year in Norway. In India, a death rate of one in eight women has been reported due to breast cancer. Efficient detection is the most effective way to reduce mortality, and currently a screening program based on mammography is considered one the best and most popular methods for detection of breast cancer. Mammography is a low-dose x-ray procedure that allows visualization of the internal structure of the breast. Mammography is highly accurate, but like most medical tests, it is not perfect. On average, mammography will detect about 80%-90% of the breast cancers in women without symptoms). Testing is somewhat more accurate in postmenopausal than in premenopausal women. The small percentage of breast cancers that are not identified by mammography may be missed for just as mammography uses x-ray machines designed especially to image the breasts (Acha, Rangayyan, & Desautels, 2006). An increasing number of countries have started mass screening programmes that have resulted in a large increase in the number of mammograms requiring interpretation. In the interpretation process radiologists carefully search each image for any visual sign of abnormality. However, abnormalities are often embedded in and camouflaged by varying densities of breast tissue structures. Estimates indicate that between 10 and 30 per cent of breast radiologists

miss cancers during routine screening. In order to improve the accuracy of interpretation, a variety of screening techniques have been developed American College of Radiology (ACR, 2003)

Breast image analysis can be performed using mammography, magnetic resonance, nuclear medicine or ultrasound. So far the most effective and economical breast imaging modality has been mammography due to its simplicity, portability and cost effectiveness. Segmentation is the fundamental process which partitions a data space into meaningful salient regions. Image segmentation essentially affects the overall performance of any automated image analysis system thus its quality is of the utmost importance (Rangayyan, Ayres, & Desautels, 2007).

Digital mammography is a technique for recording x-ray images in computer code instead of on x-ray film, as with conventional mammography. The first digital mammography system received U.S. Food and Drug Administration (FDA) approval in 2000. An example of a digital mammography system is the Senographe 2000D. The images are displayed on a computer monitor and can be enhanced (lightened or darkened) before they are printed on film. Images can also be manipulated; the radiologist can magnify or zoom in on an area. From the patient's perspective, the procedure for a mammogram with a digital system is the same as for conventional mammography

Digital mammography may have some advantages over conventional mammography. The images can be stored and retrieved electronically. Despite these benefits, studies have not yet shown that digital mammography is more effective in finding cancer than conventional mammography. Initial mammographic or MRI images themselves are not usually enough to determine the existence of a benign or malignant disease with certainty. If a finding or spot seems suspicious, your radiologist may recommend further diagnostic studies. Interpretations of mammograms can be difficult because a normal breast can appear differently for each woman. Also, the appearance of an image may be compromised if there is powder or salve on the breasts or if you have undergone breast surgery. Recent studies showed that the interpretation of the mammogram by the radiologists give high rates of false positive cases indeed the images provided by different patients have different dynamics of intensity and present a weak contrast. Moreover the size of the significant details can be very small. Several research works have tried to develop computer aided diagnosis tools. They could help the radiologists in the interpretation of the mammograms and could be useful for an accurate diagnosis.

With digital mammography the breast image is captured using a special electronic x-ray detector which converts the image into a digital mammogram for viewing on a computer monitor or storing J. (Tang, R. Rangayyan, J. Xu, I. El Naqa, Y. Yang,.2009). Each breast is imaged separately in CranioCaudal (CC) view and MedioLateral-Oblique (MLO) view shown in Figure 1(a) and Figure 1(b), respectively. The American College of Radiology (ACR) Breast Imaging Reporting And Data System (BI-RADS) suggests a standardized method for breast imaging reporting. Terms have been developed to describe breast density, lesion features and lesion classification. Screening mammography enables detection of early signs of breast cancer such as masses, calcifications, architectural distortion and bilateral asymmetry.

Figure 1. Two basic views of mammographic image: (a) CranioCaudal (CC) view, (b) Medio-LateralOblique (MLO)

 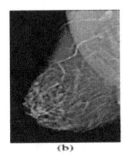

(a)　(b)

Types of Breast Cancer Images

A mass is defined as a space occupying lesion seen in at least two different projections. If a potential mass is seen in only a single projection it should be called 'Asymmetry' or 'Asymmetric Density' until its three-dimensionality is confirmed. Masses have different density (fat containing masses, low density, isodense, high density), different margins (circumscribed, microlobular, obscured, indistinct, spiculated) and different shape (round, oval, lobular, irregular). Round and oval shaped masses with smooth and circumscribed margins usually indicate benign changes. On the other hand, a malignant mass usually has a spiculated, rough and blurry boundary. However, there exist atypical cases of macrolobulated or spiculated benign masses, as well as microlobulated or well-circumscribed malignant masses (Tang, Rangayyan, Xu, El Naqa, & Yang, 2009).

Abnormalities in Breast Cancer

Calcifications are deposits of calcium in breast tissue. Calcifications detected on a mammogram are an important indicator for malignant breast disease but are also present in many benign changes. Benign calcifications are usually larger and coarser with round and smooth contours. Malignant calcifications tend to be numerous, clustered, small, varying in size and shape, angular, irregularly shaped and branching in orientation. Calcifications are generally very small and they may be missed in the dense breast tissue. Another issue is that they sometimes have low contrast to the background and can be misinterpreted as noise in the inhomogeneous background. Fine pleomorphic clustered calcifications with high probability of malignancy are shown in Figure 2(b) (Acha, Rangayyan, & Desautels, 2006).

Figure 2. Examples of abnormalities: (a) Round Mass With Circumscribed Margins, (b) Fine Pleomorphic Clustered Calcifications

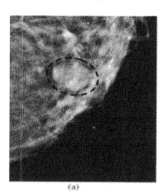 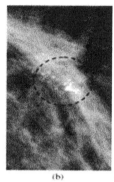

(a)   (b)

Mass Detection Algorithms

A mass is space occupying lesion seen in at least two different projections defined with wide range of features that can indicate benign changes but can also be a part of malignant changes. Masses with round, smooth and circumscribed margins usually indicate benign changes while masses with speculated, rough and blurry margins usually indicate a malignant mass. Some researchers have focused mainly on the detection of speculated masses because of their high likelihood of malignancy.

Algorithms for breast mass detection in digital mammography usually consist of several steps: segmentation, feature extraction, feature selection and classification. In the segmentation step Regions Of Interest (ROIs) that contain abnormali-

ties are segmented from the normal breast tissue. In the second stage of the algorithm each ROI is characterized with the set of features. In the feature selection step the best set of features are selected and in the classification step suspicious ROIs are classified as benign masses or malignant masses (Acha, Rangayyan, & Desautels, 2006).

For early detection of breast cancer, mammography is the best available technique. The most common breast abnormalities that may indicate breast cancer are masses and calcifications. In some cases, subtle signs that can also lead to a breast cancer diagnosis, such as architectural distortion and bilateral asymmetry, are present. Breast abnormalities are defined with wide range of features and may be easily missed or misinterpreted by radiologists while reading large amount of mammographic images provided in screening programs. To help radiologists provide an accurate diagnosis, a Computer-Aided Detection (CADe) and Computer-Aided Diagnosis (CADx) algorithms are being developed. CADe and CADx algorithms help reducing the number of false positives and they assist radiologists in deciding between follow up and biopsy. This report gives a survey of image processing algorithms that have been developed for detection of masses and calcifications. An overview of algorithms in each step (image enhancement, segmentation step, feature extraction step, feature selection step, classification step) of the mass detection algorithms is given (Tang, Rangayyan, Xu, El Naqa, & Yang, 2009; Bellotti, 2006). See Figure 3.

Figure 3. Image processing steps involved in the design of a CAD tool

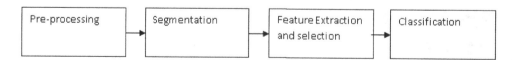

STEPS INVOLVED IN THE DESIGN OF A CAD TOOL

Pre-Processing

Enhancement of mammographic images using histogram equalization method such as Contrast Limited Histogram Equalization (CLAHE) (De Oliveira Martins, Junior, & Silva, 2009) or by the use of median filter .Here, in this study we propose to use contrast limited histogram equalization (CLAHE) technique for image enhancement. CLAHE differs from ordinary adaptive histogram equalization in its contrast limiting. This feature can also be applied to global histogram equalization, giving rise to Contrast-Limited Histogram Equalization (CLHE), which is rarely used in practice. In the case of CLAHE, the contrast limiting procedure has to be applied for each neighborhood from which a transformation function is derived. CLAHE was developed to prevent the over amplification of noise that adaptive histogram equalization can give rise to. It is advantageous not to discard the part of the histogram that exceeds the clip limit but to redistribute it equally among all histogram bins.

Segmentation

The aim of the segmentation is to extract ROIs containing all masses and locate the suspicious mass candidates from the ROI. Segmentation of the suspicious regions on a mammographic image is designed to have a very high sensitivity and a large number of false positives are acceptable since they are expected to be removed in later stage of the algorithm. Researchers have used several segmentation techniques and their combinations. Image segmentation aims at splitting an entire image into a set of regions having the following properties:

- Connectivity and compactness.
- Regularity and boundaries.
- Homogeneity in terms of color and texture.

- Differentiation from neighbor regions.

The two fundamental approaches to image segmentation include thresholding techniques and region based approach which group together pixels with similar properties combining proximity and similarity. The classification of region based segmentation is given as follows:

- Region Growing
- Split & Merge
- K-Mean Clustering
- Watershed Technique

Thresholding Techniques

Thresholding is the simplest method of image segmentation. From a greyscale image, thresholding can be used to create binary images. During the thresholding process, individual pixels in an image are marked as "object" pixels if their value is greater than some threshold value (assuming an object to be brighter than the background) and as "background" pixels otherwise. This convention is known as threshold above. Variants include threshold below, which is opposite of threshold above; threshold inside, where a pixel is labeled "object" if its value is between two thresholds; and threshold outside, which is the opposite of threshold inside . Typically, an object pixel is given a value of "1" while a background pixel is given a value of "0." Finally, a binary image is created by coloring each pixel white or black, depending on a pixel's labels.

Threshold Selection

The key parameter in the thresholding process is the choice of the threshold value (or values, as mentioned earlier). Several different methods for choosing a threshold exist; users can manually choose a threshold value, or a thresholding algorithm can compute a value automatically, which is known as automatic thresholding. A simple method would be to choose the mean or median value, the rationale being that if the object pixels are brighter than the background, they should also be brighter than the average. In a noiseless image with uniform background and object values, the mean or median will work well as the threshold, however, this will generally not be the case. A more sophisticated approach might be to create a histogram of the image pixel intensities and use the valley point as the threshold. The histogram approach assumes that there is some average value for the background and object pixels, but that the actual pixel values have some variation around these average values. However, this may be computationally expensive, and image histograms may not have clearly defined valley points, often making the selection of an accurate threshold difficult.

A simple iterative method which does not require much specific knowledge of the image, and is robust against image noise is described as follows:

Step 1: An initial threshold (T) is chosen, this can be done randomly or according to any other method desired.

Step 2: The image is segmented into object and background pixels as described above, creating two sets:
- G1 = {f(m,n):f(m,n)>T} (object pixels)
- G2 = {f(m,n):f(m,n) T} (background pixels)

where f(m,n) is the value of the pixel located in the mth column, nth row.

Step 3: The average of each set is computed.
- m1 = average value of G1
- m2 = average value of G2

Step 4: A new threshold is created that is the average of m1 and m2.
- T' = (m1 + m2)/2

Step 5: Go back to step two, now using the new threshold computed in step four, keep repeating until the new threshold matches the one before it (i.e. until convergence has been reached).

This above iterative algorithm is a special one-dimensional case of the k-means clustering algorithm, which has been proven to converge at a local minimum i.e. a different initial threshold may give a different final result.

Adaptive Thresholding

Thresholding is called adaptive thresholding when a different threshold is used for different regions in the image. This may also be known as local or dynamic thresholding . Sezgin and Sankur (2004) categorize thresholding methods into the following six groups based on the information the algorithm manipulates:

- **Histogram Shape-Based Methods:** Where, for example, the peaks, valleys and curvatures of the smoothed histogram are analyzed.
- **Clustering-Based Methods:** Where the gray-level samples are clustered in two parts as background and foreground (object), or alternately are modeled as a mixture of two Gaussians.
- **Entropy-Based Methods:** Result in algorithms that use the entropy of the foreground and background regions, the cross-entropy between the original and binarized image, etc.
- **Object Attribute-Based Methods:** Search a measure of similarity between the gray-level and the binarized images, such as fuzzy shape similarity, edge coincidence, etc.
- **Spatial Methods:** Use higher-order probability distribution and/or correlation between pixels local methods adapt the threshold value on each pixel to the local image characteristics.

Multiband Thresholding

Color images can also be thresholded. One approach is to designate a separate threshold for each of the RGB components of the image and then combine them with an AND operation. This reflects the way the camera works and how the data is stored in the computer, but it does not correspond to the way that people recognize color. Therefore, the HSL and HSV color models are more often used. It is also possible to use the CMYK color model .

Otsu's Method (Sezgin & Sankur, 2004; Otsu, 1979).

Otsu's method is used to automatically perform histogram shape-based image thresholding or, the reduction of a gray level image to a binary image. The algorithm assumes that the image to bethresholded contains two classes of pixels or bi-modal histogram (e.g. foreground and background) then calculates the optimum threshold separating those two classes so that their combined spread (intra-class variance) is minimal. In Otsu's method we exhaustively search for the threshold that minimizes the intra-class variance (within class variance), defined as a weighted sum of variances of the two classes:

$$\sigma_w^2(t) = \omega_1(t)\sigma_1^2(t) + \omega_2(t)\sigma_2^2(t)$$

Weights ω_i are the probabilities of the two classes separated by a threshold t and σ_i^2 variances of these classes.

Region Based Techniques

Region-based segmentation is a technique for determining the region directly. Split-and-merge segmentation is based on a quadtree partition of an image. It is sometimes called quadtree segmentation. This method starts at the root of the tree that represents the whole image. If it is found non-uniform (not homogeneous), then it is split into four son-squares (the splitting process), and so on so forth. Conversely, if four son-squares are homogeneous, they can be merged as several connected components (the merging process). The node in the tree is a segmented node. This process continues recursively until no further splits or merges are possible. When a special data structure is involved in the implementation of the algorithm of the method, its time complexity can reach O(nlogn), an optimal algorithm of the method.

K-Means Clustering Technique For Image Segmentation *(Arthur, Manthey, & Roeglin, 2009)*

K mean clustering is a method of cluster analysis which aims to partition n observations into k clusters in which each observation belongs to the cluster with the nearest mean. Given a set of observation(x1,x2,x3……. xn) , k mean cluster partition it into k sets(k<=n),S={s1,s2,s3…….. sk} so as to minimize the within cluster sum of squares. The algorithm for k-means clustering approach is described as follows:

Initially, we are given an initial set of k means m1,m2……mk. Then the algorithm proceeds by alternating between following two steps assignment step and update step. In assignment step, we assign each observation to the cluster with the closest mean, and in update step, we calculate the new means to be the centroid of the observation in the cluster.

Assignment Step: Assign each observation to the cluster with the closest mean i.e. partition the observations according to the Voronoi diagram generated by the means.

$$S_i^{(t)} = \left\{ x_p : \left\| x_p - m_i^{(t)} \right\| \leq \left\| x_p - m_j^{(t)} \right\| \forall 1 \leq j \leq k \right\}$$

where each x_p goes into exactly one $S_i^{(t)}$, even if it could go in two of them.

Update Step: Calculate the new means to be the centroid of the observations in the cluster.

$$m_i^{(t+1)} = \frac{1}{\left| S_i^{(t)} \right|} \sum_{x_j \in S_i^{(t)}} x_j$$

These above mentioned two steps are repeated until we get convergence point.

Fuzzy C-Means Clustering (Nock & Nielsen, 2006; Bezdek, 1981: Ahmed & Yamany, 2002)

In hard clustering, data is divided into distinct clusters, where each data element belongs to exactly one cluster. In fuzzy clustering (also referred to as soft clustering), data elements can belong to more than one cluster, and associated with each element is a set of membership levels. These indicate the strength of the association between that data element and a particular cluster. Fuzzy clustering is a process of assigning these membership levels, and then using them to assign data elements to one or more clusters. It is based on the following objective function:

$$\sum_{i-1}^{N} \sum_{j-1}^{C} U_{ij}^{m} \parallel Xi - Cj \parallel^2 \ 1 \leq m < \infty$$

where m is any real number greater than 1, U_{ij} is the degree of membership of X_i in the cluster j, X_i is the ith of d-dimensional measured data, C_j is the d- dimension centre of the cluster, and $\parallel * \parallel$ is any norm expressing the similarity between any measured data and the center.

Feature Extraction

In pattern recognition and in image processing, feature extraction is a special form of dimensionality reduction. When the input data to an algorithm is too large to be processed and it is suspected to be notoriously redundant (much data, but not much information) then the input data will be transformed into a reduced representation set of features (also named features vector). Transforming the input data into the set of features is called *feature extraction*. If the features extracted are carefully chosen it is expected that the features set will extract the relevant information from the input data in order to perform the desired task using this reduced representation instead of the full size input.

Feature extraction involves simplifying the amount of resources required to describe a large set of data accurately. When performing analysis of complex data one of the major problems stems from the number of variables involved. Analysis with a large number of variables generally requires a large amount of memory and computation power or a classification algorithm which overfits the training sample and generalizes poorly to new samples. Feature extraction is a general term for methods of constructing combinations of the variables to get around these problems while still describing the data with sufficient accuracy. After performing the image segmentation and selecting the appropriate Region Of Interest (ROI) containing micro calcifications and mass lesions from each image in image database the following features may be extracted (Baeg & Kehtarnavaz, 2002).

Histogram Based Features (Dhawan & Chitre, 1996)

The examples of histogram based features include mean, standard deviation, variance, kurtosis, skewness and moments etc. The basic definitions and their characteristics are given as follows: Mean: It extracts the fine edge structures. Mean is the mean pixel value with ROI.

$$\text{Mean} = \sum_{i=0}^{\text{Area}} \text{InputImage}[X\_ROI[i], Y\_ROI[i]]$$

Standard Deviation: It emphasizes the strong edges in the image. Standard deviation is the root mean square (RMS) deviation of the value from their arithmetic mean it is most common measure of statistical mean. It is the most common measure of statistical dispersion measuring how widely spread the values are in data set

$$\text{SD} = \sum_{i=0}^{\text{Area}} ([\text{InputImage}[X\_ROI[i], Y\_ROI[i]]] - \text{Mean})^2.$$

Skewness is defined as third order absolute moment. It measures the asymmetry of the probability distribution of a real –valued random variable .A distribution has positive skew (right –skewed) if the right (higher value) tail is longer or fatter and negative skew (left – skewed) if the left (lower value) tail is longer or fatter .tumor has left skewness which takes direction to the bright gray level.

$$\textit{Skewness} = \sum_{i=0}^{\text{Area}} ([\text{InputImage}[X\_ROI[i], Y\_ROI[i]]] - \text{Mean})$$

$$\text{Skewness} = \frac{1}{N} \frac{\sum_{i,j=0}^{N-1} [g(i,j) - \overline{g(1,J)}]^3}{\sqrt{\sum_{i,j=0}^{N-1} [g(i,j) - \overline{g(1,J)}]^3}}$$

Kurtosis=Fourth order moment-3

$$\text{Kurtosis} = \frac{1}{N} \frac{\sum_{i,j=0}^{N-1} [g(i,j) - \overline{g(1,J)}]^4}{\sqrt{\sum_{i,j=0}^{N-1} [g(i,j) - \overline{g(1,J)}]^4}}$$

$$\text{Intensity} = \overline{g(l,J)} = \frac{1}{N} \sum_{i,j=0}^{N-1} g(i,j)$$

Texture Features (Baeg & Kehtarnavaz 2002; Sheshadri & Kandaswamy, 2006)

The texture features of an image may be extracted from its gray Level concurrence matrix (GLCM), and Gray Level Difference Matrix (GLDM). Some texture features include: contrast, energy, correlation etc.

- **Contrast:** It returns a measure of the power difference between a pixel and its neighbour over the total image.

$$\sum_{i,j} |i - j|^2 p(i,j).$$

GLCM calculates the probability of pixel with the gray – level value i occurring in a specific spatial relationship to a pixel with value j.

- **Energy:** It shows sum of squared elements in the GLCM i.e. $\sum_{i,j} p(i,j)^2$.

- **Correlation:** It returns a measure of how linked a pixel is to its neighbor over the whole image.

$$\sum_{i,j} \frac{(i - \mu i)(j - \mu j) p(i,j)}{\sigma_1 \sigma_2}$$

where μ_i and μ_j (i = X, j= Y) is the mean intensity, σ_1 σ_2 (i=X, j= Y) is the standard deviation. A frequently used approach for texture analysis is based on statistical moments. The expression for the nth order moments about the mean is given by:

$$\mu_n = \sum_{i=0}^{L-1} (z_i - m)^n p(z_i)$$

where z_i is random variable indicating intensity, $p(z_i)$ is the histogram of the intensity levels in a region, L is the number of possible intensity levels and

$$m = \sum_{i=0}^{L-1} z_i p(z_i)$$

Is the mean(average) intensity.

Geometric Features

Geometric feature describe the geometric properties of the Region of the Region of Interest (ROI).It is represented as a collection of pixels in an image. Thus, for purpose of recognition we need to describe the properties of pixels[21]. The geometric properties of the region are the regional descriptors characterize, that any object must identify by features. In medical diagnose, geometric features are essential to recognize any object, regardless of breast [22].

Area (A): Area is the simplest property and by its given size. Therefore, it is the number of pixels in the number of pixels in the extracted ROI. Transformation function create array of ROI that contain pixels with 255 values. Area is defined as:

$$Area = A = \sum_i \sum_j (A_{i,j,} X\_ROI[Area] = i$$

Y_ROI[Area] =j

where i,j are the pixels within the shape. And X_ROI[] is vector contain ROI x position, Y_ROI[] is vector contain ROI y position.

Perimeter (P): Perimeter is another simple property defined by the perimeter of the region. It is the length of extracted ROI boundary.

$$Perimeter = P =$$
$$\sum_i \sum_j (P_{i,j,}(P_{i,j,} X\_edge[Perimeter] = i$$

Y_edge [Perimeter] = j

Feature Selection and Evaluation

The overall objective of this step is to use less number of selected features for classifying the mammographic images as benign, malignant or normal. If we extract the N number of features for the input image and all images in database then a feature vector is formed for each feature and all feature vectors constitute a feature space. After constituting a feature space, the next task is to select the most relevant features which best describes the image content from the overall feature space. This can be done by computing some sort of feature scores for each images and sorting or ranking them according to their relevance. The task of feature selection and evaluation, which is related to dimensionality reduction, is a major step in classification as this step has a major impact on the overall efficiency of a CAD system. The various approaches available in literature for feature selection include. Principal Component Analysis (PCA), Forward Sequential Analysis Backward analysis methods, Linear Discriminant Analysis, Majority Voting Method, Laplacian Scores method, Genetic algorithm based approaches, Particle Swarm Optimization methods, and so on.

General Algorithm for Feature Selection

Inputs:
- ◦ **S:** Data sample with features X i.e. IFS, |X|=*n*.
- ◦ **F:** Evaluation measure to be maximized
- ◦ **SG:** Successor generation operator

Output: Selected _features

Step 1:

IFS=Start_point (X); // IFS: Initial feature set

Selected _features={Best of IFS according to F}

Step 2:

Do

{IFS= Search_stategy (IFS, SG (F), X);

X'=(Best of IFS according to F);

If

$$F(X') \geq F(Selected\_features)$$

Or

(F(X')=F(Selected_features) and IX'I<ISelected_
featuresI)

And

IX'I< I Selected_featuresI)

Then

Selected_features= X';

While (*Stop(F,IFS)*) // stop when no further features can be selected from initial features set// based on evaluation function F

General Characterization of Feature Selection Algorithm

The feature selection algorithms may be based on three major criterions such as based on some evaluation measure; based on search organization; and based on the generation of successors. Some methods used for each criterion are described in Table 1.

Categories of Feature Selection Algorithms

The feature selection algorithms are divided into three categories: filters, wrappers, and hybrid methods.

Filter Based Feature Selection Methods

Filter based feature selection method use general characteristics of the data independently from the classifier for the evaluation process. See Figure 4.

The evaluation of a feature selection method is based on determining the relevancy of the generated feature subset candidate towards the classification task described as:

Rvalue = J(candidate subset)

If

(Rvalue > best_value) = Rvalue.

Types of Filter Based Evaluation Functions

- Distance measures based (Euclidean distance measure.)
- Information theoretic approach based (entropy, information gain, mutual information.)

Table 1. Feature selection characterization

Evaluation Measure	Search Organization	Generation of Successors
Distance Divergence Information Dependence Accuracy	Exponential Sequential Random	Forward Backward Compound Random Weights

Figure 4. Filter based feature selection

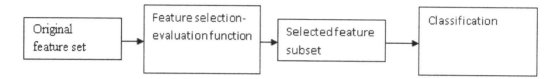

- Data dependency measures based (correlation coefficient.)
- Consistency (minimum features bias.)

Distance Measures

Example of distance measures include Euclidian distance $z^2 = x^2 + y^2$. Here, we select those features that support instances of the same class to stay within the same proximity. The instances of same class should be closer in terms of distance than those from different class.

Information Measures

Examples of information measure include entropy and information gain defined as follows:

- **Entropy:** Measurement of information content.
- **Information Gain of a Feature:** (e.g. Induction of decision tree.)

$$gain(A) = I(p,n) - E(A)$$

$gain(A)$ = before A is branched - sum of all nodes after branched

select A if $gain(A) > gain(B)$.

Mutual Information

Mutual information (MI) measures how much knowledge two variables carry about each other. It is the difference between the sum of the marginal entropies and their joint entropy. The mutual information of two independent items is always zero.

Data Dependency Measures

The dependency measure examines the correlation between a feature and a class label, and how close is the feature related to the outcome of the class label? The dependence between features is equal to the degree of redundancy. If a feature is heavily dependent on another, then it is redundant. To determine correlation, we need some physical value. The value is distance or some information. This measures the correlation between a feature and a class label. If a feature A is highly related to the class than feature B, then we select feature A. It measure how closely a feature related to the outcome of the class label. A slight variation of the definition can be used to measure the degree of redundancy between features. For example if a feature A is heavily dependent to feature B, then feature A is redundant. Since correlation is only a measure of relationship, we need some kind of physical measure in order to define such relationship.

Consistency Measure

In consistency measures, the two instances are inconsistent if they have matching feature values but group under different class label.

Here, we select feature set {F1,F2} . If in the training data set, there exist no instances as above and this heavily relies on the training data set. The objective is to find the minimum number of consistent features. See Table 2.

Wrapper Based Feature Selection Methods

In wrapper based methods, the evaluation process is classifier-dependent and uses the learning algorithm as a subroutine: The general argument in favor of this scheme is to equal the bias of both the feature selection algorithm and the learning algorithm that will be used later on to assess the goodness of the solution. The main disadvantage is the extra computational cost that comes from calling the induction/ calssifier algorithm to evaluate each subset of considered features. See Figure 5.

In wrapper based approach the classifier error rate is minimized. It is defined as follows:

error_rate = classifier (feature subset candidate)

If

(error_rate < predefined threshold) select the feature subset.

The wrapper based feature selection loss its generality, but gain accuracy towards the classification task and is computationally extensive .

Hybrid Model for Feature Selection

The hybrid models use both filtering and wrapping methods for improving the performance of the selection process. Evaluating the discrimination power of the individual feature is a key operation

Table 2. Consistency measure

	F1	**F2**	**Group/ Class**
Instance 1	A	B	C1
Instance 2	A	B	C2

in feature selection processes. Several methods may be used to evaluate the discrimination power of a feature, where mutual information is the most commonly used method .Inter cluster relations are also used for medical image feature data evaluation in . In this study, we utilize three criteria for different attributes of feature–data relations. Mutual information is used for measuring the feature and data relations. Inter cluster and inner-cluster affinity characterizes the relationship between features and classes; thus, they are for different attributes of feature–data relations.

SFS (Sequential Forward Selection) (Dash & Liu, 2012)

SFS begins with zero attributes and evaluates all features subsets with exactly one feature at a time. It selects the one with the best performance and adds to this subsets the feature that yields the best performance for subsets of next larger size . If evaluation function is a heuristics measure, the feature selection algorithm acts as a filter, extracting features to be used by the main algorithm; and if it is the actual accuracy, it acts as a wrapper around that algorithm .

SBS (Sequential Backward Selection)

SBS begins with all features and repeatedly removes a feature whose removal yields the maximal performance improvement.

Data Splitting in to Train and Test Sets

The following methods are used for data splitting:

- Holdout
- Leave One Out
- K-Fold

Figure 5. Wrapper based feature selection method

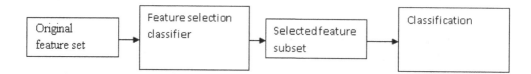

- Re-Substitution
  - **Holdout Method:** Split dataset into two groups (http://research.cs.tamu.edu/prism/lectures/iss/iss_113.pd: *Intelligent Sensor Systems Ricardo Gutierrez-Osuna Wright State University*):
    - **Training Set:** Used to train the classifier.
    - **Test Set:** Used to estimate the error rate of the trained classifier. See Figure 6.

A typical application of the holdout method is determining a stopping point for the back propagation error. See Figure 7.

The holdout method has two basic drawbacks which include i) In problems where we have a sparse dataset we may not be able to afford the cost of setting aside a portion of the dataset for testing ii) Since it is a single train-and-test experiment, the holdout estimate of error rate will be misleading if we happen to get an "unfortunate" split. The limitations of the holdout can be overcome with a family of resampling methods at the expense of more computations. See Figure 8.

- **K-Fold Cross-Validation:** This method creates a K-fold partition of the dataset. Here, for each of K experiments, K-1 folds are used for training and the remaining one for testing. See Figure 9.

K-Fold Cross validation is similar to Random Subsampling. The advantage of K-Fold Cross validation is that all the examples in the dataset are eventually used for both training and testing. The true error is estimated as the average error rate:

Figure 7. Stopping point and error

Figure 6. Holdout method

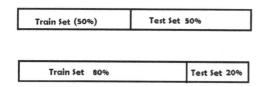

Figure 8. Holdout method

$$E = \frac{1}{k} \sum_{i=1}^{k} E_i.$$

- **Leave-One-Out:** It is the degenerate case of K-Fold cross validation, where K is chosen as the total number of examples. See Figure 10. For a dataset with N examples, it perform N experiments. For each experiment N-1 examples are used for training and the remaining example for testing. The true error is estimated as the average error rate on test examples:

$$E = \frac{1}{N} \sum_{i=1}^{N} E_i.$$

The Choice for the Selection of Number of Folds K in K-Fold Cross Validation

If large number of folds are chosen the bias of the true error rate estimator will be small and the estimator will be very accurate; the variance of the true error rate estimator will be large; and the computational time will be very large. If small number of folds are chosen the number of experiments and, therefore, computation time

Figure 9. K-Fold cross-validation

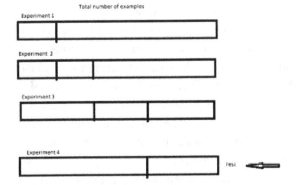

Figure 10. Leave one out method

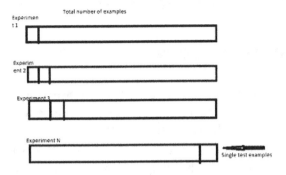

are reduced; the variance of the estimator will be small; the bias of the estimator will be large. In practice, the choice of the number of folds depends on the size of the dataset . For large datasets, even 3-Fold Cross Validation will be quite accurate. For very sparse datasets, leave-one-out may be opted in order to train on as many examples as possible. A common choice for K-Fold Cross Validation in practice is K=10.

Three-Way Data Splits

If model selection and true error estimates are to be computed simultaneously, the data needs to be divided into three disjoint sets viz train set, validation set, and test set. The training set is a set of examples used for learning to fit the parameters of the classifier. For example, in the MLP case, training set may be used to find the optimal weights with the back-propagation rule. The validation set is a set of examples used to tune the parameters of a classifier. In the MLP case, the validation set may be used to find the optimal number of hidden units or determine a stopping point for the back propagation algorithm. The test set is a set of examples used only to assess the performance of a fully-trained classifier. In the MLP case, the test is used to estimate the error rate after choosing the final model such as MLP size and actual weights. After assessing the final model with the test set, the model is not further tuned.

CLASSIFICATION

The process of comparing an unknown object with stored patterns to recognize the unknown object is called classification. It is the process of applying a label or pattern class to an unknown instance. It is the study of how machines can observe the environment, learn to distinguish patterns of interest and make reasonable decisions about the categories of the patterns. One of the important component in pattern recognition is the ability of the system to learn from the data. Learning means the development of algorithms by acquiring knowledge from the given empirical data. Various learning approaches are: supervised learning, unsupervised learning, and reinforced learning. After feature selection, the next step is image classification which consists of two phases: Training Phase, Testing Phase. In training phase, a classifier first need to be trained or better say it should learn the complex relationship between the input image features using the training data. In testing phase, after the learning process is over the classifier is called a 'learnt system' and produces a classification model, therefore the classifier assigns level either as correct or incorrect. We divide the whole image database in to two parts consisting of one set of images for training phase and another set of images for testing phase. For classification purpose we use support vector machines based classifier with linear function as a kernel function.

Support Vector Machine (SVM) (Cai, Chen, & Zhang, 2007; Sezgin & Sankur, 2004) is a powerful classification algorithm and well suited the given task. It addresses the general problem of learning to discriminate between positive and negative members of a given class of n- dimensional vectors. The algorithm operates by mapping the given training set into a possible high dimensional vectors. The algorithm operates by mapping the given training set into a possibly high dimensional feature space and attempting to learn a separating hyper plane between the positive and the negative examples for possible maximization of the margin between them. The margin corresponds to the distance between the points residing on the two edges of the hyper plane.

Some Important Classifiers

Some important classifiers used in the design of the CAD tool are:

- SVM (Support Vector Machines)
- KNN(K-Nearest Neighbor)
- Bayesian Classifier
- Neural Network Classifier

SVM (Support Vector Machine): Supervised learning

Training Instances with Known Class Labels

Support vector machine (SVM) (Cai, Chen, & Zhang, 2007; Sezgin & Sankur, 2004) is a powerful classification algorithm and well suited the given task. It addresses the general problem of learning to discriminate between positive and negative members of a given class of n- dimensional vectors. The algorithm operates by mapping the given training set into a possible high dimensional vectors. The algorithm operates by mapping the given training set into a possibly high dimensional feature space and attempting to learn a separating hyper plane between the positive and the negative examples for possible maximization of the margin between them (Otsu, 1979). The margin corresponds to the distance between the points residing on the two edges of the hyper plane.

In Figure 11, γ (gamma) is margin, **w is** weight vector, i.e. normal vector of the separating hyperplane, l *is the* number of data points $\mathbf{x}_i$ and y_i is the label of data point $\mathbf{x}_i$. In SVM based classifier, the the margin γ is defined as:

$$\gamma_i = y_i(< w.x_i > +b).$$

The margin γ_i of an example $(\mathbf{x}_i, y_i)$ is given by: If $\gamma_i > 0$ then the example is well-classified. In above model, the margin γ is the minimum of the margin distribution with respect to a training set. For maximizing the margin, the distnace between hyperplanes H and H_1 for x a point on H_1 is defined as:

$$\frac{\left|\langle w \cdot x \rangle + b\right|}{\| w \|} = \frac{1}{\| w \|}$$

In order to maximize the margin, we need to minimize the weight ‖w‖, with the condition that there are no datapoints between H_1 and H_2 i.e.

$$y_i \left(< W.X_i > +b\right) \geq 1.$$

The weight vector w is obtained by update of w in the perceptron algorithm ($w_0 = 0$):

$$W_{k+1} \leftarrow W_k + \eta y_i x_i.$$

Hence, w is a linear combination of the data points x_i i.e. $W = \sum_{i=1}^{l} \alpha_i y_i x_i$. The separating hyperplane is given by <w.x>+b = 0 which is primal and the dual one by:

$$\sum_{i=1}^{l} \alpha_i y_i < x_i.x > +b = 0$$

Kernel Function for SVM

A kernel is a symmetric function *K: X×X R* so that for all x and x' in *X*:

$$K\left(x, x'\right) = < \Phi\left(x\right).\Phi\left(x'\right) >$$

Where Φ is a non-linear mapping from the input space *X* into the Hilbert space *F* provided with the inner product. The Kernel function implicitly defines the feature space *F* and the mapping Φ.

Examples of Kernel Functions Used in SVM classifier

• Polynomial Function

$$K_{poly}(x, x') = (\lambda < x, x' > +c)^d$$

Figure 11. SVM the maximal margin classifier

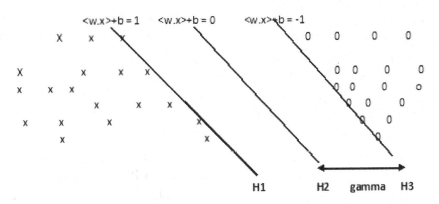

- Linear Kernel

$$K_{lin}(x, x') = <x, x'>$$

- Radial Basis Function (Feature space with infinite dimensions)

$$Krbf(x, x') = \exp(-\lambda \|x - x'\|^2 / \sigma^2)$$

- Sigmoid Kernel

$$K_{sig}(x, x') = \tanh(\lambda <x, x'> +c)$$

Classification Algorithms

- Statistical Techniques
- Non Statistical Techniques
- Hybrid Techniques

Statistical Classifiers

Statistical classifiers use statistical principles for deriving models from given training dataset using statistical learning techniques. These are of two types: Parametric classifier and Non parametric classifier.

Parametric Classifier

Parametric classifiers take a set of training data and construct a classification model. The parameters are estimated by assuming a probability distribution for each data set. Then statistical parameters such as mean and variance are found. These are of two types based on the techniques they use: Decision theoretic techniques and Probabilistic techniques

Decision Theoretic Methods

Decision theoretic methods are also referred to as discriminant function analysis. The basic idea used here is to classify the object by designing a decision boundary or discriminating functions to separate the feature vector clusters in the feature space. The decision function is designed so as to give different responses to different classes. Example includes LDA (linear discriminant analysis).

Linear Discriminant Analysis (LDA)

Fisher's LDA is a very old classification method. It assumes samples in each class follow a Gaussian distribution. The centre and covariance matrix are estimated for each class. It is assumed that the off-diagonal elements in the covariance are all zero which means different features are uncorrelated. A new sample is classified to the class with the highest probability. LDA assumes data distribution to be Gaussian.

Probabilistic Techniques

These methods use probabilistic techniques for classification. These are based on two probability concepts namely prior probability and conditional probability. Bayesian classifier is one of the most popular classifier in this category.

Bayesian Principle

The inverse probability P(A/B) can be found from P(B/A) and P(A) from Bayes theorem written as follows:

$$P(A / B) = \frac{P(B / A)P(A)}{P(B)}.$$

The Bayesian classifier requires three piece of information: P(A) which is prior probability of the class A; P(B/A) which is conditional probability that the class A has B. This can be calculated from the training data table; and P(B) which is sum of P(B/A) over the entire dataset.

Bayesian Classifier

The algorithm for finding the Bayesian classifier is described as follows:

- In first step, the Bayesian classifier is trained with the training image or labeled featured data
- In second step, the probability P(A) is computed using histogram-based estimation or using intuition based on experts opinion.
- In third step, P(A/B) is computed.
- At last step, the maximum of P(A/B) is found and the unknown instance to that class is assigned.

Advantages of using the Bayesian classifiers include: easy to use; require only one scan of the training set; are not affected much by missing values; and produce good results for datasets with simple relationships. The only disadvantage of the Bayesian classifiers is that it cannot be used for continuous data.

Naive Bayes Classifier

The Naıve Bayes (NB) is one of the oldest classifiers. It is based on the Bayes rule and assuming features (variables) are independent of each other given its class.

Types of Classifiers Based on Bayesian Principle

- Maximum Likelihood Classifier
- Minimum Distance Classifier
- Minimum Risk Classifier
- Bayesian Classifier for Multiple Features

Maximum Likelihood Classifier

According to Bayesian Maximum Likelihood classifier, the instance is assigned into a class A for which P(A/B) maximum. Suppose the attributes are many(m) independent variables, this is given as:

$$P(B \,/\, A) = \mathop{\pi}_{k=1}^{m} P(B_k \,/\, A)$$

In other words the instance having many attributes is assigned to class A and not to class C if:

P(A/B) = P (C/B)

This resultant algorithm is called Maximum Likelihood Classifier. If the attributes are assumed to be independent the same classifier is then classed Naïve Bayesian Classifier.

Minimum Distance Classifier

When the training set is of many images it is easier to approximate *P(B/A)* as a function with fewer parameters. This approximation of the input data is in the form of a Gaussian distribution and this kind of approximation is called parametric approximation. Therefore based on the distance used, there are variations in Bayesian distance classifier such as Mahalanobis distance, Euclidean distance, City block distance. Mahalanobis distance is the most reliable but computationally intensive as compared to the others.

Structural and Syntactic Classifiers

The structural methods exploit the relationships that exist among the basic elements of the objects, They use techniques such as graphs to encode the objects and the problem of recognition becomes a matching problem. The syntactic methods also known as grammar-based approach use strings or small sets of pattern primitives and grammatical rules for recognizing the object.

In syntactic classifiers, the idea is to decompose the object in terms of the basic primitives. The process of decomposing an object into a set of primitives is called Parsing. The basic primitives can then be reconstructed to the original object using formal languages to check whether the recognized pattern is obtained. The formal language theory plays an important role in syntactic classification. There are two phases involved in syntactic classifiers. In first phase, also known as training phase, the syntactic classifier is given the training dataset of valid strings of known objects. The patterns are decomposed into basic patterns and the grammar necessary for combining the primitives to reconstruct the original object is identified in the training phase. In second phase, also known as testing phase, the unknown patterns are given into the grammar of the syntactic classification system. Each unknown pattern is decomposed into the basic primitives and checked using a parser.

Rule Based Methods Based on Structural Concepts

In rule based classification methods, tree search is a popular approach that uses rules for classification. The simplest rules are IF(condition) and THEN(conclusion) . The IF part is called antecedent or precondition and the THEN part is called rule consequent. The decision rules are generated using a technique called covering algorithm where the best attribute is chosen to perform the classification based on the training data. The algorithm chooses the best attribute that minimizes the error and uses that attributes in generating a rule.

The rule based algorithm is described as follows:

- In a decision tree, every node can have only two children.
- The root is specially designated node and all the other intermediate nodes of the tree represent the rule conditions.
- The leaves of the tree are classes that are assigned to the instances.
- The unknown object or instance features are taken and their values are compared and validated with the conditions represented sequentially in the internal nodes of the tree.
- Tracing the path from the root to the assigned class gives conditions that led to the classification of that instance.
- For any tree classifier, the required feature is searched, the search is continued till the instance is assigned to a class.
- Some of the algorithms that are used include: top down search, DFS (depth first search), and BFS (Breadth First Search.)

Graph Based Methods

The graph-based approach is an extension of the tree-based approach wherein initially an object is modelled as a graph. The graph matching is then used to give the similarity measure of the objects. Two graphs can be similar even if they are structurally different. If there is a complete match, the match is declared isomorphic otherwise it's a dissimilar graph.

Performance Evaluation of Classifier Algorithms

In the case of mammographic image analysis, the results produced using a certain method can be presented in a few ways. The interpretation being mostly used is the confusion matrix (1) or just the number of True Positives (TPs) and False

Positives (FPs). The confusion matrix consists of True Negative (TN), False Positive (FP), False Negative (FN), and True Positive (TP).

$$C = \begin{bmatrix} TN & FP \\ FN & TP \end{bmatrix} \qquad (1)$$

There are some often mentioned terms such as accuracy (2), precision (3), sensitivity or True Positive Rate (TPR) (4) and False Positive Rate (FPR) (5).

$$accuracy = \frac{TP + TN}{TN + FP + FN + TP} \qquad (2)$$

$$precision = \frac{TP}{FP + TP} \qquad (3)$$

$$TPR = \frac{TP}{FN + TP} \qquad (4)$$

$$FPR = \frac{FP}{TN + FP} \qquad (5)$$

ROC (Receiver Operating Characteristic)

Area *A* under the ROC (Receiver Operating Characteristic) curve gives the information of how successful the classification is. ROC curve is determined by True Positive (TP) and False Negative (FN) results of an experiment. The larger the area (total area is 1.00) the better the classification is. In the case of *A*=1.00, the detection performance is 100% with zero false positive detected objects at the same time. ROC curves are often used for classification tasks because they can give a good description of the overall system performance. It is worth mentioning that the area under ROC curve can be maximized without really improving the

classification success. Random guessing will result in area *A*=0.5 which can be artificially boosted to some higher values close to 1.0. This will give false results and therefore results presented using only ROC curves should be taken with caution.

A CASE STUDY: DESIGN AND IMPLEMENTATION OF A CAD TOOL FOR CANCER DETECTION FROM MAMMOGRAMS

In this section, the design of a Computer Aided Diagnostic (CAD) tool for early breast cancer detection from mammograms has been proposed using Genetic Algorithm (GA) based feature selection method based on mutual information and Support Vector Machine (SVM) based classification techniques. The various steps involved in the design of a CAD tool include pre-processing, image segmentation, feature extraction, feature selection, and classification. During the pre-processing stage, the image enhancement is performed using histogram equalization based technique; image segmentation is performed using global thresholding method; histogram, geometric and texture features of input images have been extracted; for final feature selection a genetic algorithm based method based on mutual information have been used; and finally to classify the input images in to two groups viz. benign and malignant a Support Vector Machine (SVM) based classifier has been used. The performances of the CAD tool have been evaluated quantitatively as well as qualitatively.

For testing purposes, we used 322 mammogram images, grouped in two classes viz. benign and malignant, obtained from MIAS database. Total of 88 features were initially extracted resulting in to an initial feature matrix of size 322x88 and a group vector of size 322x1. In this work, we have used a genetic algorithm (GA) based feature selection technique where mutual information measure is used as a fitness function. The starting population of genes in GA is determined by:

Population=round((L-1)*rand(NumbFeat,indiv))+1;

Where L is the total number of initial features; NumbFeat is the number of features to be selected; indiv is defined as indiv=200* NumbFeat. The maximum number of generations used was 100. The fitness function is defined as the mutual information of the feature matrix data. We choose a feature in each iteration which is associated with minimum mutual information i.e. highly un-correlated feature. Finally, 50 features were selected which are as follows:

Feature_No_Selected =
[61 67 43 39 48 38 60 69 42 2
33 59 3 52 29 64 41 40 55 30 58 73
79 86 49 54 21 7 1 65 68 4 70 88
28 66 5 6 13 11 12 19 10 57 8 9
62 23 14 25]

For partitioning the data set in to train and test sets, 10-fold cross validation method have been used. Performances of the CAD tool are reported in Tables 3 and 4, Figures 12, 13, and 14.

CONCLUSION

In this chapter, an overview of recent developments in image analysis and understanding techniques for automated detection of breast cancer from digital mammograms discussed. The various steps in the design of an automated system i.e. Computer Aided Detection (CADe) and Computer Aided Diagnostics (CADx) included preparation of image database for classification, image pre-processing, mammogram image enhancement and restoration, segmentation of Region Of Interest (ROI) for cancer detection, feature extraction of selected ROIs, feature evaluation and selection, and classification of selected mammogram images in to benign, malignant, and normal. In this chapter, a detailed overview of the various methods developed in recent years for each stages required in the design of an automated system for breast cancer detection is discussed. Further, the design, implementation and performance analysis of a CAD tool presented. The various types of features extracted for classification purpose in the proposed tool included histogram features, texture features, geometric features, wavelet features, and Gabor features. The proposed CAD tool used fuzzy c-means segmentation algorithm; the feature selection algorithm based on the concepts of genetic algorithm which used mutual information as a fitness function; and linear support vector machine as a classifier.

FUTURE DIRECTIONS FOR RESEARCH

Early detection of breast cancer can increase the survival rate and increases the treatment options. Radiologists can visually search mammograms for specific abnormalities. Some of the important signs of breast cancer that radiologists can look for are clusters of micro calcifications, masses, and architectural distortions. Screening mammography, radiographic imaging of the breast can be

Table 3. Performance measures of the CAD tool using genetic algorithm based feature selection based on mutual information and SVM classifier

Classifier/ Kernel type	Precision	Recall	Sensitivity	Specificity	BCR	Accuracy (%)
SVM Linear	0.8400	0.9130	0.9130	0.5556	0.7343	81.2500

Table 4. Confusion matrix of SVM classifier for different feature sets

Classifier/ Kernel type	FP	TP	TN	FN
SVM Linear	8	42	10	4

Figure 12. Fitness function for GA_MI method

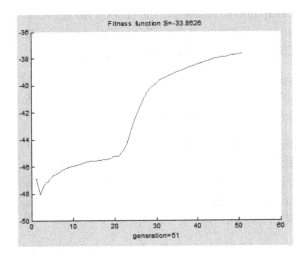

Figure 13. ROC Curve for SVM-linear classifier

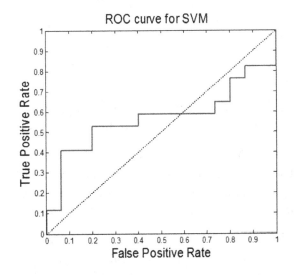

Figure 14. Confusion matrix for SVM-linear classifier using combined features

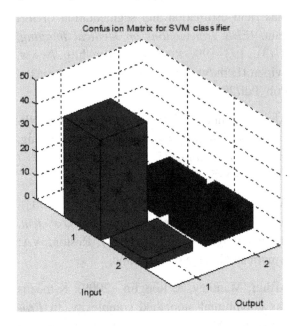

the most effective tool for early detection of breast cancer. Screening mammographic examinations with a maximum accuracy can be performed on women to detect early, clinically unsuspected breast cancer.

REFERENCES

A. C. (Ed.). (2005). *Handbook of image and video processing*. Amsterdam: Elsevier Academic Press.

Acha, B., Rangayyan, R. M., & Desautels, J. E. L. (2006). Detection of microcalcifications in mammograms. In Suri & Rangayyan (eds.), Recent Advances in Breast Imaging, Mammography, and Computer-Aided Diagnosis of Breast Cancer. Bellingham, WA: SPIE Press.

Ahmed, Yamany, Mohamed, Farag, & Moriarty. (2002). A modified fuzzy c-means algorithm for bias field estimation and segmentation of mri data. *IEEE Transactions on Medical Imaging, 21*(3), 193–199. Retrieved from http://www.cvip.uofl.edu/wwwcvip/research/publications/Pub_Pdf/2002/3.pdf.

Aloise, Deshpande, Hansen, & Popat. (2009). NP-hardness of euclidean sum-of-squares clustering. *Machine Learning, 75*, 245–249. doi:10.1007/s10994-009-5103-0.

American College of Radiology (ACR). (2003). *ACR breast imaging reporting and data system. Breast Imaging Atlas* (4th ed.). Reston, VA: American College of Radiation.

Arthur, Manthey, & Roeglin. (2009). K-means has polynomial smoothed complexity. In *Proceedings of the 50th Symposium on Foundations of Computer Science (FOCS), 2009.* Washington, DC: IEEE Press.

Baeg, S., & Kehtarnavaz, N. (2002). Classification of breast mass abnormalities using denseness and architectural distortion. *Electronic Letters on Computer Vision and Image Analysis, 1*(1), 1–20.

Bandyopadhyay. (2010). Formation of homogeneous blocks for segmentation of mammograms. *International Journal of Engineering Science and Technology, 2*(12), 7444-7448.

Bellotti. (2006). A completely automated CAD system for mass detection in a large mammographic database. *Medical Physics, 33.*

Bezdek, J. C. (1981). *Pattern recognition with fuzzy objective function algorithms.* Berlin: Springer. doi:10.1007/978-1-4757-0450-1.

Bozek, M. Delac, & Grgic. (2009). A survey of image processing algorithms in digital mammography. Zagreb, Croatia: Zagreb University.

Cai, Chen, & Zhang. (2007). Fast and robust fuzzy c-means clustering algorithm incorporating local information for image segmentation. *Pattern Recognition, 40*(3), 825–838. doi:10.1016/j.patcog.2006.07.011.

Cheng, Shi, & Min, Hu, Cai, & Du. (2006). Approaches for automated detection and classification of masses in mammograms. *Pattern Recognition, 39*(4), 646–668. doi:10.1016/j.patcog.2005.07.006.

Cristianini & Shawe-Taylor. (2000). *An introduction to support vector machines.* Cambridge, UK: Cambridge University Press.

Dash & Liu. (1997). Feature selection for classification. *Intelligent Data Analysis, 1*, 131–156. doi:10.1016/S1088-467X(97)00008-5.

De Oliveira Martins, Junior, & Silva. (2009). Detection of masses in digital mammograms using k-means and support vector machine. *Electronic Letters on Computer Vision and Image Analysis, 8*(2), 39–50.

Gunturu & Sharma. (2010). Contrast enhancement of mammographic images using wavelet transform. In *Proceedings of 3rd IEEE International Conference on Computer Science and Information Technology.* Washington, DC: IEEE Press.

Gupta, Kumar, & Sharma. (2011). Data mining classification techniques applied for breast cancer diagnosis and prognosis. *Indian Journal of Computer Science and Engineering, 2*(2).

Jain. (2006). Fundamentals of digital image processing. In *Proceedings of PHI.* India: PHI Press.

Kiyan & Yildirim. (2004). Breast cancer diagnosis using statistical neural networks. In *Proceedings of Turkish Symposium on Artificial Intelligence and Neural Networks.* Istanbul: TAINN Press.

Liao, Chen, & Chung. (2001). A fast algorithm for multilevel thresholding. *Journal of Information Science and Engineering, 17*(5), 713–727.

Maitra, Nag, & Bandyopadhyay. (2011). *Automated digital mammogram segmentation for detection of abnormal masses using binary homogeneity enhancement algorithm.* Retrieved from http://core.kmi.open.ac.uk/display/973406.

Mammographic Image Analysis Society (MIAS). (2011). *MIAS database.* Retrieved from http://www.mammoimage.org/databases/.

Mohideen, P. Krishnan, & Sathik. (2011). Image denoising and enhancement using multiwavelet with hard threshold. In Digital Mammography. Berlin: Springer.

Nock & Nielsen. (2006). On weighting clustering. *IEEE Transactions on Pattern Analysis and Machine Intelligence, 28*(8), 1–13. doi:10.1109/TPAMI.2006.157.

Otsu. (1979). A threshold selection method from gray-level histogram. *IEEE Transactions on Systems, Man, and Cybernetics, 9*(1), 62-66.

Qi, S. Head, & Elliott. (2002). detecting breast cancer from infrared images by asymmetry analysis. In *Proceedings of Second Joint Conference of the Biomedical Engineering Society.* Washington, DC: IEEE Press.

Rangayyan, R. M., Ayres, F. J., & Desautels, J. E. L. (2007). A review of computer-aided diagnosis of breast cancer: toward the detection of subtle signs. *Journal of the Franklin Institute,* 312–348. doi:10.1016/j.jfranklin.2006.09.003.

Sampat, M. P., Markey, M. K., & Bovik, A. C. (2005). Computer-aided detection and diagnosis in mammography. In Bovik, Sepehr, Jamarani, Moradi, Behnam, and Rezai Rad (Eds.), Intelligent System for Breast Cancer Prognosis Using Multiwavelet Packets and Neural Network. Washington, DC: IEEE Press.

Sezgin & Sankur. (2004). Survey over image thresholding techniques and quantitative performance evaluation. *Journal of Electronic Imaging, 13*(1), 146–165. doi:10.1117/1.1631315.

Sheshadri & Kandaswamy. (2006). *Breast tissue classification using statistical feature extraction of mammograms.* Coimbatore, India: PSG College of Technology.

Song, V., & Conant, C. Arger, & Sehgal. (2005). Artificial neural network to aid differentiation of malignant and benign breast masses by ultrasound imaging. Philadelphia: University of Pennsylvania.

Tang, Rangayyan, Xu, El Naqa, & Yang. (2009). Computer-aided detection and diagnosis of breast cancer with mammography. *IEEE Transactions on Recent Advances in Information Technology and Biomedicine, 13*(2), 236–251.

Vapnik. *Statistical Learning Theory.* Hoboken, NJ: Wiley.

Xiao & Ohya. (2008). Contrast enhancement of color images based on wavelet transform and human visual system. In *Proceedings of IASTED Conference on Graphics and Visual Engineering.* Ohkuboyama, Japan: Waseda University.

Zuiderveld. (1994). Contrast limited adaptive histogram equalization. *Graphics Gems IV.* London: Academic Press Professional, Inc.

KEY TERMS AND DEFINITIONS

Architectural Distortion: Architectural distortion is defined as distortion of normal architecture with no definite mass visible, including speculation radiating from a point and focal retraction or distortion at the edge of the parenchyma.

Breast Tumors: Breast tumors and masses usually appear in the form of dense regions in mammograms.

Cancer: Cancer is the general name for a group of more than 100 diseases in which cells in a part of the body begin to grow out of control. Although there are many kinds of cancer, they all start because abnormal cells grow out of control. Untreated cancers can cause serious illness and even death.

Classification: Calcifications are deposit of calcium in breast tissue.Calcifications detected on a mammogram are an important indicator for malignant breast disease but also in many benign changes.

Computer Aided Diagnostics Tool: A computer-aided detection (CADe) and computer-aided diagnosis (CADx).

Feature Extraction: The feature extraction is used to measure the properties from the segmented image are Area, Centriod, Major axis length, Minor axis length, Eccentricity, Orientation, Filled area, Extrema, Solidity, Equivdiameter.

Image Segmentation: The thresholding is an important step improve the detection of breast cancer segmentation subdivides an Image into its constituent regions.

Mammography: It is a low-dose x-ray procedure that allows visualization of the internal structure of the breast.

Mass: A mass is defined as a space occupying lesion.

Region of Interest (ROI): An ROI represents an area or region in a 2-D image for a particular interest.

ROC: Receiver Operating Characteristic.

Chapter 9
De-Noising, Clustering, Classification, and Representation of Microarray Data for Disease Diagnostics

Nitin Baharadwaj
Netaji Subhas Institute of Technology, India

Chanpreet Singh Arora
Netaji Subhas Institute of Technology, India

Sheena Wadhwa
Netaji Subhas Institute of Technology, India

Aviral Goel
Netaji Subhas Institute of Technology, India

Pragya Goel
Netaji Subhas Institute of Technology, India

Sonika Bhatnagar
Netaji Subhas Institute of Technology, India

Isha Sethi
Netaji Subhas Institute of Technology, India

Harish Parthasarathy
Netaji Subhas Institute of Technology, India

ABSTRACT

A microarray works by exploiting the ability of a given mRNA molecule to bind specifically to the DNA template from which it originated under specific high stringency conditions. After this, the amount of mRNA bound to each DNA site on the array is determined, which represents the expression level of each gene. Qualification of the mRNA (probe) bound to each DNA spot (target) can help us to determine which genes are active or responsible for the current state of the cell. The probe target hybridization is usually detected and quantified using dyes/flurophore/chemiluminescence labels. The microarray data gives a single snapshot of the gene activity profile of a cell at any given time. Microarray data helps to elucidate the various genes involved in the disease and may also be used for diagnosis /prognosis. In spite of its huge potential, microarray data interpretation and use is limited by its error prone nature, the sheer size of the data and the subjectivity of the analysis. Initially, we describe the use of several

DOI: 10.4018/978-1-4666-4558-5.ch009

techniques to develop a pre-processing methodology for denoising microarray data using signal process techniques. The noise free data thus obtained is more suitable for classification of the data as well as for mining useful information from the data. Discrete Fourier Transform (DFT) and Autocorrelation were explored for denoising the data. We also used microarray data to develop the use of microarray data as diagnostic tool in cancer using One Dimensional Fourier Transform followed by simple Euclidean Distance Calculations and Two Dimensional MUltiple SIgnal Classification (MUSIC). To improve the accuracy of the diagnostic tool, Volterra series were used to model the nonlinear behavior of the data. Thus, our efforts at denoising, representation, and classification of microarray data with signal processing techniques show that appreciable results could be attained even with the most basic techniques. To develop a method to search for a gene signature, we used a combination of PCA and density based clustering for inferring the gene signature of Parkinson's disease. Using this technique in conjunction with gene ontology data, it was possible to obtain a signature comprising of 21 genes, which were then validated by their involvement in known Parkinson's disease pathways. The methodology described can be further developed to yield future biomarkers for early Parkinson's disease diagnosis, as well as for drug development.

INTRODUCTION

DNA Microarrays

As a result of the rise in the number of completed genome sequencing projects, the DNA sequence present in a large number of genomes has become available. The central dogma of modern biology takes into account that the information present in the DNA is read to manufacture mRNA or messenger RNA. This, in turn, is read by the cellular machinery to manufacture proteins. The first step of this process is known as transcription (i.e., decoding of the DNA to synthesize mRNA while the second is translation or decoding of mRNA to produce functional proteins). Such a DNA fragment whose information is converted into a mRNA or a protein molecule is termed as a gene. Experimental and computational tools have helped us elucidate the presence of protein coding genes and thus map the vast, unexplored length of DNA. While all cells of the body contain the full set of DNA material (and genes), it is the subset that is transcribed or expressed that confers on the cell its unique properties. These genes are responsible for the response of the cell to its environment in both health and disease. Thus, the gene transcription profile of a cell gives an important insight into the type of genes that are transcribed under any physiological and pathological condition. The gene transcription profile reflects the response of the cell to its environment, a highly and tightly regulated process. Such a gene transcription profile can be recorded using a microarray.

The microarray capitalizes on the ability of a given mRNA molecule to bind specifically or hybridize to the DNA template from which it originated. Thus, in a microarray experiment, probes consisting of DNA are attached to a solid surface by covalent bonding to a chemical matrix like epoxy-silane, lysine, polyacrylamide, and so forth. The solid surface can be a glass or a silicon chip, commonly known as a gene chip. A gene chip consists of thousands of microscopic spots, containing a small but specific DNA sequence. In order to measure gene expression data, short section of genes are anchored to the solid surface and used as probes to detect the presence of their templates (targets) in a biological sample of interest. The target has the ability to hybridize specifically with its complementary probe mRNA under high stringency experimental conditions. Hybridization can be detected and quantified by labeling the targets with fluorophore or chemiluminescent dye materials.

The state of a disease affects the cell and changes the number/type of genes activated/ expression. This is termed as differential expression. To study the differential expression pattern of genes, mRNA is isolated from both diseased and normal samples. The mRNA is used as template to generate cDNA with a fluorescent tag attached. Use of tags of distinct colors facilitates the identification of diseased and normal samples in later stages. The two types of samples are mixed and incubated with a microarray having immobilized genes of interest. The labeled complements of these immobilized genes hybridize with them. Next, the microarray chip is placed in a reader. The samples are scanned with lasers in order to excite the fluorescent labeled tags. Upon hybridization of the probe with the target, the dye is excited with the help of laser of specific wavelength and emits a signal that can be recorded. The intensity of the signal varies proportionally with the relative abundance of the nucleic acid sequences in the target. Thus, an array containing many DNA probes can be used to determine the expression level of thousands of genes within a cell by measuring the mRNA bound to each site on the array as shown in Figure 1. The mRNA is precisely quantitated and reflects the level of activity of a gene under the conditions studied. The resulting digital image is recorded and stored in a computer for record and analysis. Since each spot in the array is associated with a specific gene, color development at each location gives information about whether the gene is present in the control or sample DNA. The intensity of the color provides an estimate of the level of expression of the gene (Deonier et al., 2005).

BACKGROUND

Applications of Microarray Data

Using microarray data, it can be shown that the type of mRNA populations produced differ both qualitatively and quantitatively in different type of tissues. The applications of microarray data are many and varied. Some of the prominent ones are:

1. To understand the role of genes involved in growth and development (Pritchard & Nelson, 2008; Diaz, 2009).
2. To explore the underlying causes of human diseases (Kim, 2010; Shih et al., 2012).

Figure 1. Schematic flowchart showing the organization of a microarray experiment

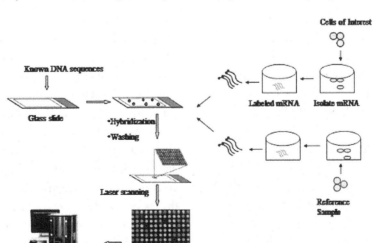

3. To characterize different types of cells in health and disease. As an example, the differential gene expression is characteristic of the distinct types of breast cancer (Perou et al., 2000; Severe et al., 2010).

4. To infer probable functions of new genes based on their expression profiles (Benoit et al., 2010; Bramswig & Kaestner, 2012).

5. To reveal how the expression of different genes is regulated (Bramswig & Kaestner, 2012).

6. To study the mechanisms involved in transformation of a normal to a cancerous cell (Severe et al., 2010).

7. To identify new drug targets by studying how the expression of different genes is affected under different conditions (Severe et al., 2010).

8. To help in disease diagnosis and prognosis (Ojha & Kostrzynska, 2008; Perry et al., 2012).

9. To study the gain and losses in the genomic expression profiles to order to identify the genes involved in tumor initiation and progression (Severi et al., 2010).

10. To study small but critical changes in the DNA sequence leading to the development of disease (Schaaf et al., 2011).

11. To study the patient response to therapy in cancer. It was shown that differential gene expression also correlates with the treatment outcome of the patient (Perou et al., 2000; Akiyoshi et al., 2012).

12. For detection and identification of micro organisms in food, feed, cell culture and patient samples (Olano & Walker, 2011).

Data Repositories

The data generated from microarray (or other) experiments that record gene expression are stored in public databases in order to support its public use and dissemination. The database of the National Centre for Biotechnology Information is known as the Gene Expression Omnibus (GEO) (http://www.ncbi.nlm.nih.gov/geo/). Other microarray databases include ArrayExpress (http://www.ebi.ac.uk/arrayexpress/) from The European Bioinformatics Institute and the UNC Microarray Database (https://genome.unc.edu/).

Limitations of Microarray Data

mRNA based microarray experiments have several limitations (Simon *et al.*, 2002). These include the small amount of mRNA in the cell, the fragility of the mRNA molecule due to degrading enzymes present, and dependence of the expression pattern on tissue handling and method of extraction of the data(Tu et al., 2004; Russo et al., 2003; Perez et al., 2004). Additionally, the expression may vary with different populations' cells in the sample as well as with distinct individuals. The experiment thus needs to be designed with great care about the technique, timing and sampling of the tissue. The mRNA needs to be precisely quantitated and duplication of experiments helps to reduce the error (Forster et al., 2003; Simon et al., 2002). Even after these issues have been dealt with satisfactorily, microarray experiment still results in the high throughput production of large amount of data. Processing, storage and analysis of this data presents a unique challenge. In the initial steps after data collection, the probe hybridization data that is stored in the form of an image needs to be quantified, processed, filtered and normalized before data interpretation can be undertaken. Several computational methods have been developed to recognize the experimental errors and to repair the erroneous data values so as to improve the significance of the study.

Even after these steps have been carried out and confirmed, the probability of their clinical correlation remains variable. A possible cause of this is proposed to be overfitting of data during supervised clustering. A solution for this problem is to leave one or more samples out during training and use it for validation of the data. In this way, it can be tested whether the pattern correctly predicts the clinical outcome. Another possible solution is to increase the sample size in order to better reflect the genetic variability (For a review, see Abdullah-Syani et al., 2006).

MAIN FOCUS OF THE CHAPTER

Issues in the Analysis of Microarray Data

In spite of the enormous promise and potential of DNA microarrays, two types of problems complicate its analysis:

1. **The inherent experimental errors associated with the system:** Both extrinsic and intrinsic. Extrinsic or experimental errors in microarray data include artifacts and contamination of the DNA samples. They interfere with the automation of the data collection process (Deonier et al., 2005). Image analysis software is first required to calculate and store the intensity of each spot. The surface of the chip is then inspected to resolve hybridization bias and to remove poorly hybridized spots from further analyses. Gene expression changes can be sensitively and reliably detected for a intermediate and higher level expression of genes, but remains problematic for genes in low abundance. The detection limit also varies with the platform and experimental material (Draghici et al., 2006; Kane et al., 2000; Dai et al., 2005). Thus, the collected data is subject to non-biological variability. Apart from this, there is divergence between various microarray platforms from different commercial sources. Therefore, it is not always straightforward to combine data from different platforms (Jarvinen et al., 2004). To be even moderately correlated across various platforms, the data needs to be denoised and

filtered (Draghici et al., 2006). Therefore, the downstream data processing and analysis are dependent on the type of platform selected. Therefore, the raw data is subjected to preprocessing involving signal adjustment, bias correction, image analysis. In different experiments, there is variation (in dye effects, sample or scanner etc). Integration of data from different experiments and platforms thus requires removal of these differences, a process known as data normalization.

In addition to the non-biological sources of error as discussed above, there is inherent variability in the biological sample. Therefore, genes that are believed to be constantly expressed across a wide variety of biological conditions are used as for normalization. Samples and observations are replicated to enhance the confidence in the data collected. Overall, the normalization procedures used vary widely with the platform and type of experiment. Further, they may not always lead to denoising and therefore yield different results during data analysis (Kokko, 2006). In conclusion, every step involved in a transcriptional profiling experiment has the capability to contribute to the 'noise' inherent in microarray data. The main factor contributing to noise is the variations in biological samples, which varies not only from one individual to another but also with respect to time/ conditions in the same individual. Other contributing factors include differences in RNA quality and target labeling. These can be minimized but not entirely removed by careful experimental design and initial calibration experiments.

1. **The handling and processing of huge amount of data to produce biologically relevant results:** The advantage of performing a microarray experiment is that the study of gene expression can be carried out at a massively parallel scale. However, this also gives rise to an enormous amount of data that requires analysis techniques combining

the image processing, principles of signal processing, statistics, computation and artificial intelligence. The result obtained after removing artifacts and inherent bias of the system is a gene expression matrix with n × m columns. Each row in n corresponds to a gene or a feature on a microarray while each column in m corresponds to a certain condition or time point at which the expression of the gene has been recorded.

Microarray data can be used to query a wide range of biological situations of interest. At one end of complexity, it can be used to query the expression pattern (and thus the function) of a single gene while at the other end, it can be used to mine regulatory and signaling networks in order to extract significant patterns. The nature and complexity of the problem determines the approach taken. Many commercial and non-commercial software tools are available for visualization, filtering, analysis, etc. of gene expression data. Some of the current software tools include Statistical Analysis of Microarrays (SAM) (Zhang et al., 2007), R and Bioconductor (Gentleman et al., 2004). Methods used in the data analysis of microarrays vary considerably. A generalized schema of the various steps involved in the analysis is shown in Figure 2. In view of the variability in experimental design and analysis, data validation is required either internally by re-sampling and recalculation of probabilities followed by comparison with original data. Experimental validation may also be done by quantitative RT-PCR.

Issues in Using Microarray Data for Molecular Classification

An important application of microarray data is for molecular classification. This allows the molecular profiles to be grouped into specified types e.g. cancerous, precancerous, drug resistant etc. A tool that can accurately classify microarray samples has immense relevance for clinical prediction and

Figure 2. Steps involved in data analysis and mining of biologically relevant information from a microarray experiment

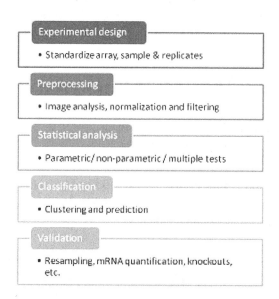

treatment. The same has been implemented previously in some methods including statistical and machine learning based feature selection methods like Linear Discriminate Analysis, Nearest Centroid Classifier, K-nearest neighbour, Probabilistic Neural Networks, Support Vector Machines, and so forth. (Ressom et al.,2008). One limitation of these methods is that feature selection has to be carried out prior to classification. Apart from being subjective and variable, this step is also a bottleneck as it is computationally intensive. Another drawback is the need for background noise removal to achieve accurate results of classification. Numerous attempts at pre-processing have been made previously to improve the quality of microarray data (Gopalappa et al., 2009; Marshall, 2004; Nadon & Shoemaker, 2002; Tu et al., 1999; Owzar et al., 2008). However, these techniques are subject to certain limitations (Gopalappa et al., 2009). Therefore, we attempted to develop a fast and efficient method for data denoising and classification that does not involve feature selection and is free from manual intervention of the investigator. Our approach is to convert the entire dataset into a signal and use it for comparison. Towards this, we describe the implementation of various signal processing techniques in this chapter.

Issues in Identifying Gene Signature from Microarray Data

Over the years, microarray data analysis has increasingly been used as a platform for finding the unique pattern of gene expression associated with a diseased condition or gene signatures. Identifying the gene signature has been carried out extensively in different types of cancer. It has previously been used to characterize tumor subtypes and to predict patient survival outcomes in B-cell lymphoma (Alizadeh et al., 2000; Mori et al., 2008), characterizing small round blue cell tumors into specific diagnostic subtypes (Khan et al., 2001; Chang et al., 2005). Multiple gene signature studies have been identified for cancers affecting different tissues e.g. lung (Boutros et al., 200; Zhu et al., 2010; Ying-Wooi et al., 2010), brain (de Tayrac et al., 2011), etc. Two predictive signatures have already been developed into clinical multi-gene panel tests (Hinestrosa et al., 2007). The study of gene signatures has also been useful for characterization of neurodegenerative diseases like Alzheimer's (Porcellini et al., 2010).

The first step of the common methodology followed for finding gene signatures is data preprocessing. This may be carried out in either of the 2 ways, namely- a) feature selection (i.e. selecting the informative genes) or b) dimensionality reduction. PCA, Principal Manifolds, Advanced algorithms like LLE (Rowels & Saul, 2000) or ISOMAP (Tenenbaum, 2000) can be used for reducing the high dimensional data. The preprocessed data is then mined for biologically pertinent information by clustering the dataset. Clustering algorithms can be broadly divided into two main types, namely Partitioning algorithms and Hierarchical algorithms (Kaufman & Rousseeuw 1990). In the partitioning algorithm, the objects of the database are partitioned into k clusters where k has to be defined during input. K-means clustering is the most often used method of this group. The drawback is that for the optimum use of these algorithms we require some prior knowledge about the database. Hierarchical algorithms, on the other hand, split the database on the lines of a tree such that each leaf of the tree contains one object and each node represents a cluster. This tree can be traversed in two ways: leaf to root, called agglomerative approach and root to leaves called divisive approach (Matej, 2005). The main disadvantage of this technique is that it is difficult to determine when to stop dividing or merging clusters. The third approach is the hybrid approach. It involves implementing multiple clustering algorithms (Chipman et al., 2005; Pirim et al., 2011) but does not always lead to an increase in efficiency. A fourth method then, is the density based approach, first explored by Jain (1988). OPTICS (Ankerst, 1999), DENCLUE (Hinneburg, 1998), CLIQUE (Agrawal, 1998) and DBSCAN (Ester, 1996) are some examples of implementations of density based clustering. This set of methods is uniquely suited for finding clusters of unknown shape and different density in a dataset full of outliers and noise (Adriano, 2005). Therefore it is of specific importance when applied to microarray data. The gene set obtained hence, by clustering, still needs to be further subjected to statistical methods like t-test (Dudoit, 2000), Significance Analysis of Microarrays (SAM) (Tusher, 2001) or combination of different variance t-tests and SAM as carried out by Wan (2010) to give the signature gene set.

SOLUTIONS AND RECOMMENDATIONS

Implementation of FFT and Autocorrelation for Denoising the Data

In view of the large amount of noise present in the microarray data, we attempted to use various signal processing techniques to represent and denoise the data. Plotting of the data allowed us to detect the presence of noise in the sample. FFT and autocorrelation were implemented using C# and database in order to handle the following datasets:

1. GDS 3217.5 taken from the Gene Expression Omnibus Database of NCBI (Ref). time variant of the relative expression of genes in 6 treated and 6 untreated cell lines expressing estrogen receptor with repetition (3 times) data of ~55000 genes. Thus the data is a matrix of 6 X 2 X 3 X 55000 points.
2. Data of gastric cancer taken from the Stanford Microarray Database (genomewww5.stanford.edu).

The results were plotted in MATLAB in order to visualize the patterns and the type of noise present in the data.

FFT

As described in the description of the first data set, the input values of the data have discrete non-zero values with finite deviation. Therefore, a FFT was employed to obtain the frequency domain DFT representation of the original time domain function. Thus, the DFT is a transform for Fourier analysis of finite-domain discrete-time functions. The sinusoidal basis functions of the decomposition have the identical properties. The DFT is widely employed in signal processing to analyze the frequencies contained in the signal.

The DFT is computed efficiently in practice using a Fast Fourier Transform (FFT) as follows:

The sequence of N complex numbers corresponding to the amplitude of the signal intensities recorded i.e. $x_0 \ldots x_{N-1}$ is transformed into the sequence of N complex numbers $X_0 \ldots X_{N-1}$ by the DFT as follows:

$$X_k = \sum_{n=0}^{N-1} x_n e^{(-2\pi ikn/N)}$$

where k=0,....,N-1.

The DFT of each column of the data is obtained as described above. This makes the data suitable for spectral analysis. It also introduces smoothening and standardization of the data. It was evident from the 3D Mesh plot of the data after FFT (Figure 3) that white noise was still present in the data. Therefore, noise removal was still incomplete. However, DFT served to smoothen the data, so that two datasets could be compared more easily.

Correlation and Auto-Correlation

Correlation is typically calculated as an indicator of the strength and direction of a linear relationship between two random variables. Thus, it reflects their departure from independence. Several types of coefficients suitable for measuring the degree of correlation may be employed, depending on the nature of the data, such as Pearson's product-moment coefficient $\rho_{X,Y}$ between two random variables X and Y with mean μ_X and μ_Y and standard deviations σ_X and σ_Y is defined as:

$$\rho_{X,Y} = \frac{Cov(X,Y)}{\sigma_X \sigma_Y} = \frac{\sum((X - \mu_X)(Y - \mu_Y))}{\sigma_X \sigma_Y} \tag{1.1}$$

The correlation matrix of n random variables $X_1, \ldots X_n$ is the n x n matrix whose i, j entry is Corr(Xi, Xj). Therefore, it is necessarily a positive semi-definite matrix. The matrix is symmetric as the correlation between Xi and Xj is the same

Figure 3. 3D mesh plot of the microarray data after FFT shows presence of white noise

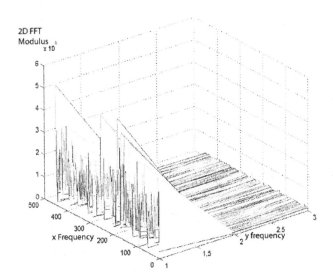

as that between Xj and Xi. The interpretation of a correlation coefficient depends on the type of data and purpose of computation (Cohen, 1988). Though it indicates the strength of a linear relationship between two variables, its value alone may not always be sufficient to evaluate this linearity, meaning there may be additional non-linear dependencies between the variables. Therefore, individual examination of the data is necessary. The assumption implicit in the calculation of a correlation coefficient is that the variables follow a normal distribution. Only then does it correctly summarize the strength of interaction.

Autocorrelation reflects the cross- correlation of a signal with itself. It is a mathematical tool for finding repeated patterns, particularly the presence of a periodic signal that has been buried under noise. It is used frequently in signal processing for analyzing functions (e.g. time domain signals). It can be understood as the similarity between observations as a function of the time separation between them. The autocorrelation function when normalized with respect to mean and variance is referred to as the autocorrelation coefficient. It can give information about periodically occurring patterns buried within the signal. Thus, the $R_{ff}(\tau)$ autocorrelation was calculated for a signal f(t) as

the continuous cross-correlation of f(t) with itself when the lag is τ.

$$R_{ff}(\tau) = \bar{f}(-\tau) * f(\tau) = \int_{-\infty}^{\infty} f(t+\tau)\bar{f}(t)dt = \int_{-\infty}^{\infty} f(t)\bar{f}(t-\tau)dt$$

(1.2)

Autocorrelation was implemented in order to find the repeating patterns in the data. The graph obtained after autocorrelation reflects the dependence of each gene over the other in the sample. However, implementation of the continuous autocorrelation causes increase in data by up to 16 times, giving a square matrix of 55000. The variation of lag values over a range of values from 100-1000 were combined with simultaneous analysis of the results was done to choose the best lag time.

However, the main problem confounding our approach were:

1.   Large data size requiring enormous computational power.
2.   Need for manual intervention in determining the best lag values.
3.   Presence of white noise in the data.

It was concluded from the denoising procedures described above that white noise is present in the data. As such noise is independently and identically distributed in the sample, it was hypothesized that it may get cancelled out during comparison of two datasets. This approach would also aid in development of a prognosis tool based on comparison of diseased and normal datasets.

Development of a Tool for Denoising and Classification

Prognosis Tool Based on Euclidean Distance Based Between the 1D-FT of the Dataset

The 1D FT of each diseased or normal dataset was computed. Euclidean Distances (ED) are calculated between all the datasets. The ratio of ED of each dataset to a predetermined reference ED was calculated. These ratios are then represented as a scatter plot. The procedure as outlined was first followed in training mode (i.e. with normal dataset). The diseased set was then used to calculate and make a combined scatterplot. The deviant position of the diseased dataset from that of the parent sample shows that this simple tool can be used to predict the occurrence of gastric cancer using the microarray gene expression dataset. The efficiency of this tool was calculated as 60%.

To improve the accuracy, as well as to eliminate the background noise, the algorithm of this tool was modified in order to consider only those quantities where the ED ration is in excess of 2.0 (i.e. double with respect to the reference ED ratio). This helps eliminate small scale variations, perhaps corresponding to the expression of housekeeping genes that do not show variation across datasets. Thereafter, more accurate and distinct results were obtained as shown in Figure 4. This figure shows the tree of the significant sum of the ED ratios. This step increased the efficiency of the prognosis tool to 75%.

Figure 4. Tree representation of the normalized relative distance of the samples from the reference line. The last leaf represents a diseased sample.

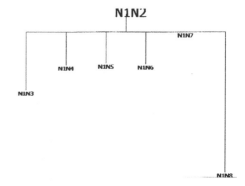

2D Multiple Signal Classification (MUSIC)

The 2D MUSIC algorithm is a MUSIC-like method. It is suitable for estimating the dominant frequency doublets complex harmonic process corrupted by noise. 2D MUSIC mathematical equivalent of the 1D MUSIC algorithm in two-dimensional space. The 1D MUSIC algorithm is a well-established technique is employed to split the M-dimensional space into signal and noise components using eigenvectors of the correlation matrix (Kay, 1999). It has been established that the 2D MUSIC algorithm gives a higher resolution as compared to the 1D MUSIC estimator function and also reduces smearing (Parthasarathy et al., 1994). This frequency estimation technique divides the signal into a signal subspace and noise subspace to extract the complex frequency components of a signal in presence of noise. By the very nature of the method, the requirement for prior pre-processing of data for noise removal is eliminated. We applied the 2D MUSIC algorithm for denoising and representation of a cancer dataset from large airway epithelial cells of smokers with and without cancer. A simple eigen vector based classifier was trained to distinguish between normal and cancerous microarray samples. The proposed methodology has the advantage that it eliminates the need for preprocessing the microarray data and subjectively selecting features from the sample. The expression data of more than 10,000 genes is represented graphically via the 2D MUSIC plot. Also, the eigenvector based classifier using the 2D MUSIC spectral estimator function is based on only the unique signal component of the genes in two distinct physiological samples. This is due to the nature of the difference function included in the classifier tool, which causes genes with similar expression levels in the two samples to be cancelled out.

2D MUSIC was implemented on the dataset of gene expression of Large airway epithelial cells from cigarette smokers with and without cancer (GDS2771) was downloaded as a .soft file from the GEO repository (http://www.ncbi.nlm.nih.gov/Geo). The data consisted of 192 samples, of which 91 were non-cancerous, 86 correspond to patients diagnosed with cancer and 5 were of patients suspected to have lung cancer. The 2D MUSIC algorithm constitutes of arranging the 2-D autocorrelation values of the data in the form of a matrix with an orthonormal eigenbasis. Based on its eigenvalues, The column space of this matrix is separated into the signal and the noise subspace, which are mutually orthogonal. For an ordered pair (ω_1, ω_2) in the two-dimensional frequency plane to be a dominant frequency doublet, the Kronecker Product of the steering vectors associated with the two frequencies ω_1 and ω_2 should lie in the signal subspace of this matrix. Therefore, a symmetric search function of two frequency variables is constructed using the signal eigenvectors. The MUSIC-like pseudobispectrum estimator is constructed using the eigenvectors. The peaks of this function lie precisely at the location of the dominant frequency doublets.

For the implementation of the function, the microarray data signal was assumed to be composed of a superposition of several complex sinusoids. The algorithm was implemented using Matlab (Version 7.8) as follows:

1. Each sample of the dataset corresponding a column was converted into a square matrix for calculation the two dimensional autocorrelation matrix.
2. The square autocorrelation matrix of complex third-order cumulants having a orthonormal eigenstructure was constructed.
3. Eigendecomposition of this matrix was done to get the eigenvalues in increasing/decreasing order and the corresponding eigenvectors for the eigenvalues were also obtained.
4. The 2D MUSIC frequency estimator function was then applied and a mesh graph was plotted as shown in Figure 5.
5. The pair of frequencies corresponding to the peaks positions was the quadratically coupled frequency pair for the given sample. This indicated the direction along which significant variation in the dataset occurred.

The (n x m) correlation matrix was constructed using the formula:

$$R(\tau_1, \tau_2) = \sum_{n,m} X[n + \tau_1, m + \tau_2] \times [n, m] \quad (1.3)$$

where $R(\tau_1, \tau_2)$ is the autocorrelation matrix calculated for the data values in matrix X, with τ_1, τ_2 are the two phase lags in the two orthonormal directions. The lexicographic ordering of R was carried out in order to give it a definite ordered matrix structure (A).

$$A[N_{i+k+1}, N_{j+l+1}] = \sum_{n,m} X(n + i, m + j) \times X(n + k, m + l) \quad (1.4)$$

where i,j,k, and l represent the loop iterants such that $\tau_1, \tau_2 \leftrightarrow (i-k),(j-l)$ and:

$$-(N - 1) \leq (i - j),(k - l) \leq (N - 1)$$

where N represents the number of rows of the matrix, n varies from 0 to:

$$\min(N - i - 1, N - k - 1)$$

and m varies from 0 to:

$$\min(N - j - 1, N - l - 1).$$

The frequency estimator function of 2D MUSIC (Parthasarathy et al., 1994) is calculated as:

$$P(\omega_1, \omega_2) = \left. 1 \middle/ \sum_{i=p+1}^{M} \left| [e(\omega_1) \otimes e(\omega_2)] \cdot v_i^H \right|^2 \right. \quad (1.5)$$

where (ω_1, ω_2) are distinct nonrandom values in $[0, 2\pi]$, M is the dimensionality of the autocorrelation matrix, separates the signal and the noise subspace and v_i are the noise eigenvectors corresponding to eigenvalues in the noise subspace.

$$e(\omega_1) = \left[1, e^{j\omega_1}, e^{j\omega_2} \ldots . e^{j(M-1)\omega_1} \right]^T \quad (1.6)$$

and,

$$e(\omega_2) = \left[1, e^{j\omega_2}, e^{2j\omega_2} \ldots . e^{j(M-1)\omega_2} \right]^T \quad (1.7)$$

where $e(\omega_1) \otimes e(\omega_2)$ represents the tensor product of $e(\omega_1)$ and $e(\omega_2)$.

The graphical representation of $P(\omega_1, \omega_2)$ shows peaks at the dominant frequency pairs in the Fourier decomposition of the signal. This was further used to calculate the frequency estimator function D as follows:

$$D = \int_0^{2\pi} \int_0^{2\pi} \left| P_{test}(\omega_1, \omega_2) - P_{trained}(\omega_1, \omega_2) \right|^2 \delta\omega_1\omega_2 \quad (1.8)$$

where $P_{test}(\omega_1, \omega_2)$ denotes the pseudospectrum for the test sample and $P_{trained}$ that of the trained sample.

2D MUSIC enables data compression. As a result, rather than storing the entire data array, we need to store/ compare only the dominant frequency doublets and their amplitudes. Time series modeling of the gene data also is a data compression technique but it may not be as accurate a model for the gene array data as the eigenvector methods like MUSIC, especially when additive white noise is present.

The 2D MUSIC frequency estimator function was calculated for 30 samples of the smokers diagnosed with cancer and 30 samples for smokers not diagnosed with cancer. In the training phase, the frequency estimator function was applied pairwise between 30 the cancerous samples, 30 non-cancerous samples and then between all possible pairs of cancerous and non-cancerous samples. Manual observation of 60 trained samples was used to determine a threshold value to distinguish between normal and diseased states. In the testing phase, the 2D MUSIC frequency estimator function was again applied to the sample. The difference function was calculated pair-wise with the trained samples (30 cancerous and 30 non-cancerous). The value of the difference function in comparison to those obtained from the training samples was used as a criterion for classification of the sample. If the value of the difference function was lesser than the threshold for majority of training cancerous samples and greater than the threshold for majority of the training non-cancerous samples, the test sample was classified as cancerous. The reverse situation was considered to indicate non-cancerous sample.

The method as outlined above was successful in classifying 59 out of the tested 80 samples

Figure 5. 3D mesh plot of the microarray data after implementation of 2D MUSIC algorithm

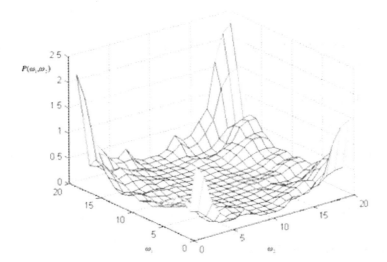

correctly. The efficiency of classification is approximately 74%. Significantly, this efficiency of prediction can be obtained even in the absence of a large number of samples for training.

Volterra Series

The Volterra series is used to model nonlinear systems. It consists of the convolution of the input signal and a series of nonlinear terms that contain products of increasing order of the correlation of the input signal with itself. These polynomial extension terms represent systems with time-invariant scalar outputs having infinite memory. The degree of the Volterra operator is determined by the number of factors in the product e.g. a first order Volterra corresponds to the weighted sum of the input signal used to describe linear systems while a second order Volterra corresponds to the weighted sum of all pairwise products of the input signals.

A discrete time-invariant system with x[i] as input and y[i] as output can be represented using the Volterra series as follows:

$$Y[i] = H_1(x[i]) + H_2(x[i]) + \ldots + Hn(x[i]) + \quad (1.9)$$

$$H_n(x[i]) = \sum_{i_1=1}^{N} \ldots \sum_{i_n=0}^{N} h_n(i_1, i_2, \ldots i_n)$$
$$x[i - i_1] x[i - i_2] \ldots x[i - i_n] \quad (2.0)$$

where h_n is n-th order Volterra kernel, or the higher-order impulse response of the system. The Least squares method can be employed to calculate the kernel. Least squares is a standard tool from linear analysis that highlights the basic property of Volterra series (i.e. a linear combination of non-linear basis functionals). For it to be estimated, the order of the original should be known, as the Volterra basis functionals are not orthogonal. Thus, it is not possible to estimate it incrementally. The reasons for choosing Volterra series for representation of the nonlinear interdependence of the gene expression pattern in each diseased and normal dataset are:

- **Non-Linearity:** The Volterra series model is suitable and widely used for representing non-linear interactions
- **Interaction:** Its capability to capture "memory" effects makes it extremely suitable to describe the dependence of genes in terms of each other.

- **Generality:** It can represent a wide range of systems.
- **Error Reduction:** Truncation of the Volterra series is expected to filter the noise and smoothen the data.

An implicit assumption of this implementation is that Volterra series are applicable only when the system is weakly non-linear i.e. the sum of the infinite term converges, preferable rapidly. In this case, the series can be truncated after some point.

The expression data GDS771 from Gene Expression Omnibus, a public domain expression data repository is being used for this project. Initially gene elimination was undertaken in order to reduce the number of genes to be processed in further steps. In this step descriptive statistical analysis of the data set was carried out. The change in the gene expression levels was plotted. From this, it could be seen that a larger expression level difference (which is more likely to provide information) is associated with a relatively few number of genes.

Boxplots are employed to display differences between populations without assuming any specific type underlying statistical distribution. Thus, they are non-parametric. The spacing between the different boxes is correlated with the degree of dispersion. It may be used to identify the skewness and outliers in the data. We used a box plot was graphically depict groups of numerical data through their five-number summaries: the smallest observation, lower quartile, median, upper quartile, and largest observation. Out of a total of 22,250 genes, only a small set of genes with a significant change in expression is required to be represented. A total of 5,554 genes with normalized expression level difference greater than 75% quartile value were obtained and used for further analysis.

The following is an illustration of the analysis procedure for a k gene system with a second order Volterra series expansion in which each

and every gene is expressed in terms of the next two genes. There are m diseased subjects and n normal subjects. The input is in the form of the expression levels of k genes for both the diseased and the normal subjects:

$$M_n = \begin{pmatrix} g^n_{11} & \cdots & g^n_{1k} \\ \vdots & \ddots & \vdots \\ g^n_{u1} & \cdots & g^n_{uk} \end{pmatrix} \quad (2.1)$$

$$M_d = \begin{pmatrix} g^d_{11} & \cdots & g^d_{1k} \\ \vdots & \ddots & \vdots \\ g^d_{v1} & \cdots & g^d_{vk} \end{pmatrix} \quad (2.2)$$

where M_n is the expression level matrix for u normal subjects and M_d is the expression level matrix for v diseased subjects. For simplicity it is assumed that only 6 genes show a marked change in their expression levels and the rest are eliminated during the gene elimination stage. This results in the following two vectors:

$$G_n = [g^n_1 g^n_2 g^n_3 g^n_4 g^n_5 g^n_6]^T \quad (2.3)$$

$$G_d = [g^d_1 g^d_2 g^d_3 g^d_4 g^d_5 g^d_6]^T \quad (2.4)$$

where g^n_i and g^d_i are calculated as:

$$g^n_i = \frac{\sum_{j=1}^{u} g^n_{ji}}{u}; 1 \leq i \leq 6 \quad (2.5)$$

$$g^d_i = \frac{\sum_{j=1}^{v} g^d_{ji}}{v}; 1 \leq i \leq 6 \quad (2.6)$$

The set of Volterra coefficient vectors A_n and A_d for normal and diseased subjects respectively can be calculated as:

$$A_n = [a_1^n a_2^n a_3^n a_4^n a_5^n a_6^n]^T \qquad (2.7)$$

$$A_d = [a_1^d a_2^d a_3^d a_4^d a_5^d a_6^d]^T \qquad (2.8)$$

The values of Ad and An can be obtained by solving the following set of equations:

$$V_n \bullet A_n = G_n \qquad (2.9)$$

$$V_d \bullet A_d = G_d \qquad (3.0)$$

where,

$$V_n = \begin{bmatrix} g_{n2} & g_{n3} & g_{n2}^2 g_{n3}^2 & g_{n2}g_{n3} \\ g_{n3} & g_{n4} & g_{n3}^2 g_{n4}^2 & g_{n3}g_{n4} \\ g_{n4} & g_{n5} & g_{n4}^2 g_{n5}^2 & g_{n4}g_{n5} \\ g_{n5} & g_{n6} & g_{n5}^2 g_{n6}^2 & g_{n5}g_{n6} \\ g_{n6} & g_{n1} & g_{n6}^2 g_{n1}^2 & g_{n6}g_{n1} \\ g_{n1} & g_{n2} & g_{n1}^2 g_{n2}^2 & g_{n1}g_{n2} \end{bmatrix} \qquad (3.1)$$

$$V_d = \begin{bmatrix} g_{d2} & g_{d3} & g_{d2}^2 g_{d3}^2 & g_{d2}g_{d3} \\ g_{d3} & g_{d4} & g_{d3}^2 g_{d4}^2 & g_{d3}g_{d4} \\ g_{d4} & g_{d5} & g_{d4}^2 g_{d5}^2 & g_{d4}g_{d5} \\ g_{d5} & g_{d6} & g_{d5}^2 g_{d6}^2 & g_{d5}g_{d6} \\ g_{d6} & g_{d1} & g_{d6}^2 g_{d1}^2 & g_{d6}g_{d1} \\ g_{d1} & g_{d2} & g_{d1}^2 g_{d2}^2 & g_{d1}g_{d2} \end{bmatrix} \qquad (3.2)$$

These Volterra series coefficients need to be computed for both the diseased and normal data sets. Thus two expression profiles are obtained. These expression profiles represent the collective behaviour of all the subjects. A similar analysis can be carried out for all the subjects to obtain their individual expression profiles. To find out if a person is diseased or not we just need to measure the closeness of the expression profile with respect to the overall diseased and normal profiles. This approach was used to distinguish between normal and diseased individuals. The entire analysis was carried out on a single data set with 90 normal and 95 diseased subjects. It was observed that the efficiency of the correct prediction increased with the order of the Volterra equations. The results for the efficiency of this method for prognosis are shown in Table 1. Thus, we could achieve a maximum efficiency of 88% with this method. However, it was not possible to compute higher order equations since the Volterra series coefficients increase to a very large number for even small values of order. Thus, the time for execution and amount of memory required to store the coefficients increases proportionately with the order and the number of genes. Additionally, the increase in accuracy validates the initial underlying assumptions of this approach (i.e. the expression of each gene depends on that of other genes and that the same can be represented as a non-linear system).

Identification of Gene Signatures

Principal Component Analysis and Density Based Clustering

Gene signature studies have been extensively carried out for various diseases. However, not many significant signature gene studies, have been done on Parkinson's Disease (PD). A chronic and progressive neurological disorder, PD affects over 3% of the world population over the age of

Table 1. Efficiency of the predictor as a function of order of the Volterra equation

Order	Total Subjects	Correct Prognosis	Incorrect Prognosis	Efficiency
1.	185	126	59	68.18%
2.	185	122	63	65.94%
3.	185	131	54	70.81%
4.	185	163	22	88.11%

65. In this the neuron cells producing dopamine get affected and as a result the patient starts having problems in coordinating movements. This quickly progresses to cognitive and behavioral problems with dementia commonly occurring in advanced stages. Though Parkinson's is mainly an age related disease, over the years it has also been found in population groups between 20 to 45 (Samii et al., 2004). At present several genes have been identified that are known to cause PD, of which the *parkin* gene (Schlitter et al., 2006) is the most important. *Parkin* has been biologically identified to be an E3 ubiquitin-protein ligase that targets specific substrates for degradation via the ubiquitin-proteasome pathway (Shimura et al., 2000). Mutations were identified in *parkin* in Japanese patients with autosomal recessive juvenile Parkinsonism (Kitada et al., 1998). But *parkin* mutations are only responsible for 1% of the PD cases. Other genes like *DJ-1*, *PINK-1*, and *UCHL-1* (Hardy et al., 2003) have also been identified over time. As yet, no comprehensive gene signature associated with PD is known.

To find the gene signature associated with PD, we have proposed a combination of PCA and DBSCAN for clustering of features in high-dimensional gene expression microarray data. Using a publicly available microarray dataset for early stage PD, we refined the gene set obtained from clustering by using inferential statistics and gene ontology data to obtain a gene signature set. Each individual gene was further validated by studying the pathway it takes part in and by establishing a relationship with the pathways known to cause PD. Hence the gene signature is established to be significant. Such a gene signature is likely to act as a future biomarker for early diagnosis of PD.

The publicly available dataset GDS2519 was downloaded from GEO (http://www.ncbi.nlm. nih.gov/geo/). It had 22 normal samples and 50 diseased samples. 22215 genes were analysed for their expression in PD samples vs normal controls. To make the data manageable both the diseased and normal datasets were treated with PCA. The

princomp function in Matlab was used to achieve the same. Both the datasets became 22215 X 5 after dimensionality reduction and were stored in the matrix SCORE. They were then subjected to DBSCAN (Daszykowski, 2001). The algorithm required 2 input parameters, namely: 1) k (the minimum number of objects in the neighborhood for it to be considered as a cluster) and 2) *eps* (the neighborhood radius). The parameter values were optimized to give the best demarcation between clusters and were finally set at k = 10, eps = 100. Three clusters were formed for both diseased (d) and normal (n) datasets, namely: 1) cluster A, 2) cluster B, 3) cluster C. It was hypothesized that in two scenarios could genes be said to be highly probably differentially expressed, namely: a) Case 1: genes belong to cluster A_n ∩ cluster C_d and b) Case 2: genes belong to cluster A_d ∩ cluster C_n. These genes formed SET I. Four cases were formulated for the less probably differentially expressed genes, namely: a) Case 3: genes belong to cluster A_n ∩ cluster B_d, b) Case 4: genes belong to cluster A_d ∩ cluster B_n, c) Case 5: genes belong to cluster B_n ∩ cluster C_d and d) Case 6: genes belong to cluster B_d ∩ cluster C_n. These genes formed SET II.

For further evaluation, value tables were constructed for both SET I and SET II using the Minitab software. Minitab 15, student version available at http://www.minitab.com/en-US/ was used for the same. Descriptive Statistical Analysis was carried out to find the distribution of data. Means and standard deviations (S.D) in expression value were calculated separately for each gene, across 50 samples for the diseased set and 22 samples for the normal set. The stringency of the statistical tests was kept high for genes belonging to SET II and medium for genes belonging to SET I. This final set of genes constituted the gene signature set. A "Leave Some Out" approach was used for validation of the signature set. The 22,215 genes were analyzed across 16 normal samples and 40 diseased samples. All the steps and parameters were kept the same. The signature set was also further validated by PDbase (Yang et al., 2009), database of Parkinson's disease related genes available at http://bioportal.kobic.re.kr/PDbase/ and literature review.

Density based clustering with DBSCAN resulted in two sets of genes. SET I contained 157 genes and SET II contained 208 genes. Descriptive statistical analysis revealed that data was normally distributed for normal and diseased expression value tables for both SET I and II genes. These distributions were used to decide the statistical tests to be performed. Inferential Statistics were then used to reduce the signature set to 21 genes which have been detailed in Table 1. This reduced signature set was verified by Leave Some Out Approach. When the reduced dataset was subjected to the same methodology, a signature set of 40 genes was obtained. An overlap of 7 genes established the significance of the original gene signature. For further validation, literature review was done to determine the biological role of the genes. Eight of the genes were found to participate in several known molecular regulatory pathways in the pathogenesis of Parkinson's disease, namely: 1) oxidative stress-induced cell responses (specifically genes were involved in extrinsic signalling events in programmed cell death (Simunovic, 2009), 2) Complement and coagulation cascades (Bonifati, 2007), 3) Toxicity to dopaminergic neurons (Simunovic, 2009), 4) Estrogen Reduction (Green and Simpkins, 2000), 5) Insulin Signalling (Morris, 2010) and 6) Signalling Cascade (Mann, 2007). Aside from these 5 more genes were either found significantly differentially expressed in previous studies undertaken on PD or found to have some function connected to PD. These genes were namely:1) a proto-oncogene 2) gene coding for topoisomerase 1 enzyme responsible for catalyzing the transient breaking and rejoining of a single strand of DNA, 3)Kelch-like21 gene responsible for modification and ubiquitination. High expression of KLHL21 in brain has been observed for PD patients. 4) ACTN4 has been known to contribute to podocyte injury, a condi-

tion observed in PD and 5) CANT1 which plays a role in nucleoside, nucleotide and nucleic acid metabolism and has been found significantly differentially expressed in PD studies on mouse (Hourani, 2010). Two of the genes identified, *MEA1* and *ACTN4* have also both been documented in PDbase. Thus, we were able to identify a 21 gene signature associated with PD using the approach as described above. Seven of the identified genes overlapped with the 40 gene signature obtained by the 'Leave Some Out' approach. Also, by carrying out gene annotation, 14 of the genes were shown to perform a function or take part in a pathway with an invariate relationship to PD. Hence on the basis of literature review, leave some out approach and use of PDbase, we conclude our gene signature is significant. Furthermore, as the dataset used in our study was of whole blood samples, we conclude that the signature set provided by us can act as biomarkers for early diagnosis of PD by the testing of whole blood samples of patients.

FUTURE RESEARCH DIRECTIONS

Linear and Volterra kernel based as well as the 2D MUSIC model are parametric models for the gene data. The 2D MUSIC algorithm estimates the dominant frequency doublets of the gene data while the time series determine the prediction coefficients, which in turn can enable us to predict furtht expression of the gene in case only partial gene information is available. There may be more effective parametrizations of the gene expression data. As an example, suppose the gene data is represented by an array:

$$((X[n,m]_{0 \leq n,m \leq N-1} \in R^{N \times N}$$

Then we construct a vector:

$$\sum_{n,m} X[n,m] e_n \otimes e_m \in R^{N^2}$$

and treat this as a 1D time series $\left((\zeta[n])\right)_{n=0}^{N^2-1}$.

We can then try a prediction model:

$$\hat{\zeta}[n+1] = \sum_{k=1}^{r} C_k \phi_k (\zeta[n], \tag{3.3}$$
$$\zeta[n-1],.,\zeta[n-p+1])$$

where ϕ_k's are known test functions and $\{C_k\}_1^r$ are coefficients determined by minimizing

$$\sum_n (\hat{\zeta}[n+1] - \zeta[n+1])^2$$

Or, more generally, we can try a parametric model of the form:

$$\hat{\zeta}[n+1] = \phi(\zeta[n], \zeta[n-1],..,$$
$$\zeta[n-p+1]; \theta_1, \theta_2, \theta_r)$$

where $\phi: \mathbb{R}^p \times \mathbb{R}^n \to \mathbb{R}$ is a known function but $\{\theta_1,..,\theta_r\}$ are unknown parameters to be estimated by minimizing

$$\sum_n (\hat{\zeta}[n+1] - \zeta[n+1])^2.$$

Different ϕ_k's or ϕ's give different minimum prediction error energies and a lot of tact has to be applied in choosing the right ϕ_k's and ϕ's. The performance of an estimator of the parameters C_k or θ_k is determined by their sample variances obtained using scatter plots.

Suppose we know that the gene data $\zeta \equiv \underline{X}$ obeys a statistical model with a probability density $p(\zeta \mid \underline{\theta})$. Then $\underline{\theta}$ may be estimated using the maximum likelihood method, as in:

$$\underline{\theta}_{ML}(\underline{\zeta}) = \overset{Arg\,max}{\underline{\theta}} \; p(\underline{\zeta} \mid \underline{\theta}) \tag{3.4}$$

where $\underline{\theta}_{ML}(\underline{\zeta})$ is the value of the parameter vector $\underline{\theta}$ for which the given gene expression data $\underline{\zeta}$ is the most probable. Any estimator $\hat{\underline{\theta}}(\underline{\zeta})$ of $\underline{\upsilon}$ will have variances

$$\left| E[(\theta_\alpha(\zeta) - \theta_\alpha)^2] \right.$$

and therefore should be small. However, according to the fundamental theorem in statistics, the variance of an estimator can not be made smaller than the Cramer-Rao lower bound (CRLB), which is defined as:

$$V_\alpha(\theta) = [J(\underline{\theta})^{-1}]_{\alpha\alpha}$$

where $\underline{J}(\underline{\theta})$ is the Fisher information matrix defined by:

$$J_{\alpha\beta}(\underline{\theta}) = \left| E \left[\begin{array}{c} \dfrac{\partial \log p(\underline{X} \mid \theta)}{\partial \theta_\alpha} \\[2mm] \dfrac{\partial \log p(\underline{X} \mid \theta)}{\partial \theta_\beta} \end{array} \right] \right.$$

$$= \int_{R^{N^2}} \frac{1}{p(\underline{X} \mid \theta)} \frac{\partial p(\underline{X} \mid \theta)}{\partial \theta_\alpha}$$
$$\frac{\partial \log p(\underline{X} \mid \theta)}{\partial \theta_\beta} \partial \underline{X} \tag{3.5}$$

We can try constructing several statistical models for the gene data, estimating the parameters by some signal processing algorithm and comparing its variance with the CRLB. Already a predictor model of the form:

$$\zeta[n+1] = \phi(\zeta[n], \zeta[n-1], \ldots, \\ \zeta[n-p+1]; \theta_1 \theta_N) + W[n+1] \tag{3.6}$$

where $\{W[n]\}$ is white noise with known pdf $p_w(\omega)$ is one such parametric model. The linear predictor and Volterra mold come under this category. For $p(\underline{\zeta} | \underline{\theta})$, we have:

$$p(\underline{\zeta} | \underline{\theta}) = \prod_{n=0}^{N^2-1} p_w(\zeta[n+1] - \\ \phi(\zeta[n], \ldots, \zeta[n-p+1], \underline{\theta})) \tag{3.7}$$

And by differentiation with respect to $\underline{\theta}$, the CRLB can be determined. This should be compared to the sample variances of our predictor coeff estimates made in this chapter using scatter plots.

The 2D MUSIC algorithm is another parametric statistical model based on assuming the data to have the form $w_{1\alpha} n + w_{2\alpha} m$

$$X[n, m] = \sum_{\alpha=1}^{\beta} A_\alpha \exp \\ \{j(w_{1\alpha} n + w_{2\alpha} m\} + w[n, m],$$

$$0 \leq n, m \leq N - 1, \tag{3.8}$$

Assuming w to have a pdf $p_{\underline{w}}(\underline{w})$ and solving:

$$\underline{X} = \sum_{n, m=0}^{N-1} X[n, m] e_n \otimes e_m,$$

$$\underline{e}_n = [\delta_{1n}, \delta_{2n}, \ldots, \delta_{Nn}] \tag{3.9}$$

$$\underline{e}(w) = [1, e^{jw}, e^{j2w}, \ldots, e^{j(N-\eta w)}]^T \tag{4.0}$$

We get:

$$\underline{X} = \sum_{\alpha=1}^{p} A_\alpha e(w_{1\alpha}) \otimes e(w_{2\alpha}) + \underline{w} \tag{4.0}$$

The parameters estimated by 2D MUSIC are only the frequency doublets

$$\{(w_{1\alpha}, w2_\alpha)\}_{\alpha=1}^{p}.$$

To estimate $\{A_\alpha\}$ in addition, we must use the 2D-ESPRTT algorithm. The pdf of the data is:

$$p(\underline{X} | \{(A_\alpha, w_{1\alpha}, w_{2\alpha})\}_1^p = \\ p_w(\underline{X} - \sum A_\alpha e(w_{1\alpha}) \otimes p_w e(w_{2\alpha})) \tag{4.1}$$

From which the CRLB for the variance, of the parameter estimate may be obtained by differentiation.

In summary, a lot more work needs to be done in order to determine the performance of our parametric models and if need be, to modify the models used in this paper to improve the performance to get better representations of gene data expression enabling, in turn, compression and feature extraction.

CONCLUSION

A large amount of gene expression data is produced by conducting a microarray data experiment. In this article, we have outlined the experimental design and the problems inherent in the microarray experiment at the level of:

1.   Design
2.   Data collection
3.   Data preprocessing, filtering and denoising
4.   Data analysis for comparison and clustering

In view of the problems outlined, various approaches signal processing have been proposed to initially identify the kind of noise present and to study the effect of various denoising procedures. White noise was found to be present in the data even though some smoothening is achieved through the implementation of FFT and autocorrelation techniques. In view of this, it was argued that the noise, being of random nature will be cancelled out during comparison of data sets. Thus, signal processing with the data sets was attempted in order to construct a simple tool for prognosis of the disease on the basis of microarray data. For this purpose, the sinusoidal form of the diseased and normal data was computed and compared. It is our conjecture that the expression values of diseased genes will be replaced by sinusoids with slightly shifted frequency doublets when compared with the frequency doublets of healthy gene data. Thus by estimating the shift in the dominant frequency doublets, we may get a clue to the nature of the disease or the degree to which it has progressed.

The data was represented using FFT, 2D MUSIC and Volterra series with increasing efficiency of prognosis. However, increase in efficiency is accompanied by compute intensiveness of the process. The techniques described were tested using various large datasets containing samples from large number of patients. The tools described are further required to be tested on a large number of different diseases and datasets in order to verify their efficacy. It was observed that the representation of the data as a signal causes loss of gene identity data, and is thus not suitable for mining the data for the presence of a gene signature. Therefore, we implemented PCA and clustering methods for to determine a gene signature for PD that could be further validated by literature and database search. In future, we intend to incorporate and test additional techniques and algorithms for development of a prognosis tool as well as for mining for gene signatures using gene expression data.

REFERENCES

Abdullah-Sayani, A., Bueno-de-Mesquita, J. M., & van de Vijver, M. J. (2006). Technology insight: Tuning into the genetic orchestra using microarrays--limitations of DNA microarrays in clinical practice. *Nature Clinical Practice. Oncology*, *3*(9), 501–516. doi:10.1038/ncponc0587 PMID:16955089.

Agrawal, R., & Srikant, R. (1994). Fast algorithms for mining association rules in large databases. In *Proceedings of 20th International Conference on Very Large Data Bases*, Santiago de Chile, Chile: Morgan Kaufmann.

Akiyoshi, T., Kobunai, T., & Watanabe, T. (2012). Predicting the response to preoperative radiation or chemoradiation by a microarray analysis of the gene expression profiles in rectal cancer. *Surgery Today*, *42*(8), 713–719. doi:10.1007/s00595-012-0223-8 PMID:22706722.

Ankerst, M., Breunig, M. M., Kriegel, H., & Sander, J. (1999). OPTICS: ordering points to identify the clustering structure. In *Proceedings of ACM SIGMOD International Conference on Management of Data* (49-60). New York: ACM Press.

Benoit, C. E., Rowe, W. B., Menard, C., Sarret, P., & Quirion, R. (2011). Genomic and proteomic strategies to identify novel targets potentially involved in learning and memory. *Trends in Pharmacological Sciences*, *32*(1), 43–52. doi:10.1016/j.tips.2010.10.002 PMID:21129790.

Bonifati, D. M., & Kishore, U. (2007). Role of complement in neurodegeneration and neuro-inflammation. *Molecular Immunology*, *44*(5), 999–1010. doi:10.1016/j.molimm.2006.03.007 PMID:16698083.

Boutros, P. C., Lau, S. K., Pintilie, M., Liu, N., Shepherd, F. A., & Jurisica, I. et al. (2009). Prognostic gene signatures for non small cell lung cancer. *Proceedings of the National Academy of Sciences of the United States of America, 106*(8), 2824–2828. doi:10.1073/pnas.0809444106 PMID:19196983.

Bramswig, N. C., & Kaestner, K. H. (2012). Organogenesis and functional genomics of the endocrine pancreas. *Cellular and Molecular Life Sciences, 69*(13), 2109–2123. doi:10.1007/s00018-011-0915-z PMID:22241333.

Brown, I., Heys, S. D., & Schofield, A. C. (2003). From peas to chips-The new millennium of molecular biology: A primer for the surgeon. *World Journal of Surgical Oncology, 1*, 21. doi:10.1186/1477-7819-1-21 PMID:14613556.

Chang, H. Y., Nuyten, D. S., Sneddon, J. B., Hastie, T., Tibshirani, R., & van de Vijver, M. J. et al. (2005). Robustness, scalability, and integration of a wound-response gene expression signature in predicting breast cancer survival. *Proceedings of the National Academy of Sciences of the United States of America, 102*(10), 3738–3743. doi:10.1073/pnas.0409462102 PMID:15701700.

Chipman, H., & Tibshirani, R. (2006). Hybrid hierarchical clustering with applications to microarray data. *Biostatistics (Oxford, England), 7*(2), 286–301. doi:10.1093/biostatistics/kxj007 PMID:16301308.

Dai, M., Wang, P., Boyd, A. D., Kostov, G., Athey, B., & Meng, F. et al. (2005). Evolving gene/transcript definitions significantly alter the interpretation of genechip data. *Nucleic Acids Research, 33*(20), e175. doi:10.1093/nar/gni179 PMID:16284200.

Daszykowski, M., Walczak, & Massart, D. L. (2001). Looking for natural patterns in data. part 1: Density based approach. *Chemometrics and Intelligent Laboratory Systems, 56*(2), 83–92. doi:10.1016/S0169-7439(01)00111-3.

de Tayrac, M., Aubry, M., Saïkali, S., Etcheverry, A., Surbled, C., & Mosser, J. et al. (2011). A 4-gene signature associated with clinical outcome in high-grade gliomas. *Clinical Cancer Research, 17*(2), 317–327. doi:10.1158/1078-0432.CCR-10-1126 PMID:21224364.

Deonier, R. C., Tavaré, S., & Waterman, M. S. (2005). Measuring expression of genome information. In Computational Genome Analysis: An Introduction. (291-327). Berlin: Springer.

Díaz, E. (2009). From microarrays to mechanisms of brain development and function. *Biochemical and Biophysical Research Communications, 385*(2), 129–131. doi:10.1016/j.bbrc.2009.05.057 PMID:19460360.

Draghici, S., Khatri, P., Eklund, A. C., & Szallasi, Z. (2006). Reliability and reproducibility issues in DNA microarray measurements. *Trends in Genetics, 22*(2), 101–109. doi:10.1016/j.tig.2005.12.005 PMID:16380191.

Dudoit, S., Yang, Y. H., Callow, M. J., & Speed, T. P. (2002). Statistical methods for identifying differentially expressed genes in replicated cDNA microarray experiments. *Statistica Sinica, 12*, 111–139.

Ester, M., Kriegel, H., Jörg, S., & Xu, X. (1996) A density-based algorithm for discovering clusters in large spatia databases with noise. In *Proceedings of 2nd International Conference on Knowledge Discovery and Data Mining (KDD-96)*. München, Germany: University of Munich Oettingenstr Institute for Computer Science.

Forster, T., Roy, D., & Ghazal, P. (2003). Experiments using microarray technology: limitations and standard operating procedures. *The Journal of Endocrinology, 178*(2), 195–204. doi:10.1677/joe.0.1780195 PMID:12904167.

Francetič, M., Nagode, M., & Nastav, B. (2005) Hierarchical clustering with concave data sets. *Metodološki zvezki, 2*(2), 173-193.

Gentleman, R. C., Carey, V. J., Bates, D. M., Bolstad, B., Dettling, M., & Zhang, J. et al. (2004). Bioconductor: Open software development for computational biology and bioinformatics. *Genome Biology*, *5*(10), R80. doi:10.1186/gb-2004-5-10-r80 PMID:15461798.

Gopalappa, C., Das, T. K., Enkemann, T., & Eschrich, S. S. (2009). Removal of hybridization and scanning noise from microarrays. *IEEE Transactions on Nanobioscience*, *8*(3), 210–218. doi:10.1109/TNB.2009.2029100 PMID:20051337.

Green, P. S., & Simpkins, J. W. (2000). Neuroprotective effects of estrogens: Potential mechanisms of action. *International Journal of Developmental Neuroscience*, *18*(4-5), 347–358. doi:10.1016/S0736-5748(00)00017-4 PMID:10817919.

Hardy, J., Cookson, M. R., & Singleton, A. (2003). Genes and parkinsonism. *The Lancet Neurology*, *2*(4), 221–228. doi:10.1016/S1474-4422(03)00350-8 PMID:12849210.

Hinestrosa, M. C., Dickersin, K., Klein, P., Mayer, M., Noss, K., & Visco, F. M. et al. (2007). Shaping the future of biomarker research in breast cancer to ensure clinical relevance. *Nature Reviews. Cancer*, *7*(4), 309–315. doi:10.1038/nrc2113 PMID:17384585.

Hinneburg, A. (2007). Denclue 2.0: Fast clustering based on kernel density estimation. In *Proceedings of the 7th International Conference on Intelligent Data Analysis* (70-80). Berlin: Springer-Verlag.

Jain, A. K. (1988). *Algorithms for clustering data*. Upper Saddle River, NJ: Prentice Hall.

Järvinen, A. K., Hautaniemi, S., Edgren, H., Auvinen, P., Saarela, J., Kallioniemi, O. P., & Monni, O. (2004). Are data from different gene expression microarray platforms comparable? *Genomics*, *83*(6), 1164–1168. doi:10.1016/j.ygeno.2004.01.004 PMID:15177569.

Kane, M. D., Jatkoe, T. A., Stumpf, C. R., Lu, J., Thomas, J. D., & Madore, S. J. (2000). Assessment of the sensitivity and specificity of oligonucleotide (50mer) microarrays. *Nucleic Acids Research*, *28*(22), 4552–4557. doi:10.1093/nar/28.22.4552 PMID:11071945.

Kaufman, L., & Rousseeuw, P. J. (1990). *Finding groups in data: An introduction to cluster analysis*. New York: John Wiley & Sons. doi:10.1002/9780470316801.

Kay, S. M. (1999). *Modern spectral estimation: Theory and application*. Upper Saddle River, NJ: Prentice Hall.

Khan, J., Wei, J. S., Ringnér, M., Saal, L. H., Ladanyi, M., & Meltzer, P. S. et al. (2001). Classification and diagnostic prediction of cancers using gene expression profiling and artificial neural networks. *Nature Medicine*, *7*(6), 673–679. doi:10.1038/89044 PMID:11385503.

Kim, E. (2010). Insulin resistance at the crossroads of metabolic syndrome: Systemic analysis using microarrays. *Biotechnology Journal*, *5*(9), 919–929. doi:10.1002/biot.201000048 PMID:20669253.

Kitada, T., Asakawa, S., Hattori, N., Matsumine, H., Yamamura, Y., & Shimizu, N. et al. (1998). Mutations in the parkin gene cause autosomal recessive juvenile parkinsonism. *Nature*, *392*(6676), 605–608. doi:10.1038/33416 PMID:9560156.

Kokko, A. (2006). *Expression Microarray Technology as a Tool in Cancer Research*. (Unpublished Doctoral Dissertation). Helsinki, Finland, Helsinki University of Technology.

Mann, F., Chauvet, S., & Rougon, G. (2007). Semaphorins in development and adultbrain: Implication for neurological diseases. *Progress in Neurobiology*, *82*(2), 57–79. doi:10.1016/j.pneurobio.2007.02.011 PMID:17537564.

Moreira, A., Santos, M. Y., & Carneiro, S. (2005). *Density-based clustering algorithms–DBSCAN and SNN*. Minho, Portugal: University of Minho.

Morris, J. K., Esteves, A. R., Bomhoff, G. L., Swerdlow, R. H., Stanford, J. A., & Geiger, P.C. (2010). Investigation of insulin signaling in parkinson's disease cytoplasmic hybrid cells. *FASEB Journal, 1053.6*.

Nadon, R., & Shoemaker, J. (2002). Statistical issues with microarrays: Processing and analysis. *Trends in Genetics, 18*(5), 265–271. doi:10.1016/S0168-9525(02)02665-3 PMID:12047952.

Ojha, S., & Kostrzynska, M. (2008). Examination of animal and zoonotic pathogens using microarrays. *Veterinary Research, 39*(1), 4. doi:10.1051/vetres:2007042 PMID:18073091.

Olano, J. P., & Walker, D. H. (2011). Diagnosing emerging and reemerging infectious diseases: The pivotal role of the pathologist. *Archives of Pathology & Laboratory Medicine, 135*(1), 83–91. PMID:21204714.

Owzar, K., Barry, W., Jung, S., Sohn, I., & George, S. (2008). Statistical challenges in preprocessing in microarray experiments in cancer. *Clinical Cancer Research, 14*(19), 5959–5966. doi:10.1158/1078-0432.CCR-07-4532 PMID:18829474.

Paik, S., Kim, C. Y., Song, Y. K., & Kim, W. S. (2005). Technology insight: application of molecular techniques to formalin-fixed paraffin-embedded tissues from breast cancer. *Nature Clinical Practice. Oncology, 2*(5), 246–254. doi:10.1038/ncponc0171 PMID:16264960.

Parthasarathy, H., Prasad, S., & Joshi, S. (1994). A music-like method for estimating quadratic phase coupling. *Signal Processing, 37*(2), 171–188. doi:10.1016/0165-1684(94)90101-5.

Perez, E. A., Pusztai, L., & Van de Vijver, M. (2004). Improving patient care through molecular diagnostics. *Seminars in Oncology, 31*, 14–20. doi:10.1053/j.seminoncol.2004.07.017 PMID:15490370.

Perou, C. M., Sørlie, T., Eisen, M. B., van de Rijn, M., Jeffrey, S. S., & Botstein, D. et al. (2000). Molecular portraits of human breast tumours. *Nature, 406*(6797), 747–752. doi:10.1038/35021093 PMID:10963602.

Perry, A. M., Mitrovic, Z., & Chan, W. C. (2012). Biological prognostic markers in diffuse large B-cell lymphoma. *Cancer Control, 19*(3), 214–226. PMID:22710897.

Pirim, H., Gautam, D., Bhowmik, T., & Perkins, A. D., Burak, Ekşioglu, B, & Alkan, A. (2011). Performance of an ensemble clustering algorithm on biological data sets. *Mathematical and Computational Applications, 16*, 87–96.

Porcellini, E., Carbone, I., Ianni, M., & Licastro, F. (2010). Alzheimer's disease gene signature says: Beware of brain viral infections. *Immunity & Ageing, 7*, 16. doi:10.1186/1742-4933-7-16 PMID:21156047.

Pritchard, C. C., & Nelson, P. S. (2008). Gene expression profiling in the developing prostate. *Differentiation, 76*(6), 624–640. doi:10.1111/j.1432-0436.2008.00274.x PMID:18462436.

Ramaswamy, S., & Golub, T. R. (2002). DNA microarrays in clinical oncology. *Journal of Clinical Oncology, 20*(7), 1932–1941. PMID:11919254.

Ressom, H., Varghese, R., Zhang, Z., Xuang, J., & Clarke, R. (2008). Classification algorithms for phenotype prediction in genomics and proteomics. *Frontiers in Bioscience, 13*, 691–708. doi:10.2741/2712 PMID:17981580.

Rowels, S., & Saul, L. (2000). Non linear dimensionality reduction by locally linear embedding. *Science, 290*(5500), 2323–2326. doi:10.1126/science.290.5500.2323 PMID:11125150.

Russo, G., Zegar, C., & Giordano, A. (2003). Advantages and limitations of microarray technology in human cancer. *Oncogene*, *22*(42), 6497–6507. doi:10.1038/sj.onc.1206865 PMID:14528274.

Samii, A., Nutt, J. G., & Ransom, B. R. (2004). Parkinson's disease. *Lancet*, *363*(9423), 1783–1793. doi:10.1016/S0140-6736(04)16305-8 PMID:15172778.

Schaaf, C. P., Wiszniewska, J., & Beaudet, A. L. (2011). Copy number and SNP arrays in clinical diagnostics. *Annual Review of Genomics and Human Genetics*, *12*, 25–51. doi:10.1146/annurev-genom-092010-110715 PMID:21801020.

Schlitter, A. M., Kurz, M., Larsen, J. P., Woitalla, D., Müller, T., Epplen, J. T., & Dekomien, G. (2006). Parkin gene variations in late-onset parkinson's disease: Comparison between norwegian and german cohorts. *Acta Neurologica Scandinavica*, *113*(1), 9–13. doi:10.1111/j.1600-0404.2005.00532.x PMID:16367892.

Shih, B., Watson, S., & Bayat, A. (2012). Whole genome and global expression profiling of Dupuytren's disease: Systematic review of current findings and future perspectives. *Annals of the Rheumatic Diseases*, *71*(9), 1440–1447. doi:10.1136/annrheumdis-2012-201295 PMID:22772327.

Shimura, H., Hattori, N., Kubo, S., Mizuno, Y., Asakawa, S., & Suzuki, T. et al. (2000). Familial parkinson disease gene product, parkin, is a ubiquitin-protein ligase. *Nature Genetics*, *25*(3), 302–305. doi:10.1038/77060 PMID:10888878.

Simon, R., Radmacher, M. D., & Dobbin, K. (2002). Design of studies using DNA microarrays. *Genetic Epidemiology*, *23*(1), 21–36. doi:10.1002/gepi.202 PMID:12112246.

Simunovic, F., Yi, M., Wang, Y., Macey, L., & Brown, L. T. (2009). Gene expression profiling of substantia nigra dopamine neurons: Further insights into parkinson's disease pathology. *Brain*, *132*(7), 1795–1809. doi:10.1093/brain/awn323 PMID:19052140.

Tenenbaum, J. B., de Silva, V., & Langford, J. C. (2000). A global geometric framework for nonlinear dimensionality reduction. *Science*, *290*(5500), 2319–2323. doi:10.1126/science.290.5500.2319 PMID:11125149.

Tu, Y., Stolovitzky, G., & Klein, U. (2002). Quantitative noise analysis for gene expression microarray experiments. *Proceedings of the National Academy of Sciences of the United States of America*, *99*(22), 14031–14036. doi:10.1073/pnas.222164199 PMID:12388780.

Tusher, V. G., Tibshirani, R., & Chu, G. (2001). Significance analysis of microarrays applied to the ionizing radiation response. *Proceedings of the National Academy of Sciences of the United States of America*, *98*(18), 5116–5121. doi:10.1073/pnas.091062498 PMID:11309499.

Wan, Y. W., Sabbagh, E., Raese, R., Qian, Y., Luo, D., & Guo, N. L. et al. (2010). Hybrid models identified a 12 gene signature for lung cancer prognosis and chemoresponse prediction. *PLoS ONE*, *5*(8). doi:10.1371/journal.pone.0012222 PMID:20808922.

Yang, J. O., Kim, W. Y., Jeong, S. Y., Oh, J. H., Jho, S., Bhak, J., & Kim, N. S. (2009). PDbase: A database of Parkinson's disease-related genes and genetic variation using substantia nigra ESTs. *BMC Genomics*, *3*. PMID:19123947.

Zang, S., Guo, R., Zhang, L., & Lu, Y. (2007). Integration of statistical inference methods and a novel control measure to improve sensitivity and specificity of data analysis in expression profiling studies. *Journal of Biomedical Informatics*, *40*(5), 552–560. doi:10.1016/j.jbi.2007.01.002 PMID:17317331.

Zhu, C. Q., Ding, K., Strumpf, D., Weir, B. A., Meyerson, M., & Tsao, M. S. et al. (2010). Prognostic and predictive gene signature for adjuvant chemotherapy in resected non-small-cell lung cancer. *Journal of Clinical Oncology*, *28*(29), 4417–4424. doi:10.1200/JCO.2009.26.4325 PMID:20823422.

ADDITIONAL REFERENCES

Abdullah-Sayani, A., Bueno-de-Mesquita, J. M., & van de Vijver, M. J. (2006). Technology insight: Tuning into the genetic orchestra using microarrays--limitations of DNA microarrays in clinical practice. *Nature Clinical Practice. Oncology*, *3*(9), 501–516. doi:10.1038/ncponc0587 PMID:16955089.

Boslaugh, S., & Watters, P. A. (2008). *Statistics in a nutshell* (Treseler, M., Ed.). Sebastopol, CA: O'Reilly Media Inc..

Brown, P., & Botstein, D. (1999). Exploring the new world of the genome with DNA microarrays. *Nature Genetics*, *21*, 33–37. doi:10.1038/4462 PMID:9915498.

Cho, S., & Won, H. (2003) Machine learning in DNA microarray analysis for cancer classification. In *Proceedings of the First Asia-Pacific bioinformatics conference on Bioinformatics* (189-198). Darlinghurst, Australia: Australian Computer Society.

Cobb, K. (2006). Microarrays: The search for meaning in a vast sea of data. *Biomedical Computation Review*. Retrieved from http://www.biomedicalcomputationreview.org/2/4/6.pdf.

Deonier, R. C., Tavaré, S., & Waterman, M. S. (2005). Measuring expression of genome information. Computational genome analysis: An introduction (291-327). Berlin: Springer.

Istepanian, R. S., Sungoor, A., & Nebel, J. C. (2011). Comparative analysis of genomic signal processing for microarray data clustering. *IEEE Transactions on Nanobioscience*, *10*(4), 225–238. doi:10.1109/TNB.2011.2178262 PMID:22157075.

Kay, S. M. (1999). *Modern spectral estimation: Theory and application*. Upper Saddle River, NJ: Prentice Hall.

Kohane, I. S., Kho, A. T., & Butte, A. J. (2005). *Microarrays for integrative genomics*. Cambridge, MA: MIT Press.

Kokko, A. (2006). *Expression Microarray Technology as a Tool in Cancer Research*. (Unpublished Doctoral Dissertation). Helsinki, Finland, Helsinki University of Technology.

McLachlan, G. J., Do, K., & Ambroise, C. (2005). *Analyzing microarray gene expression data*. Hoboken, NJ: John Wiley & Sons.

National Human Genome Research Institute. (2011). *DNA microarray technology*. Retrieved from http://www.genome.gov/10000533.

NCBI. (2007). *A science primer*. Retrieved from http://www.ncbi.nlm.nih.gov/About/primer/microarrays.html.

Papoulis, A., & Pillai, S. U. (2002). *Probability, random variables, and stochastic processes*. New York: McGraw-Hill.

Qiu, P. (2007). Genomic processing for cancer classification and prediction–A broad review of the recent advances in model-based genomoric and proteomic signal processing for cancer detection. *IEEE Signal Processing Magazine*, *24*(1), 100–110. doi:10.1109/MSP.2007.273063.

Rao, K. D., & Swamy, M. N. S. (2008). Analysis of genomics and proteomics using DSP techniques. *IEEE Transactions on Circuits and Systems, 55*(1), 370–378. doi:10.1109/TCSI.2007.910541.

Ressom, H., Varghese, R., Zhang, Z., Xuang, J., & Clarke, R. (2008). Classification algorithms for phenotype prediction in genomics and proteomics. *Frontiers in Bioscience, 13*, 691–708. doi:10.2741/2712 PMID:17981580.

Russo, G., Zegar, C., & Giordano, A. (2003). Advantages and limitations of microarray technology in human cancer. *Oncogene, 22*(42), 6497–6507. doi:10.1038/sj.onc.1206865 PMID:14528274.

Schonfeld, D., Goutsias, J., Shmulevich, I., Tabus, I., & Tewfik, A. H. (2008). Introduction to the issue on genomic and proteomic signal processing. *IEEE Journal of Selected Topics in Signal Processing, 2*(3), 257–259. doi:10.1109/JSTSP.2008.925864.

KEY TERMS AND DEFINITIONS

Autocorrelation: Mathematical representation of the cross-correlation or similarity between the two observations as a function of the time separating them.

Cancer: Cancer is the uncontrolled growth of the cells that can affect different parts of the body.

Clustering: The process of grouping a set of objects such that objects similar objects fall in the same group and differ from those in other groups.

Discrete Fourier Transform (DFT): The DFT is the equivalent of the continuous Fourier Transform for finite signals having discrete, non-zero values.

DNA: The genetic material of higher living organisms.

Expression: The process of reading of the information contained in the gene for producing a functional product.

Gene: Some stretches of the DNA that code for functional products in the cell.

Gene Signature: The expression pattern (either more or less) of a specific small set of genes that is significantly correlated with occurrence of disease.

Microarray: An experimental tool for measuring the gene expression.

mRNA: Messenger RNA is synthesized to decode the information contained in the genes and in turn serves as a template for the synthesis of the protein.

Parkinson's Disease: Neurological disorder that affects the brain and interferes with various processes involved in muscle coordination required for movement.

Principal Component Analysis: Orthogonal transformation of a set of possibly correlated variables to a set of variables called principal components. The computed principal components allow for most of the variance within the sample.

Prognosis Tool: A tool that can classify microarray data as either normal or diseased and can thus predict whether the patient from whom the microarray sample is produced is likely to develop the disease.

Volterra Series: Equation used to model the nonlinear behavior of a system.

Chapter 10
Detection of Cancer from Microscopic Biopsy Images Using Image Processing Tools

Rajesh Kumar
Indian Institute of Technology, Banaras Hindu University, India

Rajeev Srivastava
Indian Institute of Technology, Banaras Hindu University, India

ABSTRACT

Presently, most cancer diagnosis is based on human visual examination of images in a qualitative manner. Human visual grading for microscopic biopsy images is very time-consuming, subjective, and inconsistent due to inter-and intra-observer variations. A more quantitative and reproducible approach for analyzing biopsy images is highly desired. In biopsy images, the characteristics of nuclei are the key to estimate the degree of malignancy. The microscopic biopsy images always suffer from the problem of impurities, undesirable elements, and uneven exposure. Thus, there is a need of an automatic cancer diagnosis system based on microscopic biopsy images using image-processing tools. Therefore, the cancer and its type will be detected in a very early stage for complete treatment and cure. This system helps pathologists to improve the accuracy and efficiency in detection of malignancy and to minimize the inter observer variation. In addition, the method may help physicians to analyze the image cell by using classification and clustering algorithms by staining characteristics of the cells. The various image-processing steps involved for cancer detection from biopsy images include acquisition, enhancement, segmentation, feature extraction, image representation, classification, and decision-making. With the help of image, processing tools the sizes of cells, nuclei, and cytoplasm as well as the mean distance between two nearest neighboring nuclei are estimated by the system.

DOI: 10.4018/978-1-4666-4558-5.ch010

INTRODUCTION

Cancer is one of the most dangerous diseases of the human body. It is the uncontrolled growth of abnormal cells anywhere in the body. The abnormal cell is considered as either a malignant cell or tumor. The cancer is nothing but an advance stage of tumor. Cancer is easier to treat and cure if it has diagnosed early. There are about 200 types of cancer according to national cancer institute. This chapter provides the basic cancer detection techniques as well as advanced cancer diagnostic methodology with new and accurate techniques for detection of cancer from microscopic biopsy images.

What is Cancer?

Cancer is nothing but an advance stage of tumor. Cancer is easier to treat and cure if it has been diagnosed early. All cancers begin in cells, the body's basic unit of life. To understand cancer, it is helpful to know what happens when normal cells become cancer cells. Many types of cells make the body. These cells grow and divide in a controlled way to produce more cells as they needed to keep the body healthy. When cells are becoming old or damaged, are died and replaced by new cells. However, sometimes this orderly process goes wrong. The genetic material (DNA) of a cell can be damaged or changed, producing mutations that affect normal cell growth and division. See Figure 1. When this happens, cells do not die when they should and new cells form when the body does not need them. The extra cells may form a mass of tissue called a tumor. Malignant tumors are cancerous. Cells in these tumors can invade nearby tissues and spread to other parts of the body. The spread of cancer from one part of the body to another part of the body called metastasis. Some cancers do not form tumors. For example, leukemia is a cancer of the bone marrow and blood.

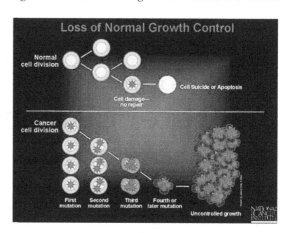

Figure 1. Understanding cancer mutation: cancer

Types of Cancer

There are about 200 type of cancer according to national cancer institute. Most of the cancer falls in following categories.

Carcinoma

The most common types of cancer arise from the cells that cover external and internal body surfaces. Lung, breast, and colon are the most frequent cancers of this type of cancer begin in the skin or tissues that line or cover internal organs.

Sarcoma

This type of cancer begins in the bones, Cartilage, fat, mussels, and blood vessels or other connectives or supportive tissues.

Leukemia

This type of cancer starts in forming blood forming tissue, such as bone marrow and causes a large number of abnormal blood cells.

Lymphoma and Myeloma

This type of Cancer begins in cell of immune systems.

Central Nervous System Cancers

This type of cancer begins in the tissues of the brain and spinal cord.

Traditional Techniques for Cancer Detection

The established technique for cancer imaging, both screening and diagnostic, is film-screen Mammography. Using film-screen mammography it is possible to detect about 85% of cancers and find these at an early enough stage to reduce mortality by approximately 50%. Mammography is the most commonly used imaging technique today throughout the world. When a patient undergoes a mammography, a beam of X-rays traverses the breast and creates a projected image on a film.

MRI Imaging

Cancer Diagnosis with High Field MRI (1.5T)

Magnetic resonance imaging uses radio waves and magnetic fields to diagnose diseases. Patients are asked to lie on a table during the test, which takes about 30 minutes. They are then advanced into the MRI machine, which contains a very strong magnetic field. The method consists of injecting a contrast enhancing dye-like material into the patient's bloodstream and using magnetic resonance imaging to monitor the way in which this material is taken up and cleared out by the tumor tissue. The ability to identify a mass in the breast requires that the mass has a different appearance (or a different contrast) from normal tissue. With MRI, the contrast between soft tissues in the breast is 10 to 100 times greater than

that obtained with x-rays (several studies have indicated that MRI can detect cancers that are not seen on mammography). The main disadvantage of breast MRI is its cost, which is about 5 times that of X-ray mammography.   .

MR Guided Biopsy with Open Systems (Mid-Field)

Open configuration MR imaging systems consists of a low-field (0.5T) superconducting magnet of an open configuration that allows access to the interventional field. The system was built with the major goal of guiding therapies: imaging may be performed during the procedure, in nearly real-time. This means that the radiologist can select the image plane during the procedure, before and during needle advancement.

Those systems are still in the experimental stage, are very expensive, and very few are actually in use throughout the world.

Digital Imaging

In digital imaging, the digital image is formed when a detector absorbs the x-rays and converts them to an electrical signal corresponding to each pixel. When images are digitally acquired and displayed, film is eliminated. This eliminates the expense, time and effort, for film processing.

Stereotactic Imaging

Stereotactic breast biopsy procedures are the only currently commercially available digital Mammography technology. Stereotactic biopsy systems use small-field digital detectors, and offer radiologists the ability to target a lesion discovered during mammography, to accurately place a needle into its center, and to remove tissue samplings. With Stereotactic biopsy, the patient has an opportunity for a less costly, less invasive, and more cosmetically acceptable procedure that she has with excisional biopsy.

Full Field Digital Mammography

When available, these will be considerably more expensive than film-screen imaging systems. The National Cancer Institute predicted that digital mammography is "the evolving technology with the greatest potential impact on management of breast cancer". The challenge for FFDM is to provide high-resolution, high-contrast images with the lowest possible radiation dose to the patient.

Single Energy X-ray Technique

This new method is called Diffraction-Enhanced Imaging (DEI). It creates significantly sharper, more detailed pictures of breast tissue, which could dramatically improve the efficacy of mammography. The new imaging method uses a single-energy X-ray source. This method is still experimental, and a lot of work needs to be done before it can be used with patients.

3D Digital Reconstruction

This 3D technique is an adaptation of a digital technology used in hospitals all over the world to guide needle biopsies to diagnose breast cancer. Stereotactic breast biopsy tables with digital detectors are commonly used to image the breast and guide the probes that obtain tissue samples. The image quality of these systems is very good, and the adapted systems can create three-dimensional or two-dimensional images of the breast. This technique can improve the accuracy of mammographic diagnoses.

Tomosynthesis

In the tomosynthesis method, multiple images are acquired as the x-ray tube is moved in an arc above the stationary breast and digital detector. the total radiation dose required for imaging the entire breast being approximately equal to the dose used for a single film-screen mammogram.

By shifting and adding the images, it is possible to bring any plane of the breast into sharp focus. Tomosynthesis has the potential to improve the specificity of mammography by reducing the contribution of normal fibro glandular breast to mask the presence of a lesion. The potential benefit will be largest in women with radio graphically dense breasts.

Computer-Aided Diagnosis

Digital mammography also offers advantages that are possible with linkage to computer aided Diagnosis (CAD) systems, because the digital information is available in a format that is usable by CAD systems. CAD may be possible with FFDM serving almost as a "second reader". The computer may automatically draw a border around areas of abnormal contrast, calling the radiologist's attention to suspicious regions. Other software techniques use pattern recognition and small object detection to detect micro calcifications in digitized mammograms.

Ultrasound Imaging

High Frequency Sonography

Sonography has the ability to demonstrate margins and internal texture, often more fully than mammography. Most importantly, this makes it possible to diagnose simple cysts within the breast. In many patients sonography also makes it possible to increase or decrease suspicion that lesions is malignant and to more accurately map the extent of tumor within the breast than is possible with mammography.

Vascular Imaging: Doppler, Power Doppler, Color Doppler

Carcinomas of the breast show remarkable changes of vascularity, which are essential for their Enhanced metabolism. Doppler imaging allows investigating normal and pathological vascularization in the breast. The technique is non-invasive, fast and easy. Color is used to encode blood velocity or volume.

Contrast Imaging

Ultrasound contrast imaging is a recent technique in which a "contrast agent" consisting in gas micro bubbles is injected intravenously. The micro bubbles act as echo-enhancers which cause the received signal to be longer and greater in the cancers than in the benign lesions. The cancers also display characteristic vascular morphologic features, with more additional vessels visualized in relation to the lesion. Contrast imaging can be effectively used with vascular imaging. The signal-to-noise ratio is markedly improved, and diagnostic confidence is increased. Ultrasound imaging using micro bubble contrast agents will definitely open up new opportunities.

Sonoelasticity

It is the use of ultrasonography to visualize in real time the hardness or stiffness of tissues and organs by depicting the tissue's motion in response to an applied vibration source. As a result, hard or dense tumors that are undetectable by conventional ultrasonography often can be visualized in sonoelasticity imaging by virtue of their altered vibration response.

Nuclear Imaging

PET Imaging

With PET, patients are injected with a glucose that has been labeled with a radioactive tracer. Cells that are undergoing more metabolic activity, such as sites of infection and cancer, will take up more glucose. Positron radioactivity emitted by the radio labeled glucose is recorded by a PET camera, processed and reconstructed by computer so that the areas of greatest metabolic

activity light up on a computer-generated image, which is much like a conventional CT scan. Due to its high cost and the limited availability of the traced isotope, widespread use of PET scanning is unlikely. PET imaging also allows doctors to predict within about a week of starting hormone therapy if women will likely respond (doctors would normally wait several months for signs of tumor shrinkage). In some countries, a PET scan is required to determine whether a cancer has spread before a patient undergoes surgery.

Sestamibi Imaging

The most frequently reported tracer applied to breast imaging has been Tc-99m-sestamibi. They are radioactive isotopes, often attached to biologically active molecules, and are usually injected into patients. These radiopharmaceuticals are designed to target the specific part of the body to by studied. A gamma camera is used to transform the radiopharmaceutical emissions into useful diagnostic images that illustrate both function and anatomy. Sestamibi scanning of the breast has only been shown to be effective in relatively large breast cancers, and its role in the diagnostic armamentarium of breast imagers remains established.

Bioelectric Imaging

This breast imaging technique is designed to assist in the detection of early stage tumors and precancerous lesions without X-rays or discomfort to the patient. Changes in cellular water content and cell membrane properties cause a significant change in tissue electrical impedance, enabling cancerous and precancerous lesions to be visualized in the image. Procedures resemble an ultra-sound with no physical discomfort nor radiation. The system should be particularly effective in detecting breast tumors in younger women (under the age of 50) who have denser breast tissue which cannot be readily examined wit traditional mammography.

Optical Diffusion Imaging

Imaging with light in the Near InfraRed (NIR) has gained increasing interest the last few years due to the very attractive potential of probing tissue oxygenation and metabolism, non-invasively, employing relatively low cost instrumentation and using non-ionizing radiation. Tissue has a low absorbing window in the NIR that allows light penetration of several centimeters employing laser power. The information obtained depends on the attenuation characteristics of breast tissues at visible and near-infrared wavelengths and can be used to determine tissue malignancy.

Tests on Blood and Other Samples

Cancer are also working on ways to test urine or other body fluids for the presence of a protein called MCM5, which can reveal cancer. The main issue with such tests is that there must be a clear difference between normal and cancerous samples.

Weaknesses of Present-Day Methods, and What Has Created the Need for New Methods

- Ability to read mammograms varies enormously among Radiologists.
- Mammography has a low specificity. The likelihood that a lesion found by mammography and sent to biopsy will be malignant is only 20 to 35%.
- Densities of tissues are similar and the lack of contrast often masks tumors. Problem with dense tissue, leads to decreased sensitivity.
- X-ray radiations are known to cause damage to DNA of cells.

Current Trends for Cancer Detection

Cancer Screening

Cancer screening detects cancers when they are at an early stage, or - in the case of cervical cancer screening - before they have developed. We know that screening saves thousands of lives each year. In the UK, we have three national screening programmers - for breast, cervical and bowel cancers.

Biopsy

A biopsy is the removal of a small amount of tissue for examination under a microscope. Other tests can suggest that cancer is present, but only a biopsy can make a definite diagnosis. A pathologist (a doctor who specializes in interpreting laboratory tests and evaluating cells, tissues, and organs to diagnose disease) analyzes the sample removed from the biopsy [33]. There are different types of biopsies, classified by the technique and/or size of needle used to collect the tissue sample.

Needle Biopsy

A biopsy uses a small needle to remove a small sample of cells.

Core Needle Biopsy

A core needle biopsy uses a larger needle to remove a larger sample of tissue. This is usually the preferred biopsy technique for finding out whether an abnormality on a physical examination or an imaging test is cancer. A vacuum-assisted biopsy removes more than one large core of tissue.

Surgical Biopsy

A surgical biopsy removes the largest amount of tissue. This biopsy may be incision (removal of part of the lump) or decisional (removal of the entire lump). Because definitive surgery is best done after a cancer diagnosis has been made, a surgical biopsy is usually not the recommended way to diagnose breast cancer. Most often, non-surgical core biopsies are recommended to diagnose breast cancer to keep surgery to one operation to remove the tumor if it is cancerous.

Image-Guided Biopsy

Image-guided biopsy is used when a distinct lump cannot be felt, but an abnormality is seen with an imaging test, such as a mammogram. During this procedure, a needle is guided to the location with the help of an imaging technique, such as mammography, ultrasound, or MRI. A stereotactic biopsy is done using mammography to help guide the needle. A small metal clip may be put into the breast to mark where the biopsy sample was taken, in case the tissue is cancerous and more surgery is needed. An image-guided biopsy can be done using a fine needle, core, or vacuum-assisted biopsy depending on the amount of tissue being removed.

RELATED WORK

Kanazawa et al., 1996 described Computer aided diagnosis system for lung cancer based on helical CT images. This technique will reduce the time complexity and increase the diagnosis confidence. This method consists of an analysis stage and a diagnosis stage. In the analysis stage, the lung and pulmonary blood vessel regions are extracted and examine the features of these regions with the help of image processing methods. In the diagnosis stage, diagnosis rules are determined according these features, and identify the tumor regions using these diagnosis rules.

Lin et al., 2002 provided a neural fuzzy model to formulate the diagnosis rules for identifying the pulmonary nodules. Initially, series of image processing methods like threshold, morphology closing, and labeling to segment the lung area and obtain the region of interest are used. Next, three main features such as circularity, size of area, and mean brightness are obtained from region of interest and the nodules are detected with diagnosis rules that are formed with the help of neural fuzzy model.

Armato et al., 2001 developed a fully automated computerized technique for the identification of lung nodules in helical computed tomography scans of the thorax. This technique is based on two-dimensional and three-dimensional analyses of the image data obtained during diagnostic CT scans. Lung segmentation carried out on a section-by-section process to create a segmented lung volume within which further analysis is carried out. Multiple gray-level thresholds are supplied to the segmented lung volume for producing a series of threshold lung volumes. An 18-point connectivity technique is implemented to detect contiguous three-dimensional structures within every threshold lung volume, and those structures that satisfy a volume criterion are chosen as initial lung nodule candidates. Morphological and gray-level features are calculated for every nodule candidate. After a rule-based technique is used to highly decrease the number of nodule candidates that corresponds to no nodules, the features of other candidates are combined through linear discriminate analysis.

The early detection and complete cure of cancer are the most challenging task for bio-medical researchers. Numerous studies have been carried out to analyze histopathological images for cancer detection. The morphological methods viz., thickness measurement, radius of curvature are proposed to analyze the normal, leukoplakia and OSF epithelium using histopathological images

(Jadhav et al., 2006; Pal et al., 2008). Textures based on wavelet (Lessmann et al., 2007; Qian et al., 2007; Sertel et al., 2008) have been used for early detection of lung cancer and neuroblastoma. Gabor filter based texture analysis was performed on mammography images and liver ultrasound images for breast and liver cancer detection (Ferrari et al., 2001; Wu et al., 1992). Other texture measures viz., fractal dimension, gray-level co-occurrence matrix (Marghani et al., 2003; Alexandratou et al., 2008; Wiltgen et al., 2007) were applied in textural classification of prostate and skin cancer. Gleason grading of prostate cancer was performed using combinations of morphological characteristics like area fraction, line length, and Euler number. The agreement of this method with visual diagnosis was 87.18% and 92.31% within the recognition of cancerous tissues from an image of a microscopic section based on the shape and the size analysis of the observed cells (Thiran & Macq, 1996). Estevez et al. designed pattern recognition system based on a Fuzzy Finite State Machine (FFSM) which was optimized by genetic algorithm. This system was used to classify normal and abnormal cells in cytological breast fine needle aspirate images and cytological peritoneal fluid images (Estevez et al., 2005). Krishnan et al. (2010b) performed a study on classifier improvement using Gaussian transformation of fractal and Brownian motion features. Al-Kadi (2010) extracted meningioma texture features by four different texture measures (model and statistical) and then corresponding features were fused together in different combinations after excluding highly correlated features to achieve higher accuracy.

According to the literature, very few automated systems for oral cancer detection using texture features are available (Krishnan et al., 2010a, 2011a). Paul et al. have used texture features using wavelet and classified normal and OSF images of transmission electron microscope with an accuracy of 95.73%. Recently, Brownian motion curve was used to depict the textural (fractal dimension)

variation of collagen fibres over normal and OSF groups. They obtained an accuracy of 96.43% using the neural network. An efficient nonparametric methodology for texture analysis based on LBP was used to extract useful information from medical images (Unay & Ekin, 2008). Unay and Ekin (2008) used LBP features from magnetic resonance images of brain. These features were used for content based image retrieval. Moreover, the authors showed that the texture with spatial context outperformed compared to intensity based texture features. Oliver et al. (2007) used LBP to extract salient micro-patterns from the mammographic masses and classified the benign and malignant masses using SVM. Experiments illustrated that LBP features were effective and efficient in the reduction of false positive even at different mass sizes. Laws masks (Gupta & Undrill, 1995; Petrou & Sevilla, 2006) are one of the widely used texture descriptors, and are used in various applications, including medical image analysis (Vince et al., 2000). In medical image analysis, they were used on intravascular ultrasound and dermatological images (Ananthaa et al., 2004). Most of the texture analyses require a filtering process to limit the influence of low-frequency variation due to soft tissue (Chappard et al., 2005). Generally, it is preferable to limit as far as possible the pre-treatment process, direct analysis offers the advantage of retaining the maximum information present in the images (Benhamou, 2007). The application of the Laws' masks requires no image pre-processing. This point constitutes one of the advantages of this technique.

Moreover, recent studies showed that Higher Order Spectra concept is useful to study the behaviour of heart and brain (Chandran et al., 1997). Higher Order Spectra invariants have been used for shape recognition and to identify different kinds of eye diseases (Acharya et al., 2008a,b; Chandran et al., 1997; Shao & Celenk, 2001). Figure 2 shows the typical normal, OSFWD and OSFD images as well as the proposed computational approach.

Figure 2. Steps involved in cancer detection from biopsy images using image processing tools

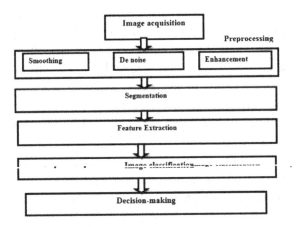

Morphological characteristics of the oral epithelial cells and tissues in 2-D histological sections were used for the histopathological diagnosis of oral premalignancy and malignancy. Cell-wise discriminant analysis using the morphometric parameters showed that 52% of the cells could be correctly classified into the original dysplasia grade (Abu-Eid & Landini, 2006). A quantitative analysis of the cyst lining architecture in radicular cysts (of inflammatory aetiology) and odontogenic keratocysts (OK) including its two counterparts: solitary and associated with the basal cell naevus syndrome was proposed (Landini, 2006). They obtained a correct discrimination of 66% (cross-validated values were 59, 60 and 82% for the solitary OK, syndrome OK and radicular cysts, respectively) for 3 classes using 150 samples. Recently, Krishnan et al. (2011a) have proposed the Brownian motion curve features for texture quantification of epithelium. They were able to classify (normal and OSFWD) the abnormalities with an accuracy of 88.83% and 96.43% using Linear Discriminant Analysis (LDA) and Back Propagation Neural Network respectively. Also, Krishnan et al. (2011c) have extracted five different texture measures (wavelet, LBP, Gabor wavelet, fractal dimension, and Brownian motion curve) and then fused them in different combina-

tions after excluding highly correlated features and achieved an accuracy of 88.38%. They have also compared the performance of HOS and LBP features for the classification of oral cancer stages (Krishnan et al., 2011d). Support vector machine classifier with HOS features was able to identify the abnormalities with an accuracy of 92.41%.

Jean-Philippe Thiran and Benoit Macq (1996), presents a new method for automatic recognition of cancerous tissues from an image of a microscopic section. Based on the shape and the size analysis of the observed cells, this method provides the physician with nonsubjective numerical values for four criteria of malignancy. This automatic approach is based on mathematical morphology, and more specifically on the use of Geodesy. This technique is used first to remove the background noise from the image and then to operate a segmentation of the nuclei of the cells and an analysis of their shape, their size and their texture. From the values of the extracted criteria, an automatic classification of the image (cancerous or not) is finally operated.

David G. Bostwick and Kenneth A. Iczkowski (1997) presented to increased clinical screening of men at risk for prostate cancer, and the realization of the benefits of performing multiple biopsies per prostate, have facilitated early detection of malignancy, while presenting the pathologist with a growing array of diagnostic findings. Interpretation of these findings requires discussion of the minimal criteria required for the diagnosis of cancer on needle biopsy within a wide spectrum of related histologic findings. This spectrum includes small acinar proliferations suspicious for but not diagnostic of cancer, benign mimics of cancer, the preinvasive entity of high-grade prostatic intraepithelial neoplasia, and various treatment effects.

Donal Downey, Jonathan Izawa, Joseph Chin, and Aaron Fenster (2006), describes the Biopsy of the prostate using 2D TransRectal UltraSound (TRUS) guidance is the current gold standard for diagnosis of prostate cancer; however, the current procedure is limited by using 2D biopsy tools to target 3D biopsy locations. We propose a technique for patient specific 3D prostate model reconstruction from a sparse collection of non-parallel 2D TRUS biopsy images. Our method conforms to the restrictions of current TRUS biopsy equipment and could be efficiently incorporated into current clinical biopsy procedures for needle guidance without the need for expensive hardware additions. In this paper, the model reconstruction technique is evaluated using simulated biopsy images from 3D TRUS prostate images of 10 biopsy patients. All reconstructed models are compared to their corresponding 3D manually segmented prostate models for evaluation of prostate volume accuracy and surface errors (both regional and global). The number of 2D TRUS biopsy images used for prostate modeling was varied to determine the optimal number of images necessary for accurate prostate surface estimation.

H. D. Cheng, Juan Shana, Wen Jua, Yanhui Guoa, and Ling Zhangb (2010), describes that breast cancer is the second leading cause of death for women all over the world. Since the cause of the disease remains unknown, early detection and diagnosis is the key for breast cancer control, and it can increase the success of treatment, save lives and reduce cost. Ultrasound imaging is one of the most frequently used diagnosis tools to detect and classify abnormalities of the breast. In order to eliminate the operator dependency and improve the diagnostic accuracy, Computer-Aided Diagnosis (CAD) system is a valuable and beneficial means for breast cancer detection and classification.

Lei He, L. Rodney Long, Sameer Antani, and George R. Thomas (2012), present an overview of the image analysis techniques in the domain of histopathology, specifically, for the objective of automated carcinoma detection and classification. As in other biomedical imaging areas such as radiology, many Computer Assisted Diagnosis (CAD) systems have been implemented to aid histopathologists and clinicians in cancer diagnosis and research, which have been attempted to significantly reduce the labor and subjectivity of traditional manual intervention with histology images. The task of automated histology image analysis is usually not simple due to the unique characteristics of histology imaging, including the variability in image preparation techniques, clinical interpretation protocols, and the complex structures and very large size of the images themselves. In this paper we discuss those characteristics, provide relevant background information about slide preparation and interpretation, and review the application of digital image processing techniques to the field of histology image analysis. In particular, emphasis is given to state-of-the-art image segmentation methods for feature extraction and disease classification. Four major carcinomas of cervix, prostate, breast, and lung are selected to illustrate the functions and capabilities of existing CAD systems.

This is an automatic cancer diagnosis system based on microscopic biopsy images using image-processing tools. Therefore, the cancer and its type will detect in very early stage for complete treatment and cure. This system helps pathologists to improve the accuracy, efficiency to detect malignancy and to minimize the inter observer variation. In addition, the method may help us to analyze the image cell by using classification and clustering algorithms by staining characteristics of the cells. Image processing tools are suitable for analyzing the biopsy images. The various image-processing steps involved for cancer detection from biopsy images include acquisition, enhancement, Segmentation, feature extraction, image representation, classification and decision-making. In this chapter an overview of the methods are proposed for the problem as discussed. In addition, we also proposed some new methods for the same. A prototype implemented and corresponding results have been discussed.

STEPS INVOLVED IN DETECTION OF CANCER FROM BIOPSY IMAGES USING IMAGE PROCESSING TOOL

There are six steps involved in detection of Cancerous images from biopsy. Image Acquisition, Pre-processing (Smoothing + Denoising +Enhancement), segmentation, feature extraction, classification and decision making, and the major steps in the image processing tools

Image Acquisition

In this work, Microscopic Biopsy images were obtained by taking the same acquisition and processing steps. The cancerous tissues will embedded in paraffin cubes after chemical processing and then cut into very thin sections. These sections were placed on glass slides and stained with colored dyes using hematoxylin and eosin solutions. Images were acquired by a set of equipment's including a high quality optical microscope, a high resolution CCD camera, and an image acquisition computer system. Each image was taken through a microscope with magnifying factor of 400. According to the characteristics for identifying HCC, the major features used for HCC grading are mainly related to nuclei; therefore, it is essential to segment nuclei from background of the image correctly. An HCC biopsy image may contain many undesirable elements such as erythrocyte, leukocyte, and impurities. Since nuclei/cells may be located in the upper or lower position of the tissue, not all nuclei/cells are focused very well at the same time. Moreover, nuclei and cytoplasm are not always transparent and the intensities in them are not always uniform. Therefore, if a segmentation method is directly applied to an HCC biopsy image without preprocessing, it will generate inaccurate edges for nuclei. To solve this problem, we propose a dual morphological gray scale reconstruction method to eliminate irrelevancies while preserving the shapes of nuclei in biopsy images.

Image Enhancement

Image enhancement refers to sharpening, of image features such as edge boundary or contrast to make the graphics display more useful for display and analysis. The enhancement process does not increase the inherent information contented in the biopsy images. Nevertheless, is increasing the dynamic range of chosen features so that they can be detected easily. Image enhancements includes gray level and contrast manipulations, noise reductions, edge christening and sharpening filtering, interpolation and magnification. The aim of image enhancement is to improve the interpretability or perception of information in images for human viewers, or to provide `better' input for other automated image processing techniques. Image enhancement techniques can be divided into two broad categories:

Spatial domain methods, which operate directly on pixels, and frequency domain methods, which operate on the Fourier transform of an image.

Unfortunately, there is no general theory for determining what `good' image enhancement is when it comes to human perception. If it looks good, it is good! However, when image enhancement techniques are used as pre-processing tools for other image processing techniques, then quantitative measures can determine which techniques are most appropriate. If it looks good, it is good. However, when image enhancement techniques are used as pre-processing tools for other image processing techniques, the quantitative measures can determine which techniques are most appropriate. Spatial domain methods the value of a pixel with coordinates (x, y) in the enhanced image $F^{\wedge}$ is the result of performing some operation on the pixels in the neighborhood of (x, y) in the input image, F. Neighborhoods can be any shape, but usually they are rectangular.

Grey Scale Manipulation

The simplest form of operation is when the operator T acts only on a 1×1 pixel neighborhood in the input image, that is F^(x, y) depends on the value of F only at (x, y). This is a grey scale transformation or mapping. The simplest case is threshold where the intensity profile is replaced by a step function, active at the chooses threshold value. In this case, any pixel with a gray level below the threshold in the input image gets mapped to the 0 in the output image other pixel are mapped to the 255.

Image Smoothing

The aim of image smoothing is to diminish the effects of camera noise, spurious pixel values, missing pixel values etc. There are many different techniques for image smoothing; we will consider neighborhood averaging and edge-preserving smoothing.

Neighborhood Averaging

Each point in the smoothed image, F^(x, y) is obtained from the average pixel value in a neighborhoods of (x, y) in the input image. For example, if we use a 3×3 neighborhood around each pixel we would use the mask:

1/9 1/9 1/9

1/9 1/9 1/9

1/9 1/9 1/9

Each pixel value is multiplied by 1/9, summed, and then the result placed in the output image. This mask is successively moved across the image until every pixel has been covered. That is, the image is convolved with this smoothing mask (also known as a spatial filter or kernel). However, one usually expects the value of a pixel to be more closely related to the values of pixels close to it than to those further away. This is because most points in an image are spatially coherent with their neighbors; indeed it is generally only at edge or feature points where this hypothesis is not valid. Accordingly it is usual to weight the pixels near the Centre of the mask more strongly than those at the edge. Some common weighting functions include the rectangular weighting function above (which just takes the average over the window), a triangular weighting function, or a Gaussian.

In practice, one does not notice much difference between different weighting functions, although Gaussian smoothing is the most commonly used. Gaussian smoothing has the attribute that the frequency components of the image are modified in a smooth manner. Smoothing reduces or attenuates the higher frequencies in the image. Mask shapes other than the Gaussian can do odd things to the frequency spectrum, but as far as the appearance of the image is concerned, we usually don't notice much.

Edge Preserving Smoothing

Neighborhood averaging or Gaussian smoothing will tend to blur edges because the high frequencies in the image are attenuated. An alternative approach is to use median filtering. Here we set the grey level to be the median of the pixel values in the neighborhoods of that pixel. The median m of a set of values is such that half the values in the set are less than m and half are greater. For example, suppose the pixel values in a 3×3 neighborhoods are (10, 20, 20, 15, 20, 20, 20, 25 and 100). If we sort the values we get (10, 15, 20, 20, j20j, 20, 20, 25, 100) and the median here is 20.

The outcome of median filtering is that pixels with outlying values are forced to become more like their neighbors, but at the same time edges are preserved. Of course, median filters are nonlinear. Median filtering is in fact a morphological operation. When we erode an image, pixel values are replaced with the smallest value in the neighborhood. Dilating an image corresponds to replacing pixel values with the largest value in the neighborhood. Median filtering replaces pixels with the median value in the neighborhood. It is the rank value of the pixel, used in the neighborhood that determines the type of morphological operation. A spatial filtering that has a high positive component at the Centre are used for sharpening is given by:

-1/9 -1/9 -1/9

-1/9 8/9 -1/9

-1/9 -1/9 -1/9

Since sum of all the weight is zero, the resulting signal will have a zero DC value (that is the average signal value of the coefficient of the zero frequency term in the Fourier expansion.

In the image enhancement stage we used the following three techniques: Gabor filter, Auto-enhancement, and Fast Fourier transform techniques.

Image Segmentation

Image segmentation refers to the decompositions of scene into its components. It is a key step of image processing. Segmentation divides an image into its constituent regions or objects. The segmentation of medical images in 2D, slice by slice has many useful applications for the medical professional: visualization and volume estimation of objects of interest, detection of Abnormalities (e.g. tumors, etc.), tissue quantification and classification, and more (H. D. Cheng, Juan Shana, Wen Jua, Yanhui Guoa, Ling Zhangb, 2010).

The goal of segmentation is to simplify and/or change the representation of an image into something that is more meaningful and easier to analyze. Image segmentation is typically used to locate objects and boundaries (lines, curves, etc.) in images. More precisely, image segmentation is the process of assigning a label to every pixel in an image such that pixels with the same label share certain visual characteristics. The result of image segmentation is a set of segments that collectively cover the entire image, or a set of contours extracted from the image (edge detection). Each of the pixels in a region is similar with respect to some characteristic or computed property, such as color, intensity, or texture. Adjacent regions are significantly different with respect to the same characteristic(s). There are two major segmentation approaches are used:

Boundary (Block)–Based Approaches

Boundary Extraction technique segments the objects based on their profiles. Thus contour following, connectivity, edge linking and graph searching, curve fitting, Hough transforms like techniques are applicable to image segmentation. The former divides high-resolution images, more than 2000×5000 pixels, using blocks of 100×100 pixels to focus the image characterization and analysis in these sub images separately. The later, split image in 64×64 pixels to analyze spatial relationships among sub-blocks using Hidden Markov Models. Note that the purposes of each strategy are completely different, from dividing the problem in many sub-problems to evaluating the influence of local features in its neighborhood. Another block-based segmentation strategy consists in divide the image in many sub-blocks of 9×9 pixels, randomly sampled from the histology image, to characterize the distribution of local features following a bag-of-features approach. This strategy does not take into account the spatial relationship between local features. The size of the blocks in these cases is related to the size of the objects or patterns that one can find in the histology image.

Region–Based Approaches

The main idea in the region based techniques is to identify various regions I the image that has similar features. One class of region-based techniques evolves region growing. The image is divided in to automatic regions of constant gray levels. Similar adjacent region are merged sequentially until the adjacent region became sufficiently different. The trick lies in selecting the criterion for merging. Instead of merging regions we can approach a segmentation problem by splitting the given region. Region based approach are generally less sensitive to the noise. Using thresholding, the algorithm can separate pixels in two classes that are set to be background and tissue. For being able to identify regions in more than two classes, the k-means clustering algorithm has been used by Sertel et al. They designed the algorithm to find 5 pixel classes, starting from the brighter, associated to background, to the darker, associated to cell nuclei. Kong et al. used a variation of the Expectation Maximization algorithm to cluster pixels following the same color distribution, and leading to a more precise segmentation. Be it the use of k-means or the EM algorithm, the color space selected to perform the analysis is La*b*. This color space is preferred, since small variations of the Euclidean distance in that space, lead to small.

Feature Extraction

Image features Extraction stage is an important stage that uses algorithms and techniques to detect and isolate various desired portions or shapes (features) of a given biopsy image. To predict the probability of cancer presence, the following methods are used.

Color

Color based features are important in histology applications since the biologists stain tissues to highlight special structures. The most common color space used to apply analysis in histology images is La*b*. Some segmentation rules can be applied on that color space, but also some features can be calculated when the particular region of interest has been already isolated. In microscopic biopsy images, features of homogeneity, energy, contrast and correlation are calcuated from a color, co-occurrence matrix representation. They are called the color texture features and are also used in.

Texture

Texture is the most used feature in histology image analysis. The following are some of the most used texture descriptors: 3.2.1 Haralick texture features Examples of histology applications using Haralick features can be found in. Not all the 14 Haralick features are used in practice, only some of them are calculated in real applications, usually up to the fourth.

Haralicks Texture Feature

These features are based on the gray level concurrences matrix G, as follows:

$$p(1,1)\ p(1,2)..\ p(1,Ng)$$

$$G=\quad p(2,1)\ p(2,2)..\ p(2,Ng)$$

$$p(Ng.1)\ p(Ng,2)..\ p(Ng,Ng)$$

Where Ng is total number of gray levels and p (i,j) is probabilities of obtaining the pixels with value i adjacent to the pixel with value j. With the help of given matrix G, Horlicks features like: Angular second moment, contrast, correlation, sum of square variants, Inverse difference moments, sum average, sum variance, sum entropy, entropy, difference variance, difference entropy measure of co relation 1, measure of correlation 2, Max correlation coefficients are detected .

Morphology

Pathologists usually describe many gland or cell characteristics in term of morphology so that they are meaningful in biopsy images feature extraction. The computations of these features are associated to segmented objects. The most common features are:

- **Area:** Number of pixels composing the object.
- **Perimeter:** Number of pixels in the frontier in the object.
- **Centroid:** Center of gravity coordinates.
- **Major and Minor Axis Length.**
- **Major Axis Direction:** Angular orientations of the line of best fits through center of gravity.
- **Size and Shape:** Of Cancer nuclei and gland.

Image Classification

After the features have been extracted and selected, they are input into a classifier to categorize the images into lesion/non-lesion or benign/malignant classes. Majority of the publications focuses on classifying malignant and benign lesions (usually called lesion classification), and some of the articles focus on classifying lesions and non-lesions (usually called lesion detection), and only a few of them focus on both. Lesion detection is necessary before lesion classification. Textures based on wavelet (Lessmann et al., 2007; Qian et al., 2007; Sertel et al., 2008) have been used for early detection of lung cancer and neuroblastoma. Gabor filter based texture analysis was performed on mammography images and liver ultrasound images for breast and liver cancer detection (Ferrari et al., 2001; Wu et al., 1992). Other texture measures viz., fractal dimension, gray-level co-occurrence matrix (et al., 2008; Wiltgen et al., 2007) were applied in textural classification of prostate and skin (Marghani et al., 2003) cancer.

In this paper, we present three classifiers, k-Nearest Neighbor (k-NN), Support Vector Machine (SVM), and SVM-based decision-graph classifiers, to grade HCC biopsy images. The k-NN classifier is well known among all nonparametric classifiers. The k-nearest neighbor decision rule classifies an observation by assigning it the label that is most frequently represented among the k-nearest neighbors. A decision is made by examining all the labels on the k-nearest neighbors and taking a vote. The following three basic steps can summarize the operation of a k-NN classifier: (Gupta & Undrill, 1995)

- Compute the distance between new sample and all previous samples already classified in to clusters.
- Sort the distance in to increasing order and select k samples with the smallest distance value.
- **Applying the Voting Principle:** A new sample is added (classified) to the cluster with the highest voting from the k selected samples.

The second classification techniques used in this paper for grading the biopsy images in the SVM method can be compared with traditional classification methods which minimize the empirical training error. The goal of SVM is to minimize the upper bound data. The theory of nonlinear SVM is described as follows.

Consider a training set of N samples in binary classification, each sample is denoted by a tuple (x_i, y_i), where $x_i = (x_{i1}, x_{i2}, x_{i3} \ldots x_{id})T$, corresponds to the feature vector of the ith sample ($i = 1, 2 \ldots N$), in d-dimensional space. And $y \in \{-1.1\}$, denotes its two class label. Any point x on hyper plane must be satisfy the decision boundary w.x+b=0; where parameter w normal to the hyper plane. Practically a nonlinear SVM is widely used for general case due to its non-linear mechanism that can effectively classify data which are non-separable by linear SVM. None linear SVM can be formulated by the following optimal problems:

$$Min_{w,b,\xi} = \frac{1}{2} \| w \|^2 + C\sum_{i=1}^{N} \xi i$$

Subject to:

$$yi((w.\Phi(xi) + b) >= 1 - \xi i, \xi i >= 0, \ i = 1,2,....N \tag{1}$$

Where the notation $\| . \|$ represents the normal of the vector. In the above objective function a training data xi is mapped to the higher dimensional space by kernel function.

And presently C is used specified parameter. By minimizing $(1/2)\|w\|2$ we can get the maximum margin between the separating hyper plane and the data. To reduce the number of training errors in linearly non-separable case the penalty term $C\sum_{i=0}^{n} \xi i$ consists of a number of positive valued stack variable ξi which can be used to construct a soft margin hyper plane. The test sample z can be classified according to the following equations.

$$f(z) = sign(w.\Phi(z) = b) =$$
$$sign(\sum_{i=1}^{N} \alpha i.yiK(xi, z) = b) \tag{2}$$

The test sample z is classified to the positive class if f(z)=+1; and is classified to the negative if if(z)=-1. In the above decision boundary equation a parameter αi are lagrange multiplier which can be obtained by using quadratic programming.

The computations of $\Phi(xi).\Phi(xj)$. (i.e. the dot product between the pair of vectors in the transformed state) is quite cumbersome and may suffer from the cause of dimensionality problems [37]. Since the kernel function k can be expressed as $K(xi, xj) = \Phi(xi).\Phi(xj)$. According to Mercre's theorem [37], the decision function of a nonlinear SVM can be written as:

$$f(z) = sign(\sum_{i=1}^{N} \alpha i.yiK(xi, z) + b) \tag{3}$$

We choose Radial Basic Function (RBF) as a kernel function for SVM due to following reason: (1)RBF kernel can handle the case where the data are not linearly separable . Besides, linear kernel is a special case of RBF kernel with specific parameters(C, Υ). (2)Compared with polynomial and sigmoid kernels, RBF kernel has fewer parameters, which need to be determined. (3) Sigmoid kernel is not valid under some parameters.

Decision Making

The accurate detection of cancerous cell from microscopic biopsy images using image-processing tools is important for prognosis and treatment of cancer. Visual detection by human being is time consuming, subjective and inconsistent while using image processing tools for detection of cancer from biopsy images is a complex task but it gives quick, objective and consistent result by which we can easily find out the level and grade of cancer.

CONCLUSION

We proposed interactive cancer detection from microscopic biopsy images using image-processing tools This system is a computer-aided system for automatically analyzing and correctly detection of cancer from biopsy images using image processing tools to provide quantitative, more objective, and consistent information for prognosis and treatment as well as planning. Therefore, the cancer and its type will detect in very early stage for complete treatment and cure. This system helps pathologists to improve the accuracy, efficiency to detect malignancy and to minimize the inter observer variation. In addition, the method may help us to analyze the image cell by using classification and clustering algorithms by staining characteristics of the cells. Image processing tools are suitable for analyzing the biopsy images. With the help of image, processing tools the sizes of cells, nuclei, and cytoplasm as well as the mean distance between two nearest neighboring of nuclei are estimated.

FUTURE DIRECTION FOR RESEARCH

The results come from the above applied tools are very helpful to the doctors and pathologists. Because it automatically determine whether the cells are cancerous. If the cells are cancerous, the biopsy results can tell your doctor where the cancer originated and the type of cancer. A biopsy also helps your doctor determine how aggressive your cancer is the cancer's grade. The grade is sometimes expressed as a number on a scale of 1 to 4, and is determined by how cancer cells look under the microscope. Grade 1, or low-grade, cancers are generally the least aggressive and grade 4, or high-grade, cancers, generally the most aggressive. This information may help guide treatment options. Other special tests on the cancer cells also can help to guide treatment choices. In certain cases, such as during surgery, a pathologist examines the sample of cells immediately and results are available to your surgeon within minutes. But in most cases, the results of your biopsy are available in one or two days. Some samples may need more time to be analyzed.

REFERENCES

Abu-Eid, R., & Landini, G. (2003). Quantification of the global and local complexity of the epithelial-connective tissue interface of normal, dysplastic, and neoplastic oral mucosae using digital imaging. *Pathology, Research and Practice*, *199*, 475–482. doi:10.1078/0344-0338-00448 PMID:14521264.

Abu-Eid, R., & Landini, G. (2006). Oral epithelial dysplasia: Can quantifiable morphological features help in the grading dilemma? In *Proceedings of First Image User and Developer Conference* (149-154). New York: ACM Press.

Asli, Selim, & Sevgen. (2012). Unsupervised segmentation and classification of cervical cell images. *Pattern Recognition*, *45*, 4150–4168.

Bostwick, G., & Iczkowski, K. (1997)...*Annals of Diagnostic Pathology*, *1*(2), 104–229. doi:10.1016/S1092-9134(97)80015-9 PMID:9869832.

Burak, Melih, Cenk, & Gunbuz. (2009). Object oriented texture analysis for the unsupervised segmentation of biopsy images for cancer detection. *Pattern Recognition*, *42*, 1104–1112. doi:10.1016/j.patcog.2008.07.007.

Chandran, V., Carswell, B., Boashash, B., & Elgar, S. L. (1997). Pattern recognition using invariants defined from higher order spectra: 2-D image inputs. *IEEE Transactions on Image Processing*, *6*, 703–712. doi:10.1109/83.568927 PMID:18282963.

Cheng, H. D., Shan Juan, Ju Wen, Guo Yanhui, & Zhang Ling. (2010). Automated breast cancer detection and classification using ultrasound images: A survey. *Pattern Recognition*, *43*, 299–317. doi:10.1016/j.patcog.2009.05.012.

Cool, Downey, & Izawa, Chin, & Fenster. (2006). D prostate model formation from non-parallel 2D ultrasound biopsy images. *Medical Image Analysis*, *10*, 875–887. doi:10.1016/j.media.2006.09.001 PMID:17097333.

Ferrari, R. J., Rangayyan, R. M., Desautels, J. E. L., & Frere, A. F. (2001). Analysis of asymmetry in mammograms via directional filtering with gabor wavelets. *IEEE Transactions on Medical Imaging*, *20*(9), 953–964. doi:10.1109/42.952732 PMID:11585211.

Gupta, R., & Undrill, P. E. (1995). The use of texture analysis to delineate suspicious masses in mammography. *Physics in Medicine and Biology*, *40*(5), 835–855. doi:10.1088/0031-9155/40/5/009 PMID:7652011.

Han, J., Kamber, M., & Pei, J. (2005). *Data mining: Concepts and techniques*. New York: Morgan Kaufmann.

Haralick, R. M., Sternberg, S. R., & Zhuang, X. (1987). Image analysis using methametical morphology. *IEEE Transactions on Pattern Analysis and Machine Intelligence*, *9*, 532–550. doi:10.1109/TPAMI.1987.4767941 PMID:21869411.

Krishnan, M. M. R., Acharya, U. R., Chakraborty, C., & Ray, A. K. (2011). Automated diagnosis of oral cancer using higher order spectra features and local binary pattern: A comparative study. *Technology in Cancer Research & Treatment*, *10*, 433–455. PMID:21895029.

Krishnan, M. M. R., Choudhary, A., Chakraborty, C., & Ray, A. K. (2011). Texture based segmentation of epithelial layer from oral histological images. *Micron (Oxford, England)*, *42*, 632–641. doi:10.1016/j.micron.2011.03.003.

Krishnan, M. M. R., Shah, P., Chakraborty, C., & Ray, A. K. (2010). Statistical analysis of textural features for improved classification of oral histopathological images. *Journal of Medical Systems*. doi: doi:10.1007/s10916-010-9550-8.

Krishnan, M. M. R., Shah, P., Chakraborty, C., & Ray, A. K. (2011). Brownian motion curve based textural classification and its application towards cancer diagnosis. *Analytical and Quantitative Cytology and Histology*, *33*(3), 158–168. PMID:21980619.

Krishnan, M. M. R., Shah, P., Choudhary, A., Chakraborty, C., Paul, R. R., & Ray, A. K. (2011). Textural characterization of histopathological images for oral sub-mucous fibrosis detection. *Tissue & Cell*; Epub ahead of print. PMID:21824635.

Krishnan, M. M. R., Shah, P., Pal, M., Chakraborty, C., Paul, R. R., Chatterjee, J., & Ray, A. K. (2010). Structural markers for normal oral mucosa and oral sub-mucous fibrosis. *Micron (Oxford, England)*, *41*(4), 312–320. doi:10.1016/j.micron.2009.12.002.

Kujan, O., Oliver, R. J., Khattab, A., Roberts, S. A., Thakker, N., & Sloan, P. (2006). Evaluation of a new binary system of grading oral epithelial dysplasia for prediction of malignant transformation. *Oral Oncology*, *42*(10), 987–993. doi:10.1016/j.oraloncology.2005.12.014 PMID:16731030.

Landini, G. (2006). Quantitative analysis of the epithelial lining architecture in odontogenic cysts. *Head & Face Medicine*, 2–4. PMID:16420691.

Landini, G., & Othman, I. E. (2003). Estimation of tissue layer level by sequential morphological reconstruction. *Journal of Microscopy*, *209*(2), 118–125. doi:10.1046/j.1365-2818.2003.01113.x PMID:12588529.

Landini, G., & Othman, I. E. (2004). Architectural analysis of oral cancer, dysplastic, and normal epithelium. *Cytometry. Part A*, *61*(1), 45–55. doi:10.1002/cyto.a.20082.

Landini, G., & Othman, I. E. (2005). Quantification of local architecture changes associated with neoplastic progression in oral epithelium using graph theory. *Fractals in Biology and Medicine*, *IV*(Part 3), 193–201. doi:10.1007/3-7643-7412-8_18.

Lessmann, B., Nattkemper, T. W., Hans, V. H., & Degenhard, A. (2007). A method for linking computed image features to histological semantics in neuropathology. *Journal of Biomedical Informatics*, *40*, 631–641. doi:10.1016/j.jbi.2007.06.007 PMID:17698418.

Marghani, K. A., Dlay, S. S., Sharif, B. S., & Sims, A. (2003). Morphological and texture features for cancers tissues microscopic images. *Medical Imaging and Image Processing*, (5032), 1757–1764.

Oliver, A., Lladó, X., Freixenet, J., & Martí, J. (2007). False positive reduction in mammographic mass detection using local binary patterns. In *Proceedings of the Medical Image Computing and Computer-assisted Intervention* (286–293). Toronto: Springer.

Pal, M., Chaudhuri, S. R., Jadav, A., Banerjee, S., Paul, R. R., & Chaudhuri, K. et al. (2008). Quantitative dimensions of histopathological attributes and status of GSTM1-GSTT1 in oral submucous fibrosis. *Tissue & Cell*, *40*(6), 425–436. doi:10.1016/j.tice.2008.04.003 PMID:18573513.

Po-Whei & Yan-Hao. (2010). Effevtive segmentation and classification of HCC biopsy images. *Pattern Recognition*, *43*, 1550–1563. doi:10.1016/j.patcog.2009.10.014.

Qian, W., Zhukov, T., Song, D. S., & Tockman, M. S. (2007). Computerized analysis of cellular features and biomarkers for cytologic diagnosis of early lung cancer. *Analytical and Quantitative Cytology and Histology*, *29*, 103–111. PMID:17484274.

Sertel, O., Kong, J., Shimada, H., Catalyurek, U., Saltz, J. H., & Gurcan, M. (2008). Computer-aided prognosis of neuroblastoma: Classification of stromal development on whole-slide images. *Medical Imaging: Computer-Aided Diagnosis*, (6915), 9150–9151.

Shao, Y., & Celenk, M. (2001). Higher-order spectra (HOS) invariants for shape recognition. *Pattern Recognition*, *34*, 112097–112113. doi:10.1016/S0031-3203(00)00148-5.

Thiran & Macq. (1996). Morphological feature extraction for the classification of digital images of cancerous tissues. *IEEE Transactions on Bio-Medical Engineering*, *43*(10), 111–120.

Unay, D., & Ekin, A. (2008). Intensity versus texture for medical image search and retrieval. In *Proceedings of the 5th IEEE International Symposium on Biomedical Imaging: From Nano to Macro* (241–244). Washingtong, DC: IEEE Press.

Vince, D. G., Dixon, K. J., Cothren, R. M., & Cornhill, J. F. (2000). Comparison of texture analysis methods for the characterization of coronary plaques in intravascular ultrasound images. *Computerized Medical Imaging and Graphics*, *24*, 221–229. doi:10.1016/S0895-6111(00)00011-2 PMID:10842046.

Vincent, L. (1993). Morphological gray scale reconstruction in image analysis: Application and efficient algorithms. *IEEE Transactions on Image Processing*, *2*, 176–201. doi:10.1109/83.217222 PMID:18296207.

Wiltgen, M., Gerger, A., Wagner, C., Bergthaler, P., & Smolle, J. (2007). Evaluation of texture features in spatial and frequency domain for automatic discrimination of histologic tissue. *Analytical and Quantitative Cytology and Histology*, *29*, 251–263. PMID:17879634.

KEY TERMS AND DEFINITIONS

Adenocarcinoma: An adenocarcinoma is a type of carcinoma that starts in glandular tissue (tissue that makes and secretes a substance).

Biopsy: A biopsy is a procedure to remove a piece of tissue or a sample of cells from your body so that it can be analyzed in a laboratory.

Carcinoma: This is a term used to describe a cancer that begins in the lining layer (epithelial cells) of organs like the breast.

Core Needle Biopsy: A larger needle with a cutting tip is used during core needle biopsy to draw a column of tissue out of a suspicious area.

Fibrosis and Cysts: Most lumps turn out to be caused by fibrosis and/or cysts, benign changes in the breast tissue that happen in many women at some time in their lives. (This is sometimes called *fibrocystic changes* and used to be called *fibrocystic disease*.)

Lymph Nodes: Lymph nodes are small, bean-shaped collections of immune system cells (cells that are important in fighting infections) that are connected by lymphatic vessels.

Malignant Tumor: A malignant tumor is a group of cancer cells that can grow into (invade) surrounding tissues or spread (metastasize) to distant areas of the body.

Sarcoma: Sarcomas are cancers that start in connective tissues such as muscle tissue, fat tissue, or blood vessels.

Segmentation: Segmentation is the process of partitioning the image in to meaningful regions based on having similar behavior of pixels.

Chapter 11
Digital Image Watermarking:
Impact on Medical Imaging Applications in Telemedicine

Ruchira Naskar
Indian Institute of Technology Kharagpur, India

Rajat Subhra Chakraborty
Indian Institute of Technology Kharagpur, India

Dev Kumar Das
Indian Institute of Technology Kharagpur, India

Chandan Chakraborty
Indian Institute of Technology Kharagpur, India

ABSTRACT

With the advent of telemedicine, Digital Rights Management of medical images has become a critical issue pertaining to security and privacy preservation in the medical industry. The technology of telemedicine makes patient diagnosis possible for physicians located at a remote site. This technology involves electronic transmission of medical images over the internet, thus raising the need for ensuring security and privacy of such information. Digital watermarking is a widely used technique for the authentication and protection of multimedia data such as images and video against various security and privacy threats. But such digital rights management practices as watermarking often lead to considerable distortion or information loss of the medical images. The medical images being highly sensitive and legally valuable assets of the medical industry, such information loss are often not tolerable. Most importantly, such information loss may lead to incorrect patient diagnosis or reduced accuracy of disease detection. In this chapter we investigate the impact of digital watermarking, and its effect on the accuracy of disease diagnosis, specifically diagnosis of malarial infection caused by Plasmodium vivax parasite. We have used a computer–aided, automatic diagnostic model for our work in this chapter. Our experimental results show that although general (lossy) digital watermarking reduces the diagnostic accuracy, it can be improved with the use of reversible (lossless) watermarking. In fact, the adverse effect(s) of watermarking on the diagnostic accuracy can be completely mitigated through the use of reversible watermarking.

DOI: 10.4018/978-1-4666-4558-5.ch011

INTRODUCTION

Telemedicine (Stanberry, 2001) is the technology dealing with electronic transmission of medical images, from one location to another remote location, for the purpose of interpretation of those images by physicians, clinical experts, as well as medical researchers, at the remote location. Pathological patient imaging, radiological patient imaging and nuclear patient imaging, are some of the significant medical imaging techniques contributing to telemedicine. Over the past few decades, telemedicine has evolved from the need to improve the existing quality of health care services to patients. With the help of telemedicine, physicians are able to extend medical diagnostic help to patients in a remote location. This technique removes the required constraint of pathologist, physicians, or even surgeons, to be present at the same location as the patient for correct medical diagnosis and treatment. Telemedicine allows the patient images to be analyzed and interpreted at a remote location, and the test reports to be electronically sent back to the patient's location.

In telemedicine, the medical images of a patient are often transmitted across the world, often over public communication infrastructure such as the internet, and thus such communications are often insecure. Due to regular transmission of medical images in large numbers, issues of security and privacy preservation have arisen in the medical industry. Thus, a major concern of the present day medical industry is to maintain the security and privacy of medical information (Eid, 1995). Therefore, with the advent of telemedicine, Digital Rights Management (DRM) of medical images has become a necessity in the present day medical industry.

DRM has been in wide use over the past couple of decades, for content protection and authentication of security sensitive medical data. One significant instance of DRM, often used to protect such security sensitive medical images, is Digital Watermarking. However, sometimes the acts of DRM, specifically watermarking, causes some information loss of the medical images. In most cases, medical images and their integrity are assets of high legal value for the patients as well as hospitals. Therefore, such medical information losses are ideally highly undesirable, many times due to legal causes.

An example from the medical industry will clearly demonstrate how distortions are induced into medical images, due to watermarking. Most hospitals today, maintain patient records in form of digital data. Patient records include results of clinical tests, as well as patients' personal information such as medical history. In hospitals patients' personal information or medical history, also known as Electronic Patient Records (EPRs) (Berger & Cepelewicz, 1996) are used by professionals such as doctors, clinical researchers and insurance companies. Many times, the EPRs are kept embedded in form of watermark, into medical images, for example ultrasonography, Computed Tomography (CT), and Magnetic Resonance Images (MRI). This causes some distortion of the medical images. Moreover, patient records change over time, and this phenomenon requires the embedded EPRs to be updated from time to time. Repeated extraction and embedding of EPRs, in order to update them, causes the distortion of the medical images to accumulate. Such cumulative distortion effects adversely affect the quality of the medical images, so that it becomes difficult to make the correct diagnosis.

Our goal in this chapter is to investigate the effects of DRM on sensitive medical information, specifically, the effects of digital watermarking on medical image interpretation and disease diagnosis. In this chapter we carry out a computer–aided, automated diagnosis of malarial infection from a set of patient blood smear images, and investigate the effects of digital watermarking on those images, in terms of diagnostic accuracy. In summary, we investigate the impact of digital watermarking, on automated diagnosis of malarial infection.

Rest of the chapter has been organized as follows. In Section Background we present the required background related to digital watermarking, as well as the existing techniques for automated diagnosis systems for malaria. In Section Investigation Methodology we describe our malarial infection diagnostic system along with an experiment carried out to demonstrate the effect of watermarking on the accuracy of malaria diagnosis. Our experimental results have been presented in Section Results. Finally, we present some future research directions in Section Future Research Directions and conclude the chapter in Section Conclusion.

BACKGROUND

In this section we present the necessary background related to (a) digital watermarking, and (b) computer–aided automatic diagnosis of malaria.

Digital Watermarking

Digital watermarking (Cox et al., 2000; Wang et al., 2000) is the act of hiding information in multimedia data (images, audio, or video), for the purpose of content protection or authentication. In digital watermarking, the secret information (usually in the form of a bit stream), the watermark, is embedded into a multimedia data (cover data), in such a way that distortion of the cover data due to watermarking is almost negligible perceptually. General application domains of digital watermarking include broadcast monitoring, owner identification, transaction tracking, content authentication, copy control and many more.

In general, watermarking systems are lossy, that is, a minimum distortion or information–loss of the cover data is bound to occur due to watermark embedding. A primary requirement of general watermarking systems is imperceptibility, that is, the distortion of the cover data caused due to watermarking should be minimal and the water-mark should be perceptually negligible. (However a special class of watermarking, known as the visible or perceptual watermarking [Cox et al., 2000], demands that the watermark embedded into the cover data be perceptible.) In application domains such as the medical industry, where data integrity is of utmost importance, the cover data distortion introduced due to watermarking is intolerable, however minimal or perceptually negligible the distortion is.

Least Significant Bit (LSB) substitution based watermarking is the most widely used, computationally simple method of general watermarking. In LSB–substitution based watermark embedding algorithm, the cover image pixels are scanned sequentially, and the LSB of each pixel is substituted by the next watermark bit to be embedded. While extraction, the watermark bits are extracted sequentially from the LSB positions of the cover image pixels. But the original cover image pixel LSBs, once substituted, are permanently lost in the process. Hence LSB–substitution based watermarking is a lossy watermarking algorithm.

However, another class of digital watermarking, called the reversible watermarking (Feng et al., 2006), allows complete recovery of original cover data information from the watermarked data. In reversible watermarking, the original cover data can be restored back to its original form, bit–by–bit, after watermark extraction. This class of watermarking is useful in applications dealing with highly sensitive data, where integrity of data is of utmost importance. Apart from the medical industry, other application domains of reversible watermarking are the military and legal industries. In general, the watermark embedded into the cover data by reversible watermarking is a keyed hash of the cover data. Thus, the purpose of reversible watermarking is two–fold: (1) authentication of cover data, (2) distortion–free recovery of the cover data after watermark extraction. Several classes of reversible watermarking algorithms have been proposed in the past decade, the most commonly studied among them are based on Difference

Expansion (Tian, 2003), Histogram Bin Shifting (Ni et al., 2006), Pixel Value Interpolation (Luo et al., 2010), Integer DCT (Yang at al., 2004), and so forth.

In this chapter, we investigate the impact of digital watermarking, both general and reversible, on malarial infection diagnostic accuracy by an automatic diagnostic model. The effects of both the approaches have been shown in Section Results.

Automated Diagnosis of Malaria

In the last few decades, malaria has become a leading cause of death worldwide, having caused 1.5-2.7 million deaths per year (Raviraja et al., 2008), more significantly in the sub–African and Asian countries (Frean, 2010). In today0s diagnostic circumstances, pathologists diagnose malarial infection from peripheral blood smear images, under microscope, based on their clinicopathological knowledge and expertise. This manual procedure is error–prone as well as time–consuming and tedious. To reduce the error probability and time complexity of malaria diagnosis, computer–assisted, automated diagnostic systems are being developed, which automatically detect malarial infection from peripheral blood smear images with a high degree of prediction accuracy.

The present state–of–the–art for the existing automatic malaria diagnosis approaches can be traced from the following works. A quantification and classification scheme for *Plasmodium falciparum* infected erythrocytes has been presented in (Diaz et al., 2009). Tek et al. proposed a color histogram based malaria parasite detection in (Tek et al., 2006). A gray level thresholding technique for malaria parasite detection was used in (Toha & Ngah, 2007). Further, Ross et al. (Ross et al., 2006) used a morphological thresholding technique for identification of malaria infected erythrocytes. Makkapati and Rao (2009) proposed segmentation in the HSV (Hue Saturation Value) color space for the identification of malaria parasite. A mathematical morphology and granulometry based approach

for the estimation of malarial parasitemia was proposed in Dempster & Ruberto (1999).

In this chapter, we deal specifically with the diagnosis of Malaria caused by *Plasmodium vivax*. We have used the morphological and textural information based probabilistic model, recently proposed by in (Das et al., 2011). Our experimental procedure has been presented in Section Investigation Methodology.

INVESTIGATION METHODOLOGY

Watermark Embedding and Extraction

In our work, first the original test images were subjected to the automated diagnosis system, and the prediction accuracy was measured. Next, the same images were watermarked using a LSB-substitution (Wang et al., 2000) based general watermarking algorithm. We considered the watermark to be a stream of bits, and substituted the LSBs of the test image pixels by the watermark bits, sequentially. The automatic malarial infection prediction mechanism was then applied to the watermark extracted test images, which contain the residual distortions caused due to the lossy watermarking, and the prediction accuracy was again noted.

In the second phase of our work, the same set of original, undistorted images were reversibly watermarked using the interpolation–based reversible watermarking algorithm, proposed in (Luo et al., 2010). In this technique, some of the cover image pixels are interpolated based on their neighboring pixels. Such interpolation gives rise to interpolated pixel values as well as interpolation errors. The watermark bits are embedded into the interpolation errors by additive expansion of the errors. The modified errors and the interpolated pixels are combined to produce the watermarked pixels. For watermark extraction, the interpolation errors are computed from the watermarked pixels and the watermark bits are extracted from the errors. Those retrieved errors when combined with the interpolated pixel values, restore the original cover image pixels, bit–by–bit. For details of the reversible watermarking technique, the readers are requested to consult the original work by Luo et al. (2010). Our working methodology has been represented in form of a block diagram in Figure 1.

Note here that, watermark transparency being a primary requirement of any watermarking algorithm, the residual cover–image distortions are considerably low. However, due to the image distortions introduced by watermarking, the prediction accuracy can be adversely affected in case of the images once lossily watermarked, as compared to the original images. Reversible watermarking is expected to provide a solution to this problem. With reversible watermarking, the images can be used in their watermarked form, as well as their original forms, retrieved from the watermarked images. In the above scenario, with the use of reversible watermarking, we can restore

Figure 1. Work methodology

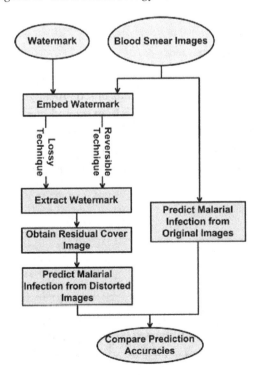

the watermarked blood smear images back to their original forms before the prediction. Since this reversal is error–free, that is every bit of the original cover images can be restored to its original form after watermark extraction by reversible watermarking, the prediction accuracy should be as high as what was obtained with the original images. Our experimental results demonstrating the effects of the aforementioned watermarking algorithms on malarial infection prediction accuracy have been presented in Section Results. Next we describe the automated Malaria diagnosis system.

Automated Malaria Diagnosis

For our experiment we collected the peripheral blood smear images of 250 patients, from Midnapore Medical College & Hospital and Medipath Laboratory, West Bengal, India. According to doctors' suggestions, out of those 250 blood smear images, we used 50 as our test images, which were the least noisy and whose slides were the best prepared. Median filtering (Mitra & Sicuranza, 2001) was applied on our 50 test images, specifically on their green (G) component, to their reduce impulse noise further. Since the green (G) channel of a color image provides more information than its red (R) or blue (B) channels, we used the green component of the test images, in our experiment.

Erythrocytes being the area of interest for detection of Plasmodium vivax infection in blood, the erythrocytes were segmented from the blood smear images, by the using gray level thresholding method proposed by Otsu (1979). Next, the unwanted cells like leukocyte and platelets were eliminated from the blood smear images by morphological operators. Finally the overlapping erythrocytes were segmented by the marker controlled watershed algorithm (Gonzalez & Woods, 2002).

After the segmentation was complete, we extracted some features from the processed test images, to identify the infected and non–infected erythrocytes. We selected a total of 26 different features, significant enough to discriminate the two classes. Those features include geometrical features such as area, parameter, compactness, circularity etc.; as well as Haralick (Haralick & Sternberg, 1987) textural features such as difference entropy, contrast, correlation, dissimilarity etc. The erythrocytes were predicted to be healthy or Plasmodium vivax infected from those 26 geometrical and textural features, by the use of multivariate logistic regression model (Rastogi, 2008). The entire experimental procedure has been shown in Figure 2, with the help of a block diagram. We have carried out the experiment on three different data sets, as described in the previous subsection:

- Firstly, on the set of 50 original blood smear images.
- Secondly, the images obtained by watermarking those 50 blood smear images by LSB substitution (Wang et al., 2000), and subsequently extracting the watermark from those images.
- Finally, on the images reversibly watermarked by Luo et al.'s (2010) interpolation based algorithm, and subsequently restored to their original forms after watermark extraction.

The total numbers of healthy and infected erythrocytes were constant for all three test image sets. Our test data consisted of total 90 infected and 186 healthy erythrocytes, for each of the three sets.

For each of the three above cases, we measured the prediction accuracy and compared them. The prediction accuracy of the healthy erythrocytes is measured as $(P_{healthy}/N_{heathy}) \times 100\%$, where $P_{healthy}$ is the number of erythrocytes predicted as healthy by our experiment, and N_{heathy} is the actual number of healthy erythrocytes. Similarly, the prediction accuracy of the infected erythrocytes is measured as $(P_{infected}/N_{infected}) \times 100\%$, where $P_{infected}$ is the number of erythrocytes predicted as infected by our experiment, and $N_{infected}$ is the actual number of healthy erythrocytes. The overall prediction accuracy is computed as the average:

$$\frac{\left(\dfrac{P_{healthy}}{N_{healthy}}\right) + \left(\dfrac{P_{infected}}{N_{infeceted}}\right)}{2} \times 100\%$$

For our test data sets, $N_{heathy} = 186$ and $N_{infected} = 90$.

The main steps of our evaluation methodology can be summarized by the flowchart shown in Figure 1. We present our experimental results in the next section.

RESULTS

Figure 3 shows an original blood smear image, along with its watermark extracted versions containing residual distortions, by both LSB–substitution based lossy watermarking and interpolation based reversible watermarking schemes.

Figure 2. Experimental procedure

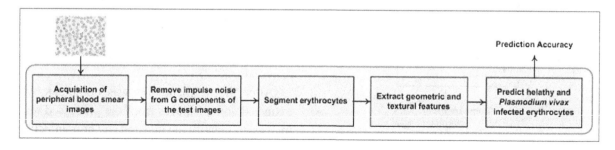

Figure 3. (a) An original blood smear image; (b) image containing residual distortions after lossy watermark extraction; (c) image restored after watermark extraction by reversible watermarking

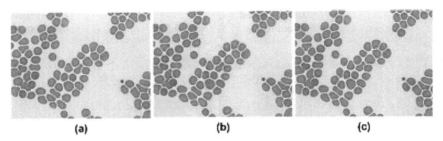

(a)   (b)   (c)

The size of watermark embedded and the cover image residual distortion, averaged across all 50 test images, have been presented in Table 1. The images restored by reversible watermarking after watermark extraction, contain zero residual distortions, according to inherent property of reversible watermarking. In our experiment, the erythrocytes are segmented from the G component of the blood smear images. Hence the distortion and the amount of information embedded into the G component of the test images play an important role in our experimental results. These data have also been specified in Table 1. All data presented in Table 1 are the averages over all 50 test images. We have measured the watermark size in terms of bits–per–pixel (bpp) and the image distortion in terms of Peak–Signal–to–Noise–Ratio (PSNR).

In Figures 4–7 we have presented the class–condition density plots (Rastogi, 2008) of the healthy and Plasmodium vivax infected erythrocytes, corresponding to four arbitrarily selected features. The class–condition density plots represent the likelihood area of the healthy and infected erythrocytes in form of their probability density functions. The four features selected by us are, entropy, homogeneity, difference entropy and inverse difference normalized, which are represented by dimensionless numeric values, as shown on the X–axes of the plots in Figures 4–7. For detailed procedure of calculation of those Haralick textural features, the readers are requested to consult the referred work in (Haralick & Sternberg, 1987). Y–axes of the plots in Figures 4–7, represent the probability density values of the four features, estimated by Kernel Density Estimation (Scott, 1992). For each feature, the class–condition density plots for the original test images and test images containing residual distor-

Table 1. Watermarked image distortions, residual distortions (after watermark extraction) and embedded watermark size[†]

Algorithm	Watermarked Image Distortion (PSNR)		Residual Distortion (PSNR)		Embedded bpp	
	Entire Image	G Component	Entire Image	G Component	Entire Image	G Component
LSB substitution based lossy watermarking	51.14 dB	55.91 dB	51.14 dB	55.91 dB	3.00	1.00
Interpolation based reversible watermarking	49.84 dB	54.10 dB	Zero distortion	Zero distortion	2.17	0.78
†All data averaged over 50 test images						

Figure 4. Class–condition density plots of feature entropy, for (a) original and (b) distorted test images

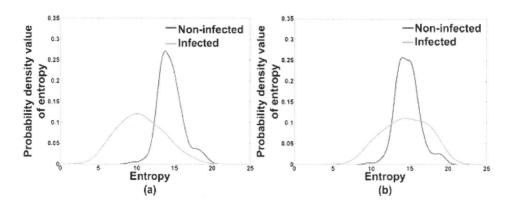

Figure 5. Class–condition density plots of feature homogeneity, for (a) original and (b) distorted test images

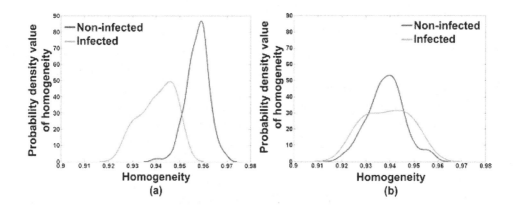

Figure 6. Class–condition density plots of feature difference entropy, for (a) original and (b) distorted test images

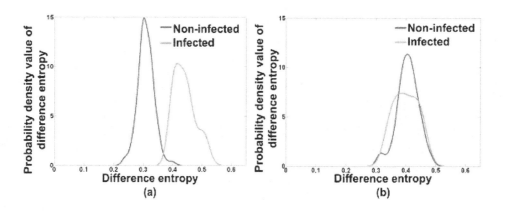

Figure 7. Class–condition density plots of feature inverse difference normalized, for (a) original and (b) distorted test images

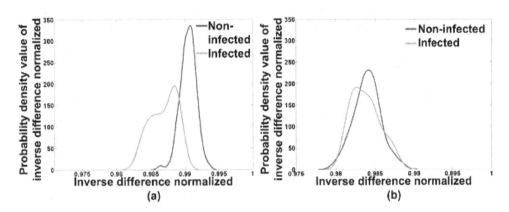

tions after lossy watermark extraction have been presented in subfigures (a) and (b) respectively. From the class–condition density plot of a particular feature, the overlap between the likelihood areas of the infected and non–infected classes of erythrocytes is observed. Larger the area of overlap, lower is the overall prediction accuracy. It can be observed that for all four features shown in Figures 4–7, the area of overlap is higher for the distorted images, compared to the original images. Hence, when all 26 features are combined to predict the healthy and infected erythrocytes in our experiment, the prediction accuracy is considerably higher for the original images, as compared to the images containing some residual distortions (remaining even after the watermark was extracted), caused by lossy watermarking.

The accuracy of predicting the healthy and infected erythrocytes, for the original and distorted sets of test images have been reported in Table 2 and Table 3, respectively. Table 2 and Table 3 show that the overall prediction accuracy for the original test images is 91.74%; whereas the overall prediction accuracy for the distorted test images is 87.88%. Thus our experimental results prove that the prediction accuracy is considerably lower for the distorted blood smear images, as compared to the original images. In order to avoid erroneous diagnosis of diseases,

Table 2. Prediction statistics of healthy and Plasmodium vivax infeceted erythrocytes, for original test images

		Actual		Prediction Accuracy (%)
		Infected	Healthy	
Predicted	Infected	79	11	87.78
	Healthy	8	178	95.70
Overall Prediction Accuracy (%)				91.74

Table 3. Prediction statistics of healthy and Plasmodium vivax infected erythrocytes, for test images containing residual distortion, caused due to lossy watermarking and subsequent watermark extraction

		Actual		Prediction Accuracy (%)
		Infected	Healthy	
Predicted	Infected	74	16	82.22
	Healthy	12	174	93.54
Overall Prediction Accuracy (%)				87.88

the prediction accuracy of such clinical tests need to be high enough. Hence, from these experimental results we conclude that LSB–replacement based and similar lossy watermarking schemes might not be the best choice for medical records for which accuracy is a crucial issue.

To demonstrate the effect of reversible watermarking, we watermarked the same set of 50 blood smear images using Luo et al.'s (2010) interpolation based reversible watermarking algorithm. Next, the watermark was extracted from the reversibly watermarked images and they were restored to their original forms by Luo et al.'s (2010) reversible watermark extraction algorithm. Our experimental procedure described in Section Investigation Methodology, was applied to those restored test images. The restored test images contained zero residual distortion, according to the inherent property of reversible watermarking; and the prediction accuracy achieved was the same as that obtained in case of the original, non–watermarked images, as expected. The prediction accuracy achieved with the test images restored by reversible watermarking, has been presented in Table 4. Hence we conclude that reversible watermarking, in spite of being generally computationally more involved than lossy watermarking schemes, is a better choice for medical imaging where accuracy is crucial.

FUTURE RESEARCH DIRECTIONS

In this chapter we have studied the adverse effects of digital rights managements, specifically digital watermarking, on the prediction accuracy

Table 4. Prediction statistics of healthy and Plasmodium vivax infected erythrocytes, for test images reversibly watermarked and subsequently restored to their original forms after watermark extraction

		Actual		Prediction Accuracy (%)
		Infected	Healthy	
Predicted	Infected	79	11	87.78
	Healthy	8	178	95.70
Overall Prediction Accuracy (%)			91.74	

of a malarial disease diagnostic system, and how such effects can be minimized with the help of reversible watermarking. For a significant future research in this direction, with respect to the medical industry in current times, the proposed method may be used to survey the impact of distortion caused by general digital watermarking, on the diagnostic accuracy of various important and common diseases, diagnosed from medical images in their digital forms. Additionally, it will also be investigated how the impact of such distortion may be minimized by the use of reversible watermarking. These investigations will make this research complete and its results useful for the present-day medical industry.

Further future work will be directed towards theoretical analysis of the effects of Digital Rights Management techniques on sensitive medical imaging applications. Also the effect of repeated watermark embedding and extraction on medical images will be investigated in the future.

CONCLUSION

We have investigated the effects of digital watermarking on medical images. Specifically, we showed the adverse effect of information–loss caused by a simple lossy watermarking scheme on the prediction accuracy of malarial infection, vis-a-vis the effect of a lossless reversible watermarking scheme. It was observed from our experimental results that the information–loss caused by a lossy watermarking scheme results in reduced accuracy of an automated diagnosis scheme for malaria. Such information–loss, residual even after watermark extraction is undesirable in the medical industry, since it deals with highly sensitive data. On the other hand, reversible watermarking provided a solution to this problem, as the original cover image can be losslessly restored by reversible watermarking. Thus we conclude that the use of reversible watermarking in medical imaging is more suitable as it allows maximized accuracy of disease diagnosis.

REFERENCES

Berger, S. B., & Cepelewicz, B. B. (1996). Medical-legal issues in teleradiology. *American Journal of Roentgenolo, 166*(3), 505–510. doi:10.2214/ajr.166.3.8623616 PMID:8623616.

Cox, I. J., Miller, M. L., Bloom, J. A., Fridrich, J., & Kalker, T. (2008). *Digital watermarking and steganography*. New York: Morgan Kaufmann Publishers.

Das, D., Ghosh, M., Chakraborty, C., Maiti, A. K., & Pal, M. (2011). Probabilistic prediction of malaria using morphological and textural information. In *Proceedings of International Conference on Image Information Processing (ICIIP)*. Wahington, DC: IEEE Press.

Dempster & Ruberto. C. D. (1999). Morphological processing of malarial slide images. In *Proceedings of Matlab DSP Conference*. Natick, MA: MathWorks.

Diaz, G., Gonzalez, F. A., & Romero, E. (2009). A semi automatic method for quantification and classification of erythrocytes infected with malaria parasites in microscopic image. *Journal of Biomedical Informatics, 42*(2), 296–307. doi:10.1016/j.jbi.2008.11.005 PMID:19166974.

Eid, T. A. (1995). Privacy protection for patient-identifiable medical information. *Action Report. Western Governors Association, 1995*, 42–47.

Feng, J. B., Lin, I. C., Tsai, C. S., & Chu, Y. P. (2006). Reversible watermarking: Current status and key issues. *International Journal of Network Security, 2*(3), 161–171.

Frean, J. (2010). Microscopic determination of malaria parasite load: Role of image analysis. *Microscopy: Science, Technology, Application, and Education, 3*, 862–866.

Gonzalez, R. C., & Woods, R. E. (2002). *Digital image processing*. New York: Prentice Hall.

Haralick, R. M., & Sternberg, S. R. (1987). Image analysis using mathematical morphology. *IEEE Transactions on Pattern Analysis and Machine Intelligence, 9*(4), 532–550. doi:10.1109/TPAMI.1987.4767941 PMID:21869411.

Luo, L., Chen, Z., Chen, M., Zeng, X., & Xiong, Z. (2010). Reversible image watermarking using interpolation technique. *IEEE Transactions on Information Forensics and Security, 5*(1), 187–193. doi:10.1109/TIFS.2009.2035975.

Makkapati, V. V., & Rao, R. M. (2009). Segmentation on malaria parasites in peripheral blood smear images. *IEEE International Conference on Acoustics, Speech, and Signal Processing* (1361–1364).

Mitra, S., & Sicuranza, J. (2001). *Nonlinear image processing*. San Diego: Academic Press.

Ni, Z., Shi, Y. Q., Ansari, N., & Su, W. (2006). Reversible data hiding. *IEEE Transactions on Circuits and Systems for Video Technology, 16*(3), 354–362. doi:10.1109/TCSVT.2006.869964.

Otsu, N. (1979). A threshold selection method from gray-level histograms. *IEEE Transactions on Systems, Man, and Cybernetics, 9*(1), 62–66. doi:10.1109/TSMC.1979.4310076.

Rastogi. (2008). *Fundamentals of biostatistics*. New Dehli: Ane Books.

Raviraja, S., & Osman, S. S., & Kardman. (2008). A novel technique for malaria diagnosis using invariant moments and by image compression. *IFMBE Proceedings, 21*(3), 730–733. doi:10.1007/978-3-540-69139-6_182.

Ross, N. E., Pritchard, C. J., & Rubin, D. M. (2006). Automatic image processing method for the diagnosis and classification of malaria on thin blood smears. *Medical & Biological Engineering & Computing, 44*, 427–436. doi:10.1007/s11517-006-0044-2 PMID:16937184.

Scott, D. W. (1992). *Multivariate density estimation*. New York: Wiley. doi:10.1002/9780470316849.

Stanberry, B. (2001). Legal ethical and risk issues in telemedicine. *Computer Methods and Programs in Biomedicine*, *64*(3), 225–233. doi:10.1016/S0169-2607(00)00142-5 PMID:11226620.

Tek, F. B., Dempster, A. G., & Kale, I. (2006). Malaria parasite detection in peripheral blood images. In *Proceedings of British Machine Vision Conference*. Berlin: Springer-Verlag.

Tian, J. (2003). Reversible data embedding using a difference expansion. *IEEE Transactions on Circuits and Systems for Video Technology*, *13*(8), 890–896. doi:10.1109/TCSVT.2003.815962.

Toha, S. F., & Ngah, U. K. (2007). Computer aided medical diagnosis for the identification of malaria parasites. *IEEE ICSCN*, *2007*, 521–522.

Wang, R. Z., Lin, C. F., & Lin, J. C. (2000). Image hiding by optimal LSB substitution and genetic algorithm. *Pattern Recognition*, *34*(3), 671–683. doi:10.1016/S0031-3203(00)00015-7.

Yang, B., Schmucker, M., Funk, W., Busch, C., & Sun, S. (2004). Integer DCT–based reversible watermarking technique for images using companding technique. *Proceedings of the Society for Photo-Instrumentation Engineers*, *5306*, 405–415. doi:10.1117/12.527216.

ADDITIONAL REFERENCES

Bandyopadhyay, S., Naskar, R., & Chakraborty, R. S. (2011). Reversible watermarking using priority embedding through repeated application of integer wavelet transform. *International Conference on Security Aspects in Information Technology, High-performance Computing, and Networking, Lecture Notes in Computer Science, 7011*, 45-56.

Celik, M. U., Sharma, G., Tekalp, A. M., & Saber, E. (2002). Reversible data hiding. In *Proceedings of International Conference on Image Processing* (III-157-III-160). Washington, DC: IEEE Press.

Celik, M. U., Sharma, G., Tekalp, A. M., & Saber, E. (2003). Localized lossless authentication watermark (LAW). *International Society for Optical Engineering*, *5020*, 689–698.

Celik, M. U., Sharma, G., Tekalp, A. M., & Saber, E. (2004). Lossless generalized-LSB data embedding. *IEEE Transactions on Image Processing*, *14*(2), 253–266. doi:10.1109/TIP.2004.840686 PMID:15700530.

Fallahpour, M., Megias, D., & Ghanbar, M. (2011). Reversible and high-capacity data hiding in medical images. *IET Image Process*, *5*(2), 190–197. doi:10.1049/iet-ipr.2009.0226.

Fridrich, J., Goljan, M., & Du, R. (2001). Distortion free data embedding. In *Proceedings of 4th Information Hiding Workshop* (27–41). Pittsburgh, PA: Springer.

Fridrich, J., Goljan, M., & Du, R. (2002). Lossless data embedding–New paradigm in digital watermarking. *EURASIP Journal of Signal Processing*, *2002*(2), 185–196.

Kim, K. S., Lee, M. J., Lee, H. Y., & Lee, H. K. (2009). Reversible data hiding exploiting spatial correlation between sub–sampled images. *Pattern Recognition*, *42*(11), 3083–3096. doi:10.1016/j.patcog.2009.04.004.

Naskar, R., & Chakraborty, R. S. (2011). Reversible image watermarking through coordinate logic operation based prediction. *International Conference on Information Systems Security, Lecture Notes on Computer Science, 7093*, 190-203.

Naskar, R., & Chakraborty, R. S. (2012). Performance of reversible digital image watermarking under error-prone data communication: A simulation-based study. *IET Image Processing*, *6*(6), 728–737. doi:10.1049/iet-ipr.2011.0160.

Naskar, R., & Chakraborty, R. S. (2012). Reversible watermarking utilizing weighted–median based prediction. *IET Image Processing*, *6*(5), 507–520. doi:10.1049/iet-ipr.2011.0244.

Naskar, R., & Chakraborty, R. S. (2012). Fuzzy Inference rule based reversible watermarking for digital images. *International Conference on Information Systems Security, Lecture Notes on Computer Science. 7671*, 149-163.

Ni, Z., Shi, Y. Q., Ansari, N., & Su, W. (2003). Reversible data hiding. In *Proceedings of International Symposium on Circuits and Systems* (II-912-II-915). Washington, DC: IEEE Press.

Vleeschouwer, C. D., Delaigle, J. F., & Macq, B. (2001) Circular interpretation of histogram for reversible watermarking. In *Proceedings of the IEEE 4th Workshop on Multimedia Signal Processing* (345–350). Washington, D: IEEE Press.

KEY TERMS AND DEFINITIONS

Automated Medical Diagnosis: Computer-aided, rule-based expert systems to diagnose medical conditions of patients, without human intervention.

Digital Rights Management (DRM): Techniques to manage the rights of accessing digital multimedia data, enforced by their owners or distributors.

Digital Watermarking: Act of embedding valuable information (watermark) into multimedia data such as text, image, audio, video etc for the purpose of security and protection of multimedia data.

Image Filtering: Techniques generally used to remove noise from an image, example, mean filtering, median filtering etc.

Image Segmentation: The process of partitioning an image into separate areas of adjoining pixels. In digital image processing, segmentation techniques are generally used for identifying useful objects or regions-of-interest within an image.

Interpolation Based Reversible Watermarking: A specialized reversible watermarking technique where the grayscale values of some selected pixel locations are estimated (as accurately as possible) from their neighboring pixels; and the watermark bits are reversibly embedded by modification of the estimation errors.

Multimedia Security: Security and protection of digital media such as text, image, audio, video etc. against cyber crimes and frauds; used for the protection of intellectual property.

Peak-Signal-to-Noise-Ratio (PSNR): A metric used to define the quality of digital images, after the application of common image processing operations such as compression; represented as the ratio of the maximum image signal power to the noise.

Reversible Watermarking: The class of digital watermarking where the cove r data can be restored back to its original form in a distortion-free way, after watermark extraction by the user.

Telemedicine: Technology dealing with electronic transmission of medical images from one location to another remote location; mainly used to provide remote clinical care.

Chapter 12
Biomedical Watermarking:
An Emerging and Secure Tool for Data Security and Better Tele-Diagnosis in Modern Health Care System

Koushik Pal
University of Calcutta, India

Goutam Ghosh
University of Calcutta, India

Mahua Bhattacharya
Indian Institute of Information Technology and Management, India

ABSTRACT

The proposed chapter describes the need of data security and content protection in the modern health care system. A digital watermarking technique is used as a strong and secure tool to achieve ultimate security. In this chapter the authors discuss some existing watermarking techniques and also describe some new types of data hiding techniques using biomedical watermarking techniques in both spatial and frequency domain which would help keep the authenticity and secure the contents of the hidden biomedical information for accurate tele-diagnosis. These techniques use multiple copies of the same information that is to be hidden in the cover image. The bandwidth requirement is greater, but reconstruction of hidden information is more accurate at the time of recovery even under several unintentional attacks. Some new types of embedding and recovery processes have also been employed for better results and success of the different proposed schemes. The Modified Bit Replacement (MBR) embedding process and the Bit Majority Algorithm (BMA) technique for recovery of the hidden information are the newer approaches that are also described here.

DOI: 10.4018/978-1-4666-4558-5.ch012

INTRODUCTION

Recent innovations and advancements in Medical Science not only increase the quality of the treatment, it also has introduced some new concepts like tele-diagnosis, tele-medicine and tele-surgery. These new concepts in modern health care system can give the facility of remote patient monitoring and helps patients to have a better diagnosis and treatment without actually going to the treatment center. A number of expert doctors from different locations can give their views and suggestions in the form of Electronic Patient Record (EPR) (Pal et al., 2012). The digitization of patient information such as EPR (electronic patient records), clinical and diagnostic images offers significant flexibility in medical diagnosis. In modern health care systems, HIS (Hospital Information System) and PACS (Picture Archiving and Communications System) (Cao et al., 2003), has formed the latest information technology infrastructure for a hospital based on the DICOM (Digital Imaging and COmmunication in Medicine) standard. And even this EPR can be stored for any future correspondence or reference.

As per the existing regulations prescribed by DICOM (Kobayashi et al., 2009), all patient records need to be secured and information confidentiality maintained. For biomedical images, modifications should not occur during data transfer over networks for both legal reasons and accurate treatment. If medical data is illegally obtained and the content is changed, it may lead to wrong diagnosis. Therefore, different protection mechanisms have evolved through several encryption and authentication techniques. Digital watermarking is one of the safest and popular methods that can embed medical data in a cover image without violating the DICOM format and enhancing medical data security. However, medical image watermarking requires extreme care when embedding additional information within medical images, because the additional information should not degrade the medical image quality (Liew et al., 2010).

Therefore appropriate biomedical image watermarking technique can introduce a new security layer that we expect to be preserved by continuous protection of the information during data storage, transmission.

Biomedical image watermarking is the process of embedding information imperceptibly into a medical image without changing image size or format such that the hidden information or the watermark can be extracted or recovered later. When applied for medical images, the watermarked image can still conform to the DICOM format. Some of the necessity for applying watermarking techniques to medical images is mentioned (Huang et al., 2011).

1. Watermarking technique should be invertible or reversible means once the image has been verified, the watermarked image should be reverted to the original image by removing the watermark.
2. There should be minimal perceptible changes in the watermarked image. The watermarked image should visually be the same as the original image.
3. There should be no impact on the stored images in the PACS server due to introduction of watermark.
4. Modification of the watermarked image may lead to unsuccessful verification. So proposed watermarking schemes should not change the amount of data that needs to be transferred.
5. Watermarking technique for authentication should be applied while transferring image data in DICOM format over the network.

A watermarking method is usually designed depending on a compromise between different requirements: capacity robustness privacy and imperceptibility. A biomedical image watermarking technique can be characterized by the following four features: imperceptibility, robustness, security, and capacity (Zain et al., 2007).

1. **Imperceptibility:** Refers to the perceptual transparency of the watermark. Ideally, no perceptible difference between the watermarked and original image should be perceived by the human visual system.
2. **Robustness:** Is the capability of the watermark to survive unwanted alterations or manipulations known as attacks. A watermark needs only to survive the attacks that are likely to occur when the watermarked signal is being transmitted. Not all watermarking applications require a watermark to be robust enough to survive all attacks. In an extreme case, robustness may be completely irrelevant where fragility is desirable.
3. **Security:** In watermarking implies that the watermark should be difficult to remove or alter without damaging the host image. It is the most important figure of merit for a medical image assuring secrecy and integrity of the watermarked information.
4. **Watermarking Capacity:** Normally refers to the amount of information that can be embedded into the cover image. Higher the strength of the watermark signal, the more it is robust or of higher capacity albeit perceptibility is compromised. A robust watermark is desirable to authenticate the image origins, while at the same time the watermark should not interfere with the image content interpretation.

Applications of Watermarking

As previously stated, watermarking can be really useful in several areas of interest involving digital images (Gonzalez, Woods, et al., 2008). In order to fully understand the main challenges involved in the development of watermarking related tools, some applications of invisible watermarks are listed here:

1. **Fingerprinting:** In order to trace the source of illegal copies the owner can embed different watermarking keys in the copies that are supplied to different customer. For the owner, embedding a unique serial number-like watermark is a good way to detect customers who break their license agreement by copying the protected data and supplying it to a third party.
2. **Indexing:** Watermarking offers a wide range of new capabilities to multimedia applications. It allows the indexing of video mail by permitting the insertion of comments in video content as well as the indexing of movies or news items by making available the utilization of markers that can be exploited in search engines. As the number of online images and videos increases a lot faster than the capabilities of today's search engine, it is important to plan ahead for new ways to allow quick access to multimedia data and watermarking is certainly a promising way to do so.
3. **Owner Identification:** To protect its intellectual property, the data owner can embed a watermark representing copyright information of his data. This application can be a really helpful tool in settling copyright disputes in court. It is probably the most widely spread use of digital images watermarking and it is also the application we have worked on in the present project.
4. **Broadcast Monitoring:** In order to help the automated identification of broadcasted programs, original watermarks can be inserted in any type of data to be widely broadcasted on a network. It could assure that advertisers received the airtime they have paid for or make certain that musicians' property is not rebroadcast by pirate stations (or at least, if so, that it can be detected).

5. **Copy Protection:** The watermarked information can directly control digital recording device. The embedded key can represent a copy-permission bit stream that is detected by the recording device which then decide if the copying procedure should go on (allowed) or not (prohibited).

6. **Data Authentication:** Fragile watermarks are used to detect any corruption of an image or any other type of data. If the watermark is detected, the data is genuine, if not; the data has been corrupted and cannot be considered.

7. **Data Hiding or Covert Communication:** The transmission of private data is probably one of the earliest applications of watermarking. As one would probably have already understood, it consists of implanting a strategic message into an innocuous one in a way that would prevent any unauthorized person to detect it.

Types of Watermarking

Digital image watermarking may be classified in several ways, viz. visible and invisible, robust and fragile, reversible and irreversible, and so on. Watermarking can be applied in the spatial domain or in the frequency domain. Spatial domain techniques, such as the Least Significant Bit (LSB) method, embed the message by altering the coefficients of the LSB of some image pixels. The frequency domain technique embeds the message by modulating the coefficients in the frequency domain, such as in Discrete Cosine Transform (DCT) and Discrete Wavelet Transform (DWT) cases. Here, values of certain frequencies are altered from their original. Typically, these frequency alterations are done in the lower frequency levels, since alternations at the higher frequencies are lost during compression. Spatial domain watermarking schemes have a higher level of invisibility than frequency domain schemes. However, since frequency domain techniques can embed more bits of information and provide ease of compression it is more popular (Cox et al., 2002).

LSB Watermarking

The Least Significant Bit (LSB) algorithm in spatial domain, is very simple, strong, and less perceptible. The embedding of the watermark is performed choosing a subset of image pixels and substituting the LSB of each of the chosen pixels with the watermark bits. This algorithm takes as inputs a cover image and a watermark logo while the output function takes as input the watermarked image and gives the extracted watermark as its output. For a gray scale 8- bit image, we need to read the cover image and information logo and then add the data of the information logo to the least significant bits of each pixel of the cover image, in every 8-bit pixel. The cover image is generally a gray scale image where each pixel is represented by 1 byte. It can represent 256 gray colors between the black which is 0 to the white which is 255. The information logo is generally a binary image and it can be represented by black (0) or white (1). Recovery of the hidden information or watermark is done by extracting the least significant bit of each of the selected image pixels. If the extracted bits match the inserted bits, then the watermark is reconstructed (Pal et al., 2012).

Though LSB watermarking schemes have a higher level of invisibility and a less computational overhead, modifications of LSB data is highly sensitive to noise and is easily destroyed. This technique is not resistant enough to image compression and other image processing techniques. Furthermore, image quality may be degraded by the watermark

DCT Watermarking

The classic and still most popular domain for image processing is that of the Discrete-Cosine-Transform, or DCT. The DCT allows an image to be broken up into different frequency bands, making it much easier to embed watermarking information into the middle frequency bands of an image. The middle frequency bands are chosen such that they have minimize they avoid the most visual important parts of the image (low frequencies) without over-exposing themselves to removal through compression and noise attacks (high frequencies). A DCT expresses finite number of data points in terms of sum of cosine functions oscillating at different frequencies. The method that we used for digital image watermarking is based on DCT, where the 2D DCT of the images are determined and added to watermark an image. This needs the 2-dimensional DCT of the images for the watermarking to be performed. 2-D DCT is represented by the equation:

$$X(k1, k2) = \sum_{n1=0}^{N_1} \sum_{n2=0}^{N_2} x(n1, n2)\text{Cos}((\frac{\pi}{N1}) + 0.5)k1)\text{Cos}\left(\left(\frac{\pi}{N2}\right) + 0.5\right)k2) \qquad (1)$$

where the value of n1, n2 and constants k1, k2 vary from 0 to 7 for a 8x8 block of data.

The digital data of the image is made into several 8X8 blocks and the 1D DCT of each block is found out. Then the transpose of the 8x8 block is taken and again the 1D DCT is found out, which when applied to all the blocks of the image gives the 2D DCT of the whole image. In other words, the row wise block DCT is first found, followed by the column wise DCT which gives the 2D DCT. Suppose that the image under consideration is of size 512x512, and then the image, when divided into 8x8 blocks gives, 4096 blocks. The block wise DCT is found out for each block.

From the above explanation it is quite evident that the implementation of digital watermarking needs an efficient algorithm to find the 2D DCT/IDCT.

Watermarking of an image can be done using the DCTs of the images to be used. The DCT of both the images are taken and the intensity of the image that has to appear as the watermark can be varied by the proportion in which the DCT is added. The basic process that takes place is the addition of DCTs followed by the IDCT of the result, which gives the watermarked image.

$$Vi' = Vi * (1 + \alpha * (Xi + \beta * Wi)) \qquad (2)$$

where Vi' is the result of the added DCT of the two images. Xi is the DCT value of the image on which the watermarking is done and Wi is the DCT of the logo, which is watermarked on the image. The constants α, β, affect the visibility of the watermark. For very small β value, a watermark is invisible and as the visibility increases by growth of β value. For extraction of a watermark, the values of α and β have to be known and hence the extraction of the watermarking cannot be done by anyone who does not know these values. To increase security, there are methods where in the values of α, β are varied for each block, which are known only to the owner. This is the principle used in image authentication or copyright.

DWT Watermarking

Another possible domain for watermark embedding is that of the wavelet domain. The DWT (Discrete Wavelet Transform) separates an image into a lower resolution approximation image (LL) as well as horizontal (HL), vertical (LH), and diagonal (HH) detail components. The process can then be repeated to computes multiple "scale" wavelet decomposition, as in the 2 scale wavelet transform shown in Figure 1.

Figure 1. Two scale 2-dimensional discrete wavelet transform

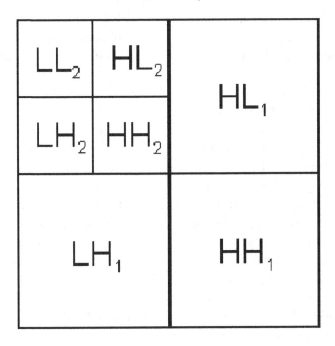

One of the many advantages over the wavelet transform is that that it is believed to more accurately model aspects of the HVS as compared to the FFT or DCT. This allows us to use higher energy watermarks in regions that the HVS is known to be less sensitive to, such as the high resolution detail bands {LH, HL, HH}. Embedding watermarks in these regions allow us to increase the robustness of our watermark, at little to no additional impact on image quality (Pal et al., 2012).

Unwanted alterations known as attacks may be performed intentionally on a watermarked document to destroy or degrade the quality of the hidden watermark. These distortions also introduce degradation on the performance of the watermark extraction algorithm. The watermarking technique should be robust enough to survive the attacks so that after extraction the watermark should resemble the original image.

The measurement of the quality of a watermarked image and the recovered information logo is very important to indicate its strength and integrity of the watermarking technique. The amount of visual quality degradation between the original and watermarked images is generally described by different types of image quality metrics.

GENERALISED BIO-MEDICAL IMAGE WATERMARKING FRAMEWORK

The purpose of watermarking is the insertion of a message, known as content or watermark or information logo, in a document, also called carrier or cover image. Unlike steganography, which also has the same objective, watermarking explicitly requires that the data remains hidden to any unauthorized user and be resistant to any attempt to suppress it.

Three types of watermarking methods were identified for medical images. A first class regroups methods that embed information within Region Of Non-Interest (RONI) in order not to compromise the diagnosis capability. Various experiments suggest that RONI generally corresponds to the black background of the image. Since there is no interference with the image content, invisibility is less strict; consequently one can revert to methods with higher capacity and robustness.

The second approach corresponds to reversible watermarking. Once the embedded content is read, the watermark can be removed from the image allowing retrieval of the original image. But the embedding capacity is still way below that of the nonreversible watermarking technique. Because of the fragility of reversible methods, such methods are used for the integrity purpose and data hiding. Medical tradition is very strict with the quality of biomedical images, in that it is often not allowed to alter in any way the bit field representing the image. Thus the watermarking method must be reversible, in that the original pixel values must be exactly recovered (Velumani et al., 2010).

The third approach consists in using classical watermarking methods while minimizing the distortion. In that case, the watermark replaces some image details such as the least significant bit of the image. In all the cases properties of the Human Visual System (HVS) are exploited to control the quality of the image.

A generalized medical image watermarking system may be devised in Figure 2.

Step 1: Acquisition of raw medical image treated as cover data, I, which must be processed inside Encoder Block.

Step 2: In the Encoder Block, copyright information is hidden inside the original piece of work in an encrypted form. The other input to this block is the copyright information (also known as signature) or the watermark, W to be embedded inside I using the secret key, K.

Step 3: The final image available in from the encoder block is composite image, I_w containing the encrypted logo inside the original image. This composite image has to be stored in Health Information Network for medical diagnosis.

Step 4: The composite image available in Health Information Network has every possibility of being attacked by the hackers in a bid to destroy the watermark embedded inside it, to generate the hacked version, $<I_w>$ of the composite image. Once the hackers become successful in destroying the watermark the original piece of work becomes susceptible to all kinds of fraud.

Step 5: The primary aim of present research is to design the watermarking decoder block to extract an estimate of the copyright information, $<W>$, from the hacked version $<I_w>$. The better the watermarking system the more $<W>$ resembles W.

ATTACKS AND DISTORTIONS

The watermarked image may be altered either intentionally or inadvertently. Different types of attacks can be performed to degrade the image quality. An attack may be performed intentionally on a watermarked document in order to destroy or degrade the quality of the hidden watermark. These distortions also introduce degradation on the performance of the watermark extraction algorithm. The watermarking technique should be robust enough to survive the attacks so that after extraction the watermark should resemble the original image.

Attack may be classified as Active, Passive, Collusion, Forgery, and so forth. In Active attacks, the hacker tries deliberately to remove the watermark or simply make it undetectable. This is a big issue in copyright protection. In Passive attacks, the attacker is not trying to remove the watermark but simply attempting to determine the presence of the mark. Protection against passive attacks is of the utmost importance in covert communications where the simple knowledge of the presence of watermark is often more than one want to grant. In Collusion attacks, the goal of the hacker is the same as for the active attacks but the

Figure 2. Medical Image Watermarking Framework

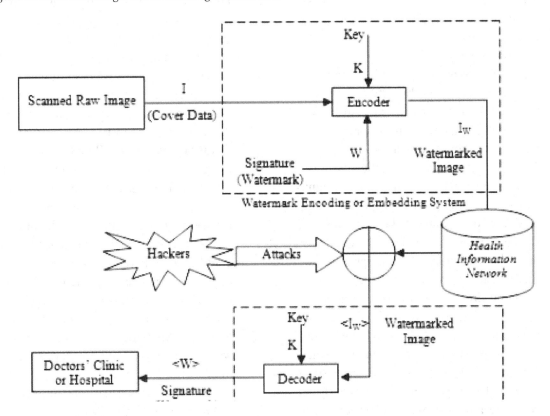

method is slightly different. In order to remove the watermark, the hacker uses several copies of the same data, containing each different watermark, to construct a new copy without any watermark. This attack is not widely spread because the attacker must have access to multiple copies of the same data. Forgery attack is probably the main concern in data authentication. In forgery attacks, the hacker aims at embedding a new, valid watermark rather than removing one. By doing so, it allows him to modify the protected data as he wants and then, re-implants a new given key to replace the fragile one, thus making the corrupted image seems genuine.

Some of the popular attacks mentioned here are Salt and Pepper Noise, Image Compression, Gaussian Noise, Multiplicative Noise, Erosion, Dilation, Low pass filtering, High pass filtering, Image Cropping, Rotation and Scaling, Image Averaging, Multiple watermarking (Pal et al., 2012).

1. **Salt and Pepper Noise:** Salt and Pepper Noise is a form of noise that replaces the intensity levels of some of the pixels of an image resulting in loss of information from those pixels. "Impulsive" noise falls under this category. An image containing salt-and-pepper noise represents itself as randomly occurring dark pixels in bright regions and bright pixels in dark regions. This type of noise can be caused by analog-to-digital converter errors, bit errors in transmission, and others.

2. **Image Compression:** High quality images like BMP images are often converted to JPEG images to reduce their size. Compression is a common form of attack, as data transferred via a network is often compressed using JPEG. The degree of compression can be adjusted, allowing a selectable tradeoff between storage size and image quality.

The compression method is usually lossy, meaning that some original image information is lost and cannot be restored, possibly affecting image quality.

3. **Gaussian Noise:** Gaussian noise is statistical in nature that has its probability density function equal to that of the normal distribution. It can degrade the watermark image quality and may destroy the watermark.

4. **Multiplicative Noise:** Multiplicative noise, also known as speckle noise, is a signal dependent form of noise whose magnitude is related to the value of the original pixel. This noise can also degrade the quality of the watermark image by manipulating the hidden information or watermark.

5. **Erosion:** Erosion is one of the fundamental operations in morphological image processing from which all other morphological operations are based. It was originally defined for binary images, later being extended to gray scale images, and subsequently to complete lattices. Erosion process will allow thicker lines to get skinny and detect the hole inside any contour of an image.

6. **Dilation:** Dilation is another basic operation in morphological image processing. Originally developed for binary images, it has been expanded first to gray scale images, and then to complete lattices. The dilation operation usually uses a structuring element for probing and expanding the shapes contained in the input image. Dilation is the dual operation of the erosion. Figures that are very lightly drawn get thicker when "dilated."

7. **Low Pass Filtering:** Low pass filtering is the process by which we can reject the higher frequency components by passing only the low frequencies. This is generally used to blur the image. As this type of filter temper the frequency component of the image it can also be used as an attack.

8. **High Pass Filtering:** High pass filter rejects the low frequencies and increases the sharpness of the image. It may reduce the information of the image.

9. **Image Cropping:** Cropping of any image is also treated as an attack as it manipulates the original image and thus information in the image may be lost.

10. **Rotation and Scaling:** Rotation and resizing of any image may reduce the quality of the image. So it can also be treated as an attack which is also known as geometrical attack.

11. **Image Averaging:** Averaging the intensity levels of several pixels of an image may degrade the quality of an image. It either may increase or decrease the intensity levels of several pixels of the original image which is also responsible for information loss.

12. **Multiple Watermarking:** If more than one watermarking is done one after another on the same image then it is known as multiple watermarking which may cause information by degradation of the original image.

IMAGE QUALITY METRICS

The measurement of the quality of a watermarked image and the recovered information logo is very important to indicate its strength and integrity of the watermarking technique. The amount of visual quality degradation between the original and watermarked images are generally described by different types of image quality metrics such as Peak Signal to Noise Ratio (PSNR), Structural Similarity Index Measurement (SSIM), Bit Error Rate (BER), Normalized Absolute Error (NAE), Mean Average Error (MAE), Universal Image Quality Index (UIQI) while the quality and similarity of the recovered information with the original are determined by the BER, SSIM, Normalized Cross Correlation (NCC), Mutual Information (MI), Structural Content (SC), and UIQI. Higher value of PSNR, SSIM, NCC, MI, and UIQI represents image of good quality while lower values of BER, NAE, MAE, SC represent less error and consequently good quality image (Eskicioglu et al., 1995).

Measurement of the quality of a watermarked image and recovered information logo is very important for the watermarking technique to prove its strength and successfulness.

To measure the amount of visual quality degradation between the original and watermarked images different types of image quality metrics such as

Peak Signal-to-Noise Ratio (PSNR), Structural Similarity Index Measure (SSIM), Bit Error Rate (BER), Normalized Absolute Error (NAE), Mean Average Error (MAE), Universal Image quality index (UIQI) are used while the quality and similarity of the recovered information logo with the original may be measured using Bit Error Rate (BER), Structural Similarity Index Measure (SSIM), Normalized Cross Correlation (NCC), Mutual information (MI), Structural Content (SC) and Universal Image quality index (UIQI) (Pal et al., 2012).

Peak Signal-To-Noise Ratio (PSNR)

It is the ratio between the maximum possible power of a signal and the power of corrupting noise that affects the fidelity of its representation. PSNR is usually expressed in terms of dB for a wide range of signals The PSNR is most commonly used as a measure of quality of reconstruction for lossy compression. The cover image in this case is the original data, and the information logo is the error introduced by watermarking. A higher PSNR would normally indicate that the reconstruction is of higher quality. A small value of PSNR indicates poor quality.

It is most easily defined as the Mean Square Error (MSE) of two monochrome images x (m, n) and x^ (m, n), where one of the images is considered a noisy approximation of the other.

M and N are the number of pixels in the row and column directions respectively.

MSE is defined as:

$$MSE = \frac{1}{MN \sum_{m=1}^{M} \sum_{n=1}^{N} (x(m,n) - x^{m,n}))^2} \quad (3)$$

The PSNR is defined as:

$$
\begin{aligned}
PSNR &= 10 * \log_{10}\left(\frac{MAX_1^2}{MSE}\right) \\
&= 20 * \log_{10}\left(\frac{MAX_1}{\sqrt{MSE}}\right)
\end{aligned} \quad (4)
$$

Here, MAX_1 is the maximum possible pixel value of the image. When the pixels are represented using 8 bits per sample, MAX_1 is 255.

Structural Similarity Index Measure (SSIM)

SSIM is a method for measuring the similarity between two images. It is a full reference metric, where the measure of the image quality is based on an initial distortion-free image as reference. SSIM is designed to improve on traditional methods like PSNR and MSE, which have proved to be inconsistent with human eye perception. The resultant SSIM index is a decimal value between -1 and 1. The value 1 is only attainable in the case of two identical sets of data. The SSIM metric is calculated on various windows of an image. The measure between two windows x and y of common size $N \times N$ is:

$$SSIM(x,y) = \frac{(2\mu_x\mu_y + c_1)(2\sigma_{xy} + c_2)}{(\mu_x^2 + \mu_y^2 + c_1)(\sigma_x^2 + \sigma_y^2 + c_2)} \quad (5)$$

where μ_x is the average of x; μ_y the average of y; σ_x^2 the variance of x; σ_y^2 the variance of y; σ_{xy} the covariance of x and y; $c_1 = (k_1 L)^2$, $c_2 = (k_2 L)^2$ are two variables to stabilize the division with weak denominator; L the dynamic range of the pixel-values (typically this is $2^{\#bits\ per\ pixel}-1$); k_1=0.01 and k_2=0.03 by default.

Mean Average Error (MAE)

The large value of Mean Average Error (MAE) means that the image is of poor quality.

MAE is defined as:

$$MAE = \frac{1}{MN \sum_{m=1}^{M} \sum_{n=1}^{N} \left| x(m,n) - x^\wedge(m,n) \right|} \tag{6}$$

Structural Content (SC)

Structural Content is the measure of information content in the image and is defined as the ratio of the structural information content of the original to the recovered information logo. A large value of Structural Content (SC) thus means that the image is of poor quality. SC is defined by:

$$SC = \frac{\sum_{m=1}^{M} \sum_{n=1}^{N} x(m,n)^2}{\sum_{m=1}^{M} \sum_{n=1}^{N} x^\wedge(m,n)^2} \tag{7}$$

Normalized Absolute Error (NAE)

A large value of Normalized Absolute Error (NAE) means that image is poor quality. NAE is defined as follows:

$$NAE = \frac{\sum_{M=1}^{M} \sum_{n=1}^{N} \left| x(m,n) - x^{m,n} \right|}{\sum_{M=1}^{M} \sum_{n=1}^{N} \left| x(m,n) \right|} \tag{8}$$

Bit Error Rate (BER)

The bit error rate or Bit Error Ratio (BER) is the number of bit errors divided by the total number of transferred bits during a studied time interval. BER is a unit less performance measure, often expressed as a percentage. The BER can be considered as an approximate estimate of the bit error probability. This estimate is accurate for a long time interval and a high number of bit errors.

$$BER = 1/2 \ \text{erfc}(\sqrt{\frac{2Eb}{N0}}) \tag{9}$$

Normalized Cross Correlation (NCC)

Visually recognizable patterns as watermarks and extracted messages may be judged subjectively. However, the subjective measurement depends on various factors such as the expertise of the viewers, the experimental conditions, etc. and an objective measure becomes essential to quantify the fidelity of the extracted message. One common measure for quality assessment of the decoded data is the normalized cross correlation (NCC) is represented as follows:

$$NCC = \frac{\sum_X \sum_Y w(x,y) w'(x,y)}{\sum_X \sum_y \left[w(x,y) \right]^2} \tag{10}$$

Here $W(x, y)$ and $W'(x, y)$ represent the hidden watermark and the extracted watermark respectively.

Universal Image Quality Index (UIQI)

The Universal Image Quality Index is defined as:

$$Q = \frac{4\sigma_{xy} \overline{xy}}{\left(\sigma_x^2 + \sigma_y^2 \right) \left[(\overline{x})^2 + (\overline{y})^2 \right]} \tag{11}$$

where

$$\bar{x} = \frac{1}{N} \sum_{I=1}^{N} x_i, \bar{y} = \frac{1}{N} \sum_{I=1}^{N} y_i, \sigma_x^2 = \frac{1}{N-1}$$

$$\sum_{i=1}^{N} (x_i - \bar{x})^2, \sigma_y^2 = \frac{1}{N-1} \sum_{i-1}^{N} (y_i - \bar{y})^2,$$

$$\sigma_{xy} = \frac{1}{N-1} \sum_{i=1}^{N} (x_i - \bar{x})(y_i \bar{y})$$

Q can also be defined as the product of three components:

$$Q = \frac{\sigma_{xy}}{\sigma_x \sigma_y} \cdot \frac{2\overline{xy}}{(\bar{x})^2 + (\bar{y})^2} \cdot \frac{2\sigma_x \sigma_y}{\sigma_x^2 + \sigma_y^2}$$
$$[\text{I}] \qquad\quad [\text{II}] \qquad\quad [\text{III}]$$

where

[I] Defines the degree of correlation between $\bar{x}$ and $\bar{y}$ with dynamic range between -1 and 1.

[II] Measures how close the luminance is between $\bar{x}$ and $\bar{y}$, the range being between 0 and 1.

[III] Measures how similar the contrasts of the image between $\bar{x}$ and $\bar{y}$ are.

Mutual Information (MI)

Mutual information value $I(X; Y)$ can be used as a measure to quantify the robustness efficiency against various image degradations. The reason for considering the mutual information $I(X; Y)$ as an objective measure stems from the fact that if there were no image impairments the average amount of information received would be $H(X)$ bits (entropy of the source) per received symbol. But because of the channel noise due to the various attacks, an average of $H(X/Y)$ bits of information per symbol is lost and in this process the amount of information the receiver receives is, on the average, $I(X;Y)$ bits per symbol, where $I(X;Y) = H(X) - H(X/Y)$

Let random variables X and Y represent the watermark image and its decoded version obtained from the distorted watermarked image. If $p(x_i)$ represents the probability of occurrence of the ith pixel value in watermark image and $p(y_i / x_i)$ represents the channel transition matrix, $I(X; Y)$ can be expressed as follows:

$$I(X;Y) = \sum_i \sum_j p(x_i)p(y_i / x_i)$$
$$\log \frac{p(y_i / x_i)}{\sum_i p(x_i)p(y_i / x_i)} \qquad (12)$$

OVERVIEW OF THE PREVIOUS WORK

Focusing on a brief overview it can be found that Anand et al., proposed, to insert an encrypted version of the EPR in the LSB (Least Significant Bit) of the gray levels of medical-image pixels. Although the damage to the diagnostic image quality is minimal, the limitations and fragility of LSB watermarking is well-known.

Miaou et al. have similarly proposed an LSB technique. The image carrier authenticates the origin of the transmission and the message to be embedded is composed of an ECG record, the diagnosis report and the doctor's seals.

As Macq and Dewey, he gives attention to trusted header by watermarking the root part in the image data.

Tirkel et al. presented one of the first used techniques for image watermarking to hide data in the spatial domain of images based on the pixel value's Least Significant Bit modifications.

Kurah and McHughes proposed an algorithm to embed in the LSB and it was known as image downgrading.

Hao Luo et al, proposed a self-embedding digital image watermarking technique where they used the cover image as a watermark. It generates the watermark by half toning the cover image into a halftone image. Then, the watermark is created and embedded in the LSB of the cover image. The watermark is recovered from the LSB of the suspicious image and inverse permuted.

Wen-Chao Yang et al used the Public-Key Infrastructure, Public-Key Cryptography and watermarking techniques to design a novel testing and verifying method of digital images. The main idea of their algorithm was to embed encrypted watermarks in the LSB of cover images.

Sung-Cheal Byun et al., proposed a fragile watermarking technique where they used singular values of singular value decomposition of images to check the integrity of images. In order to make authentication data, the singular values are changed to the binary bits using modular arithmetic. Then, they inserted the binary bits into the randomly selected LSBs of the cover image.

Gil-Je Lee et al. proposed a new LSB watermarking technique by embedding watermark randomly in the coordinates of the cover image by using random function to be more robust than the traditional LSB technique.

Saeid Fazli et al presented trade-off between imperceptibility and robustness of LSB watermarking using SSIM Quality Metrics. In their algorithm, they put significant bit-planes of the watermark image instead of lower bit-planes of the cover image.

NEW TYPES OF BIOMEDICAL IMAGE WATERMARKING TECHNIQUES

In this chapter we also describe some new biomedical watermarking techniques in both spatial and frequency domain. These techniques use multiple copies of the same information that is to be hidden in the cover image. The bandwidth requirement is more but reconstruction of hidden information is more accurate at the time of recovery even under several unintentional attacks. Some new types of embedding and recovery processes have also been employed for better results and successfulness of

the different proposed schemes. The Modified Bit Replacement (MBR) embedding process and the Bit Majority Algorithm (BMA) technique for recovery of the hidden information are the newer approaches that are described.

Biomedical Image Watermarking in Spatial Domain: MBR (Modified Bit Replacement) Technique

In this biomedical image watermarking technique, modified bit replacement algorithm in spatial domain is used which is much better than the conventional simple LSB technique. In this scheme, multiple copies of the same information are hidden in several bits of the cover image starting from the lower order to the higher orders. So even if some of the information is lost due to an attack, we can still collect the remaining information and recover the watermark from the cover image using the bit majority algorithm (Pal, 2012).

Embedding Watermark

The gray scale cover image is divided into several parts according to the size of the information logo and the number of the same information that are to be hidden. Then the lowest pixel value of each sub division is taken as the starting index for the embedding process and this value gradually increases up to the limit equal to the maximum number of information blocks of the watermark. The number of information blocks is the total number of black pixels of the binary logo. This number is also used as a random key which is also sent along with the watermarked image and two other keys which hold the information about the dimensions of the watermark.

Step 1: Take the gray scale cover image and the binary information logo as input.
Step 2: Determine the size of both the cover image and information logo.

Step 3: Convert both cover image and information logo from 2 D array to 1D array.

Step 4: Calculate the number of pixels of the binary information logo having lowest intensity (0) and store the positions of those pixels in an array.

Step 5: Calculate the minimum intensity value of the gray scale cover image.

Step 6: Create an array for storing the positions of pixels in increasing order starting from the minimum intensity of the cover image.

Step 7: Calculate the size of the divisions of the cover image and store the value.

Step 8: Divide the above obtained array into some parts according to how many times the same logo is to be hidden. Each part will have a length equal to the size of the divisions.

Step 9: Reshape the positional information of the logo whose intensity value is zero.

Step 10: Calculate the length of the zero intensity position of logo and store as a random key.

Step 11: XOR of the key with the positional information of the 0 intensity pixels of logo and save it as information bit for security reasons.

Step 12: Set the 2nd to 5th bit of the cover image having lower intensity value by the stored information bits up to the times equal to the number of zero intensity of the information logo.

Step 13: Repeat the process for how many times the same logo is to be hidden.

Step 14: Reshape the final watermarked image from 1D array to 2 D array.

Step 15: Write the watermarked image to a file and display it.

Recovery of Watermark

The watermarked image is compared with the original cover image to find the difference in pixel values depending on the three hidden keys. The first key indicates the information block of the information logo and the remaining two indicate the row size and column size of the information block respectively. After getting the three correct keys from the user the different hidden sets of information logo from the watermarked image are found. These different sets are built using the positional information of the hidden pixels and the information obtained from those three keys. The final information logo is then reconstructed by a number of comparisons between these different recovered sets using the proposed bit majority algorithm. This algorithm provides a method to find the closest twin by several comparisons between different sets of data. After recovering the different sets from the attacked watermarked image, the best sets of pixels which are closest to the original information logo, are taken. The rest of the portions of black dots are replaced by white dots. Every set of the recovered logo is checked with one another to find the similarity between the pixels.

Step 1: Take the watermarked image and the original cover image as input.

Step 2: Determine the size of both the cover image and watermarked image.

Step 3: Convert both cover image and watermarked image from 2 D array to 1D array.

Step 4: Obtain the 3 keys from the user: Key 1 must be equal to the amount of information, Key 2 and Key 3 must be equal to the row and column size of the hidden information logo.

Step 5: Calculate the minimum intensity value of the gray scale cover image.

Step 6: Create an array for storing the positions of pixels in increasing order starting from the minimum intensity of the cover image.

Step 7: Calculate the size of the divisions of the cover image and store the value.

Step 8: Divide the above obtained array into some parts according to how many times the same logo is to be hidden. Each part will have a length equal to the size of the divisions.

Step 9: Extract the encrypted positional information of the logo or message.

Step 10: Find the majority of information pixels and construct different sets of recovered logo.

Step 11: Reconstruct the outline of final recovered watermark or logo according to the total majority by comparing all the recovered sets of information logo using bit majority algorithm.

Step 12: Reshape the final watermark or information logo from 1D array to 2 D array.

Step 13: Write the information logo to a file and display it.

Bit Majority Algorithm

Bit Majority algorithm is a technique to find the closest twin by several comparisons between different sets of data. After recovering 8 different sets from attacked watermarked image we have to find the best sets of pixel which is much closer to the original information logo. The rest portions' black dots are replace by white dots. For this every sets of recovered logo is checked with each other to find the similarity. From obtained results it can be easily understand that recovered 8 sets are practically not recognizable but the final derived logo is quite recognizable and the quality matrices also reflect the strength of this new algorithm.

Biomedical Image Watermarking in Wavelet Domain

A new type of medical image watermarking scheme has been introduced here that uses multiple copies of information logo hidden in several bits of the cover image starting from lower order to higher order to hide the information logo in wavelet domain (Pal et al., 2012). Discrete Wavelet Transform (DWT) separates the image into lower resolution approximation image (LL) as well as horizontal (HL), vertical (LH), and diagonal (HH) detail components. The whole process is repeated to compute multiple scale wavelet decomposition. Here we generally hide several sets of the same information logo into the cover image. So even if some of the information is lost due to an attack, we

can still collect the remaining information from the cover image using the bit majority algorithm so as to reconstruct the hidden information resembling the original one very closely.

Embedding the Digital Watermark

Step 1: First, a gray scale medical image of size 256 X 256 or 512 X 512 is taken where we can hide the information logo. Then a binary image basically a sequence of 0's and 1's is taken as information or logo of size 16 X 16 or 32 X 32 as another input.

Step 2: Next to make the program compatible to run for any size of the cover image and information logo keeping in mind the data carrying capacity of the cover image, the dimensions of the respective images are extracted and stored in to two variables.

Step 3: After normalizing the information logo, it is reshaped into one dimension.

Step 4: The cover image is then transformed to wavelet domain using Discrete Wavelet Transform (DWT) by application of the 'haar' transform. Here, the 1st level DWT was used to obtain more capacity for hiding the information. The cover image is decomposed into 4 sub-domains as HH, HL, LH and LL according to different frequencies of the cover image.

Step 5: The length of transformed cover image and information logo in one dimension is then calculated.

Step 6: The size of each decomposed sub-domain cover image is calculated and reshaped into one dimension.

Step 7: The maximum coefficient value of each of the 4 sub-domains is then determined.

Step 8: The position where the information logo can be hidden into the transformed cover image should be such that the position for hiding the binary logo in each sub domain must be between zero and the maximum coefficient value of that sub-domain.

Step 9: More than one set of the same information (8 sets in our case) is being hidden in HL and LH bands or domains for easier and good quality recovery. The hiding process in each of these domains follows a specific formula. The black pixels in each set of the one dimension information logo are hidden in a position of the information logo from where a constant value is subtracted.

Step 10: Three secret keys are also hidden in the cover image which is used to recover the information. Here we use the row and column size of the information logo as two secret keys and the total number of black dots (0's) in the one dimension logo which is actually the information to be hidden separately in the transformed cover image.

Step 11: At the end, the decomposed image is reshaped back to its normal dimension and the watermarked image is written to a file for transmission for future use.

Recovery of Watermark

We assume that the cover image that is hiding the watermark is available at the receiving end. So again in the process of recovery we first take the original image that has been used to hide the information. Along with that we also send the receiver of the message, 3 keys which essentially act as private keys. These keys are required to decrypt and to extract the encrypted, embedded messages. The steps in the recovery process are as follows:

Step 1: The watermarked and original image is taken at first as input.

Step 2: The first level decomposition of both the two inputs using DWT is to be found as we are using first level Discrete Wavelet Transform (DWT).

Step 3: Size of each sub domain of both the decomposed cover and original image is to be found for further calculations.

Step 4: Each of the decomposition of both watermarked and original cover image is reshaped into one dimension.

Step 5: The two input keys are taken from the user equal to the dimension of logo to find the size of the 4 decompositions of logo.

Step 6: The remaining input key from the user is taken which is the number of black dots that was hidden in the watermarked image.

Step 7: After that we have to determine the maximum coefficient values of original cover image.

Step 8: Those positions are then found that were used to hide the logo for each of the 4 decompositions.

Step 9: Positional sets for different sets of logo from each decomposition are extracted.

Step 10: Finally, different sets of logo are recovered from each of the sub bands using bit majority algorithm and the final logo is constructed from the different recovered sets.

RESULTS AND DISCUSSIONS:

Biomedical Image Watermarking in Spatial Domain

In Table 1, four sets of biomedical cover images along with the information logos and the obtained watermarked images are shown as the outcome of our proposed embedding technique. The calculated value of the quality metrics such as PSNR and SSIM UIQI, BER, MAE, NAE are also given to find the image quality. It is observed that the difference between the watermarked image and the cover image by the Human Visual System appear to be identical. From Table 1 we observe that the value of SSIM in all the cases is close to 1 and

Table 1. Cover image, Watermarked image, watermark and image quality measurements

	Cover Image	Information Logo	watermarked image	Image quality measures		
SET 1	Knee Douglass Lucas MRI	**S** S Logo No of Information Blocks: 93		PSNR	SSIM	UIQI
				42.29	0.97293	0.90468
				BER	MAE	NAE
				0.04465	0.33777	0.00666
SET 2	Pelvis Gynae MRI	**E** E Logo No of Information Block: 140		PSNR	SSIM	UIQI
				40.5349	0.98105	0.96866
				BER	MAE	NAE
				0.06819	0.50885	0.00869
SET 3	Foot Ankle MRI	**B** B Logo No of Information Block: 130		PSNR	SSIM	UIQI
				40.8229	0.96193	0.84927
				BER	MAE	NAE
				0.06337	0.47525	0.00753
SET 4	Brain MRI (Top View)	**KP** KP Logo No of Information Block: 109		PSNR	SSIM	UIQI
				41.2924	0.97498	0.86849
				BER	MAE	NAE
				0.05563	0.42175	0.00878

BER is close to 0 which are proof of the similarity between the original and watermarked cover image. The values of the other quality metrics also indicate that the watermarked images are quite similar to the original cover images without any distortions or visual deformities. The value of Universal Image Quality Index (UIQI) is also close to 1 which is proof of the good quality of the watermarked image.

In Table 2 through Table 7, the successful recovery of hidden information from the altered watermarked image is shown under several attacks. The results are shown for some biomedical images (MRI) subjected to different types of attacks such as salt and pepper noise, image compression, Gaussian noise, multiplicative noise, erosion and dilation. The recovered logos are visually similar to the original one. The values of SSIM and BER of the recovered logo indicate that they are much closer to the embedded one. Moreover NCC and UIQI also prove the quality of the recovered watermark or information logo.

In Table 8, reconstruction of the final logo from the different recovered hidden sets of information logo using bit majority algorithm is shown. Here two sets of results are given considering Gaussian noise and 40% of salt and pepper noise. From this table it is clear that the proposed methodology is strong enough to reconstruct the information closer to the original one.

Table 2. Watermarked image, attacked watermarked image, recovered logo and image quality metrics for Salt and Pepper Noise

Watermarked Image	Amount	Noisy Image	PSNR	Recovered Logo	Image Quality Measures		
	20%		10.9805	KP	BER	SSIM	NCC
					0.00391	0.99683	1.0000
				KP	MI	SC	UIQI
					0.95027	0.99324	0.9922
	30%		9.24336	B	BER	SSIM	NCC
					0.03906	0.91396	0.9841
				B	MI	SC	UIQI
					0.77205	0.95455	0.8965
	40%		8.28448	E	BER	SSIM	NCC
					0.14453	0.65472	0.9139
				E	MI	SC	UIQI
					0.43845	0.88520	0.6596

Table 3. Watermarked image, attacked watermarked image, recovered logo and image quality metrics for JPEG Compression

Watermarked Image	Amount	Noisy Image	PSNR	Recovered Logo	Image Quality Measures		
	2%		54.9002	KP	BER	SSIM	NCC
					0.00000	1.00000	1.0000
				KP	MI	SC	UIQI
					0.98405	1.0000	1.0000
	3%		40.4657	B	BER	SSIM	NCC
					0.05469	0.80754	0.9603
				B	MI	SC	UIQI
					0.69693	0.96923	0.8320
	5%		41.9293	S	BER	SSIM	NCC
					0.06250	0.87479	0.9698
				S	MI	SC	UIQI
					0.66550	0.96399	0.8668

Biomedical Image Watermarking in Wavelet Domain

In this section several experimental results are given to demonstrate the outcomes of the proposed biomedical image watermarking technique.

In Table 9, five sets of biomedical cover images along with information logos and the obtained watermarked images are shown as the outcome of our proposed embedding technique. The calculated value of the quality metrics such as PSNR and SSIM are also given to find the image

Table 4. Watermarked image, attacked watermarked image, recovered logo and image quality metrics for Gaussian Noise

Watermarked Image	Noisy Image	PSNR	Recovered logo	Image Quality Measures		
		49.0898	KP	BER	SSIM	NCC
				0.02344	0.95255	0.9863
			KP	MI	SC	UIQI
				0.82424	0.98658	0.9516
		40.1825	B	BER	SSIM	NCC
				0.00391	0.95005	1.0000
			B	MI	SC	UIQI
				0.96691	0.99213	0.9755
		40.0208	E	BER	SSIM	NCC
				0.05469	0.93935	0.9570
			E	MI	SC	UIQI
				0.72331	0.98272	0.9253

Table 5. Watermarked image, attacked watermarked image, recovered logo and image quality metrics for Erosion

Watermarked Image	Noisy Image	PSNR	Recovered Logo	Image Quality Measures		
		20.4966	KP	BER	SSIM	NCC
				0.08594	0.71682	0.9659
			KP	MI	SC	UIQI
				0.56838	0.92453	0.8182
		18.4799	B	BER	SSIM	NCC
				0.11328	0.81104	0.9285
			B	MI	SC	UIQI
				0.49918	0.91971	0.7771
				0.29688	0.46485	0.7471
		22.3705	S	BER	SSIM	NCC
				0.10547	0.67195	0.9450
			S	MI	SC	UIQI

quality. It is impossible to distinguish between the watermarked image and the cover image by the Human Visual System as they look very similar. From the Table 1 we can find the value of SSIM in all the cases is closer to 1 which is the proof of similarity or original and watermarked cover image. The values of the quality metrics also indicate that the watermarked images are quite similar to the original cover images without any distortions or visual deformities.

In Table 10, results using the same recovery technique are shown on some more biomedical images like X-Ray, MRI, CT scan etc. under presence of attacks known as salt and pepper noise and JPEG compression. From this table it is clear that the proposed algorithm can withstand 40%

Table 6. Watermarked image, attacked watermarked image, recovered logo and image quality metrics for Dilation

Watermarked Image	Noisy Image	PSNR	Recovered Logo	Image Quality Measures		
		17.0916	KP	BER	SSIM	NCC
				0.00000	1.00000	1.0000
			KP	MI	SC	UIQI
				0.98405	1.00000	1.0000
		14.1056	B	BER	SSIM	NCC
				0.00000	1.00000	1.0000
			B	MI	SC	UIQI
				0.99982	1.00000	1.0000
		16.8831	E	BER	SSIM	NCC
				0.00781	1.00000	1.000
			E	MI	SC	UIQI
				0.99365	0.99966	1.0000

Table 7. Watermarked image, attacked watermarked image, recovered logo and image quality metrics for Multiplicative Noise

Watermarked Image	Noisy Image	PSNR	Recovered Logo	Image Quality Measures		
		46.5546	KP	BER	SSIM	NCC
				0.01953	0.98918	0.9863
			KP	MI	SC	UIQI
				0.84527	0.99324	0.9702
		39.2459	B	BER	SSIM	NCC
				0.04688	0.90073	0.9682
			B	MI	SC	UIQI
				0.73051	0.96923	0.8869
		34.5861	S	BER	SSIM	NCC
				0.03516	0.83182	0.9820
			S	MI	SC	UIQI
				0.78671	0.99356	0.9100

salt and pepper attack and 5% JPEG compression attack with ease and the information logo that is recovered from the 8 different hidden sets using bit majority algorithm closely resembles the original information logo.

In Table 11, the quality metrics of different sets of recovered logo are compared under different types of noise attacks. The SSIM index indicates that the proposed algorithm is quite efficient for salt and pepper noise up to 40% and JPEG compression up to 5% as the SSIM is close to 1.

Table 8. Reconstruction of final logo using Bit Majority Algorithm

Type of Attack	Embedded Logo	8 different sets of recovered logo and reconstructed final logo using bit majority algorithm in spatial domain				
40 % Salt and pepper noise	E					
Gaussian Noise	E					

Table 9. Watermark embedding and resulting quality metrics

Cover Image (256X256)	Message Image (16X16)	Watermarked Image	PSNR in dB	SSIM
Brain CT	M Logo	Watermarked Brain CT	42.34	0.988
Side Face	R Logo	Watermarked Side Face	41.81	0.978
Abdomen MRI	JS Logo	Watermarked Abdomen MRI	41.51	0.985
Ankle Joint X-Ray	S Logo	Watermarked Ankle Joint X-Ray	42.16	0.981
Knee Joint MRI	K Logo	Watermarked Knee Joint MRI	41.19	0.969

CONCLUSION

Biomedical image watermarking has a lot of potential in latest and improved digital healthcare system. The relevance of watermarking for biomedical image analysis has been analyzed in Healthcare and Telemedicine. It provides an ultimate guarantee of data authentication or content protection that no other techniques ensure. Careful selection of the watermarking techniques should

Table 10. Recovery of information from watermarked image under several attacks

Watermarked image (256X256)	Altered or Attacked Watermarked image	8 different recovered sets and derived final logo using bit majority algorithm			
Watermarked Abdomen MRI	2% JPEG compression	SSIM 0.8574			
Watermarked Brain CT	5%JPEG compression	SSIM 0.7842			
Watermarked Ankle Joint X-Ray	5%JPEG compression	SSIM 0.7689			
Watermarked Brain CT	20% salt & pepper noise	SSIM 0.9673			
Watermarked Side Face	30% salt & pepper noise	SSIM 0.9351			
Watermarked Abdomen MRI	40% Salt & Pepper noise	SSIM 0.79874			
Watermarked Knee Joint MRI	20% Salt & Pepper noise	SSIM 0.9432			

Table 11. SSIM Value for different sets of recovered information logo

Used Logo	Types of Attack	Amount of Distortion	SSIM
M Logo	JPEG Compression	1%	0.9872
		2%	0.8731
		5%	0.7842
S Logo	JPEG Compression	1%	0.8975
		2%	0.8512
		5%	0.7689
K Logo	Salt and Pepper Noise	20%	0.9432
		30%	0.9378
		40%	0.7664
R Logo	Salt and Pepper Noise	20%	0.9532
		30%	0.9351
		40%	0.7762
JS Logo	Salt and Pepper Noise	20%	0.9614
		30%	0.9182
		40%	0.7987

be made to guarantee the acceptability of this new technique in biomedical field. The capability to embed maximum amount of data without image quality degradation satisfies the criteria of frequent applications in bio-medical data protection, safety and management.

The results obtained show satisfying statistics of the performance of the proposed algorithm. The biomedical image watermarking scheme in both the spatial domain and wavelet domain include procedures for data embedding, extraction and verification of quality using several quality metrics for both watermarked image and the recovered watermark. Experimental results show that these watermarking schemes have high robustness, embedding capacity, low distortion and enhanced security. Moreover these can also resist several moderately strong attacks. It is also observed that the original information can be reconstructed by the bit majority algorithm whose integrity can be strictly verified. A number of image quality metrics support the quality, strength and satisfy the high performance of the biomedical watermarking algorithms mentioned in this chapter.

So we can conclude that recently developed watermarking algorithm in both spatial and wavelet domain can be used for secure patient record storage and transmission purpose for tele-diagnosis as advancement in modern healthcare system to ensure more batter and accurate treatment.

FUTURE DIRECTIONS FOR RESEARCH

Various watermarking techniques discussed in this chapter have been performed on gray scale images. Recently, color imaging is being used in biomedical diagnosis. Therefore, the algorithm for watermarking methodologies mentioned here is to be modifying so that it can also be adopted for use with color images. In this discussion the wavelet domain has been used for frequency domain watermarking. So some other methodologies in the frequency domain using other different transforms like DCT can also be developed. Therefore the future direction is to upgrade the watermarking algorithms in such a way that they can be more strong and robust against more intensified and varied attacks.

REFERENCES

Cao, F., Huang, H. K., & Zhou, X. Q. (2003). Medical image security in a HIPAA mandated PACS environment. *Computerized Medical Imaging and Graphics, 27*(2-3), 185–196. doi:10.1016/S0895-6111(02)00073-3 PMID:12620309.

Cox, I. J., Miller, M., & Bloom, J. (2002). *Digital watermarking*. New York: Morgan Kaufmann Publishers.

Eskicioglu, M., & Fisher, P. S. (1995). Image quality measures and their performance. *IEEE Transactions on Communications, 43*(12), 2959–2965. doi:10.1109/26.477498.

Gonzalez, Woods, & Eddins. (2003). *Digital Image Processing Using MATLAB*. Upper Saddle River, NJ: Pearson Prentice Hall.

Huang, H., Coatrieux, G., Shu, H. Z., Luo, L. M., & Roux, C. (2011). Medical image integrity control and forensics based on watermarking- Approximating local modifications and identifying global image alterations. In *Proceedings of the Annual International Conference of the IEEE on Engineering in Medicine and Biology Society* (8062-8065). Washington, DC: IEEE Press.

Kobayashi, L. O. M., Furuie, S. S., & Barreto, P. S. L. M. (2009). Providing integrity and authenticity in DICOM images: A novel approach. *IEEE Transactions on Information Technology in Biomedicine, 13*(4), 582–589. doi:10.1109/TITB.2009.2014751 PMID:19244022.

Liew & Zain. J. M. (2010). Reversible medical image watermarking for tamper detection and recovery. In *Proceedings of the 3rd IEEE International Conference on Computer Science and Information Technology, 5*, 417–420. Washington, DC: IEEE Press.

Pal, K., Ghosh, G., & Bhattacharya, M. (2012)d. A novel digital image watermarking scheme for data security using bit replacement and majority algorithm technique. Watermarking, 1, (979-953). Rijecka, Croatia: INTECH Publications.

Pal, K., Ghosh, G., & Bhattacharya, M. (2012a). Biomedical image watermarking in wavelet domain for data integrity using bit majority and multiple copies of hidden information. *American Journal of Biomedical Engineering, 2*(2), 29–37. doi:10.5923/j.ajbe.20120202.06.

Pal, K., Ghosh, G., & Bhattacharya, M. (2012b). Reversible digital image watermarking using bit replacement and majority algorithm technique. *Journal of Intelligent Learning Systems and Applications, 4*(3), 199–206. doi:10.4236/jilsa.2012.43020.

Pal, K., Ghosh, G., & Bhattacharya, M. (2012c). Relevance of bio-medical image watermarking for data authentication and security in telemedicine and healthcare. In *Proceedings of the National Conference on Pervasive Computing & Communications* (131-135). Kolkata, India: IEEE Press.

Pal, K., Ghosh, G., & Bhattacharya, M. (2012e). Biomedical image watermarking for medical data security using modified bit replacement algorithm in spatial domain. *International Journal of Applied Engineering, 2*(3), 158–169.

Velumani, R., & Seenivasagam, V. (2010). A reversible blind medical image watermarking scheme for patient identification, improved telediagnosis, and tamper detection with a facial image watermark. In *Proceedings of IEEE International Conference on Computational Intelligence and Computing Research* (1-8). Washington, DC: IEEE Press.

Zain, J. M., & Fauzi, A. R. M. (2007). Evaluation of medical image watermarking with tamper detection and recovery. In *Proceedings of 29th Annual International Conference of the IEEE on Engineering in Medicine and Biology Society* (5661–5664). Washington, DC: IEEE Press.

ADDITIONAL REFERENCES

Allaert & Dusserre. (1994). Security of Health System in France. What we do will no longer be different from what we tell. *International Journal of Bio-Medical Computing, 35*(1), 201–204. PMID:8188415.

Anand & Niranjan. (1998). Watermarking medical images with patient information. In *Proceedings of IEEE/EMBS Conference* (703-706). Hong Kong: IEEE Press.

Arnold, Schmucker, & Wolthusen. (2006). *Techniques and applications of digital watermarking and content protection*. Boston: Artech House.

Coatrieux, Maitre, Sankur, Rolland, & Collorec. (2000). Relevance of watermarking in medical imaging. In *Proceedings of the IEEE EMBS Conference on Information Technology Applications in Biomedicine* (250-255). Arlington, VA: IEEE Press.

Fazli & Khodaverdi. (2009). Trade-off between imperceptibility and robustness of LSB watermarking using SSIM quality metrics. In *Proceedings of IEEE Conference*. Washington, DC: IEEE Press.

Giakoumaki, A., Pavlopoulos, S., & Koutsouris, D. (2006). Multiple image watermarking applied to health information management. *IEEE Transactions on Information Technology in Biomedicine, 10*(4), 722–732. doi:10.1109/TITB.2006.875655 PMID:17044406.

Hartung & Kutter. (1999). Multimedia watermarking techniques. *Proceedings of the IEEE, 87*(7), 1079–1107. doi:10.1109/5.771066.

Katzenbeisser & Petitcolas. (2000). *Information hiding techniques for steganography and digital watermarking*. Boston: Artech House.

Kutter & Petitcolas. (1999). A fair benchmark for image watermarking systems. [San Jose, CA: SPIE Press.]. *Proceedings of SPIE Security and Watermarking of Multimedia Contents, 3657*, 226–239. doi:10.1117/12.344672.

Langelaar, Setyawan, & Lagendijk. (2000). Watermarking digital image and video data. *IEEE Signal Processing Magazine, 17*, 20–46. doi:10.1109/79.879337.

Lee, G. J., Yoon, E. J., & Yoo, K. Y. (2008). A new LSB based digital watermarking scheme with random mapping function. In *Proceedings of IEEE Conference*. Washington, DC: IEEE Press.

Lin & Delp. (1999). A review of fragile image watermarks. In *Proceedings of the Multimedia and Security Workshop* (35-39). Orlando, FL: ACM Press.

Macq & Dewey. (1999). Trusted headers for medical images. In *Proceedings of DFG VIII-DII Watermarking Workshop*. Erlangen, Germany: IEEE Press.

Maeder & Ecker. (1999). Medical image compression: Quality and performance issues. New Approaches in Medical Image Analysis, 3747, 93–101. Bellingham, WA: SPIE Press.

Miller, C. Linnartz, & Kalker. (1999). A review of watermarking principles and practices. In K. K. Parhi & T. Nishitani (Eds.), Digital Signal Processing for Multimedia Systems (461-485). New York: CRC Press.

Pal, K., & Bhar, A. Ghosh. G., & Bhattacharya, M. (2009). A review on digital watermarking schemes using several LSB techniques. In *Proceedings of National Conference on Ubiquitous Computing* (76-89). Washington, DC: IEEE Press.

Pal, K., Das, T. S., & Mankar, V. H. (2009). Contour detection and recovery through bio-medical watermarking for tele-diagnosis. *International Journal of Tomography & Statistics*, *14*(S10), 109–119.

Pal, K., Ghosh, G., & Bhattacharya, M. (2012f). A comparative study between LSB and modified bit replacement (MBR) watermarking technique in spatial domain for biomedical image security. *International Journal of Computer Applications and Technology*, *1*(1), 30–39. doi:10.7753/2012.1007.

Pal, K., Ghosh, G., & Bhattacharya, M. (2012g). Biomedical image watermarking for content protection using multiple copies of information and bit majority algorithm in wavelet domain. In *Proceedings of IEEE Students' Conference On Electrical, Electronics And Computer Sciences* (1-6). Bhopal, India: IEEE Press.

Podilchuk & Delp. (2001). Digital watermarking algorithms and applications. *IEEE Signal Processing Magazine*, *18*(4).

Rey & Dugelay. (2002). A survey of watermarking algorithms for image authentication. *EURASIP Journal on Applied Signal Processing*, 613–621.

Sheikh, Sabir, & Bovik. (2006). A statistical evalution of recent full reference image quality assessment algorithms. *IEEE Transactions on Image Processing*, *15*(11), 3441–3456. doi:10.1109/TIP.2006.881959.

Tian, J. (2003). High capacity reversible data embedding and content authentication. In *Proceedigns of IEEE International Conference on Acoustics, Speech, and Signal Processing* (517-520). Washington, DC: IEEE Press.

Wong, P. W. (1998). A public key watermark for image verification and authentication. In *Proceedings of the IEEE International Conference on Image Processing* (455-459). Chicago: IEEE Press.

Wong, P. W. (1999). A watermark for image integrity and ownership verification. In *Proceedings of the IS&T PICS 99* (374-379). Bellingham, WA: SPIE Press.

Zhao, Hsu, & Miaou. (2002). A data-hiding technique with authentication, integration, and confidentiality for electronic patient records. *IEEE Transactions on Information Technology in Biomedicine*, *6*, 46–53. doi:10.1109/4233.992161 PMID:11936596.

KEY TERMS AND DEFINITIONS

Attack: Unwanted manipulation or alteration of image causing image quality degradation.

Cover Image: It is the image where the information is being stored hidden.

Electronic Patient Record: (EPR): Is the various medical document of patient in digital format.

Embedding: This is the process for putting the information to a cover image.

Logo: Information or message that is to be stored.

Recovery: This is the process by which hidden information can be retrieve from watermarked image.

Robust: This is the strength by which any system can protect itself from unwanted alteration.

Watermarking: This is a process to hide some information visibly or invisibly into an image.

Quality Metrics: Some standard measures to check the image quality degradation after processing.

Chapter 13

Electrical Impedance Tomography (EIT):
A Harmless Medical Imaging Modality

Tushar Kanti Bera
Indian Institute of Science, India

J. Nagaraju
Indian Institute of Science, India

ABSTRACT

Looking into the human body is very essential not only for studying the anatomy and physiology, but also for diagnosing a disease or illness. Doctors always try to visualize an organ or body part in order to study its physiological and anatomical status for understanding and/or treating its illness. This necessity introduced the diagnostic tool called medical imaging. The era of medical imaging started in 1895, when Roentgen discovered the magical powerful invisible rays called X-rays. Gradually the medical imaging introduced X-Ray CT, Gamma Camera, PET, SPECT, MRI, USG. Recently medical imaging field is enriched with comparatively newer tomographic imaging modalities like Electrical Impedance Tomography (EIT), Diffuse Optical Tomography (DOT), Optical Coherence Tomography (OCT), and Photoacaustic Tomography (PAT). The EIT has been extensively researched in different fields of science and engineering due to its several advantages. This chapter will present a brief review on the available medical imaging modalities and focus on the need of an alternating method. EIT will be discussed with its physical and mathematical aspects, potentials, and challenges.

INTRODUCTION

Visualizing the interior of the human body is very essential for studying its anatomy as well as physiology but also for diagnosing a disease or illness. Doctors have always been interested to visualize the organs or body parts for study-ing their physiological and anatomical status for diagnosing and treating its illness which insisted the doctors to search for a diagnostic tool called medical imaging. The era of medical imaging started in 1895, when Roentgen discovered the magical and powerful invisible rays called X-rays which were unexpectedly found in his laboratory to be useful for visualizing the tissue contrast on photography plates called planar radiography.

DOI: 10.4018/978-1-4666-4558-5.ch013

After that the medical imaging field introduced X-Ray Computed Tomography (X-Ray CT), Gamma Camera, Positron emission tomography (PET), Single-Photon Emission Computed Tomography (SPECT), Magnetic Resonance Imaging (MRI), UltraSonoGraphy (USG). Recently medical imaging field is enriched with comparatively newer tomographic imaging modalities with electric current and light signals. The computed tomography which use the electric signal is called Electrical Impedance Tomography (EIT) whereas the other tomographic methods which use the light signal can be found in form of Diffuse Optical Tomography (DOT), Optical Coherence Tomography (OCT), PhotoAcaustic Tomography (PAT), and others. The EIT has been extensively researched in different field of science and engineering for more than three decades due to its several advantages over other tomographic imaging modalities. Being a very fast, low-cost, radiation free, nonionizing, noninvasive, portable tomographic imaging technique EIT is studied and applied in medical imaging, industrial process tomography, chemical engineering, civil engineering, defense field, geosciences, oceanography, manufacturing technology, MEMS and thin film technology, microbiology and biotechnology and so on. This chapter will present the physical and mathematical aspects of the EIT technology along with its potentials and challenges. The chapter will start with a brief introduction to the medical imaging technologies and summarize the available conventional medical imaging techniques. Starting from the invention of X-rays, the chapter will discuss about few of the main imaging modalities in brief to understand their working principle, advantages and limitations. The chapter emphasizes on the medical imaging modalities working on the Computed Tomography (CT) principle. The computed tomography is discussed in detail considering the X-Ray CT as the basic CT imaging modality. The present scenario of the medical imaging is discussed with their own advantages and disadvantages. The chapter also discusses about the

nuclear medicine technologies with the examples of the available emission tomographic modalities used in clinics and hospitals. After a brief review on the available medical imaging modalities the chapter summarizes their advantages and limitations and focuses on the need of an alternating method. As an alternating medical imaging modality Electrical Impedance Tomography (EIT) is proposed and discussed in detail. It's working principle, methodology, physical significance are discussed along with its advantages over the existing medical imaging techniques.

BACKGROUND

Doctors always looked for a safe, effective, reliable, low cost and fast imaging modality to visualize human body parts for studying its physiological and anatomical status for clinical diagnosis. A number of medical imaging modalities have been introduced for better visualization or for a particular advantage in medical or clinical aspects. The imaging modalities such as X-Ray Planner Radiography, X-Ray CT, Gamma Camera, SPECT, PET, MRI, USG, and so forth have been employed for clinical investigations and diagnosis and treatments since for long while. All these imaging methods have their own advantages and limitations. Although the above mentioned techniques are found very popular in modern medical diagnosis but still all of these techniques are found with several limitations and challenges which are still under research. Researcher are also trying to invent a medical imaging modality with most of the desired advantages as not a single of these available modalities is found with all required advantages sought by clinicians and doctors. Moreover all the methods are always found with a number of disadvantages or some limitations which direct the doctors to study the patient with a number of imaging modality for better diagnosis. CT, SPECT, PET, though provide better image quality, use the ionizing radiation and hence those methods are not medically safe. Although the imaging modalities with ionizing radiation are essential in modern medical imaging field for their higher resolution, yet they are not the safe techniques and hence, sometimes, they create some complications. Therefore a alternating imaging modality is found required which will provide the most essential advantages as well as with some distinct features which are still not available in conventional medical imaging modalities. In this direction Electrical Impedance Tomography (EIT) is introduced with a lot of advantages over other medical imaging methods. The main limitation of EIT is the low spatial resolution which needs more research and hence it is being studied with a number of research groups all around the world.

MEDICAL IMAGING

Introduction

Biological subjects (animals and plants) are complex living structures developed by several cells and tissues spatially distributed in three dimensions. A human body is a three dimensional living object with very complex anatomical and physiological structures having several body parts (tissues and organs) performing their own works essential for keeping the whole body alive. The mal functioning of any of the body parts due to their abnormal anatomical or physiological changes (called illness or disease) or any sudden damages or disordered state (temporary or permanent) may harm the body and the life may be in danger. If the necessary steps (diagnosis and treatment) are not taken immediately the illness may cause even death. In these conditions the visualization of the interior of the body parts becomes very much essential for the diagnosis of the illness, its causes and the proper treatment. The body interior visualization procedure called medical imaging (Bankman, 2000) is considered as a strong diagnostic modality which is essentially

required in this case to visualize the interior of the body or any body parts. Thus, medical imaging is a powerful diagnostic modality by which doctors and clinicians can observe the body interiors along with the information related to their physiological, anatomical structures and/or functional aspects which help them to diagnose, treat and cure the disease. In medical science, the medical imaging technology is used to create the images of human subjects (or their body parts and function thereof) with an invasive or noninvasive visualization approaches (medical procedures to evaluate, diagnose or examine the physiological or biophysical status). Biomedical imaging is the procedure applied in biological as well as in the medical science whereas the imaging procedures applied in medical science is called the medical imaging. Medical imaging can be a 2D or 3D visualizations process of the Domain Under Test (DUT) representing its anatomical and/or functional profile. According to Slobodanka Stankovic and Olivera Klisuric, "Medical imaging refers to the techniques and processes used to create images of the human body (or parts thereof) for clinical purposes (medical procedures seeking to reveal, diagnose or examine disease) or medical science (including the study of normal anatomy and function)" (Stankovic and Olivera Klisuric, 2007). Medical imaging procedures apply energy to the SUT and produce the image of the living tissues in terms of their properties obtained from the observed signal generated by an applied signal. As the human body is a complex 3D structure composed of different types of muscles and tissues oriented on the skeleton and hence images taken at different views (such as anterior, posterior, lateral, dorsal, ventral, etc.) carry their own importance and useful information. Moreover, as a particular organ or body part of the human body has its particular geometry and position in the body, the imaging of the human body in different planes (transverse, coronal, sagittal etc.) and angles is very important.

History of Medical Imaging

As the human body is an opaque structure, looking inside is generally difficult and hence before the medical imaging comes (before the invention of X-rays), anatomical surgery was one only means to look inside the patient's body. To avoid the invasive procedures (surgery), the doctors, medical scientists and engineers and clinicians always looked for a means by which the body parts and the organs can be visualized without surgery (non-invasively). The era of medical imaging started with the great invention of X-rays by Professor W. C. Roentgen in 1895. W. C. Roentgen, a professor of physics in Worzburg, Bavaria, discovered the X-rays in his laboratory when he was working with an electromagnetic radiation. X-rays, as called by its inventor due to their unknown nature at the time of discovery, were discovered from the electromagnetic radiation.

In 1895, Roentgen was conducting an electromagnetic experiment in a dark room with an induction coil placed inside a partially evacuated glass tube which was totally covered by a black paper. Suddenly he noticed that a screen covered in fluorescent material was illuminated by some unknown rays. After observing the repetitive experimentation he concluded that a number of objects could be penetrated by these unknown rays called X-rays. He applied the X-rays on the left hand of his wife, Anna Bertha Ludwig. The image of his wife's hand was taken on a photographic plate which showed the clear contrast between the opaque bones and the translucent flesh including the clear image of the ring his wife had. In 1896, the X-ray image was presented to Professor Ludwig Zehnder of the Physik Institut, University of Freiburg. In this way an extraordinary discovery, that the internal structures of the body could be made visible without any surgery, was made.

Dr. John Macintyre, the head of the X-ray department (established in 1896 and which was one of the first radiology departments in the world), Glasgow Royal Infirmary, produced a number of remarkable X-rays images (British Library, 2013) like: the first X-ray of a kidney stone; an X-ray showing a penny in the throat of a child, and an image of a frog's legs in motion. Dr Hall-Edwards, in the same year, became one of the first people to use an X-ray to make a diagnosis by visualizing a needle embedded in a woman's hand (British Library, 2013). After that, in the first twenty years following the Roentgen's discovery, X-rays were successfully used to treat soldiers by visualizing the bone fractures and imbedded bullets (British Library, 2013).

After the invention of X-rays in 19th century, a new path called medical imaging is opened in the field of medical sciences. X-ray planar radiography (Figure 1) is the first medical imaging modality which totally changed the scenario of the medical diagnosis. *X-ray planar radiography* (Figure 1) is a method of shadowing of a Subject Under Test (SUT) by using the X-rays passing through the SUT composed of different body parts having different absorption coefficients. The X-rays coming out from the SUT (after absorption) are exposed to an X-ray receptor either may be a X-ray sensitive screen or a radiographic cassette. X-ray planar radiography either may be direct radiogra-

Figure 1. X-ray planar radiography: X-ray planar radiography schematic (X-rays are passed through the patient's body and received on the radiographic plate/film which is developed to obtain the image)

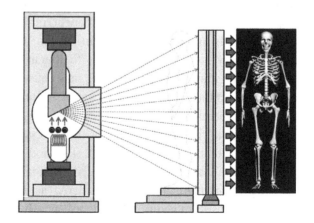

phy (DR) which is sometimes called screen/film radiography or Computed Radiography (CR). After that, the other medical imaging techniques like X-rays Computed Tomography, MRI scanners, ultrasound, nuclear medicine etc. came gradually due to the different types of needs to visualize the human body. Each of these techniques has their own advantages and disadvantages that make them essential and useful for different conditions and suitability for different parts of the complex anatomy and physiology of the patient body.

Medical Imaging Modalities

Medical imaging is the procedure which is essentially required to visualize the anatomical or physiological interiors of human body or human parts for the clinical investigations or medical diagnoses of the diseases (or abnormal physiological status) of human subjects as well as for studying and understanding the internal physiological status of normal anatomy and physiology. It applies some form of energy (Bushberg et al., 2001) as an input signal and measures the signal developed after interacting with the body tissue under test. Different types of medical imaging procedures can be obtained by varying the types of energies used and the data acquisition technologies (Bushberg *et al.*, 2001). The different modes or procedures used for obtaining the medical images are termed as the *medical imaging modalities*. Each medical imaging modality has its own applications and advantages in medicine. Depending on the modalities, the medical imaging can be broadly classified as: X-ray radiography, Computed Tomography (CT), MRI, Nuclear medicine, Ultrasound Imaging, and other medical imaging modalities (Endoscopy, Microscopy, etc).

COMPUTED TOMOGRAPHY (CT)

Introduction to CT

Computed Tomography (CT) (Rockett & Wang, 2001), also known as Computed Axial Tomography (CAT) is a computation technique which produces the cross sectional view (image) of the spatial distribution of a particular parameter of an object by calculating the parameters from the signals acquired at the domain boundary generated by injecting a suitable signal at the boundary. Hence the computed tomography can be defined as the solution of mathematical inverse problems in which the properties of living tissue of the Domain Under Test (DUT) is inferred from the observed (at the domain boundary) signal generated by an applied signal at the domain boundary. The word "tomography", derived from the Greek words *"tomos"* (which means "part" or "section"), and *"graphein"* (to write), represents the imaging by sections or sectioning, through the use of any kind of penetrating energy. The device which conducts the tomography is called a tomograph and the image produced in tomography is termed as a tomogram. The mathematical algorithm or the computer programme which calculates the parameters (solution of the problem) of the tomographic imaging from the measured data, using some known information (boundary conditions) some assumptions and approximations, is called *tomographic reconstruction technique*. As the tomography needs a lot of mathematical matrix calculations which is generally performed in a Personal Computer (PC) it is "often termed as the 'Computed Tomography'."

CT vs. Planner Radiography

Radiography is a procedure in which a shadow or impression is created using a radiation based on the transparency or attenuation properties of the object under test. Hence the X-ray planar radiography gives only the two dimensional projection of the object on the plane perpendicular to the path of the radiation applied. The planar radiographic images, called radiograms, record only the *mean* absorption by the various tissues situated along the path of X-ray penetration (Hounsfield, 1979). Whereas the computed tomograph reconstructs the picture of the body interiors with a spatial distribution of the tissue properties (X-ray attenuation co-efficient) by measuring the attenuation of X-ray beams passing through the sections of the body at different angles called projections angles (Hounsfield, 1979). Also, applying the X-rays at different parallel planes (plane of interest or imaging domain) a number of cross sectional views called "CT image slice" are obtained for a particular body part. Combining these "image slices" a three-dimensional view and its related information of the body part is virtually obtained (Hounsfield, 1979). The computed tomography not only gives the structural information of the object but also it provides the spatial distribution of the object parameters carrying a lot of information about the object.

History of CT

As the planar X-radiographs were not satisfactory to the clinicians who urged the radiologists to provide them with more effective and more informative images, a strong driving force with clinical motivation started to act for developing a technology capable of providing more information about the patient body parts than what X-radiograph provides (Seynaeve & Broos, 1995). In 1914, Mayer first suggests the idea of tomography, then Bocage, Grossman and Vallebona all developed the idea further and built their own tomographic equipments (Seynaeve & Broos, 1995). After that, Ziedses des Plantes published the most extensive and thorough study on tomography (Seynaeve & Broos, 1995) in 1931 and Frank and Takahashi published the basic principles of axial tomography in the mid forties. British engineer Godfrey Hounsfield of EMI Laboratories, Eng-

land and South African physicist Allan Cormack, Tufts University, Massachusetts, developed and commercialized the first axial computer tomography in 1972 (EMI-Scanner) with a necessary developments in electronics (Seynaeve & Broos, 1995; Internet Article, 2011). Both of them got the Nobel Prize for their brilliant contributions to medicine and science.

Application of CT

CT imaging technology has been very popular over the last few decades in all over the world. Although most common in medicine, due to its several advantages, CT is also being applied in different field of science and technology such as: in medical, biology, biotechnology, chemical sciences, geophysics, oceanography, materials science, astrophysics, rock science, archaeology and other sciences, engineering and technologies.

Modern CT Scanners

A modern CT scanner looks like a big, square doughnut with a patient aperture (opening) which is around 60 cm to 70 cm (24" to 28") in diameter (Advanced Veterinary Medical Images, 2011) Inside the CT scanner a rotating X-ray tube is mounted on one side of the gantry and the banana shaped X-ray detector is mounted on the opposite side. The detector in a CT scanner is the device that measures or detects the amount of attenuated X-ray (X-ray that passes through the object being scanned) being scanned. A rotating beam of X-ray (either parallel beam, fan beam or cone beam, or else) is passed through the object and the attenuated X-rays are detected by the detectors. For a complete rotation (360° rotation) of the X-ray tube and detector, CT scanner produces an "image slice" which is then collimated (focused) to a thickness between 1 mm and 10 mm using lead shutters in front of the X-ray tube and X-ray detector (Advanced Veterinary Medical Images, 2011). The number of slices per rotation is equal to the number of detectors the scanner has and hence the more the detectors in a CT scanner, more slices per rotation. If a CT scanner has 16 detectors, it is able to take 16 slices per rotation; if the scansner has 64 detectors, it acquires 64 slices of the object per rotation and so on.

Tomographic Reconstruction Basics

In computed tomographic imaging of the SUT (the human body) some kind of energy (such as ionizing radiation, optical, electrical, sound, ultrasound, near infrared or else) is applied on the SUT (or passed through the SUT) and the transformed form of the energy is collected or detected to compare with the incident one for reconstruction of the parameter of interest which is the material property of the system (SUT). The parameter of interest of SUT may be the transfer function of the system or a function of a number of material properties and it gives the anatomical, physiological (bio-physiological or physiochemical) or pathological information. Hence, in the medical tomographic imaging, the energy used to produce the image must penetrate the body tissues (Bushberg et al., 2001). If the energy passed through the SUT does not experience any type of interaction (e.g. absorption, attenuation, scattering), the detected energy would not contain any useful information about the internal anatomy of SUT (Bushberg et al., 2001). Therefore, it would not be possible to construct an image of the anatomy using that information. In computed tomographic technique a power signal (either X-rays or optical or electrical or else) is applied to the boundary of the object under test and the signal generated at the boundary are collected for the different projections angle to obtain a complete scan around a 360° rotation. Thus the CT involves gathering the output signal (Y) generated by applying an input signal (X) at the boundary from multiple directions and reconstructing the domain parameter relating the Y to X (parameter of interest) using a software called reconstruction algorithm processed in a PC.

Figure 2. 2D-Computed tomography principle: X-Ray projections at different angles for looking into the patient body at a particular plane (image plane or image slice) through the 2D computed tomographic imaging

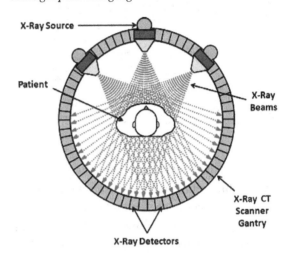

2D Computed Tomography (CT)

In 2D computed tomography X-Rays are passed through the object under test at different angles called projection angle (Theta_suffix_n) within a particular plane (Figure 2). The X-ray data collection process conducted for a particular projection angle (Theta_suffix_n) is called a projection (P_suffix_n) and the (P_suffix_n) is given by 360 degree/(Theta_suffix_n). The attenuated X-Ray beams are received by the X-Ray detectors placed at the scanner gantry and the data are sent to the PC for image reconstruction process. By 2D computed tomography the doctors and the clinicians can visualize the anatomical profiles at a particular 2D plane (plan of interest) inside the patient body.

3D Computed Tomography (CT)

Though the CT scanners in earlier age are used only to generate the images in the transverse plane, the modern scanners now allow us to image the body in various planes. 3D Computed Tomography

Figure 3. 3D-Computed tomography principle in transverse planes: X-rays are applied in three transverse planes S1, S2 and S3

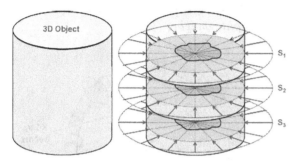

(3DCT) is a medical imaging method employing tomographic technique to reconstruct the 3D image of the subject image under test by computer processing of large amount of boundary data using 3D image reconstruction algorithm (Herman, 2009). In 3D X-ray computed tomography, the 3D image reconstruction algorithm is used to generate a three-dimensional image of the inside of the object from a large series of two-dimensional X-ray images taken around a single axis of rotation (Smith-Bindman et al., 2009) for complex structures (Figure 3).

PRESENT SCENARIO OF MEDICAL IMAGING

In this section, the most of the available medical imaging techniques which are being used as regular medical and clinical imaging modalities in clinics and hospitals are discussed with their working principle, applications, advantages and limitations.

The most important aspect of the modern medical imaging technology is to obtain the better and more informative internal views of the human body interiors called human anatomy (CBS, 2005), its organs and body parts. Medical imaging (Suetens, 2009) is the most important and most essential tool of the modern medical

diagnostics which allows us to look into the human body parts noninvasively (SUNY, 2006) or minimal invasively (SUNY, 2006). The journey of the Medical Imaging began in November 1895 with discovery of the X-rays (Assmus, 1995; Bradley, 2008) by Wilhelm Conrad Roentgen (Assmus, 1995; Bradley, 2008). The era of the medical imaging was initiated by W. C. Röntgen when he invented X-Rays and produced an X-ray radiographic planner image of his wife's left hand in 1985 (Assmus, 1995). Actually it is told that, "The discovery of X rays in 1895 was the beginning of a revolutionary change in our understanding of the physical world" (Assmus, 1995). The discovery of X-rays revolutionized the field of medical diagnosis and the doctors got a very strong and effective diagnostic modality to visualize the human anatomy noninvasively. X-rays are of short wavelength (0.1 to 1 Å) and not deflected by the object it passes through (Noor, 2007).

In 1970, the concept of the medical imaging is remarkably changed by the invention of the X-ray computed tomography (CT scan) (Muller et al., 2012; Kak & Slaney, 1999; Hsieh, 2009) which provided the 2D cross sectional images (Hendee, 1989) of the human body representing the spatial distribution of the body tissue parameter. Rotating X-ray beams are applied on the patient body at different projection angles and the attenuated X-rays are collected by the X-ray detectors (Guerra, 2004; Iniewski, 2009). Comparing the incidental X-rays with the attenuated X-rays collected for different projections throughout a complete scan, the image reconstruction algorithm reconstruct the spatial distribution of the X-ray attenuation co-efficient of the body tissue and provides the 2D tomographic images of the body parts.

After that, the nuclear imaging technique (Lima, 2011) called the nuclear medicine (Lima, 2011) or Emission Computed Tomography (ECT) (Lima, 2011) was introduced to visualize the metabolic functions of the body tissue. A radiopharmaceutical (Lima, 2011) is administered to the body tissue and the radiations produced by the decaying of the short life radio isotopes (Lima, 2011) are detected by the radiation detectors (Guerra, 2004; Iniewski, 2009; Lima, 2011) to obtain the tomographic images of the spatial distribution of the radiopharmaceutical which represents the metabolic functions (Guerra, 2004; Iniewski, 2009; Lima, 2011) of the body tissue under test. The automated process of this technique was invented by Cassen et al. (1950) in early 50's after he built his rectilinear scanner (Noor, 2007; Cassen, 1998). Depending on the methods and type of radiations produced by the radionuclide used, ECT is developed in two branches (Guerra, 2004; Iniewski, 2009; Lima, 2011; Elliott, 2005): Single-Photon-Emission Computed Tomography (SPECT) and Positron Emission Computed Tomography (PET) (Guerra, 2004; Iniewski, 2009; Lima, 2011; Elliott, 2005). SPECT detects gamma rays emitted singly, and sequentially, by the radionuclide tracer (Noor, 2007; Guerra, 2004; Iniewski, 2009; Lima, 2011; Elliott, 2005) whereas the PET detects the two coincident 511-keV annihilated photos from position emitters such as ^{11}C, ^{13}N, ^{15}O, and ^{18}F (Noor, 2007; Guerra, 2004; Iniewski, 2009; Lima, 2011; Elliott, 2005). The CT-scan and ECT rely on ionizing radiation; therefore they carry some finite potential disadvantage which imposes the limitations on their usage especially for pregnant women and children (Noor, 2007).

Donald et al. (1958) introduced the Ultrasonography or USG technique in mid 50's which is based on the sonar principle and employs ultrasound waves (frequencies from 1 MHz to 20 MHz) transmitted by an ultrasonic transducer to reconstruct the image from the returning echoes. Except the local thermal effect and bubble formation the USG is considered as the safe medical imaging modality but the main disadvantage of USG provides very low resolution medical images (Barber, 1992).

In 1973, Paul C. Lauterbur (1973a, 1973b) and Sir Peter Mansfield (Mansfield & Grannell, 1973) introduced the Magnetic Resonance Imaging (MRI) technique to reconstruct the tomographic image of the body tissue using Nuclear Magnetic Resonance (NMR) and received The Nobel Prize in Physiology or Medicine in 2003 for their remarkable contribution in MRI. The NMR technique was first described by Edward Mills Purcell (Purcell et al., 1946) and Felix Bloch (Bloch et al., 1946) in 1946 and they received the Nobel Prize in Physics in 1952. Lauterbur and Mansfield used the principles of NMR and demonstrated a technique to reconstruct the physical structure in form of a tomographic image. Since then Magnetic Resonance Imaging (MRI) has been used in many biomedical, chemical and several engineering fields. MRI imaging method (Stuart, 1997; Bushong, 2003; Kuperman, 2000) reconstructs the magnetic properties of matter from the radio frequency energy released by protons of hydrogen atoms in the body tissue by applying a Radio Frequency (RF) pulse on the protons aligned with a strong magnetic field generated by a super conducting magnet (Stuart, 1997; Bushong, 2003). The image is obtained by displacing the equilibrium magnetization vector using a radio frequency pulse and observing the signal emitted by the proton as they returns to equilibrium. The images of a human organs produced by CT and MR techniques have better spatial resolutions (Hero et al., 1999) than the images obtained with radiopharmaceutical techniques. Though the MRI provides the radiation free tomographic image with considerably good resolution, yet the method is quite expensive. Large magnetic field of the MRI technique limits the application on patient in several conditions. The patients with metal implants, pacemaker, and other medical implants are not allowed to go through the MRI procedure.

A number of medical imaging modalities such as X-Ray Planner Radiography, X-Ray CT, Gamma Camera, SPECT, PET, MRI, USG etc. have been employed for clinical investigations and diagnosis and treatments. Although the above mentioned techniques are very essential in modern medical field but not a single method is found with all required advantages sought by clinicians and doctors. Moreover all the methods are always found with a number of disadvantages or some limitations which direct the doctors to study the patient with a number of imaging modality. CT, SPECT, PET use the ionizing radiation and hence those methods are not medically safe. Though the imaging modalities with ionizing radiation are essential in modern medical imaging field, yet they are not the safe techniques and hence, sometimes, they create some complications. In 2011, the Cochrane collaboration (Gøtzsche, 2011) concluded that the X-Ray mamography reduce mortality from breast cancer by 15 percent but also result in unnecessary surgery and anxiety, resulting in their view that it is not clear whether mammography screening does more good or harm (Gøtzsche, 2011). The U.S. Preventive Services Task Force (U. S. Preventive Services Task Force, 2013) pointed out that in addition to unnecessary surgery and anxiety, the risks of more frequent mammograms include a small but significant increase in breast cancer induced by radiation (U. S. Preventive Services Task Force, 2013). Though, very often the results of noninvasive examination such as mammography (Feig & Hendrick, 1997) helps us to diagnose the lump in breast, yet, the cumulative effect of the mammography radiation, sometimes, cause cancer (Feig & Hendrick, 1997). Both mammography and clinical breast exam, also used for screening, can indicate an approximate likelihood that a lump is cancer, and may also detect some other lesions (Saslow et al., 2004). The X-Ray CT, mammography, ultrasound imaging gives only the geometrical (position and shape) anatomy of the tumor which is not sufficient to identify the malignancy and hence sometimes the surgery (lumpectomy (Litière et al., 2012) or mastectomy (Majid et al., 2012) with or without lymph node removal) and the post surgery biopsy (Kothari et al., 2012) may appeared as unimportant when they are already performed (U. S. Preventive Services Task Force, 2013). Also, mammography cannot be efficiently applied to the patient with

dense breast and hence the procedure has poor efficiency for young women. MRI uses very strong magnetic field which imposes a lot of restrictions and precautions during the procedures. USG does not use any ionizing radiation and hence it is assumed as a safe technique and it is also portable. CT, SPECT, PET gives better resolution but use ionizing radiation and hence it is found as a safe technique and it is also portable, although it provides a very low resolution images. CT, SPECT, PET gives better resolution compared to USG, but use ionizing radiations and hence they are not always medically safe. Though the functional imaging (Frank & Kaye, 2012) can be obtained from SPECT and PET, yet, ordinary CT does not provide any functional information about the subject. SPECT and PET are not noninvasive as these techniques need some radiopharmaceuticals to be injected to the body. Functional MRI (Stuart, 1997) also gives the metabolic function of the region under test. CT, SPECT, PET, MRI methods are expensive and non-portable. As the CT, MRI, SPECT, PET machines are not portable the bedside imaging and imaging of critical ill patient is a tough task in these modalities. Also, the long term monitoring and ambulatory monitoring (Kubiak & Stone, 2012) are not possible for CT, Gamma Camera, SPECT, PET, USG and MRI. Although the USG is portable, but this method provides the low contrast (Singh et al., 2012) and low resolution images with insufficient information. As the MRI uses very strong magnetic field and provides high resolution and high contrast image. But due to the strong magnetic field, it imposes a lot of restrictions and precautions during the procedures. Therefore, the MRI technique has a lot of precautions and limitation for its strong magnetic fields and radio pulses which can affect metal implants (Abtahi et al., 2012), cochlear implants (Chena et al., 2012), cardiac pacemakers (Korpinen et al., 2012) etc. Due to the huge and heavy structure of CT and MRI machine with fixed gantry openings, the extremely obese persons may face problems to fit into traditional scanners. CT, SPECT, PET uses ionizing radiations and the SPECT and PET are invasive. Hence, although the above mentioned available techniques carry some superiority in terms of spatial resolutions, they also possess some disadvantages and limitations. Therefore, a low cost, radiation free, noninvasive, compact, portable and medically safe imaging modality is found essential and hence the Electrical Impedance Tomography (EIT) is introduced. The EIT technique injects a low amplitude low frequency alternating current which cannot be even felt by the patients and hence the technique is assumed as harmless and medically safe.

Hence, from the above summary it is concluded that, the available imaging modalities used for medical imaging applications either apply the ionizing radiations or provide insufficient diagnostic information or expensive or invasive or non-portable or provide low resolution image. Hence a low cost, portable, medically safe, radiation free, noninvasive diagnostic tool is essentially required which will not only give the geometrical (position and shape) anatomy of the tumor but also can provide the functional information of the tumor required to identify the malignancy and other physiological status of the tumor.

ELECTRICAL IMPEDANCE TOMOGRAPHY (EIT)

Introduction to EIT

Electrical Impedance Tomography (EIT) (Webster, 1990; Holder, 2005; Seo & Woo, 2012; Barber, 2000; Cheney et al., 1999; Borcea, 2002; Denyer, 1996; Graham, 2007; Grootveld, 1996; Bera & Nagaraju, 2011a) is an image reconstruction technique in which the electrical conductivity or resistivity of a conducting domain (Ω) is reconstructed from the surface potential developed by a current signal injected (Figure 4a) at the domain boundary ($\partial\Omega$). An EIT system is developed with mainly three parts (Figure 4b): EIT sensors or surface electrodes (Webster, 1990), electronic instrumentation (Denyer, 1996; Bera & Nagaraju, 2009a) and a personal computer (PC) with reconstruction algorithm (Yorkey, 1986; Lionheart, 2004; Bera et al., 2011b; Bera et al., 2011c). An array of EIT sensors or electrodes (Bera & Nagaraju 2011a) are attached to the boundary of the domain under test and a low frequency sinusoidal constant amplitude current is injected through the current electrodes using a particular current protocol or current pattern (Webster, 1990; Malmivuo& Robert, 1995; Bera & Nagaraju 2012a). Boundary potentials are

Figure 4. A modern EIT system with phantom and electrodes (a) A closed domain (Ω) under EIT scanning with current injection at the domain boundary ($\partial\Omega$) and the surface potential measurements, (b) An EIT system schematic

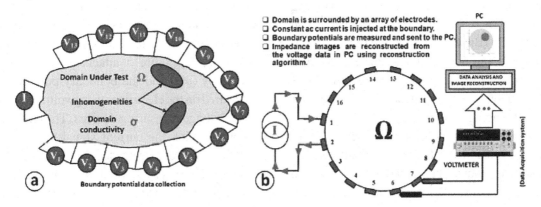

measured using a data acquisition system (Wei & Soleimani, 2012) and the processed data are stores in the PC for computation and image reconstruction (Graham, 2007; Bera et al., 2011b; Bera et al., 2011c). Being a non-invasive, non-radiating, non-ionizing and inexpensive methodology, electrical impedance tomography has been extensively researched in medical science (Metherall, 1998; Chen et al., 2009; Fabrizi1 et al., 2009; Bagshaw et al., 2003; Murphy et al., 1987; Noordegraaf et al., 1996; Hope & Iles, 2004; Calvetti1 et al., 2012; Josue´ et al., 2004; Jaume & Lluís, 2012; Frerichs et al., 2007; Smith et al., 1995; Tehrani et al., 2012; Edd et al., 2005), industrial process control (Bolton et al., 2002), geotechnology (Chambers *et al.*, 2012), defence sector (Church et al., 2006), material engineering (Hou et al., 2007), civil engineering (Karhunen et al., 2010), chemical engineering (Davidson et al., 2004), nondestructive testing (Djamdji et al., 1996), environmental science (D'Antona & Rocca, 2002), biotechnology (Sun et al., 2010), and so on due to its several advantages (Bayford, 2006; Lionheart et al., 1997; Riera et al., 2011) over other computed tomographic techniques (Kalender, 2011). EIT is a fast portable non-radiating, non-ionizing, noninvasive, low-cost, safe medical imaging modality. As EIT uses a low magnitude alternating current it does not have any side effect on the patient and hence is considered as harmless. Though the EIT technology has been studied in different fields of science and technology, yet EIT has shown it maximum advantages in medical science and hence a number of research groups are working on it in this field. But due to poor Signal to Noise Ratio (SNR) (Brown, 2001) of the boundary potential data and poor spatial resolution (Hou & Mo, 2002), the EIT technology needs some more developmental studies to make EIT as a regular medical imaging modality.

A medical EIT system has a number of advantages over other medical imaging modalities. One big challenge that ever attracted the researcher to overcome it is its image resolution and hence a lot of scope is there to explore the EIT technology in different clinical applications with better spatial resolution. A medical EIT system developed for a particular application is never prescribed to apply on the human subject until unless it is tested calibrated and certified as a safe medical imager. Practical phantoms (Holder et al., 1996; Bera & Nagaraju, 2012b; Soni et al., 2003; Bera & Nagaraju, 2009b; Ahn et al., 2010; Bera & Nagaraju, 2009c; Bera & Nagaraju, 2009d; Bera & Nagaraju, 2009e; Bera & Nagaraju, 2009f; Bera & Nagaraju, 2011d; Bera & Nagaraju, 2011e; Bera & Nagaraju, 2011f) are essential to study the EIT image reconstruction process, its performance and efficiency to test, calibrate and assess the EIT systems. It is, also, highly recommended to conduct a profound study on the system's efficiency, reliability and factor of safety prior to conduct the diagnostic imaging (Holder, 2005) on the patients. Multifrequency impedance imaging (Robitaille, et al., 2009; Kerner, et al., 2000) is found advantageous in medical Electrical Impedance Tomography (EIT) as the frequency response of the biological tissues depend on the signal frequency (Bera & Nagaraju, 2011g). SNR of the boundary potential data increases with the amplitude of the current signal but the maximum current limit is restricted below a certain level for patient safety (Webster, 1990).

How EIT Works

In electrical impedance tomography, a low frequency constant sinusoidal current is injected to the domain under test (Ω) through the surface electrodes (shown in rectangles on the domain periphery in Figure 5 attached to the domain boundary ($\partial\Omega$) and the boundary potentials are measured on the electrodes using voltmeter or any other voltage measuring devices. The electrodes, through which the current signal is injected is called the current electrodes (shown in red color) and the electrodes on which the voltage data are measured are termed as voltage electrodes (shown

Figure 5. Current paths in homogeneous and inhomogeneous medium (a) current flux in homogeneous medium, (b) current flux in medium with inhomogeneity

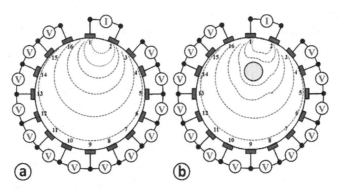

in blue color). The voltage data are transferred to PC for data analysis and image reconstruction. The spatial distribution of the electrical resistivity or the conductivity is reconstructed from the boundary data using a mathematical algorithm or computer program called the image reconstruction algorithm (Lionheart, 2004).

When a constant current is injected to the domain under test in electrical impedance tomography, the current lines or paths called current fluxes will be produced within the domain and the current is conducted through the domain. The profile of the current fluxes produced within the domain depend on the domain electrical properties i.e. its impedance profile. If the domain is homogeneous (Figure 1-5a), the current flux lines will be symmetric for a circular domain; whereas the inhomogeneous domain (domain with inhomogeneity) (Figure 1-5b) will distort the current flux. As the current flux will develop the voltages at each point of the domain, the profile of the potential distribution within the domain depends on the current flux profile. Similarly, the voltages develop at the domain boundary will also depend on the profile of the current flux. As the profile of the current flux depends on the profile of the impedance or conductivity distribution of the domain, the boundary voltage profile will also depend on the impedance profile. Therefore, the

voltage developed at the boundary for a homogeneous medium will be different from the boundary voltages for a domain with inhomogeneity. If we have an idea of the boundary voltage profile of the homogenous medium, then we can obtain (reconstruct) the impedance (or conductivity or resistivity) profile of the domain by comparing the voltage data collected from the boundary of an inhomogeneous medium.

CT vs. EIT

In CT X-Ray is passed through the subject under test and the beam is rotated in space to get the attenuated X-Ray data received by the X-Ray detectors at all the projection angles and the measured data are processed in PC to reconstruct the spatial distribution of the particular properties (X-ray attenuation coefficient) of the body tissue using the image reconstruction algorithm. In EIT the electrical current is injected to the body and the boundary potentials are measured on the surface electrodes attached to the body and the measured voltage data are processed in PC to reconstruct the spatial distribution of the particular properties (electrical resistivity or conductivity) of the body tissue using the image reconstruction algorithm. Hence the CT is a tomographic imaging with X ray and EIT is the tomography with electric current.

Advantages of EIT

Electrical impedance tomography has several advantages over other medical imaging techniques. The major advantages are summarized below:

- Noninvasive
- Radiation free
- Low cost
- Portable: One laptop with 16 or more electrode probes
- Bedside measurement
- Suitable for ambulatory monitoring
- No patient preparation no precautions
- Suitable for infants, children, and critically ill patients

Four Probe Measurement in EIT

In electrical impedance tomography a low frequency constant sinusoidal current is injected to the domain under test and the boundary potentials are measured. The current injection and voltage measurement is, generally, conducted using four electrode method or tetrapolar method (Bera & Nagaraju, 2011g; Guimera et al., 2012; Barber & Brown, 1984) in EIT. The four electrode method is an impedance measurement technique in which a constant current is injected through two electrodes (outer electrodes) called current electrodes and the voltages are measured on other two electrodes (inner electrodes) named as voltage electrodes (Bera & Nagaraju, 2011g). On the contrary, the two probe or two electrode method uses only two electrodes both for current injection and voltage measurement. As the same electrode pair is used for current injection and voltage measurement in two electrode method it has some disadvantages (Barber & Brown, 1984).

In two-electrode systems, the contact impedance reduces the system accuracy. As the voltages are measured on the current carrying electrodes, the voltage drop (developed due to the high current magnitude) for the electrode contact impedance is also included with the measured value. So, in two probe method the electrode impedance cannot be neglected. In four electrodes method the current injection and voltage measurement are done with two separate electrode pairs and hence the electrode contact impedance problem is neglected and the measurement accuracy is improved remarkably.

Boundary potentials in EIT are measured by injecting the current signal through the different current electrode pairs. The current injection and voltage measurement for a particular current electrode pair is known as a current projection (P_i: i = 1 though 16 for a 16-electrode EIT system). The voltage data are collected for all the possible projections (P_1 through P_{16}) for obtaining the full set of independent data. Hence the voltage data are collected for different projections (injecting current through the different current electrode pairs) to obtain a full data set from a complete scan of the object similar to the data collection process conducted at different projection angles in CT. In all the current projection all the single voltage data measurement is conducted with a four electrode configuration. For a particular current projection (say P_1: current injected through, say, E_1 and E_2), the voltage data are measured from all the possible voltage electrode pairs with four electrode method keeping the current electrode unchanged. And after completing the P_1, current electrode pair is changed to start the data collection through the P_2 (In P_2: current injected through, say, E_2 and E_3), and all the voltage data are collected with four electrode method. Hence the EIT data collection is conducted using a repetitive four electrode method.

Current Patterns in EIT

In EIT a low frequency constant sinusoidal current is injected to the domain under test through the electrodes called driving electrodes or current electrodes (E_1). The boundary potentials are measured on the electrodes called sensing electrodes or voltage electrodes (E_v). The current injection through a particular current electrode pair and corresponding voltage data collection from all the possible voltage electrode pairs is known as a current projection (P_1). The method or pattern in which the current in injected to the object under imaging is called the current pattern or current injection method or current injection protocol (Malmivuo & Plonsey, 1995; Bera & Nagaraju, 2012a; Bera & Nagaraju, 2011f; Bera & Nagaraju, 2011h). In a particular current pattern in EIT, the boundary data collection are generally collecting by selecting the combinations of current electrode pairs and the voltage electrode pairs in each projection. Depending of the selection of the geometric positions of the current electrodes in the current electrode pair and the voltage electrode pairs the data collection procedure or strategy is named. In this section the four famous current injection protocols as reported by the researchers are summarized below. In general, the differential potentials are measured across the different electrodes excluding the current electrodes to avoid the contact impedance problem. In the present study, however, in spite of the problem of skin impedance, to obtain the greatest sensitivity to changes in the resistivity of the body, voltages on current electrodes are also measured.

Neighbouring Method

Brown and Segar (Brown & Segar, 1987) suggested the neighbouring or adjacent current injection method in which the current signal is applied through two neighbouring or adjacent electrodes and the voltage is measured successively from all other adjacent electrode pairs excluding the pairs containing one or both the current electrodes. Figure 6 illustrates the neighbouring method for a 16-electrode EIT system with a circular domain under test (within a cylindrical volume conductor) surrounded by sixteen surface electrodes denoted as the electrode-1 through electrode-16 (E_1, E_2, E_3, E_4, E_5, E_6, E_7, E_8, E_9, E_{10}, E_{11}, E_{12}, E_{13}, E_{14}, E_{15} and E_{16}). In neighbouring method, for the first current projection (P_1), the current is injected through electrode-1 (E_1) and electrode-2 (E_2) and the differential potentials (V_d: V_1, V_2, V_3, ... V_{13}) are measured successively with thirteen electrode pairs E_3-E_4, E_4-E_5, ... and E_{15}-E_{16} (Figure 6a). Hence the first current projection yields thirteen differential voltage data viz. V_1 or V_{3-4} (measured between E_3 and E_4), V_2 or V_{4-5} (measured between E_4 and E_5), ... and V_{13} or V_{15-16} (measured between E_{15} and E_{16}). The thirteen differential voltage data obtained in this process are assumed to represent the impedance between the equipotential lines intersecting their corresponding measurement

Figure 6. Neighbouring or adjacent current method of boundary potential data collection illustrated for a cylindrical volume conductor and 16 equally spaced electrodes. (a) projection-1 (P_1), (b) projection-2 (P_2)

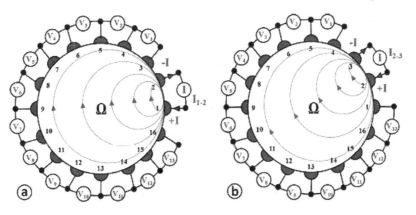

electrodes (Webster, 1990) and are all independent to each other (Webster, 1990). In neighbouring method, the current density is, of course, the highest between the current electrodes (E_1 and E_2 for the projection-1), decreasing rapidly as a function of distance (Webster, 1990).

In current projection-2 (P_2), the set of other thirteen differential voltage measurements is obtained by feeding the current through electrodes 2 (E_2) and 3 (E_3) as shown in (Figure 6b). Therefore, in this current projection, the current is injected through electrodes 2 (E_2) and 3 (E_3) and the differential potentials (V_d: V_1, V_2, V_3, ... V_{13}) are measured successively with thirteen electrode pairs E_4-E_5, E_5-E_6, ... and E_{16}-E_1. Hence the second current projection (P_2) yields thirteen differential voltage data viz. V_1 or V_{4-5} (measured between E_4 and E_5), V_2 or V_{5-6} (measured between E_5 and E_6), and V_{13} or V_{16-1} (measured between E_{16} and E_1) as shown in Figure 6b.

Similarly, in current projection-16 (P_{16}), another set of thirteen differential voltage measurements is obtained with a current injection through electrodes 16 (E_{16}) and 1 (E_1). Therefore, in this current projection, the current is injected through electrodes 16 (E_{16}) and 1 (E_1) and the differential potentials (V_d: V_1, V_2, V_3, ... V_{13}) are measured successively with thirteen electrode pairs E_2-E_3, E_3-E_4, ... and E_{14}-E_{15}. Hence the P_{16} yields thirteen differential voltage data viz. V_1 or V_{2-3} (measured between E_2 and E_3), V_2 or V_{3-4} (measured between E_3 and E_4), ... and V_{13} or V_{14-15} (measured between E_{14} and E_{15}).

Therefore, for a 16-electrode system, the neighbouring current injection method yields sixteen current projections (P_1, P_2, P_3,..., P_{15} and P_{16}) each of which will produce thirteen differential voltage data. Therefore, in neighbouring method, a complete scan on a 16-electrode EIT system yields $16 \times 13 = 208$ voltage measurements. But, due to the reciprocity (Malmivuo & Plonsey, 1995), the measurements made on the boundary yield identical voltage data in which the current electrodes and voltage electrodes are interchanged (Webster, 1990). Therefore, among the 208 differential voltage measurements only 104 data are independent to each other. In the neighbouring method, the measured voltage is at a maximum with adjacent electrode pairs while in the opposite electrode pairs, the voltage is only about 2.5% of that (Webster, 1990).

Opposite Method

Another alternative current injection method called the *opposite method* was proposed by Hua et al (1987). In this method current is injected through two diametrically opposed electrodes in each current projection (Figure 7) and hence the method is known as the opposite method. Dif-

Figure 7. Opposite method of boundary potential data collection: (a) projection-1, (b) projection-2

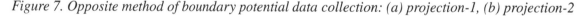

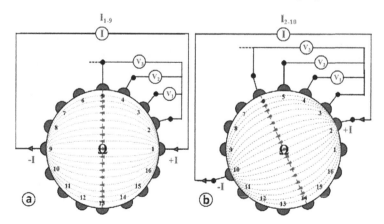

ferential potentials are measured on the voltage electrodes with respect to the electrode (called as the voltage reference electrode) adjacent to the current-injecting electrode (Figure 7).

In the first current projection (P_1) of the opposite method, the current is injected through electrodes 1 (E_1) and 9 (E_9) and the differential potentials (V_d: V_1, V_2, V_3, ... V_{13}) are measured successively from thirteen electrode pairs E_2-E_3, E_2-E_4, . . and E_2-E_{16} (Figure 7a) considering the electrode 2 (E_2) as the reference. Hence the P_1 yields thirteen differential voltage data viz. V_1 or V_{2-3} (measured between E_2 and E_3), V_2 or V_{2-4} (measured between E_2 and E_4), ... and V_{13} or V_{2-16} (measured between E_2 and E_{16}). In opposite method, the current distribution is more uniform and, therefore, has a good sensitivity (Webster, 1990).

The current projection-2 (P_2), the set of other thirteen differential voltage measurements is obtained by injecting the current signal through electrodes 2 (E_2) and 10 (E_{10}) as shown in Figure 7b. Therefore, in P_2, the current is fed through the electrodes 2 (E_2) and 10 (E_{10}) and the differential potentials (V_d: V_1, V_2, V_3, ... V_{13}) are measured successively from the thirteen electrode pairs E_3-E_4, E_3-E_5, ... and E_3-E_1 (Figure 7b) considering electrode 3 (E_3) as the voltage reference electrode. Hence the second current projection yields thirteen differential voltage data viz. V_1 or V_{3-4} (measured between E_3 and E_4), V_2 or V_{3-5} (measured between E_3 and E_5), ... and V_{13} or V_{3-1} (measured between E_3 and E_1).

Similarly, in the current projection-16 (P_{16}), the set of thirteen differential voltage measurements is obtained by feeding the current through electrodes 16 (E_{16}) and 8 (E_8). Therefore in this current projection the current is injected through electrodes 16 (E_{16}) and 8 (E_8) and the differential potentials (V_d: V_1, V_2, V_3, ... V_{13}) are measured successively with thirteen electrode pairs E_1-E_2, E_1-E_3, ... and E_1-E_{15} considering electrode 1 (E_1) as the voltage reference. Hence the P_{16} yields thirteen differential voltage data viz. V_1 or V_{1-2} (measured between E_1 and E_2), V_2 or V_{1-3} (measured between E_1 and E_3), ... and V_{13} or V_{1-15} (measured between E_1 and E_{15}).

Therefore, for a 16-electrode system, the opposite current injection method yields sixteen current projections each of which produces thirteen differential voltage data. Thus, in opposite method, a complete scan of a 16-electrode EIT system yields $16 \times 13 = 208$ voltage measurements. But, due to the reciprocity (Malmivuo & Plonsey, 1995), the measurements made on the boundary yield identical voltage data in which the current electrodes and voltage electrodes are interchanged (Webster, 1990; Bera & Nagaraju, 2009a). Therefore, among the 208 differential voltage measurements, only 104 data are independent to each other (Webster, 1990).

Cross Method

Hua et al. (1987) suggested a current injection method called the *cross method* (Figure 8) in which a more uniform current distribution is obtained when the current is injected between a pair of more distant electrodes. In this method, adjacent electrodes E_{16} and E_1 are first selected for current and voltage reference electrodes respectively (Figure 8). The positive terminal of the current source is connected to the electrode E_2 (positive current injecting electrode). The thirteen voltage data are measured successively for all other 13 electrodes starting from E_3 with the aforementioned electrode E_1 as the reference (Figure 8). Figure 8a shows the detail data collection procedures of the cross method in which the thirteen differential voltage measurements are obtained by injecting the positive current through electrode 2 (E_2) keeping the electrode 16 (E_{16}) as the current reference (Figure 8a). Hence, the current is injected through electrodes 16 (E_{16}) and 2 (E_2) and the differential potentials (V_d: V_1, V_2, V_3, ... V_{13}) are measured successively with thirteen electrode pairs E_1-E_3, E_1-E_4, ... and E_1-E_{15} considering electrode 1 (E_1) as the voltage reference (Figure 8a). Therefore the

Figure 8. Cross method of boundary data collection: four different steps of the cross method are illustrated here from Figures a to d

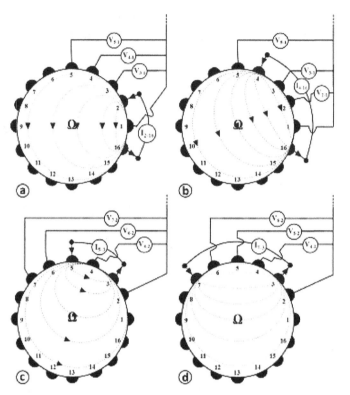

cross method yields thirteen differential voltage data viz. V_1 or V_{1-3} (measured between E_1 and E_3), V_2 or V_{1-4} (measured between E_1 and E_4), ... and V_{13} or V_{1-15} (measured between E_1 and E_{15}).

After collecting the first thirteen differential voltage data, the next thirteen differential voltage measurements are obtained by injecting by injecting the positive current through electrode 4 (E_4) keeping the electrode 16 (E_{16}) as the current reference (Figure 8b). Therefore, the current is injected through electrodes 16 (E_{16}) and 4 (E_4) and the differential potentials (V_d: V_1, V_2, V_3, ... V_{13}) are measured successively with thirteen electrode pairs E_1-E_2, E_1-E_3, E_1-E_5, ... and E_1-E_{15} again considering electrode 1 (E_1) as the voltage reference. Hence, this current projection yields another set of thirteen differential voltage data viz. V_1 or V_{1-2} (measured between E_1 and E_2), V_2 or

V_{1-3} (measured between E_1 and E_3), V_3 or V_{1-5} (measured between E_1 and E_5), ... and V_{13} or V_{1-15} (measured between E_1 and E_{15}). By repeating this procedure by connecting the positive terminal of the current source to the electrodes E_6, E_8, ... E_{14}, the entire procedure thus yields $7 \times 13 = 91$ measurements. The measurement sequence is then repeated with electrodes E_3 and E_2 as current and voltage reference electrodes, respectively (Figure 8c). Connecting the positive terminal of the current source to the E_5, the cross method then yields thirteen voltage data measured successively on all other 13 electrode pairs using the E_2 as the voltage reference (Figure 8c).

After obtaining the first set of thirteen data with the current injection through the electrodes E_5 and E_3 (taking E_2 as the voltage reference), the procedure is just repeated by connecting the positive terminal of the current source to the electrodes E_7 (Figure 8d) and the another set of thirteen differential voltage data is collected (taking the same electrodes as the current and voltage references). Similarly, by connecting the positive terminal of the current source successively to the electrodes E_9, E_{11}, ..., E_1, the cross method gives thirteen voltage data successively for other 13 electrodes with the aforementioned electrodes as the current and voltage references and another set of $7 \times 13 = 91$ differential voltage measurements is obtained. From these $91 + 91 = 182$ measurements, only 104 data are independent. It is to be noted that the cross method does not have as good a sensitivity in the periphery as does the neighbouring method, but has better sensitivity over the entire domain under test (Webster, 1990).

Adaptive or Trigonometric Method

In the aforementioned methods, current has been injected with a pair of electrodes and the differential voltage data have been measured between different pairs of electrodes excluding the current electrodes. Gisser et al. (1987) proposed a current injection method called the adaptive method or trigonometric method (Figure 9), in which the current is injected through all electrodes. Because current flows through all electrodes simultaneously, as many independent current injectors are needed as are the electrodes used in EIT system and hence a 16-electrode EIT system needs sixteen

current injectors. The electrodes can be fed a current from $-I$ to $+I$ (I is any suitable R.M.S. amplitude of the current), allowing different current distributions. Homogeneous current distribution may be obtained only in a homogeneous volume conductor and hence, if the volume conductor is cylindrical with circular cross-section, the injected current must be proportional to $\cos\theta$ to obtain a homogeneous current distribution (Figure 9). In trigonometric method, the boundary potentials are measured with respect to a single grounded electrode and hence, a 16-electrode EIT system, the trigonometric current injection method yields fifteen voltage measurements as shown in projection 1 (Figure 9a) and projection 2 (Figure 9b). The desired current distribution (or projection) is then rotated one electrode increment ($22.5°$ for a 16-electrode system) and other projections are obtained. Thus, for a 16-electrode EIT system, the trigonometric current injection method produces 8 different current distributions yielding $8 \times 15 = 120$ independent voltage data.

CLASSIFICATIONS EIT

EIT is classified in three types: Electrical Impedance Tomography (EIT), Electrical Capacitance Tomography (ECT) and Electrical Resistance Tomography (ERT)

Figure 9. Adaptive or the trigonometric current injection method of voltage data collection: (a) projection-1, (b) projection 2

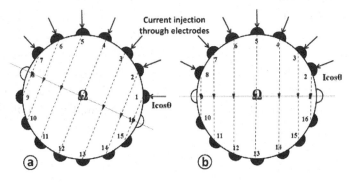

- **Electrical Conductance or Impedance Tomography (EIT):** Conductivity is reconstructed.
- **Electrical Capacitance Tomography (ECT):** Permittivity is reconstructed.
- **Electrical Resistance Tomography (ERT):** Resistivity is reconstructed using D.C. current.

APPLICATIONS OF EIT

EIT is a low cost, portable, medically safe, radiation free, noninvasive diagnostic tool which is being extensively studied in medical imaging research. It can be used to provide the spatial distribution of the tissue conductivity carrying the functional information including malignancy and other physiological status of the tumor. Due to its several advantages, EIT has also been studied in different fields like:

- Medical Imaging and Clinical Diagnosis (Holder, 1993).
- Industrial Process Application (Bolton et al., 2002).
- Chemical Engineering (Davidson et al., 2004).
- Material Science and Engineering (Hou et al., 2007).
- NonDestructive Testing (NDT) in Manufacturing Technology (Djamdji et al., 1996).
- Civil Engineering (Karhunen et al., 2010).
- Earth Science and Geophysics and Geoscience (Chambers et al., 2012).
- Microbiology and Biotechnoloy (Sun et al., 2010).
- Defense Fields (Church et al., 2006).
- MEMS and Thin Films (Hou et al., 2007).
- Archaeology (Ullrich et al., 2007).
- Oceanography (Ingham et al., 2008).

- Environmental Engineering (D'Antona & Rocca, 2002) and other Applied Physics and Applied Sciences.

A BASIC EIT SYSTEM

A basic EIT system has three main parts and SUT:

- EIT-Instrumentation
- Electrode Array or EIT Sensors
- PC with Reconstruction Algorithm
- Subject Under Test (SUT)

A brief discussion on EIT Instrumentation, in general, is presented below whereas the details of the Multifrequency Multifunction Electrical Impedance Tomography (MfMf-EIT) instrumentation developed in the present research work will be discussed in Chapter 3 along with its components, operating principles and performance analysis.

EIT-Instrumentation

EIT-Instrumentation is developed with four main parts:

- Constant Current Injector (CCI)
- Signal Conditioner Block (SCB)
- Electrode Switching Module (ESM)
- Data Acquisition System (DAS)

Constant Current Injector (CCI) is used to inject a constant current signal to the boundary of the object under test through the EIT electrodes. The developed voltage signal is processed by Signal Conditioner Block (SCB). Electrode Switching Module (ESM) is used to switch the current and voltage electrodes for required current injection and voltage measurement as per the current pattern used in EIT study. Finally the data are collected from the complete scan of the object using DAS.

Electrode Array or EIT Sensors

EIT electrode array or EIT sensors are very important part of EIT. These are used to inject current to the body under test and collecting the voltage data at the boundary. The sensor array actually makes the interface between the SUT and the EIT-Instrumentation. The following parameters of the EIT electrodes are very important in EIT studies:

- Electrode Number
- Electrode Material
- Electrode Size
- Electrode Type

PC with Reconstruction Algorithm

Personal Computer (PC) with image reconstruction algorithm is a very important part of the EIT system. The measured boundary data are stored in PC and then processed to reconstruct the EIT images using reconstruction algorithm. The image reconstruction algorithms are generally developed with two main parts:

- Forward Solver (FS)
- Inverse Solver (IS)

The forward solver solves the characteristic equation or governing equation of EIT and calculates the boundary potentials for a constant current simulation in PC. The calculated potential data (V_c) data are then compared with the measured potential data (V_m) in inverse solver and the domain conductivity distribution is reconstructed for which the difference between V_m and V_c is minimized.

Mathematical Modeling of EIT

The EIT system is applied to a DUT with a particular characteristic equation called governing equation which establishes the relation between the domain conductivity and the potentials at the points in DUT. The forward solver solves the characteristic equation or governing equation of EIT and calculates the boundary potentials for a constant current simulation in PC. The calculated potential data (V_c) data are then compared with the measured potential data (V_m) in inverse solver and the domain conductivity distribution is reconstructed for which the difference between V_m and V_c is minimized.

Governing Equation of EIT

The conductivity of the domain under test is reconstructed in inverse solver using the from the measured boundary potentials developed for the current injection and the calculated boundary potentials obtained from the forward solution of the EIT characteristics equation called governing equation. The governing equation of EIT represents the relation between the conductivity of the DUT and the developed potential for a constant current injection. If the electrical potential (ϕ) developed by a low frequency sinusoidal current applied to a homogeneous and isotropic medium with low magnetic permeability (biological tissue) and electrical conductivity (σ), the EIT governing equation can be represented as (Holder, 2005):

$$\nabla \cdot \sigma \nabla \phi = 0 \qquad (1)$$

where, ∇ is the gradient operator in the same system. The Equation 1 is a nonlinear partial differential equation which represents the relationship between the conductivity distribution and the potential distribution developed for a particular current injection at the boundary and is known as the Governing Equation of EIT (Graham, 2007). Boundary conditions (Webster, 1990) are applied to restrict these solutions of the Equation 1.

Forward Solver

The forward solver solves the forward problem in which the conductivity distribution matrix [σ] and the current injection matrix [C] are known and the potential distribution matrix [Φ] is unknown. The image reconstruction algorithm tries to reconstruct the conductivity distribution of DUT from the boundary potential data (developed for a known constant current injection at the domain boundary) for which the difference between the measured potential data and the computer predicted data (for same current simulation) calculated by forward solver. Hence, in order to solve the inverse problem of EIT, a forward model is required to be developed to calculate the voltages from the injected current for a known conductivity distribution.

The forward model present the mathematical relation between the applied signal (electric current) and the developed signal (electrical voltage) through a function of the system inherent parameter (which can be assumed as the transfer function of the system). The forward solver works on the governing equation and constructs the forward model which is used to solve the governing equation to calculate the boundary potentials. Forward solver applies a numerical technique like Finite Element Method (FEM) and discretized the DUT with a finite element mesh containing a finite number or elements and nodes. FS works on the discretized domain and derives a forward model which is a matrix equation relating the calculated potential data matrix [V_c] and the current injection matrix [**C**] through a transformation matrix called global stiffness matrix developed with the elemental conductivities and the nodal coordinates. Forward solver then solves the governing equation of the domain under test (DUT) which relates the known and unknown parameters of the DUT.

$$\Phi = \left[\mathrm{K}\left(\sigma\right) \right]^{-1} \left[\mathrm{C} \right] \qquad (2)$$

Inverse Solver

The inverse solver solves the inverse problem in which the measured potential data matrix [V_m], calculated potential data matrix [V_c], Jacobian matrix [J] (calculated from the forward solution for a known current injection) the current injection matrix [C] are known and the conductivity distribution matrix [σ] is unknown. In inverse solver, the calculated boundary potentials are then compared to the measured voltage data in an iterative approach for finding the unknown conductivity for which the difference between the measured data and the calculated data is minimized.

The forward model also provides the capability to calculate the interior electric fields to construct the Jacobian matrix using a particular Jacobian calculation method such as the adjacent field method (Bahrani, 2012). The Jacobian matrix is developed in the inverse modeling for EIT to solve the unknown conductivity given measured voltage and is necessary to solve the inverse problem (Bahrani, 2012). Hence, the forward solution data are used to construct the Jacobian and to solve the inverse problem using the calculate boundary data and Jacobian matrix provided by the forward solver.

If K(σ) and C are known, Equation 2 can be solved numerically using Finite Element Method (FEM) (Yorkey, 1986; Bagshaw et al., 2003) to calculate the nodal potentials of the domain for the known conductivity (**σ**). It is known as the "forward problem". Using Gauss-Newton method (Yorkey, 1986; Bagshaw et al., 2003; Bera et al., 2011b; Bera et al., 2011c; Grootveld, 1996; Graham, 2007; Bera et al., 2012c; Bera et al., 2012d; Bahrani, 2012; Arridge, 1999; Soleimani, 2005), update vector of **σ** can be expressed as:

$$\Delta\sigma = f\left(\left[\mathrm{Q} \right]^{-1}, \left[\mathrm{V_d} \right] \right) \qquad (3)$$

where, f is a function of $\mathbf{Q}$ and V_d. $\mathbf{Q}$ is a function of Jacobian matrix ($\mathbf{J}$) (Yorkey, 1986; Bagshaw et al., 2003; Bera et al., 2011b; Bera et al., 2011c; Grootveld, 1996; Graham, 2007; Bera et al., 2012c; Bera et al., 2012d) and regularization parameters (Yorkey, 1986; Bagshaw et al., 2003; Bera et al., 2011b; Bera et al., 2011c; Grootveld, 1996; Graham, 2007; Bera et al., 2012c; Bera et al., 2012d) and V_d is the mismatch vector $[\Delta V]$ defined as the difference between calculated boundary potential (V_c) and measured boundary potential (V_m). That means if the matrix $\mathbf{Q}$ and the surface potentials (V_c and V_m) are known then the elemental conductivity (σ) can be mapped. This is known as the "inverse problem" which is discussed in the next section.

Image Reconstruction in EIT

The response matrix $[J^TJ]$ in the electrical conductivity imaging has a rank deficiency. There are no direct analytical methods by which we can get the unique solution of this inverse problem. EIT, being a problem of several variables, minimization algorithm is the best way to obtain the approximate solution. In minimization algorithm (Yorkey, 1986; Bagshaw et al., 2003; Bera et al., 2011b; Bera et al., 2011c; Grootveld, 1996; Graham, 2007; Bera et al., 2012c; Bera et al., 2012d), we minimize the objective function that is formed by taking the difference between the computationally predicted data and the experimental measurement data is minimized. Generally this objective function is minimized by Newton's method. Among the various Newton's methods, Gauss-Newton method is, frequently, used for finding the approximate solution (Arridge, 1999). In inverse problem a least square solution of a minimized object function (s) obtained from the calculated and measured voltage data is searched by a numerical approximation algorithm.

If $\mathbf{V_m}$ is the measurement voltage matrix and $\mathbf{f}$ as a function mapping an E-dimensional (E is the number of element in the FEM mesh) imped-ance distribution into a set of M (number of the measured data available) measured voltage, then, the Gauss-Newton algorithm (Yorkey, 1986; Bagshaw et al., 2003; Bera et al., 2011b; Bera et al., 2011c; Grootveld, 1996; Graham, 2007; Bera et al., 2012c; Bera et al., 2012d; Bahrani, 2012; Arridge, 1999; Soleimani, 2005) tries to find a least square solution of the minimized object function s defined as (Yorkey, 1986; Bagshaw *et al.*, 2003; Bera et al., 2011b; Bera et al., 2011c; Grootveld, 1996; Graham, 2007; Bera et al., 2012c; Bera et al., 2012d):

$$s = \frac{1}{2}\left\| V_m - f \right\|^2 = \frac{1}{2}\left(V_m - f \right)^T \left(V_m - f \right) \quad (4)$$

By Gauss-Newton method, the conductivity update vector $[\Delta\sigma]$ is given by:

$$\Delta\sigma = \left[\left[f' \right]^T \left[f' \right] \right]^{-1} J^T \left[V_m - f \right] \quad (5)$$

where the term $J = f'$ is known as the Jacobin matrix.

By the inherent ill-posed nature of EIT, $\left[f' \right]^T$ matrix in Equation 5 is always ill-conditioned (Hou & Mo, 2002), and hence small measurement errors will make the solution of Equation 5 change drastically. Regularization method is incorporated to make the inverse problem well-posed by reforming the equation and the conductivity update vector with regularization (Levenberg, 1944; Marquardt, 1963; Jinchuang et al., 2002; Cohen-Bacrie, 1997) terms is defined as:

$$\Delta\sigma = \left(J^T J + \lambda I \right)^{-1} \left(J^T \left(V_m - f \right) \right) \quad (6)$$

where, λ is regularization parameter and $\mathbf{I}$ is an Identity matrix,

EIT algorithm starts with an initial guessed conductivity $[\sigma_o]$ and the forward solution is obtained and Jacobian (J) is calculated. In inverse, using the $[V_c]$ and $[J]$ the conductivity update vector ($[\Delta\sigma]$) is calculated using a minimization algorithm such as using modified Gauss-Newton based Minimization Algorithm (GNMA) (Bera et al., 2011b; Bera et al., 2011c; Bera et al., 2012c; Bera et al., 2012d). Using an iterative technique such as modified Newton Raphson Iterative Technique (NRIT) (Bera et al., 2011b; Bera et al., 2011c; Bera et al., 2012c; Bera et al., 2012d), the inverse solver repetitively update the conductivity matrix $[\sigma_1 = \sigma_0 + \Delta\sigma]$ and tries to find out a desired conductivity distribution for which the voltage mismatch vector $[\Delta V]$ is minimized. The detail discussion about the EIT reconstruction algorithm using Gauss-Newton method will be discussed in Chapter 4.

Why EIT is Tough

EIT is a nonlinear ill-posed inverse problem (Kolehmainen et al., 1998; An et al., 2002). Hence the solution or the reconstruction process is highly dependent on the nonlinearity and ill-posedness of the problem. The following characteristics of the EIT are discussed in brief in the following sections:

- EIT is an Inverse Problem
- EIT is Non-Linear
- EIT is Ill-Posed
- 3D Current conduction is assumed as 2D Current conduction in EIT

EIT: An Inverse Problem

An inverse problem (Aster et al., 2012; Yu, 1991) is a general framework that is used to obtain the information (transfer function) about a physical object or system under test by using the system response measured at the boundary (data measured at the boundary of the system) developed by applying a know signal. If for a system S, the measured data is d, a model of the system is m and G is an operator (called forward operator)

describing the explicit relationship between d and the model parameters, then the objective of an inverse problem is to find the best model M such that (approximately) (Wikipedia, 2013):

$$d = G\left(m\right) \tag{7}$$

where, G is the forward operator is sometimes called as observation operator or observation function. In the most general context, G represents the governing equations that relate the model parameters to the observed data (i.e. the governing physics) (Wikipedia, 2013).

Very few of the physical systems are actually linear with respect to the model parameters. As for example of such linear system is Earth's gravitational field. In the case of linear inverse problems, d (the model parameters) and M are vectors, and the problem can be written as (Wikipedia, 2013):

$$d = Gm \tag{8}$$

where, G is a matrix (an operator), often called the observation matrix (Wikipedia, 2013).

In EIT the internal profile (information of the inside of the system) of a subject under test is reconstructed from the data measured at the system boundary (outside of the system). Therefore it is tried to obtain an insight picture from the outside measurements and hence it is called as an inverse problem.

EIT: Nonlinear Inverse Problem

Non-Linear Inverse Problems (NLIP) are inherently more difficult family of inverse problems in which G is a non-linear operator and cannot be separated to represent a linear mapping of the model parameters that form M into the data. NLIP have a more complex relationship between data and model, represented by the Equation 8. The nonlinearity can be understood from the governing equation (Equation 1) as expressed below. Now, using the Equation 2 in Equation 1 we get,

$$\nabla . \sigma \nabla \left[\left[K \left(\sigma \right) \right]^{-1} \left[C \right] \right] = 0 \qquad (9)$$

$$\nabla \sigma . \nabla \left[\left[K \left(\sigma \right) \right]^{-1} \left[C \right] \right] + \sigma \nabla^2 \left[\left[K \left(\sigma \right) \right]^{-1} \left[C \right] \right] = 0 \qquad (10)$$

Now, the Equation 10 will be simplified to a linear equation called the Laplace's equation if and only if the conductivity is constant (Grootveld, 1996). In EIT, however, the conductivity is not constant and hence the Equation 10 becomes a nonlinear partial differential equation representing the nonlinear inverse problem of EIT.

EIT: An Ill-Posed Inverse Problem

EIT seeks to reconstruct the interior electrical conductivity of an inhomogeneous object by measuring the voltage data generated by a low-frequency current injection at the boundary. EIT is a nonlinear ill-posed inverse problem (Dai et al., 1994). Like any other nonlinear inverse problems, Electrical impedance tomography is also an ill-posed inverse problem. According to Jacques Hadamard for a well-posed problem will have three properties existence, uniqueness, stability of the solution or solutions. The ill-posedness implies that the solution of the system under test does not depend continuously on the measured boundary data and a small variation in the data measured at the system can lead to large errors in the solution (reconstruction of the conductivity distribution) of the system (Dai et al., 1994). Since the data measured at the boundary are, generally, not exact because of measurement error produced by system noise, there is no exact solution to the ill posed inverse problem of EIT (Dai et al., 1994).

Consequently, the effort is to be given to find a method to stabilize the ill posed EIT, and then to find an approximate solution to that stabilized

problem (Dai et al., 1994). The first attempts in the direction of the stabilization of EIT problems are to linearize the ill posed problem in which the filtered back-projection algorithm proposed by Barber (Barber, 1990) is considered as the most representative method. Due to their mathematical simplicity and computational rapidity, these linearization methods are very attractive (Dai et al., 1994; Barber, 1990), although they have the defect of ignoring the non-linearity of EIT (Dai et al., 1994). The approaches to reformulate the EIT problem as a non-linear optimization problem by treating the non-linearity and ill posedness of EIT (without linearization), which requires the solution of the direct problem at each step of the iteration procedure used to obtain a solution have also been proposed by Yorkey et al. (1987).

EIT: Current Conducts in 3D

A constant current is injected at the object boundary and the generated surface potentials are measured in EIT. In EIT, it is often assumed that the currents injected to the object under test are confined in the electrode plane (2D plane of interest) and hence the solution obtained from the reconstruction process is based on these assumptions. Though the injected current produces current fluxes in three dimensional space in a real object, it is assumed that the current is confined in the plane of interest. As, the currents conduct in three dimensional (3D) space in a real object, the off-plane structures have significant effect on the reconstructed images (Vauhkonen et al., 1999). Hence the assumption produces an error in calculation. The error in the boundary data measurement in a practical phantom of a 2D EIT system produces error in the reconstruction (Wang, 1999).

Multifrequency EIT System

Electrical Impedance Tomograph is a low cost, portable, medically safe, radiation free, noninvasive diagnostic tool which provides the spatial distribution of the tissue conductivity carrying the functional information including malignancy and other physiological status of the tumor. The different biological tissues have different frequency responses (Bera & Nagaraju, 2011g) and hence the multifrequency EIT (Romsauerova et al., 2006; Soni et al., 2004; Wi et al., 2012; Oh et al., 2008; Griffiths, 1988) is found more suitable in medical diagnosis of diseases in human subject. EIT can be potentially used to obtain the spatial distribution of the electrical conductivity which carries the anatomical, physiological and the functional information about the disease. Being a low cost, noninvasive, non-ionizing, radiation free and portable imaging modality, EIT can be suitably applied in diagnosis and treatment of the breast cancer. Moreover, multifrequency EIT will potentially provide all the parameters in the frequency domain which will add another advancement in the diagnosis and treatment of the disease.

3D Electrical Impedance Tomography (3D EIT)

2D Electrical Impedance Tomography (2D-EIT) reconstructs the approximate spatial distribution of the internal impedance profile from the measurements of boundary voltage data developed by a known constant current injected to the surface electrodes placed in a certain 2D plane within the patient's body. 2D EIT assumes that the electrical current conducts within a 2D plane whereas the electrical currents are not confined in the plane of electrode array rather it spread over a three dimensional space within the volume conductor. Eventually, the 2D EIT suffers from the errors contributed by this 3D conduction of electrical current. Moreover 2D EIT provides only the two dimensional distribution of the electrical impedance of the tissue in its tomograms in which the 3D anatomical and physiological information are not available. 3D EIT provides better and more scientific visualization of the tissue insight in terms of its electrical impedance distribution in 3D.

Subject Under Test (SUT)

EIT instrument called electrical impedance tomograph is applied to an object or Subject Under Test (SUT) which may be a patient or laboratory animal or tissue mimicking model called "phantom". The domain of interest within the SUT is called the Domain Under Test (DUT).

Practical Phantoms

Practical phantoms (Bera & Nagaraju, 2009a; Bera & Nagaraju, 2012a; Bera & Nagaraju, 2012b; Holder et al., 1996; Bera & Nagaraju, 2009f; Bera & Nagaraju, 2011d; Bera & Nagaraju, 2011e; Griffiths,1988; Sperandio et al., 2012; Paulson et al., 1992; Bera et al., 2012c; Bera et al., 2012d) with surface electrodes (Webster, 2009) are essential to assess the performance of Electrical Impedance Tomography (EIT) systems for their validation, calibration and comparison purposes. To assess an EIT system, studying of the performance of reconstruction algorithm or instrumentation or both is essential which is generally performed with a practical phantom mimicking the patient body parts. Researchers have reported several types of phantoms for studying their EIT systems such as saline-insulator phantoms (Bera & Nagaraju, 2011a; Bera & Nagaraju, 2011d; Bera & Nagaraju, 2011f; Bera & Nagaraju, 2011h; Bera & Nagaraju, 2011i; Bera & Nagaraju, 2010; Bera et al., 2012c; Bera et al., 2012d; Bera & Nagaraju, 2012e), saline-agar phantom (Soni et al., 2003; Qiao et al., 2007; Conway, 1987), saline-vegetable phantom (Holder et al., 1996; Ahn et al., 2010; Bera & Nagaraju, 2011i; Bera & Nagaraju, 2012e), passive or active element phantoms (Schneider et al., 2000; Griffiths, 1988). All the phantoms have their own advantages and disadvantages. Phantoms are generally of two types: practical phantom and network phantom. Practical phantoms are developed with two or more material with different conductivities. Network phantoms are developed with circuit elements. Practical phantoms are developed with mainly three parts:

phantom tank, surface electrodes and phantom materials. Network phantoms are developed with two parts: electronic circuit elements and electronic element base or PCB board. Network phantoms do not require any electrodes, only electronic connections are sufficient to interface the phantom with the EIT system. The phantoms with electrical components are sometime advantageous for their long life, rigidity, stability and ease of control. But they, generally, suffer from their own limitations as they cannot be assumed to be mimicking the biological tissues.

Phantoms with saline and solid inorganic (plastic, wood, or metal rod) or organic (vegetables or other biological tissues) materials are very popular in EIT as they are low cost, easy to develop and can be developed in any shape. But they cannot be assumed as a perfect mimic of the body parts as the background medium is a pure saline solution (purely resistive) whereas none of the human body parts are purely resistive. Hence, the impedance response over frequency of purely resistive saline solution is constant but the response of the real tissue varies with frequency according to their physiological and physiochemical compositions contributing the reactive part to their complex impedance. Moreover, the evaporation of the saline solution makes them unstable over the time which makes the assessment erroneous in real case. Also, it is quite difficult to reconstruct the actual resistivity of the insulator inhomogeneity in a saline background because of their large resistivity difference. Hence the saline phantoms and the phantoms with circuit elements sometimes fail to calibrate a medical EIT system properly as the responses of inorganic solution and the insulator inhomogeneity differ from the living tissues in several aspects. Hence, the practical biological phantoms consisting two different materials with low resistivity difference are more suitable for impedance imaging study. Real tissue phantoms (Bera & Nagaraju, 2011e; Bera & Nagaraju, 2012a) are found more suitable for studying EIT systems.

Dynamic vs. Static Imaging in EIT

Depending on the *imaging modalities* Electrical Impedance Tomography can be classified in two categories: *dynamic imaging* and *static imaging*. Though the present EIT technologies are practically applicable only in dynamic imaging and feature extraction of anomalies yet the static imaging seems to be still far from medical and clinical applications primarily due to the fundamental ill-posedness of the inverse problem. It is little bit too early to say that, however, static imaging in EIT is not to be pursued since active researchers are still looking for innovative algorithms and new measurement technologies.

Dynamic Imaging in EIT

The dynamic imaging, introduced by Barber and Brown (1984) yields differential images whereas the static imaging yields absolute images. The differential imaging produces the images of the conductivity changes of a region between two different time intervals (Molinary, 2003). The dynamic imaging allows us to monitor the changes such as gastric emptying or long-term observation of body functions/volume changes (Molinary, 2003). Imaging physiological function within the body largely relies on this technique which is relatively simple to implement. A more recent meaning of "dynamic imaging" has been introduced by the work of the Kuopio group (Vauhkonen, 1997), which is looking at imaging and tracking objects in the fluid flow within a pipe (Molinary, 2003). Dynamic imaging techniques have been applied to visualize physiological activities in a human body such as respiration, breast cancer detection, cardiac circulation, brain function, stomach emptying, fracture healing, bladder filling, and others. It can also be used in corrosion detection, crack detection, electric field sensing, bubble detection, and other nondestructive testing. The reasons that EIT is not yet a well-established tool in the biomedical sector are (Molinary, 2003):

- Sensitive to electrode positioning.
- Provides rather low image resolution due to noise in the measurements.
- Low image resolution due to the discretization.
- Time-consuming non-linear numerical reconstruction.
- Lack of dedicated easy-to-use software.

FUTURE RESEARCH DIRECTIONS

EIT has been extensively researched in several fields of science and engineering for obtaining the tomographic imaging noninvasively. It has been applied to visualize several system properties in terms of electrical parameters like conductivity, resistivity and permittivity. Though EIT has a lot of advantages over other tomographic imaging modalities still it is suffering from the low spatial resolution problem. The researchers and scientists are engaged in their scientific research on EIT to make it more effective, efficient and reliable. During the last three decades the EIT has been studied extensively and time difference EIT and frequency difference EIT has been introduces for reducing the system noise. Regularization techniques are also required to be studied for better impedance imaging. 3D EIT with larger number of finite element needs more advanced computing facilities which will help to reconstruct the fast real time EIT image in 3D. Though the difference imaging does not provide the functional imaging the absolute EIT is required to obtain the function properties of body tissue. But the absolute EIT is highly difficult as it extremely depends on modeling error and electrode arrangement errors. For obtaining the successful absolute EIT imaging with high resolution we have to study and research the EIT technology more. We hope that the EIT technology will be applied in lot of new scientific and technological areas with better resolution and higher speed in near future.

CONCLUSION

The medical imaging is an essential tool to medical doctors and clinicians for clinical diagnosis of several diseases. X-Ray planar radiography, X-Ray CT, Gamma Camera, PET, SPECT, MRI, and USG all are considered as the conventional medical imaging modalities where as the EIT, DOT, and OCT are new and promising technologies which are still being researched for improved performance. Among the new and promising technologies EIT is one of the most safe, fast, portable and clinical hazards free technique. The first electrical impedance imaging system was introduced by J. G. Webster and Ross P. Henderson in 1978 for medical imaging purpose. Since then the EIT technology is researched not only in medical imaging field but also it has been studied in several field of applied sciences and engineering. Being a low-cost, portable, fast, non-radiating, non-ionizing, non-invasive methodology EIT is found as a suitable imaging modality in medical imaging, mechanical engineering, material engineering, chemical engineering, biomedical and biotechnological engineering. It is also studied for nondestructive evaluation of materials and objects in archeology, oceanography, civil engineering and geotechnology. Several electrical parameters like electrical conductivity, electrical resistivity, and electrical permittivity are reconstructed in different forms of electrical impedance imaging suitable for different applications. For reducing the system and errors difference imaging (time difference and frequency difference) are also studied by several research groups.

REFERENCES

Abtahi, J., Tengvall, P., & Aspenberg, P. (2012). A bisphosphonate-coating improves the fixation of metal implants in human bone. A randomized trial of dental implants. *Bone*, *50*(5), 1148–1151. doi:10.1016/j.bone.2012.02.001 PMID:22348981.

Advanced Veterinary Medical Images. (2011). Computed tomography. CAT scan. *Advanced Veterinary Imaging*. Retrieved from http://www.avmi.net/newfiles/CT/CT.html.

Ahn, S., Jun, S. C., Seo, J. K., Lee, J., Woo, E. J., & Holder, D. (2010). Frequency-difference electrical impedance tomography: Phantom imaging experiments. *Journal of Physics: Conference Series, 224*.

An, L. T. H., Pham Dinh Tao, P. D., & Hàob, D. N. (2002). Towards tikhonov regularization of non-linear ill-posed problems: A DC programming approach. *Comptes Rendus Mathematique*, *335*(12), 1073–1078. doi:10.1016/S1631-073X(02)02611-0.

Arridge, S. R. (1999). Optical tomography in medical imaging, Topical review. *Inverse Problems*, *15*, R41–R93. doi:10.1088/0266-5611/15/2/022.

Assmus, A. (1995). Early history of X rays. *University of Stanford Beam Line Periodical*, *25*(2), 11–24.

Aster, R. C., Borchers, B., & Thurber, C. H. (2012). *Parameter estimation and inverse problems* (2nd ed.). New York: Academic Press.

Bagshaw, A. P., Liston, A. D., Bayford, R. H., Tizzard, A., Gibson, A. P., & Holder, D. S. et al. (2003). Electrical impedance tomography of human brain function using reconstruction algorithms based on the finite element method. *NeuroImage*, *20*, 752–764. doi:10.1016/S1053-8119(03)00301-X PMID:14568449.

Bahrani, N. (2012). *2½D Finite Element Method for Electrical Impedance Tomography Considering the Complete Electrode Model.* (Master of Applied Science Thesis). Ottawa, Ontario, Carleton University.

Bankman, I. N. (2000). *Handbook of medical imaging: Processing and analysis* (1st ed.). New York: Academic Press.

Barber, D. C. (1990). Quantification in impcdanee imaging. *Clinical Physics and Physiological Measurement*, *11*, 45–56. doi:10.1088/0143-0815/11/4A/306 PMID:2286047.

Barber, D. C. (1992). Registration of low resolution medical images. *Physics in Medicine and Biology*, *37*(7), 1485–1498. doi:10.1088/0031-9155/37/7/002 PMID:1631194.

Barber, D. C. (2000). Electrical impedance tomography. In Bronzino, J. D. (Ed.), *The Biomedical Engineering Handbook* (2nd ed.). Boca Raton, FL: CRC Press.

Barber, D. C., & Brown, B. H. (1984). Applied potential tomography, Review article. *Journal of Physics. E, Scientific Instruments*, *17*, 723–734. doi:10.1088/0022-3735/17/9/002.

Bayford, R. H. (2006). Bioimpedance tomography (Electrical impedance tomography). *Annual Review of Biomedical Engineering*, *8*, 63–91. doi:10.1146/annurev.bioeng.8.061505.095716 PMID:16834552.

Bera, T. K., Biswas, S. K., Rajan, K., & Nagaraju, J. (2011b). Improving conductivity image quality using block matrix-based multiple regularization (BMMR) technique in EIT: A simulation study. *Journal of Electrical Bioimpedance*, *2*, 33–47.

Bera, T. K., Biswas, S. K., Rajan, K., & Nagaraju, J. (2011c). Improving image quality in electrical impedance tomography (EIT) using projection error propagation-based regularization (PEPR) technique: A simulation study. *Journal of Electrical Bioimpedance*, *2*, 2–12.

Bera, T. K., Biswas, S. K., Rajan, K., & Nagaraju, J. (2012c). Improving the image reconstruction in electrical impedance tomography (EIT) with block matrix-based multiple regularization (BMMR): A practical phantom study. In *Proceedings of the IEEE World Congress on Information and Communication Technologies 2011* (1346-1351). Mumbai, India: IEEE Press.

Bera, T. K., Biswas, S. K., Rajan, K., & Nagaraju, J. (2012d). Image reconstruction in electrical impedance tomography (EIT) with projection error propagation-based regularization (PEPR): A practical phantom study. *Advanced Computing, Networking, and Security. Lecture Notes in Computer Science, 7135*, 95–105. doi:10.1007/978-3-642-29280-4_11.

Bera, T. K., & Nagaraju, J. (2009a) A study of practical biological phantoms with simple instrumentation for electrical impedance tomography (EIT), In *Proceedings of IEEE International Instrumentation and Measurement Technology Conference* (511-516). Singapore: IEEE Press.

Bera, T. K., & Nagaraju, J. (2009b). A simple instrumentation calibration technique for electrical impedance tomography (EIT) using A 16 electrode phantom. In, *Proceedings of The Fifth Annual IEEE Conference on Automation Science and Engineering* (347-352). Bangalore, India: IEEE Press.

Bera, T. K., & Nagaraju, J. (2009c). A reconfigurable practical phantom for studying the 2 D electrical impedance tomography (EIT) using a FEM based forward solver. In *Proceedings of 10th International Conference on Biomedical Applications of Electrical Impedance Tomography.* Manchester, UK: Oxford University Press.

Bera, T. K., & Nagaraju, J. (2009d). A FEM-Based forward solver for studying the forward problem of electrical impedance tomography (EIT) with a practical biological phantom. In *Proceedings of IEEE International Advance Computing Conference' 2009* (1375–1381). Patiala, India: IEEE Press.

Bera, T. K., & Nagaraju, J. (2009e). Studying the boundary data profile of a practical phantom for medical electrical impedance tomography with different electrode geometries. In *Proceedings of the World Congress on Medical Physics and Biomedical Engineering-2009* (925–929). Munich, Germany: Springer.

Bera, T. K., & Nagaraju, J. (2009f). A stainless steel electrode phantom to study the forward problem of electrical impedance tomography (EIT). *Sensors & Transducers Journal, 104*(5), 33–40.

Bera, T. K., & Nagaraju, J. (2010). A multifrequency constant current source for medical electrical impedance tomography. In *Proceedings of the IEEE International Conference on Systems in Medicine and Biology 2010* (278-283). Kharagpur, India: IEEE Press.

Bera, T. K., & Nagaraju, J. (2011a). Resistivity imaging of a reconfigurable phantom with circular inhomogeneities in 2d-electrical impedance tomography. *Measurement, 44*(3), 518–526. doi:10.1016/j.measurement.2010.11.015.

Bera, T. K., & Nagaraju, J. (2011d). Gold electrode sensors for electrical impedance tomography (EIT) studies. In *Proceedings of IEEE Sensors Application Symposium 2011* (24-28) San Antonio, TX: IEEE Press.

Bera, T. K., & Nagaraju, J. (2011e). A chicken tissue phantom for studying an electrical impedance tomography (EIT) system suitable for clinical imaging. *Sensing and Imaging: An International Journal, 12*(3-4), 95–116. doi:10.1007/s11220-011-0063-4.

Bera, T. K., & Nagaraju, J. (2011f). Studying the 2D resistivity reconstruction of stainless steel electrode phantoms using different current patterns of electrical impedance tomography (EIT). In Biomedical Engineering (163-169). New Dehli, India: Narosa Publishing House.

Bera, T. K., & Nagaraju, J. (2011g). Electrical impedance spectroscopic study of broiler chicken tissues suitable for the development of practical phantoms in multifrequency EIT. *Journal of Electrical Bioimpedance, 2*, 48–63.

Bera, T. K., & Nagaraju, J. (2011h). Common ground method of current injection in electrical impedance tomography. In *Proceedings of the Fourth International Conference on Recent Trends in Computing, Communication, & Information Technologies 2011*, (593-605). Tamil Nadu, India: ITC Press.

Bera, T. K., & Nagaraju, J. (2011i). Studying the 2D-image reconstruction of non biological and biological inhomogeneities in electrical impedance tomography (EIT) with EIDORS. In *Proceedings of International Conference on Advanced Computing, Networking, and Security 2011* (132-136). Mangalore, India: ACM Press.

Bera, T. K., & Nagaraju, J. (2012a). Studying the resistivity imaging of chicken tissue phantoms with different current patterns in electrical impedance tomography (EIT). *Measurement, 45*, 663–682. doi:10.1016/j.measurement.2012.01.002.

Bera, T. K., & Nagaraju, J. (2012b). A gold sensors array for imaging the real tissue phantom in electrical impedance tomography. In *Proceedings of the International Conference on Materials Science and Technology 2012*. Kerala, India: ASM Press.

Bera, T. K., & Nagaraju, J. (2012e). A multifrequency electrical impedance tomography (EIT) System for biomedical imaging. In *Proceedings of International Conference on Signal Processing and Communications* (1-5). Bangalore, India: IEEE Press.

Bloch, F., Hansen, W. W., & Packard, M. (1946). Nuclear induction. *Physical Review, 69*, 127. doi:10.1103/PhysRev.69.127.

Bolton, G. T., Qiu, C. H., & Wang, M. (2002). A novel electrical tomography sensor for monitoring the phase distribution in industrial reactors. In *Proceedings of the 7th UK Conference on Mixing*. Bradford, UK: Ametys.

Borcea, L. (2002). Electrical impedance tomography, Topical review. *Inverse Problems, 18*, R99–R136. doi:10.1088/0266-5611/18/6/201.

Bradley, W. G. (2008). History of medical imaging. *Proceedings of the American Philosophical Society, 152*(3), 349–361. PMID:19831232.

British Library. (2013). Roentgen's discovery of the X-Ray, learning, bodies of knowledge. *British Library*. Retrieved from http://www.bl.uk/learning/cult/bodies/xray/roentgen.html.

Brown, B. H. (2001). Medical impedance tomography and process impedance tomography: A brief review. *Measurement Science & Technology, 12*(8), 991–996. doi:10.1088/0957-0233/12/8/301.

Brown, B. H., & Segar, A. D. (1987). The sheffield data collection system. *Clinical Physics and Physiological Measurement, 8*, 91–97. doi:10.1088/0143-0815/8/4A/012 PMID:3568577.

Bushberg, J. T., Seibert, J. A., Leidholdt, E. M. Jr, & Boone, J. M. (2001). *The essential physics of medical imaging* (2nd ed.). Riverwoods, Il.: Lippincott, Williams, & Wilkins.

Bushong, S. C. (2003). *Magnetic resonance imaging: Physical and biological principles* (3rd ed.). Philadelphia: Mosby & Saunders.

Calvetti, D., McGivney, D., & Somersalo, E. (2012). Left and right preconditioning for electrical impedance tomography with structural information. *Inverse Problems*, *28*, 26. doi:10.1088/0266-5611/28/5/055015.

Cassen, B. (1998). The rectilinear scanner and an enduring legacy of education and research. *Journal of Nuclear Medicine*, *39*(5), 16N. PMID:9591566.

Cassen, B., Curtis, L., & Reed, C. W. (1950). A sensitive directional gamma-ray detector. *Nucleonics*, 78–81. PMID:15398050.

CBS. (2005). *The encyclopedia atlas of the human body: A visual guide to the human body*. New York: CBS Publishers & Distributors Pvt. Ltd..

Chambers, J. E., Wilkinson, P. B., Wardrop, D., Hameed, A., Hill, I., & Gunn, D. A. et al. (2012). Bedrock detection beneath river terrace deposits using three-dimensional electrical resistivity tomography. *Geomorphology*, *177–178*, 17–25. doi:10.1016/j.geomorph.2012.03.034.

Chen, Z., Brown, E. N., & Barbieri, R. (2009). assessment of autonomic control and respiratory sinus arrhythmia using point process models of human heart beat dynamics. *IEEE Transactions on Electromagnetic Compatibility*, *56*(7), 1791–1802. PMID:19272971.

Chena, C. F., Liub, Z. H., Xiea, J., Xiao-Bo Maa, X. B., Lia, Y., & Gonga, S. S. (2012). Cochlear implant challenges encountered in tuberculous otitis media. *Asian Pacific Journal of Tropical Medicine*, *5*(5), 416–419. doi:10.1016/S1995-7645(12)60071-6 PMID:22546663.

Cheney, M., Isaacson, D., & Newell, J. C. (1999). Electrical impedance tomography. *SIAM Review*, *41*(1), 85–101. doi:10.1137/S0036144598333613.

Church, P., McFee, J. E., Gagnon, S., & Wort, P. (2006). Electrical impedance tomographic imaging of buried landmines. *IEEE Transactions on Geoscience and Remote Sensing*, *44*(9), 2407–2420. doi:10.1109/TGRS.2006.873208.

Cohen-Bacrie, C., Goussard, Y., & Guardo, G. (1997). Regularized reconstruction in electrical impedance tomography using a variance uniformization constraint. *IEEE Transactions on Medical Imaging*, *16*(5), 562–571. doi:10.1109/42.640745 PMID:9368111.

Conway, J. (1987). Electrical impedance tomography for thermal monitoring of hyperthermia treatment: an assessment using in vitro and in vivo measurements. *Clinical Physics and Physiological Measurement*, *8*, 141–146. doi:10.1088/0143-0815/8/4A/018 PMID:3568563.

D'Antona, G., & Rocca, L. (2002). Electrical impedance tomography for underground pollutant detection and polluted lands reclaiming monitoring. In *Proceedings of IEEE Instrumentation and Measurement Technology Conference* (1035-1038). Anchorage, AK: IEEE Press.

Dai, W. W., Mmili, P. M., Martinez, E., & Morucci, J.-P. (1994). Using the hilbert uniqueness method in a reconstruction algorithm for electrical impedance tomography. *Physiological Measurement*, *15*, A161–A168. doi:10.1088/0967-3334/15/2A/021 PMID:8087039.

Davidson, J. L., Ruffino, L. S., Stephenson, D. R., Mann, R., Grieve, B. D., & York, T. A. (2004). Three-dimensional electrical impedance tomography applied to a metal-walled filtration test platform. *Measurement Science & Technology*, *15*(1), 2263–2274. doi:10.1088/0957-0233/15/11/012.

Denyer, C. W. L. (1996). *Electronics for Real-Time and Three-Dimensional Electrical Impedance Tomographs*. (PhD Thesis). Oxford, UK, Oxford Brookes University.

Djamdji, F., Gorvin, A. C., Freeston, I. L., Tozer, R. C., Mayes, I. C., & Blight, S. R. (1996). Electrical impedance tomography applied to semiconductor wafer characterization. *Measurement Science & Technology*, *7*(3), 391–395. doi:10.1088/0957-0233/7/3/021.

Donald, I., MacVicar, J., & Brown, T. G. (1958). Investigation of abdominal masses by pulsed ultrasound. *Lancet*, *271*(7032), 1188–1195. doi:10.1016/S0140-6736(58)91905-6 PMID:13550965.

Edd, J. F., Horowitz, L., & Rubinsky, B. (2005). Temperature dependence of tissue impedivity in electrical impedance tomography of cryosurgery. *IEEE Transactions on Bio-Medical Engineering*, *52*(4), 695–701. doi:10.1109/TBME.2005.844042 PMID:15825871.

Elliott, A. (2005). Medical imaging. *Nuclear Instruments & Methods in Physics Research. Section A, Accelerators, Spectrometers, Detectors and Associated Equipment*, *546*(1), 1–13. doi:10.1016/j.nima.2005.03.127.

Fabrizi1, L., McEwan, A., Oh, T., Woo, E. J., & Holder, D. S. (2009). An electrode addressing protocol for imaging brain function with electrical impedance tomography using a 16-channel semi-parallel system. *Physiological Measurement*, *30*, S85–S101.

Feig, S. A., & Hendrick, R. E. (1997). Radiation risk from screening mammography of women aged 40–49 years. *Journal of the National Cancer Institute. Monographs*, *22*(22), 119–124. PMID:9709287.

Frank, G. K. W., & Kaye, W. H. (2012). Current status of functional imaging in eating disorders. *The International Journal of Eating Disorders*, *45*(6), 723–736. doi:10.1002/eat.22016 PMID:22532388.

Frerichs, I., Schmitz, G., Pulletz, S., Schadler, D., Zick, G., Scholz, J., & Weiler, N. (2007). Reproducibility of regional lung ventilation distribution determined by electrical impedance tomography during mechanical ventilation. *Physiological Measurement*, *28*, S261–S267. doi:10.1088/0967-3334/28/7/S19 PMID:17664640.

Gisser, D. G., Isaacson, D., & Newell, J. C. (1987). Current topics in impedance imaging. *Clinical Physics and Physiological Measurement*, *8*, 39–46. doi:10.1088/0143-0815/8/4A/005 PMID:3568569.

Gøtzsche, P. C. (2011). Screening for breast cancer with mammography. *Cochrane Database of Systematic Reviews*, *1*.

Graham, B. M. (2007). *Enhancements in Electrical Impedance Tomography (EIT) Image Reconstruction for 3D Lung Imaging*. (PhD thesis). Ottawa, Ontario, University of Ottawa.

Griffiths, H. (1988). A phantom for electrical impedance tomography. *Clinical Physics and Physiological Measurement*, *9*, 15–20. doi:10.1088/0143-0815/9/4A/003 PMID:3240643.

Grootveld, C. J. (1996). *Measuring and Modeling of Concentrated Settling Suspensions Using Electrical Impedance Tomography*. (PhD Thesis). Delft, Netherlands, Delft University of Technology.

Guerra, A. D. (2004). *Ionizing radiation detectors for medical imaging*. Singapore: World Scientific Pub. Co. Inc..

Guimera, A., Gabriel, G., Plata-Cordero, M., Montero, L., Maldonado, M. J., & Villa, R. (2012). A non-invasive method for an in vivo assessment of corneal epithelium permeability through tetrapolar impedance measurements. *Biosensors & Bioelectronics*, *31*, 55–61. doi:10.1016/j.bios.2011.09.039 PMID:22019100.

Hendee, R. W. (1989). Cross sectional medical imaging: A history. *Radiographics, 9*(6), 1155–1180. PMID:2685939.

Herman, G. T. (2009). *Fundamentals of computerized tomography: Image reconstruction from projection* (2nd ed.). Berlin: Springer. doi:10.1007/978-1-84628-723-7.

Hero, A. O., Piramuthu, R., Fessler, J. A., & Titus, S. R. (1999). Minimax emission computed tomography using high-resolution anatomical side information and B-Spline models. *IEEE Transactions on Information Theory, 45*(3), 920–938. doi:10.1109/18.761333.

Holder, D. S. (1993). *Clinical and physiological applications of electrical impedance tomography* (1st ed.). Philadelphia: Taylor & Francis.

Holder, D. S. (Ed.). (2005). *Electrical impedance tomography: Methods, history, and applications. Series in Medical Physics and Biomedical Engineering* (1st ed.). London: Institute of Physics Publishing Ltd..

Holder, D. S., Hanquan, Y., & Rao, A. (1996). Some practical biological phantoms for calibrating multifrequency electrical impedance tomography. *Physiological Measurement, 17*, A167–A177. doi:10.1088/0967-3334/17/4A/021 PMID:9001615.

Hope, T. A., & Iles, S. E. (2004). Technology review: The use of electrical impedance scanning in the detection of breast cancer. *Breast Cancer Research, 6*, 69–74. doi:10.1186/bcr744 PMID:14979909.

Hou, T. C., Loh, K. J., & Lynch, J. P. (2007). Spatial conductivity mapping of carbon nanotube composite thin films by electrical impedance tomography for sensing applications. *Nanotechnology, 18*, 9. doi:10.1088/0957-4484/18/31/315501.

Hou, W. D., & Mo, Y. L. (2002). New regularization method in electrical impedance tomography. *Journal of Shanghai University, 6*(3), 211–215. doi:10.1007/s11741-002-0036-x.

Hou, W. D., & Mo, Y. L. (2002). Increasing image resolution in electrical impedance tomography. *Electronics Letters, 38*, 701–702. doi:10.1049/el:20020477.

Hounsfield, G. N. (1979). Computed medical imaging (568-586). London: The Medical Systems Department of Central Research Laboratories EMI.

Hsieh, J. (2009). *Computed tomography: Principles design artifacts and recent advances.* Bellingham, WA: SPIE Press.

Hua, P., Webster, J. G., & Tompkins, W. J. (1987). Effect of the measurement method on noise handling and image quality of EIT imaging. In *Proceedings of Ninth International Conference of IEEE Engineering in Medicine and Biology Society* (1429-1430). New York: IEEE Press.

Ingham, M., Pringle, D., & Eicken, H. (2008). Cross-borehole resistivity tomography of sea ice. *Cold Regions Science and Technology, 52*, 263–277. doi:10.1016/j.coldregions.2007.05.002.

Iniewski, K. (2009). *Medical imaging: Principles, detectors, and electronics.* Hoboken, NJ: John Wiley & Sons, Inc..

Jaume, C., & Lluís, G. (2012). The dark side of the lung: Unveiling regional lung ventilation with electrical impedance tomography. *Anesthesiology, 116*(6), 1186–1188. doi:10.1097/ALN.0b013e318256ef0a PMID:22546963.

Jinchuang, Z., Wenli, F., Taoshen, L., & Shi, W. (2002). An image reconstruction algorithm based on a revised regularization method for electrical capacitance tomography. *Measurement Science & Technology, 13*(4), 638–640. doi:10.1088/0957-0233/13/4/329.

Kak, A. C., & Slaney, M. (1999). *Principle of computerized tomographic imaging.* Washington, DC: IEEE Press.

Kalender, W. A. (2011). *Computed tomography* (3rd ed.). London: Publicis.

Karhunen, K., Seppänen, A., Lehikoinen, A., Monteiro, P. J. M., & Kaipio, J. P. (2010). Electrical resistance tomography imaging of concrete. *Cement and Concrete Research, 40,* 137–145. doi:10.1016/j.cemconres.2009.08.023.

Kerner, T. E., Williams, D. B., Osterman, K. S., Reiss, F. R., Hartov, A., & Paulsen, K. D. (2000). Electrical impedance imaging at multiple frequencies in phantoms. *Physiological Measurement, 21,* 67–77. doi:10.1088/0967-3334/21/1/309 PMID:10720001.

Kolehmainen, V., Somersalo, E., Vauhkonen, P. J., Vauhkonen, M., & Kaipio, J. P. (1998). A bayesian approach and total variation priors in 3D electrical impedance tomography. In *Proceedings of the 20th Annual International Conference of the IEEE Engineering in Medicine and Biology Society* (1028-1031). Hong Kong: IEEE Press.

Korpinen, L., Kuisti, H., Elovaara, J., & Virtanen, V. (2012). Cardiac pacemakers in electric and magnetic fields of 400-kV power lines. *Pacing and Clinical Electrophysiology, 35*(4), 422–430. doi:10.1111/j.1540-8159.2011.03327.x PMID:22309463.

Kothari, M. S., Rusby, J. E., Agusti, A. A., & MacNeill, F. A. (2012). Sentinel lymph node biopsy after previous axillary surgery: A review. *European Journal of Surgical Oncology, 38*(1), 8–15. doi:10.1016/j.ejso.2011.10.003 PMID:22032909.

Kubiak, T., & Stone, A. A. (2012). Ambulatory monitoring of biobehavioral processes in health and disease. *Psychosomatic Medicine, 74*(4), 325–326. doi:10.1097/PSY.0b013e31825878da PMID:22582329.

Kuperman, V. (2000). *Magnetic resonance imaging: Physical principles and applications.* New York: Academic Press.

Lauterbur, P. C. (1973). Image formation by induced local interactions: Examples employing nuclear magnetic resonance. *Nature, 242,* 190–191. doi:10.1038/242190a0.

Levenberg, K. (1944). A method for the solution of certain problems in least squares. *Quarterly of Applied Mathematics, 2,* 164–168.

Lima, J. J. P. (2011). *Nuclear medicine physics series in medical physics and biomedical engineering.* Philadelphia: Taylor & Francis.

Lionheart, W. R. B. (2004). EIT reconstruction algorithms: Pitfalls, challenges, and recent developments. *Physiological Measurement, 25,* 125–142. doi:10.1088/0967-3334/25/1/021 PMID:15005311.

Lionheart, W. R. B., Lidgey, F. J., McLeod, C. N., Paulson, K. S., Pidcock, M. K., & Shi, Y. (1997). Electrical impedance tomography for high speed chest imaging. *Physica Medica, 13,* 247–249.

Litière, S., Werutsky, G., Fentiman, I. S., Rutgers, E., Christiaens, M. R., & Bartelink, H. et al. (2012). Breast conserving therapy versus mastectomy for stage I—II breast cancer: 20 year follow-up of the EORTC 10801 phase 3 randomised trial. *The Lancet Oncology, 13*(4), 412–419. doi:10.1016/S1470-2045(12)70042-6 PMID:22373563.

Majid, M., Mohiuddin, M. M., Nichols, E. M., Marter, K. J., & Flannery, T. W. (2012). Decrease of the lumpectomy cavity volume after whole-breast irradiation affects small field boost planning. *Medical Dosimetry, 37*(3), 339–343. doi:10.1016/j.meddos.2011.11.008 PMID:22305933.

Malmivuo, J., & Plonsey, R. (1995). *Bioelectromagnetism: Principles and Applications of Bioelectric and Biomagnetic Fields*. New York: Oxford University Press. doi:10.1093/acprof:oso/9780195058239.001.0001.

Mansfield, P., & Grannell, P. K. (1973). NMR `diffraction' in solids? *Journal of Physical Chemistry*, *6*, L422–L426.

Marquardt, D. (1963). An algorithm for least-squares estimation of nonlinear parameters. *SIAM Journal on Applied Mathematics*, *11*, 431–441. doi:10.1137/0111030.

Metherall, P. (1998). *Three Dimensional Electrical Impedance Tomography of the Human Thorax*. (PhD Thesis). Sheffield, UK: University of Sheffield.

Molinary, M. (2003). *High Fidelity Imaging in Electrical Impedance Tomography*. (PhD Thesis). Southampton, UK: University of Southampton.

Muller, P., Hiller, J., Cantatore, A., & De Chiffre, L. (2012). A study on evaluation strategies in dimensional X-ray computed tomography by estimation of measurement uncertainties. *International Journal of Metrology and Quality Engineering*, *3*, 107–115. doi:10.1051/ijmqe/2012011.

Murphy, D., Burton, P., Coombs, R., Tarassenko, L., & Rolfe, P. (1987). Impedance imaging in the newborn. *Clinical Physics and Physiological Measurement*, *8*, 131–140. doi:10.1088/0143-0815/8/4A/017 PMID:3568562.

Noor, J. A. E. (2007). *Electrical Impedance Tomography at Low Frequencies*. (PhD Thesis). Kensington, Australia, University Of New South Wales.

Noordegraaf, A. V., Faes, T. J. C., Janse, A., Marcus, J. T., Heethaar, R. M., Postmus, P. E., & Vries, P. M. J. M. (1996). Improvement of cardiac imaging in electrical impedance tomography by means of a new electrode configuration. *Physiological Measurement*, *17*, 179–188. doi:10.1088/0967-3334/17/3/004 PMID:8870058.

Oh, T. I., Koo, H., Lee, K. H., Kim, S. M., Lee, J., & Woo, E. J. et al. (2008). Validation of a multi-frequency electrical impedance tomography (mfEIT) system KHU Mark1: Impedance spectroscopy and time-difference imaging. *Physiological Measurement*, *29*, 295–307. doi:10.1088/0967-3334/29/3/002 PMID:18367806.

Paulson, K., Breckon, W., & Pidcock, M. (1992). A hybrid phantom for electrical impedance tomography. *Clinical Physics and Physiological Measurement*, *13*, 155–159. doi:10.1088/0143-0815/13/A/030 PMID:1587092.

Purcell, E. M., Torrey, H. C., & Pound, R. V. (1946). Resonance absorption by nuclear magnetic moments in a solid. *Physical Review*, *69*, 37–38. doi:10.1103/PhysRev.69.37.

Qiao, G., Wang, W., Wang, L., He, Y., Bramer, B., & Al-Akaidi, M. (2007). Investigation of biological phantom for 2D and 3D breast EIT images. In *Proceedings of the 13th International Conference on Electrical Bioimpedance and the 8th Conference on Electrical Impedance Tomography* (328-331). Graz, Austria: Springer.

Riera, J., Riu, P. J., Casan, P., & Masclans, J. R. (2011). Electrical impedance tomography in acute lung injury. *Medicina Intensiva*, *35*(8), 509–517. doi:10.1016/j.medin.2011.05.005 PMID:21680060.

Robitaille, N., Guardo, R., Maurice, I., Hartinger, A. E., & Gagnon, H. (2009). A multi-frequency EIT system design based on telecommunication signal processors. *Physiological Measurement*, *30*, S57–S71. doi:10.1088/0967-3334/30/6/S04 PMID:19491440.

Rockett, P., & Wang, G. (2001). The principles of X-ray computed tomography. In Kutz, M. (Ed). Standard Handbook of Biomedical Engineering and Design (26.1-26.52). New York: McGraw-Hill.

Romsauerova, A., McEwan, A., Horesh, L., Yerworth, R., Bayford, R. H., & Holder, D. S. (2006). Multi-frequency electrical impedance tomography (EIT) of the adult human head: Initial findings in brain tumours, arteriovenous malformations, and chronic stroke, development of an analysis method and calibration. *Physiological Measurement, 27,* S147–S161. doi:10.1088/0967-3334/27/5/S13 PMID:16636407.

Saslow, D., Hannan, J., Osuch, J., Alciati, M. H., Baines, C., & Coates, R. et al. (2004). Clinical breast examination: Practical recommendations for optimizing performance and reporting. *CA: a Cancer Journal for Clinicians, 54*(6), 327–344. doi:10.3322/canjclin.54.6.327 PMID:15537576.

Schneider, I. D., Kleffel, R., Jennings, D., & Courtenay, A. J. (2000). Design of an electrical impedance tomography phantom using active elements. *Medical & Biological Engineering & Computing, 38*(4), 390–394. doi:10.1007/BF02345007 PMID:10984936.

Seo, J. K., & Woo, E. J. (2012). Electrical impedance tomography, Chapter 7. Nonlinear Inverse Problems in Imaging (195-250). Hoboken, NJ: Wiley-Blackwell.

Seynaeve, P. C., & Broos, J. I. (1995). The history of tomography. *Journal Belge de Radiologie, 78*(5), 284–288. PMID:8550391.

Singh, S. S., Devi, H. M., Singh, T. T., & Singh, O. I. (2012). A new easy method of enhancement of low contrast image using spatial domain. *International Journal of Computers and Applications, 40*(1), 32–34. doi:10.5120/4922-7149.

Smith, R. W. M., Freeston, I. L., & Brown, B. H. (1995). A real-time electrical impedance tomography system for clinical use-design and preliminary results. *IEEE Transactions on Bio-Medical Engineering, 42*(2), 133–140. doi:10.1109/10.341825 PMID:7868140.

Smith-Bindman, R., Lipson, J., & Marcus, R. (2009). Radiation dose associated with common computed tomography examinations and the associated lifetime attributable risk of cancer. *Archives of Internal Medicine, 169*(22), 2078–2086. doi:10.1001/archinternmed.2009.427 PMID:20008690.

Soleimani, M., & Lionheart, W. R. B. (2005). Nonlinear image reconstruction for electrical capacitance tomography using experimental data. *Measurement Science & Technology, 16*(10), 1987–1996. doi:10.1088/0957-0233/16/10/014.

Soni, N. K., Dehghani, H., Hartov, A., & Paulsen, K. D. (2003). A novel data calibration scheme for electrical impedance tomography. *Physiological Measurement, 24,* 421–435. doi:10.1088/0967-3334/24/2/354 PMID:12812427.

Soni, N. K., Hartov, A., Kogel, C., Poplack, C. S., & Paulsen, K. D. (2004). Multi-frequency electrical impedance tomography of the breast: new clinical results. *Physiological Measurement, 25,* 301–314. doi:10.1088/0967-3334/25/1/034 PMID:15005324.

Sperandio, M., Guermandi, M., & Guerrieri, R. (2012). A four-shell diffusion phantom of the head for electrical impedance tomography. *IEEE Transactions on Bio-Medical Engineering, 59*(2), 383–389. doi:10.1109/TBME.2011.2173197 PMID:22027364.

Stankovic, S., & Klisuric, O. (Eds.). (2007). Medical imaging-Indispensable medical tools, Chapter 1. Environmental, health, and humanity issues in the down danubian region: Multidisciplinary approaches. In *Proceedings of the 9th International Symposium on Interdisciplinary Regional Research.* Novi Sad, Serbia: University of Novi.

Stuart, C. S. (1997). *Functional MRI: Methods and Applications.* (PhD Thesis). Nottingham, UK, University of Nottingham.

Suetens, P. (2009). *Fundamentals of medical imaging* (2nd ed.). Cambridge, UK: Cambridge University Press. doi:10.1017/CBO9780511596803.

Sun, T., Tsuda, S., Zauner, K. P., & Morgan, H. (2010). On-chip electrical impedance tomography for imaging biological cells. *Biosensors & Bioelectronics*, *25*(5), 1109–1115. doi:10.1016/j.bios.2009.09.036 PMID:19850464.

SUNY. (2006). News update: The department of surgery. *University Hospital and Health Sciences Center at Stony Brook*, *19*, 1–20.

Tehrani, J. N., Jin, C., & McEwan, A. L. (2012). Modelling of an oesophageal electrode for cardiac function tomography. *Computational and Mathematical Methods in Medicine*. doi:10.1155/2012/585786 PMID:22481975.

U. S. Preventive Services Task Force. (2013). Screening for breast cancer: U.S. preventive services task force recommendation statement. *Annals of Internal Medicine*. Retrieved from http://www.uspreventiveservicestaskforce.org/uspstf09/breastcancer/brcanrs.pdf.

Ullrich, B., Günther, T., & Rücker, C. (2007). Electrical resistivity tomography methods for archaeological prospection. In A. Posluschny, K. Lambers, & I. Herzog (Ed.), *Layers of Perception. Proceedings of the 35th International Conference on Computer Applications and Quantitative Methods in Archaeology (CAA)* (1-7). Berlin: Koll.

Vauhkonen, M. (1997). *Electrical Impedance Tomography and Prior Information*. (PhD Thesis). Joensuu, Finland, Kuopio University.

Vauhkonen, P. J., Vauhkonen, M., Savolainen, T., & Kaipio, J. P. (1999). Three-dimensional electrical impedance tomography based on the complete electrode model. *IEEE Transactions on Bio-Medical Engineering*, *46*(9), 1150–1160. doi:10.1109/10.784147 PMID:10493078.

Victorino, Borges, & Okamoto, Matos, Tucci, ... & Amato. (2004). Imbalances in regional lung ventilation: A validation study on electrical impedance tomography. *American Journal of Respiratory and Critical Care Medicine*, *169*(7), 791–800. doi:10.1164/rccm.200301-133OC PMID:14693669.

Wang, M. (1999). Three- dimensional effects in electrical impedance tomography. In *Proceedings of 1st World Congress on Industrial Process Tomography* (410-415). Buxton, UK: OLIL.

Webster, J. G. (Ed.). (1990). *Electrical impedance tomography. Adam Hilger Series of Biomedical Engineering*. New York: Adam Hilger.

Webster, J. G. (2009). *Medical instrumentation: Application and design* (3rd ed.). Singapore: John Wiley & Sons.

Wei, H. Y., & Soleimani, M. (2012). Hardware and software design for a national instrument-based magnetic induction tomography system for prospective biomedical applications. *Physiological Measurement*, *33*(5), 863–879. doi:10.1088/0967-3334/33/5/863 PMID:22531316.

Wi, H., Kim, T. E., Oh, T. I., & Woo, E. J. (2012). Expandable multi-frequency EIT system for clinical applications. In *Proceedings of Progress in Electromagnetics Research Symposium* (49-52). Kuala Lumpur, Malaysia: PIERS Press.

Wikipedia. (2013). *Inverse problem*. Retrieved from http://en.wikipedia.org/wiki/Inverse_problem.

Yorkey, T. J. (1986) *Comparing Reconstruction Methods for Electrical Impedance Tomography*. (PhD Thesis). Madison, WI, University of. Wisconsin at Madison.

Yorkey, T. J., Webster, J. G., & Tompkins, W. J. (1987). Comparing reconstruction algorithms for electrical impedance tomography. *IEEE Transactions on Bio-Medical Engineering, 34,* 843–852. doi:10.1109/TBME.1987.326032 PMID:3692503.

Yu, W. (1991). On the existence of an inverse problem. *Journal of Mathematical Analysis and Applications, 157*(1), 63–74. doi:10.1016/0022-247X(91)90137-O.

KEY TERMS AND DEFINITIONS

Computed Tomography (CT): Computed Tomography (CT) is a computer aided imaging technique which produces the cross sectional view (image) of the spatial distribution of a particular parameter of an object by calculating the parameter from the signals acquired at the domain boundary generated by the injecting a suitable signal at the boundary.

Electrical Impedance Tomography (EIT): Electrical Impedance Tomography (EIT) is an image reconstruction technique in which the electrical conductivity or resistivity of a conducting domain (Ω) is reconstructed from the surface potentials developed by current signals injected at the domain boundary ($\partial\Omega$).

Forward Solver: Forward solver is a part of the image reconstruction algorithm which computes the boundary data for a simulated object geometry and known properties of the object under test and known applied signal.

Illposed Inverse Problem: Illposed inverse problem is the inverse problem in which a small error in measurement data produces a large error in reconstructed image.

Image Reconstruction: Image reconstruction is the process of producing or developing the image of the properties of an object under test in an inverse problem from its boundary data.

Image Reconstruction Algorithm: Image reconstruction algorithm is a computer program or software which calculates and computes the properties of an object under test in an inverse problem from its boundary data.

Inverse Problem: Inverse problem is the mathematical problem in which the spatial distribution of a particular property or the properties of an object under test is computed from the boundary data developed by applying a input energy signal at the domain boundary.

Inverse Solver: Inverse solver is a part of the image reconstruction algorithm which iteratively computes the object properties using the calculated boundary data and measured boundary data to obtain an optimum property distribution for which the difference between the measured and calculated data becomes minimum.

Medical Imaging: Medical imaging is a procedure which produce two dimensional or three dimensional images of the tissue organ or body parts of patients or normal human subject to study their anatomy as well as the structural and functional physiology for diagnostic purposes.

Safe Medical Imaging Modality: Safe medical imaging modality is that medical imaging procedure which has no or negligible side effect to the patients.

Chapter 14
Research and Developments in Medical Image Reconstruction Methods and its Applications

Shailendra Tiwari
Indian Institute of Technology, India

Rajeev Srivastava
Indian Institute of Technology, India

ABSTRACT

Image reconstruction from projection is the field that lays the foundation for Medical Imaging or Medical Image Processing. The rapid and proceeding progress in medical image reconstruction, and the related developments in analysis methods and computer-aided diagnosis, has promoted medical imaging into one of the most important sub-fields in scientific imaging. Computer technology has enabled tomographic and three-dimensional reconstruction of images, illustrating both anatomical features and physiological functioning, free from overlying structures. In this chapter, the authors share their opinions on the research and development in the field of Medical Image Reconstruction Techniques, Computed Tomography (CT), challenges and the impact of future technology developments in CT, Computed Tomography Metrology in industrial research & development, technology, and clinical performance of different CT-scanner generations used for cardiac imaging, such as Electron Beam CT (EBCT), single-slice CT, and Multi-Detector row CT (MDCT) with 4, 16, and 64 simultaneously acquired slices. The authors identify the limitations of current CT-scanners, indicate potential of improvement and discuss alternative system concepts such as CT with area detectors and Dual Source CT (DSCT), recent technology with a focus on generation and detection of X-rays, as well as image reconstruction are discussed. Furthermore, the chapter includes aspects of applications, dose exposure in computed tomography, and a brief overview on special CT developments. Since this chapter gives a review of the major accomplishments and future directions in this field, with emphasis on developments over the past 50 years, the interested reader is referred to recent literature on computed tomography including a detailed discussion of CT technology in the references section.

DOI: 10.4018/978-1-4666-4558-5.ch014

INTRODUCTION

Images and Visualization have become increasingly important in many areas of Science and technology. Advances in hardware and software have allowed computerized image processing to become a standard tool in many scientific applications. Applications include, although are not restricted to, remote sensing when imaging the earth or a planet, electrical resistivity imaging as a geophysical method to image the underground, SONAR as a sound navigation ranging imaging, Radar imaging, and medical imaging (Chan & Shen, 2005).

Medical imaging technologies provide several of the most powerful diagnostic tools available to modern medical science, Since the introduction of X-ray machines at the end of the 19th century, and the development of imaging devices using internally relating radio nuclides in the middle of the 20th century, diagnostic imaging has been an important tool. Such important innovations are nowadays taking place, however, that they should be characterised as emerging technologies.

Computed Tomography (CT), Single Photon Emission Computed Tomography (SPECT), Positron Emission Tomography (PET), Magnetic Resonance Imaging (MRI), Optical imaging, ultrasound, and Electrical Impedance Tomography: all of these techniques have advantages and disadvantages in terms of resolution, cost, safety, sensitivity, specificity, as well as the physiological and metabolic features they can detect. More recently, however, big steps have been taken by integrating different imaging modalities in one system. Combining pathophysiological imaging with high resolution anatomic data allows the result to be much more than the sum of the parts. (Strauss, 2006) describes some of the opportunities and concerns that this marriage of imaging techniques is presenting to future medical practice.

Computerized Tomography (CT) is a major method of biomedical imaging, as well as of industrial non-destructive testing, geophysics, and other areas. Nevertheless, in the last few decades it has observed fast and major new challenges in the field of Medical Imaging. The present CT modalities (X-ray CT, PET, SPECT, MRI, and Ultrasound) have been going through improvements, due to technical and numerical problems. On the other hand, brand new techniques were being developed. The reasons for this advancement are manifold.

For instance, new physiological and metabolic parameters of biological tissues (e.g. stiffness, electrical conductivity, or hemoglobin oxygenation) are attempted to be imaged (Geertsma et al., 2007). Besides, some previously addressed optical and electric parameters (e.g., optical absorption, or electric conductivity) could not bestably imaged by already existing techniques, such as Optical Tomography (OT) or Electrical Impedance Tomography (EIT). Thus, a variety of novel imaging modalities are being developed. A heterogeneity of the so called "hybrid methods" are being introduced and studied. In such techniques, scientist have been developing novel hybrid methods that combine two or more physical types of signals (in most cases, ultrasound and electromagnetic), in the hope of alleviating the deficiencies of each of the types, while taking advantage of their strengths. The most successful example of such a combination is the thermoacoustic tomography also known as Opto-or Photo-Acoustic Tomography (PAT) (Peter & Lenoid, 2008). In the clinical context, medical imaging is generally equated to radiology or "clinical imaging". Research into the application and interpretation of medical images is usually the preserve of radiology and the medical sub-discipline relevant to medical condition or area of medical science (neuroscience, cardiology, psychiatry, psychology) under investigation. Many of the techniques developed for medical imaging also have scientific and industrial applications.

Although the mathematical sciences were used in a general way for image processing, they were of little importance in bio-medical work until the development of Computed Tomography (CT) for the imaging of X-rays (leading to computer assisted tomography or CAT) and isotope emission tomography (leading to Positron Emission Tomography or PET scans and single Positron Emission Computed Tomography or SPECT scans), then MRI (magnetic resonance imaging) ruled over the other modalities in many ways as the most informative medical imaging methodology.

Besides all these well established techniques computer based methods are being explored in application of ultrasound and electroencephalography as well as new techniques of optical imaging, impedance tomography and magnetic source imaging. Though the final images obtained from many techniques have similarities but the technologies used and the parameters represented in the images are very different in characteristics as well as in medical usefulness, even different mathematical and statistical models have been used.

Several techniques have been developed to enable CT, MRI, and ultrasound scanning software to produce 3D images for the physician. Traditionally CT and MRI scans produced 2D static output on film then to produce 3D images many scans are made and then produced a 3D model which can be manipulated by physician (Andrew et al., 2009). In this chapter, we have tried to present a detail survey on Medical Imaging and tomographic reconstruction algorithms; we hope that this work will definitely provide a concrete overview on the past, present and future aspects in this field.

Medical Imaging Systems Overview

Medical imaging (see Figure 1) is considered as a part of biological imaging, which has been developed from 19th century onwards. A brief overview of medical imaging is as follows (Webb, 2003). In 1895 Roentgen accidentally discovered X-rays. Conventional radiography has been the most widespread medical imaging technique ever science. From 1896 radionuclides were for therapy and for metabolic tracer studies rather than imaging. Then γ- ray imaging rectilinear scanner was

invented. During World War 2 Sonar Technology and in 1970's ultrasound became widely available in medicine.

In 20th century the mathematical principles behind tomographic reconstruction have been understood and Positron Emission Tomography (PET) and X-ray Computed Tomography (CT) have been developed. Nuclear magnetic resonance has been using for imaging in Magnetic Resonance Imaging (MRI).

In 21st century X-rays, MRI, ultrasound kept dominating but more interesting techniques especially imaging is getting included with microscopic as well as macroscopic biological structures (thermal imaging, electrical impedance tomography, scanned probe techniques etc). In future the emphasis will be increased on obtaining functional and metabolic information along with structural (image) information. This can be done to some extent with radioactive tracers (e.g. PET) and magnetic resonance spectroscopy (Ogawa et al., 1990).

Medical imaging systems are based on the physical interaction between some energy source and the human body. (Exceptions, such as phono-

Figure 1. Emerging medical imaging modalities

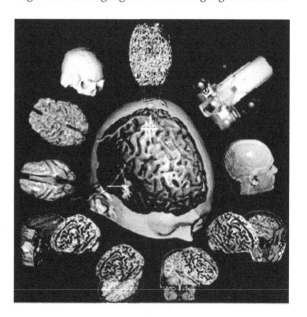

cardiography and thermography, that use *internal* energy sources within the body are rare and represent very few applications). The following Figure 2 gives a generic block diagram of a typical modern electronic medical imaging system.

Biomedical Imaging Modalities

With the evolutionary progress in engineering and computing technologies in the last century, medical imaging technologies have witnessed a tremendous growth that has made a major impact in diagnostic radiology. These advances have revolutionarized healthcare through fast imaging techniques; data acquisition, storage and analysis systems; high resolution picture archiving and communication systems; information mining with modeling and simulation capabilities to enhance our knowledge base about the diagnosis, treatment and management of critical diseases such as cancer, cardiac failure, brain tumors, and cognitive disorders.

Medical imaging is highly multidisciplinary and interdisciplinary with a wide coverage of physical, biological, engineering and medical sciences. Figure 3 provides a conceptual notion of the medical imaging process from determination of principle of imaging based on the target pathological investigation to acquiring data for image reconstruction, processing and analysis for diagnostic, treatment evaluation, and/or research applications. There are many medical imaging modalities and techniques that have been developed in the past years. Anatomical structures can be effectively imaged today with X-ray Computed Tomography (CT), Magnetic Resonance Imaging (MRI), ultrasound, and optical imaging methods. Furthermore, information about physiological structures with respect to metabolism and/or functions can be obtained through nuclear medicine (Single Photon Emission Computed Tomography (SPECT) and Positron Emission Tomography (PET)), ultrasound, optical fluorescence, and several derivative protocols of MRI such as fMRI, MRI, etc.

Figure 2. Generic block diagram of a typical modern electronic medical imaging system

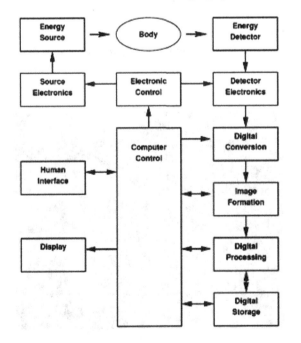

Figure 3. A schematic block diagram of medical imaging process

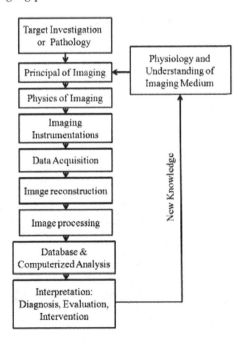

Emerging Medical Imaging Modalities

New and emerging medical technologies will offer patients improved and personalised treatments, better prognosis and reduced recovery times. Consequently, new risks will also emerge. Advances in imaging technology, biosensors and lab-on-a-chip devices will enable more precise diagnosis, at an earlier disease stage and at the point of care. Minimally invasive surgery techniques combined with sophisticated implant systems, constructed from innovative materials and possibly using state-of-the-art software and telemetry, provide continuously improving therapy options. New generations of medical technology products are more and more resulting from so-called "converging technologies", i.e. the combination of different technologies which leads to the crossing of borders between traditional categories of medical products such as medical devices, pharmaceutical products or human tissues (see Figure 4.)

Furthermore, the trend can be observed that a growing number of diseases and disorders can be treated with technological solutions instead of medicines.

Multimodality Imaging

Multimodality imaging is the combination of images derived from different modalities like Computed X-ray Tomography (CT), Magnetic Resonance Imaging (MRI), Positron Emission Tomography (PET), Single Photon Emission Computed Tomography (SPECT), Ultrasound (US), and many more. It helps to obtain more reliable diagnoses and more effective therapeutics. Thus the outcome for the patient quite often is better when treated/diagnosed with a multi-modality device compared to a single modality device. In Figure 5, images of some possible combinations are shown.

Compressed Sensing Based CT Reconstruction

Computed Tomography (CT) is considered as a radiation-intensive procedure, yet it becomes more and more common. The risk of radiation induced disease makes a strong need to reconstruct Computed Tomography (CT) images with practically useful quality using as low radiation as possible (Andrew et al., 2009). One strategy is to use limited number of projections. To reduce the radiation dose, the projection images are only acquired at few views. The major challenging is that the number of observation is much less than

Figure 4. Converging technologies

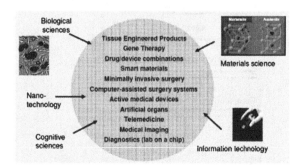

Figure 5. Fusion FDG-PET/MRI (top left), Fusion FET-PET/MRI (top right), Fusion FDG-PET/CT (bottom left), Fusion DPD-SPECT/CT (bottom right)

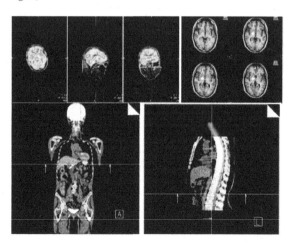

the number of unknowns. Recently, Candes, Romberg, and Tao proposed a new mathematical theory, Compressed Sensing (CS), which can perform nearly exact image reconstruction with only few measurements. Based on this theory, new developed CT reconstruction method required as few projection images as possible. According to the framework of compressed sensing, the image should firstly be sparsifying and then be reconstructed by a constrained l1 norm minimization method. We used total variation as the sparsifying transform and tested the algorithm using Shepp-Logan phantom. The reconstructed image is almost the same with the original image with only 20 projection images.

Spectral Computed Tomography

Spectral Computed Tomography (spectral CT) is a newly emerging, medical imaging modality. It extends CT by acquiring multiple datasets over different x-ray energy bins. As the x-ray absorption of materials is energy dependent, the energy bins together provide significantly more information about the composition of the subject. (Tang, de Ruiter, Mohr, Butler, Butler,

& Aamir, 2012). The Simultaneous Algebraic Reconstruction Technique (SART) has been used for spectral reconstruction and will be extended in the near future.

Spatial Resolution Properties of Motion-Compensated Tomographic Image Reconstruction Methods

This paper presents the Motion-Compensated Image Reconstruction (MCIR) methods that have been proposed to correct for subject motion in medical imaging. MCIR (see Figure 6) methods incorporate motion models to improve image quality by reducing motion artifacts and noise. The spatial resolution properties of MCIR methods can lead to non-uniform and anisotropic spatial resolution for conventional quadratic regularizers. This undesirable property is akin to the known effects of interactions between heteroscedastic log-likelihoods (e.g., Poisson likelihood) and quadratic regularizers. This effect may lead to quantification errors in small or narrow structures (such as small lesions or rings) of reconstructed images. (Chun & Fessler, 2013)

Figure 6. Classifications of Tomographic Image Reconstruction Techniques

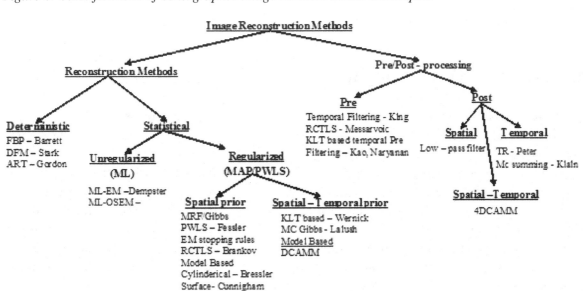

Optical Fiber Imaging Based Tomographic Reconstruction of Burner Flames

This paper presents the design, implementation, and evaluation of an optical fiber imaging based tomographic system for the 3-D visualization and characterization of a burner flame. Eight imaging fiber bundles coupled with two RGB charge coupled device cameras are used to acquire flame images simultaneously from eight different directions around the burner. The fiber bundle has 30k picture elements and an objective lens with a 92^0 angle of view. The characteristic evaluation of the imaging fiber bundles and the calibration of the system were conducted to ensure the accuracy of the system. A new tomographic algorithm that combines the logical filtered back-projection and the simultaneous algebraic reconstruction technique is proposed to reconstruct the flame sections from the images. A direct comparison between the proposed algorithm and other tomographic approaches is conducted through computer simulation for different test templates and numbers of projections. The 3-D reconstruction of the cross- and longitudinal-sections of a burner flame from image projections obtained from the imaging system was also performed. The effectiveness of the imaging system and computer algorithm is assessed through experimental tests (Hossain, Lu, & Yan, 2012).

Technical Concepts of Tomography

The word $\tau o'\mu o\sigma$ (tomos) is Greek and means a slice or a cut and $\gamma\rho\alpha\varnothing\hat{o}(graph\hat{o})$ means a drawing. Thus tomography is the science of drawing slices. By making many cuts through an object, a 3D description of the target can be obtained.

Tomography is a non-invasive imaging technique allowing for the visualization of the internal structures of an object without the superposition of over- and under-lying structures that usually plagues conventional projection images.

- For example, in a conventional chest radiograph, the heart, lungs, and ribs are all superimposed on the same film, whereas a Computed Tomography (CT) slice captures each organ in its actual three-dimensional position.

- Tomography has found widespread application in many scientific fields, including physics, chemistry, astronomy, geophysics, and, of course, medicine.

- While X-ray CT may be the most familiar application of tomography, tomography can be performed, even in medicine, using other imaging modalities, including ultrasound, magnetic resonance, nuclear-medicine, and microwave techniques.

- Each tomographic modality measures a different physical quantity:
  - **CT:** The number of x-ray photons transmitted through the patient along individual projection lines.
  - **Nuclear Medicine:** The number of photons emitted from the patient along individual projection lines.
  - **Ultrasound Diffraction Tomography:** The amplitude and phase of scattered waves along a particular line connecting the source and detector.

- The task in all cases is to estimate from these measurements the distribution of a particular physical quantity in the object. The quantities that can be reconstructed are:
  - **CT:** The distribution of linear attenuation coefficient in the slice being imaged.
  - **Nuclear Medicine:** The distribution of the radiotracer administered to the patient in the slice being imaged.
  - **Ultrasound Diffraction Tomography:** The distribution of refractive index in the slice being imaged.

- Remarkably, under certain conditions, the measurements made in each modality can be converted into samples of the Radon transform of the distribution that we wish to reconstruct. For example, in CT, dividing the measured photon counts by the incident photon counts and taking the negative logarithm yields samples of the Radon transform of the linear attenuation map.

- The Radon transform and its inverse provide the mathematical basis for reconstructing tomographic images from measured projection or scattering data.

Transmission and Emission Tomography

Transmission tomography and Emission tomography are the two main families of medical imaging. X-rays belongs to the first family, where the radiation source is outside the patient, while Nuclear medicine belongs to the second family, where the radiation source is inside the patient. Transmission tomography investigates a semi-transparent object by sending radiation through it from a number of angles. The projections are then fed to a computer and the amount of absorption is reconstructed. X-ray CT (Computed Tomography) uses transmission measurements to estimate a cross-sectional image within the patient body. X-rays have very high energy, and they are able to penetrate the patient body. However, not every X-ray can make it through the patient body. Some X-rays get scattered within the body, and their energy gets weakened. During X-ray scattering, an X-ray photon interacts with an electron within the patient, transfers' part of its energy to that electron, and dislodges the electron. The X-ray is then bounced to a new direction with decreased energy. Some other X-rays completely disappear within the body, converting their energy to the tissues in the body, for example, via the photoelectric conversion. The photoelectric effect is a process in which the X-ray photon energy is completely absorbed by an atom within the patient. The absorbed energy ejects an electron from the atom. Energy deposition within the body can damage DNA if the X-ray dose is too large.

Emission tomography is a medical imaging modality that can provide unique functional information about physiological processes in the body. Typically, a small amount of a radioactive compound (or radiotracer) is introduced into a subject via injection or inhalation. Sometimes the radiotracer itself is of physiological interest as in ^{15}O imaging in the brain. In other situations, the radioisotope is attached to a molecule that is selectively taken up in different anatomical regions, such as ^{18}F labeled FluoroDeoxyGlucose (FDG) in tumors. After allowing the radiotracer to distribute throughout the body, an image of the radiotracer distribution can be made. This image indicates the concentration of the radiotracer in different anatomical regions. This is important for diagnosis, for example, in cancer studies, since tumors tend to use more glucose than other regions in the body. Therefore, FDG images often show "hot spots" or regions of higher concentration where tumors lie. In other studies physicians are interested in "cold spots" due to improper blood circulation (Joseph, 2003).

In transmission tomography, X-ray tomography for instance, the source's position is known so that every collected photon yields exact information about the projection line that is the line joining the detection incidence and the source. This is not the case in emission tomography where the activity distribution, the emitting source of photons, is the unknown. To extract information about the spatial distribution of the activity, a collimator is used.

Another difference between X –ray imaging and nuclear medicine imaging is that we have a smaller amount of detected photons in the latter (Sustens, 2002). Thus noise is a big player in this process and must be taken care of; hence stochastic modelling becomes very useful. We cannot predict the exact amount at which the atom will disintegrate; however we know the decay probability as:

$$\frac{dN(t)}{dt} = \hat{a}N(t)$$

where $\hat{a}$ is an isotope dependent decay constant and N(t) is the activity at time t. This differential equation gives away the expected value as:

$$N(t) = N(t_0)e^{-\hat{a}(t-t_0)}$$

Since the process is statistical, we usually measure only an approximation to the true N(t).

Some Applications Areas of Biomedical Imaging

The imaging methods used in biomedical applications include:

- X-ray projection imaging
- X-ray Computed Tomography (CT)
- Magnetic Resonance Imaging (MRI) and Magnetic Resonance Spectroscopy (MRS)
- Single Photon Emission Computed Tomography (SPECT)
- Positron Emission Tomography (PET)
- Ultrasonic
- Electrical Source Imaging (ESI)
- Electrical Impedance Tomography (EIT)
- Magnetic Source Imaging (MSI)
- Medical Optical Imaging

In this section, we discuss to present some applications areas of biomedical imaging that play a vision of the research work in the world of biomedical imaging, wherein medical imaging plays an expanded role in diagnosis and therapy processing and high quality images gives medical personnel access to much greater insight into their patients' conditions.

Although this report emphasizes methodologies for visualizing internal body anatomy and function, some mention is warranted of the importance of improving techniques for the evaluation of human biology and disease processes through visualization of external features and functions. For example, sequential image-based descriptions of skin texture or color, gait, flexibility, and so on would require the development of convenient observation systems, perhaps with greater sensitivities than the human eye, and mathematical methods (e.g., artificial intelligence) for identifying significant changes. Applications of Medical Imaging in different fields are discussed here:

Computer-Aided Diagnosis

Computer-Aided Diagnosis (CAD) has become one of the major research areas in medical imaging. It assists radiologists by acting as a "second opinion"; the performance of the computer does not have to be equal or better than that of the radiologist, just complementary. The majority of CAD research has been concerned with three organs-breast, chest and colon-although research has been undertaken on other organs such as the brain, liver, and skeletal and vascular systems.

Mammography is the single most important technique in the investigation of breast cancer, the most common malignancy in women. It can detect disease at an early stage when therapy or surgery is most effective. However the interpretation of screening mammograms is a repetitive task involving subtle signs, and suffers from a high rate of *false negatives* (10-30%), and *false positives* (10-20%). Computer-Aided Diagnosis (CAD) aims to increase the predictive value of the technique by pre-reading mammograms to indicate the locations of suspicious abnormalities, and analyze their characteristics, as an aid to the radiologist.

Tumour Imaging and Treatment

Multi-modality imaging is essential in the diagnosis and treatment of cancer. Once a tumour is characterized, imaging is used in guiding surgical resection and Radiation Treatment Planning (RTP) and assessment. It is important to be able to distinguish benign from malignant tumours, and this can be achieved by studying the microcirculation and/or oxygenation status. High tumour perfusion is indicative of a high blood and oxygen supply to the tumour, which are key elements in its growth. With hybrid CT/PET scanners the PET scan picks up the metabolic signal of actively growing cancer cells, and the CT scan provides the size and shape of the abnormal cancerous growths.

Bone Strength and Osteoporosis

Osteoporosis is a prevalent bone disease characterized by a loss of bone strength and consequent fracture risk. Because it tends to be asymptomatic until fractures occur, relatively few people are diagnosed in time for effective therapy to be administered. Although bone mineral density, BMD, is widely used clinically, it has been increasingly realized that internal bone architecture is also an important determinant of the mechanical strength of bone and can lead to an earlier and more accurate diagnosis of osteoporosis. The limited resolution of commercial CT scanners precludes proper resolution of the trabecular structure; however, CT images retain some of this architectural information, albeit degraded by the inadequate Modulation Transfer Function (MTF) of the imaging system, and this can be characterized by the fractal signature of the trabecular bone (viz. its fractal dimension as a function of spatial frequency).

Tortuosity

The clinical recognition of elevated *tortuosity* or integrated curvature is important in the diagnosis of many diseases. Increased vascular tortuosity, for example, affects the flow haemodynamics and can lead to *aneurysm* (rupture of the blood vessels), and the tortuosity of retinal blood vessels can be an early indicator of systemic diseases.

Agriculture and Forestry Application

Cruvinel et al. (1990) and Vaz et al. (1989) developed a portable X ray and gamma ray mini tomograph for application in soil science and used the scanner to measure water content and bulk density of soil samples Soil related studies address the identification of features such as fracture wormhole and roots and assist in studies of flow of various contaminants in soil.

Forestry applications of CT have appeared in the literature in the form of scanning of live trees to measure growth rings and detect decay using a portable X ray CT scanner and monitoring tree trunks or logs in the timber and lumber industry.

Microtomography

The resolution of common CT devices used in medical and other applications varies from the common figure of 1x1 *mm* to about 200x200 $i\,m$ in cross-section, and 1-5 mm between slices. Special systems have been built to image small samples of the order of 1cm^3 in volume with resolution of the order of 5-10 $i\,m$ in cross-section. Such an imaging procedure is called Microtomography, microCT, or iCT, being a hybrid of tomography and microscopy. Most iCT studies are performed with finally focused and nearly monochromatic X-ray beams produced by a particle accelerator (such as a synchrotron). Stock provides a review of the basic principles techniques and applications of iCT whereas most iCT studies have been limited to small excised sample (Sasov, 2001) discusses the design of a iCT to image whole small animals with resolution of the order of 10 $i\,m$.

Application Analysis of the Tumor in Neuroblastoma

Neuroblastoma is a malignant tumor of neural-crest origin that may arise anywhere along the sympathetic ganglia or within the adrenal medulla (Alexender, 2000). There are three types of ganglion cell lesions that form a spectrum of neo plastic disease. Neuroblastoma is the most immature and malignant form of the three, usually presenting before the age of five years. Ganglioneuroblastoma is a more mature form that retains some malignant characteristics with peak incidence between five and years of age Ganglioneuroma is well differentiated and benign typically presenting after years of age (Abramson, 1997).

Tissue Characterization Using CT

The linear attenuation coefficient i of tissue is the physical entity that is measured in CT. The linear attenuation coefficient varies with two material properties: density and elemental composition (Fullerton & Zagzebski, 1980).The value of i has been measured and tabulated for several materials, including human and animal tissues, at different X-ray energies (including measurements with multiple energies, such as dual-energy imaging [Phelps et al., 1975]).However, it is not common to display CT images in terms of the linear attenuation coefficient which is dependent on the energy used. Instead, normalized CT units that are more convenient and independent to a certain extent, of the X-ray energy are used.

Medical Image Reconstruction Algorithms: Review

Image reconstruction from projection is the field that lays the foundation for medical Imaging or Medical Image Processing. The rapid and proceeding progress in medical image reconstruction, and the related developments in analysis methods and computer-aided diagnosis, has promoted medical imaging into one of the most important sub-fields in scientific imaging. Computer technology has enabled tomographic and three-dimensional reconstruction of images, illustrating both anatomical features and physiological functioning, free from overlying structures.

An image lifetime goes through three stages, acquisition, processing, and interpretation. Image reconstruction, which belongs to the second stage, processing. Processing involves contrast enhancing, denoising, deblurring, inpainting, coregistration, segmentation, or reconstruction of an image. To reconstruct an image, we first obtain or record data via some form of sensing. We need then to link the data to the object we aim to image via physical models, usually in a simplified form. Mathematical tools such as Fourier transforms, matrix theory, optimization techniques, probability and statistics are essential in imaging. Image analysis, for instance, uses mathematical tools such as geometry of curves and surfaces and Bounded Variations (BV) functions. It utilizes also elements from Bayesian statistical inference, wavelets, and iterative optimization techniques. Image modelling employs tools such as distributions, L^p and Sobelev H^n (Ω) spaces, Markov and Gibbs random fields and processes, level sets, PDEs, and Mumford-Shah free boundary (Chan, Shen, Epstein, & Sustens, 2005, 2008, 2002)

The mathematics behind image reconstruction has seen early developments. Radon published his famous paper in (1917) linking any function f to its sinogram p (s, `e). It is called the Radon transform operator that associates with each line its line integral. It saw its first application in Computed Tomography (CT) in 1970, and later on in nuclear medical imaging. The matrix C, in this case, is modelled as a transform operator. The projected data can be represented as follows:

$$g(s, `e) = Rf(r)$$

where $\mathcal{R}$ is the Radon transform operator and f is the activity function, usually used in a discrete form as a vector x; $\grave{e}$ is the position angle of the camera head and s is the distance between the camera and the object. We need to find $f(r)$ given the sinogram g (s,`e); that is we must invert the Radon transform as follow:

$$f(r) = R^{-1}\{g(s, `e)\}$$

A less used way to solve for f is by direct inversion of the Radon operator using the Hilbert transform operator (Hilbert, 1953). A very important operator in signal processing is the Fourier transform. There exists a useful relationship between the Fourier transform and the Radon transform known as central slice theorem or the projection theorem. In the 2-dimensional case for instance, the projection-slice theorem states that the Fourier transform of the projection function $f(r)$ onto a line is equal to a slice through the origin of the 2D Fourier transform of that function which is parallel to the projection line. As a consequence f can be reconstructed by performing first a 1D FT of g at different angles, followed by a 2D inverse FT, The Filtered Back-Projection algorithm (FBP) is the earliest reconstruction method tailored to medical imaging. It is the most widely used analytical reconstruction method in tomography and is a numerical implementation of the inverse formula of the Radon transform. Roughly speaking, the back-projection step produces a blurred version of f and the filtering step aims to reduce this blur; some useful references are in (Louis & Natterer, 1992, 2001). If we had the line integrals for every line, then we could use that data to determine the activity, with some precision. In practice through, we have available only finitely many noisy line integral values, so using the central slice theorem gives us only approximate solutions. Nonetheless, the main advantage of this approach is its time efficiency.

An alternative to analytical approaches is to use iterative approaches. The Maximum Likelihood Expectation Maximization (MLEM) or just EM algorithm, introduced in 1982 (Shepp & Vardi), is the most popular algorithm; it is based on a Bayesian model. It yields anatomically non-negative solutions, a desirable feature in medical imaging which is lacking in FBP solutions. This statistical view sees the activity x_j as the expected number of emitted photons at the jth location during the scanning time. Thereby the location values can be seen as parameters to be estimated. Thus the expected number of detected photons at the ith detector is:

$$E(y_i) = \sum_j C_{ij} x_j$$

However, the actual count y_i replaces the expected count $E(y_i)$. Hence we do not seek an exact solution, rather, an approximate one. We have only noisy data and as the number of iterations increases, we obtain projections closer and closer to this noisy data. This phenomenon has been observed in the EM algorithm. Thus EM is only semi-convergent; that is noise is amplified at high iteration numbers (Peters, 2005). A remedy is to ameliorate our comparison criteria between the measured data and the projections of the actual approximate. An improved criterion could be to have the projections of the actual approximate as close as possible to the measured data and the reconstructed image not being too noisy. Thereby we might introduce a prior knowledge as a constraint into our optimization problem. This operation is called *regularization*. The prior, based on our assumption of what the true image should be like, is usually chosen to penalize noisy images. Maximizing both criteria has been done for EM and a One-Step-Late (OSL) algorithm was introduced by Green (1990).

We can say that there exist mainly two classes of reconstruction methods in tomography. The first class corresponds to non-iterative methods that include the analytical deterministic approach like convolution techniques; FBP is one of these (Amini, Bjrklund, Dror, Nygren, Kak, Slaney, Natterer, & Wubbeling, 1997, 1999, 2001). The second class corresponds to the iterative approaches that include the stochastic methods based on Bayesian analysis. Statistical criteria that have been utilized in devising these methods include the Minimum Mean Squares Error (MMSE), Weighted Least Squares (WLS), Maximum Entropy (ME), Maximum Likelihood (ML), and Maximum A Posteriori (MAP). The Algebraic Reconstruction Technique (ART) and Multiplicative ART (MART) were first introduced by Gordon et al (1970); although it was noticed later on that ART is but a particular case of Kaczmarz's algorithm (1937) introduced earlier. ART and MART are two examples of this second class of iterative methods. Other iterative approaches have been used such as Gauss-Seidel, Conjugate Gradient (CG), EM and OSEM (ordered subsets EM), a faster variant of EM (Hudson & Larkin, 1994). Even though CG can be quicker than EM, it is still slow for the large problem that we face in image reconstruction (Tsui, Zhao, Frey, & Gulberg, 1991). It is also harder to find pre-conditioners for this ill-conditioned image reconstruction problem except when we deal with extremely structured matrices, which is not usually the case. Time consuming convergence of EM has restricted its use clinically although it produces acceptable reconstructions early in the iterative process.

- **Abbreviations:**
  - **ART:** Algebraic Reconstruction Technique
  - **CAMM:** Content Adaptive Mesh Modelling
  - **DCAMM:** Deformable CAMM
  - **DFM:** Direct Fourier Method
  - **EM:** Expectation Maximization
  - **FBP:** Filtered Back Projection
  - **KLT:** Karhunen – Loeve Transform
  - **MAP:** Maximum a Posterior
  - **MC:** Motion Compensation
  - **MRF:** Markov Random Field
  - **ML:** Maximum Likelihood
  - **OSEM:** Ordered Subsets EM
  - **PWLS:** Penalized Weighted Least Squares
  - **RCTLS:** Regularized Total Least Square
  - **TR:** Temporal Regression

Iterative reconstruction algorithms produce accurate images without streak artifacts as in filtered backprojection. They allow improved incorporation of important corrections for image degrading effects, such as attenuation, scatter and depth-dependent resolution. Only some corrections, which are important for accurate reconstruction in positron emission tomography and single photon emission, computed tomography, can be applied to the data before filtered backprojection. The main limitation for introducing iterative algorithms in nuclear medicine has been computation time, which is much longer for iterative techniques than for filtered backprojection. Modern algorithms make use of acceleration techniques to speed up the reconstruction. These acceleration techniques and the development in computer processors have introduced iterative reconstruction in daily nuclear medicine routine. We give an overview of the most important iterative techniques and discuss the different corrections that can be incorporated to improve the image quality (Vandenberghe, D'Asseler, Van de Walle, Kauppinen, Koole, Bouwens, Van Laere, Lemahieu, & Dierckx, 2001).

Iterative algorithms can be classified into two classes. The first class contains the conventional iterative algebraic methods, which reconstruct the images by solving the aforementioned set of linear equations. Examples are the Algebraic Reconstruction Technique (ART) (Gordon, Bender, & Herman, 1970, 1974), the Simultaneous Iterative Reconstruction Technique (SIRT) (Gilbert, 1972) and the Iterative Least-Squares Technique (ILST) (Goitein, 1972). The second class contains the iterative statistical reconstruction methods, which reconstruct images by iteratively maximizing a likelihood function.

They take the noise on the measurement data into account. Therefore they use a statistical modelling of the measurement process. The best known example is the ML-EM algorithm. The projection data are Poisson variables with a mean equal to the line integral, perpendicular to the projection bin, through the activity distribution. For a large number of photons, the measured data is relatively close to the value of the line integral. For low count statistics, the measured data can have a large deviation of the mean. This is the reason why analytical algorithms (e.g. FBP), which assume the measured data are equal to the line integral, perform quite good in the case of high photon statistics, but bad for low count acquisitions. The Maximum Likelihood Expectation Maximization (ML-EM) (Shepp, Vardi, & Kaufman, 1982, 1985) algorithm, takes the Poisson nature of the data into account.

The statistical algorithms (Liang, Hart, & Green, 1988, 1990) can be further subdivided into one group which does not use a priori information, and a second group which takes into account a priori information (Herbert, Leahy, Girodias, Barrett, & Shoemaker, 1989, 1991). This is useful to constrain the number of possible solutions to the ones which are acceptable. The positivity constraint is the best known. It ensures that all pixels have a non-negative value, which is reasonable because they should represent activity distribution. This is not guaranteed by FBP. There are more sophisticated priors as Median Root Prior (Alenius & Ruotsalainen, 1997, 1998), mostly used to guarantee good noise reduction and edge preservation.

Another advantage of the iterative methods is the possibility to incorporate image degrading effects into the projection matrix. Scatter, attenuation, depth-dependent resolution and geometrical weighting can be incorporated into matrix. These effects results in a quantitatively improved reconstruction image. The difference between the different classes of iterative reconstruction

techniques, which are used in PET and SPECT, was described. The main disadvantage (long reconstruction times) of iterative reconstruction has been minimized by the recent developments in processors and optimization of the algorithms. This allowed its introduction into nuclear medicine: first it was used for PET reconstruction, where the correction for attenuation and PSF are easier to include than in SPECT. Further developments in iterative reconstruction will include the further development of simultaneous attenuation and emission map reconstruction [60] and better and faster scatter correction techniques. The diagrammatically classification of Image reconstruction methods are shown below.

Drawbacks and Limitations of Computed Tomography

When Computed Tomography (CT) became available in the 1970s, it enabled us to establish diagnoses with unprecedented speed and accuracy. But it also affected the way we practice and teach medicine, shifting our focus from the bedside to the laboratory and giving rise to a malady that has slowly pervaded medical profession.

I emphasize here the drawbacks of the CT test—its expense, the high dose of radiation it delivers, the laziness it promotes, and the havoc it can wreak when misinterpreted. I also highlight certain limitations of CT and suggest ways to reduce its radiation dose and curtail its ever increasing misuse.

Drawbacks

Exorbitantly Expensive

How Much Does a CT Examination Cost? In a survey of 4 major hospitals in Houston, I found that the charge for CT of the head, chest, or abdomen—including contrast, but excluding the radiologist's

Fee—ranges from $1,400 to $2,500. The same studies without contrast average $100 to $200 less.

Scans of the head are slightly cheaper than those of the chest or abdomen. One of the hospitals automatically includes the pelvis in abdominal CTs, which raises the cost to $4,079 (abdomen, $2,112; pelvis, $1,967).

Comment: These prices can create a significant financial burden for patients, especially those who undergo multiple CT examinations. And for those without medical insurance, the burden can be devastating. Yet, the medical literature and teachers in medical schools remain silent when it comes to the monetary specifics of CT. No wonder physicians know so little about the expense of this test.

Delivers High Dose of Radiation

How Much Radiation Does a Patient Receive from a CT Examination? Several factors determine the radiation dose a patient receives from CT. These include the design of the scanner, size of the patient, anatomic volume scanned, scanning protocol, technique used, and quality of the x-ray beam.

Typical effective radiation doses in adults range from about 2 mSv (0.2 rad) for head CTs to about 8 to 10 mSv for CTs of the chest, abdomen, or pelvis.4 These latter doses are high compared to those of natural background radiation, which is about 3 mSv/year.5 Thus, it would take a person 3.3 years to get the same amount of background radiation that an abdominal CT delivers in less than a minute.

Even more striking, one chest CT gives an effective dose of radiation equivalent to that of about 400 posteroanterior chest films.

Comment: Although CT has been with us for more than 3 decades, only in recent years have radiologists and allied radiology personnel focused attention on the amount and potential risks of radiation that CT delivers. Clearly, CT is a costly and relatively high dose procedure, with levels of radiation often approaching and sometimes exceeding those known to increase the probability of cancer. Furthermore, the radiation dose per

procedure has not diminished with the advent of helical, fluoroscopic, and multi-slice techniques. Yet the use of CT continues to spiral upwards. Many patients undergo 2 or 3 CT examinations in the same day and then have serial scans during follow-up. Disturbingly, I recently saw a patient who had undergone 12 CT examinations during the previous 3 months and was in the hospital to have another one. While evidence linking CT with cancer has not been established, the carcinogenic potential of this test is real. About 40% of the collective dose of radiation in diagnostic radiology results from CT procedures, 4% of which involve children 0 to 15 years old, Moreover, the radiation dose in children often exceeds the level necessary for diagnostic information, and the proportion of CT examinations in children is increasing rapidly. Even worse, a panel of expert pediatric radiologists concluded that up to 30% of CTs in children are unnecessary. Given the fact that children are more sensitive to radiation than are middle-aged adults by a factor of 10, pediatric radiologists wisely are leading the crusade against the unnecessary or indiscriminate use of CT.

Promotes Laziness

Physicians order CTs for a variety of reasons, from my vantage point, the most common reason is "fishing"—scanning the body part thought to be the source of the patient's complaint or problem, in the hope that a diagnosis will somehow be reeled in. In such cases, the physician takes a brief medical history, may or may not examine the patient, and, guided by the chief complaint, proceeds directly to CT scanning. This approach has many attractive features. It takes little of the physician's time, requires no special expertise, demands no discriminate thought, and serves as an easy, convenient way to obtain a lot of information quickly. In fact, the physician need not even see the patient before ordering the test.

Comment: There appear to be two basic reasons why physicians use CT to fish for diagnoses—convenience and necessity. With regard to convenience, we have a large group of well-trained doctors who once were capable of using their minds and sensory faculties to make correct diagnoses. Through CT, however, they have found an easy way to reduce their busy workloads. And by using CT over and over again in this manner, they gradually, but unwittingly, become victims of technologic tenesmus.

Limitations

There are several factors that limit the accuracy of tomography reconstructions. These limitations are caused both by the approximations that must be made in the derivation of the reconstruction process and the experimental factors.

- Resolution limited to about 1000-2000x the object cross-section diameter; high resolution requires small objects.
- Finite resolution causes some blurring of material boundaries.
- Calibration of gray levels to attenuation coefficients complicated by polychromatic X-rays.
- Large (dm-scale) geological specimens cannot be penetrated by low-energy X-rays, reducing resolving capability.
- Not all features have sufficiently large attenuation contrasts for useful imaging (carbonate fossils in carbonate matrix; quartz vs. plagioclase)
- Image artifacts (beam hardening) can complicate data acquisition and interpretation
- Large data volumes (gigabytes+) can require considerable computer resources for visualization and analysis.

The mathematical and experimental effects limit the reconstruction in different ways. The most severe mathematical limitations are im-

posed by the Born and the Rytov approximations (Slaney & Kak, 2001). These approximations are fundamental to the reconstruction process and limit the range of objects that can be examined. On the other hand, it is only possible to collect a finite amount of data and this gives rise to errors in the reconstruction which can be attributed to experimental limitations. Up to the limit in resolution caused by evanescent waves, and given a perfect reconstruction algorithm, it is possible to improve a reconstruction by collecting more data. It is important to understand the experimental limitations so that the experimental data can be used efficiently.

Experimental Limitations

In addition to the limits on the reconstructions imposed by the Born and the Rytov, approximations (Li, 2008), there are also the following experimental limitations to consider:

- Limitations caused by ignoring evanescent waves.
- Sampling the data along the receiver line.
- Finite receiver length.
- Limited views of the object.

Each of the first three factors can be modeled as a simple constant low pass filtering of the scattered field. Because the reconstruction process is linear the net effect can be modeled by a single low pass filter with a cutoff at the lowest of the three cutoff frequencies. The experiment can be optimized by adjusting the parameters so that each low pass filter cuts off at the same frequency. The effect of a limited number of views also can be modeled as a low pass filter. In this case, though, the cutoff frequency varies with the radial direction.

4D and 5D Computed Tomography Reconstruction

Four-dimensional Computed Tomography (4D-CT) is one of the most important topics in medical imaging field that attract tremendous interests nowadays. The use of 4D (spatio-temporal) image processing algorithms, and continues to study their use in improving image quality in cardiac SPECT, a standard imaging procedure to assess coronary artery disease. In 4D techniques, image sequences are treated as fully four-dimensional signals, consisting of three spatial dimensions plus time. In addition to providing three dimensional volumetric anatomical information as in conventional CT, 4D-CT is capable of resolving organ motions due to, for example, patient respiration by reconstructing a set of CT images corresponding to different respiratory phases in a breathing cycle. Such an imaging modality is particularly of use in many clinical applications regarding thorax or upper abdomen area, where a considerable amount of blurring artifacts would appear, if conventional CT is used instead.

A logical and clinically important extension of the gated (4D) reconstruction problem is the problem of reconstructing nuclear cardiac imaging studies using agents for which both the tracer distribution and cardiac function change during the course of imaging. We call this five dimensional (5D) reconstruction because the data are described by two different time axes, one conveying information on the time scale of a single cardiac cycle (as in gated imaging), the other on a time scale that shows gradual changes occurring after injection and stress (as in dynamic imaging).

In new 5D methods, the time axis is split into a dynamic dimension (for large-scale time evolution) and a gated dimension (which captures a single cardiac cycle). The 5D approach may pave the way for alternative imaging protocols in which cardiac patients are evaluated in a single imaging session that provides information about cardiac perfusion, wall motion, and tracer kinetics simultaneously.

Research and Development in Medical Imaging Science and Technology

Advances in medical imaging are assisting with the earlier detection of a range of diseases including cardiovascular disease, stroke, cancers and neurodegenerative diseases such as Alzheimer's disease.

Photoacoustic Imaging

Photoacoustic imaging, as a hybrid biomedical imaging modality, is developed based on the photoacoustic effect. In photoacoustic imaging, non-ionizing laser pulses are delivered into biological tissues (when radio frequency pulses are used, the technology is referred to as thermoacoustic imaging). Some of the delivered energy will be absorbed and converted into heat, leading to transient thermoelastic expansion and thus wideband (e.g. MHz) ultrasonic emission. The generated ultrasonic waves are then detected by ultrasonic transducers to form images. It is known that optical absorption is closely associated with physiological properties, such as haemoglobin concentration and oxygen saturation. As a result, the magnitude of the ultrasonic emission (i.e. photoacoustic signal), which is proportional to the local energy deposition, reveals physiologically specific optical absorption contrast. 2D or 3D images of the targeted areas can then be formed. Figure.7 is a schematic illustration showing the basic principles of photoacoustic imaging.

Modern generations of CT scanners employ multiple rows of detector arrays allowing rapid scanning and wider scan coverage. Computed tomography, as a medical diagnostic technique, is a mature field. However, in the last decade it has experienced fast and major new developments. All new CT systems are MDCT, and a number of new dose reduction tools have become available commercially. There are a number of new influencing parameters specific to MDCT which systematically increase or decrease patient dose

Figure 7. Schematic illustration of photoacoustic imaging (left), 3D photoacoustic imaging of melanoma (right) (Source: http://en.wikipedia.org/wiki/Photoacoustic_imaging_in_biomedicine)

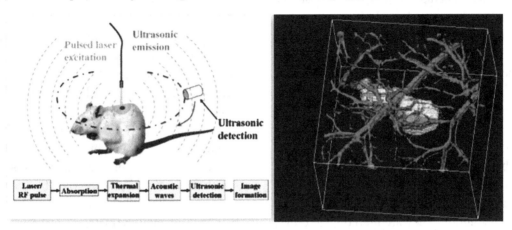

compared to Single-Detector row CT scanners (SDCT). On one hand, the older CT modalities (X-ray CT, PET, SPECT, MRI, and Ultrasound) have been going through improvements, due to technological and mathematical progress. On the other hand, brand new techniques were being developed. The reasons for this advance are manifold. For instance, new physiological and metabolic parameters of biological tissues, e.g. stiffness, electrical conductivity, or haemoglobin oxygenation are attempted to be imaged. Besides, some previously addressed optical and electric parameters (e.g., optical absorption, or electric conductivity) could not be stably imaged by already existing techniques, such as Optical Tomography (OT) or Electrical Impedance Tomography (EIT). Thus, a variety of novel imaging modalities are being developed.

MDCT was in its infancy at the time of the 2000 report (ICRP, 2000) and thus there was brief mention in the report of its impact on radiation dose. The concrete data and experience was insufficient to make any judgement. In the following years there has been a phenomenal increase in use of MDCT and technology has been advancing very rapidly to move from 4 slices to 8, 16, 32, 40, and 64-slice. Furthermore, dual source MDCT has been recently made available and 256-slice MDCT is expected to be released soon. The improved speed of MDCT scanning has also meant new applications (cardiac CT, whole body scanning) as well as improved patient throughput and workflow. In the last two decades, use of CT scanning has increased by more than 800% globally (Frush, 2003). In the United States, over the period of 1991 to 2002, a 19% growth per year in CT procedures has been documented. Also in the United States during this period, CT scanning for vascular indications has shown a 235% growth, followed by a 145% growth in cardiac applications An increase has also been demonstrated in abdominal (25%), pelvic (27%), thoracic (26%), and head & neck (7%) applications (Fox, 2003). With 64-slice MDCT a further substantial increase is expected in cardiac applications. A 10% annual growth in the global CT market was reported in the year 2002 and this trend seems to continue.

A variety of the so called "hybrid methods" are being introduced and studied. In such techniques, two or more types of physical waves (in most cases, ultrasound and electromagnetic) are involved, in order to overcome the individual deficiencies of each of them and to combine their strengths. Probably the most developed, both experimentally and mathematically; among these is the so called ThermoAcoustic Tomography (TAT), also known as Opto- or Photo-Acoustic Tomography (PAT). This technique attempts to use the high contrast between cancerous and healthy tissues when irradiated by a radiofrequency electromagnetic wave or a laser beam. In TAT, a brief broad homogeneous microwave pulse irradiates the object. As the result, small portions of the EM energy are absorbed throughout the tissue. The absorption coefficient, and thus amount of energy absorbed, is known to be several times higher in cancerous areas than in the healthy ones, which leads to a wonderful contrast.

However, the waves used are too long to allow for high resolution. They are used only to create energy absorption and thus minute heating of the tissues. In PAT, the same heating is achieved by irradiating by a broadened short laser pulse. However, light is also not suitable for imaging, since at the depth of several centimetres photons enter diffusion regime and the resolution is lost. Imaging in TAT/PAT is achieved by using the thermo-acoustic effect: local heating generates a propagating pressure wave, which can be detected by ultrasound transducers placed around the object of interest. These pressure measurements over a period of time allow one to recover the initial pressure distribution, directly linked to (in a crude approximation proportional to) energy absorbed. The experimental work on TAT/PAT has been going on for about 15 years, resulting in some devices industrially manufactured. However, the sorely needed mathematics of this technique has started being developed in earnest in the last 5-6 years. Major work has been done on describing the forward operator, resolving uniqueness issues, devising inversion algorithms, obtaining stability estimates and range descriptions, and considering reconstructions from incomplete data and related deterioration of images. In spite of these achievements, several important issues remain not completely resolved. One of them is recovering the actual optical properties of the tissues, rather than the initial pressure activated by heating. Another is accounting for and eliminating effect of the ultrasound attenuation. Still another is recovery of the unknown acoustic properties of the medium (in most initial studies the medium is assumed acoustically homogeneous, which might be an acceptable approximation for breast imaging, but not for imaging through a skull).

Another recently developing medical imaging modality is elastography, which attempts to image mechanical properties (e.g., stiffness) of tissues, which are known to provide valuable medical information. Although this field is in early stages of both experimental and mathematical development, the initial experimental and mathematical studies show a high potential for medical applications. There are manifold other novel techniques, such as for instance Electron Microscope Tomography (ET) and Cryo-Imaging, which are actively being developed for small (nano)scale imaging of biological samples, including protein imaging. ET still faces manifold technological and even more mathematical challenges and is being actively developed.

RECENT ADVANCES IN BIOMEDICAL IMAGING SYSTEMS

In Imaging in 2020: 2012, we will explore the use of molecular imaging to understand complex biology. New links between molecular imaging and systems biology will be developed. Understanding the biological systems at play in both normal and diseased physiology will play a critical role in the creation, monitoring and control of new, highly potent interventions. With new therapeutic technologies such as RNA interference, nanotherapeutics and stem cells entering the clinic, a more in depth understanding of underlying systems biology, that can only be attained through molecular imaging technology is increasingly needed.

Medical Imaging in 2020?

The recent advances in X-ray technology provide high contrast and spatiotemporal resolution, which offer new potential for evaluation of cardiac kinetics with 4D dynamic sequences. In this special issue, Garreau et al. propose a new method for cardiac motion extraction in multislice CT based on a 4D hierarchical surface-volume matching process (Andrew et al, 2009). Their aim is to detect the left heart cavities along the acquired sequence and estimate their 3D surface velocity fields. (See Figure 8.)

Transducer Electronics

This is enabling technology for real-time 3D ultrasound imaging, as well as pocket size ultrasound devices. The goal is to increase understanding of fundamental limitations of noise and power dissipation in the transducer readout and driver electronics and to develop new hardware technologies where the performance power dissipation ratio is improved compared to current solutions (MI Lab, 2011).

New Beamformer Strategies for Real-Time 3D Imaging

Beamformer hardware with improved computational capacity enables new possibilities for

Figure 8. Medical imaging in 2020

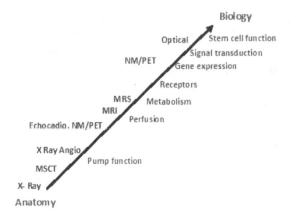

increased frame-rate in 3D ultralsound imaging. The object (e.g. human heart) can be sufficiently illuminated by a reduced number of transmit beams with limited diffraction to avoid loss in signal to noise ratio.

Quantification of Valvular Regurgitation

This is an ongoing project, where the regurgitant jet crossectional area is visualized and estimated by a newly developed 3D ultrasound technique.

Biomechanical Modeling Linked with Ultrasound Imaging

In the development of new image modalities, a proper method validation before clinical trials is important to 1) establish the true potential and limitations of the given modality, 2) save time, patient discomfort, and human resources, and cost by avoiding unnecessary clinical investigations. This task has previously been done using simplified computer simulations and in vitro models, providing an important but limited answer. Recent work has shown that by linking advanced biomechanical models with ultrasound imaging simulations, new and existing modalities can be tested for more realistic scenarios. Biomechanical models will specifically be (further) developed to aid in the development and validation of new potential tissue deformation and flow imaging modalities. Examples include models of mitral regurgitation and vulnerable plaque deformation.

Improved Flow Imaging and Quantification

With recent advances in ultrasound imaging technology, the image acquisition rate can be increased substantially for a broad range of clinical applications. A real-time high-frame rate imaging was developed at MI Lab based on emitting plane ultrasound waves and generating 16 image lines in parallel. This setup provides the means to increase both the frame rate and image quality in conventional Doppler modalities, and also provides opportunities for new modalities overcoming the traditional limitations in Doppler imaging, such as angle-dependencies and aliasing. Improvements of both conventional colour-Doppler imaging as well as the recently introduced Blood Flow Imaging modality will be investigated. Further, using a high rate acquisition new quantitative flow imaging modalities overcoming well-known Doppler imaging limitations (aliasing and angle-dependencies) become feasible and will be investigated(MI Lab,2011).

Nonlinear Wave Propagation in Heterogeneous Soft Tissue

This activity will be focused on fast numerical simulations to be used for evaluation of new transducer design, and beamformer strategies for real-time 3D imaging.

Integration of 2D/3D Echo and Cardiac MRI

New probe- and acquisition technology in ultrasound can give detailed functional measurements from anatomically specified regions in the heart, and due to the 3D nature of the datasets, fusion of this information with detailed functional and morphological information from cardiac MRI will be possible.

Ultrasound 3D Heart Model

This subproject is an extension of an existing Kalman filter-based image segmentation and tracking framework to support new modes of operation, as well as applying the framework to new and innovative applications within 3D echocardiography. The model adaption can be performed in real-time, which enables immediate feedback to the user, and optimized data acquisition. The underlying motivation is to increase the clinical value of 3D

New Imaging Methods in Paediatric Echocardiography

Clinical studies will continue on the use of Blood Flow Imaging (BFI), an angle-independent flow visualization supplemented to conventional colour-Doppler imaging. This includes both transthoracic imaging during the normal examination, as well as using BFI in transesophageal imaging during catheter intervention.

3D Echo and Cardiac MRI in Patients with Non-ST Elevation Myocardial Infarction (NSTEMI)

This study will investigate the effects of a new interleukin-6 antagonist on inflammatory markers and left ventricular function in patients with NSTEMI undergoing revascularization.

Cardiac Ultrasound in the HUNT Population Study

In the HUNT3 (Health Survey of North-Trøndelag) population advanced cardiac ultrasound was performed in a subgroup of app. 1300. This unique database will be used in several studies. A first study was to establish normal values for two dimensional deformation measurements, and a planned activity is to use the data to modify normal values according to heart rate, blood pressure and body size, as well as cardiac risk factors and fitness data.

To Validate if the Use of Pocket Sized Ultrasound in General Practice Will Improve Diagnosis of Heart Failure Among Risk Patient Groups

Assessment of left ventricular global contractility with echocardiography is mandatory in patients with suspected heart failure.

Improved Intraoperative 2-D and 3-D Imaging of Flow in Neurosurgery

Research on new ultrasound methods for intraoperative blood flow visualization and quantification in the cerebral vascular system in general, and tailored to specific needs for arterio-venous malformations, aneurysms and in tumour resection.

R&D on Automatic Real-Time Brain Shift (Brain Deformation) Correction and Display During the Operation

Including mathematic modelling of the brain deformation, use of ultrasound angiography for co-registration with preoperative MR angiography, and development of robust algorithms for the real-time image warping.

Clinical Evaluation of the Benefits of Ultrasound Angiography for Surgery of Intracranial Aneurysms

Evaluation of aneurysm morphology and to what extent vessels related to the aneurysm can be identified, and if there is flow in the vessels after aneurysm clipping. Evaluation of the technology for this purpose.

Research on Comparison between Volume Measurments of Gliomas Based on MRI and Ultrasound Imaging

The measured volumes based on the different techniques are currently used as if they were similar, although this is not known. Comparing the volumes of preoperative MRI and peri-operative ultrasound with accurate tools would help the surgeon in the resection of tumours with a diffuse growth pattern. The project will include research on new methods for improved tumor rim detection both with MR and ultrasound, and also study potential methods for detection of peri-tumour cancer infiltration and islets.

Development and Evaluation of Non-Invasive Echocardiography Indexes that can be Used During Cardiac Surgery to Optimize Stroke Work and Cardiac Output In Failing Hearts

Specifically, we evaluate echocardiography derived indexes that reflects, and can replace, ventricular elastance as a description of ventricular function in the equation defining ventriculoarterial coupling, thus making it possible to optimize stroke work without the present invasive measurements (requiring intra-arterial catheterisation). This index must detect alterations in ventriculoarterial coupling during different physiological and pathological settings, such as volume-load, alterations in vascular resistance, heart failure and inotropic stimulation.

Clinical Feasibility Studies of New Equipment for Perioperative Integrated Anatomical and Functional Quality Assessment of Cardiac Bypass Grafts

This is based on perioperative blood flow measurements and high-resolution visualisation of vessel lumen. This equipment also has numerous other potential applications that need to be evaluated, like perioperative use of the high resolution imaging modality on the native coronary vessels to locate ideal landing zones for bypass grafts, perioperative quality assessment of the ascending aorta before cannulation for cardiopulmonary bypass etc. These applications of this novel equipment need to be investigated in a clinical setting.

Improved Vascular Imaging Modalities

Research on how recent advances in high frame rate ultrasound imaging can be used to improve non-invasive plaque characterization, vessel wall stiffness, and flow related parameters such as wall shear stress.

Clinical Utility and Feasibility of MRI in More Precise Diagnosis and Prediction of Outcome and Potential Benefit of Rehabilitation in Moderate to Severe Traumatic Brain Injury (TBI)

This is part of a large interdisciplinary follow-up study of a cohort of >100 moderate to severe TBI patients and 60 matched controls. On the behavioural level extensive neuropsychological, psychiatric, and motor function tests have been performed repeatedly from acute to chronic phase. The imaging research integrates several advanced methods: Diffusion Tensor Imaging, attention task fMRI, resting state fMRI, mapping of vascular response, and automatic segmentation of MRI based brain volumes & brain morphometry including use of NeuroQuant software.

Clinical Utility and Feasibility of MRI in More Precise Diagnosis and Prediction of Outcome and Potential Benefit of Rehabilitation After Premature Birth

Premature birth is connected to significant risk for neurocognitive problems and reduced academic performance. Furthermore, there is an increase in the prevalence of psychiatric symptoms. By combining extensive clinical and neuropsychological testing, MRI and EEG, we explore the effect of premature birth and factors adversely affecting the longterm consequences of it.

Vascular Response/Hemodynamic Response Function

The activity includes both research on changed hemodynamic response (altered neurovascular coupling) as a cause of false negatives in fMRI, and the use of the vascular response as a possible diagnostic method and/or imaging biomarker. The main patient groups are Traumatic Brain Injury, brain tumour and carotid artery stenosis.

MR-Sequences for High-Resolution fMRI

A main aim is to develop tools for functional MRI at 3T with sufficient spatial resolution and sufficient precise anatomical localization to fully explore different memory functions in the medial temporal lobe (including hippocampus) in order to gain new knowledge about impaired memory functions and dementia, and use this knowledge to develop MR based early (subclinical) diagnosis and new imaging biomarkers for Alzheimer's disease. The two main areas of technology research are optimization and validation of a balanced SSFP (Steady State Free Precession) sequence for fMRI and optimization and validation of different methods for correction of geometrical distortions and magnetic susceptibility artefacts both in balanced SSFP and in Single-shot Echo Planar Imaging sequences.

Compressed Sensing in MRI and Ultrasound

The main focus is to be an additional approach to obtain functional MRI at 3T with sufficient spatial resolution and sufficient precise anatomical localization to fully explore different memory functions in the medial temporal lobe (see point above).

Multimodal MRI for Image Guidance of Transplant-Mediated Repair of Brain and Spinal Cord White Matter Degeneration and Injury

The main imaging methods are Manganese-Enhanced MRI (MEMRI), tracking of transplanted cells labelled with MR sensitive contrast agents and Diffusion Tensor Imaging. The transplant-mediated repair integrates stem cells, scaffolding cells (Olfactory Ensheathing Cells) and alginate scaffolds and the ability of the MR imaging for monitoring and guidance of the repair will be optimized and validated in three rat models of brain and spinal cord degeneration/injury.

Research on Multi-Modal and Multi-Functional Nanoparticles for MR Imaging Including Image-Guided Drug Delivery

The chosen nanoparticles are "oil-in-water nanoemulsions" type with multi-modality for both MR Imaging and optical imaging (fluorescence) resepcti and with ligands binding to intravascular and tissue receptors. A window chamber model of rat tumours allow excellent co-localization between the MR and optical images, and will be used to focus on research on some basic mechanisms: what size of the nanoparticles gives optimal MR sensitivity, the ability and the reproducibility of the nanoparticles to cross the biological barriers between the main tissue compartments, and mechanisms for binding to the receptors (MI Lab, 2011).

Local/Interior CT

There is a long track record for the exact reconstruction of an ROI from a minimum dataset, starting from the work on half-scan fan-beam reconstruction. The benefits include shorter data acquisition time, less radiation dose and more imaging flexibility. The most remarkable recent finding is the work by Katsevich in 2002 that demonstrates the feasibility of the exact regional reconstruction within a long object from longitudinally truncated data collected along a PI-turn of a helical scanning trajectory. The subsequent backprojection filtration variant and generalization into the quite arbitrary scanning case significantly enriched the local CT theory. It is highly desirable to establish a unified theory for exact local/interior reconstruction that covers the exact reconstruction schemes and methods from a minimum dataset in the two-dimensional 2D and three-dimensional 3Dcases

from parallel- and divergent-beam geometries. It should be valuable to refine the reported stability analysis and reflect the sampling geometry and data noise in an optimal fashion.

Also, it is critical to design numerically stable, robust and efficient algorithms for this purpose. The state-of-the-art framework for local/interior reconstruction is the Hilbert transform analysis. Perhaps other possibilities exist for us to gain a thorough understanding of this amazing problem.

Flat-Panel Based CT

Flat-panel volume Computed Tomography (CT) systems have an innovative design that allows coverage of a large volume per rotation, fluoroscopic and dynamic imaging, and high spatial resolution that permits visualization of complex human anatomy such as fine temporal bone structures and trabecular bone architecture. In simple terms, flat-panel volume CT scanners can be thought of as conventional multidetector CT scanners in which the detector rows have been replaced by an area detector (Gupta et al., 2008).

Dual-Source CT

Dual-source CT improves temporal resolution, and theoretically improves the diagnostic image quality of coronary artery examinations without requiring pre-examination beta-blockade. The purpose of our study was to show the improved diagnostic image quality of dual-source CT compared with single-source CT despite the absence of pre-examination beta-blockade in the dual-source CT group (Donnino et al. 2009). (See Figure 9.)

Multi-Source CT

Multiple-source cone-beam scanning is a promising mode for dynamic volumetric CT/micro-CT. The first dynamic CT system is the Dynamic Spatial Reconstructor (DSR) built in 1979. The pursuance for higher temporal resolution has

Figure 9. The flat panel detector (top left), Dual source CT (DSCT) systems (top right), extremely sensitive detector allows working with low energy x-ray source (bottom left), the Nano – CT scanner (bottom right) (Source: http://www.european-radiology.org)

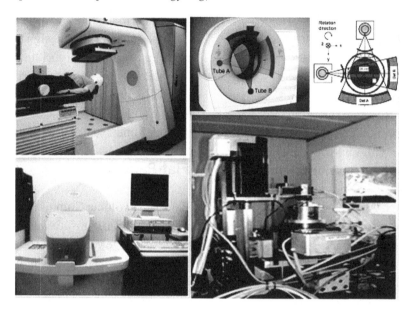

largely driven the development of CT technology, and recently led to the emergence of Siemens dual-source CT scanner. Given the impact and limitation of dual-source cardiac CT, triple-source cone-beam CT seems a natural extension for future cardiac CT. Our work shows that trinity (triple-source architecture) is superior to duality (dual-source architecture) for helical cone-beam CT in terms of exact reconstruction. In particular, a triple-source helical scan allows a perfect mosaic of longitudinally truncated cone-beam data to satisfy the Orlov condition and yields better noise performance than the dual-source counterpart. In the (2N+1)-source helical CT case, the more sources, the higher temporal resolution. In the N-source saddle CT case, a triple-source scan offers the best temporal resolution for continuous dynamic exact reconstruction of a central volume. The recently developed multi-source cone-beam algorithms include an exact BackProjection-Filtration (BPF) approach and a "slow" exact Filtered-BackProjection (FBP) algorithm for (2N+1)-source helical CT, two

fast quasi-exact FBP algorithms for triple-source helical CT, as well as a fast exact FBP algorithm for triple-source saddle CT. Some latest ideas will be also discussed, such as multi-source interior tomography and multi-beam field-emission x-ray CT (Zhao et al., 2010).

Energy-Sensitive CT

An energy-sensitive computed tomography system is provided. The energy-sensitive computed tomography system includes an X-ray source configured to emit an X-ray beam resulting from electrons impinging upon a target material. The energy-sensitive computed tomography system also includes an object positioned within the X-ray beam. The energy-sensitive computed tomography system further includes a detector configured to receive a transmitted beam of the X-rays through the object, the filter configured to facilitate measuring projection data that can be used to generate low-energy and high-energy spectral information (Peter et al., 2011).

Nano-CT

The world's first and only sub-100 nm nano-CT scanner nanoXCT™98 was recently developed by the Xradia company (Concord, CA). This system is a revolutionary microscope for non-invasive investigations involving semiconductor analysis, drug discovery, molecular imaging, stem-cell research and materials development. It allows 50 nm resolution using proprietary condenser and objective optics. For most samples in nano-technology, the x-ray attenuation length for low Z materials is very long, resulting in poor image contrast. The Xradia system can significantly increase image contrast in the Zernike phase contrast mode. Since this century, nanotechnology has gained tremendous momentum through both governmental and private investments. Clearly, nano-CT may be a strategic enabling component for the immediate future research and education. In a broad range of nano-CT applications, interior tomography is not only valuable but also necessary. *For example*, in the case of *in-situ* imaging of cells or tissue specimens at the cellular/molecular level, we require little morphological changes and minimum radiation exposure, have the water or air component as reference and a Volume Of Interest (VOI) much smaller than the specimen. Since the recent theoretical and numerical results demonstrated that the interior problem can be solved in a theoretically exact and stable fashion assuming that a small sub region within the interior region is known it becomes now feasible to meet the abovementioned interior reconstruction need for nano-CT. In the next decade, we believe that the existing nano-CT scanners will be further advanced, unique reconstruction algorithms will be developed with multi-scale and interior imaging capabilities, and more nano-CT applications will be identified in the fields including but not limited to life science, preclinical and clinical imaging studies *in vitro*, pharmaceutical research, and so on.

Artifact Reduction

Reduction of image artifacts has been a central topic in the CT field. The paradigm shift towards volumetric CT, novel architectures and dynamic and quantitative imaging demands a more effective reduction of various artifacts. The well-known scattering artifacts become more and more serious with the increasing cone angle and dual-source CT configurations. Beam hardening artifacts must be suppressed to extract energy-dependent information. Motion artifacts remain a main challenge for cardiac CT and contrast-enhanced studies. More than a dozen types of artifacts are well known to the field (Figure. 10), most of which assume new forms and present new problems associated with the

Figure 10. Representative CT image artifacts. (a) A shoulder phantom image with streaks caused by photon starvation, (b) a patient with spine implants generating metal artifacts, and (c) a moving head leading to motion artifacts (http://www.imaging.sbes.vt.edu/BIDLib/CT/C146-Outlook-CT.pdf)

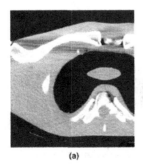 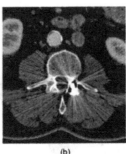 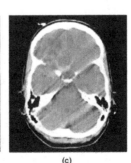

(a)　　　　　(b)　　　　　(c)

development of new CT technologies. Therefore, the fight against these artifacts remains active and requires new tools. While many traditional artifact reduction algorithms are *ad hoc* and approximate, the future efforts may rely on more solid physical models and more rigorous inherent data integrity. In this context, data consistency conditions were proposed to suppress motion artifacts, minimize beam hardening and so on. The invariance of the integral was suggested as a possible mechanism for this purpose. Nevertheless, much more work is required to advance this frontier. To a large degree, artifact reduction is very similar to image reconstruction. In both cases, the goal is to find an optimum subject to a set of constraints. Given the complexities imposed by the artifact-related constraints, the iterative approach will play a more important role. Several iterative schemes have been well studied so far. New iterative schemes deserve major attention and refinement, such as the alternating iteration scheme for metal artifact reduction. Only with optimized reduction of various artifacts, the future CT technology will deliver its ultimate performance that should be spatially, dynamically, spectrally and quantitatively correct.

Modality Fusion

A distinguished trend in modern biomedical imaging is the area of multi-modal imaging, in which two or more imaging systems are syner-gistically integrated for much better performance, improving or enabling biomedical applications. A primary example is the Positive Emission Tomography (PET)/CT systems. Another example is the hybrid optical tomography systems such as those proposed for Magnetic Resonance Imaging (MRI) based diffuse optical tomography, CT/MRI integration, and CT-based bioluminescence tomography. Recently, the Siemens micro-CT-PET-Single Photon Emission Computed Tomography (SPECT) system Inveon (Figure 11) became commercially available as an integrated preclinical imaging platform. From the perspective of x-ray CT research and development, an unprecedented potential would be unlocked by identifying new combinations of complementary imaging modes and improving the existing multi-modal systems, such as hybrid CT-angio and CT-cardiac systems. There are good possibilities for one-stop imaging centres or suites to emerge where all the imaging tasks can be streamlined in a task specific fashion, which is in some sense an extension of the currently already available trail based multi-modal small animal imager. In addition to the architectural issues, we emphasize that there are excellent opportunities for algorithm development in this area. Traditionally, each component modality of a fusion-based system can be independently considered for image reconstruction. Then, all reconstructed images are retrospectively combined via post-processing for further analysis. However, there is generally some

Figure 11. Imaging platform Inveon for fusion of CT (left), PET and SPECT in preclinical applications Preclinical X-ray phase-contrast CT scanner. "X-Ray phase-contrast imaging (right) (Source: http://www.imaging.sbes.vt.edu)

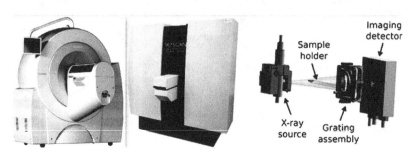

or strong correlation among the datasets acquired by multiple imaging tools applied to study the same individual object. Ideally, we should not solve the imaging problems for these modalities separately but couple these imaging problems with implicit or explicit relationships describing dependence among the involved datasets. Such an integrated inverse problem may require an iterative solution containing several loops each of which assumes other image reconstructions known and refines an intermediate image, or have more sophisticated forms like a truly simultaneous iterative solution. Theoretical studies are needed to establish the solution existence, uniqueness and stability with new iterative reconstruction schemes. In the cases of no unique solutions, regularization issues must be addressed with the aid of *a priori* knowledge in the form of constraints, penalty terms and so on.

Phase-Contrast CT

Phase-contrast x-ray Computed Tomography (CT) is an emerging imaging technique that can be implemented at third generation synchrotron radiation sources or by using a micro focus x-ray tube. X-ray Computed Tomography (CT) using phase contrast can provide images with greatly enhanced soft-tissue contrast in comparison to conventional attenuation-based CT. We report on the first scan of a human specimen recorded with a phase-contrast CT system based on an x-ray grating interferometer and a conventional x-ray tube source. Feasibility and potential applications of preclinical and clinical phase-contrast CT are discussed (Andrei, 2009)

THE FUTURE OF MEDICAL VISUALISATION

Medicine has been revolutionised by 3D imaging techniques. Medical visualisation (shown in Figure 12) is the use of computers to create 3D images from medical imaging data sets. It's a relatively young field of science, relying heavily on advances in computing for its horsepower. (Charl Botha et al., 2012)

Despite its youth, these techniques have revolutionised medicine. Much of modern medicine relies on the 3D imaging that is possible with magnetic resonance imaging scanners and Computed Tomography (CT) scanners, which make 3D images out of 2D slices. Almost all surgery and cancer treatment in the developed world relies on it. Perhaps the most important factor in medical visualisation is the way the data is taken and here there are numerous advances in the pipeline. In the last five years, commercial CT scanners have become available that can take five 320 slice volumes in a single second. That's fast enough to make 3D videos of a beating heart.

Figure 12. The future of medical visualization (Source:http://www.technologyreview.com/view/428134/the-future-of-medical-visualisation/)

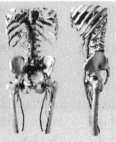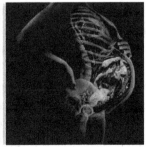

There are also various new diffusion imaging techniques which reveal the diffusion of water through the body. That's important because water tends to follow otherwise hard-to-image structures such as nerve bundles and muscle fibres. Images of these structures are opening important new areas of study in neuroscience and biomechanics. Then there are the imaging techniques that work on the level of molecules and genes. The great potential of these is that they can reveal pathological processes at work long before they become apparent on the larger scale, in the form of tumours, for example.

Collecting the data is just one part of the challenge, of course. Representing it visually in a way that allows the most effective analysis is also hugely difficult but again there have been huge advances. One of the most spectacular is the representation of medical data topologically, in other words showing the surfaces of objects. That makes it possible to more easily see the shapes of organs and to plan interventions such as surgery.

What's more, the most recent image processing techniques allow the addition of realistic lighting effects creating photo-realistic images. Beyond this, hyper-realistic images can show what lies beneath certain layers. The images at the top of this page are recent examples of this. These kinds of images are crucial for reconstructive surgery but a huge challenge for the future and the subject of much current research is to create images of the potential outcome of interventions that show the result of the surgery.

Another area of growing importance is the visualisation of multi-subject data sets. The idea here is to take images of a particular condition from lots of different patients and to combine them in a way that shows the progression of the disease or how it varies between different population groups, for example. Clearly, the challenges here are manifold.

The final piece in this puzzle is the way medical practitioners view images and once again this is changing rapidly. The technology driving this change is essentially the iPad. It's easy to forget that this device hit the shops only in 2010, practically yesterday in the timeline of medical visualisation technology. And yet it has already transformed the way many doctors access and interacts with images, not least because it frees them from desk-based computers.

CONCLUSION

Biomedical imaging has seen truly exciting advances in recent years. New imaging methods can now reflect internal anatomy and dynamic body functions, Not only can technological advances create new and better ways to extract information about our bodies, but they also offer the promise of making some existing imaging tools more convenient and economical.

While exponential improvements in computing power have contributed to the development of today's biomedical imaging capabilities, computing power alone does not account for the dramatic expansion of the field, nor will future improvements in computer hardware is a sufficient springboard to enable the development of the biomedical imaging tools described in this chapter. That development will require continued research in physics and the mathematical sciences, fields that have contributed greatly to biomedical imaging and will continue to do so. Many of the envisioned innovations in medical imaging are fundamentally dependent on the mathematical sciences. Equations that link imaging measurements to quantities of interest must be sufficiently complex to be realistic and accurate and yet simple enough to be capable of solution, either by a direct "inversion formula" or by an appropriate iterative algorithm. In the early 1970s computer methods and algorithms became powerful enough to allow some equations to be solved for practical situations. But there is invariably noise in the measurements, and errors also arise because of the impossibility of giving an exact inversion solution to the equations, either because the equations are only approximate or because the solution technique involves approximation. The development of mathematical methods for producing images from projections thus also requires a capability for overcoming errors or artefacts of the reconstruction method that arise from different sources, and much remains to be done. The result is the need for approximate reconstruction strategies or the incorporation of prior or side information. In addition, computer simulation of imaging methods plays an essential role in separating errors of noise from errors in the design of the mathematical methods, and simulation allows the mathematician and physicist to critically evaluate new ideas in the emerging field of dynamic biomedical imaging.

Early diagnosis of disease must be accompanied by effective treatments. As technological advances occur in identifying diseases and disorders early in their development, increasingly innovative treatments, well validated by outcome studies, also are required. The continued quest for improvement in health care undoubtedly will produce many unimaginable, innovative new diagnostic imaging techniques. In essence, the major task for this new field of medical imaging science is to translate the knowledge about image interpretation accumulated in radiologists' brains into concepts and terminologies understandable by physicists, computer scientists and engineers. It is, therefore, necessary to have close collaboration among researchers in multiple disciplines.

As indicated earlier, this chapter is meant to be suggestive and not exhaustive. As a result, the citations are not comprehensive relative to the huge related literature base. Nevertheless, to the best of our knowledge it reflects the current trends in CT and, while our insights are unavoidably biased, the reality should not be too far from the targets we hope for and believe in. It is our intension to keep refining our predictions in this framework as time goes by and to update this report in a few years. Thus, we highly welcome comments and critiques from colleagues and peers.

FUTURE DIRECTIONS FOR RESEARCH

In the future, researchers hope Medical imaging techniques can be developed to show the progress of disease as shown in multiple individuals or how it differs between different groups. Other imagery advances may be able to help create potential images of surgical outcomes.

Healthcare is rising in quality; complexity and cost, as a range of new advances in previously disparate fields start to appear in the clinic. The challenge for researchers, industry and policymakers is to understand how these converging technologies will change the patient experience in years to come, and how they will be funded. Point-of-care diagnostics, low-cost genome sequencing, improved imaging technologies – all are striking examples of medical progress; but it makes no sense to apply them case-by-case. There needs to be a strategic view of how they can all come together to change the medical paradigm from treatment after illness begins to prediction and prevention before it begins. What is needed is a process of interdisciplinary innovation to promote the adoption of new medical technologies. Medicine needs to be targeted to the individual. General practitioner records should be searchable by researchers, and disease mechanisms modeled in silica. Telemedicine–for expert reading of scans and operating theatre technique–should move from experiment to practice.

Medical imaging is changing how doctors see patients but how doctors actually view the images have also changed. Tablet devices, such as an iPad, are providing portable methods that can improve a doctor's productivity. With photo-realistic images, molecular image and other developments, the future is in focus thanks to advances in medical imaging.

Of course, there are various issues with privacy but it's fair to say that the future of medical Imaging & visualisation is firmly tied to slate-type devices. One area that does not cover in their future is the cost of these imaging techniques and how they can be made cheaper. That's an unforgivable omission but perhaps a reflection of the narrow focus of medicine in the 21st century. Many of the techniques describe are available only to the richest 1 per cent or so of the world's population. For the other 99 percent, these techniques are essentially science fiction. That's clearly unacceptable. The biggest challenge of all is to find ways of making powerful medical visualisation techniques cheap enough for everyone.

All in all, development of medical imaging may not bring a positive impact on the societal healthcare. We have to concern how the service is delivering to the clients and whether the target group can really benefit from the new technology. Advanced technologies do provide better healthcare if everyone is able to use it. The government should put more subsidies for the R&D Project of developing medical imaging so that the cost is reduced and hence the price will be lower.

REFERENCES

Abramson, S. J. (1997). Adrenal neoplasm in children. *Radiologic Clinics of North America, 35*(6), 1415–1453. PMID:9374997.

Alenius, S., & Ruotsalainen, U. (1997). Bayesian image reconstruction for emission tomography based on median root prior. *European Journal of Nuclear Medicine, 24*, 258–265. doi:10.1007/BF01728761 PMID:9143462.

Alenius, S., Ruotsalainen, U., & Astola, J. (1998). Using local median as the location of the prior distribution in iterative emission tomography image reconstruction. *IEEE Transactions on Nuclear Science, 45*, 3097–3104. doi:10.1109/23.737670.

Alexander, F. (2000). Neuroblastoma. *The Urologic Clinics of North America, 27*(3), 383–392. doi:10.1016/S0094-0143(05)70087-2 PMID:10985139.

Amini, B. Dror, &Nygren. (1997). *Tomographic reconstruction of SPECT data*. Retrieved from http://www.owlnet.rice.edu/elect539/projects97/cult/report.html.

Aster, R., Borchers, B., & Thurber, C. (2004). *Parameter estimation and inverse problems*. Amsterdam: Elsevier.

Bankman, I. N. (2000). *Handbook of medical imaging, processing, and analysis*. New York: Academic Press.

Barrett, H. H. & Swindell, W. (n.d.). *Radiological imaging volumes*. New York: Academic Press.

Beister, Kolditz, & Kalender. (2012). Iterative reconstruction methods in X-ray CT. *Physica Medica, 28*, 94–108. doi:10.1016/j.ejmp.2012.01.003 PMID:22316498.

Berry, P., & Midgley, G. Hall, & Lewis. (2009). Recent advances in biomedical imaging systems. ISIC 2009 (183-186). Washington, DC: IEEE Press.

Bronnikov, A. V. (2009). *Phase-contrast CT: Fundamental theorem and fast image reconstruction algorithms*. Retrieved from http://www.bronnikov-algorithms.com/downloads/SPIE631827.pdf

Buchanan, R. A., Finkelstein, S. I., & Wickersheim, K. A. (1976). X-ray exposure reduction using rare earth oxysulfide intensifying screens. *Radiology, 118*, 183–188. PMID:1244656.

Censor, Y., & Zenios, S. A. (1997). *Parallel optimization: Theory, algorithms, and applications*. New York: Oxford University Press.

Chan & Shen. (2005). *Image processing and analysis: Variational, PDE, wavelet, and stochastic methods*. Philadelphia: SIAM.

Charl, B. (2012). *The future of medical visualisation*. Retrieved from http://www.technologyreview.com/view/-428134/the-future-of-medical-visualisation.

Cho, Z. H., Jones, J. P., & Singh, M. (1993). *Foundations of medical imaging*. New York: Wiley.

Cruvinel, P. E., Cesareo, R., Crestana, S., & Mascarenhas, S. (1990). X and gamma rays computerized minitomograph scanner for soil science. *IEEE Transactions on Instrumentation and Measurement, 39*(5), 745–750. doi:10.1109/19.58619.

Devaney. (1982). Filtered backpropagation algorithm for diffraction tomography. *Ultrasonic Imaging, 4*, 336-350.

Donnino, R., Jacobs, J. E., Doshi, J. V., Hecht, E. M., Kim, D. C., Babb, J. S., & Srichai, M. B. (2009). Dual-source versus single-source cardiac CT angiography: Comparison of diagnostic image quality. *AJR. American Journal of Roentgenology, 192*(4), 1051–1056. doi:10.2214/AJR.08.1198 PMID:19304713.

Dougherty. (1998). Computerized evaluation of mammographic image quality using phantom images. *Computerized Medical Imaging and Graphics, 22*, 365-373.

Dougherty. (2009). *Digital image processing for medical applications* (10-13). Cambridge, UK: Cambridge University Press.

Edic, S. Tkaczyk, & Wu. (2011). System and method for energy sensitive computed tomography. *US 7885372 B2*. Retrieved from http://www.google.com/patents/US7885372.

Epstein. (2008). *Introduction to the mathematics of medical imaging* (2nd ed.). Philadelphia: SIAM Press.

Fantini, S., Aggarwal, P., Chen, K., & Franceschini, M. A. (2001). Monitoring brain activity using near-infrared light. *American Laboratory*, 15–17.

Fullerton, G. D. (1980). Fundamentals of CT tissue characterization. In G. D. Fullerton and J. A. Zagzebski (eds.), Medical Physics of CT and Ultrasound: Tissue Imaging and Characterization (125-162). New York: American Association of Physicists in Medicine.

Garreau, Simon, & Boulmier, & Coatrieux, & Le Breton. (2006). Assessment of left ventricular function in cardiac MSCT imaging by a 4D hierarchical surface volume matching process. *International Journal of Biomedical Imaging*. doi:10.1155/IJBI/2006/37607 PMID:23165027.

Geertsma, de Bruijn, Hilbers-Modderman, Hollestelle, Bakker, & Roszek. (2007). New and emerging medical technologies: A horizon scan of opportunities and risks. *Report 360020002*. Bilthoven, Netherlands: Rijksinstituut voor Volksgezondheid en Milieu. Retrieved from http://www.rivm.nl/bibliotheek/rapporten/360020002.html.

Gevins, A. (1998). The future of electroencephalography in assessing neurocognitive functioning. *Electroencephalography and Clinical Neurophysiology, 106*, 165–172. doi:10.1016/S0013-4694(97)00120-X PMID:9741778.

Gilbert, P. (1972). Iterative methods for the three-dimensional reconstruction of an object from projections. *Journal of Theoretical Biology, 36*, 105–117. doi:10.1016/0022-5193(72)90180-4 PMID:5070894.

Girodias, K. A., Barrett, H. H., & Shoemaker, R. L. (1991). Parallel simulated annealing for emission tomography. *Physics in Medicine and Biology, 36*(7), 921–938. doi:10.1088/0031-9155/36/7/002 PMID:1886927.

Goitein, M. (1972). Three-dimensional density reconstruction from a series of two-dimensional projections. *Nuclear Instruments and Methods in Physics, 101*, 509–518. doi:10.1016/0029-554X(72)90039-0.

Gordon, Bender, & Herman. (1970). Algebraic reconstruction technique (ART) for three dimensional electron microscopy and X-ray photography. *Journal of Theoretical Biology, 29*, 471–481. doi:10.1016/0022 5193(70)90109 8 PMID:5492997.

Gordon, R. (1974). A tutorial on ART. *IEEE Transactions on Nuclear Science, 21*, 78–93.

Gordon, R., Bender, R., & Herman, G. T. (1970). Algebraic reconstruction techniques (ART) for three-dimensional electron microscopy and x-ray photography. *Journal of Theoretical Biology, 29*, 471–481. doi:10.1016/0022-5193(70)90109-8 PMID:5492997.

Green, P. J. (1990). Bayesian reconstructions from emission tomography data using a modified EM algorithm. *IEEE Transactions on Medical Imaging, 9*, 84–93. doi:10.1109/42.52985 PMID:18222753.

Gupta, R., Cheung, A. C., Bartling, S. H., Lisauskas, J., Grasruck, M., & Brady, T. J. et al. (2008). Flat-panel volume CT: Fundamental principles, technology, and applications. *Radiographics, 28*(7). doi:10.1148/rg.287085004 PMID:19001655.

Herbert, T., & Leahy, R. (1989). A generalized EM algorithm for 3-D bayesian reconstruction from poisson data using gibbs priors. *IEEE Transactions on Medical Imaging, 8*, 194–202. doi:10.1109/42.24868 PMID:18230517.

Herman, G. T. (1980). *Image reconstruction from projections: The fundamentals of computed tomography*. New York: Academic.

Herman, G. T. (2009). *Fundamentals of computerized tomography: Image reconstruction from projection* (2nd ed.). Berlin: Springer. doi:10.1007/978-1-84628-723-7.

Hilbert. (1953). *Grundzuge einer allgemeinen theorie der linearen integralgleichungen*. New York: Chelsea Publishing Company.

Huda, W., & Slone, R. (1995). *Review of radiologic physics*. Baltimore: Williams and Wilkins.

Hudson & Larkin. (1994). Accelerated image reconstruction using ordered subsets of projection data. *IEEE Transactions on Medical Imaging, 13*, 601–609. doi:10.1109/42.363108 PMID:18218538.

Jin, Wernick, Yang, Brankov, Gravier, Feng, & King. (2006). 5D image reconstruction for tomographic image sequences. In *Proceedings of Fortieth Asilomar Conference on Signals, Systems, and Computers*. Pacific Grove, CA: IEEE Press.

Kaczmarz. (1937). Angenaherte auflosunf, von systemen linearer gleichungen. *Bulletin de l'Academie des Sciences et Letters, A, 35*, 355-357.

Kak & Slaney. (2001). *Principles of computerized tomographic imaging*. Retrieved from http://www.slaney.org/pct/pct-toc.html.

Kuchment & Kunyansky. (2008). A survey in mathematics and industry-Mathematics of thermoacoustic tomography. *European Journal of Applied Mathematics, 19*, 191–224. doi: doi:10.1017/S095679250800735.

Larsson, S. A. (1980). Gamma camera emission tomography. *Acta Radiologica. Supplementum*, 363. PMID:6267902.

Law, S. K., Nunez, P. L., Westdorp, A. F., Nelson, A. V., & Pilgreen, K. L. (1991). Topographical mapping of brain electrical activity, 194-200. Washington, DC: IEEE Press.

Li, Zhang, & Li. (2008). *Tomographic* Reconstruction using the distorted rytov iterative method with phaseless data. *IEEE Geoscience and Remote Sensing Letters, 5*(3).

Liang, Z., & Hart, H. (1988). Bayesian reconstruction in emission computerized tomography. *IEEE Transactions on Nuclear Science, 35*, 788–792. doi:10.1109/23.12833.

Mueller, Yagel, & Wheller. (1998). A fast and accurate projection algorithm for 3-D cone-beam reconstruction with the algebraic reconstruction technique (ART). In *Proceedings of SPIE Medical Imaging Conference*. San Diego: SPIE Press.

Natterer & Wubbeling. (2001). *Mathematical Methods in image reconstruction*. Philadelphia: SIAM.

Ogawa, Lee, Kay, & Tank. (1990). Brain magnetic resonance imaging with contrast dependent on blood oxygenation. *Proceedings of the National Academy of Sciences of the United States of America*, *87*, 9868–9872. doi:10.1073/pnas.87.24.9868 PMID:2124706.

Pan & Kak. (1983). A computational study of reconstruction algorithms for diffraction tomography: Interpolation vs. filtered-back propagation. *IEEE Transactions on Acoustics, Speech, and Signal Processing*, *31*, 1262–1275. doi:10.1109/TASSP.1983.1164196.

Peters. (2005). *Signal processing, A mathematical approach*. Wellesley, MA: Dexter Publishing Company.

Phelps, M. E., Homan, E. J., & Ter-Pogossian, M. M. (1975). Attenuation coefficients of various body tissues, fluids, and lesions at photon energies of 18 to 136 keV. *Radiology*, *117*, 573–583. PMID:810827.

Rehani, K. McCollough, & Nagel. (2006). *Managing patient dose in multi-detector computed tomography (MDCT)*. Retrieved from http://www.icrp.org/docs/icrp-mdct-for_web_cons_32_219_06.pdf.

Rennie, J. M. (2005). *Roberton's textbook of neonatology* (4th ed.). Amsterdam: Elsevier.

Sasov, A. (2001). High-resolution in-vivo micro-CT scanner for small animals. In Proceedings of SPIE 4320: Medical Imaging 2001-Physics of Medical Imaging (705-710). San Diego: SPIE Press.

Shepp, L. A., & Vardi, Y. (1982). Maximum likelihood reconstruction for emission tomography. *IEEE Transactions on Medical Imaging*, *1*, 113–122. doi:10.1109/TMI.1982.4307558 PMID:18238264.

Shepp & Vardi. (1982). Maximum likelihood reconstruction for emission tomography. *IEEE Transactions on Medical Imaging*, *1*, 113–122. doi:10.1109/TMI.1982.4307558 PMID:18238264.

Soumekh, Kaveh, & Mueller. (1986). Algorithms and experimental results in acoustic tomography using Rytov's approximation. In *Proceedings of International Conference On Acoustics, Speech, and Signal Processing* (135-138). Washington, DC: IEEE Press.

Soumekh & Kaveh. (1984). Image reconstruction from frequency domain data on arbitrary contours. In *Proceedings of the Conference on Acoustics, Speech, and Signal Processing* (12A.2.1-12A.2.4). Washington, DC: IEEE Press.

Srinivasan, R. (1999). Methods to improve the spatial resolution of EEG. *International Journal of Bioelectromagnetism*, *1*(1), 102–110.

Stayman. (2003). *Spatial Resolution in Penalized-Likelihood Image Reconstruction*. (PhD. Thesis). Ann Arbor, MI, University of Michigan.

Strauss, H. W. (2006). Nuclear medicine 2020. *The Quarterly Journal of Nuclear Medicine and Molecular Imaging*, *50*, 1–3. PMID:16557198.

Sustens. (2002). *Fundamentals of medical imaging*. New York: Cambridge University Press.

Teplan, M. (2002). Fundamentals of EEG measurement. *Measurement Science Review, 2*.

Tsui, Zhao, Frey, & Gulberg. (1991). Comparison between ML-EM and WLS-CG algorithm for SPECT image reconstruction. *IEEE Transactions on Nuclear Science, 38*, 1766–1772.

Vandenberghe, D'Asseler, Van de Walle, Kauppinen, Koole, ... & Dierckx. (2001). Iterative reconstruction algorithms in nuclear medicine. *Computerized Medical Imaging and Graphics, 25*, 105-111.

Vardi, Y., Shepp, L. A., & Kaufman, L. (1985). A statistical model for positron emission tomography. *Journal of the American Statistical Association, 80*, 8–20. doi:10.1080/01621459.1 985.10477119.

Vaz, C. M. P., Crestana, S., Mascarenhas, S., Cruvinel, P. E., Reichardt, K., & Stolf, R. (1989). Using a computed tomography miniscanner for studying tillage induced soil compaction. *Soil Technology, 2*, 313–321. doi:10.1016/0933-3630(89)90015-9.

Vo-Dinh, T. (2003). *Biomedical photonics handbook*. New York: CRC Press. doi:10.1201/9780203008997.

Wang & Yu. (2008). An outlook on x-ray CT research and development. *Medical Physics, 35*(3).

Webb, A. (2003). *Introduction to biomedical imaging*. Washington, DC: IEEE Press.

Webb, S. (2000). *The physics of medical imaging*. London: Institute of Physics.

Xu & Wang. (2006). Photoacoustic imaging in biomedicine. *The Review of Scientific Instruments, 77*(4).

Zhao, J., Lu, Y., Zhuang, T., & Wang, G. (2010). Overview of multisource CT systems and methods. In S. R. Stuart (Ed.) *Proceedings of the SPIE: Developements in X-Ray Tomography VII* (78040H-78040H-14). Bellingham, WA: SPIE Press.

Zhou, X., & Gordon, R. (1989). Detection of early breast cancer. *An overview and future prospects. Critical Reviews in Biomedical Engineering, 17*(3), 203–255. PMID:2673660.

KEY TERMS AND DEFINITIONS

Anatomy: The body's structure, parts and organs.

Angiography: An examination of arteries and veins using a contrast medium to differentiate them from surrounding organs. The contrast medium is introduced through a catheter to show the blood vessels and the structures they supply, including organs.

Artifact: Image quality Signal intensities in the Medical images that do not correspond to the spatial distribution of tissue in the image plane. They result mainly from physiological as well as system-related influences. Aliasing artifact, Distortion artifact, Flow artifact, Motion artefact.

Back-Projection: $y \rightarrow A^T y$ where A is the system matrix.

Biopsy: A medical procedure that involves obtaining a tissue sample for analysis to establish a precise diagnosis.

Cardiology: The clinical study and practice of treating the heart.

Chest X-Ray: Pictures of the inside of the chest, mainly of the lungs, taken using high energy rays. Please refer to the Patient Information section on X-ray for further information.

Coincidence: Event selection consisting of the detection of two high-energy photons within some selected time interval.

Computed Tomography (CT, CAT): CT stands for Computed Tomography, an imaging technique used to visualise both the soft tissue and bone inside your body. CT uses special x-rays to obtain image data from different angles around the body. A powerful computer is then used to process the information to show a cross-section of body tissues and organs - much like viewing the slices of a loaf of bread. CT imaging can show bones, as well as surrounding tissues such as muscle and blood vessels with great clarity. Using this technique, Radiologists can more easily diagnose problems such as cancer, cardiovascular disease, infectious disease, trauma and musculoskeletal disorders. Please refer to our CT information page for further information.

Electrocardiogram: Medical test of the heart. Small pads are stuck onto the chest around the heart. Wires are attached to the pads and these connect to a machine that takes an electrical recording of the heart beat. Doctors can examine the trace of the heart beat to see if the heart is working normally.

FluoroDeoxyGlucose (FDG): Also commonly referred to as FDG; compound used widely in PET imaging and which behaves in a similar (analogous) way to Glucose and therefore reflects metabolism in the body. Cancer cells have an increased metabolism and therefore show increased uptake of FDG, reflected in PET images.

Forward-Projection: $x \rightarrow Ax$ where A is the system matrix.

Gamma Camera: A camera that records the distribution of a radiopharmaceutical containing a radionuclide that is attracted or taken up by a specific organ or tissue of interest.

Gamma Ray: A very high frequency form of electromagnetic radiation that consists of photons emitted by radioactive elements. Gamma rays can injure and destroy body cells and tissue, especially cell nuclei.

Image Fusion: Method for displaying two images of the same patient from different scanners simultaneously, for example PET and CT images. This gives doctors more information allowing them to more accurately locate where disease may be.

Imaging: Tests that produce pictures of areas inside the body.

Interventional Radiology: A specialised area of radiology that uses various imaging techniques to guide the insertion of small instruments and tools through the body to identify and treat a medical disorder without requiring conventional surgery.

Isotope: One of two or more atoms having the same atomic number but differing in atomic weight and mass number. The concept of isotope was introduced to explain aspects of radioactivity. A radioactive isotope or radioisotope is a natural or artificially created isotope of a chemical element having an unstable nucleus that decays, emitting alpha, beta, or gamma rays until stability is reached.

Magnetic Resonance Imaging: An imaging technique used to visualise the soft tissue inside your body. MRI combines a powerful magnet with radio-frequency pulses. These collect signals that are then processed by a sophisticated computer to form pictures of the inside of your body. MRI gives highly detailed pictures of the soft tissues within the body, for example muscles and ligaments. This capability means Doctors can use MRI in a wide range of investigations: from slipped discs and brain tumours, to painful or injured joints, to the assessment of blood flow. Please refer to our MRI information page for further details.

Mammography: An examination method using x-rays to detect cancer in the breast.

Medical Imaging: Use of electromagnetic radiation to produce images of internal body structures for diagnosis.

Nuclear Medicine: Medical speciality using radioactive elements or isotopes for diagnosis and treatment of disease. A radioisotope is introduced into the body (usually by injection). The radiation it emits, detected by a scanner and recorded, reflects its distribution in different tissues and can reveal the presence, size, and shape of abnormalities in various organs. The isotopes used have short half-lives and decay before radioactivity causes any damage.

PET/CT: Combines PET and CT images using image fusion to better localise lesions. PET/CT significantly improves sensitivity and specificity of lesion identification over either modality. Most new PET scanners now have an integrated CT.

Positron Emission Tomography: An imaging technique that uses small quantities of a radioactive tracer similar to sugar (18Fluorodeoxyglucose) to produce images showing how your body is functioning. PET visualises active tissue and cells as opposed to the body's anatomy and structure. You will be injected with a non-harmful radioactive tracer that acts like glucose and travels all around the body. This tracer collects in active areas of your body, such as cancer cells and is imaged using a PET scanner. PET is primarily used in imaging cancer and can provide doctors with useful information at many stages of the disease process, such as diagnosis, staging or treatment evaluation. Applications for PET in cardiology and neurology are also on the increase.

Radiation: The process of emitting energy as waves or particles. The energy thus radiated. Frequently used for ionising radiation except when it is necessary to avoid confusion with non-ionising radiation. Sunlight is a form of radiation. Without that radiation, we would not exist. Thus radiation is necessary for life on our planet, as we know it.

Radioactivity: The spontaneous emission of radiation from unstable atoms. Radionuclides lose particles (e.g., alpha or beta) and energy through radioactive decay.

Radioisotope/Radionuclide: In a group of atoms with the same number of protons but different numbers of neutrons, the atoms with an unstable number of neutrons that disintegrate, releasing rays of subatomic particles, are called radioisotopes.

Reconstructed Image: A 3-D array, where each cell is an estimate of the tracer distribution in the patient.

Scanner: A medical device with which images of the body are obtained.

Scattered Coincidence: Background coincidence event in which one or both photons have scattered one or more times before being detected

Sensitivity: Statistical term specifying how many of the diseased will be detected by the test - usually expressed as a percentage. The higher the better.

Single Photon Emission Computed Tomography (SPECT or SPET): A nuclear medicine imaging technique which produces a 3 dimensional reconstruction of radio-pharmaceutical distribution in an organ. The image may be viewed either as slices through the organ or as a pseudo 3 dimensional image.

Sinogram: Data structure in which the measurements are ordered by projection angle and radial distance.

SPECT/CT: A nuclear medicine imaging device with an integral CT scanner. This type of image fuses Nuclear Medicine images with X-ray CT images improving disease and lesion localisation.

Tomography: From the Greek words "to cut or section" (tomos) and "to write" (graphein). In Nuclear Medicine, it is a method of separating interference from the area of interest by imaging a cut section of the object.

Ultrasound: (Ultrasound Scan, Ultrasound Scans): Scan using sound waves to build up a picture of the inside of the body. A gel is put on the skin and a microphone passed back and forth over the area to be scanned. A computer converts the reflected sound waves into a picture on a screen. Please refer to our Ultrasound information page for further information.

Voxel: The same as a pixel but with the additional description of the thickness of slice used. Thus voxels might measure 2 mm by 2 mm by 5mm (2 mm sized pixels, 5 mm thick).

X-Ray: Photons or electromagnetic radiation produced by the de-excitation of bound atomic electrons. The energy of an x-ray is equivalent to the difference in energy of the initial and final atomic state minus the binding energy of the electron.

APPENDIX: LINKING WITH OTHER IMAGING MODALITIES

1. Medical Image Analysis–Atam Dhawan. Wiley-IEEE Press; 2003. Available at Fenwick: http://magik.gmu.edu/cgi-bin/Pwebrecon.cgi?BBID=1559656
2. Diagnostic Ultrasound Imaging: Inside Out–Thomas Szabo. Elsevier Academic Press; 2004. Electronic resource available through GMU Libraries: http://magik.gmu.edu/cgi-bin/Pwebrecon.cgi?BBID=1312573
3. Handbook of Medical Imaging: Processing and Analysis–Isaac N. Bankman. Academic Press; 2000. Available at Fenwick: http://magik.gmu.edu/cgi-bin/Pwebrecon.cgi?BBID=882057
4. Medical imaging at the Open Directory Project http://www.dmoz.org/Health/Medicine/Imaging//
5. MedPix Free Medical Image Database, Search & Download Images http://rad.usuhs.edu/medpix/parent.php3?mode=home_page
6. IPRG Open group related to image processing research resources http://iprg.co.in/
7. Research Material in medical imaging, tomography, nonparametric estimation, and inverse problems, with current and past projects in X-ray CT, MRI, PET, SPECT, radiation therapy, and image registration. http://web.eecs.umich.edu/~fessler/
8. Overview over the medical and budget advantages of medical imaging www.medicalimaging.org/
9. Medical Imaging News http://www.sciencedaily.com/news/health_medicine/medical_imaging/
10. IEEE Transactions on Medical Imaging http://www.ieee-tmi.org/
11. BMC Medical Imaging is an open access, peer-reviewed journal that considers articles on the development, evaluation, and use of imaging techniques and image processing tools to diagnose and manage disease.http://www.biomedcentral.com/bmcmedimaging/
12. Computed Tomography –http://www.unene.ca/un805-2004/assign_group/Group1.doc
13. Principles of Computerized Tomographic Imaging http://cobweb.ecn.purdue.edu/~malcolm/pct/pct-toc.html
14. Parallel Implementation of the Filtered Back Projection Algorithm for Tomographic Imaging – http://www.sv.vt.edu/xray_ct/parallel/Parallel_CT.html
15. M611 – Tomography Project http://www.math.udel.edu/~monk/Classes/m611/tomo.pdf
16. Natterer, Frank (1986). *The mathematics of computerized tomography*. John Wiley. ISBN 0471909599
17. C. L. Epstein, Introduction to the Mathematics of Medical Imaging. Prentice Hall, 2003
    a. C. Kak and M. Slaney, Principles of Computerized Tomographic Imaging. IEEE Press, 1987
    b. http://www.slaney.org/pct/
    c. http://www.freetechbooks.com/principles-of-computerized-tomographic-imaging-t707.html
    d. http://www.slaney.org/pct/pct-toc.html
18. The Algebraic Reconstruction Technique (ART) is an iterative algorithm for the reconstruction of
    a. A two-dimensional image from one-dimensional input data (a sinogram), used in Computed Tomography scanning. In numerical linear algebra the method is called Kaczmarz method[1].
19. The radon transform and some of its applications. http://www.owlnet.rice.edu/~elec431/projects96/DSP/bpanalysis.html
    http://www.mathworks.com/access/helpdesk_r13/help/toolbox/images/transfo9.html
20. Medical Imaging Links. http://www-ee.uta.edu/Online/Alavi/ee4328Fall10/
21. The Visible Human Project. http://www.nlm.nih.gov/research/visible/getting_data.html

22. Sta 4274h -- Statistical Inverse Problems. http://fisher.utstat.toronto.edu/andrey/courses/inverse.htm

23. Introduction to the Mathematics of Computed Tomography. http://oregonstate.edu/~faridana/preprints/AFintroct.ps

24. Computed Tomography and Nuclear Magnetic Resonance with Mathematical Applications. http://www.yale.edu/ynhti/curriculum/units/1983/7/83.07.04.x.html

25. Using Mathematics to Improve CAT scans. http://math.fullerton.edu/apineda/Angelwebfiles/X-Ray_Talk.pdf

26. Adel Faridani's Research Page: Computed Tomography and Sampling matlab image Reconstruction http://oregonstate.edu/~faridana/preprints/preprints.html

27. Single Photon Emission Computed Tomography. http://physics.wm.edu/physicsnew/undergrad/2001/Kevin_Knott.pdf

28. Computerized Tomography: An Introduction. ftp://ftp.cs.colorado.edu/pub/HPSC/TomographyTutorial.ps.Z

29. General Geometry CT Reconstruction. http://www.cs.uwaterloo.ca/~jorchard/academic/Ramotar_IPCV06.pdf

30. CTSim - The Open Source Computed Tomography Simulator. http://www.ctsim.org/

31. UK's CT scanner evaluation centre. http://www.impactscan.org/index.htm

32. University of California, Berkeley. EE225B, spring 2006 - Digital Image Processing

33. Different Imaging Methods. http://ns.ph.liv.ac.uk/~arm/public/presentations/Imaging%20Progress%20-%20July%202004.pdf

34. The Shepp-Logan phantom. http://server.oersted.dtu.dk/31655//?ct_data/shepp_logan.html

35. Make projected data for Shepp-Logan phantom for CT reconstruction. http://server.oersted.dtu.dk/ftp/jaj/31655/ct_programs/shepp_logan.m

36. 3D Shepp-Logan phantom. http://tomography.o-x-t.com/2008/04/13/3d-shepp-logan-phantom/

37. Algebraic Reconstruction Algorithms. http://www.nada.kth.se/~szepessy/tomografi.pdf

38. The Algebraic Reconstruction Technique (Art). http://accelconf.web.cern.ch/accelconf/pac97/papers/pdf/2P057.PDF

39. Imaging systems rely on reconstruction. http://www.owlnet.rice.edu/~elec539/Projects97/cult/node1.html

40. Image Processing Learning Resources. http://homepages.inf.ed.ac.uk/rbf/HIPR2/hipr_top.htm

Chapter 15
Automatic MRI Brain Image Segmentation Using Gravitational Search-Based Clustering Technique

Vijay Kumar
JCDM College of Engineering, India

Jitender Kumar Chhabra
National Institute of Technology, India

Dinesh Kumar
GJUS&T, India

ABSTRACT

Image segmentation plays an important role in medical imaging applications. In this chapter, an automatic MRI brain image segmentation framework using gravitational search based clustering technique has been proposed. This framework consists of two stage segmentation procedure. First, non-brain tissues are removed from the brain tissues using modified skull-stripping algorithm. Thereafter, the automatic gravitational search based clustering technique is used to extract the brain tissues from the skull stripped image. The proposed algorithm has been applied on four simulated T1-weighted MRI brain images. Experimental results reveal that proposed algorithm outperforms the existing techniques in terms of the structure similarity measure.

INTRODUCTION

The rapid advancement in the technology has lead to the design and development of medical tools that are in use for analyzing the human body and detecting diseases with good accuracy. Magnetic Resonance Imaging (MRI) and Computed Tomography (CT) are most widely used techniques so far

as analysis of the human brain is concerned. MRI is preferred over CT because it provides better contrast between different soft tissues of the brain (Gao & Xie, 2009). MRI Brain image provides a way of observing brain anatomy and helps in the diagnosis of brain irregularities.

With the increasing number of MRI brain images, the use of computers has become neces-

DOI: 10.4018/978-1-4666-4558-5.ch015

sary. Computer algorithms have been developed for analyzing the anatomical structures in brain image, called image segmentation algorithms (Pham et al., 1998).The segmentation of MRI brain plays a crucial role in neuro image analysis. Automatic brain image segmentation is of great importance in neurological research. The accurate segmentation of MRI brain image into different brain tissues like white matter, gray matter, and cerebrospinal fluid, is an important task (Riad et al, 2010). The accurate estimation of these brain tissues provides valuable information for disease diagnosis. However, the automatic brain image segmentation remains a persistent problem. The overlapping of magnetic resonance intensities of different brain tissues further complicates the segmentation process.

It is difficult to design an automatic segmentation algorithm without any prior knowledge of an organ being imaged. To alleviate this problem, a framework for automatic brain image segmentation using gravitational search based clustering has been proposed in this chapter. It consists of two main stages. The first stage is the extraction of brain tissues from non-brain tissues using the skull stripping procedure. The skull stripping procedure consists of anisotropic diffusion filtering, edge detection and morphological operations. In the second stage, the proposed gravitational search based clustering is applied on the skull stripped image to form the clusters with optimized cluster centroids without any prior knowledge. In the proposed work, the algorithm would be applied on different MRI brain images to extract brain tissues like white matter, gray matter and cerebrospinal fluid.

This chapter aims to formulate the image segmentation of MRI brain images as a soft computing problem, and segment the brain tissues using gravitational search based clustering technique. It includes a general overview of brain image segmentation with emphasis on recently introduced segmentation techniques followed by proposed Gravitational Search Algorithm based brain image segmentation technique. The performance evaluation has been done using brain images. It also suggests some future research directions.

BACKGROUND

In this section, we first define the terminology that will be used and brief description of recently developed segmentation methods.

Definitions

Image segmentation is an important process for medical image analysis. It is defined as the process of subdividing the image into constituent regions. These regions have two main properties: 1.) homogeneity within a region, 2.) heterogeneity between the regions. The mathematical formulation of segmentation is defined as follows (Raut et al., 2009):

Let I be the set of all image pixels. By applying segmentation on I, it is partitioned into n different non-overlapping regions $\{R_1, R_2, ..., R_n\}$ such that:

$$\bigcup_{i=1}^{n} R_i = I, \quad where \, R_i \cap R_j = \phi \qquad (1)$$

The main goal of segmentation is to change the representation of an image into something that is more meaningful and easier to analyze (Shapiro & Stockman, 2001). Image segmentation is often treated as pattern recognition problem since it requires classification of pixels (Li et al., 2005). The role of segmentation in medical imaging is to study anatomical structure of brain, identify the brain tissues, measure the growth of tumor and help in radiation dose calculation.

Related Work

A lot of research has been done on automatic segmentation of normal tissues in the brain and its surrounding structures. There are many approaches available in literature for image segmentation such as threshold method (Mardia & Hainsworth, 1988), edge-based methods (Perona & Malik, 1990), region-based methods (Haris et al., 1998), graph-based methods (Felzenszwalb & Huttenlocher, 2004), and clustering methods. Threshold techniques use the local pixel information for taking the decision of segmenting the image. Its main drawbacks are computation of threshold and sensitivity towards noise (Forghani et al., 2007). The threshold calculation in brain image is difficult due to complex distribution of tissue intensities. Some variations in thresholding techniques are used in medical imaging that are based on either local intensity (Li et al., 1995) or connectivity (Lee et al., 1998). Next, edge-based technique uses the concept of connecting the broken contour lines together. But, it is prone to failure in the presence of blurring (Jiao, 2011). Region-based method partitions an image into connected regions by grouping neighboring pixels of similar intensity levels. Adjacent regions are then merged under some characteristics. But, it requires precise anatomical information to locate seed pixels for each region and together with their associated homogeneities (Robb, 2000). The hybridization of edge and region based methods are used in MRI brain image segmentation (Tang et al, 2000). In graph based method, the problem is formulated in terms of graph terminology. Each node corresponds to pixel intensity in the image and an edge connects a pair of neighbouring pixels having similar feature value. It is also suffer from the same problem as edge based technique. It has been applied in MRI brain imaging.

Due to the heuristic nature of segmentation methods, segmentation problem can be formulated as an optimization problem. Using this fact, clustering techniques have been widely used in image segmentation (Bezdek et al., 1993). The three widely used clustering techniques are K-means, Fuzzy C-Means (FCM) and Expectation-Maximization algorithm. They are sensitive towards parameter initialization and noise. To get the rid off this problem, metaheuristic techniques are used with clustering. Some of metaheuristic techniques are genetic algorithm, ant colony optimization, particle swarm optimization, harmony search and gravitational search algorithm. They have been investigated for MRI segmentation in (Bhadarkar & Zhang, 1999; Veenman et al., 2003; Melkemi et al., 2006; Saha & Bandyopadhyay, 2007; Maulik, 2009).

In this chapter, skull stripping and Gravitational Search Algorithm (GSA) based automatic clustering have been proposed. The proposed GSA based clustering applied on MRI brain image for segmentation.

MAIN FOCUS OF THE CHAPTER

Problems and Challenges of MRI Brain Image Segmentation

There are a large number of image segmentation techniques. Most of segmentation techniques are not applicable to MRI brain imaging due to the complex structure of the brain and the inaccuracy of brain tissue estimation. There is no standard MRI Brain image segmentation technique that can produce satisfactory results. Optimal selection of brain and non-brain tissues play major role in brain segmentation. Accurate segmentation of brain image is difficult due to overlapping of skull intensity with brain tissues and noise sensitivity. The main challenge of brain image segmentation using clustering is sensitivity towards initialization of cluster centroids.

Figure 1. The proposed framework of automatic MRI brain image segmentation

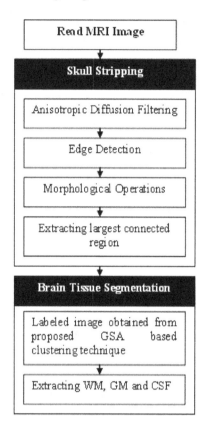

Solution and Recommendations

Recently, hybridization of metaheuristic and clustering techniques have been used to solve issues mentioned in the above section. To solve the automatic image segmentation problem, we formulated it as a soft computing problem. Our proposed framework tries to alleviate problems occurred during brain image segmentation. The first stage of the framework is a skull stripping procedure which removes the skull from brain image to prevent the overlapping of skull intensity with brain tissues. Another issue of global cluster centroid computation associated with clustering is solved using proposed GSA based clustering technique. It is able to extract the skull from the brain image and separate the brain tissues ac-

curately. Figure 1 shows the proposed automatic MRI brain image segmentation framework. It consists of two major stages: skull stripping and GSA based clustering technique. The details of these stages are given below.

Skull Stripping

Skull stripping is an important preprocessing step in neuro imaging. The subsequent image analysis steps are affected from results obtained from skull stripping procedure. Here we have modified the brain extraction algorithm proposed by Gao & Xie (2009). Three modifications are proposed in Gao and Xie's method. First, the faculas removal step is eliminated, as there is no need of this step in the skull stripping procedure. Instead of Marr-hilderth, Sobel edge detector has been used as it is able to find edge orientations. This property is absent in the Marr-hilderth detector. Last, there is no need to apply morphological operations after extracting the largest connected components. The modified skull stripping algorithm is given below:

Step 1: Apply anisotropic diffusion filtering on the brain image to reduce the noise.

Step 2: Use sobel edge detector to find edges in the diffused image.

Step 3: Apply opening morphological operation on edge sets using structuring element. R_2 is the size 8 disk structuring element.

$$X_{os} = X_s * R_2 \tag{2}$$

Where X_{os} is opened image and X_s is edge sets.

Step 4: Retain the largest connected region as brain tissue after opened image.

$$X_l = S_c\left(X_{os}\right) \tag{3}$$

where S_c is the procedure for selecting the largest connected component in the image and X_l is the largest connected region.

Step 5: Multiply the extracted largest connected component with original image to get skull stripped brain image.

Segmentation Using Proposed GSA Based Clustering Technique

The main goal of MRI brain image segmentation is to extract brain tissues accurately. Conventional image segmentation methods are not preferred, as they require human interaction for accurate segmentation (Riad et al., 2010). In this section, we briefly describe the gravitational search algorithm followed by proposed GSA based clustering technique.

Gravitational Search Algorithm

Gravitational Search Algorithm (GSA) was first introduced by Rashedi et al.(2009). It is a metaheuristic optimization algorithm based on the laws of gravitation and motion. In GSA, each agent is considered as an object and its performance is measured by its mass (Rashedi et al, 2009). All these objects attract each other with a force that is directly proportional to the product of their masses and inversely proportional to the square of the distance between them. This force causes a global movement of all objects towards the objects having heavier masses. The heavy masses correspond to good solutions of the problem. In GSA, each mass presents a solution, and it is navigated by adjusting the gravitational and inertia masses (Rashedi et al, 2010). Masses are attracted by the heaviest mass. This mass will present an optimal solution in the search space.

Proposed GSA Based Clustering Technique

In this section, the GSA based clustering technique is proposed for automatically determining the optimal partitioning of image data. The goodness of partitioning is determined by the DB cluster validity index. The technique is described below:

Step 1: Solution representation and population initialization. In the proposed approach, the feature values of cluster centroids are encoded into a real-coded string. Each chromosome (or agent) consists of the K cluster centroids. Here K is the number of clusters. An example of chromosome structure in our approach is illustrated as follows, where it represents a partition of an image into three regions, and associated gray levels are 39, 112 and 189 respectively.

$$Chromosome_i = \begin{bmatrix} 39 & 112 & 189 \end{bmatrix}$$

GSA requires a population of potential solutions to be initialized at the beginning of GSA process. In our approach, we randomly select a few gray levels from as the initial cluster centroids.

Step 2: While (objective function is not optimized)
- **Objective Function Computation:** The fitness of agent/ chromosome is computed using DB index (Davies & Bouldin, 1979). The objective function of i-th chromosome in GSA-based clustering can be formulated as:

$$F(X_i) = \frac{1}{DB_i(K)} \qquad (4)$$

where DB_i is the DB index, evaluated on the partitions formed by the i-th string in GSA and K is the number of clusters.

The objective of GSA-based clustering is to maximize this fitness function to obtain optimal clustering.

- **Update Masses of Agents Using Fitness Function:** The gravitational and inertia masses of GSA are calculated using objective function. These are given by following equations (Rashedi et al., 2009).

$$m_i(t) = \frac{fit_i(t) - worst(t)}{best(t) - worst(t)} \qquad (5)$$

$$M_i(t) = \frac{m_i(t)}{\sum\limits_{j=1}^{n} m_j(t)} \qquad (6)$$

where $fit_i(t)$ represents the fitness value of agent i at time t. $best(t)$ and $worst(t)$ are defined as follows:

$$best(t) = \max_{j=1}^{n} fit_j(t) \qquad (7)$$

$$worst(t) = \min_{j=1}^{n} fit_j(t) \qquad (8)$$

- **Calculate the Total Force of Each Agent:** The force acting on mass i from mass j at a time t in a dimension d, $F_{ij}^d(t)$, is defined as:

$$F_{ij}^d(t) = G(t) \frac{M_i(t) \times M_j(t)}{R_{ij}(t) + \varepsilon} \left(x_j^d(t) - x_i^d(t) \right) \qquad (9)$$

where $M_i(t)$ is the gravitational mass related to agent i, $G(t)$ is gravitational constant at time t, ε is a small constant, and $R_{ij}(t)$ is the euclidean distance between two agents i and j.

The total force acts on agent i in the dimension d can be defined as:

$$F_i^d(t) = \sum_{\substack{j \in Kbest \\ j \neq i}} rand_j \times F_{ij}^d(t) \qquad (10)$$

where $Kbest$ is the set of first K agents with best fitness and biggest mass.

- **Calculate Acceleration and Velocity of Each Agent:** The acceleration of agent i at time t in direction d, $a_i^d(t)$, is defined as follows:

$$a_i^d(t) = \frac{F_i^d(t)}{M_i(t)} \qquad (11)$$

The velocity of agent i in direction d is defined as:

$$v_i^d(t+1) = rand_i \times v_i^d(t) + a_i^d(t) \qquad (12)$$

- **Update the Position of Agents According to Velocity and Position of Agent:** The next position of agent is determined by the current position added to its next velocity. The position of agent i in direction d is defined as:

$$x_i^d(t+1) = x_i^d(t) + v_i^d(t) \qquad (13)$$

Step 3: Cluster the feature space using GSA optimized cluster centroids.

Step 4: Separate the brain tissues from skull stripped image using the cluster feature space.

VALIDATION AND DISCUSSIONS

Dataset Used

To evaluate the performance of the proposed framework, it has been applied to four T1 weighted MRI brain images. The simulated MRI brain images have been obtained from simulated brain dataset (http://www.bic.mni.mcgill.ca/brainweb/). The advantage of using Brainweb dataset was the availability of ground truth for brain tissues. This dataset contains several subsets of images with different noise and inhomogeneities levels (Kwon et al., 1999). The four normal T1-weighted MRI brain images and their manual segmentations were utilized in our experimentation. The in-plane voxel size and slice thickness of these images was 1.0 mm and 3.0 mm respectively.

Performance Assessment Metrics

Quantitative performance measurement for skull stripped image is computed by comparing the results with the corresponding ground truth image. The manually skull stripped image served as the ground truth image. The Jaccard Similarity Coefficient (JSC) and the Dice Similarity Coefficient (DSC) have been used as performance assessment metrics as they are widely accepted performance metrics. These measures ranged from 0 (for no overlap) to 1 (for perfect overlap). These are mathematically formulated as (Zou et al., 2004; Dice, 1945):

$$JSC = \frac{Vol\left(S_A \cap S_M\right)}{Vol\left(S_A \cup S_M\right)} \qquad (14)$$

and

$$DSC = \frac{2 \times Vol\left(S_A \cap S_M\right)}{Vol\left(S_A + S_M\right)} = \frac{2 \times JSC}{1 + JSC} \qquad (15)$$

where S_A is automatically skull stripped region by algorithm, S_M is the brain region of manually stripped image and $Vol\left(X\right)$ denotes the volume of the region X.

The performance of segmentation algorithms is quantitatively evaluated by recently proposed Structure-SIMilarity (SSIM) index. SSIM is preferred over widely used quality assessment measures such as Mean Squared Error (MSE) and Peak Signal to Noise Ratio (PSNR). The reason behind is that MSE and PSNR do not perceive the visual quality (Wang et al., 2004). The value of SSIM lies in the range [-1, 1]. The value 1 indicates the identical set of data.

Evaluation and Discussion

Two experiments were performed on simulated MRI brain images. In the first experiment, the modified skull stripping algorithm has compared with Gao and Xie (2009) method. To evaluate the performance of the modified skull stripping algorithm, its accuracy was measured. Regarding the accuracy, the Jaccard coefficent and the Dice similarity coefficient were measured. The four images of T1-weighted have been tested on skull stripping techniques and evaluated the results against manual skull-stripped image that has been taken as a 'ground truth'. Figure 2 shows skull stripped images using Gao & Xie method and our

Figure 2. Skull Stripped images obtained from and proposed method

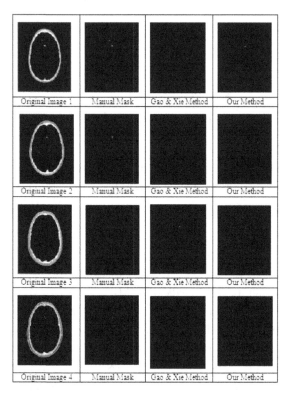

method with ground truth image. The quantitative results of the skull stripping procedure are summarized in Table 1.

In the second experiment, the segmentation of intracranial brain tissues on stripped image obtained from modified skull stripping algorithm

is defined. The comparison of proposed GSA based clustering has been done with existing techniques such as K-Means (KM), Fuzzy C-Means (FCM). These techniques are applied on MRI brain images to form clustered image. Thereafter, clustered image is decomposed into three images corresponding to three clusters. These clustered images are corresponding to gray matter, white matter, and cerebrospinal fluid. The segmentation accuracy of KM, FCM, and GSA based clustering algorithms are compared with reference images obtained from Brainweb dataset. Four T1-weighted images have been used to evaluate the performance of the above-said techniques. Figures 3-6 show the best brain tissues obtained from K-means, fuzzy c-means and GSA based clustering technique applied on four T1-weighted images under 10 independent runs.

Tables 2-5 show the average structure similarity measure between segmented images using above-mentioned techniques and ground truth images for 10 runs. The results reveal that proposed method performs better than K-means and fuzzy c-means. The white and gray matters extracted from the brain image using the proposed method have a higher structural similarity index than the K-means and Fuzzy c-means. The SSIM value of CSF extracted using the proposed method is better than K-means.

Table 1. Performance evaluation of skull stripping algorithms

		JSC	DSC
Image 1	Gao & Xie Method	0.9200	0.9583
	Our Method	**0.9298**	**0.9636**
Image 2	Gao & Xie Method	0.9194	0.9580
	Our Method	**0.9271**	**0.9621**
Image 3	Gao & Xie Method	0.9256	0.9613
	Our Method	**0.9323**	**0.9649**
Image 4	Gao & Xie Method	0.9278	0.9625
	Our Method	**0.9373**	**0.9676**

Figure 3. Segmented tissues of image 1 using K Means, FCM and proposed technique

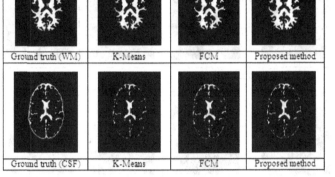

Figure 4. Segmented tissues of image 2 using K Means, FCM and proposed technique

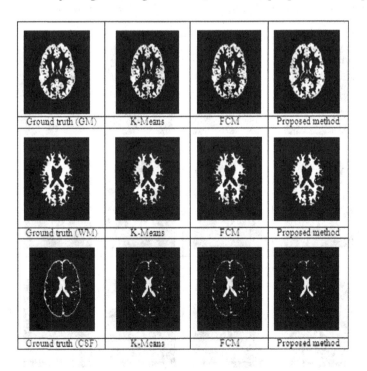

Figure 5. Segmented tissues of image 3 using K Means, FCM and proposed technique

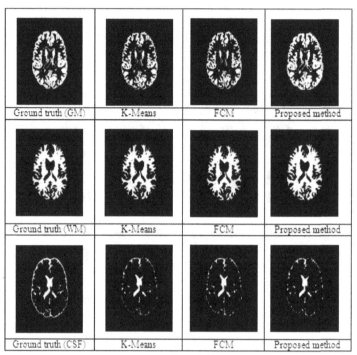

Figure 6. Segmented tissues of image 4 using K Means, FCM and proposed technique

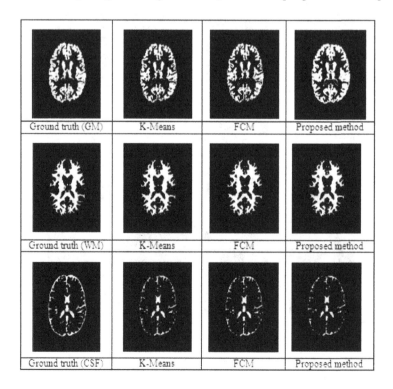

Table 2. Structure similarity measure for image 1

	Gray Matter	White Matter	CSF
K-Means	0.7562	0.8453	0.6305
Fuzzy C-Means	0.7475	0.8490	**0.7118**
Proposed Technique	**0.7566**	**0.8492**	0.6956

Table 3. Structure similarity measures for image 2

	Gray Matter	White Matter	CSF
K-Mean	0.7602	0.8217	0.5763
Fuzzy C-Mean	0.7498	0.8374	**0.7265**
Proposed Technique	**0.7697**	**0.8385**	0.6992

Table 4. Structure similarity measures for image 3

	Gray Matter	White Matter	CSF
K-Means	0.7386	0.8202	0.5617
Fuzzy C-Means	0.7291	0.8436	**0.7181**
Proposed Technique	**0.7434**	**0.8454**	0.6814

Table 5. Structure similarity measures for image 4

	Gray Matter	White Matter	CSF
K-Mean	0.7470	0.8299	0.5853
Fuzzy C-Means	0.7479	0.8527	**0.7048**
Proposed Technique	**0.7549**	**0.8578**	0.6831

FUTURE RESEARCH DIRECTIONS

The spatial information integrated with proposed framework may increase the performance of segmentation. One possible direction for future

research is selecting robust features. These features should be independent of registration algorithms used, scanning parameters etc. The other recently proposed metaheuristic techniques such as cuckoo search, galaxy-based, and firefly search may also be applied for automatic image segmentation. Although the euclidean distance is widely used in clustering techniques for similarity measures, the possibility, that other existing distance measures such as cosine similarity, Manhattan, and correlation based distances may provide better results, can not be ignored.

Another open research concerns intensity inhomogeneity. Due to this, different tissues at different locations may have similar intensity appearance, while same tissues at different locations may have different intensity appearance. So, if inhomogeneity is properly dealt with prior to segmentation operation may increase the accuracy of segmentation algorithms.

CONCLUSION

In this chapter, a framework for automatic MRI brain image segmentation has been proposed. The proposed framework, firstly extracts the non-brain tissues from the brain image using the modified skull stripping method. Thereafter the skull stripped image is segmented into white matter, gray matter and cerebrospinal fluid using proposed GSA based clustering technique. The search capability of the Gravitational Search Algorithm (GSA) has been used for segmentation of MRI images. The partitions generated from GSA are optimized using the cluster validity index, DB- index. The utility of proposed framework is demonstrated on four T1-weighted brain images. We have compared the modified skull-stripping algorithm with Gao and Xie's method. The results reveal that modified skull stripping method out perform Gao and Xie's method. The comparison of three segmentation algorithms-K-means, Fuzzy C-means and GSA based clustering have been performed. The results depict that GSA based clustering technique outperforms the K-Means and Fuzzy C-means. Simulation results show that proposed framework is able to identify the brain tissues accurately.

REFERENCES

Atkins, M. S., & Mackiewich, B. T. (1998). Fully automatic segmentation of the brain in MRI. *IEEE Transactions on Medical Imaging*, *17*(1), 98–107. doi:10.1109/42.668699 PMID:9617911.

Bezdek, J. C., Hall, L. O., & Clarke, L. P. (1993). Review of MR image segmentation techniques using pattern recognition. *Medical Physics*, *20*(4), 1033–1048. doi:10.1118/1.597000 PMID:8413011.

Bhandarkar, S. M., & Zhang, H. (1999). Image segmentation using evolutionary computation. *IEEE Transactions on Evolutionary Computation*, *3*(1), 1–21. doi:10.1109/4235.752917.

Davis, D. L., & Bouldin, D. W. (1979). A cluster separation measure. *IEEE Transactions on Pattern Analysis and Machine Intelligence*, *1*, 224–227. doi:10.1109/TPAMI.1979.4766909 PMID:21868852.

Dice, L. R. (1945). Measures of the amount of ecologic association between species. *Ecology*, *26*(3), 297–302. doi:10.2307/1932409.

Felzenszwalb, P. F., & Huttenlocher, D. P. (2004). Efficient graph-based image segmentation. *Journal of Computer Vision*, *59*(2), 167–181. doi:10.1023/B:VISI.0000022288.19776.77.

Forghani, N., Forouzanfar, M., & Forouzanfar, E. (2007). MRI fuzzy segmentation of brain tissue using IFCM algorithm with particle swarm optimization. In *Proceedings of the International Symposium on Computer and Information Science* (1-4). Tehran, Iran: Springer.

Gao, J., & Xie, M. (2009). Skull-stripping MR brain images using anisotropic diffusion filtering and morphological processing. In *Proceedings of the International Symposium on Computer Network and Multimedia Technology* (1-4). Wuhan, China: IEEE Press.

Gonzalez, R. C., & Woods, R. E. (2002). *Digital image processing*. Upper Saddle River, NJ: Prentice-Hall, Inc..

Haris, K., Efstratiadis, S. N., Maglaveras, N., & Katsaggelos, A. K. (1998). Hybrid image segmentation using watersheds and fast region merging. *IEEE Transactions on Image Processing*, *7*(12), 1684–1699. doi:10.1109/83.730380 PMID:18276235.

Jiao, L. (2011). Evolutionary based image segmentation methods. In P.-G. Ho (Ed.), Image Segmentation (179-224). Rijecka, Croatia: InTech Publishing.

Kole, D. K., & Halder, A. (2012). Automatic brain tumor detection and isolation of tumor cells from MRI images. *International Journal of Computers and Applications*, *39*(16), 26–30. doi:10.5120/4905-7416.

Kwan, R. K.-S., Evans, A. C., & Pike, G. B. (1999). MRI simulation-based evaluation of image-processing and classification methods. *IEEE Transactions on Medical Imaging*, *18*, 1085–1097. doi:10.1109/42.816072 PMID:10661326.

Lee, C., Huh, S., Ketter, T. A., & Unser, M. (1998). Unsupervised connectivity-based thresholding segmentation of midsaggital brain MR images. *Computers in Biology and Medicine*, *28*, 309–338. doi:10.1016/S0010-4825(98)00013-4 PMID:9784966.

Li, C., Goldgof, D. B., & Hall, L. O. (1993). Automatic segmentation and tissue labelling of MR brain images. *IEEE Transactions on Medical Imaging*, *12*(4), 672–682.

Li, C. M., Xu, C. Y., Gui, C. F., & Fox, M. D. (2005). Level set evolution without re-initialization: A new variational formulation. In *Proceedings of IEEE Computer Society Conference on Computer Vision and Pattern Recognition* (430-436). Washington, DC: IEEE Press.

Li, H. D., Kallergi, M., Clarke, L. P., Jain, V. K., & Clark, R. A. (1995). Markov random field for tumour detection in digital mammography. *IEEE Transactions on Medical Imaging, 14*(3), 565–576. doi:10.1109/42.414622 PMID:18215861.

Mardia, K. V., & Hainsworth, T. J. (1998). A spatial thresholding method for image segmentation. *IEEE Transactions on Pattern Analysis and Machine Intelligence, 10*(6), 919–927. doi:10.1109/34.9113.

Maulik, U. (2009). Medical image segmentation using genetic algorithms. *IEEE Transactions on Information Technology in Biomedicine, 13*(2), 166–173. doi:10.1109/TITB.2008.2007301 PMID:19272859.

Melkemi, K. E., Batouche, M., & Foufou, S. (2006). A multiagent system approach for image segmentation using hybrid genetic algorithm-extremal optimization heuristics. *Pattern Recognition Letters. Special Issue on Evolutionary Computer Vision and Image Understanding, 27*(11), 1230–1238.

Perona, P., & Malik, J. (1990). Scale-space and edge detection using anisotropic diffusion. *IEEE Transactions on Pattern Analysis and Machine Intelligence, 12*, 629–639. doi:10.1109/34.56205.

Pham, D. L., Xu, C., & Prince, J. L. (1998). A survey of current methods in medical image segmentation. *Technical Report JHU/ECE 99-01* (315-338). Baltimore: The Johns Hopkins University.

Rashedi, E., Nezamabadi-pour, H., & Saryazdi, S. (2009). GSA: A gravitational search algorithm. *Information Sciences, 179*(13), 2232–2248. doi:10.1016/j.ins.2009.03.004.

Rashedi, E., Nezamabadi-pour, H., & Saryazdi, S. (2010). BGSA: Binary gravitational search algorithm. *Natural Computing, 9*(3), 727–745. doi:10.1007/s11047-009-9175-3.

Riad, A. M., Atwan, A., El-Bakry, H. M., Mostafa, R. R., Elminir, H. K., & Mastorakis, N. (2010). A new approach for segmentation of brain MR image. In *Proceedings of WSEAS International Conference on Environment, Medicine and Health Sciences* (74-83). Stevens Point, WI: WSEAS Press.

Robb, A. R. (2000). *Biomedical imaging, visualization, and analysis*. New York: Wiley.

Saha, S., & Bandyopadhyay, S. (2007). MRI brain image segmentation by fuzzy symmetry based genetic clustering technique. In *Proceedings of the IEEE Congress on Evolutionary Computation, 4417-4424*. Washington, DC: IEEE Press.

Shapiro, L. G., & Stockman, G. C. (2001). *Computer Vision*. Upper Saddle River, NJ: Prentice-Hall.

Tang, H., Wu, E. X., Ma, Q. Y., Gallagher, D., Perera, G. M., & Zhuang, T. (2000). MRI brain image segmentation by multi-resolution edge detection and region selection. *Computerized Medical Imaging and Graphics, 24*(6), 349–357. doi:10.1016/S0895-6111(00)00037-9 PMID:11008183.

Veenman, C. J., Reinders, M. J. T., & Backer, E. (2003). A cellular coevolutionary algorithm for image segmentation. *IEEE Transactions on Image Processing, 12*(3), 304–313. doi:10.1109/TIP.2002.806256 PMID:18237910.

Wang, Z., Bovik, A. C., Sheikh, H. R., & Simoncelli, E. P. (2004). Image quality assessment: From error visibility to structural similarity. *IEEE Transactions on Image Processing*, *13*(4), 600–612. doi:10.1109/TIP.2003.819861 PMID:15376593.

Zou, K. H., Warfield, S. K., Bharatha, A., Tempany, C. M. C., Kaus, M. R., & Kikinis, R. et al. (2004). Statistical validation of image segmentation quality based on a spatial overlap index. *Academic Radiology*, *11*(2), 178–189. doi:10.1016/S1076-6332(03)00671-8 PMID:14974593.

KEY TERMS AND DEFINITIONS

Brain: It is the portion of the vertebrate central nervous system that is enclosed within the cranium and is composed of gray and white matters.

Cerebrospinal Fluid (CSF): It surrounds the spinal cord and brain.

Clustering: It is an unsupervised technique for grouping the data based upon some similarity measure that minimizes within-group variability and maximizes the between-group variability.

Image Segmentation: It is the process of partitioning an image into separate regions, which correspond to different real-world objects.

Magnetic Resonance Imaging: It is a technique that uses a magnetic field and radio waves to create detailed images of organs and tissues within body.

Metaheuristic: It is a general algorithmic framework which can be applied to different optimization problems with relatively few modifications to make them adapted to a specific problem.

Skull Stripping: It is the process of extracting brain tissues from extracerebral tissues such as skull.

Chapter 16
Survey of Medical Image Compression Techniques and Comparative Analysis

P. Geetha
Anna University Chennai, India

ABSTRACT

Today digital imaging is widely used in every application around us like Internet, High Definition TeleVision (HDTV), satellite communications, fax transmission, and digital storage of movies and more, because it provide superior resolution and quality. Recently, medical imaging has begun to take advantage of digital technology, opening the way for advanced medical imaging and teleradiology. However, medical imaging requires storing, communicating and manipulating large amounts of digital data. Applying image compression reduces the storage requirements, network traffic, and therefore improves efficiency. This chapter provides the need for medical image compression; different approaches to image compression, emerging wavelet based lossy-lossless compression techniques, how the existing recent compression techniques work and also comparison of results. After completing this chapter, the reader should have an idea of how to increase the compression ratio and at the same time maintain the PSNR level compared to the existing techniques, desirable features of standard compression techniques such as embededness and progressive transmission, how these are very useful and much needed in the interactive teleradiology, telemedicine and telebrowsing applications.

INTRODUCTION

Medical images are widely used in disease diagnosis. Currently, the following modalities such as 1) Computerized Tomography (CT); 2) Magnetic Resonance Imaging (MRI); 3) Positron Emission Tomography (PET) and 4) X radiographs, etc are used to produce images in digital form. Those modalities provide flexible means for viewing anatomical cross sections and physiological states.

The improvement of diagnosis and the development of interventional procedures have been facilitated by digital enhanced displays and immediate reviewing. However, medical images have large storage requirements. Medical diagnostic digital data produced by hospitals have increased exponentially. In an average-sized hospital, many terabytes of digital data are generated each year, almost all of which have to be kept and archived, which require a large amount of memory storage.

DOI: 10.4018/978-1-4666-4558-5.ch016

Transmitting such an image over a network could take minutes to transfer; because it may be slow for interactive teleradiology, telemedicine and telebrowsing applications. Therefore there is a need to reduce the storage and the transmission requirements with the help of image compression techniques. So, Image compression plays a critical role in telematics applications and especially in telemedicine and teleradiology. The two basic types of compression techniques are

1. Lossless Compression
2. Lossy Compression

The lossless compression technique allows for perfect reconstruction of the original image and yields a modest compression rate of at most two. The lossy compression technique yields higher compression rates, but the resulting image is only approximately similar to the original image where the quality of the image is measured in terms of Peak Signal to Noise Ratio (PSNR). Several lossless and lossy compression techniques with different compression rates have been developed.

Measuring Compression Effectiveness

The effectiveness of compression schemes can be described using a relative measure, Compression Ratio (CR) or by describing an absolute measure, the Bit Rate of an image, PSNR, and complexity. The bit rate is the average number of bits required to encode a pixel and is computed from the total number of bits encoded divided by the number of pixels. Such a value is useful when comparing different schemes applied to one image, or multiple images with the same bit depth. Accordingly, a relative measure, the compression ratios are computed from comparing the number of bits in the uncompressed image to the number of bits in the encoded image.

Compression ratio =

$$\frac{\text{size of the original file}}{\text{size of the compressed file}} = \frac{N \cdot k}{C} \quad (1)$$

$$\text{Bit rate} = \frac{\text{size of the compressed file}}{\text{pixels in the image}} = \frac{C}{N}$$
(bits per pixel) $\quad (2)$

The other parameter used for comparison is peak signal to noise ratio and it is defined as follows:

$$\text{MSE} = \frac{1}{N} \sum_{i=1}^{N} \left(y_i - x_i \right)^2 \quad (3)$$

where
Mean Square Error

$$P(x,y) = r1.P(x-1,y) - r1.r2.P$$
$$(x-1,y-1) + r2.P(x,y-1) \quad (4)$$

The number of arithmetic operations required to perform both encoding and decoding process measures the complexity of an image compression algorithm. This is an important parameter for applications involving online image compression and decompression where speed is crucial.

Traditional and state of the art Lossless/Lossy to lossless coding are given in next section. Main focus of this chapter gives comparison of various coding techniques, problems and issues in standard image compression techniques and also solutions to the problem. Future direction and conclusions are given in the last section.

BACKGROUND

This section attempts to discuss and evaluate the performance of traditional and state of the art Lossless/Lossy to Lossless compression techniques as applied to medical images. Emphasis is placed on those techniques that have been adopted or proposed as international standards. Lossless image coding is important in medical applications where no information loss is allowed during compression. All the approaches for lossless/near lossless coding of images can be classified into four main categories, and they are listed as

1. Ad hoc schemes
2. Dictionary based schemes
3. Prediction schemes
4. Transform based approaches

AD HOC COMPRESSION TECHNIQUES

Ad hoc compression techniques are lossless coding techniques. Lossless coding is based on Information Theory given by Shannon. The major approaches under this category of lossless codes are:

1. Huffman Coding
2. Arithmetic Coding
3. Run Length Coding

And they are discussed in this section.

Huffman Coding

Huffman coding is one of the oldest simple lossless compression methods. It is based on data statistics, and it represents the symbols of the alphabet by variable code length, depending on their probability of occurrence. The more probable a symbol is, the shorter the code it is assigned. Huffman coding is an optimal way of generating such variable length codes (Knuth, 1985).

Algorithmic Steps in Huffman coding:

- Each symbol is a leaf node in a tree.
- Combining the two symbols with the least probabilities to form a new parent node,

this has the combined probabilities. Assign a bit 0 and 1 to the two symbols.
- Continue this process until all symbols merged into one root node. For each symbol, the sequence of the 0s and 1s from the root node to the symbol is the code word.

This method requires the statistical knowledge. For decoding the algorithm, the coding table (the statistics) is sent before the data. This overhead may become negligible for large files. Hence Huffman coding method is only applicable for offline compression. Huffman's algorithm takes $O(n \log n)$ time. Huffman codes are optimal in the sense that no other lossless fixed-to-variable length code has a lower average rate. The maximum compression ratio achieved by this technique is 2.72:1. This compression algorithm is mainly efficient in compressing text or program files. Images are better handled by other compression algorithms. Huffman compression is mainly used in compression programs like pkZIP, lha, gz, zoo, and arj. Also, Huffman method is used in one of the two basic versions of the JPEG standard. Many Modifications to Huffman coding is found in the literature, one such modification is given in (Gopal Lakhani, 2003). Compared to arithmetic coding it is simple but the compression ratio achieved is less. Next the arithmetic coding technique is explained below.

Arithmetic Coding

This method approaches very close the theoretical limit of compression efficiency. It is based on data statistics like Huffman's method, but it is usually more efficient. Its basic advantage is that unlike Huffman coding, it does not have the limitation that each codeword has to be at least one-bit long. However, its implementation is complicated and is very computationally intensive.

The basic idea in arithmetic coding is to divide the interval between 0 and 1 into a number of smaller intervals corresponding to the probabilities of the message's symbols. Then the first input symbol selects an interval, which is further divided into smaller intervals. The next input symbol selects one of these intervals, and the procedure is repeated. In this way, the selected interval narrows with every symbol, and at the end, any number inside the final interval can be used to represent the message. The limitation of this technique is the precision required in performing the calculations and arriving at the code word, which will represent the entire sequence correctly.

Arithmetic coding is more powerful than Huffman coding in compression ratio, but arithmetic coding requires more computational power and memory. Huffman coding is more attractive than arithmetic coding when simplicity is the major concern (Huffman, 1952). The maximum compression ratio achieved by this method is 3:1. The main usefulness of arithmetic coding is in obtaining maximum compression in conjunction with an adaptive model (Witten, 1987). Arithmetic coding gives optimal compression, but its slow execution can be problematical. One of the other popular techniques used in adaptive scheme is run length encoding and the same is explained below.

Run Length Encoding

The image is viewed as a sequence of bits it can often detect long runs of zeros followed by ones, due to the presence of large uniform regions in most images. Run Length Coding (Jain, 2011) (RLE) tries to exploit such inherent uniformity by using numbers to count the repetitions of zeros or ones. In its simpler implementation, Run-Length Encoding replaces repeated data by a {length, value} pair, where "value" is the repeated data value and "length" is the number of repetitions. The disadvantage of Run Length Coding is that it only deals with 1D correlation within the image, and ignores spatial (2D) correlation.

If the image having number of consecutive sequences of repeated pixels, this method results in high performance; otherwise this method gives

poor performance i.e. this method will make the file bigger. This technique is especially successful in compressing bi-level images, and it is widely used in FACSimile (FAX) systems. If direct application of Run-Length Encoding on a gray-scale image does not produce satisfactory compression, then the image can be decomposed into bit planes and every bitplane can be compressed separately. Many modified versions of RLE are found in the literature, one such modification is given in (Geetha, 2005). The above-mentioned three techniques achieve an average compression ratio of 2:1 to 3:1. The various approaches under dictionary-based scheme are explained in the next section.

DICTIONARY BASED SCHEMES

In Dictionary based scheme, strings of symbols are replaced with shorter code words. Dictionary based schemes are widely used for text compression. Many text compressors have been presented so far. They are word-based Lempel-Ziv-Welch (LZW), word-based PPM (Portable Pixel Map), and Burrows Wheeler Transform (BWT) compression on words. One of the most popular dictionary based schemes such as LZW technique is discussed below.

Lempel-Ziv-Welch (LZW)

This original approach is given by Ziv & Lempel (1977). Welch's refinements to the algorithm were published in 1984. LZW is a lossless compression technique that is an optional part of the GIF and TIFF image file formats. A LZW compressor modeled by reading through the input data token by token and then constructing a dictionary of observed sequences and looking for repetitions as it goes.

LZW compressor does not do any analysis of the incoming text. Instead, when it sees a new string it just adds the new string to the dictionary and also writing the string to the output stream. When a repetition is encountered it writing the number of the dictionary entry to the output stream. The output thus consists of appropriately labeled new data and references to old data. The corresponding LZW decompressor reads through the output data, reconstructing the dictionary created during compression. When it sees a new data, it adds it to the dictionary just as the compressor did, as well as sending it to its uncompressed output. When it sees a code for a repetition of a dictionary item, it copies that item to its output. In this way, its dictionary always matches the dictionary that the compressor had at the same point in the data stream, and its output replicates the original input by expanding the repetition codes.

The compression performance of this algorithm is poor. However as strings are re-encountered and replaced with dictionary codeword, performance increases rapidly. For a small set of data, the dictionary does not build up, but as the data gets larger, dictionary builds up long strings and hence compression is better. There are three best-known applications of LZW: UNIX compress (file compression), GIF (image compression), and V4.2 bis (compression over Modems). GZIP is a combination of LZW and Huffman coding. The SZIP scheme is a simple approach that uses LZW and the same fast entropy coder Rice-Golomb coder (Seroussi 1997) as used in JPEG-LS. The

maximum compression ratio achieved by this method is 2.5:1. In order to increase the compression ratio further, prediction based coding techniques are used. Various types of prediction based coding techniques are explained below.

PREDICTION BASED CODING TECHNIQUES

It is a simple method for lossless/near lossless image compression. This method divides an image into small blocks and chooses the optimal predictor among a set of predictors for each block based on the information from previously processed blocks. Two basic parts of predictive compression scheme are prediction of the current pixel from the information of the previously encoded pixels and coding of the prediction errors by using entropy coders such as Huffman coders or Arithmetic coders. There are prediction schemes that adapt the predictor and/or correct the prediction errors (bias cancellation) based on the information obtained from previously encoded pixels (context for error modeling). Most of the prediction techniques need a lot of context data for error modeling and need a lot of memory. General block diagram for the prediction based schemes is shown in Figures 1, where f is input pixel f' is predicted coefficients and e is error.

Figure 1. Block diagram of prediction-based encoder and decoder

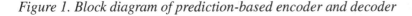
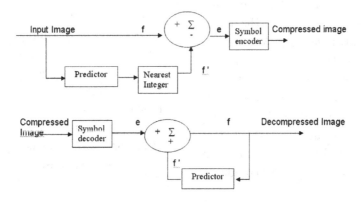

The popular lossless compression techniques under prediction based are 1.) DPCM, 2.) LOCO-I / JPEG-LS, 3.) CALIC and 4.) FELICS. In this section some of the prediction-based techniques are discussed.

Differential Pulse Code Modulation (DPCM)

In DPCM, predict the value of each pixel by using the values of its neighboring pixels, and then store only the prediction error. Typically, the errors are small; therefore fewer bits are required to store them. Depending on how many neighboring pixels are used, DPCM is classified as 1st order (1 pixel), 2nd order (2 pixels), 3rd order (3 pixels), and so forth. A prediction model that is often used for 3rd order DPCM is the following:

$$2^{\left\lfloor \log_2 (\max(image(x,y))) \right\rfloor} \tag{5}$$

In the above Equation, the values used for the coefficients r1 and r2 can vary, and usually they are image-dependent. A set of values that works well for many cases, and can simplify the calculations is $r1 = r2 = 1$. Usually, different regions in the same image have different optimal prediction coefficients. Adaptive prediction has been used which splits the image into blocks and then computes independently the prediction coefficients for each block. Netravali in (Netravali, 1980) presented a review of predictive coding techniques. In lossless prediction coding, the differential image has a greatly reduced variance compared to the original image, is significantly less correlated. The difference between lossy and lossless DPCM lies in the handing of the differential image. In order to lower the bit rate, the differential image in lossy DPCM is quantized prior to encoding and transmission.

Adaptive Differential Pulse Code Modulation, a form of Pulse Code Modulation (PCM) that produces a digital signal with a lower bit rate than standard PCM. ADPCM (Wong, 1995) produces a lower bit rate by recording only the difference between samples and adjusting the coding scale dynamically to accommodate large and small differences. In ADPCM quantization step size adapts to the current rate of change in the waveform, which is being compressed. The good side of the ADPCM method is minimal CPU load, but it has significant quantization noise. In old lossless JPEG algorithm, encoding is based on Differential Pulse Code Modulation (DPCM) followed by Huffman coding. The first lossless JPEG algorithm never gained much popularity because the compression rates achieved by this method can be only (3.5:1) (Wong, 1995). In JPEG-LS the low complexity context based lossless image compression is used and it is explained below.

Low Complexity Context Based Lossless Image Compression (LOCO-I)

Two basic parts of predictive compression scheme are modeling and coding. The main objective driving the design of LOCO-I is to systematically project the image modeling principles outlined in (Weinberger, 1996) and further developed in (Weinberger,1997), into a low complexity plane, both from a modeling and coding perspective. The LOCO algorithm combines good performance with efficient implementation, without arithmetic coding. It also allows for a near-lossless mode, where the compression level depends on the maximum reconstruction error specified. The LOCO algorithm employs nonlinear predictors with rudimentary edge detecting capability, and is based on a very simple context model, determined by quantized gradients. It has two modes: lossless and near-lossless. In lossless mode there is no information loss in the reconstructed image. In near-lossless mode, every sample value in a reconstructed image component is guaranteed to differ from the corresponding value in the original image by up to a preset (small) amount.

JPEG-LS is the basis for lossless/near-lossless compression standard for compressing continuous-tone, grayscale, or color digital still images. The standard is based on the LOCO-I algorithm (Low COmplexity LOssless COmpression for Images). JPEG-LS has a number of advantages over other standards (e.g., JPEG). First, it is capable of producing lossless compression, this is not just important but mandatory for Medical databases. Secondly, JPEG-LS include a near-lossless mode through which the maximal error in pixel value can be controlled, thereby limiting the maximal error in the reconstructed image. This is fundamental for applications such as teleconferencing. A major side effect of undertaking this standards activity was that some of the other contenders such as CALIC, FELICS, and Ricoh's CREW algorithm in particular had some very attractive features-for example, in the ability to provide a single code stream, which could provide lossy and lossless images without additional processing. Although outside the direct scope of JPEG-LS, these features and the discussions they provoked directly led to the development of the architectural approach of the JPEG2000 standard.

The research leading to the CALIC algorithm (Wu, 1996), conducted in parallel to the development of LOCO-I. CALIC avoids some of the optimizations performed in (Xiong, 1997), but by tuning the model more carefully to the image compression application, some compression gains are obtained. Yet, the improvement is not dramatic, even for the most complex version of the algorithm. The Context-based Adaptive Lossless Image Coding (CALIC) algorithm is explained in the next section.

Context-Based Adaptive Lossless Image Coding (CALIC)

In lossless JPEG standard and JPEG-LS a simple fixed linear predictor is used. The weakness of linear predictors is that their performance is not robust in the areas of edges. In fact a pitfall that optimal linear predictor in least squares sense actually led to higher entropy of prediction errors than some naive predictors. This conflict of least square prediction and entropy reduction was observed often on images of many sharp edges such as multimedia images in which texts, graphics and photographs are mixed. Whereas in CALIC, an adaptive non-linear predictors or gradient adjusted predictor is used. If edges exit, it can adjust its parameters according to the local edge strengths and orientations. The adjustment of predictor parameters can be made very efficient since it is based on local information. The CALIC algorithm was a strong candidate for consideration as lossless JPEG 2000 compression standard (Wu, 1996).

The context adaptive nonlinear predictor operates in either binary or continuous-tone modes, depending on the context of the current pixel. In the continuous-tone gradient adjusted prediction takes place and is further improved by error feedback, where prediction errors are modeled under different contexts, resulting in reduced conditional entropies. CALIC uses complex predictor and also it uses only few contexts. For coding, either Huffman or Arithmetic coding is used. CALIC performance is comparable to that of state of the art transform based compression techniques but it is too slow for most practical applications. In order to increase the speed a Fast, Efficient, Lossless Image Compression System (FELICS) is used in predictive scheme, and it is explained below.

Fast, Efficient, Lossless Image Compression System (FELICS)

The Fast, Efficient, Lossless Image Compression System (FELICS) (Howard, 1993) combines the prediction and error modeling steps by utilizing the two nearest neighbors of a pixel in a raster scan order to estimate the probability distribution of the pixel intensity. Based on a parameter estimation method, the most suitable error model is chosen from a set, and also the Rice code of the model is used to encode the intensity. The resulting compressor runs out of five times as fast as an implementation of the lossless mode of the JPEG 2000 standard while obtaining slightly better compression on many images. Compare to CALIC and LOCO-I, its compression ratio is slightly less but it is faster.

Most of the prediction techniques need a lot of context data for error modeling and need a lot of memory. In order to increase the compression ratio and execution speed transform based coding techniques are introduced. The state of the art transform based coding techniques are explained in the next section.

TRANSFORM BASED CODING TECHNIQUES

Transform based coding in which images are transferred into frequency or wavelet domain prior to modeling and coding. Block diagram of transform-based coder is shown in the Figure 2. Such a coder operates by transforming data to remove redundancy, then quantizing the transform coefficients, and finally entropy coding the quantizer output. The decoder side is the reverse of the coder side. Over the years, a variety of linear transforms have been developed which include Discrete Fourier Transform (DFT), Discrete Cosine Transform (DCT) (Ahmed, 1974), Discrete Wavelet Transform (DWT) (Vetterli, 1995), and many more, each with its own advantages and disadvantages.

An excellent analysis of DCT and related transforms and their applications can be found in Rao (1990). In 1992, JPEG established the first international standard for still image compression

where the encoders and decoders are DCT-based. The advantages of JPEG compression schemes based on DCT are simplicity, satisfactory performance, and availability of special purpose hardware for implementation. The disadvantage of this compression is this results in noticeable and annoying ``blocking artifacts'' particularly at low bit rates. Lapped Orthogonal Transforms (LOT) attempts to solve this problem by using smoothly overlapping blocks. Blocking effects are reduced in LOT compressed images, but the increased computational complexities of such algorithms do not justify wide replacement of DCT by LOT.

Over the past several years, the wavelet transform has gained widespread acceptance in image compression. Wavelets are outperforming traditional DCT compression, as used in the prevailing JPEG standard, for four main reasons.

1. They have non-uniform frequency spectra, which facilitate multiscale analysis.
2. The multiresolution (Mallat, 1989) property of the wavelet transform can be used to exploit the fact that the human eye's capacity to detect noise deteriorates at high and low frequencies. This is because most of the energy of wavelet-transformed data is concentrated in the low frequency region.
3. The DWT can be applied to an entire image without imposing a block structure as used by the DCT, so there is less distortion.
4. Compression strategies in the DWT domain produces better results than quantization in the DCT domain.

Wavelets have attracted a great deal of both academic and commercial interest because their

Figure 2. Block diagram of transform based coder

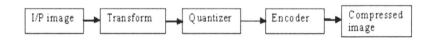

properties are simultaneously of theoretical and practical significance. The practical use of wavelets is demonstrated by their incorporation into the emerging JPEG2000 standard for image compression and the MPEG-4 video coding standard. JPEG2000 coding is given in Gonzalez and Wood (2011).The DWT is useful in image processing because it can simultaneously localize signals in time and scale, whereas the DFT or DCT localize only in the time or frequency.

Different families of wavelets exist, the most well known being the Haar and Daubechies wavelets. Two-dimensional DWT's and IDWT's are formed by successively applying one-dimensional transforms to the rows and columns of an image. In most cases, the wavelet transform produces floating-point coefficients and although this allows perfect reconstruction of the original image in theory, the use of finite-precision arithmetic, together with quantization, results in a lossy scheme. Recently, Integer wavelet transform, i.e. wavelet transforms that transform integer to integer have been introduced (Calderbank, 1998; Daubechies, 1996; Sweldens, 1996). In (Daubechies, 1996), it was shown that an integer version of every wavelet transform with finite filters could be obtained using the lifting scheme of (Sweldens, 1996). Lifting allows a wavelet transform to be computed quickly through a series of individual lifting steps and fully in place calculation. Integer wavelet transform is used to reduce the memory demands of the compression algorithm as integers are used instead of real numbers. More detailed information on lifting can be found in Calderbank (1998), Daubechies (1996), and Sweldens (1996). Various integer wavelet transforms found in the literature are (4,2) (6,2) (2,4) (2,2) (2,2+2) and S (Calderbank, 1998). Biorthogonal multiwavelets can be found in Yu Shen (2011).The image is decomposed by any one of the above-mentioned transforms. The decomposed images of various transforms are given in Figure 3.

Figure 3. Decomposed image of various transforms

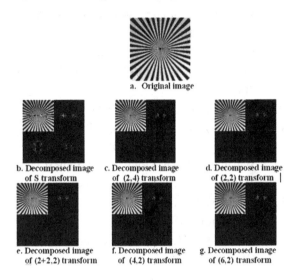

a. Original image

b. Decomposed image of S transform

c. Decomposed image of (2,4) transform

d. Decomposed image of (2,2) transform

e. Decomposed image of (2+2,2) transform

f. Decomposed image of (4,2) transform

g. Decomposed image of (6,2) transform

One of the most successful applications of wavelet methods is transform-based image compression. Because of the superior energy compaction properties of wavelet, wavelet compression methods have produced better results. The multiresolution nature of wavelet transform makes it ideal candidate for progressive transmission. Using lifting scheme the Reversible lossless integer wavelet transforms are developed. In this section for coding the transform coefficient the following state of the art Lossy to lossless compression techniques are going to be discussed. Now-a-days various algorithms are developed based on the following state of the art transform based compression techniques.

1. Embedded Zero tree Wavelet (EZW) (Shapiro, 1993).
2. Set-Partitioning In Hierarchical Trees (SPIHT) (Said, 1996).
3. Set Partitioned Embedded bloCK coder (SPECK) (Said, 2004).
4. Space Frequency Quantization (SFQ) (Xiong, 1997).
5. Compression with Reversible Embedded Wavelet (CREW) (Boliek, 1997).

6. Stack Run coding (Tsai, 1996).
7. Embedded Predictive Wavelet Image Coder (EPWIC) (Buccigrossi, 1997).
8. Embedded Block Coding with Optimized Truncation (EBCOT)/JPEG2000 (Taubman, 2000).
9. Hybrid Block Coder (HBC) (Wheeler, 2000).
10. Subband Block Hierarchical Partitioning (SBHP) (Chrysafis, 2000).
11. Wavelet Difference Reduction (WDR) (Tian, 1998).
12. Adaptively Scanned Wavelet Difference Reduction (ASWDR) (Walker, 2000).
13. Embedded Zero Block Coding (EZBC) (Wei-na Du, 2004).

Embedded Zero Tree Coding (EZW)

Shapiro (Shapiro, 1993) proposed a very clever method to combine bit-plane coding, applied to the wavelet coefficients, and with a tree based partitioning similar to the one developed by Lewis and Knowles. Shapiro's Embedded Zero tree Wavelet coding (EZW) (1993) as a simple and remarkably effective image compression algorithm, having the property that the bit streams are generated in order of importance, yielding a fully embedded code. Using an embedded coding algorithm, an encoder can terminate the encoding at any point thereby allowing a target rate or target distortion metric to be met exactly. In addition to producing a fully embedded bit stream, EZW consistently produces compression results that are competitive with other compression algorithms such as LOCO or CALIC on standard test images.

Shapiro (1993) states that, in a hierarchical subband system every coefficient at a given scale can be related to a set of coefficients at the next finer scale of similar orientation. The coefficients at the coarse scale are called the parent, and all coefficients corresponding to the same spatial location at the next finer scale of similar orientation are called children. Parent child relation and scanning order for subband encoding are given in Figure 4. Zerotree coding which provides a compact multiresolution representation of significance maps, which are binary maps indicating the positions of the significant coefficients. Zerotrees allow the successful prediction of insignificant coefficients across scales to be efficiently represented as part of exponentially growing trees. The zero tree is based on the hypothesis that if a wavelet coefficient at a coarse scale is insignificant with respect to a given threshold T, then all wavelet coefficients of the same spatial location at finer scales are surely to be insignificant with respect to T.

The EZW algorithm supports both lossy and lossless coding. The image compression and reconstruction addressed in this method involves the following steps.

Step 1: The given image is decomposed using Discrete wavelet transform.

Figure 4. Scanning order and parent–child relation

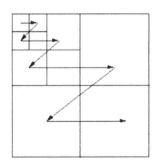
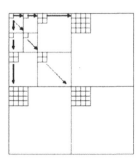

Step 2: An initial threshold value T is chosen based on the below equation

$$\begin{cases} 1, if \left| C_{i,j} \right| \geq T \\ \quad\quad (i,j) \in X \\ 0, else \end{cases} \tag{6}$$

The coefficient $C_{i,j} \in$ Image is significant if $| C_{i,j} | \geq$ Threshold. The significance set function is defined as

$$SG_n(T) = \begin{cases} 1, if \left| C_{i,j} \right| \geq T \\ \quad\quad (i,j) \in X \\ 0, else \end{cases} \tag{7}$$

The Morton (Zig-zag) scanning order is used to scan the transformed image from the lowest to the highest subbands.

Step 3: Two passes are used to encode the coefficients of significant map: i) Dominant and ii) Subordinate pass (refinement pass). During dominant pass, the coefficients are scanned in zig-zag order and the significant test using the threshold is performed. To encode the coefficients of significant map, the following four symbols are used in EZW:- a.) Zerotree root (Z), b.) Isolated zero(I), c.) Positive significant(P) and d.) Negative significant (N). If the coefficient value is greater than the threshold T, 'P' is transmitted to code bitstream. Character 'P' indicates that the pixel location has significant positive coefficient. If the coefficient is negative and if the magnitude of the coefficient value is greater than the threshold T, 'N' is transmitted to code bitstream. Character 'N' indicates that the location has significant negative coefficient. Isolated zero (I) means that the coefficient is insignificant but has some significant descendent. If the coefficient is insignificant and also all of its descendents

are insignificant with respect to T, 'Z' can be transmitted. The character 'Z' indicates that the pixel location is insignificant and also all its descendents are insignificant.

Dominant pass list provides a compact multiresolution representation of significance map indicating the positions of the significant coefficients. The subordinate list contains the magnitudes of those coefficients that have been found to be significant with respect to threshold T. All the significant coefficients in the dominant pass are refined by refinement pass. In refinement pass, each magnitude on the subordinate list has been encoded using a binary alphabet with a '1' symbol indicating that the value fall in the upper half of the interval meaing, [max_value (pixel), threshold+ ((max_value-threshold)/2)]. A binary alphabet with a '0' symbol indicates that the value fall in the lower half of the interval i.e. [threshold, threshold+ ((max_value-threshold)/2)].

Step 4: In EZW, the dominant pass symbols and subordinate pass symbols are encoded by the adaptive arithmetic coding technique. The compressed data is transmitted through the transmission line. In decoding, decompressed data is obtained by applying the arithmetic decoding procedure.

Step 5: In Inverse zerotree-decoding method, during dominant pass the symbols are passed in the same scanning order. So in dominant pass, it is easy to find the positions of the decoded symbols and decompress the wavelet coefficients of the significant map. The refinement pass, refines all the significant coefficients in the dominant pass.

Step 6: Threshold is decreased by half, and goes back to step 3, and the procedure is repeated until the required bit rate/compression ratio of the image is reached.

Step 7: Inverse Integer wavelet transform is applied to the decompressed data obtained in the previous step so that the original image be reconstructed.

The EZW algorithm produces excellent results without any pre-stored tables or codebooks, no training or no knowledge of the image source. A family of tree based wavelet coders such as EZW, SPIHT, SFQ and CREW, exploits the dependencies across subbands, and is explained in following sections. There are various modifications in EZW coding to improve its performance is found in Geetha (2004) and Ouafi (2008). Said and Pearlman introduced a popular variation of EZW, is called SPIHT which has achieved better compression and performance than EZW.

Set Partitioning in Hierarchical Trees (SPIHT) Coding

The SPIHT coder (Said, 1996; Walker 2001) is a highly refined version of the EZW algorithm and is a powerful image compression algorithm that produces an embedded bit stream from which some of the best results—highest PSNR values for given compression ratios—for a wide variety of images have been obtained with SPIHT. In SPIHT, the coefficients of the wavelet transform are grouped into spatial orientation trees that are, linked according to spatial orientation in subbands across scales. One of the main features of the SPIHT algorithm is that the ordering data is not explicitly transmitted. Instead, it is based on the scanning order and the results of magnitude comparisons. So, if the encoder and decoder have the same sorting algorithm, then the decoder can duplicate the encoder's execution path if it receives the results of the magnitude comparisons, and the ordering information can be recovered from the execution path. The transmitted code or compressed image file is completely embedded, so that a single file for an image at a given rate can be truncated at various points and decoded to give a serious of reconstructed images at various rates.

Said (1996) states that, normally, most of the image's energy is concentrated in the low frequency components. Consequently, the variance decreases as one move from the highest to the lowest of the subband pyramid. Furthermore, it has been observed that there is a spatial self-similarity between subbands, and the coefficients are expected to be better magnitude-ordered as one move downward in the pyramid following the same spatial orientation. A tree structure, called spatial orientation tree, naturally defines the spatial relationship on the hierarchical pyramid. Figure 4 shows how the spatial orientation tree is defined in a pyramid constructed with recursive four-band splitting. Each node of the tree corresponds to a pixel, and is identified by the pixel coordinate. Its direct descendants correspond to the pixels of the same spatial orientation in the next finer level of the pyramid. The tree is defined in such a way that each node has either no child or four children's, which always form a group of 2x2 adjacent pixels. The pixels in the highest level of the pyramid are the tree roots and are also grouped in 2x2 adjacent pixels.

For the implementation of the algorithm, the following three lists are used: List of Insignificant Sets (LIS), List of Insignificant Pixels (LIP) and List of Significant Pixels (LSP). Two passes are needed to encode the coefficients of significant map: Sorting pass and Refinement pass. The SPIHT coding algorithm is given below.

The outline of the full coding algorithm is as follows:

1. **Initialization:** Output
   $n = \lfloor \log_2 (\text{image}_{(i,j)} | c_{i,j}|) \rfloor$, where $c_{i,j}$ is the coefficient value in location i,j.

Set the list of significant points (LSP) as empty. Set the roots of similarity trees in the lists of insignificant points (LIP) and insignificant sets (LIS). Actually, an algorithm which simply selects the coefficients such that $2^n < |C_{i,j}| \leq 2^{n+1}$, with

n decremented in each pass. Given n, if $\left| C_{i,j} \right| \geq 2^n$ then the coefficient is said to be significant; otherwise it is called insignificant.

2. **Sorting Pass:** Using the set partitioning algorithm distribute the appropriate indices of the coefficients to the LIP, LIS, and LSP. The sorting algorithm divides the sets of pixels into partitioning subsets Tm and performs the magnitude test. If the decoder receives a "0", that is the subset is insignificant, then it knows that all coefficients in Tm are insignificant. If it receives is "1", that is the subset is significant, then a certain rule shared by the decoder and encoder is used to partition Tm into new subsets and the significance test is then applied to the new subsets. This set division process continues until the magnitude test is done to all single coordinate significant subsets in order to identify each significant coefficient. To reduce the number of magnitude comparisons, a set partitioning rule that uses the following strategy: To create new partitions such that subsets expected to be insignificant contain a large number of elements, and subsets expected to be significant contain only one element.

3. **Refinement Pass:** For each entry in the LSP significant for higher n, send the nth most significant bit to the decoder.

4. Decrement n by one and return to step 2 until the specified bit rate is reached.

Similar to EZW, with this algorithm the rate can be precisely controlled because the transmitted information is formed of single bits. The encoder can estimate the progressive distortion reduction and stop at a desired distortion value. In SPIHT, all branching conditions based on the significance data S_n, which can be calculated with the knowledge of image coefficient $C_{i,j}$ are output by the encoder. The ordering information is recovered when the coordinates of the significant coefficients are added to the end of the LSP, that is, the coefficients pointed by the coordinates in the LSP are sorted. But whenever the decoder inputs data, its three control lists (LIS, LIP, and LSP) are identical to the ones used by the encoder at the moment it outputs that data, which means that the decoder indeed recovers the ordering from the execution path.

From the experimental results, it can be seen that the compression ratio increase, when the levels of decomposition is increased. This is because, when the levels of decomposition are increased, coefficients with higher magnitude concentrate mostly on the root levels. Also most of the coefficients will have low magnitudes. These coefficients require only less number of bits to be transmitted. Hence the compression ratio will increase when the decomposition level is increased. But the resolution of the reconstructed image will reduce for higher decomposition levels. The PSNR value in a higher level of decomposed image is increased, when the number of iteration or passes is increased in the coding technique.

Efficiency of the algorithm can be improved by entropy coding its output, but at the expense of a larger coding/decoding time. There are various modified SPIHT coding techniques are developed to improve its performance is found in (Geetha, 2006; Geetha, 2007; Ouafi, 2008). The need for reducing the number of lists used in this scheme and also to increase the compression ratio, led to the forming of the next algorithm, called SPECK.

Set Partitioned Embedded Block Coder (SPECK)

The image-coding scheme SPECK (Said, 2004) is different from some of the above-mentioned schemes in that it does not use trees, which span and exploit the similarity, across different subbands; rather, it makes use of sets in the form of blocks. The main idea is to exploit the clustering of energy in frequency and space in hierarchical structures of transformed images. The SPECK algorithm (Said, 2004) belongs to the class of scalar quantized significance testing schemes. It has its roots primarily in the ideas developed in the SPIHT, and few block coding image coding algorithms.

The SPECK encoding algorithm can directly replace the JPEG-2000 entropy coding of the wavelet subband subblocks. Consider an image *X,* which has been adequately transformed using a discrete wavelet transform. The transformed image is said to exhibit a hierarchical pyramidal structure defined by the levels of decomposition, with the top most level being the root. The finest pixels lie at the bottom level of the pyramid while the coarsest pixels lie at the top level.

In SPECK, two linked lists-List of Insignificant Sets (LIS) and List of Significant Pixels (LSP) are maintained. LIS contains sets of type S of varying sizes, which have not yet been found significant against threshold T. LSP contains pixels, which are found to be significant against threshold T. After finding the threshold value, the image X is processed using SPECK algorithm considering rectangular regions of image. The regions or sets referred to as sets of type S, can be of varying dimensions. The other type of sets used in the SPECK algorithm is referred to as sets of type I. These 2 sets (type S and type I) are obtained by applying the 3 set splitting rules on the image. Using first rule the given image X is divided into 2 sets. One is type S and other is type I. These sets are obtained by chopping off a small square block (2x2) from the top left portion of the image and this is called as set S and stored in the list LIS. The remaining region in the image is known as sets of type I and stored in the list LIS. First apply the significance test for coefficients. If the set S is significant, contains one or more significant values then the set is further partitioned into four of equal size using quad-tree partitioning (i.e. rule 2.) Each of these offspring sets O (S) is tested for significance for same T and, if significant, it is further partitioned once more and the procedure is repeated recursively until all the sets are processed. If all the coefficients happen

to be insignificant no further splitting is required and the set stays in the LIS.

The set/block I is processed next, by testing it against the same threshold T. If it is found to be significant then it is partitioned by another partitioning scheme-the octave band partitioning (i.e. set splitting rule 3.) Set I is partitioned into four sets-three sets of type S and one of type I. The size of each of these three S type sets is the same as that of the chopped portion of X. The new set I that is formed by this partitioning process is now reduced in size. A set I is always partitioned into S sets in a prescribed way, so as to progress through the transformed image from coarser to finer resolution subbands. The binary result of every significant test is sent to the code bitstream. Then the bit plane order n is decremented by 1 and the sets in the LIS are tested from top to bottom (smallest to largest) in the same way as before, finding pixels significant for n - 1 and moving them to the end of the LSP and finding pixels and sets insignificant for n-1 and putting their identifiers at the bottom of the LIS. The outcome of every test, '1' or '0', is put into the code bit stream. When a single pixel is found significant, a '1' and a sign bit are put into the bit stream. Also, once the LSP is complete for n - 1, the n -1 bits of all coefficients in the LSP found significant at all higher thresholds (the refinement bits) are put into the bitstream. The bit plane order n continues to be decremented until the required bit rate has been satisfied.

Without further entropy coding this method is still efficient. The decoder uses the same mechanism as the encoder. It receives significance test results from the coded bit stream and builds up the same list structure during the execution of the algorithm. Hence, it is able to follow the same execution paths for the significance tests of the different sets, and reconstructs the image progressively as the algorithm proceeds. From the experimental results, it can be seen that SPECK gives higher compression ratios compared to other EZW and SPIHT. However, the significance bits for four quadrants produced by recursive splitting can be Huffman or arithmetic coded to obtain a small improvement in efficiency.

So when entropy coding is enacted in SPECK, it is far simpler than that of JPEG-2000. The SPECK calculations for coding are just finding highest order bits in a set, which can be implemented by a bitwise OR of all its coefficients. So nothing more complicated than bitwise operations is needed for SPECK coding.

Space Frequency Quantization for Wavelet Image Coding

Space Frequency Quantization (SFQ) (Xiong, 1997) is an image coding algorithm coupling standard scalar quantization of frequency coefficients with tree-structured quantization. Despite the basic form of the two quantizers considered, the resulting algorithm often outperforms EZW algorithm. A variety of more complex coding algorithms have been proposed that are based on models of block interdependence, composite source models, image segmentation models, etc. Contrasting with the early coders, SFQ exploits both the frequency and spatial compaction property of the wavelet transform through the use of two simple quantization methods- Zerotree quantization and scalar quantization. The wavelet coefficients from the wavelet transform are sent to zerotree quantization. The non-zeroed coefficients are scalar quantized. Compared to EZW in SFQ instead of subordinate pass scalar quantization is used. The main advantage of going to scalar quantization rather than subordinate pass is that, the user can reduce the step size for better refinement.

Integration of zerotree quantization and scalar quantization yields better performance than using them separately. Scalar quantization done after each dominant pass of EZW coder enhances the refinement to a greater extent. Experimental results showed that the SFQ coder performance is slightly better (0.2 dB to 0.8 dB) than SPIHT on standard test images at various compression rates,

but the method is very complex, since it tries to jointly optimize the actual rate-distortion trade in the quantization and construction of zerotrees. SPIHT with arithmetic coding outperforms SFQ. The popular wavelet based image coder CREW is also based on EZW algorithm and it is explained in the following subsection(s).

Compression with Reversible Embedded Wavelet (CREW)

Compression with Reversible Embedded Wavelets (CREW) (Boliek, 1997) is a unified lossless and lossy continuous-tone still image compression developed at the RICOH California Research Center in Menlo Park, California. It is wavelet based using a "reversible" approximation of one of the best wavelet filters. For coding of coefficient, CREW uses a method similar to Shapiro's Zero tree coding, and Horizon coding. Horizon coding is a context based coding takes the advantage of spatial and spectral information available in the wavelet domain. It uses wavelet transform technology and also It is pyramidal (similar to hierarchical) and progressive by nature. CREW was the stimulus for a JPEG 2000 standard.

The features make CREW an ideal choice for applications that require high quality and flexibility for multiple input and output environments, such as, medical imagery, fixed-rate and fixed-size applications (ATM, frame store, etc.), pre-press images, continuous-tone facsimile documents, World Wide Web image or graphic type, satellite images. Three technologies are combined in CREW, they are:

1. **The Reversible Wavelet Transforms:** Nonlinear filters that have exact reconstruction implemented in minimal integer arithmetic.
2. **The Embedded Code Stream:** A method of implying quantization in the code stream.
3. **High-Speed:** High-compression binary entropy coder.

The same CREW code stream can be used for both lossless and lossy applications due to embedded quantization. The wavelet transform produces pyramidally ordered data and a natural means for interpolation. The bit-significance coding allows for bitplane progressive transmission. CREW performs better than EZW. Furthermore, CREW compression is idempotent and CREW encoding and decoding can be simply and efficiently implemented in either hardware or software. All of these features combine to make a flexible "device-independent" compression system.

Stack-Run (SR)

Stack-run coding is an alternative to zero-trees which maintains independence between subbands. Stack Run image coding (SR) representation of (Tsai, 1996) partitions the quantized transform coefficients into two groups containing zero valued and nonzero valued, referred to as significant coefficients. In stack-run coding, where run-lengths of zeros and quantized values are mapped into a four-letter alphabet code which is then further entropy-coded with an arithmetic code. The efficiency of this algorithm depends on the presence of runs of zeroes, so requires a transform such as DCT or wavelet prior to quantization. This algorithm works by raster scanning within subbands.

SR is relatively simple and does not need to maintain any list of coefficients, as is the case with EZW (Shapiro, 1993) and SPIHT (Said, 1996). Despite its simplicity this algorithm is competitive with best enhancements of zero tree coding. Its overall complexity is about the same or perhaps slightly larger than SPIHT, due to its heavy reliance on adaptive arithmetic coding, and its performance is slightly inferior in tests on standard test images at rates of 0.25 and 0.50 bpp. The comparison will probably not stand up at higher rates, as shorter runs of zeroes occur more frequently and the entropy of these runs increase. Also stack-run coding does not deliver an embedded bit stream.

Embedded Predictive Wavelet Image Coder (EPWIC)

EPWIC (Buccigrossi, 1997; Buccigrossi, 1999) is an embedded image coder based on a statistical characterization of natural images in the wavelet transform domain. The joint distribution between pairs of coefficients at adjacent spatial locations, orientations, and scales are defined. Although the raw coefficients are nearly, uncorrelated, their magnitudes are highly correlated. A linear magnitude predictor coupled with both multiplicative and additive uncertainties, provides a reasonable description of the conditional probability densities. In EPWIC, subband coefficients are encoded one bit-plane at a time using a non-adaptive arithmetic encoder. Bit-planes are ordered using an algorithm that considers the MSE reduction per encoded bit. The overall ordering of bit-planes is determined by the ratio of their encoded variance to compressed size. The coder is inherently embedded, and should prove useful in applications requiring progressive transmission. EPWIC surpasses EZW at nearly all compression levels, and approaches the encoding capability of SPIHT at the higher compression rates. EPWIC outperforms EZW by 0.5 dB at 1 kB, and nearly 1.5 dB at 16 kB and above. EZW would have a transmission time roughly 15% higher than EPWIC for an image quality of 26 dB.

Embedded Block Coding with Optimized Truncation (EBCOT) Coding

The method of entropy coding of the subblocks is called Embedded Block Coding with Optimized Truncation (EBCOT) (Taubman, 2000). Prior to entropy coding, the image is transformed into subbands by a wavelet (or wavelet packet) decomposition. The subbands are then subdivided into as many subblocks, nominally of dimensions 64x64 or 32x32, as possible. Generally there will be partial-size subblocks for subband dimensions not divisible by 32 or 64 or smaller than 32 or 64.

They will be treated similarly to the square sub-blocks with the appropriate modifications. Entropy coding is progresses from lowest to highest scale among subbands and in raster order within subbands. Every subblock is encoded independently via context-based bit plane arithmetic coding. The wavelet coefficients are first finely quantized to a sign and magnitude representation of the bin indices. Encoding of the binary expansion of the bin index magnitudes starts from the highest order non-all-zero bit plane in each subblock and proceeds in order through the lower bit planes until the target bit budget is reached for the subblock. Three passes through each bit plane are made together contexts of bits in three categories for adaptive arithmetic coding. There is also passage through the sign plane for context-based adaptive arithmetic coding prior to the magnitude passes.

The decoder must be informed of the number of leading all-zero bit planes for each subblock. The array of such numbers, one for each subblock, is encoded by a quadtree technique and sent as overhead information. In order to encode the image to a given target bit rate, the encoding algorithm calculates, for each subblock, several actual points of the rate-distortion curve and uses them to assign the optimal number of bits to each subblock. This requires encoding each subblock to a high rate, usually 3 bits per pixel, and truncating each subblock's bit stream to the point determined by the rate assignment calculation. One can determine a set of optimal truncation points for each subblock corresponding to a set of target bit rates. Once the subblock bitstreams have been truncated for a certain target rate, they are merged and interleaved by common order bit planes to form an embedded composite bit stream. Note that for efficient implementation without disk swapping, the bitstreams of all subblocks must be held in memory to achieve this embedded compressed bit stream. The emerging JPEG-2000 still image compression standard uses a memory-saving line-based wavelet transform and bit plane entropy coding of subblocks of wavelet subbands (EBCOT).

Hybrid Block Coder (HBC)

A low-memory cache efficient Hybrid Block Coder (HBC) (Wheeler, 2000) for images in which, an image subband decomposition is partitioned into a combination of spatial blocks and subband blocks, which are independently coded. Spatial blocks contain hierarchical trees spanning subband levels, and are each encoded using the SPIHT algorithm. Subband blocks contain a block of coefficients from within a single subband, and are each encoded by the SPECK algorithm. The decomposition may have the dyadic or a wavelet packet structure. Rate is allocated amongst the sub-bitstreams produced for each block and they are packetized. The partitioning structure supports resolution embedding. The final bitstream may be progressive in fidelity or in resolution.

In previous reports, SPIHT (Said, 1996) was generally superior to SPECK (Said, 2004) considering rate vs. distortion performance. However, SPECK has been found to be most competitive in images with elevated high spatial frequency energy, such as the Barbara image. Hybrid Block Coder (HBC) is attempting to capitalize on this difference. HBC applies tree-based SPIHT to low-frequency bands and block based SPECK to high-frequency bands. From the results, the performance of subband block SPECK is better than spatial block SPIHT for all images and all rates. The results for HBC fall close to, but slightly below the SPECK results.

Subband-Block Hierarchical Partitioning (SBHP) Coder

SBHP (Chrysafis, 2000) coder is a low-complexity entropy coder, originally designed to work in the JPEG2000 image compression standard framework. The algorithm is meant for embedded and non-embedded coding of wavelet coefficients inside a subband. SBHP is a SPECK variant implemented in the JPEG2000 platform. SPECK was incorporated into the JPEG2000 coding framework, where a simple command line switch initiated the SPECK coding engine in place of EBCOT (Taubman 2000). This implementation was named Subband Hierarchical Block Partitioning (SBHP). SBHP used a very simple fixed Huffman code of 15 symbols for encoding the significance map bits sent by the SPECK algorithm. As with SPECK, the other types of bits, the magnitude refinement and sign bits, were not further encoded.

Chrysafis (2000) states that, from a functional point of view, SBHP does exactly the same tasks executed by the entropy coding routines used on the JPEG 2000 Verification Model (VM). In consequence, every single feature and mode of operation supported by the VM continues to be available with SBHP. Like EBCOT and other encoders, SBHP is applied to blocks of wavelet coefficients extracted from inside subbands. It produces a fully embedded bit stream that is suitable for several forms of progressive transmission, and for one-pass rate control. Except for the fact that it does not use the arithmetic encoder, it does not require any change in any of the VM functions outside entropy coding. The SBHP performance was measured after its integration into VM 4.2. From the reports, it was found that the SBHP encoder runs about 4 times faster, and the decoder is about 6 to 8 times faster, depending on the platform. SBHP yield a significant reduction in the complexity of entropy coding, with a small loss in compression performance. Furthermore, it is able to support all JPEG2000 features.

Wavelet Difference Reduction (WDR)

One of the defects of SPIHT is that it only implicitly locates the position of significant coefficients. This makes it difficult to perform operations, which depend on the position of significant transform values, such as region selection on compressed data. This method produces an embedded bit stream with region-of-interest capability. Region selection or Region Of Interest (ROI), means a portion of a compressed image that requires increased resolution. For example, with a portion of a low-resolution medical image that has been

sent at a low bpp rate in order to arrive quickly. Such compressed data operations are possible with the WDR algorithm of (Tian & Wells, 1998). The term difference reduction refers to the way in which WDR encodes the locations of significant wavelet transform values.

Although WDR will not produce higher PSNR values than SPIHT, as observed from experiment reports, it can produce perceptually superior images, especially at high compression rates. The only difference between WDR and bit-plane encoding is the significant pass. In WDR, the output from the significance pass consists of the signs of significant values along with sequences of bits, which concisely describe the precise locations of significant values. In order to improve the rate-distortion performance of WDR led to the forming of the next algorithm called Adaptively Scanned Wavelet Difference Reduction is explained below.

Adaptively Scanned Wavelet Difference Reduction (ASWDR)

While WDR (Tian, 1998) employs a fixed order on scanning of the coefficients in a wavelet pyramid, the ASWDR (Walker, 2000, 2001) employs an adaptive scanning order in order to predict locations of significant transform values at half thresholds. These methods retain all of the important features of WDR: low-complexity, region of interest, embeddedness, and progressive SNR. They improve the rate-distortion performance of WDR so that it is essentially equal to that of the SPIHT algorithm of Said and Pearlman (1996). When arithmetic compression is not employed. When arithmetic compression is used, then the rate-distortion performance of the ASWDR algorithms is only slightly worse than SPIHT. The perceptual quality of ASWDR images is clearly superior to SPIHT.

Embedded Zero Block Coding (EZBC)

A higher complexity variant of SPECK, called EZBC (Embedded Zero Block Coding), was reported by Hsiang and Woods in 2000. EZBC uses the SPECK algorithm to produce the significance map, magnitude refinement and sign bits, but then uses the context-based adaptive, arithmetic coding of EBCOT to encode all these kinds of bits. EZBC outperformed SPECK, on the average over several natural images and rates up to 1.0 bit per pixel by about 0.45 dB, because of this additional encoding. In fact, it also outperformed JPEG2000 Verification Model (VM 3.1A) in most cases. Although higher in complexity than basic SPECK, EZBC is still somewhat lower in complexity than JPEG2000, because at each threshold it only needs to pass through coefficients that have previously become significant. The JPEG2000 coder requires passage through all coefficients at each threshold.

OTHER COMPRESSION TECHNIQUES

Fractal Compression

The application of fractals in image compression started with Barnsley and Jacquin (1988). Fractal image compression is a process to find a small set of mathematical equations that can describe the image. By sending the parameters of these equations to the decoder, reconstruct the original image. In general, the theory of fractal compression is based on the contraction mapping theorem in the mathematics of metric spaces. The Partitioned Iterated Function System (PIFS), which is essentially a set of contraction mappings, is formed by analyzing the image. Those mappings can exploit the redundancy that is commonly present in most images. This redundancy is related to the similarity of an image with itself, that is, part *A* of a certain image is similar to another part *B* of the image,

by doing an arbitrary number of contractive transformations that can bring *A* and *B* together. These contractive transformations are actually common geometrical operations such as rotation, scaling, skewing and shifting. By applying the resulting PIFS on an initially blank image iteratively, it can completely regenerate the original image at the decoder. Since the PIFS often consists of a small number of parameters, a huge compression ratio (e.g. 500 to 1000 times) can be achieved by representing the original image using these parameters. However, fractal image compression has its disadvantages. Because fractal image compression usually involves a large amount of matching and geometric operations, it is time consuming. Zhao Xiu-Ying and Zhai Lin-Pei (2005) states that Wavelet-fractal based compression is used to improve the real-time performance of the fractal coding algorithm.

This section will give an idea of how the existing recent compression techniques work and its results. The next section gives an idea for the researchers to increase the compression ratio and at the same time maintain the PSNR level compared to the existing techniques for gray scale medical images.

MAIN FOCUS OF THIS CHAPTER

Issues, Controversies, Problems

In this chapter the various commonly used image compression techniques are put into four categories and discussed. Extensive experiments and survey were conducted for the existing standard compression techniques. From the results the Ad hoc schemes such as Run length encoding, Arithmetic coding and Huffman coding techniques achieve a maximum average compression ratio of 2:1 to 3:1. The performance of such methods is insufficient for dealing with the storage requirements of imaging systems, partly due to the fact that they are 1D algorithms that treat the data as being a bit stream and are unable to take advantage of spatial correlation of image data in 2D or 3D. However, the advantage of ad hoc scheme is that the raw data can be reconstructed for use without any change in the original data. Schemes that take advantage of spatial correlation include bit-plane processing and predictive coding.

The second category is dictionary based lossless compression algorithms, they are commonly found in text compression. The compression performance of this algorithm is poor. The maximum compression ratio achieved by this method is 2.5:1. The dictionary schemes such as GZIP (CR=2.38) performed poorly for a set of images. The third category is prediction- based lossy/lossless coding technique. In this category we observed that CALIC algorithm performed consistently well for all the images. JPEG-LS/LOCO technique performed equally well (3.81), almost as well as CALIC (3.91). Both out-performed existing JPEG (3.04 with optimum predictor choice per image). LOCO-I/JPEG-LS uses similar principles to CALIC, but requires only one pass through the image. CALIC uses complex predictor and the coding step may involve either Huffman or arithmetic coding. CALIC gives high compression in a reasonable time, whereas JPEG-LS is nearly as effective and very fast. For example, an images of size 512 x 512 with 16 bits word size the average compression and decompression times for CALIC were 3.25 and 4.51 seconds respectively, compared with 0.85 and 0.92 seconds for JPEGLS, and 1.91 and 1.62 seconds for lossless JPEG.

LOCO-I differs significantly from FELICS in that it follows a more traditional predictor-modeler-coder structure. Compared to CALIC and LOCO-I, FELICS compression ratio is slightly less but it is faster. FELICS running about five times as fast as JPEG Lossless. Most of the prediction techniques need a lot of context data for error modeling and need a lot of memory. CALIC performance is comparable to that of state of the art transform based compression techniques but it is too slow for most practical applications. In

order to increase the compression ratio and execution speed transform based coding techniques are introduced.

The fourth category is state of the art transform based coding techniques. For still image compression, the DCT based Joint Photographic Experts Group' or JPEG standard has been established by ISO (International Standards Organization) and IEC (International Electro-Technical Commission). The performance of these coders generally degrades at low bit-rates mainly because of the underlying block-based Discrete Cosine Transform (DCT) (Xiong, 1996) scheme. Nowadays the wavelet transform has emerged as a cutting edge technology, within the field of image compression. The advantage of wavelet-based techniques is the ability to achieve an embedded bit stream. So based on the application, the user can fix the desired bit rate.

Some of the wavelet transform based lossy to lossless coding techniques found in the literature are discussed in the previous section. Among the different compression techniques wavelet based coding outperforms the others in image compression. From the experimental results, the higher complexity variant of SPECK called EZBC is the best showing the lowest rate on set of images. EZBC uses the SPECK algorithm to produce the significant map, magnitude refinement and sign bits, but then uses the context-based adaptive, arithmetic coding of EBCOT to encode all these kinds of bits. Referring to (Said, 2004), average over all rates (0.125, 0.25, 05, 1.0, 2.0bpp) for a set of images, EZBC outperforms JPEG2000 by 0.25 dB, while JPEG 2000 outperforms SPIHT and SPECK by 0.1 dB and 0.18 dB respectively. SPECK outperforms SBHP by 0.2 dB. The rate-distortion performance of the WDR is slightly worse than SPIHT and the rate-distortion performance of the ASWDR algorithms is equal to SPIHT. SPIHT-AC outperforms WDR and AS-WDR by 0.43 dB and 0.26dB respectively. WDR outperforms EZW by 0.32 dB. The results for HBC fall close to, but slightly below the SPECK results. The rate-distortion performance of the EZW, CREW and EPWIC algorithms are slightly worse than SPIHT and SPECK. EPWIC surpasses EZW at nearly all compression levels, and approaches the encoding capability of SPIHT at the higher compression rates. SFQ coder performance is slightly better (0.2dB to 0.8dB) than SPIHT on standard test images at various compression rates, but the method is very complex. CREW outperforms EZW and EPWIC by 0.3dB and 0.2dB respectively. SR performance is slightly inferior in tests on standard images compared to SPIHT.

Considering the complexity, JPEG2000 is not as efficient as SPECK or SPIHT and is only more efficient than SBHP, for lossless coding. EZBC is higher in complexity than SPECK and SPIHT, but lower in complexity than JPEG2000, because at each threshold it only needs to pass through coefficients that have previously become significant. The JPEG2000 coder requires passage through all coefficients at each threshold. The application will dictate whether the increase in coding performance is worth for the added complexity. SPECK and SPIHT algorithms have given excellent coding performance with very low computational complexity compared to other techniques such as SFQ, CREW, EPWIC, WDR and ASWDR. Execution time of SPIHT-AC for a set of images is 0.325s. Almost all the wavelet transform based coding techniques takes only 0.32s to 0.52 seconds to execute. Wavelet transform based coding techniques takes less time to execute than prediction based techniques.

Medical image applications require still higher compression for good quality images. So the required coding approaches should have an optimal PSNR with reduced complexity and also should reduce the storage requirements. In order to improve the performance of the lossy to lossless compression techniques I have proposed few algorithms which produce better compression ratio and good quality of reconstructed images comparable with that of the conventional approaches. Proposed algorithms are given next.

Solutions and Recommendations

All the conventional wavelet based image compression techniques mentioned above concentrate on how to minimize the number of bits needed to represent the insignificant coefficients. The proposed techniques given below not only minimize the number of bits needed to represent insignificant coefficient but also efficiently minimize the bits needed to represent the significant coefficients. So I have analyzed various conventional lossy to lossless compression approaches and necessary modifications are proposed to further increase the compression ratios and maintaining the PSNR close to 30dB with less computational complexity.

Based on the above concepts two methods were proposed and they are:

1. Embedded Significant and Zero Set Coding in Hierarchical Trees (ESZSCHT).
2. Embedded Set Partitioning Significant and Zero Block Coding (ESPSZBC).

THE PROPOSED FAST EMBEDDED SIGNIFICANT AND ZERO SET CODING IN HIERARCHICAL

Trees (ESZSCHT) Algorithm for Medical Image Compression

Tree based Set partitioning techniques for coding bit planes of image subband decompositions have received much attention recently. In a hierarchical tree based subband system, every coefficient at a given scale can be related to a set of coefficients at the next finer scale of similar orientation. The two fundamental techniques for tree based set partitioning are EZW (Shapiro, 1993) and SPIHT (Said, 1996). These tree-based algorithms are designed to exploit the correlation of coefficient magnitudes that occur across bands of decomposition. The proposed Embedded Significant and Zero Set Coding in Hierarchical Trees (ESZSCHT) algorithm is one such set partitioning technique and it is rooted from SPIHT. Block diagram of the proposed compression technique is shown in Figure 5.

The proposed compression system is based on reversible integer wavelet transform, Embedded Significant and Zero Set Coding in Hierarchical Trees (ESZSCHT) algorithm and arithmetic coding. The use of the lifting scheme allows the generation of truly lossless integer-to-integer wavelet transforms. Images are compressed/decompressed by the proposed ESZSCHT algorithm. The compression ratio of the proposed coding method is further increased by arithmetic coding technique.

After analyzing the decomposition results of various transforms, normally most of the image's energy is concentrated in the low frequency components. Consequently, the variance decreases as one move from the highest to the lowest of the subband pyramid. Furthermore, it has been observed that there is a spatial self similarity between subbands, and the coefficients are expected to be better magnitude-ordered as one move downward in the pyramid following the same spatial orientation. A tree structure, called spatial orientation tree, naturally defines the spatial relationship on the hierarchical pyramid as shown in Figure 4. In ESZSCHT, the coefficients of the wavelet transform are grouped into spatial orientation trees (i.e. linked according to spatial orientation in subbands across scales). The objective of this approach is to create new partitions such that subsets expected to be insignificant contain a large number of ele-

ments in HL,LH and HH subbands, and subsets expected to be significant contain large number of elements in LL subband.

In SPIHT, during encoding, each coefficient's significance is checked and if significant, the coefficients sign is checked for transmission. Whereas in proposed ESZSCHT, for coding coefficients in the LL subband, each set (i.e. it is having four pixels) as a whole is considered for significance test. In other subbands, during encoding each coefficient's significance is checked and if significant, the coefficient's sign is checked for transmission. Both the compression methods need to visit all the coefficients, so its complexity is propositional to the number of pixels or coefficients. Most of the coefficients in LL subband are found to be significant and positive, so only a single bit is needed to code the entire set in proposed ESZSCHT. So the compression ratio is increased extensively in ESZSCHT algorithm but the computational complexity and PSNR ratio is maintained to the same level of SPIHT algorithm.

One of the main features of the tree-based algorithm is that the ordering data is not explicitly transmitted. Instead, it is based on the fact that the execution path of the algorithm depends on significance test result. So, if the encoder and decoder have the same sorting algorithm, then the decoder can duplicate the encoder's execution path if it receives the results of the magnitude comparisons. And if the same scanning method is applied, the execution path can be recovered. The transmitted code or compressed image file is completely embedded, so that a single file for an

Figure 5. Block diagram of the proposed compression technique

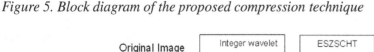

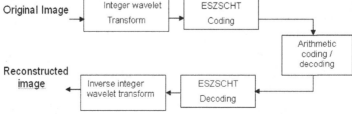

image at a given rate can be truncated at various points and decoded to give a series of reconstructed images at lower rates. For lossless application, the rate should be low and for lossy application such as telebrowsing, the compression rate is high, and using this lossy to lossless approach the user can fix the compression rate. The PSNR ratio of both SPIHT and the proposed ESZSCHT are same but the average increase in compression ratio ranges from 2 to 4 in proposed ESZSCHT. The maximum compression ratio achieved in the proposed approach is 19 for good quality images (PSNR=30 dB). At various compression ratios, the proposed ESZSCHT has given better results (i.e. PSNR is increased by a factor of 0.5dB to 6dB) than the conventional SPIHT. In order to increase the compression ratio further, an Embedded Set Partitioning Significant and Zero Block Coding (ESPSZBC) was proposed and it is explained in Geetha (2008).

The proposed compression techniques are implemented and tested using the database of Computed Tomography (CT) and Magnetic Resonance (MR) images [33, 34] and results are compared with conventional approaches. From the results it is found that the proposed coders are competitive

with other state of the coders such as EZW, SPIHT, SPECK, JPEG2000, and EZBC on compression performance and also computational complexity for standard test images. The proposed algorithms are applied to various images after applying the 1st, 2nd and 3rd level of decomposition of (2,4) integer wavelet transform. The results obtained after 3rd iteration in various coding techniques are given in Table 1.

The execution time of conventional and proposed compression/decompression algorithm at various compression ratios is shown in Table 2. The results indicate that the proposed coder execution time is comparable with the conventional techniques, although such comparisons strongly depend on the underlying machine, processor, bus and cache. From the results, at various compression ratios for a set of images the proposed techniques encoding time or decoding time is lesser than the conventional techniques, and also for all images there is a significant improvement in image quality. The results show that the proposed wavelet methods for coding medical datasets perform favorably for both lossy and lossless compression. They are also very competitive with other state-of-the-art compression techniques and

Table 1. Comparison of proposed approaches with existing standard compression techniques after 1st, 2nd and 3rd level of decomposition of (2,4) transform and the results obtained after 3rd iteration in various coding techniques

Gray scale ImagesCR	SPIHT Level-1		Proposed ESZSCHT		SPECK		Proposed ESPSZBC	
	PSNR	CR	PSNR	CR	PSNR	CR	PSNR	
I Level Decomposition –After 3rd Iteration								
Saturm	13.51	32.09	17.54	32.09	17.46	32.09	**28.05**	32.10
Brain3d 512	8.43	32.46	10.35	32.46	9.60	32.50	**13.08**	32.50
CAROTID	7.12	28.74	9.57	28.74	7.70	29.07	**12.90**	29.07
Zelda 512	6.1	32.14	7.71	32.14	6.56	32.14	**9.93**	32.14
Ct-lungs 256	5.66	30.60	7.22	30.60	6.11	30.60	**8.85**	30.60
Ct-lomb	6.01	27.54	7.91	27.54	6.61	27.54	**10.40**	27.54
Graygoldhill	6.76	27.71	7.44	27.71	7.46	27.62	**8.62**	27.62
Ct34a	6.27	28.28	7.99	28.28	6.90	28.17	**10.17**	28.17

Table 2. Comparison of execution (encoding and decoding) time's and measured in seconds, PSNR ratio at various compression ratios

Images (512X512)	SPIHT			Proposed ESZSCHT			SPECK			Proposed ESPSZBC		
	Enc	Dec	PSNR	Enc	Dec	PSNR	Enc	Dec	PSNR	Enc	Dec	PSNR
At the Compression Ratio of 8												
Brain3d	2.766	1.469	34.32	2.687	**1.604**	**34.34**	2.856	1.659	34.81	2.768	1.769	**34.83**
Carotid	2.422	1.297	32.33	**2.359**	**1.282**	32.37	2.251	**1.127**	33.91	**2.156**	1.198	**33.94**
Zelda	1.542	1.203	33.53	1.50	1.187	33.54	**1.612**	1.245	32.96	1.615	1.245	**33.25**

the image qualities obtained from these techniques are found to be significantly good. If the size of the images used is large, the proposed algorithms offer excellent compression ratio and also the restored image quality is found to be better than the conventional approaches.

List of features for developing new wavelet based compression systems include the following:

- Low Mean Squared Error (MSE) for a given bit rate.
- Rate scalability and Resolution scalability.
- Random access decoding.
- Enhanced Region-Of-Interest (ROI) encoding.
- Idempotency.
- Robustness/resilience to channel errors and packet loss.
- Low memory usage.
- Fast, simple encoding and decoding.

The first point above is, achieving the lowest possible MSE or highest possible PSNR for a given bit rate. The wavelet-based methods can provide fine-grain rate scalability and resolution scalability in several octave steps. But scalability in rate and spatial/temporal resolution can only be achieved in a limited way for the DCT-based methods. Enabling bit plane coding of DCT coefficients would be one ingredient to accomplish fine grain rate scalability (Xiong, 1996), but it is not allowed in the current coding standards. Random

access decoding is the ability to select for decoding portions of the bit stream corresponding to a given region of the image. Since JPEG encodes 8x8 image blocks independently, it is easy to select the portions of the bit stream belonging to a region that is comprised of a union of 8x8 blocks. It is harder to do in principle for a wavelet coder, but certainly quite feasible if one can identify the bits of wavelet coefficients belonging to a given region. Region of interest (ROI) encoding can be achieved by identifying a given region at encoding time and assigning more bits per pixel to this region than to the remainder of the image. The wavelet coding methods can integrate ROI enhancement very naturally into the encoding process. Idempotency means perfect reversibility of decompression from compressed bitstream to reconstruction.

One way to create a less error-sensitive bit stream is to encode the source in many independent units, so that an error in one unit will not affect others. A method's memory usage is an important issue, especially for large images and implementation in small devices, such as cameras. The most common method is to partition the image into stripes or tiles and encode these partitions independently. JPEG and MPEG encode 8x8 blocks independently, so their coding algorithms do use a small memory space. The disadvantage of this method is that the partition boundaries become noticeable, as bit rate drops below some value, so these methods are not suitable for low rate applications. A wavelet transform requires a full image transform, but the full image is not required in memory since the filters are finite in length. For computing a transform coefficient one needs only as many rows or columns in memory to cover the extent of the filters for each level of decomposition. There are such memory-saving transforms based on putting into memory at any instant a minimum numbers of image lines or a minimum numbers of rows and columns in a block. They are called line-based (Chrysafis, 2000) and block-based (Xiaozhen Zhong, 2000) transforms, respectively. They yield the same coefficients as a full image transform, at the expense of some extra processing.

A fast, low complexity decoder has always been a crucial requirement, but it becomes increasingly difficult with state of the art efficiency for large images. Now there is a call for real-time encoding for cameras, medical images in teleconferencing and digital cinema. That requires fast and simple compression, which again is difficult to attain with state-of-the-art efficiency for large images. So concentrate the attention on low-complexity compression techniques that meet these requirements and possess the features itemized above.

FUTURE RESEARCH DIRECTIONS

- ROI based image compression.
- Document contains both text and image.
- Trend toward algorithms to handle large, multidimensional images.
- Low complexity encoding for image transmission.
- Background is same only the object is moving (robot and also remote sensing applications).

CONCLUSION

Clinical Picture Archiving and Communication Systems (PACS), and telemedicine networks require the storage and transmission of a large amount of medical image data. To preserve these data lossy or lossless/near lossless compression is used. For most of the medical image diagnosis applications the total information must be preserved even the images are subjected to compression techniques for storing the images or for quick transmission. On the other hand for browsing applications the lossy techniques can be employed without any difficulties. Based upon the application, an integrated scheme is employed, which can control the compression from lossy to lossless. The proposed integrated lossy-lossless wavelet transform based image compression methods have given higher compression ratio, better image quality and reduced computational complexity compared to the standard wavelet coding techniques. In order to reconstruct the image without any loss, the integer wavelet transform is used to decompose the image.

From the experimental results, the higher complexity variant of SPECK called EZBC is the best, showing the lowest rate on set of images. Referring to Said and Pearlman (2004), average over all rates (0.125, 0.25, 0.5, and 1.0bpp) for a set of images, EZBC method's PSNR ratio is better than other techniques like EZW, SFQ, CREW, EPWIC, JPEG2000, SPECK, SPIHT WDR and ASWDR. Compared with EZBC technique the proposed compression techniques with arithmetic coding have shown significant improvement in performance in terms of Peak Signal-to-Noise Ratio and CR and therefore these methods provide a powerful, efficient, fast and flexible approach to image compression. The low cost effective, faster and simpler implementation highly satisfies the good candidate for telemedicine applications and also retains the option of lossless transmission and archiving of the image. So the proposed coding techniques are highly suitable for fast consultation and transmission of losslessly archived large medical images. Also the proposed techniques have given better results when compared to other lossy techniques (i.e. JPEG) in browsing applications.

REFERENCES

Ahmed, N., Natarajan, T., & Rao, K. R. (1974). Discrete cosine transform. *IEEE Transactions on Computers*, (C-23), 90–93. doi:10.1109/T-C.1974.223784.

Barnsley, M. F. & Sloan, A. D. (1988). A better way to compress images. *Byte*, 215-223.

Boliek, M., Gormish, M. J., Schwartz, E. L., & Keith, A. (1997). Next generation image compression and manipulation using CREW. *Proceeding of IEEE ICIP, 3*, 567-572.

Buccigrossi, R., & Simoncelli, E. P. (1997). EPWIC: Embedded predictive wavelet image coder. In *Proceedings of 4th IEEE International Conference on Image Processing,* (pp. 640-648). Santa Barbara, CA: IEEE Press.

Calderbank, R., Daubechies, I., Sweldens, W., & Yeo, B.-L. (1998). Wavelet transforms that map integers to integers. *Journal of Applied and Computational Harmonic Analysis,* (5), 332-369.

Chrysafis, C., & Ortega, A. (2000). Line based, reduced memory, wavelet image compression. *IEEE Transactions on Image Processing, 9*, 378–389. doi:10.1109/83.826776 PMID:18255410.

Chrysafis, C., Said, A., Drukarev, A., Islam, A., & Pearlman, W. A. (2000). SBHP-A low complexity wavelet coder. In *Proceedings of IEEE International Conference on Acoustics, Speech, and Signal Processing* (2035-2038). Washington, DC: IEEE Press.

Daubechies, I., & Sweldens, W. (1998). Factoring wavelet transforms into lifting steps. *Journal of Fourier Analysis and Applications, 4*(3), 245–267. doi:10.1007/BF02476026.

Du, Sun & Sima. (2004). Improved EZBC algorithm with low complexity. *IEICE Electronics Express, 1*(15), 447–452. doi:10.1587/elex.1.447.

Geetha, P., & Annadurai, S. (2004a). Fast, efficient, and secured lossless coding of medical images using reversible integer wavelet transform. In *Proceedings of 3rd FAE International Conference of European University of Lefke* (320-325). Turkish Republic of Northern Cyprus: FAE Press.

Geetha, P., & Annadurai, S. (2004b). Fast and efficient secured lossless coding of medical images-Use of the lifting scheme. In *Proceedings of IEEE International Conference on Signal Processing and Communications* (23-25). Bangalore, India: IEEE Press.

Geetha, P., & Annadurai, S. (2005). efficient secured lossless compression of medical images–Using modified run-length coding for character representation. In *Proceedings of IEEE Indicon-2005* (66-68). Washington, DC: IEEE Press.

Geetha, P., & Annadurai, S. (2006). Efficient secured lossless coding of medical images-Using region based modified SPIHT and modified run-length coding for character representation. *International Journal on Graphics Vision and Image Processing, 9*, 40–47.

Geetha, P., & Annadurai, S. (2007). Efficient secured lossless coding of medical images-using a new fast embedded significant and zero set coding in hierarchical trees. *AMSE Journal, 50*(1), 18–35.

Geetha, P., & Annadurai, S. (2008). Medical image compression using a novel embedded set partitioning significant and zero block coding (ESPSZBC). *International Arab Journal of Information Technology, 5*(2), 132–139.

Gonzalez, R. C., & Wood, R. E. (2011). *Digital image processing using MATLAB* (2nd ed.). New York: McGraw Hill Companies.

Horspool, N., & Cormack, G. (1992). Constructing word-based text compression algorithms. In *Proceedings of the IEEE Data Compression Conference* (62-71). Washington, DC: IEEE Press.

Howard, P. G., & Vitter, J. S. (1993). Fast and efficient lossless image compression. In *Proceedings of IEEE Data Compression Conference* (351-360). Washington, DC: IEEE Press.

Hsiang, S. T., & Woods, J. W. (2000). Embedded image coding using zeroblocks of subband/wavelet coefficients and context modeling. *Proceeding of IEEE ISCAS, 3,* 662-665.

Huffman, D. A. (1952). A method for the construction of minimum redundancy codes. *Proceeding of IRE,* (40), 1098-1101.

Jain, A. K. (2011). *Fundamentals of digital image processing*. Upper Saddle River, NJ: Prentice Hall.

Knuth, D. E. (1985). Dynamic huffman coding. *Journal of Algorithms*, 6, 163–180. doi:10.1016/0196-6774(85)90036-7.

Lakhani, G. (2003). Modified JPEG huffman coding. *IEEE Transactions on Image Processing*, 12, 159–169. doi:10.1109/TIP.2003.809001 PMID:18237897.

Mallat, S. G. A. (1989). Theory for multiresolution signal decomposition: The wavelet representation. *IEEE Transactions on PAMI*, 11, 674–693. doi:10.1109/34.192463.

Netravali, A. N., & Limb, J. O. (1980). Picture coding a review. *Proceedings of the IEEE*, 68, 366–406. doi:10.1109/PROC.1980.11647.

Ouafi, A., Taleb, A., Baarir, Z., & Zitouni, A. (2008). A modified embedded zerotree wavelet (MEZW) algorithm for image compression. *Journal of Mathematical Imaging and Vision*, 30, 298–307. doi:10.1007/s10851-007-0057-y.

Pearlman, W. A. (2001). Trends of tree-based, set partitioning compression techniques in still and moving image systems. In *Proceedings of Picture Coding Symposium 2001* (1-8). Seoul, Korea: IEEE Press.

Pearlman, W. A., & Said, A. (1998). A survey of the state of the art and utilization of embedded, tree-based coding. In *Proceeding of 1998 IEEE International Symposium on Circuits and Systems*. Monterey, CA: IEEE Press.

Rao, K. R., & Yip, P. (1990). *Discrete cosine transforms-Algorithms, advantages, applications*. San Diego: Academic Press Professional, Inc..

Said, A., & Pearlman, W. A. (1996). A new, fast, and efficient image codec based on set partitioning in hierarchical trees. *IEEE Transactions on Circuits and Systems for Video Technology*, 6, 243–250. doi:10.1109/76.499834.

Said, A., & Pearlman, W. A. (1997). Low-complexity waveform coding via alphabet and sample set partitioning in hierarchical trees. *IEEE Transactions on Circuits and Systems for Video Technology*, 3024, 25–37.

Said, A., & Pearlman, W. A. (2004). Efficient, low-complexity image coding with a set-partitioning embedded block coder. *IEEE Transactions on Circuits and Systems for Video Technology*, 14(11), 1219–1235. doi:10.1109/TCSVT.2004.835150.

Seroussi, G., & Weinberger, M. J. (1997). On adaptive strategies for an extended family of Golomb-type codes. In *Proceedings of Data Compression Conference* (131-140). Snowbird, UT: IEEE Press.

Shapiro, J. (1993). Embedded image coding using zerotrees of wavelet coefficients. *IEEE Transactions on Signal Processing*, *41*, 3445–3462. doi:10.1109/78.258085.

Shen, Gao, Pu, Linlangliu, & Cao. (2011).construct the biorthogonal balanced multiwavelets by lifting scheme. In *Proceedings of the IEEE International Conference on Computer Science and Automation Engineering* (484-488). Washington, DC: IEEE Press.

Sweldens, W. (1996). The lifting scheme: A custom-design construction of biorthogonal wavelets. *Journal of Applied and Computational Harmonic Analysis*, *3*, 186–200. doi:10.1006/acha.1996.0015.

Taubman, D. (2000). High performance scalable image compression with EBCOT. *IEEE Transactions on Image Processing*, *9*, 1158–1170. doi:10.1109/83.847830 PMID:18262955.

Tian, J., & Wells, R. O. (1998). Embedded image coding using wavelet difference reduction. In P. Topiwala (Ed.), Wavelet Image and Video Compression (289-301). Norwell, MA: Kluwer Academic Publishers.

Tsai, M. J., Villasenor, J. D., & Chen, F. (1996). Stack-run image coding. *IEEE Transactions on Circuits and Systems for Video Technology*, *6*, 519–521. doi:10.1109/76.538934.

Vetterli, M., & Kovacevic, J. (1995). *Wavelets and subband coding*. Englewood Cliffs, NJ: Prentice Hall.

Walker, J. S. (2000). A lossy image codec based on adaptively scanned wavelet difference reduction. *Optical Engineering (Redondo Beach, Calif.)*, *39*(7), 1891–1897. doi:10.1117/1.602573.

Walker. (2001). Wavelet-based image compression. *The Transform and Data Compression*. New York: CRC Press LLC.

Weinberger, M. J., & Seroussi, G. (1997). Sequential prediction and ranking in universal context modeling and data compression. *IEEE Transactions on Information Theory*, *43*, 1697–1706. doi:10.1109/18.623176.

Weinberger, M. J., Seroussi, G., & Sapiro, G. (1996). LOCO-I: A low complexity, context-based lossless image compression algorithm. In *Proceedings of IEEE Data Compression Conference* (140-149). Snowbird, UT: IEEE Press.

Weinberger, M. J., Seroussi, G., & Sapiro, G. (2000). The LOCO-I lossless image compression algorithm: Principles and standardization into JPEG-LS. *IEEE Transactions on Image Processing*, *9*, 1309–1324. doi:10.1109/83.855427 PMID:18262969.

Wheeler, F. W., & Pearlman, W. A. (2000). Combined spatial and subband block coding of images. *IEEE International Conference on Image Processing (ICIP2001)*. Vancouver, BC: IEEE Press.

Witten, I. H., Neal, R. M., & Cleary, J. G. (1987). Arithmetic coding for data compression. *Communications of the ACM*, *30*(6), 520–540. doi:10.1145/214762.214771.

Wong, S., Zaremba, L., Gooden, D., & Huang, H. K. (1995). Radiologic image compression–A review. *Proceedings of the IEEE*, *83*, 194–219. doi:10.1109/5.364466.

Wu, X., & Menon, N. (1996). CALIC-A context based adaptive lossless image codec. In *Proceedings of International Conference on Acoustics, Speech, and Signal Processing* (1890-1893). Washington, DC: IEEE Press.

Xiong, Z., Guleryuz, O., & Orchard, M. T. (1996). A DCT based embedded Image coder. *IEEE Signal Processing Letters*, *3*, 289–290. doi:10.1109/97.542157.

Xiong, Z., Ramachandran, K., & Orchard, M. T. (1997). Space-frequency quantization for wavelet image coding. *IEEE Transactions on Image Processing*, *6*(5), 677–693. doi:10.1109/83.568925 PMID:18282961.

Zhao, X., & Zhai, L.-P. (2005). Wavelet-fractal based compression of ophthalmic image. [Bellingham, WA: SPIE Press.]. *Proceedings of the Society for Photo-Instrumentation Engineers*, *ICO20*, 35–42.

Zhong, X. (2000). *Block based wavelet transform image coding based on set partitioning in hierarchical algorithm. Project Report*. Sydney, Australia: Motorola Australia Research Center.

Ziv, J., & Lempel, A. (1977). A universal algorithm for sequential data compression. *IEEE Transactions on Information Theory*, *IT-23*(3), 337–343. doi:10.1109/TIT.1977.1055714.

ADDITIONAL REFERENCES

Andrew, J. (1997). A simple and efficient hierarchical image coder. In *Proceedings of IEEE International Conference on Image Processing (ICIP)* (658-661). Washington, DC: IEEE Press.

Clunie, D. (2000). Lossless compression of grayscale medical images-Effectiveness of traditional and state of the art approaches. *Proceedings of the Society for Photo-Instrumentation Engineers*, 3980.

Dewritte & Cornelis. (1997). Lossless integer wavelet transform. *IEEE Signal Processing Letters*, *4*, 158–160. doi:10.1109/97.586035.

Dvorsky, J., Pokorny, J., & Snasel, V. (1999). Word-based compression methods and indexing for text retrieval systems. *Lecture Notes in Computer Science*, *1691*, 75–84. doi:10.1007/3-540-48252-0_6.

Knuth, D. E. (1985). Dynamic huffman coding. *Journal of Algorithms*, *6*, 163–180. doi:10.1016/0196-6774(85)90036-7.

Kovacevic, J., & Vetterli, M. (1991). Perfect reconstruction filter banks with rational sampling rate changes. *International Conference on Acoustics, Speech, and Signal Processing*, *3*, 1785-1788.

Langdon, G. G. (1984). An introduction to arithmetic coding. *IBM Journal of Resource and Development*, *28*(2), 135–149. doi:10.1147/rd.282.0135.

Langdon, G. G., & Haidinyak, C. A. (1995). Experiments with lossless and virtually lossless image compression algorithms. *Proceedings of the Society for Photo-Instrumentation Engineers*, *2418*, 21–27. doi:10.1117/12.204135.

Lewis, A. S., & Knowles, G. (1992). Image compression using the 2-D wavelet transform. *IEEE Transactions on Image Processing*, *1*(2), 244–250. doi:10.1109/83.136601 PMID:18296159.

Mallat, S. G. A. (1989). Theory for multiresolution signal decomposition: The wavelet representation. *IEEE Transaction on PAMI*, *11*(7), 674–693. doi:10.1109/34.192463.

Martucci, S. A. (1990). Reversible compression of HDTV images using median adaptive prediction and arithmetic coding. In *Proceedings of the IEEE International Symposium on Circuits and Systems* (1310-1313). Washington, DC: IEEE Press.

Moffat, A., Neal, R., & Witten, I. H. (1995). Arithmetic coding revisited. In *Proceedings of the IEEE Data Compression Conference*. Snowbird, UT: IEEE Press.

Wallace, G. K. (1991). The JPEG still picture compression standard. *Communications of the ACM*, 30–44. doi:10.1145/103085.103089.

Wang & Haung. (1996). Medical image compression by using three-dimensional wavelet transformation. *IEEE Transactions on Medical Imaging*, *15*, 547–554. doi:10.1109/42.511757 PMID:18215935.

Weinberger, M. J., Rissanen, J., & Arps, R. B. (1996). Applications of universal context modeling to lossless compression of gray-scale images. *IEEE Transactions on Image Processing*, *5*, 575–586. doi:10.1109/83.491334 PMID:18285146.

Welch, T. A. (1984). A technique for high performance data compression. *IEEE Computer*, *17*(6), 8–19. doi:10.1109/MC.1984.1659158.

Xiong, Z., Wu, X., Cheng, S., & Hua, J. (2003). Lossy-to-lossless compression of medical volumetric data using three-dimensional integer wavelet transforms. *IEEE Transactions on Medical Imaging*, *22*, 459–470. doi:10.1109/TMI.2003.809585 PMID:12760561.

KEY TERMS AND DEFINITIONS

Compression: An algorithm that is applied to reduce the actual file size required to store an image. Compression can be either lossy or lossless.

Digital Image: A matrix that hold digital colour and/or brightness information, when viewed at suitable distance, form an image.

Gray Scale: A range of shades of gray between black to white.

JPEG 2000: Wavelet based image compression standard, which offers high compression ratio without image distortion compared to standard JPEG compression.

Pixel: Picture element, smallest element of a digital image.

Quantization: Mapping a range of values to single quantum value.

Transform Coding: Used to convert spatial image pixel values to transform coefficient value. Number of coefficients produced is equal to the number of pixels.

Wavelet Transform: Basically the representation of an image using wavelet functions at different locations and scales.

Chapter 17
Analysis of Blood Smear and Detection of White Blood Cell Types Using Harris Corner

Nilanjan Dey
JIS College of Engineering, India

Bijurika Nandi
CIEM, Tollygunge, India

Anamitra Bardhan Roy
JIS College of Engineering, India

Debalina Biswas
JIS College of Engineering, India

Achintya Das
Kalyani Government Engineering College, India

Sheli Sinha Chaudhuri
Jadavpur University, India

ABSTRACT

Blood cell smears contain huge amounts of information about the state of human health. This chapter proposes a Fuzzy c-means segmentation based method for the evaluation of blood cells of humans by counting the presence of Red Blood Cells (RBCs) and recognizing White Blood Cell (WBC) types using Harris corner detection. Until now hematologists gave major priority to WBCs and spent most of the time studying their features to reveal various characteristics of numerous diseases. Firstly, this method detects and counts the RBCs present in the human blood sample. Secondly, it assesses the detected WBCs to minutely scrutinize its type. It is a promising strategy for the diagnosis of diseases. It is a very tedious task for pathologists to identify and treat diseases by manually detecting, counting, and segmenting RBCs and WBCs. Simultaneously the analysis of the size, shape, and texture of every WBC and its elements is a very cumbersome process that makes this system vulnerable to inaccuracy and generates trouble. Hence, this system delivers a precise methodology to extract all relevant information for medical

DOI: 10.4018/978-1-4666-4558-5.ch017

diagnosis with high germaneness maintaining pertinence. This present work proposes an algorithm for the detection of RBCs comparing the results between expert ophthalmologists' hand-drawn ground-truths and the RBCs detected image as an output. Accuracy is used to evaluate overall performance. It is found that this work detects RBCs successfully with accuracy of 82.37%.

INTRODUCTION

The number of WBCs present in human blood depends on several factors like coagulation and thickness of blood that in turn depends on age, tiredness and fatigue. The whole process of counting WBC from human blood samples is cumbersome and is in immense need for automation to lessen the burden of the hematologists in maintaining accuracy, while working within a stipulated time frame. This method proposes a new approach of time conscious methodology to detect, study and determine the shape, contour and type of the WBCs and its elements. Proper and accurate diagnosis of the peripheral and marginal elements of the blood cells results in determination of diseases ranging from inflammation to leukemia. In general, achieving the same desired result until now was a dreary and monotonous process for trained and expert professionals in the field of biomedical sciences. Along with these factors, the microscopic review also seeks a large time span that slows down the process of disease detection and treatment of the same increasing fatal consequences. White blood cells or leukocytes play major role in defending the body against both infectious disease and foreign materials. There are normally approx. 7000 white blood cells per μL of blood. White Blood Cells are of mainly two types:

1. Granulocytes
2. Agranulocytes

Those WBCs having granules in the cytoplasm are called granulocytes (neutrophil, basophil, eosinophil), and those devoid of granules are agranulocytes (monocyte, lymphocyte, macro-phage). See Figure 1. Neutrophils have multilobed nucleus, basophils have bi or trilobed nucleus, eosinophils have bilobed nucleus, lymphocytes have highly stained, eccentric nucleus and monocytes have kidney shaped nucleus. Neutrophils make about 55%-70% of WBC, lymphocytes around 20%-40%, monocytes and macrophages about 2%-8%, eosinophils 1%-4% and basophils make up less than 1% of WBC. Any disbalance in the proportion or count of various components of WBC may indicate the presence of a disease. Neutrophils fight bacterial germs. Low count of neutrophil, called Neutropenia is caused due to chemotherapy, or viral infections and high count due to blood cancer Leukemia. Lymphocytes are of 2 types: The T-lymphocytes kill germs and the B-lymphocytes produce antibodies. Chronic infections and hereditary disorders lead to reduced number of lymphocytes (Lymphocytopenia). AIDS (Acquired Immunodeficiency Syndrome) cause CD4[+] T-lymphocytes to decrease drastically. Patients receiving chemotherapy or corticosteroids have low level of monocytes. Allergic reactions or Parasitosis elevate the level of eosinophil, resulting in Eosinophilia.

Also in this algorithm, the presence of the Red Blood Cells (RBCs) in the blood is counted. RBC (Harms, et.al., 1986; Bandyopadhyay et. al., 2012) is the chief component of human blood. RBCs give blood its characteristic red color. An RBC is a biconcave disc, without any nucleus. Its anomalies are the causes of many severe or fatal diseases. RBC maintains the hemoglobin level of humans and is responsible for oxygen supply to the entire body. The variations in human genetic or enzymatic pigments like Triglycerides lead to coagulation of RBCs and may be fatal causing heart blockages. Proper monitoring of the level

Figure 1. Types of WBC. (a) neutrophil (b) eosinphil (c) basophil (d) lymphocyte (e) monocyte. Picture courtesy: Wikipedia

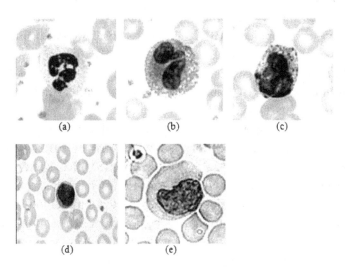

and nature of RBC in human blood can check cerebral thrombosis. The ranges for a normal RBC count (expressed in million red cells per micro liter {μL} of blood) are:

- **Children:** 3.8 - 5.5 million
- **Newborns:** 4.8 - 7.2 million
- **Adult (Males):** 4.6 - 6.0 million
- **Adult (Females):** 4.2 - 5.0 million

Abnormality in RBC count stems from a number of factors. Low count of RBC (anemia) might be due to trauma (a physical or mental injury). Another reason for RBC destruction is Hemolytic Anemia, caused due to abnormal breakdown of the RBC that results from autoimmunity or various other defects such as Sickle Cell Anemia(RBC is abnormally sickle or crescent shaped), Thalassemia (a structural abnormality of hemoglobin) or enzyme defects (like G6PD deficiency). In chronic Anemia, due to lack of oxygen, the heart pumps harder and harder to produce more blood, making itself enlarged. Acute bleeding from the digestive tract (caused due to ulcers, polyps or colon cancer) or from uterus in women (due to heavy menstrual bleeding) lowers the RBC count.

Iron deficiency, Vitamin B12 deficiency etc. also result in low RBC count. In many cases, Vitamin B12 deficiency results from Pernicious Anemia, when the body immunity system mistakenly destroys these vitamins. Various inflammatory diseases result in low RBC count. Kidney produces hormone erythropoietin which stimulates RBC production by bone marrow. So chronic kidney diseases hamper the production of RBCs. Bone marrow failure caused due to a rare genetic disease Fanconi Anemia, also inhibits the production of RBC. In white blood cell cancer, Leukemia, the normal bone marrow cells are overtaken by the cancerous cell, resulting in low RBC count or anemia. In many cases, donating blood above a desired level may cause low RBC count in the donor. It is however normal to have low RBC count during pregnancy. Increased RBC count (polycythemia) may be due to several reasons. Polycythemic Vera is a rare disease that inappropriately increases the RBC count. In lung diseases, adequate oxygen intake and absorption becomes difficult for the patient, and in congenital heart diseases the heart inefficiently pumps blood resulting in low oxygen absorption. In both cases body compensates by producing more blood that elevates the RBC count. Loss of blood plasma is another reason for increased RBC count. When bone marrow produces more than sufficient erythrocytes or when the kidney produces more erythropoietin, RBC count increases. Hemoglobinopathies, a condition present in human at birth impairing oxygen carrying capacity of blood, results in more RBC count. Kidney cancers, kidney transplants, Dehydration, smoking are some other factors. However, at high altitudes, elevated RBC count is normal, due to presence of less oxygen in air.

This methodology incorporates the ventures of detecting and counting RBCs in human blood sample and its comparison with the ground truth to detect various diseases.

This method provides the method for analyzing the blood sample with high precision and sensitivity for detecting, counting the number of RBC and determining the shape & pattern of the WBC. This result is to help radically with efficient time management in the field of hematology tackling large number of diseases.

LITERARY REVIEW

A number of works have been done in fields of image processing for counting and detection of both RBC and WBC. A brief summary of some of them have been discussed below.

In the paper 'Precise Segmentation of White Blood Cells by using Multispectral Imaging analysis Techniques', Quiongshui Wu, Libo Zeng, Hong Zheng and Ningning Guo have introduced multispectral imaging techniques for detection of WBC. The methodology involves acquiring a high quality image, whose each pixel spectrum is given input to the trained Support Vector Machine (SVM) for classification purpose. Subsequently morphological binary operations are performed to correct small error classified regions and thus satisfactory detection of WBC has been done (Wu et. al., 2008).

In another work 'White Blood Cell Detection using a Novel Fuzzy Morphological Shared-Weight Neural Network', author Cheng Ke has treated background influence, cell reunion and occlusion as fuzziness present in an image. On this basis a fuzzy morphological hit/miss operator and thereafter a morphological shared-weight neural network have been designed that has been shown to locate WBC (Ke, 2008).

Detection of WBC based on Boundary Support Vector (BSV) has been proposed by Min Wang and Rong Chu in the paper 'A Novel White Blood Cell Detection Method based on Boundary support Vectors'. The authors have presented a novel approach where v-Support Vector Regression (v- SVR) has been introduced in the beginning, followed by sparse BSV obtained while fitting 1D histogram by v-SVR. The threshold value has then been directly shifted from these limited support vectors. Finally segmentation of the entire connective WBC regions has been done from the original cell image. This method has been found to detect WBC, reducing effects of illumination and staining (Wang et.al., 2009).

Two image processing techniques, edge detection and segmentation have been used to classify RBC in the work 'Red Blood Cells Classification using Image Processing' prepared by Navin D. Jambhekar. The methodology steps include image detection, feature extraction, image segmentation, histogram analysis and finally classification under artificial neural network. All these steps have been used for the classification of RBC (Jambhekar, 2011).

The importance of image processing in RBC detection has been shown in another paper 'Red Blood Cell Segmentation using Masking and Watershed Algorithm: A Preliminary Study' put forward by J. M. Shariff, M. F. Miswan, M. A. Nagadi, and Sah Haj Salam. The steps involved to detect RBC are Ycbcr color conversion, masking, morphological operators and watershed algorithm. The formation of segmented White

Blood Cell (WBC) nucleus has resulted from the combination of Ycbcr color conversion and morphological operator. It has then been used as a mask to remove WBC from the blood cell image. The resulted RBC segmentation has been subsequently passed through marker controlled watershed algorithm which handles overlapping cells (Shariff et al., 2012).

In their work 'Computerized Hematology Counter', by S. T. Khot and R. K. Prasad, various image processing techniques have been incorporated in the counting of RBC and detection of WBC. For counting RBC, the initial RGB (Red Green Blue) image has been converted to HSV (Hue Saturation Value) image which is then sharpened. The thresholding of the resulting image has then been performed and thereafter passed through median filter. Hole filling and Labeling help to count RBC. For the detection of WBC, before conversion from RGB to HSV, background has been eliminated. After that S-Plane thresholding, noise removal and dilation have been performed. Finally contour tracking help to determine WBC (Khot et al., 2012).

In another approach, the image containing RBCs has undergone histogram equalization and segmentation as steps of image preprocessing in the paper 'Automated Red Blood Cell Counting' presented by Alaa Hamouda, Ahmed Y. Khedr and Rabie A. Ramadan. A binary mask using the segmented cell has then been created by the application of a threshold. Edge detection has been done using Sobel Operator. Experimenting with four methods for the extraction of RBC, among K-means Clustering, Classification, Hybrid of Clustering and Classification and Learning using Decision Tree, the last method have been found to be the most accurate for counting of RBC (Hamouda et al., 2012).

The proposed approach is much simpler than the aforementioned method in respect to speed, cost and robustness. Manual individual detection and marking of RBC cells for better diagnosis are the main advantages of our approach.

METHODOLOGY

Fuzzy C-Means Segmentation

In pattern recognition, a clustering method known as Fuzzy C-Means (FCM) is widely used. FCM was proposed by Bezdek in 1973 (Bezdek, 1981). FCM is also known as Fuzzy ISODATA (Dunn, 1973). In this clustering technique one piece of data belongs to two or more clusters. FCM based segmentation is nothing but fuzzy pixel classification. FCM allows data points or pixels to belong to multiple classes with varying degree of membership function between 0 and 1.

FCM possesses unique advantage of grading linguistic variables to fit for appropriate analysis in discrete domain on pro-rata basis.

FCM computes cluster centers or Centroids by minimizing the dissimilarity function with the help of iterative approach. By updating the cluster centers and the membership grades for individual pixel, FCM (Dey et al., 2012) shifts the cluster centers to the "right" location within set of pixels.

To accommodate the introduction of fuzzy partitioning, the membership matrix (U) = [u_{ij}] is randomly initialized according to Equation 1, where u_{ij} being the degree of membership function of the data point of ith cluster x_i.

$$\sum_{i=1}^{c} u_{ij} = 1, \forall j = 1, ..., n \qquad (1)$$

The performance index (PI) for membership matrix U and c_is used in FCM is given in Equation 2:

$$J(U, c_1, c_2, ... c_c) = \sum_{i=1}^{c} J_i = \sum_{i=1}^{c} \sum_{j=1}^{n} u_{ij}^{m} d_{ij}^{2} \qquad (2)$$

u_{ij} is between 0 and 1. c_i is the centroid of cluster i.

d_{ij} is the Euclidian distance between i^{th} centroid (c_i) and j^{th} data point.

m ϵ [1, ∞] is a weighting exponent. To reach a minimum of dissimilarity function there are two conditions. These are given in Equation 3 and Equation 4:

$$c_i = \frac{\sum_{j=1}^{n} u_{ij}^{m} x_j}{\sum_{j=1}^{n} u_{ij}^{m}} \qquad (3)$$

$$u_{ij} = \frac{1}{\sum_{k=1}^{c} \left(\dfrac{d_{ij}}{d_{kj}}\right)^{2/(m-1)}} \qquad (4)$$

The algorithm of FCM is as follows:

Step 1: The membership matrix (U) that has constraints in Equation 1is randomly initiated.
Step 2: Centroids (ci) are calculated by using Equation 3
Step 3: Dissimilarity between centroids and data points is computed using Equation 2. Stop if its improvement over previous iteration is below a threshold.
Step 4: A new U is computed using Equation 4 go to Step 2.

In this section, Fuzzy C-Means clustering method is used as a pre-processing technique for Basic Region Growing Segmentation. The basic difference from other approaches is the extension of feature space which results in better segmentation.

Stationary Wavelet Transform (SWT)

The wavelet transform describes a multi-resolution decomposition process in terms of expansion of an image onto a set of wavelet basis functions. Discrete Wavelet Transformation (DWT) has its own excellent space frequency localization prop-

erty (see Figure 2.) Application of DWT in 2D signals corresponds to 2D filter image processing in each dimension. The input image is divided into 4 non-overlapping multi-resolution sub-bands by the filters, namely LL1 (Approximation coefficients), LH1 (vertical details), HL1 (horizontal details) and HH1 (diagonal details). The sub-band (LL1) is processed further to obtain the next coarser scale of wavelet coefficients, until some final scale "N" is reached. When "N" is reached, 3N+1 sub-band are obtained consisting of the multi-resolution sub-bands. Which are LLX and LHX, HLX and HHX where "X" ranges from 1 until "N." Generally, most of the image energy is stored in the LLX sub-bands.

Stationary Wavelet Transform (SWT) is modification of the Discrete Wavelet Transform (Dey et al., 2012) to make it a translation-invariant in nature that does not decimate coefficients at every transformation level (see Figure 3.)

Translation-invariance is achieved by removing the down samplers and up samplers in the DWT and up sampling the filter coefficients by a factor of $2^{(j-1)}$ in the jth level of the algorithm

It is an inherently redundant scheme as the output of each level contains the same number of

Figure 2. Three phase decomposition using DWT

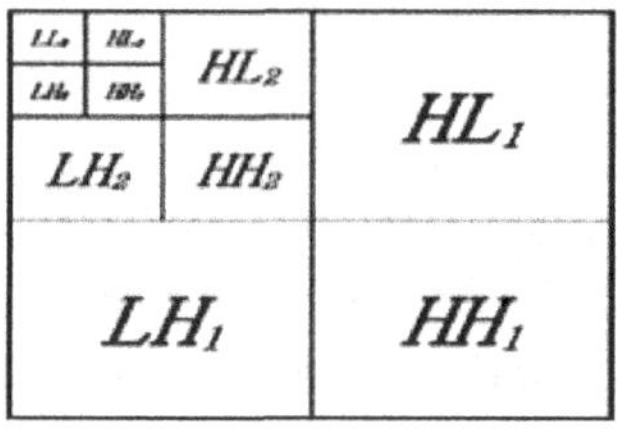

LL₂	HL₂	HL₂	HL₁
LH₂	HH₂		
LH₁		HH₁	

Figure 3. Three phase decomposition using SWT

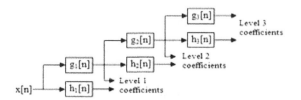

samples as the input. Therefore, for a decomposition of N levels there are a redundancy of N in the wavelet coefficients. This algorithm, proposed by Holdschneider is also known as "algorithme à trous," refers to inserting zeros in the filters.

Haar wavelet is not continuous, and therefore not differentiable. This property can, however, be an advantage for the analysis of signals with sudden transitions.

The results obtained at each step of Discrete Wavelet Transformation (DWT) are half the size of the original Image. Contrary to this, Stationary Wavelet Transform (SWT) does not sub-sample the signal. Rather, the corresponding low-pass and high-pass filters are padded with zeros to up-sample the signal at each level of decomposition. The primary advantage of SWT over DWT is that spatial information of the original image at each step is restored, which aids in achieving translation invariance that remains impossible to be carried out with the conventional DWT.

Harris Corner Detection

Harris corner detector is based on the local auto-correlation function of a signal that measures the local changes of the signal with patches shifted by a small amount in different directions. Given a shift $(\Delta x, \Delta y)$ to a point (x, y) the auto-correlation function is defined in Equation 5 as:

$$c(x,y) = \left[\Delta x \; \Delta y\right] \begin{bmatrix} \sum_w (I_x(x_i,y_i))^2 & \sum_w I_x(x_i,y_i)I_y(x_i,y_i) \\ \sum_w I_x(x_i,y_i)I_y(x_i,y_i) & \sum_w (I_y(x_i,y_i))^2 \end{bmatrix} \begin{bmatrix} \Delta x \\ \Delta y \end{bmatrix}$$

$$= \left[\Delta x \; \Delta y\right] C\left(x,y\right) \begin{bmatrix} \Delta x \\ \Delta y \end{bmatrix}$$

$$(5)$$

$C(x, y)$ the auto-correlation matrix captures the intensity structure of the local neighborhood.

For α_1 and α_2 be Eigen values of $C(x, y)$, three cases may be considered as:

1. Both Eigen values are small signifying uniform region (constant intensity).

2. Both Eigen values are high signifying Interest point (corner).
3. One Eigen value is high signifying contour (edge).

To find out the points of interest, corner response H(x, y) is characterized by Eigen values of C(x, y).

- C(x, y) is symmetric and positive definite that is α_1 and α_2 are >0
  ° $\alpha_1 \alpha_2 = \det(C(x, y)) = AC - B^2$
- $\alpha_1 + \alpha_2 = \text{trace}(C(x, y)) = A + C$
- Harris suggested the corner response:
  ° $H_{cornerResponse} = \alpha_1 \alpha_2 - 0.04(\alpha 1 + \alpha 2)^2$

Finally, it is needed to find out corner points as local maxima of the corner response.

PROPOSED ALGORITHM

RBC Count

Step 1: Sample Image is converted into grey image from the red channel.

Step 2: Fuzzy C-means Segmentation is applied on pre-processed gray image.

Step 3: Segmented Image is binarized followed by filtering.

Step 4: Binary area open is used to remove small objects from filtered image.

Step 5: RBCs are extracted from the binarized image by applying watershed transformation.

Step 6: Centroids of the RBCs are determined from the watershed image followed by labeling.

Step 7: RBC count is determined from the labeled Sample Image.

Step 8: A single RBC is selected.

Step 9: Sobel Edge detection is applied on the binarized image.

Step 10: Harris Corner Detection Algorithm (Harris, C., et. al, 1988) (Derpanis, K.G., 2004) is applied.

Step 11: Maximum Harris Diameter is calculated and based on the Harris points the center is determined.

Step 12: A circle is drawn based on the centre point and diameter on the sample image to mark the RBC. See Figure 4.

WBC Types Detection

Step 1: Sample image is converted into grey image from the red channel.

Step 2: Static Wavelet Transformation is applied on the grey image and the approximation coefficient (Ca) is extracted.

Step 3: Fuzzy C-means Segmentation is applied on the Ca.

Step 4: Segmented Image is binarized followed by filtering.

Step 5: Binary area open is used to remove small objects from filtered image.

Step 6: WBC type is detected from the binarized image.

Step 7: Sobel Edge detection is applied on the binarized image.

Figure 4. RBC marking and count

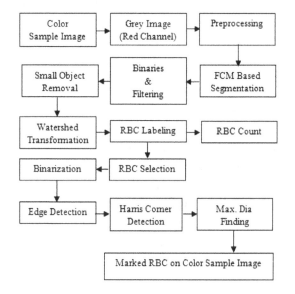

Step 8: Harris Corner Detection Algorithm is applied on the edge detected image followed by maximum Harris Diameter calculation.

Step 9: A circle is drawn based on the centre point and diameter on the sample image to mark the WBC. See Figure 5.

EXPLANATION OF THE PROPOSED METHOD

RBC Count

For RBC Counting, the sample image is converted into grey image from the red channel one. In RGB images, the best contrast between the foreground and the background is exhibited by the green channel, whereas the red and blue channels tend to be noisier. To increase the level of robustness of our proposed method against noise the red channel is selected. The reason behind not selecting the blue channel is because that the noise in the blue channel is a combination of cascading effects that work together to make the blue appear the worst.

The pre-processed grey image is then subjected to Fuzzy C-means Segmentation, due to the expansion of feature space, which results in better segmentation. Thereafter binarization of image is performed, followed by filtering. Median filtering is a nonlinear operation often used to reduce

Figure 5. WBC type detection and marking

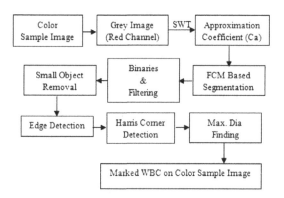

"salt and pepper" noise in image processing. In our proposed method median filtering is used. To eliminate small objects from the filtered mage, Binary area open is used. To remove all connected components from a binary image, Binary area open is implemented as a part of morphological filtering process. Watershed Transformation is applied on the binarized image for the extraction of RBC intended to split the clustered objects. Marker-Controlled Watershed Segmentation Watershed transform originally proposed by Digabel and Lantuejoul is widely endorsed in image segmentation (Digabel et al., 1978; Lantuéjoul, 1978). Watershed Transform (Wang, 1997; Kim et al., 2003; Dey et al., 2011) draws its inspiration from the geographical concept of Watershed. A Watershed is the area of land where all the water that is under it or drains off of it, goes into the same place. Simplifying the picture, a watershed can be assumed as a large bathtub. The bathtub defines the watershed boundary. On land, that boundary is determined topographically by ridges, or high elevation points. The watershed transform computes the catchment basins and ridgelines in a gradient image and generates closed contours for each region in the original image. A potent and flexible method for segmentation of objects with closed contours, where the extremities are expressed as ridges is the Marker-Controlled Watershed Segmentation. In Watershed Segmentation, the Marker Image used is a binary Image comprising of either single marker points or larger marker regions. In this, each connected marker is allocated inside an object of interest. Every specific watershed region has a one-to-one relation with each initial marker; hence the final number of watershed regions determines the number of markers. Post Segmentation, each object is separated from its neighbors as the boundaries of the watershed regions are arranged on the desired ridges. The markers can be manually or automatically selected, automatically generated markers being generally preferred. In a single word, Watershed transform can be classified as a region-based image seg-

mentation approach, results generated by which can be taken as pre-processes for further Image analysis. After determination of the centroids of RBC from the watershed image, labeling is done. RBC count is determined from the labeled sample image. RBC is manually selected from the labeled sample image. Sobel Edge Detection, and subsequently Harris Corner Detection are applied on the binarized image. Then maximum Harris Corner diameter is calculated, and the centre is determined based on the Harris points. A circle is drawn with the detected centre point and diameter is drawn to mark RBC.

WBC Types Detection

Similar to the RBC Count, WBC Type Detection also undergoes conversion of red channel image into the grey one in the beginning. The explanation for selecting the red channel is already discussed in the RBC detection section. Then Static Wavelet Transformation is applied on the image, followed by approximation coefficient (Ca) extraction. SWT has been employed to reduce information loss due to the down sampling in DWT. This is followed by combining all high frequency sub-band images in order to generate improved and corrected high frequency sub-band images. The key purpose of SWT is de-noising. On the other hand, it gives a better estimate than Discrete Wavelet Transform (DWT) given that; it is redundant, linear and shift invariant. In this section, SWT is used to decompose sample image. This is because the multi-resolution analysis permits to decrease the amount of noise and remove small details from the image allowing only large objects to remain. For ease, Haar wavelet is used, since it is orthogonal and symmetric. After application of Fuzzy C-means segmentation on Ca, the image is binarized and thereafter filtered. As in the RBC Count, here also Binary area open is used to remove small objects from the filtered image. WBC type is then detected form the binarized image. Sobel edge Detection, Harris Corner Detection and maximum Harris diameter detection are step by step performed. Finally a circle is drawn around the detected centre point and the WBC is marked.

RESULT AND DISCUSSION

MATLAB 7.0.1 Software is extensively used for the study of count and type analysis of red and white blood cells. Sample image of human blood is taken under consideration. Concerned images obtained in the result are shown in Figure 6 and 7

The detected results are compared with hand-drawn ground truth provided by hematologists' based on five performance measurements, namely, True Positive (TP, a number of RBCs correctly detected), False Positive (FP, a number of non-RBCs which are detected wrongly as RBCs),

Figure 6. (a) sample image (b) red component (c) fuzzy c-mean segmented image (d) binarized image (e) watershed transformed image (f) RBC labeled image (g) RBC labeled as sixth (h) harris corner detected sixth RBC (i) maximum harris diameter (j) marked sample image(RBC)

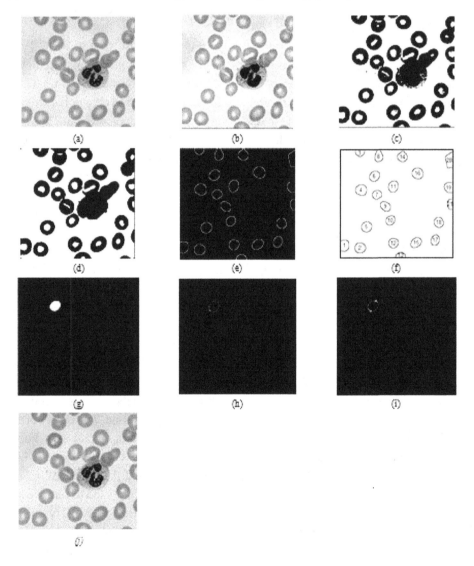

Figure 7. (a) sample image (b) red component (c) SWT decomposed image (d) fuzzy c-mean segmented binarized image (e) edge detected image (f) harris corner detected image (g) maximum harris diameter (h) marked sample image(WBC)

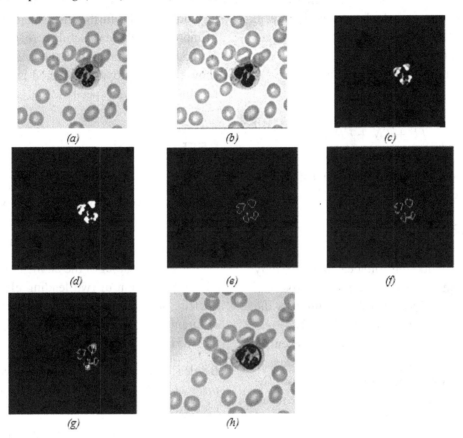

Figure 8. The proposed method (a) hand-drawn ground truth (b) detected RBCs

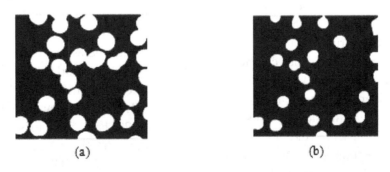

False Negative (FN, a number of RBCs that are not detected), True Negative (TN, a number of non- RBCs which are correctly identified as non-RBCs), accuracy are calculated. See Figure 8. The specified parameters are individually calculated for the above test case.

Accuracy is defined by Equation 6:

$$Accuracy\ (\%) = \frac{TP + TN}{TP + TN + FP + FN} \quad (6)$$

It is found that this work detects RBCs successfully with an accuracy of 82.37%,

CONCLUSION

This approach works on biological image to study and analyze the basic characteristics associated with them. Very specifically, it scrutinizes the number count of Red Blood Cells (RBCs) and types of White Blood Cells (WBCs) present in sample image of human blood. RBCs are primarily responsible for carrying oxygen throughout the human body. Its change in count and nature result in many types of health issues that may be fatal in some cases. WBCs, consisting of five different types of components, are the immunity builders of human body. The method proposed in this chapter delivers with the scope of locating and counting RBCs with higher accuracy. The performance of the algorithm is measured against ophthalmologists' hand-drawn ground-truth. Accuracy is used to evaluate overall performance which combines both true positive and false positive rates. Types of WBCs are also determined by the method to identify their presence in the sample. This advancement has huge impact on the biomedical field enhancing the detection approaches of many hematological diseases. Since the application of wavelet transformation in signal processing is relatively a new field of research, many methodological aspects (Choice of the mother wavelet, values of the scale parameters) of the wavelet technique require further investigations in order to improve the clinical usefulness of this proposed method. The simulation result and its analysis show that this proposed method is economical, reliable, robust and speedy.

REFERENCES

Aids.org. (2013). Complete blood count (CBC). Retrieved from http://www.aids.org/topics/complete-blood-count.

Bandyopadhyay, S. K., & Roy, S. (2012). Detection of sharp contour of the element of the WBC and segmentation of two leading elements like nucleus and cytoplasm. *International Journal of Engineering Research and Applications*, 2(1), 545–551.

Bezdek, J. C. (1981). *Pattern recognition with fuzzy objective function algorithms*. New York: Plenum Press. doi:10.1007/978-1-4757-0450-1.

Buzzle. (2012). White blood cells: Diseases and disorders. Retrieved from http://www.buzzle.com/articles/white-blood-cells-diseases-and-disorders.html.

Derpanis, K. G. *(2004). The harris corner detector.* Retrieved from http://www.google.com/url?sa=t&rct=j&q=&esrc=s&source=web&cd=1&ved=0CC0QFjAA&url=http%3A%2F%2Fwinda ge.googlecode.com%2Fsvn%2Ftrunk%2FMind map%2FTracking%2FPapers%2F%255B2004%255D%2520The%2520Harris%2520Corner%2520Detector.pdf&ei=gSXTUYXxBszc4APp64D QDA&usg=AFQjCNGlKM3AVlhJGehehVhW NfbwDDaOeg&sig2=xUs4oAo0UCCQlD97G vf86Q&bvm=bv.48705608,d.dmg.

Dey, N., Pal, M., & Das, A. (2012). A session based watermarking technique within the NROI of retinal fundus images for authentication using DWT, spread spectrum and harris corner detection. *International Journal of Modern Engineering Research*, 2(3), 749–757.

Dey, N., Roy, A. B., Pal, M., & Das, A. (2012). FCM based blood vessel segmentation method for retinal images. *International Journal of Computer Science and Network*, 1(3).

Dey, N., Sinha, A., & Rakshit, P. (2011). A novel approach of watershed segmentation of noisy image using adaptive wavelet threshold. *International Journal of Computer Science and Information Technologies*, 2(6), 2686–2690.

Digabel, H., & Lantuéjoul, C. (1978). Iterative algorithms. In J.-L. Chermant (Ed.), *Actes du Second Symposium Européen d'Analyse Quantitative des Microstructure es en Sciences des Matériaux, Biologie et Médecine* (85-99). Stuttgart, Germany: Riederer Verlag.

Dunn, J. C. (1973). A fuzzy relative of the ISO-DATA process and its use in detecting compact well separated clusters. *Journal of Cybernetics*, 3, 32–57. doi:10.1080/01969727308546046.

Hamouda, A., Khedr, A. Y., & Ramadan, R. A. (2012). Automated red blood cell counting. *International Journal of Computing Science*, 1(2), 1366–1374.

Harms, H., Aus, H., Haucke, M., & Gunzer, U. (1986). Segmentation of stained blood cell images measured at high scanning density with high magnification and high numerical aperture optics. *Cytometry*, 7, 522–531. doi:10.1002/cyto.990070605 PMID:2430764.

Harris, C., & Stephens, M. (1988). A combined corner and edge detector. In *Proceedings of 4th Alvey Vision Conference*. Manchester, UK: Manchester University Press.

Jambhekar, N. D. (2011). Red blood cells classification using image processing. *Science Research Reporter*, 1(3).

Ke, C. (2008). White blood cell detection using a novel fuzzy morphological shared-weight neural network. In *Proceedings of the International Symposium on Computer Science and Computational Technology*. Washington, DC: IEEE Press.

Khot, S. T., & Prasad, R. K. (2012). Computerized hematology counter. *International Journal of Medical and Clinical Research*, 3(6), 190–194.

Kim, J. B., & Kim, H. J. (2003). Multi-resolution–based watersheds for efficient image segmentation. *Pattern Recognition Letters*, 24, 473–488. doi:10.1016/S0167-8655(02)00270-2.

Lab Tests Online. (2013). Red blood cell count. Retrieved from http://labtestsonline.org/understanding/analytes/rbc/tab/test.

Lantuéjoul, C. (1978). *La Squelettisation et Son Application aux Mesures Topologiques des Mosaiques Polycristallines*. (PhD thesis). Paris, Ecole des Mines.

Shariff, J. M., Miswan, M. F., Nagadi, M. A., & Salam, S. H. (2012). Red blood cell segmentation using masking and watershed algorithm: A preliminary study. In *Proceedings of the International Conference on Biomedical Engineering*. Penang, Malaysia: IEEE Press.

Wang, D. (1997). A multiscale gradient algorithm for image segmentation using watersheds. *Pattern Recognition*, 30(12), 2043–2052. doi:10.1016/S0031-3203(97)00015-0.

Wikipedia. (2013a). Stationary wavelet transform. Retrieved from http://en.wikipedia.org/wiki/Stationary_wavelet_transform.

Wikipedia. (2013b). White blood cell. Retrieved from http://en.wikipedia.org/wiki/White_blood_cell.

Wu, Q., Zeng, L., Zheng, H., & Guo, N. (2008). precise segmentation of white blood cells by using multispectral imaging analysis techniques. In *Proceedings of the International Conference on Intelligent Networks and Intelligent Systems*. Washington, DC: IEEE Press.

KEY TERMS AND DEFINITIONS

Fuzzy C-Means (FCM): Segmentation algorithm is used for segmentation using fuzzy pixel classification.

Harris Corner Detection: The Harris corner detector is a mathematical operator for feature and corner detection and is largely acceptable due to its strong invariance to rotation, scale, illumination variation and image noise.

Red Blood Cells (RBC): Disk-shaped, biconcave cells in the blood that contains hemoglobin, lacks a nucleus, and transports oxygen and carbon dioxide to and from the tissues.

Stationary Wavelet Transformation (SWT): A wavelet transform algorithm designed to overcome the lack of translation-invariance of the discrete wavelet transformation.

White Blood Cells (WBC): A form of blood cell that lacks hemoglobin, are colorless and contain a nucleus; these cells are involved in the body's immune system and protects the body against invading microorganisms and foreign particles.

Compilation of References

A. C. (Ed.). (2005). *Handbook of image and video processing*. Amsterdam: Elsevier Academic Press.

Abadi & Nikbakht. (2011). Image denoising with two-dimensional adaptive filter algorithms. *Iranian Journal of Electrical & Electronic Engineering, 7*(2).

Abd-Elmoniem, Youssef, & Kadah. (2002). Real-time speckle reduction and coherence enhancement in ultrasound imaging via nonlinear anisotropic diffusion. *IEEE Transactions on Bio-Medical Engineering, 49*(9), 997–1014. doi:10.1109/TBME.2002.1028423 PMID:12214889.

Abdullah-Sayani, A., Bueno-de-Mesquita, J. M., & van de Vijver, M. J. (2006). Technology insight: Tuning into the genetic orchestra using microarrays--limitations of DNA microarrays in clinical practice. *Nature Clinical Practice. Oncology, 3*(9), 501–516. doi:10.1038/ncponc0587 PMID:16955089.

Abramson, S. J. (1997). Adrenal neoplasm in children. *Radiologic Clinics of North America, 35*(6), 1415–1453. PMID:9374997.

Abtahi, J., Tengvall, P., & Aspenberg, P. (2012). A bisphosphonate-coating improves the fixation of metal implants in human bone. A randomized trial of dental implants. *Bone, 50*(5), 1148–1151. doi:10.1016/j.bone.2012.02.001 PMID:22348981.

Abu-Eid, R., & Landini, G. (2006). Oral epithelial dysplasia: Can quantifiable morphological features help in the grading dilemma? In *Proceedings of First Image User and Developer Conference* (149-154). New York: ACM Press.

Abu-Eid, R., & Landini, G. (2003). Quantification of the global and local complexity of the epithelial-connective tissue interface of normal, dysplastic, and neoplastic oral mucosae using digital imaging. *Pathology, Research and Practice, 199*, 475–482. doi:10.1078/0344-0338-00448 PMID:14521264.

Acha, B., Rangayyan, R. M., & Desautels, J. E. L. (2006). Detection of microcalcifications in mammograms. In Suri & Rangayyan (eds.), Recent Advances in Breast Imaging, Mammography, and Computer-Aided Diagnosis of Breast Cancer. Bellingham, WA: SPIE Press.

Achim & Bezerianos. (2003). SAR image denoising via bayesian wavelet shrinkage based on heavy-tailed modelling. *IEEE Transactions on Geoscience and Remote Sensing, 41*(8).

Advanced Veterinary Medical Images. (2011). Computed tomography. CAT scan. *Advanced Veterinary Imaging*. Retrieved from http://www.avmi.net/newfiles/CT/CT.html.

Agarwal, S., Snavely, N., Simon, I., Seitz, S. M., & Szeliski, R. (2009). Building rome in a day. In *Proceedings of International Conference on Computer Vision*. Kyoto, Japan: IEEE Press.

Agrawal, R., & Srikant, R. (1994). Fast algorithms for mining association rules in large databases. In *Proceedings of 20th International Conference on Very Large Data Bases*, Santiago de Chile, Chile: Morgan Kaufmann.

Ahmed, Yamany, Mohamed, Farag, & Moriarty. (2002). A modified fuzzy c-means algorithm for bias field estimation and segmentation of mri data. *IEEE Transactions on Medical Imaging, 21*(3), 193–199. Retrieved from http.//www.cvip.uofl.edu/wwwcvip/research/publications/Pub_Pdf/2002/3.pdf.

Ahmed, N., Natarajan, T., & Rao, K. R. (1974). Discrete cosine transform. *IEEE Transactions on Computers*, (C-23), 90–93. doi:10.1109/T-C.1974.223784.

Ahn, S., Jun, S. C., Seo, J. K., Lee, J., Woo, E. J., & Holder, D. (2010). Frequency-difference electrical impedance tomography: Phantom imaging experiments. *Journal of Physics: Conference Series, 224*.

Aids.org. (2013). Complete blood count (CBC). Retrieved from http://www.aids.org/topics/complete-blood-count.

Akiyoshi, T., Kobunai, T., & Watanabe, T. (2012). Predicting the response to preoperative radiation or chemoradiation by a microarray analysis of the gene expression profiles in rectal cancer. *Surgery Today, 42*(8), 713–719. doi:10.1007/s00595-012-0223-8 PMID:22706722.

Alenius, S., & Ruotsalainen, U. (1997). Bayesian image reconstruction for emission tomography based on median root prior. *European Journal of Nuclear Medicine, 24*, 258–265. doi:10.1007/BF01728761 PMID:9143462.

Alenius, S., Ruotsalainen, U., & Astola, J. (1998). Using local median as the location of the prior distribution in iterative emission tomography image reconstruction. *IEEE Transactions on Nuclear Science, 45*, 3097–3104. doi:10.1109/23.737670.

Alexander, F. (2000). Neuroblastoma. *The Urologic Clinics of North America, 27*(3), 383–392. doi:10.1016/S0094-0143(05)70087-2 PMID:10985139.

Aloise, Deshpande, Hansen, & Popat. (2009). NP-hardness of euclidean sum-of-squares clustering. *Machine Learning, 75*, 245–249. doi:10.1007/s10994-009-5103-0.

American College of Radiology (ACR). (2003). *ACR breast imaging reporting and data system. Breast Imaging Atlas* (4th ed.). Reston, VA: American College of Radiation.

Amini, B. Dror, &Nygren. (1997). *Tomographic reconstruction of SPECT data*. Retrieved from http://www.owlnet.rice.edu/elect539/projects97/cult/report.html.

Ankerst, M., Breunig, M. M., Kriegel, H., & Sander, J. (1999). OPTICS: ordering points to identify the clustering structure. In *Proceedings of ACM SIGMOD International Conference on Management of Data* (49-60). New York: ACM Press.

An, L. T. H., Pham Dinh Tao, P. D., & Hàob, D. N. (2002). Towards tikhonov regularization of non-linear ill-posed problems: A DC programming approach. *Comptes Rendus Mathematique, 335*(12), 1073–1078. doi:10.1016/S1631-073X(02)02611-0.

Antonini, Barlaud, Mathieu, & Daubechies. (1992). Image coding using wavelet transform. *IEEE Transactions on Image Processing, 1*(2), 205–220. doi:10.1109/83.136597 PMID:18296155.

Arlimatti. (2012). Window based method for automatic classification of apple fruit. *International Journal of Engineering Research and Applications, 2*(4), 1010-1013.

Arnold-Bos, A., Malasset, J.-P., & Kervern, G. (2005). Towards a model-free denoising of underwater optical images. In *Proceedings of the IEEE Europe Oceans Conference, 1,* 527-532. Brest, France: IEEE Press.

Arnold-Bos, A., Malkasse, J. P., & Kerven, G. (2005). A pre-processing framework for automatic underwater images denoising. In *Proceedings of the European Conference on Propagation and Systems*. Brest, France: IEEE Press.

Arridge, S. R. (1999). Optical tomography in medical imaging, Topical review. *Inverse Problems, 15*, R41–R93. doi:10.1088/0266-5611/15/2/022.

Arthur, Manthey, & Roeglin. (2009). K-means has polynomial smoothed complexity. In *Proceedings of the 50th Symposium on Foundations of Computer Science (FOCS), 2009*. Washington, DC: IEEE Press.

Asli, Selim, & Sevgen. (2012). Unsupervised segmentation and classification of cervical cell images. *Pattern Recognition, 45*, 4150–4168.

Assmus, A. (1995). Early history of X rays. *University of Stanford Beam Line Periodical, 25*(2), 11–24.

Aster, R. C., Borchers, B., & Thurber, C. H. (2012). *Parameter estimation and inverse problems* (2nd ed.). New York: Academic Press.

Aster, R., Borchers, B., & Thurber, C. (2004). *Parameter estimation and inverse problems*. Amsterdam: Elsevier.

Atkins, M. S., & Mackiewich, B. T. (1998). Fully automatic segmentation of the brain in MRI. *IEEE Transactions on Medical Imaging*, *17*(1), 98–107. doi:10.1109/42.668699 PMID:9617911.

Aziz, M. Z., & Mertsching, B. (2007). An attentional approach for perceptual grouping of spatially distributed patterns. In *Proceedings of 29th DAGM Conference on Pattern Recognition* (345–354). Berlin: Springer.

Aziz, M. Z., & Mertsching, B. (2008). Fast and robust generation of feature maps for region-based visual attention. *IEEE Transactions on Image Processing*, *17*(5), 633–644. doi:10.1109/TIP.2008.919365 PMID:18390370.

Babu & Alamelu. (2009). Wavelet based medical image compression using ROI EZW. *International Journal of Recent Trends in Engineering*, *1*(3).

Backer, G., Mertsching, B., & Bollmann, M. (2001). Data- and model-driven gaze control for an active-vision system. *IEEE Transactions on Pattern Analysis and Machine Intelligence*, *23*, 1415–1429. doi:10.1109/34.977565.

Baeg, S., & Kehtarnavaz, N. (2002). Classification of breast mass abnormalities using denseness and architectural distortion. *Electronic Letters on Computer Vision and Image Analysis*, *1*(1), 1–20.

Bagshaw, A. P., Liston, A. D., Bayford, R. H., Tizzard, A., Gibson, A. P., & Holder, D. S. et al. (2003). Electrical impedance tomography of human brain function using reconstruction algorithms based on the finite element method. *NeuroImage*, *20*, 752–764. doi:10.1016/S1053-8119(03)00301-X PMID:14568449.

Bahrani, N. (2012). *2½D Finite Element Method for Electrical Impedance Tomography Considering the Complete Electrode Model*. (Master of Applied Science Thesis). Ottawa, Ontario, Carleton University.

Ballaster, C., & Sapiro, V. (2000). Filling-in by joint interpolation of vector fields and gray levels. *IEEE Transactions on Image Processing*, *9*, 1200–1211. PMID:18262958.

Baluja, S., & Pomerleau, D. (1997). Dynamic relevance: Vision-based focus of attention using artificial neural networks. *Artificial Intelligence*, *97*, 381–395. doi:10.1016/S0004-3702(97)00065-9.

Bandyopadhyay. (2010). Formation of homogeneous blocks for segmentation of mammograms. *International Journal of Engineering Science and Technology*, *2*(12), 7444-7448.

Bandyopadhyay, S. K., & Roy, S. (2012). Detection of sharp contour of the element of the WBC and segmentation of two leading elements like nucleus and cytoplasm. *International Journal of Engineering Research and Applications*, *2*(1), 545–551.

Bankman, I. N. (2000). *Handbook of medical imaging: Processing and analysis* (1st ed.). New York: Academic Press.

Barber, D. C. (1990). Quantification in impcdanee imaging. *Clinical Physics and Physiological Measurement*, *11*, 45–56. doi:10.1088/0143-0815/11/4A/306 PMID:2286047.

Barber, D. C. (1992). Registration of low resolution medical images. *Physics in Medicine and Biology*, *37*(7), 1485–1498. doi:10.1088/0031-9155/37/7/002 PMID:1631194.

Barber, D. C. (2000). Electrical impedance tomography. In Bronzino, J. D. (Ed.), *The Biomedical Engineering Handbook* (2nd ed.). Boca Raton, FL: CRC Press.

Barber, D. C., & Brown, B. H. (1984). Applied potential tomography, Review article. *Journal of Physics. E, Scientific Instruments*, *17*, 723–734. doi:10.1088/0022-3735/17/9/002.

Barnsley, M. F. & Sloan, A. D. (1988). A better way to compress images. *Byte*, 215-223.

Barrett, H. H. & Swindell, W. (n.d.). *Radiological imaging volumes*. New York: Academic Press.

Bato, P. M. M., Nagata, Q., Cao, B. P., Shrestha, R., & Nakashima. (1999). Strawberry sorting using machine vision. *ASAE Paper No. 993162*. St. Joseph, MI: ASAE.

Bayford, R. H. (2006). Bioimpedance tomography (Electrical impedance tomography). *Annual Review of Biomedical Engineering*, *8*, 63–91. doi:10.1146/annurev.bioeng.8.061505.095716 PMID:16834552.

Bazeille, S., Quidu, I., Jaulin, L., & Malkasse, J. P. (2006). Automatic underwater image pre-processing. In *Proceedings of the Caracterisation du Milieu Marin (CMM'06)*. Brest, France: IEEE Press.

Begum, M., Mann, G. K. I., & Gosine, R. G. (2006). A biologically inspired bayesian model of visual attention for humanoid robots. In *Proceedings of 6th IEEE-RAS International Conference on Humanoid Robots* (587–592). Washington, DC: IEEE Press.

Beister, Kolditz, & Kalender. (2012). Iterative reconstruction methods in X-ray CT. *Physica Medica, 28*, 94–108. doi:10.1016/j.ejmp.2012.01.003 PMID:22316498.

Bell & Sejnowski. (1997). The "independent components" of natural scenes are edge filters. *Vision Research, 37*(23), 3327–3338. doi:10.1016/S0042-6989(97)00121-1 PMID:9425547.

Bellotti. (2006). A completely automated CAD system for mass detection in a large mammographic database. *Medical Physics, 33*.

Bennedsen, B. S., Peterson, D. L., & Tabb, A. (2005). Identifying defects in images of rotating apples.[Amsterdam: Elesevier.]. *Computers and Electronics in Agriculture*, 92–102. doi:10.1016/j.compag.2005.01.003.

Benoit, C. E., Rowe, W. B., Menard, C., Sarret, P., & Quirion, R. (2011). Genomic and proteomic strategies to identify novel targets potentially involved in learning and memory. *Trends in Pharmacological Sciences, 32*(1), 43–52. doi:10.1016/j.tips.2010.10.002 PMID:21129790.

Bera, T. K., & Nagaraju, J. (2009a) A study of practical biological phantoms with simple instrumentation for electrical impedance tomography (EIT), In *Proceedings of IEEE International Instrumentation and Measurement Technology Conference* (511-516). Singapore: IEEE Press.

Bera, T. K., & Nagaraju, J. (2009b). A simple instrumentation calibration technique for electrical impedance tomography (EIT) using A 16 electrode phantom. In, *Proceedings of The Fifth Annual IEEE Conference on Automation Science and Engineering* (347-352). Bangalore, India: IEEE Press.

Bera, T. K., & Nagaraju, J. (2009c). A reconfigurable practical phantom for studying the 2 D electrical impedance tomography (EIT) using a FEM based forward solver. In *Proceedings of 10th International Conference on Biomedical Applications of Electrical Impedance Tomography*. Manchester, UK: Oxford University Press.

Bera, T. K., & Nagaraju, J. (2009d). A FEM-Based forward solver for studying the forward problem of electrical impedance tomography (EIT) with a practical biological phantom. In *Proceedings of IEEE International Advance Computing Conference' 2009* (1375–1381). Patiala, India: IEEE Press.

Bera, T. K., & Nagaraju, J. (2009e). Studying the boundary data profile of a practical phantom for medical electrical impedance tomography with different electrode geometries. In *Proceedings of the World Congress on Medical Physics and Biomedical Engineering-2009* (925–929). Munich, Germany: Springer.

Bera, T. K., & Nagaraju, J. (2010). A multifrequency constant current source for medical electrical impedance tomography. In *Proceedings of the IEEE International Conference on Systems in Medicine and Biology 2010* (278-283). Kharagpur, India: IEEE Press.

Bera, T. K., & Nagaraju, J. (2011d). Gold electrode sensors for electrical impedance tomography (EIT) studies. In *Proceedings of IEEE Sensors Application Symposium 2011* (24-28) San Antonio, TX: IEEE Press.

Bera, T. K., & Nagaraju, J. (2011f). Studying the 2D resistivity reconstruction of stainless steel electrode phantoms using different current patterns of electrical impedance tomography (EIT). In Biomedical Engineering (163-169). New Dehli, India: Narosa Publishing House.

Bera, T. K., & Nagaraju, J. (2011h). Common ground method of current injection in electrical impedance tomography. In *Proceedings of the Fourth International Conference on Recent Trends in Computing, Communication, & Information Technologies 2011*, (593-605). Tamil Nadu, India: ITC Press.

Bera, T. K., & Nagaraju, J. (2011i). Studying the 2D-image reconstruction of non biological and biological inhomogeneities in electrical impedance tomography (EIT) with EIDORS. In *Proceedings of International Conference on Advanced Computing, Networking, and Security 2011* (132-136). Mangalore, India: ACM Press.

Bera, T. K., & Nagaraju, J. (2012b). A gold sensors array for imaging the real tissue phantom in electrical impedance tomography. In *Proceedings of the International Conference on Materials Science and Technology 2012*. Kerala, India: ASM Press.

Bera, T. K., & Nagaraju, J. (2012e). A multifrequency electrical impedance tomography (EIT) System for biomedical imaging. In *Proceedings of International Conference on Signal Processing and Communications* (1-5). Bangalore, India: IEEE Press.

Bera, T. K., Biswas, S. K., Rajan, K., & Nagaraju, J. (2012c). Improving the image reconstruction in electrical impedance tomography (EIT) with block matrix-based multiple regularization (BMMR): A practical phantom study. In *Proceedings of the IEEE World Congress on Information and Communication Technologies 2011* (1346-1351). Mumbai, India: IEEE Press.

Bera, T. K., Biswas, S. K., Rajan, K., & Nagaraju, J. (2011b). Improving conductivity image quality using block matrix-based multiple regularization (BMMR) technique in EIT: A simulation study. *Journal of Electrical Bioimpedance, 2*, 33–47.

Bera, T. K., Biswas, S. K., Rajan, K., & Nagaraju, J. (2011c). Improving image quality in electrical impedance tomography (EIT) using projection error propagation-based regularization (PEPR) technique: A simulation study. *Journal of Electrical Bioimpedance, 2*, 2–12.

Bera, T. K., Biswas, S. K., Rajan, K., & Nagaraju, J. (2012d). Image reconstruction in electrical impedance tomography (EIT) with projection error propagation-based regularization (PEPR): A practical phantom study. *Advanced Computing, Networking, and Security. Lecture Notes in Computer Science, 7135*, 95–105. doi:10.1007/978-3-642-29280-4_11.

Bera, T. K., & Nagaraju, J. (2009f). A stainless steel electrode phantom to study the forward problem of electrical impedance tomography (EIT). *Sensors & Transducers Journal, 104*(5), 33–40.

Bera, T. K., & Nagaraju, J. (2011a). Resistivity imaging of a reconfigurable phantom with circular inhomogeneities in 2d-electrical impedance tomography. *Measurement, 44*(3), 518–526. doi:10.1016/j.measurement.2010.11.015.

Bera, T. K., & Nagaraju, J. (2011e). A chicken tissue phantom for studying an electrical impedance tomography (EIT) system suitable for clinical imaging. *Sensing and Imaging: An International Journal, 12*(3-4), 95–116. doi:10.1007/s11220-011-0063-4.

Bera, T. K., & Nagaraju, J. (2011g). Electrical impedance spectroscopic study of broiler chicken tissues suitable for the development of practical phantoms in multifrequency EIT. *Journal of Electrical Bioimpedance, 2*, 48–63.

Bera, T. K., & Nagaraju, J. (2012a). Studying the resistivity imaging of chicken tissue phantoms with different current patterns in electrical impedance tomography (EIT). *Measurement, 45*, 663–682. doi:10.1016/j.measurement.2012.01.002.

Berger, S. B., & Cepelewicz, B. B. (1996). Medical-legal issues in teleradiology. *American Journal of Roentgenolo, 166*(3), 505–510. doi:10.2214/ajr.166.3.8623616 PMID:8623616.

Berry, P., & Midgley, G. Hall, & Lewis. (2009). Recent advances in biomedical imaging systems. ISIC 2009 (183-186). Washington, DC: IEEE Press.

Bezdek, J. C. (1981). *Pattern recognition with fuzzy objective function algorithms*. Berlin: Springer. doi:10.1007/978-1-4757-0450-1.

Bezdek, J. C., Hall, L. O., & Clarke, L. P. (1993). Review of MR image segmentation techniques using pattern recognition. *Medical Physics, 20*(4), 1033–1048. doi:10.1118/1.597000 PMID:8413011.

Bhandarkar, S. M., & Zhang, H. (1999). Image segmentation using evolutionary computation. *IEEE Transactions on Evolutionary Computation, 3*(1), 1–21. doi:10.1109/4235.752917.

Bloch, F., Hansen, W. W., & Packard, M. (1946). Nuclear induction. *Physical Review, 69*, 127. doi:10.1103/PhysRev.69.127.

Blunt, S. D. (2011). The reiterative superresolution (RISR) algorithm. *IEEE Transactions on Aerospace and Electronic Systems, 47*(1), 332–346. doi:10.1109/TAES.2011.5705679.

Bogdanova, I., Bur, A., & Hugli, H. (2008). Visual attention on the sphere. *IEEE Transactions on Image Processing*, *17*(11), 2000–2014. doi:10.1109/TIP.2008.2003415 PMID:18854253.

Boliek, M., Gormish, M. J., Schwartz, E. L., & Keith, A. (1997). Next generation image compression and manipulation using CREW. *Proceeding of IEEE ICIP, 3*, 567-572.

Bolton, G. T., Qiu, C. H., & Wang, M. (2002). A novel electrical tomography sensor for monitoring the phase distribution in industrial reactors. In *Proceedings of the 7th UK Conference on Mixing*. Bradford, UK: Ametys.

Bonifati, D. M., & Kishore, U. (2007). Role of complement in neurodegeneration and neuroinflammation. *Molecular Immunology*, *44*(5), 999–1010. doi:10.1016/j.molimm.2006.03.007 PMID:16698083.

Boracchi & Foi. (2011). Uniform motion blur in poissonian noise: Blur/noise trade-off. *IEEE Transactions on Image Processing*, *20*(2).

Borcea, L. (2002). Electrical impedance tomography, Topical review. *Inverse Problems*, *18*, R99–R136. doi:10.1088/0266-5611/18/6/201.

Borman, S., & Stevenson, R. L. (1998). Super-resolution from image sequences-A review. In *Proceedings of Midwest Symposium on Circuits and Systems* (374-378). Washington, DC: IEEE Press.

Bostwick, G., & Iczkowski, K. (1997).. . *Annals of Diagnostic Pathology*, *1*(2), 104–229. doi:10.1016/S1092-9134(97)80015-9 PMID:9869832.

Boutros, P. C., Lau, S. K., Pintilie, M., Liu, N., Shepherd, F. A., & Jurisica, I. et al. (2009). Prognostic gene signatures for non small cell lung cancer. *Proceedings of the National Academy of Sciences of the United States of America*, *106*(8), 2824–2828. doi:10.1073/pnas.0809444106 PMID:19196983.

Bovik. (2009). *The essential guide to image processing.* Amsterdam: Elsevier Inc.

Boyd, S., & Vandeberghe, L. (2004). *Convex optimization.* New York: Cambridge University Press.

Bozek, M. Delac, & Grgic. (2009). A survey of image processing algorithms in digital mammography. Zagreb, Croatia: Zagreb University.

Bradley, A. P., & Stentiford, W. M. (2003). Visual attention for region of interest coding in jpeg 2000. *Journal of Visual Communication and Image Representation*, *14*(3), 232–250. doi:10.1016/S1047-3203(03)00037-3.

Bradley, W. G. (2008). History of medical imaging. *Proceedings of the American Philosophical Society*, *152*(3), 349–361. PMID:19831232.

Bramswig, N. C., & Kaestner, K. H. (2012). Organogenesis and functional genomics of the endocrine pancreas. *Cellular and Molecular Life Sciences*, *69*(13), 2109–2123. doi:10.1007/s00018-011-0915-z PMID:22241333.

British Library. (2013). Roentgen's discovery of the X-Ray, learning, bodies of knowledge. *British Library*. Retrieved from http://www.bl.uk/learning/cult/bodies/xray/roentgen.html.

Bronnikov, A. V. (2009). *Phase-contrast CT: Fundamental theorem and fast image reconstruction algorithms.* Retrieved from http://www.bronnikov-algorithms.com/downloads/SPIE631827.pdf

Brown, B. H. (2001). Medical impedance tomography and process impedance tomography: A brief review. *Measurement Science & Technology*, *12*(8), 991–996. doi:10.1088/0957-0233/12/8/301.

Brown, B. H., & Segar, A. D. (1987). The sheffield data collection system. *Clinical Physics and Physiological Measurement*, *8*, 91–97. doi:10.1088/0143-0815/8/4A/012 PMID:3568577.

Brown, I., Heys, S. D., & Schofield, A. C. (2003). From peas to chips-The new millennium of molecular biology: A primer for the surgeon. *World Journal of Surgical Oncology*, *1*, 21. doi:10.1186/1477-7819-1-21 PMID:14613556.

Bruce, C., Desimone, R., & Gross, C. (1981). Visual properties of neurons in a polysensory area in the superior temporal sulcus of the macaque. *Journal of Neurophysiology*, *46*, 369–384. PMID:6267219.

Bruce, N. D. B. (2005). Features that draw visual attention: an information theoretic perspective. *Neurocomputing*, *65-66*, 125–133. doi:10.1016/j.neucom.2004.10.065.

Bruce, N. D. B., & Tsotsos, J. K. (2009). Saliency, attention, and visual search: An information theoretic approach. *Journal of Vision (Charlottesville, Va.)*, *9*(3), 1–24. doi:10.1167/9.3.5 PMID:19757944.

Buccigrossi, R., & Simoncelli, E. P. (1997). EPWIC: Embedded predictive wavelet image coder. In *Proceedings of 4th IEEE International Conference on Image Processing*, (pp. 640-648). Santa Barbara, CA: IEEE Press.

Buchanan, R. A., Finkelstein, S. I., & Wickersheim, K. A. (1976). X-ray exposure reduction using rare earth oxysulfide intensifying screens. *Radiology*, *118*, 183–188. PMID:1244656.

Bur, A., Tapus, A., Ouerhani, N., Siegwart, R., & Hugli, H. (2006). Robot navigation by panoramic vision and attention guided fetaures. In *Proceedings of 18th International Conference on Pattern Recognition* (695–698). Washington, DC: IEEE Press.

Burak, Melih, Cenk, & Gunbuz. (2009). Object oriented texture analysis for the unsupervised segmentation of biopsy images for cancer detection. *Pattern Recognition*, *42*, 1104–1112. doi:10.1016/j.patcog.2008.07.007.

Bushberg, J. T., Seibert, J. A., Leidholdt, E. M. Jr, & Boone, J. M. (2001). *The essential physics of medical imaging* (2nd ed.). Riverwoods, IL: Lippincott, Williams, & Wilkins.

Bushong, S. C. (2003). *Magnetic resonance imaging: Physical and biological principles* (3rd ed.). Philadelphia: Mosby & Saunders.

Buzzle. (2012). White blood cells: Diseases and disorders. Retrieved from http://www.buzzle.com/articles/white-blood-cells-diseases-and-disorders.html.

Cai, Chen, & Zhang. (2007). Fast and robust fuzzy c-means clustering algorithm incorporating local information for image segmentation. *Pattern Recognition*, *40*(3), 825–838. doi:10.1016/j.patcog.2006.07.011.

Calderbank, R., Daubechies, I., Sweldens, W., & Yeo, B.-L. (1998). Wavelet transforms that map integers to integers. *Journal of Applied and Computational Harmonic Analysis*, (5), 332-369.

Calvetti, D., McGivney, D., & Somersalo, E. (2012). Left and right preconditioning for electrical impedance tomography with structural information. *Inverse Problems*, *28*, 26. doi:10.1088/0266-5611/28/5/055015.

Candes, E. J., & Romberg, J. K. (2004). Practical signal recovery from random projections. In *Proceedings of SPIE Conference on Wavelet Application in Signal and Image Processing XI, 5914*. Bellingham, WA: SPIE Press.

Candes, E. J., & Romberg, J. K. (2005). *L1-magic: Recovery of sparse signals via convex programming*. Retrieved from http://users.ece.gatech.edu/~justin/l1magic/downloads/l1magic.pdf.

Candes, E. J., Wakin, M. B., & Boyd, S. P. (2008). Enhancing sparsity by reweighted l1 minimization. *The Journal of Fourier. Analysis and Applications*, *14*(5), 877–905.

Candes, Romberg, & Tao. (2006). Stable signal recovery from incomplete and inaccurate measurements. *Communications on Pure and Applied Mathematics*, *59*(8), 1207–1223. doi:10.1002/cpa.20124.

Cao, F., Huang, H. K., & Zhou, X. Q. (2003). Medical image security in a HIPAA mandated PACS environment. *Computerized Medical Imaging and Graphics*, *27*(2-3), 185–196. doi:10.1016/S0895-6111(02)00073-3 PMID:12620309.

Cao, Q., Lu, T., & Masatera, N. (1997). Development of the strawberry sorting robot. *Journal of Shanghai Jiaotong University*, *7*(7), 881–884.

Cassen, B. (1998). The rectilinear scanner and an enduring legacy of education and research. *Journal of Nuclear Medicine*, *39*(5), 16N. PMID:9591566.

Cassen, B., Curtis, L., & Reed, C. W. (1950). A sensitive directional gamma-ray detector. *Nucleonics*, 78–81. PMID:15398050.

Cater, K., Chalmers, A., & Ledda, P. (2002). Selective quality rendering by exploiting human inattentional blindness: Looking but not seeing. In *Proceedings of the ACM symposium on Virtual Reality Software and Technology* (17–24). New York: ACM Press.

CBS. (2005). *The encyclopedia atlas of the human body: A visual guide to the human body*. New York: CBS Publishers & Distributors Pvt. Ltd..

Censor, Y., & Zenios, S. A. (1997). *Parallel optimization: Theory, algorithms, and applications.* New York: Oxford University Press.

Cerf, M., Frady, E. P., & Koch, C. (2008). Using semantic content as cues for better scanpath prediction. In *Proceedings of Symposium on Eye tracking Research & Applications* (143–146). New York: ACM Press.

Chalmers, A., Cater, K., & Maflioli, D. (2003). Visual attention models for producing high fidelity graphics efficiently. In *Proceedings of 19th Spring Conference on Computer Graphics* (39–46). New York: ACM Press.

Chambah, M., Semani, D., Renouf, A., Courtellement, P., & Rizzi, A. (2004). Underwater color constancy: Enhancement of automatic live fish recognition. In Proceedings of SPIE (157-168). San Jose, CA: SPIE Press.

Chambers, J. E., Wilkinson, P. B., Wardrop, D., Hameed, A., Hill, I., & Gunn, D. A. et al. (2012). Bedrock detection beneath river terrace deposits using three-dimensional electrical resistivity tomography. *Geomorphology, 177–178,* 17–25. doi:10.1016/j.geomorph.2012.03.034.

Chan & Shen. (2005). *Image processing and analysis: Variational, PDE, wavelet, and stochastic methods.* Philadelphia: SIAM.

Chandler & Hemami. (2007). VSNR: A wavelet-based visual signal-to-noise; ratio for natural images. *IEEE Transactions on Image Processing, 16*(9).

Chandran, V., Carswell, B., Boashash, B., & Elgar, S. L. (1997). Pattern recognition using invariants defined from higher order spectra: 2-D image inputs. *IEEE Transactions on Image Processing, 6,* 703–712. doi:10.1109/83.568927 PMID:18282963.

Chang, H., Yeung, D., & Xiong, Y. (2004). Super-resolution through neighbor embedding. In *Proceedings of IEEE Conference on Computer Vision and Pattern Recognition (CVPR 2004)* (I-275-I-282). Washington, DC: IEEE Press.

Chang, H. Y., Nuyten, D. S., Sneddon, J. B., Hastie, T., Tibshirani, R., & van de Vijver, M. J. et al. (2005). Robustness, scalability, and integration of a wound-response gene expression signature in predicting breast cancer survival. *Proceedings of the National Academy of Sciences of the United States of America, 102*(10), 3738–3743. doi:10.1073/pnas.0409462102 PMID:15701700.

Chang, S. G., Yu, B., & Martin Vetterli, M. (2000). Adaptive wavelet thresholding for image denoising and compression. *IEEE Transactions on Image Processing, 9*(9), 1532–1546. doi:10.1109/83.862633 PMID:18262991.

Charl, B. (2012). *The future of medical visualisation.* Retrieved from http://www.technologyreview.com/view/-428134/the-future-of-medical-visualisation.

Chen & Liu. (2000). Mixed kalman filter. *Journal of the Royal Statistical Society. Series B. Methodological, 62*(3), 493–508. doi:10.1111/1467-9868.00246.

Chen, D.-Y., Tyan, H.-R., Hsiao, D.-Y., Shih, S.-W., & Liao, H.-Y. M. (2008). Dynamic visual saliency modeling based on spatiotemporal analysis. In *Proceedings of IEEE International Conference on Multimedia and Expo* (1085-1088). Washington, DC: IEEE Press.

Chen, H.-Y., & Leou, J.-J. (2008). A new visual attention model using texture and object features. In *Proceedings of IEEE 8th International Conference on Computer and Information Technology Workshops* (374–378). Washington, DC: IEEE Press.

Chena, C. F., Liub, Z. H., Xiea, J., Xiao-Bo Maa, X. B., Lia, Y., & Gonga, S. S. (2012). Cochlear implant challenges encountered in tuberculous otitis media. *Asian Pacific Journal of Tropical Medicine, 5*(5), 416–419. doi:10.1016/S1995-7645(12)60071-6 PMID:22546663.

Cheney, M., Isaacson, D., & Newell, J. C. (1999). Electrical impedance tomography. *SIAM Review, 41*(1), 85–101. doi:10.1137/S0036144598333613.

Cheng, H. D., Shan Juan, Ju Wen, Guo Yanhui, & Zhang Ling. (2010). Automated breast cancer detection and classification using ultrasound images: A survey. *Pattern Recognition, 43,* 299–317. doi:10.1016/j.patcog.2009.05.012.

Cheng, Shi, & Min, Hu, Cai, & Du. (2006). Approaches for automated detection and classification of masses in mammograms. *Pattern Recognition, 39*(4), 646–668. doi:10.1016/j.patcog.2005.07.006.

Chen, Z., Brown, E. N., & Barbieri, R. (2009). assessment of autonomic control and respiratory sinus arrhythmia using point process models of human heart beat dynamics. *IEEE Transactions on Electromagnetic Compatibility, 56*(7), 1791–1802. PMID:19272971.

Chipman, H., & Tibshirani, R. (2006). Hybrid hierarchical clustering with applications to microarray data. *Biostatistics (Oxford, England)*, *7*(2), 286–301. doi:10.1093/biostatistics/kxj007 PMID:16301308.

Choi, S.-B., Ban, S.-W., & Lee, M. (2004). Biologically motivated visual attention system using bottom-up saliency map and top-down inhibition. *Neural Information Processing-Letters and Reviews, 2.*

Cho, Z. H., Jones, J. P., & Singh, M. (1993). *Foundations of medical imaging*. New York: Wiley.

Chrysafis, C., Said, A., Drukarev, A., Islam, A., & Pearlman, W. A. (2000). SBHP-A low complexity wavelet coder. In *Proceedings of IEEE International Conference on Acoustics, Speech, and Signal Processing* (2035-2038). Washington, DC: IEEE Press.

Chrysafis, C., & Ortega, A. (2000). Line based, reduced memory, wavelet image compression. *IEEE Transactions on Image Processing*, *9*, 378–389. doi:10.1109/83.826776 PMID:18255410.

Church, P., McFee, J. E., Gagnon, S., & Wort, P. (2006). Electrical impedance tomographic imaging of buried landmines. *IEEE Transactions on Geoscience and Remote Sensing*, *44*(9), 2407–2420. doi:10.1109/TGRS.2006.873208.

Cohen-Bacrie, C., Goussard, Y., & Guardo, G. (1997). Regularized reconstruction in electrical impedance tomography using a variance uniformization constraint. *IEEE Transactions on Medical Imaging*, *16*(5), 562–571. doi:10.1109/42.640745 PMID:9368111.

Coifman & Donoha. (1995). *Translation-invariant denoising. Wavelets and Statistics*. Berlin: Springer-Verlag.

Coifman & Wickerhauser. (1992). Entropy-based algorithms for best basis selection. *IEEE Transactions on Information Theory*, *38*(2), 713–718. doi:10.1109/18.119732.

Conway, J. (1987). Electrical impedance tomography for thermal monitoring of hyperthermia treatment: an assessment using in vitro and in vivo measurements. *Clinical Physics and Physiological Measurement*, *8*, 141–146. doi:10.1088/0143-0815/8/4A/018 PMID:3568563.

Cool, Downey, & Izawa, Chin, & Fenster. (2006). D prostate model formation from non-parallel 2D ultrasound biopsy images. *Medical Image Analysis*, *10*, 875–887. doi:10.1016/j.media.2006.09.001 PMID:17097333.

Cox, I. J., Miller, M. L., Bloom, J. A., Fridrich, J., & Kalker, T. (2008). *Digital watermarking and steganography*. New York: Morgan Kaufmann Publishers.

Cox, I. J., Miller, M., & Bloom, J. (2002). *Digital watermarking*. New York: Morgan Kaufmann Publishers.

Cristianini & Shawe-Taylor. (2000). *An introduction to support vector machines*. Cambridge, UK: Cambridge University Press.

Cruvinel, P. E., Cesareo, R., Crestana, S., & Mascarenhas, S. (1990). X and gamma rays computerized minitomograph scanner for soil science. *IEEE Transactions on Instrumentation and Measurement*, *39*(5), 745–750. doi:10.1109/19.58619.

Dai, M., Wang, P., Boyd, A. D., Kostov, G., Athey, B., & Meng, F. et al. (2005). Evolving gene/transcript definitions significantly alter the interpretation of genechip data. *Nucleic Acids Research*, *33*(20), e175. doi:10.1093/nar/gni179 PMID:16284200.

Dai, W. W., Mmili, P. M., Martinez, E., & Morucci, J.-P. (1994). Using the hilbert uniqueness method in a reconstruction algorithm for electrical impedance tomography. *Physiological Measurement*, *15*, A161–A168. doi:10.1088/0967-3334/15/2A/021 PMID:8087039.

D'Antona, G., & Rocca, L. (2002). Electrical impedance tomography for underground pollutant detection and polluted lands reclaiming monitoring. In *Proceedings of IEEE Instrumentation and Measurement Technology Conference* (1035-1038). Anchorage, AK: IEEE Press.

Das, D., Ghosh, M., Chakraborty, C., Maiti, A. K., & Pal, M. (2011). Probabilistic prediction of malaria using morphological and textural information. In *Proceedings of International Conference on Image Information Processing (ICIIP)*. Wahington, DC: IEEE Press.

Dash & Liu. (1997). Feature selection for classification. *Intelligent Data Analysis*, *1*, 131–156. doi:10.1016/S1088-467X(97)00008-5.

Daszykowski, M., Walczak, & Massart, D. L. (2001). Looking for natural patterns in data. part 1: Density based approach. *Chemometrics and Intelligent Laboratory Systems, 56*(2), 83–92. doi:10.1016/S0169-7439(01)00111-3.

Daubechies, I., & Sweldens, W. (1998). Factoring wavelet transforms into lifting steps. *Journal of Fourier Analysis and Applications, 4*(3), 245–267. doi:10.1007/BF02476026.

Davidson, J. L., Ruffino, L. S., Stephenson, D. R., Mann, R., Grieve, B. D., & York, T. A. (2004). Three-dimensional electrical impedance tomography applied to a metal-walled filtration test platform. *Measurement Science & Technology, 15*(1), 2263–2274. doi:10.1088/0957-0233/15/11/012.

Davis, D. L., & Bouldin, D. W. (1979). A cluster separation measure. *IEEE Transactions on Pattern Analysis and Machine Intelligence, 1*, 224–227. doi:10.1109/TPAMI.1979.4766909 PMID:21868852.

De Leeuw & de Carvalho. (2009). Performance evaluation of several adaptive speckle filters for SAR imaging. In *Proceedings of Anais XIV Simpósio Brasileiro de Sensoriamento Remoto (7299-7305)*. Natal, Brasil: INPE.

De Oliveira Martins, Junior, & Silva. (2009). Detection of masses in digital mammograms using k-means and support vector machine. *Electronic Letters on Computer Vision and Image Analysis, 8*(2), 39–50.

de Tayrac, M., Aubry, M., Saïkali, S., Etcheverry, A., Surbled, C., & Mosser, J. et al. (2011). A 4-gene signature associated with clinical outcome in high-grade gliomas. *Clinical Cancer Research, 17*(2), 317–327. doi:10.1158/1078-0432.CCR-10-1126 PMID:21224364.

Demanet & Ying. (2007). Wave atoms and sparsity of oscillatory patterns. *Applied and Computational Harmonic Analysis, 23*(3), 368–387. doi:10.1016/j.acha.2007.03.003.

Dempster & Ruberto. C. D. (1999). Morphological processing of malarial slide images. In *Proceedings of Matlab DSP Conference*. Natick, MA: MathWorks.

Denyer, C. W. L. (1996). *Electronics for Real-Time and Three-Dimensional Electrical Impedance Tomographs*. (PhD Thesis). Oxford, UK, Oxford Brookes University.

Deonier, R. C., Tavaré, S., & Waterman, M. S. (2005). Measuring expression of genome information. In Computational Genome Analysis: An Introduction. (291-327). Berlin: Springer.

Derpanis, K. G. *(2004). The harris corner detector.* Retrieved from http://www.google.com/url?sa=t&rct=j&q=&esrc=s&source=web&cd=1&ved=0CC0QFjAA&url=http%3A%2F%2Fwindage.googlecode.com%2Fsvn%2Ftrunk%2FMindmap%2FTracking%2FPapers%2F%255B2004%255D%2520The%2520Harris%2520Corner%2520Detector.pdf&ei=gSXTUYXxBszc4APp64DQDA&usg=AFQjCNGlKM3AVlhJGehehVhWNfbwDDaOeg&sig2=xUs4oAo0UCCQlD97Gvf86Q&bvm=bv.48705608,d.dmg.

Devaney. (1982). Filtered backpropagation algorithm for diffraction tomography. *Ultrasonic Imaging, 4*, 336-350.

Devcic & Loncaric. (n.d.). *Non-linear image noise filtering algorithm based on SVD block processing*. Washington, DC: IEEE Press.

Dey, N., Pal, M., & Das, A. (2012). A session based watermarking technique within the NROI of retinal fundus images for authentication using DWT, spread spectrum and harris corner detection. *International Journal of Modern Engineering Research, 2*(3), 749–757.

Dey, N., Roy, A. B., Pal, M., & Das, A. (2012). FCM based blood vessel segmentation method for retinal images. *International Journal of Computer Science and Network, 1*(3).

Dey, N., Sinha, A., & Rakshit, P. (2011). A novel approach of watershed segmentation of noisy image using adaptive wavelet threshold. *International Journal of Computer Science and Information Technologies, 2*(6), 2686–2690.

Díaz, E. (2009). From microarrays to mechanisms of brain development and function. *Biochemical and Biophysical Research Communications, 385*(2), 129–131. doi:10.1016/j.bbrc.2009.05.057 PMID:19460360.

Diaz, G., Gonzalez, F. A., & Romero, E. (2009). A semi automatic method for quantification and classification of erythrocytes infected with malaria parasites in microscopic image. *Journal of Biomedical Informatics, 42*(2), 296–307. doi:10.1016/j.jbi.2008.11.005 PMID:19166974.

Dice, L. R. (1945). Measures of the amount of ecologic association between species. *Ecology, 26*(3), 297–302. doi:10.2307/1932409.

Digabel, H., & Lantuéjoul, C. (1978). Iterative algorithms. In J.-L. Chermant (Ed.), *Actes du Second Symposium Européen d'Analyse Quantitative des Microstructure es en Sciences des Matériaux, Biologie et Médecine* (85-99). Stuttgart, Germany: Riederer Verlag.

Dimitris, P. (2000). Hill climbing algorithms for content-based retrieval of similar configurations. In *Proceedings of the ACM Conference on Information Retrieval*. Athens, Greece: ACM Press.

Djamdji, F., Gorvin, A. C., Freeston, I. L., Tozer, R. C., Mayes, I. C., & Blight, S. R. (1996). Electrical impedance tomography applied to semiconductor wafer characterization. *Measurement Science & Technology, 7*(3), 391–395. doi:10.1088/0957-0233/7/3/021.

Donald, I., MacVicar, J., & Brown, T. G. (1958). Investigation of abdominal masses by pulsed ultrasound. *Lancet, 271*(7032), 1188–1195. doi:10.1016/S0140-6736(58)91905-6 PMID:13550965.

Donnino, R., Jacobs, J. E., Doshi, J. V., Hecht, E. M., Kim, D. C., Babb, J. S., & Srichai, M. B. (2009). Dual-source versus single-source cardiac CT angiography: Comparison of diagnostic image quality. *AJR. American Journal of Roentgenology, 192*(4), 1051–1056. doi:10.2214/AJR.08.1198 PMID:19304713.

Donoho, D. L. (1995). De-noising by soft-thresholding. *IEEE Transactions on Information Theory, 41*(3), 613–626. doi:10.1109/18.382009.

Donoho, D. L., & Johnstone, I. M. (1994). Ideal spatial adaptation via wavelet shrinkage. *Biometrika, 81*(3), 425–455. doi:10.1093/biomet/81.3.425.

Dougherty. (1998). Computerized evaluation of mammographic image quality using phantom images. *Computerized Medical Imaging and Graphics, 22*, 365-373.

Dougherty. (2009). *Digital image processing for medical applications* (10-13). Cambridge, UK: Cambridge University Press.

Draghici, S., Khatri, P., Eklund, A. C., & Szallasi, Z. (2006). Reliability and reproducibility issues in DNA microarray measurements. *Trends in Genetics, 22*(2), 101–109. doi:10.1016/j.tig.2005.12.005 PMID:16380191.

Driscoll, J. A., Peters, R. A., II, & Cave, K. R. (1998). A visual attention network for a humanoid robot, In *Proceedings of IEEE/RSJ International Conference on Intelligent Robots and Systems* (1968–1974). Washington, DC: IEEE Press.

Driver, J. S., & Baylis, G. C. (1989). Movement of visual attention: The spotlight metaphor breaks down. *Journal of Experimental Psychology. Human Perception and Performance, 15*, 448–456. doi:10.1037/0096-1523.15.3.448 PMID:2527954.

Du. (2005). Wavelet-based illumination normalization for face recognition. In *Proceedings of IEEE International Conference on Image Processing* (954-957). Washington, DC: IEEE Press.

Duarte, M. F., Wakin, M. B., & Baraniuk, R. G. (2008). Wavelet-domain compressive signal reconstruction using a hidden Markov tree model. In *Proceedings of International Conference on Acoustics, Speech, and Signal Processing* (5137-5140). Washington, DC: IEEE Press.

Dudoit, S., Yang, Y. H., Callow, M. J., & Speed, T. P. (2002). Statistical methods for identifying differentially expressed genes in replicated cDNA microarray experiments. *Statistica Sinica, 12*, 111–139.

Duncan, J. (1984). Selective attention and the organization of visual information. *Journal of Experimental Psychology. General, 113*, 501–517. doi:10.1037/0096-3445.113.4.501 PMID:6240521.

Dunn, J. C. (1973). A fuzzy relative of the ISO-DATA process and its use in detecting compact well separated clusters. *Journal of Cybernetics, 3*, 32–57. doi:10.1080/01969727308546046.

Du, Sun & Sima. (2004). Improved EZBC algorithm with low complexity. *IEICE Electronics Express, 1*(15), 447–452. doi:10.1587/elex.1.447.

Edan, Y., Pastermak, H., Shmulevich, I., Rachmani, D., Guedalia, D., Grinberg, A., & Fallik, E. (1997). Colour and firmness classification of tomatoes. *Journal of Food Science, 62*(4), 793–796. doi:10.1111/j.1365-2621.1997.tb15457.x.

Edd, J. F., Horowitz, L., & Rubinsky, B. (2005). Temperature dependence of tissue impedivity in electrical impedance tomography of cryosurgery. *IEEE Transactions on Bio-Medical Engineering, 52*(4), 695–701. doi:10.1109/TBME.2005.844042 PMID:15825871.

Edic, S. Tkaczyk, & Wu. (2011). System and method for energy sensitive computed tomography. *US 7885372 B2*. Retrieved from http://www.google.com/patents/US7885372.

Egly, R., Driver, J., & Rafal, R. D. (1994). Shifting visual attention between objects and locations: Evidence from normal and parietal lesion subjects. *Journal of Experimental Psychology. General, 123*(2), 161–177. doi:10.1037/0096-3445.123.2.161 PMID:8014611.

Eid, T. A. (1995). Privacy protection for patient-identifiable medical information. *Action Report. Western Governors Association, 1995*, 42–47.

Elliott, A. (2005). Medical imaging. *Nuclear Instruments & Methods in Physics Research. Section A, Accelerators, Spectrometers, Detectors and Associated Equipment, 546*(1), 1–13. doi:10.1016/j.nima.2005.03.127.

Epstein. (2008). *Introduction to the mathematics of medical imaging* (2nd ed.). Philadelphia: SIAM Press.

Eskicioglu, M., & Fisher, P. S. (1995). Image quality measures and their performance. *IEEE Transactions on Communications, 43*(12), 2959–2965. doi:10.1109/26.477498.

Ester, M., Kriegel, H., Jörg, S., & Xu, X. (1996) A density-based algorithm for discovering clusters in large spatia databases with noise. In *Proceedings of 2nd International Conference on Knowledge Discovery and Data Mining (KDD-96)*. München, Germany: University of Munich Oettingenstr Institute for Computer Science.

Fabrizi1, L., McEwan, A., Oh, T., Woo, E. J., & Holder, D. S. (2009). An electrode addressing protocol for imaging brain function with electrical impedance tomography using a 16-channel semi-parallel system. *Physiological Measurement, 30,* S85–S101.

Fantini, S., Aggarwal, P., Chen, K., & Franceschini, M. A. (2001). Monitoring brain activity using near-infrared light. *American Laboratory*, 15–17.

Faraji & MacLean. (2006). CCD noise removal in digital images. *IEEE Transactions on Image Processing, 15*(9).

Fazli, S. (2010). Complex PDE image denoising based on particle swarm optimization. In *Proceedings of 2010 International Congress Ultra-Modern Telecommunications and Control Systems and Workshops* (364–370). Washington, DC: IEEE Press.

Feig, S. A., & Hendrick, R. E. (1997). Radiation risk from screening mammography of women aged 40–49 years. *Journal of the National Cancer Institute. Monographs, 22*(22), 119–124. PMID:9709287.

Felzenszwalb, P. F., & Huttenlocher, D. P. (2004). Efficient graph-based image segmentation. *Journal of Computer Vision, 59*(2), 167–181. doi:10.1023/B:VISI.0000022288.19776.77.

Feng, B. (2002). *Study on the method of computer vision information processing and fruit gradation and detection technology*. Beijing: China Agricultural University.

Feng, J. B., Lin, I. C., Tsai, C. S., & Chu, Y. P. (2006). Reversible watermarking: Current status and key issues. *International Journal of Network Security, 2*(3), 161–171.

Ferrari, R. J., Rangayyan, R. M., Desautels, J. E. L., & Frere, A. F. (2001). Analysis of asymmetry in mammograms via directional filtering with gabor wavelets. *IEEE Transactions on Medical Imaging, 20*(9), 953–964. doi:10.1109/42.952732 PMID:11585211.

Forghani, N., Forouzanfar, M., & Forouzanfar, E. (2007). MRI fuzzy segmentation of brain tissue using IFCM algorithm with particle swarm optimization. In *Proceedings of the International Symposium on Computer and Information Science* (1-4). Tehran, Iran: Springer.

Forster, T., Roy, D., & Ghazal, P. (2003). Experiments using microarray technology: limitations and standard operating procedures. *The Journal of Endocrinology, 178*(2), 195–204. doi:10.1677/joe.0.1780195 PMID:12904167.

Francetič, M., Nagode, M., & Nastav, B. (2005) Hierarchical clustering with concave data sets. *Metodološki zvezki, 2*(2), 173-193.

Franconeri, S. L., Hollingworth, A., & Simons, D. J. (2005). Do new objects capture attention? *Psychological Science, 16*(4), 275–281. doi:10.1111/j.0956-7976.2005.01528.x PMID:15828974.

Franconeri, S. L., & Simons, D. J. (2003). Moving and looming stimuli capture attention. *Perception & Psychophysics, 65*(7), 999–1010. doi:10.3758/BF03194829 PMID:14674628.

Frank, G. K. W., & Kaye, W. H. (2012). Current status of functional imaging in eating disorders. *The International Journal of Eating Disorders, 45*(6), 723–736. doi:10.1002/eat.22016 PMID:22532388.

Frean, J. (2010). Microscopic determination of malaria parasite load: Role of image analysis. *Microscopy: Science, Technology, Application, and Education*, *3*, 862–866.

Frerichs, I., Schmitz, G., Pulletz, S., Schadler, D., Zick, G., Scholz, J., & Weiler, N. (2007). Reproducibility of regional lung ventilation distribution determined by electrical impedance tomography during mechanical ventilation. *Physiological Measurement*, *28*, S261–S267. doi:10.1088/0967-3334/28/7/S19 PMID:17664640.

Fullerton, G. D. (1980). Fundamentals of CT tissue characterization. In G. D. Fullerton and J.A. Zagzebski (eds.), Medical Physics of CT and Ultrasound: Tissue Imaging and Characterization (125-162). New York: American Association of Physicists in Medicine.

Funk, C., Bryant, S., & Heckman, P. (1972). Handbook of underwater imaging system design. *Techical Report TR303*. San Diego, CA: Naval Undersea Center

Furukawa Y. & Ponce J. (2010). Accurate, dense, and robust multiview stereopsis. *IEEE Transactions on Pattern Analysis & Machine Intelligence, 32*(8). doi:1362-1376 2010.

Gao & Zheng. (2008). Quality constrained compression using DWT-based image quality metric. *IEEE Transactions on Circuits and Systems for Video Technology*, *18*(7), 910–922. doi:10.1109/TCSVT.2008.920744.

Gao, J., & Xie, M. (2009). Skull-stripping MR brain images using anisotropic diffusion filtering and morphological processing. In *Proceedings of the International Symposium on Computer Network and Multimedia Technology* (1-4). Wuhan, China: IEEE Press.

Gao, K., Lin, S., Zhang, Y., Tang, S., & Zhang, D. (2009). Logo detection based on spatio-spectral saliency and partial spatial context. In *Proceedings of IEEE International Conference on Multimedia and Expo* (322–329). Washington, DC: IEEE Press.

Garcia, R., Nicosevici, T., & Cufi, X. (2002). On the way to solve lighting problems in underwater imaging. In *Proceedings of the IEEE Oceans Conference* (263-266). Washington, DC: IEEE Press.

Garreau, Simon, & Boulmier, Coatrieux, & Le Breton. (2006). Assessment of left ventricular function in cardiac MSCT imaging by a 4D hierarchical surface volume matching process. *International Journal of Biomedical Imaging*. doi:10.1155/IJBI/2006/37607 PMID:23165027.

Geertsma, de Bruijn, Hilbers-Modderman, Hollestelle, Bakker, & Roszek. (2007). New and emerging medical technologies: A horizon scan of opportunities and risks. *Report 360020002*. Bilthoven, Netherlands: Rijksinstituut voor Volksgezondheid en Milieu. Retrieved from http://www.rivm.nl/bibliotheek/rapporten/360020002.html.

Geetha, P., & Annadurai, S. (2004a). Fast, efficient, and secured lossless coding of medical images using reversible integer wavelet transform. In *Proceedings of 3rd FAE International Conference of European University of Lefke* (320-325). Turkish Republic of Northern Cyprus: FAE Press.

Geetha, P., & Annadurai, S. (2004b). Fast and efficient secured lossless coding of medical images-Use of the lifting scheme. In *Proceedings of IEEE International Conference on Signal Processing and Communications* (23-25). Bangalore, India: IEEE Press.

Geetha, P., & Annadurai, S. (2005). efficient secured lossless compression of medical images–Using modified run-length coding for character representation. In *Proceedings of IEEE Indicon-2005* (66-68). Washington, DC: IEEE Press.

Geetha, P., & Annadurai, S. (2006). Efficient secured lossless coding of medical images-Using region based modified SPIHT and modified run-length coding for character representation. *International Journal on Graphics Vision and Image Processing*, *9*, 40–47.

Geetha, P., & Annadurai, S. (2007). Efficient secured lossless coding of medical images-using a new fast embedded significant and zero set coding in hierarchical trees. *AMSE Journal*, *50*(1), 18–35.

Geetha, P., & Annadurai, S. (2008). Medical image compression using a novel embedded set partitioning significant and zero block coding (ESPSZBC). *International Arab Journal of Information Technology*, *5*(2), 132–139.

Gentleman, R. C., Carey, V. J., Bates, D. M., Bolstad, B., Dettling, M., & Zhang, J. et al. (2004). Bioconductor: Open software development for computational biology and bioinformatics. *Genome Biology*, *5*(10), R80. doi:10.1186/gb-2004-5-10-r80 PMID:15461798.

Gesu, V. D., Valenti, C., & Strinati, L. (1997). Local operators to detect regions of interest. *Pattern Recognition Letters*, *18*, 1077–1081. doi:10.1016/S0167-8655(97)00084-6.

Gevins, A. (1998). The future of electroencephalography in assessing neurocognitive functioning. *Electroencephalography and Clinical Neurophysiology*, *106*, 165–172. doi:10.1016/S0013-4694(97)00120-X PMID:9741778.

Gezici, Yilmaz, Gerek, Enis, & Etin. (2001). *Image denoising using adaptive subband decomposition*. Washington, DC: IEEE Press.

Ghazanfari, A. J., & Irudayaraj, K. A. (1996). Grading pistachio nuts using a neural network approach. *Transactions of the ASAE. American Society of Agricultural Engineers*, *39*(6), 2319–2324.

Gilbert, P. (1972). Iterative methods for the three-dimensional reconstruction of an object from projections. *Journal of Theoretical Biology*, *36*, 105–117. doi:10.1016/0022-5193(72)90180-4 PMID:5070894.

Gilboa, Sochen, & Zeevi. (2004). Image enhancement and denoising by complex diffusion. *IEEE Transactions on Pattern Analysis and Machine Intelligence*, *26*(8). doi:10.1109/TPAMI.2004.47 PMID:15641732.

Girodias, K. A., Barrett, H. H., & Shoemaker, R. L. (1991). Parallel simulated annealing for emission tomography. *Physics in Medicine and Biology*, *36*(7), 921–938. doi:10.1088/0031-9155/36/7/002 PMID:1886927.

Gisser, D. G., Isaacson, D., & Newell, J. C. (1987). Current topics in impedance imaging. *Clinical Physics and Physiological Measurement*, *8*, 39–46. doi:10.1088/0143-0815/8/4A/005 PMID:3568569.

Goitein, M. (1972). Three-dimensional density reconstruction from a series of two-dimensional projections. *Nuclear Instruments and Methods in Physics*, *101*, 509–518. doi:10.1016/0029-554X(72)90039-0.

Gonzalez, Woods, & Eddins. (2003). *Digital Image Processing Using MATLAB*. Upper Saddle River, NJ: Pearson Prentice Hall.

Gonzalez. (2011). *Digital image processing* (3rd Ed.). Upper Saddle River, NJ: Pearson publication.

Gonzalez, R. C., & Wood, R. E. (2011). *Digital image processing using MATLAB* (2nd ed.). New York: McGraw Hill Companies.

Gonzalez, R. C., & Woods, R. E. (2002). *Digital image processing*. New York: Prentice Hall.

Gopalakrishnan, V., Hu, Y., & Rajan, D. (2009). Random walks on graphs to model saliency in images. In *Proceedings of IEEE Computer Society Conference on Computer Vision and Pattern Recognition* (1698–1705).

Gopalappa, C., Das, T. K., Enkemann, T., & Eschrich, S. S. (2009). Removal of hybridization and scanning noise from microarrays. *IEEE Transactions on Nanobioscience*, *8*(3), 210–218. doi:10.1109/TNB.2009.2029100 PMID:20051337.

Gordon, Bender, & Herman. (1970). Algebraic reconstruction technique (ART) for three dimensional electron microscopy and X-ray photography. *Journal of Theoretical Biology*, *29*, 471–481. doi:10.1016/0022-5193(70)90109-8 PMID:5492997.

Gordon, R. (1974). A tutorial on ART. *IEEE Transactions on Nuclear Science*, *21*, 78–93.

Gordon, R., Bender, R., & Herman, G. T. (1970). Algebraic reconstruction techniques (ART) for three-dimensional electron microscopy and x-ray photography. *Journal of Theoretical Biology*, *29*, 471–481. doi:10.1016/0022-5193(70)90109-8 PMID:5492997.

Gottlieb, J. P., Kusunoki, M., & Goldberg, M. E. (1998). The representation of visual salience in monkey parietal cortex. *Nature*, *391*, 481–484. doi:10.1038/35135 PMID:9461214.

Gøtzsche, P. C. (2011). Screening for breast cancer with mammography. *Cochrane Database of Systematic Reviews*, 1.

Graham, B. M. (2007). *Enhancements in Electrical Impedance Tomography (EIT) Image Reconstruction for 3D Lung Imaging*. (PhD thesis). Ottawa, Ontario, University of Ottawa.

Green, P. J. (1990). Bayesian reconstructions from emission tomography data using a modified EM algorithm. *IEEE Transactions on Medical Imaging*, *9*, 84–93. doi:10.1109/42.52985 PMID:18222753.

Green, P. S., & Simpkins, J. W. (2000). Neuroprotective effects of estrogens: Potential mechanisms of action. *International Journal of Developmental Neuroscience*, *18*(4-5), 347–358. doi:10.1016/S0736-5748(00)00017-4 PMID:10817919.

Griffiths, H. (1988). A phantom for electrical impedance tomography. *Clinical Physics and Physiological Measurement*, *9*, 15–20. doi:10.1088/0143-0815/9/4A/003 PMID:3240643.

Grootveld, C. J. (1996). *Measuring and Modeling of Concentrated Settling Suspensions Using Electrical Impedance Tomography*. (PhD Thesis). Delft, Netherlands, Delft University of Technology.

Grossberg, S. (1976a). Adaptive pattern classification and universal recoding. I. Parallel development and coding of neural feature detectors. *Biological Cybernetics*, *23*, 121–134. doi:10.1007/BF00344744 PMID:974165.

Grossberg, S. (1976b). Adaptive pattern classification and universal recoding. ii. feedback, expectation, olfaction, and illusions. *Biological Cybernetics*, *23*, 187–202. PMID:963125.

Guerra, A. D. (2004). *Ionizing radiation detectors for medical imaging*. Singapore: World Scientific Pub. Co. Inc..

Guimera, A., Gabriel, G., Plata-Cordero, M., Montero, L., Maldonado, M. J., & Villa, R. (2012). A non-invasive method for an in vivo assessment of corneal epithelium permeability through tetrapolar impedance measurements. *Biosensors & Bioelectronics*, *31*, 55–61. doi:10.1016/j.bios.2011.09.039 PMID:22019100.

Guironnet, M., Guyader, N., Pellerin, D., & Ladret, P. (2005). Spatio temporal attention model for video content analysis. In *Proceedings of IEEE International Conference on Image Processing* (1156-1159). Washington, DC: IEEE Press.

Gunturu & Sharma. (2010). Contrast enhancement of mammographic images using wavelet transform. In *Proceedings of 3rd IEEE International Conference on Computer Science and Information Technology*. Washington, DC: IEEE Press.

Guo, Y., Mu, Z., Zeng, H., & Wang, K. (2010). Fast rotation-invariant DAISY descriptor for image keypoint matching. ISM, 183-190.

Gupta & Gupta. (n.d.). *Wavelet domain image enhancement using local regularity*. Pilani, India. *BITS Pilani.*.

Gupta, Kumar, & Sharma. (2011). Data mining classification techniques applied for breast cancer diagnosis and prognosis. *Indian Journal of Computer Science and Engineering*, *2*(2).

Gupta, R., Cheung, A. C., Bartling, S. H., Lisauskas, J., Grasruck, M., & Brady, T. J. et al. (2008). Flat-panel volume CT: Fundamental principles, technology, and applications. *Radiographics*, *28*(7). doi:10.1148/rg.287085004 PMID:19001655.

Gupta, R., & Undrill, P. E. (1995). The use of texture analysis to delineate suspicious masses in mammography. *Physics in Medicine and Biology*, *40*(5), 835–855. doi:10.1088/0031-9155/40/5/009 PMID:7652011.

Hafizah & Supriyanto. (2011). Comparative evaluation of ultrasound kidney image enhancement techniques. *International Journal of Computers and Applications*, *21*(7).

Haidekker. (2011). *Advanced biomedical image analysis*. Hoboken, NJ: John Wiley and Sons.

Hamouda, A., Khedr, A. Y., & Ramadan, R. A. (2012). Automated red blood cell counting. *International Journal of Computing Science*, *1*(2), 1366–1374.

Han, J., Kamber, M., & Pei, J. (2005). *Data mining: Concepts and techniques*. New York: Morgan Kaufmann.

Hao & Sun. (2010). A modified retinex algorithm based on wavelet transformation. In *Proceedings of International Conference on Multimedia and Information Technology* (306-309). New York: ACM Press.

Haralick, R. M., & Sternberg, S. R. (1987). Image analysis using mathematical morphology. *IEEE Transactions on Pattern Analysis and Machine Intelligence*, *9*(4), 532–550. doi:10.1109/TPAMI.1987.4767941 PMID:21869411.

Hardy, J., Cookson, M. R., & Singleton, A. (2003). Genes and parkinsonism. *The Lancet Neurology*, *2*(4), 221–228. doi:10.1016/S1474-4422(03)00350-8 PMID:12849210.

Harel, J., Koch, C., & Perona, P. (2006). Graph-based visual saliency. *Advances in Neural Information Processing Systems*, 19.

Haris, K., Efstratiadis, S. N., Maglaveras, N., & Katsaggelos, A. K. (1998). Hybrid image segmentation using watersheds and fast region merging. *IEEE Transactions on Image Processing*, *7*(12), 1684–1699. doi:10.1109/83.730380 PMID:18276235.

Harms, H., Aus, H., Haucke, M., & Gunzer, U. (1986). Segmentation of stained blood cell images measured at high scanning density with high magnification and high numerical aperture optics. *Cytometry*, *7*, 522–531. doi:10.1002/cyto.990070605 PMID:2430764.

Harris, C., & Stephens, M. (1988). A combined corner and edge detector. In *Proceedings of 4th Alvey Vision Conference*. Manchester, UK: Manchester University Press.

Hartley, R. I. (1998). Chierality. *International Journal of Computer Vision*, *26*(1), 4161. doi:10.1023/A:1007984508483.

Hartley, R., & Zisserman, A. (2000). *Multiview geometry in computer vision*. Cambridge, UK: Cambridge University Press.

Hartline, H. K. (1938). The response of single optic nerve fibers of the vertebrate eye to illumination of the retina. *The American Journal of Physiology*, *121*, 400–415.

He, D. (1998). *Color classification of fresh fruits by neural network*. Shanxi, China: Xibei Agricultural University.

Heinen, M. R., & Engel, P. M. (2009). Evaluation of visual attention models under 2D similarity transformations. In *Proceedings of ACM Symposium on Applied Computing* (1156–1160). New York: ACM Press.

Hendee, R. W. (1989). Cross sectional medical imaging: A history. *Radiographics*, *9*(6), 1155–1180. PMID:2685939.

Herbert, T., & Leahy, R. (1989). A generalized EM algorithm for 3-D bayesian reconstruction from poisson data using gibbs priors. *IEEE Transactions on Medical Imaging*, *8*, 194–202. doi:10.1109/42.24868 PMID:18230517.

Herman, G. T. (1980). *Image reconstruction from projections: The fundamentals of computed tomography*. New York: Academic.

Herman, G. T. (2009). *Fundamentals of computerized tomography: Image reconstruction from projection* (2nd ed.). Berlin: Springer. doi:10.1007/978-1-84628-723-7.

Hero, A. O., Piramuthu, R., Fessler, J. A., & Titus, S. R. (1999). Minimax emission computed tomography using high-resolution anatomical side information and B-Spline models. *IEEE Transactions on Information Theory*, *45*(3), 920–938. doi:10.1109/18.761333.

Herrero-Langreo. (2012). Combination of optical and non-destructive mechanical techniques for the measurement of maturity in peach. *Journal of Food Engineering*, *108*, 150–157. doi:10.1016/j.jfoodeng.2011.07.004.

Hilbert. (1953). *Grundzuge einer allgemeinen theorie der linearen integralgleichungen*. New York: Chelsea Publishing Company.

Hinestrosa, M. C., Dickersin, K., Klein, P., Mayer, M., Noss, K., & Visco, F. M. et al. (2007). Shaping the future of biomarker research in breast cancer to ensure clinical relevance. *Nature Reviews. Cancer*, *7*(4), 309–315. doi:10.1038/nrc2113 PMID:17384585.

Hinneburg, A. (2007). Denclue 2.0: Fast clustering based on kernel density estimation. In *Proceedings of the 7th International Conference on Intelligent Data Analysis* (70-80). Berlin: Springer-Verlag.

Ho, C.-C., Cheng, W.-H., Pan, T.-J., & Wu, J.-L. (2003). A user-attention based focus detection framework and its applications. In *Proceedings of the Joint Conference of the 4th International Conference on Information, Communications, and Signal Processing, and the 4th Pacific Rim Conference on Multimedia* (1315–1319). Washington, DC: IEEE Press.

Hogue, A., German, A., & Jenkin, M. (2007). Underwater environment reconstruction using stereo and inertial data. *IEEE International Conference on Systems, Man and Cybernetics* (2372–2377). Washington, DC: IEEE Press.

Holder, D. S. (1993). *Clinical and physiological applications of electrical impedance tomography* (1st ed.). Philadelphia: Taylor & Francis.

Holder, D. S. (Ed.). (2005). *Electrical impedance tomography: Methods, history, and applications. Series in Medical Physics and Biomedical Engineering* (1st ed.). London: Institute of Physics Publishing Ltd..

Holder, D. S., Hanquan, Y., & Rao, A. (1996). Some practical biological phantoms for calibrating multifrequency electrical impedance tomography. *Physiological Measurement*, *17*, A167–A177. doi:10.1088/0967-3334/17/4A/021 PMID:9001615.

Hope, T. A., & Iles, S. E. (2004). Technology review: The use of electrical impedance scanning in the detection of breast cancer. *Breast Cancer Research*, *6*, 69–74. doi:10.1186/bcr744 PMID:14979909.

Horspool, N., & Cormack, G. (1992). Constructing word-based text compression algorithms. In *Proceedings of the IEEE Data Compression Conference* (62-71). Washington, DC: IEEE Press.

Hou, W., & Weidemann, A. D. (2007). Objectively assessing underwater image quality for the purpose of automated restoration. In *Proceedings of SPIE Visual Information Processing XVI*. Orlando, FL: SPIE Press.

Hou, W., Gray, D. J., Weidemann, A. D., Fournier, G. R., & Forand, J. L. (2007). Automated underwater image restoration and retrieval of related optical properties. In *Proceedings of the IEEE International Geoscience and Remote Sensing Symposium* (1889–1892).

Hou, X., & Zhang, L. (2007). Saliency detection: A spectral residual approach. In *Proceedings of IEEE Conference on Computer Vision and Pattern Recognition* (1–8). Washington, DC: IEEE Press.

Hounsfield, G. N. (1979). Computed medical imaging (568-586). London: The Medical Systems Department of Central Research Laboratories EMI.

Hou, T. C., Loh, K. J., & Lynch, J. P. (2007). Spatial conductivity mapping of carbon nanotube composite thin films by electrical impedance tomography for sensing applications. *Nanotechnology*, *18*, 9. doi:10.1088/0957-4484/18/31/315501.

Hou, W. D., & Mo, Y. L. (2002). Increasing image resolution in electrical impedance tomography. *Electronics Letters*, *38*, 701–702. doi:10.1049/el:20020477.

Hou, W. D., & Mo, Y. L. (2002). New regularization method in electrical impedance tomography. *Journal of Shanghai University*, *6*(3), 211–215. doi:10.1007/s11741-002-0036-x.

Howard, P. G., & Vitter, J. S. (1993). Fast and efficient lossless image compression. In *Proceedings of IEEE Data Compression Conference* (351-360). Washington, DC: IEEE Press.

Hsiang, S. T., & Woods, J. W. (2000). Embedded image coding using zeroblocks of subband/wavelet coefficients and context modeling. *Proceeding of IEEE ISCAS, 3,* 662-665.

Hsieh, J. (2009). *Computed tomography: Principles design artifacts and recent advances.* Bellingham, WA: SPIE Press.

Hu, Y., Rajan, D., & Chia, L. T. (2005). Adaptive local context suppression of multiple cues for salient visual attention detection. In *Proceedings of IEEE International Conference on Multimedia and Expo* (346-349). Washington, DC: IEEE Press.

Hu, Y., Xie, X., Ma, W.-Y., Chia, L.-T., & Rajan, D. (2004). Salient region detection using weighted feature maps based on the human visual attention model. In *Proceedings of Pacific-Rim Conference on Multimedia* (993–1000). Washington, DC: IEEE Press.

Hua, P., Webster, J. G., & Tompkins, W. J. (1987). Effect of the measurement method on noise handling and image quality of EIT imaging. In *Proceedings of Ninth International Conference of IEEE Engineering in Medicine and Biology Society* (1429-1430). New York: IEEE Press.

Huang, H., Coatrieux, G., Shu, H. Z., Luo, L. M., & Roux, C. (2011). Medical image integrity control and forensics based on watermarking-Approximating local modifications and identifying global image alterations. In *Proceedings of the Annual International Conference of the IEEE on Engineering in Medicine and Biology Society* (8062-8065). Washington, DC: IEEE Press.

Huda, W., & Slone, R. (1995). *Review of radiologic physics.* Baltimore: Williams and Wilkins.

Hudson & Larkin. (1994). Accelerated image reconstruction using ordered subsets of projection data. *IEEE Transactions on Medical Imaging, 13*, 601–609. doi:10.1109/42.363108 PMID:18218538.

Huffman, D. A. (1952). A method for the construction of minimum redundancy codes. *Proceeding of IRE, (40)*, 1098-1101.

Hurvich, L. M., & Jameson, D. (1957). An opponent-process theory of color vision. *Psychological Review, 64*, 384–404. doi:10.1037/h0041403 PMID:13505974.

Ingham, M., Pringle, D., & Eicken, H. (2008). Cross-borehole resistivity tomography of sea ice. *Cold Regions Science and Technology, 52*, 263–277. doi:10.1016/j.coldregions.2007.05.002.

Iniewski, K. (2009). *Medical imaging: Principles, detectors, and electronics*. Hoboken, NJ: John Wiley & Sons, Inc..

Iqbal, K., Abdul Salam, R., Osman, A., & Zawawi Talib, A. (2007). Underwater image enhancement using an integrated color model. *International Journal of Computer Science, 34*(2).

Itti, L., & Koch, C. (1999a). A comparison of feature combination strategies for saliency based visual attention systems. In *Proceedings of SPIE Human Vision and Electronic Imaging* (473-482). Bellingham, WA: SPIE Press.

Itti, L., & Koch, C. (1999b). Target detection using saliency-based attention. In *Proceedings of RTO/SCI-12 Workshop on Search and Target Acquisition (NATO Unclassified)* (3.1–3.10). Washington, DC: NATO.

Itti, L. (2004). Automatic foveation for video compression using a neurobiological model of visual attention. *IEEE Transactions on Image Processing, 13*, 1304–1318. doi:10.1109/TIP.2004.834657 PMID:15462141.

Itti, L., & Koch, C. (2001). Computational modeling of visual attention. *Nature Reviews. Neuroscience, 2*, 194–203. doi:10.1038/35058500 PMID:11256080.

Itti, L., Koch, C., & Niebur, E. (1998). A model of saliency-based visual attention for rapid scene analysis. *IEEE Transactions on Pattern Analysis and Machine Intelligence, 20*(11), 1254–1259. doi:10.1109/34.730558.

Jaffe, J. S. (1990). Computer modeling and the design of optical underwater imaging systems. *IEEE Journal of Oceanic Engineering, 15*(2), 221–231. doi:10.1109/48.50695.

Jain. (2006). Fundamentals of digital image processing. In *Proceedings of PHI*. India: PHI Press.

Jain, A. K. (1988). *Algorithms for clustering data*. Upper Saddle River, NJ: Prentice Hall.

Jain, A. K. (2011). *Fundamentals of digital image processing*. Upper Saddle River, NJ: Prentice Hall.

Jambhekar, N. D. (2011). Red blood cells classification using image processing. *Science Research Reporter, 1*(3).

Järvinen, A. K., Hautaniemi, S., Edgren, H., Auvinen, P., Saarela, J., Kallioniemi, O. P., & Monni, O. (2004). Are data from different gene expression microarray platforms comparable? *Genomics, 83*(6), 1164–1168. doi:10.1016/j.ygeno.2004.01.004 PMID:15177569.

Jaume, C., & Lluís, G. (2012). The dark side of the lung: Unveiling regional lung ventilation with electrical impedance tomography. *Anesthesiology, 116*(6), 1186–1188. doi:10.1097/ALN.0b013e318256ef0a PMID:22546963.

Jiao, L. (2011). Evolutionary based image segmentation methods. In P.-G. Ho (Ed.), Image Segmentation (179-224). Rijecka, Croatia: InTech Publishing.

Jin, Wernick, Yang, Brankov, Gravier, Feng, & King. (2006). 5D image reconstruction for tomographic image sequences. In *Proceedings of Fortieth Asilomar Conference on Signals, Systems, and Computers*. Pacific Grove, CA: IEEE Press.

Jinchuang, Z., Wenli, F., Taoshen, L., & Shi, W. (2002). An image reconstruction algorithm based on a revised regularization method for electrical capacitance tomography. *Measurement Science & Technology, 13*(4), 638–640. doi:10.1088/0957-0233/13/4/329.

Jing, F., Li, M., Zhang, H.-J., & Zhang, B. (2002). An effective region-based image retrieval framework. In *Proceedings of ACM Multimedia*. New York: ACM Press.

Jing, Z., Li, Z., Jingjing, G., & Zhixing, L. (2009). A study of top-down visual attention model based on similarity distance. In *Proceedings of 2nd International Congress on Image and Signal Processing* (1–5). Berlin: Springer.

Jonides, J., & Yantis, S. (1988). Uniqueness of abrupt visual onset in capturing attention. *Perception & Psychophysics, 43*(4), 346–354. doi:10.3758/BF03208805 PMID:3362663.

Joo & Kim. (2003). *PDE-based image restoration, I: Anti-staircasing and anti-diffusion. Technical Report #2003-07.* Lexington, KY: University of Kentucky.

Kaczmarz. (1937). Angenaherte auflosunf, von systemen linearer gleichungen. *Bulletin de l'Academie des Sciences et Letters, A, 35,* 355-357.

Kak & Slaney. (2001). *Principles of computerized tomographic imaging.* Retrieved from http://www.slaney.org/pct/pct-toc.html.

Kak, A. C., & Slaney, M. (1999). *Principle of computerized tomographic imaging.* Washington, DC: IEEE Press.

Kalender, W. A. (2011). *Computed tomography* (3rd ed.). London: Publicis.

Kane, M. D., Jatkoe, T. A., Stumpf, C. R., Lu, J., Thomas, J. D., & Madore, S. J. (2000). Assessment of the sensitivity and specificity of oligonucleotide (50mer) microarrays. *Nucleic Acids Research, 28*(22), 4552–4557. doi:10.1093/nar/28.22.4552 PMID:11071945.

Karhunen, K., Seppänen, A., Lehikoinen, A., Monteiro, P. J. M., & Kaipio, J. P. (2010). Electrical resistance tomography imaging of concrete. *Cement and Concrete Research, 40,* 137–145. doi:10.1016/j.cemconres.2009.08.023.

Kaufman, L., & Rousseeuw, P. J. (1990). *Finding groups in data: An introduction to cluster analysis.* New York: John Wiley & Sons. doi:10.1002/9780470316801.

Kaur, L., Gupta, S., & Chauhan, R. C. (2002). Image denoising using wavelet thresholding. In *Proceedings of Indian Conference on Computer Vision, Graphics, and Image Processing.* Ahmedabad, India: ICVGIP Press.

Kay, S. M. (1999). *Modern spectral estimation: Theory and application.* Upper Saddle River, NJ: Prentice Hall.

Kazuhiro, N. (1997). Application of neural networks to the color grading of apples. *Computers and Electronics in Agriculture, 18*(2–3), 105–116.

Ke, C. (2008). White blood cell detection using a novel fuzzy morphological shared-weight neural network. In *Proceedings of the International Symposium on Computer Science and Computational Technology.* Washington, DC: IEEE Press.

Kerner, T. E., Williams, D. B., Osterman, K. S., Reiss, F. R., Hartov, A., & Paulsen, K. D. (2000). Electrical impedance imaging at multiple frequencies in phantoms. *Physiological Measurement, 21,* 67–77. doi:10.1088/0967-3334/21/1/309 PMID:10720001.

Khan, J., Wei, J. S., Ringnér, M., Saal, L. H., Ladanyi, M., & Meltzer, P. S. et al. (2001). Classification and diagnostic prediction of cancers using gene expression profiling and artificial neural networks. *Nature Medicine, 7*(6), 673–679. doi:10.1038/89044 PMID:11385503.

Khare & Tiwary. (2005). Soft-thresholding for denoising of medical images, A multiresolution approach. *International Journal of Wavelets, Multresolution, and Information Processing, 3*(4), 477–496. doi:10.1142/S021969130500097X.

Khot, S. T., & Prasad, R. K. (2012). Computerized hematology counter. *International Journal of Medical and Clinical Research, 3*(6), 190–194.

Kienzle, W., Wichmann, F. A., Scholkopf, B., & Franz, M. O. (2006). A non-parametric approach to bottom-up visual saliency. *Advances in Neural Information Processing Systems, 19.*

Kim & Ra. (2005). Improvement of ultrasound image based on wavelet transform: Speckle reduction and edge enhancement in medical imaging, image processing. *Processing of SPIE, 5747.*

Kim, E. (2010). Insulin resistance at the crossroads of metabolic syndrome: Systemic analysis using microarrays. *Biotechnology Journal, 5*(9), 919–929. doi:10.1002/biot.201000048 PMID:20669253.

Kim, J. B., & Kim, H. J. (2003). Multi-resolution–based watersheds for efficient image segmentation. *Pattern Recognition Letters, 24,* 473–488. doi:10.1016/S0167-8655(02)00270-2.

Kitada, T., Asakawa, S., Hattori, N., Matsumine, H., Yamamura, Y., & Shimizu, N. et al. (1998). Mutations in the parkin gene cause autosomal recessive juvenile parkinsonism. *Nature, 392*(6676), 605–608. doi:10.1038/33416 PMID:9560156.

Kiyan & Yildirim. (2004). Breast cancer diagnosis using statistical neural networks. In *Proceedings of Turkish Symposium on Artificial Intelligence and Neural Networks.* Istanbul: TAINN Press.

Klein, R., Kingstone, A., & Pontefract, A. (1992). Orienting of visual attention, In K. Rayner (Ed.), Eye Movements and Visual Cognition: Scene Perception and Reading (46-65). New York: Springer.

Knuth, D. E. (1985). Dynamic huffman coding. *Journal of Algorithms, 6*, 163–180. doi:10.1016/0196-6774(85)90036-7.

Kobayashi, L. O. M., Furuie, S. S., & Barreto, P. S. L. M. (2009). Providing integrity and authenticity in DICOM images: A novel approach. *IEEE Transactions on Information Technology in Biomedicine, 13*(4), 582–589. doi:10.1109/TITB.2009.2014751 PMID:19244022.

Koch, C., & Ullman, S. (1985). Shifts in selective visual attention: towards the underlying neural circuitry. *Human Neurobiology, 4*, 219–227. PMID:3836989.

Kokko, A. (2006). *Expression Microarray Technology as a Tool in Cancer Research.* (Unpublished Doctoral Dissertation). Helsinki, Finland, Helsinki University of Technology.

Kole, D. K., & Halder, A. (2012). Automatic brain tumor detection and isolation of tumor cells from MRI images. *International Journal of Computers and Applications, 39*(16), 26–30. doi:10.5120/4905-7416.

Kolehmainen, V., Somersalo, E., Vauhkonen, P. J., Vauhkonen, M., & Kaipio, J. P. (1998). A bayesian approach and total variation priors in 3D electrical impedance tomography. In *Proceedings of the 20th Annual International Conference of the IEEE Engineering in Medicine and Biology Society* (1028-1031). Hong Kong: IEEE Press.

Korpinen, L., Kuisti, H., Elovaara, J., & Virtanen, V. (2012). Cardiac pacemakers in electric and magnetic fields of 400-kV power lines. *Pacing and Clinical Electrophysiology, 35*(4), 422–430. doi:10.1111/j.1540-8159.2011.03327.x PMID:22309463.

Kothari, M. S., Rusby, J. E., Agusti, A. A., & MacNeill, F. A. (2012). Sentinel lymph node biopsy after previous axillary surgery: A review. *European Journal of Surgical Oncology, 38*(1), 8–15. doi:10.1016/j.ejso.2011.10.003 PMID:22032909.

Krishnan, M. M. R., Acharya, U. R., Chakraborty, C., & Ray, A. K. (2011). Automated diagnosis of oral cancer using higher order spectra features and local binary pattern: A comparative study. *Technology in Cancer Research & Treatment, 10*, 433–455. PMID:21895029.

Krishnan, M. M. R., Choudhary, A., Chakraborty, C., & Ray, A. K. (2011). Texture based segmentation of epithelial layer from oral histological images. *Micron (Oxford, England), 42*, 632–641. doi:10.1016/j.micron.2011.03.003.

Krishnan, M. M. R., Shah, P., Chakraborty, C., & Ray, A. K. (2010). Statistical analysis of textural features for improved classification of oral histopathological images. *Journal of Medical Systems.* doi: doi:10.1007/s10916-010-9550-8.

Krishnan, M. M. R., Shah, P., Chakraborty, C., & Ray, A. K. (2011). Brownian motion curve based textural classification and its application towards cancer diagnosis. *Analytical and Quantitative Cytology and Histology, 33*(3), 158–168. PMID:21980619.

Krishnan, M. M. R., Shah, P., Choudhary, A., Chakraborty, C., Paul, R. R., & Ray, A. K. (2011). Textural characterization of histopathological images for oral sub-mucous fibrosis detection. *Tissue & Cell*; Epub ahead of print. PMID:21824635.

Krishnan, M. M. R., Shah, P., Pal, M., Chakraborty, C., Paul, R. R., Chatterjee, J., & Ray, A. K. (2010). Structural markers for normal oral mucosa and oral sub-mucous fibrosis. *Micron (Oxford, England), 41*(4), 312–320. doi:10.1016/j.micron.2009.12.002.

Kubiak, T., & Stone, A. A. (2012). Ambulatory monitoring of biobehavioral processes in health and disease. *Psychosomatic Medicine, 74*(4), 325–326. doi:10.1097/PSY.0b013e31825878da PMID:22582329.

Kuchment & Kunyansky. (2008). A survey in mathematics and industry-Mathematics of thermoacoustic tomography. *European Journal of Applied Mathematics, 19*, 191–224. doi: doi:10.1017/S095679250800735.

Kujan, O., Oliver, R. J., Khattab, A., Roberts, S. A., Thakker, N., & Sloan, P. (2006). Evaluation of a new binary system of grading oral epithelial dysplasia for prediction of malignant transformation. *Oral Oncology*, *42*(10), 987–993. doi:10.1016/j.oraloncology.2005.12.014 PMID:16731030.

Kuperman, V. (2000). *Magnetic resonance imaging: Physical principles and applications*. New York: Academic Press.

Kutulakos, K. N., & Seitz, S. M. (2000). A theory of shape by space carving. *International Journal of Computer Vision*, *38*(3), 199–218. doi:10.1023/A:1008191222954.

Kwan, R. K.-S., Evans, A. C., & Pike, G. B. (1999). MRI simulation-based evaluation of image-processing and classification methods. *IEEE Transactions on Medical Imaging*, *18*, 1085–1097. doi:10.1109/42.816072 PMID:10661326.

Lab Tests Online. (2013). Red blood cell count. Retrieved from http://labtestsonline.org/understanding/analytes/rbc/tab/test.

LaBerge, D. (1983). Spatial extent of attention to letters and words. *Journal of Experimental Psychology. Human Perception and Performance*, *9*, 371–379. doi:10.1037/0096-1523.9.3.371 PMID:6223977.

Lagarias, Reeds, Wright, & Wright. (1998). Convergence properties of the nelder-mead simplex method in low dimensions. *SIAM Journal on Optimization*, *9*(1), 112–147. doi:10.1137/S1052623496303470.

Lai & Kuo. (1997). Image quality measurement using the haar wavelet. In *Proceedings of SPIE: Wavelet Applications in Signal and Image Processing V*. Bellingham, WA: SPIE Press.

Lakhani, G. (2003). Modified JPEG huffman coding. *IEEE Transactions on Image Processing*, *12*, 159–169. doi:10.1109/TIP.2003.809001 PMID:18237897.

Landi. (2007). A truncated lagrange method for total variation-based image restoration. *Journal of Mathematical Imaging and Vision, 28*, 113–123.

Landini, G. (2006). Quantitative analysis of the epithelial lining architecture in odontogenic cysts. *Head & Face Medicine*, 2–4. PMID:16420691.

Landini, G., & Othman, I. E. (2003). Estimation of tissue layer level by sequential morphological reconstruction. *Journal of Microscopy*, *209*(2), 118–125. doi:10.1046/j.1365-2818.2003.01113.x PMID:12588529.

Landini, G., & Othman, I. E. (2004). Architectural analysis of oral cancer, dysplastic, and normal epithelium. *Cytometry. Part A*, *61*(1), 45–55. doi:10.1002/cyto.a.20082.

Landini, G., & Othman, I. E. (2005). Quantification of local architecture changes associated with neoplastic progression in oral epithelium using graph theory. *Fractals in Biology and Medicine*, *IV*(Part 3), 193–201. doi:10.1007/3-7643-7412-8_18.

Lantuéjoul, C. (1978). *La Squelettisation et Son Application aux Mesures Topologiques des Mosaiques Polycristallines*. (PhD thesis). Paris, Ecole des Mines.

Larsson, S. A. (1980). Gamma camera emission tomography. *Acta Radiologica. Supplementum*, 363. PMID:6267902.

Lauterbur, P. C. (1973). Image formation by induced local interactions: Examples employing nuclear magnetic resonance. *Nature*, *242*, 190–191. doi:10.1038/242190a0.

Law, S. K., Nunez, P. L., Westdorp, A. F., Nelson, A. V., & Pilgreen, K. L. (1991). Topographical mapping of brain electrical activity, 194-200. Washington, DC: IEEE Press.

Laykin, S., Alchanatis, V., & Fallik, E., & Edany. (2002). Image processing algorithms for tomatoes classification. *Transactions of the American Society of Agricultural Engineers*, *45*(3), 851–858.

Lee, C., Huh, S., Ketter, T. A., & Unser, M. (1998). Unsupervised connectivity-based thresholding segmentation of midsaggital brain MR images. *Computers in Biology and Medicine*, *28*, 309–338. doi:10.1016/S0010-4825(98)00013-4 PMID:9784966.

Lessmann, B., Nattkemper, T. W., Hans, V. H., & Degenhard, A. (2007). A method for linking computed image features to histological semantics in neuropathology. *Journal of Biomedical Informatics*, *40*, 631–641. doi:10.1016/j.jbi.2007.06.007 PMID:17698418.

Levenberg, K. (1944). A method for the solution of certain problems in least squares. *Quarterly of Applied Mathematics*, *2*, 164–168.

Li, C. M., Xu, C. Y., Gui, C. F., & Fox, M. D. (2005). Level set evolution without re-initialization: A new variational formulation. In *Proceedings of IEEE Computer Society Conference on Computer Vision and Pattern Recognition* (430-436). Washington, DC: IEEE Press.

Li, Q., Wang, M., & Gu, W. (2002). Computer vision based system for apple surface defect detection. Computers and Electronics in Agriculture (215-223). Amsterdam: Elsevier.

Li, Y., Ma, Y.-F., & Zhang, H.-J. (2003). Salient region detection and tracking in video. In *Proceedings of International Conference on Multimedia and Expo* (269–272). Washington, DC: IEEE Press.

Liang, Z., & Hart, H. (1988). Bayesian reconstruction in emission computerized tomography. *IEEE Transactions on Nuclear Science, 35*, 788–792. doi:10.1109/23.12833.

Liao, Chen, & Chung. (2001). A fast algorithm for multilevel thresholding. *Journal of Information Science and Engineering, 17*(5), 713–727.

Li, C., Goldgof, D. B., & Hall, L. O. (1993). Automatic segmentation and tissue labelling of MR brain images. *IEEE Transactions on Medical Imaging, 12*(4), 672–682.

Li, C., & Heinemann, P. H. (2007). ANN-integrated electronic nose and znose system for apple quality evaluation. *Transactions of the ASABE, 50*(6), 2285–2294.

Liew & Zain. J. M. (2010). Reversible medical image watermarking for tamper detection and recovery. In *Proceedings of the 3rd IEEE International Conference on Computer Science and Information Technology, 5*, 417–420. Washington, DC: IEEE Press.

Li, H. D., Kallergi, M., Clarke, L. P., Jain, V. K., & Clark, R. A. (1995). Markov random field for tumour detection in digital mammography. *IEEE Transactions on Medical Imaging, 14*(3), 565–576. doi:10.1109/42.414622 PMID:18215861.

Lima, J. J. P. (2011). *Nuclear medicine physics series in medical physics and biomedical engineering*. Philadelphia: Taylor & Francis.

Lionheart, W. R. B. (2004). EIT reconstruction algorithms: Pitfalls, challenges, and recent developments. *Physiological Measurement, 25*, 125–142. doi:10.1088/0967-3334/25/1/021 PMID:15005311.

Lionheart, W. R. B., Lidgey, F. J., McLeod, C. N., Paulson, K. S., Pidcock, M. K., & Shi, Y. (1997). Electrical impedance tomography for high speed chest imaging. *Physica Medica, 13*, 247–249.

Li, Q., Zhang, M., & Wang, M. (2000). Real-time apple colour grading based on genetic neural network. *Journal of Image and Graphics, 5A*(9), 779–784.

Li, S., & Lee, M.-C. (2007). An efficient spatiotemporal attention model and its application to shot matching. *IEEE Transactions on Circuits and Systems for Video Technology, 17*(10), 1383–1387. doi:10.1109/TCSVT.2007.903798.

Litière, S., Werutsky, G., Fentiman, I. S., Rutgers, E., Christiaens, M. R., & Bartelink, H. et al. (2012). Breast conserving therapy versus mastectomy for stage I—II breast cancer: 20 year follow-up of the EORTC 10801 phase 3 randomised trial. *The Lancet Oncology, 13*(4), 412–419. doi:10.1016/S1470-2045(12)70042-6 PMID:22373563.

Liu, H., Xie, X., Ma, W.-Y., & Zhang, H.-J. (2003). Automatic browsing of large pictures on mobile devices. In *Proceedings of ACM International Conference on Multimedia* (148–150). New York: ACM Press.

Liu, T., Sun, J., Zheng, N. N., Tang, X., & Shum, H. Y. (2007). Learning to detect a salient object. In *Proceedings of the Conference on Computer Vision and Pattern Recognition* (1-8). Washington, DC: IEEE Press.

Liu, Z., Yu, Y., Zhang, K., & Huang, H. (2001). Underwater image transmission and blurred image restoration. *Optical Engineering (Redondo Beach, Calif.), 40*(6), 1125–1131. doi:10.1117/1.1364500.

Li, Zhang, & Li. (2008). *Tomographic* Reconstruction using the distorted rytov iterative method with phaseless data. *IEEE Geoscience and Remote Sensing Letters, 5*(3).

Loftus, G. R., & Mackworth, N. H. (1978). Cognitive determinants of fixation location during picture viewing. *Journal of Experimental Psychology. Human Perception and Performance, 4*, 565–572. doi:10.1037/0096-1523.4.4.565 PMID:722248.

Longfei, Z., Yuanda, C., Gangyi, D., & Yong, W. (2008). A computable visual attention model for video skimming. In *Proceedings of Tenth IEEE Symposium on Multimedia* (667-672). Washington, DC: IEEE Press.

Lourakis, M. I. A., & Argyros, A. A. (2009). SBA: A software package for generic sparse bundle adjustment. *ACM Transactions on Mathematical Software*, *36*(1). doi:10.1145/1486525.1486527.

Lowe, D. G. (2004). Distinctive image features from scale-invariant keypoints. *International Journal of Computer Vision*, *60*(2), 91–110. doi:10.1023/B:VISI.0000029664.99615.94.

Luo, J., & Singhal, A. (2000). On measuring low-level saliency in photographic images. In *Proceedings of IEEE Conference on Computer Vision and Pattern Recognition* (84–89). Washington, DC: IEEE Press.

Luo, L., Chen, Z., Chen, M., Zeng, X., & Xiong, Z. (2010). Reversible image watermarking using interpolation technique. *IEEE Transactions on Information Forensics and Security*, *5*(1), 187–193. doi:10.1109/TIFS.2009.2035975.

Lysaker, Osher, & Tai. (2004). Noise removal using smoothed normals and surface fitting. *IEEE Transactions on Image Processing*, *13*(10). doi:10.1109/TIP.2004.834662 PMID:15462144.

Ma, Y.-F., & Zhang, H.-J. (2003). Contrast-based image attention analysis by using fuzzy growing. In *Proceedings of 11th ACM International Conference on Multimedia* (374–381). New York: ACM Press.

Mackworth, N. H., & Morandi, A. J. (1967). The gaze selects informative details within pictures. *Perception & Psychophysics*, *2*, 547–552. doi:10.3758/BF03210264.

Mairal, J., Elad, M., & Sapiro, G. (2008). Sparse representation for color image restoration. *IEEE Transactions on Image Processing*, *17*(1), 53–69. doi:10.1109/TIP.2007.911828 PMID:18229804.

Maitra, Nag, & Bandyopadhyay. (2011). *Automated digital mammogram segmentation for detection of abnormal masses using binary homogeneity enhancement algorithm*. Retrieved from http://core.kmi.open.ac.uk/display/973406.

Ma, J., Chang, C. C.-W., & Cangers, F. (2012). An operational superresolution approach for multi-temporal and multi-angle remotely sensed imagery. *IEEE Journal of Selected Topics in Applied Earth Observations and Remote Sensing*, *5*(1), 110–124. doi:10.1109/JSTARS.2011.2182505.

Majid, M., Mohiuddin, M. M., Nichols, E. M., Marter, K. J., & Flannery, T. W. (2012). Decrease of the lumpectomy cavity volume after whole-breast irradiation affects small field boost planning. *Medical Dosimetry*, *37*(3), 339–343. doi:10.1016/j.meddos.2011.11.008 PMID:22305933.

Makkapati, V. V., & Rao, R. M. (2009). Segmentation on malaria parasites in peripheral blood smear images. *IEEE International Conference on Acoustics, Speech, and Signal Processing* (1361–1364).

Malfait & Roose. (1997). Wavelet-based image denoising using a markov random field a priori model. *IEEE Transactions on Image Processing*, *6*(4), 549–565. doi:10.1109/83.563320 PMID:18282948.

Mallat, S. G. A. (1989). Theory for multiresolution signal decomposition: The wavelet representation. *IEEE Transactions on PAMI*, *11*, 674–693. doi:10.1109/34.192463.

Malmivuo, J., & Plonsey, R. (1995). *Bioelectromagnetism: Principles and Applications of Bioelectric and Biomagnetic Fields*. New York: Oxford University Press. doi:10.1093/acprof:oso/9780195058239.001.0001.

Mammographic Image Analysis Society (MIAS). (2011). *MIAS database*. Retrieved from http://www.mammoimage.org/databases/.

Mannan, S. K., Ruddock, K. H., & Wooding, D. S. (1997). Fixation patterns made during brief examination of two-dimensional images. *Perception*, *26*, 1059–1072. doi:10.1068/p261059 PMID:9509164.

Mann, F., Chauvet, S., & Rougon, G. (2007). Semaphorins in development and adultbrain: Implication for neurological diseases. *Progress in Neurobiology*, *82*(2), 57–79. doi:10.1016/j.pneurobio.2007.02.011 PMID:17537564.

Mansfield, P., & Grannell, P. K. (1973). NMR ʻdiffraction' in solids? *Journal of Physical Chemistry*, *6*, L422–L426.

Mardia, K. V., & Hainsworth, T. J. (1998). A spatial thresholding method for image segmentation. *IEEE Transactions on Pattern Analysis and Machine Intelligence*, *10*(6), 919–927. doi:10.1109/34.9113.

Marghani, K. A., Dlay, S. S., Sharif, B. S., & Sims, A. (2003). Morphological and texture features for cancers tissues microscopic images. *Medical Imaging and Image Processing*, (5032), 1757–1764.

Margos. (2004). Morphological filtering for image enhancement and feature detection. *Image and Video Processing Handbook* (2nd edition). Amsterdam: Academic Press.

Marquardt, D. (1963). An algorithm for least-squares estimation of nonlinear parameters. *SIAM Journal on Applied Mathematics, 11,* 431–441. doi:10.1137/0111030.

Masatera, N., & Osamu, K. (1997). Studies on automatic sorting system for strawberry. *Journal of Japanese Society of Agricultural Machinery, 59*(1), 43–48.

Maulik, U. (2009). Medical image segmentation using genetic algorithms. *IEEE Transactions on Information Technology in Biomedicine, 13*(2), 166–173. doi:10.1109/TITB.2008.2007301 PMID:19272859.

Maybank, S. (1992). *Theory of reconstruction from image motion.* Berlin: Springer-Verlag.

McGlamery, B. (1980). A computer model for underwater camera systems.[Bellingham, WA: SPIE Press.]. *Proceedings of SPIE Ocean Optics, VI,* 221–231. doi:10.1117/12.958279.

Melkemi, K. E., Batouche, M., & Foufou, S. (2006). A multiagent system approach for image segmentation using hybrid genetic algorithm-extremal optimization heuristics. *Pattern Recognition Letters. Special Issue on Evolutionary Computer Vision and Image Understanding, 27*(11), 1230–1238.

Metherall, P. (1998). *Three Dimensional Electrical Impedance Tomography of the Human Thorax.* (PhD Thesis). Sheffield, UK: University of Sheffield.

Meur, O. L., Callet, P. L., Barba, D., & Thoreau, D. (2004). Performance assessment of a visual attention system entirely based on a human vision modeling. In *Proceedings of International Conference on Image Processing* (2327–2330). Washington, DC: IEEE Press.

Meur, O. L., Callet, P. L., Barba, D., & Thoreau, D. (2006). A coherent computational approach to model bottom-up visual attention. *IEEE Transactions on Pattern Analysis and Machine Intelligence, 28*(5). PMID:16640265.

Meyer. (2002). Oscillating patterns in image processing and nonlinear evolution equations. *University Lecture Series 22.* Providence, RI: AMS.

Mikolajczyk, K., & Schmid, C. (2004). Scale and affine invariant interest point detectors. *International Journal of Computer Vision, 60*(1), 63–86. doi:10.1023/B:VISI.0000027790.02288.f2.

Milanese, R., Wechsler, H., Gil, S., Bost, J., & Pun, T. (1994). Integration of bottom-up and top-down cues for visual attention using nonlinear relaxation. In *Proceedings of IEEE Computer Society Conference on Computer Vision and Pattern Recognition* (781-785). Washington, DC: IEEE Press.

Milindkumar & Deshmukh. (2011). Performance evaluation of noise reduction algorithm in magnetic resonance images. *International Journal of Computer Science Issues, 8*(2).

Mitra, S., & Sicuranza, J. (2001). *Nonlinear image processing.* San Diego: Academic Press.

Mohideen, P. Krishnan, & Sathik. (2011). Image denoising and enhancement using multiwavelet with hard threshold. In Digital Mammography. Berlin: Springer.

Molinary, M. (2003). *High Fidelity Imaging in Electrical Impedance Tomography.* (PhD Thesis). Southampton, UK: University of Southampton.

Monahan, J. S., & Lockhead, G. R. (1977). Identification of integral stimuli. *Journal of Experimental Psychology. General, 106,* 94–110. doi:10.1037/0096-3445.106.1.94.

Moreira, A., Santos, M. Y., & Carneiro, S. (2005). *Density-based clustering algorithms–DBSCAN and SNN.* Minho, Portugal: University of Minho.

Morris, J. K., Esteves, A. R., Bomhoff, G. L., Swerdlow, R. H., Stanford, J. A., & Geiger, P.C. (2010). Investigation of insulin signaling in parkinson's disease cytoplasmic hybrid cells. *FASEB Journal, 1053.6.*

Motwani, Gadiya, & Motwani. (n.d.). Survey of image denoising techniques. *International Arab Journal of e-Technology, 2*(1).

Mueller, Yagel, & Wheller. (1998). A fast and accurate projection algorithm for 3-D cone-beam reconstruction with the algebraic reconstruction technique (ART). In *Proceedings of SPIE Medical Imaging Conference.* San Diego: SPIE Press.

Muller, P., Hiller, J., Cantatore, A., & De Chiffre, L. (2012). A study on evaluation strategies in dimensional X-ray computed tomography by estimation of measurement uncertainties. *International Journal of Metrology and Quality Engineering*, *3*, 107–115. doi:10.1051/ijmqe/2012011.

Mundy, J. L., & Zisserman, A. (Eds.). (1992). *Geometric invariance in computer vision*. Cambridge, MA: The MIT Press.

Murphy, D., Burton, P., Coombs, R., Tarassenko, L., & Rolfe, P. (1987). Impedance imaging in the newborn. *Clinical Physics and Physiological Measurement*, *8*, 131–140. doi:10.1088/0143-0815/8/4A/017 PMID:3568562.

Mustafa, O., & Ediz, P. (2007). A color image segmentation approach for content-based image retrieval. *Pattern Recognition*, *40*, 1318–1325. doi:10.1016/j.patcog.2006.08.013.

Nabil. (2009). SAR image filtering in wavelet domain by subband depended shrink. *International Journal of Open Problems of Computational Mathematics, 2*(1).

Nadon, R., & Shoemaker, J. (2002). Statistical issues with microarrays: Processing and analysis. *Trends in Genetics*, *18*(5), 265–271. doi:10.1016/S0168-9525(02)02665-3 PMID:12047952.

Nakagaki, R., & Katsaggelos, A. K. (2003). A VQ-based blind image restoration algorithm. *IEEE Transactions on Image Processing*, *12*(9), 1044–1053. doi:10.1109/TIP.2003.816007 PMID:18237976.

Natterer & Wubbeling. (2001). *Mathematical Methods in image reconstruction*. Philadelphia: SIAM.

Navalpakkam, V., & Itti, L. (2006). Optimal cue selection strategy. *Advances in Neural Information Processing Systems*, *19*, 987–994.

Negahdaripour, S., & Firoozfam, P. (2006). An ROV stereovision system for ship-hull inspection. *IEEE Journal of Oceanic Engineering*, *31*(3), 551–564. doi:10.1109/JOE.2005.851391.

Nelder & Mead. (1965). A simplex method for function minimization. *The Computer Journal*, *7*, 308–313. doi:10.1093/comjnl/7.4.308.

Netravali, A. N., & Limb, J. O. (1980). Picture coding a review. *Proceedings of the IEEE*, *68*, 366–406. doi:10.1109/PROC.1980.11647.

Ngau, C. W. H., Ang, L.-M., & Seng, K. P. (2009). Comparison of colour spaces for visual saliency. In *Proceedings of International Conference on Intelligent Human-Machine Systems and Cybernetics* (278–281). Washington, DC: IEEE Press.

Nhat, V. D. M., & Vo, D. (2008). Efficient projection for compressed sensing. In *Proceedings of International Conference on Computer and Information Science* (322-327). Washington, DC: IEEE Press.

Nimesh, S., Delwiche, M. J., & Scott Johnson, R. (1993). Image analysis methods for realtime color grading of stone fruit. *Computers and Electronics in Agriculture*, *9*(1), 71–84. doi:10.1016/0168-1699(93)90030-5.

Ni, Z., Shi, Y. Q., Ansari, N., & Su, W. (2006). Reversible data hiding. *IEEE Transactions on Circuits and Systems for Video Technology*, *16*(3), 354–362. doi:10.1109/TCSVT.2006.869964.

Nock & Nielsen. (2006). On weighting clustering. *IEEE Transactions on Pattern Analysis and Machine Intelligence*, *28*(8), 1–13. doi:10.1109/TPAMI.2006.157.

Noor, J. A. E. (2007). *Electrical Impedance Tomography at Low Frequencies*. (PhD Thesis). Kensington, Australia, University Of New South Wales.

Noordegraaf, A. V., Faes, T. J. C., Janse, A., Marcus, J. T., Heethaar, R. M., Postmus, P. E., & Vries, P. M. J. M. (1996). Improvement of cardiac imaging in electrical impedance tomography by means of a new electrode configuration. *Physiological Measurement*, *17*, 179–188. doi:10.1088/0967-3334/17/3/004 PMID:8870058.

Ogawa, Lee, Kay, & Tank. (1990). Brain magnetic resonance imaging with contrast dependent on blood oxygenation. *Proceedings of the National Academy of Sciences of the United States of America*, *87*, 9868–9872. doi:10.1073/pnas.87.24.9868 PMID:2124706.

Oh, T. I., Koo, H., Lee, K. H., Kim, S. M., Lee, J., & Woo, E. J. et al. (2008). Validation of a multi-frequency electrical impedance tomography (mfEIT) system KHU Mark1: Impedance spectroscopy and time-difference imaging. *Physiological Measurement*, *29*, 295–307. doi:10.1088/0967-3334/29/3/002 PMID:18367806.

Ojha, S., & Kostrzynska, M. (2008). Examination of animal and zoonotic pathogens using microarrays. *Veterinary Research*, *39*(1), 4. doi:10.1051/vetres:2007042 PMID:18073091.

Olano, J. P., & Walker, D. H. (2011). Diagnosing emerging and reemerging infectious diseases: The pivotal role of the pathologist. *Archives of Pathology & Laboratory Medicine, 135*(1), 83–91. PMID:21204714.

Oliver, A., Lladó, X., Freixenet, J., & Martí, J. (2007). False positive reduction in mammographic mass detection using local binary patterns. In *Proceedings of the Medical Image Computing and Computer-assisted Intervention* (286–293). Toronto: Springer.

Omer, O. A., & Tanaka, T. (2008). Joint blur identification and high-resolution image estimation based on weighted mixed-norm with outlier rejection. In *Proceedings of IEEE International Conference on Acoustics, Speech, and Signal Processing* (1305-1308). Washington, DC: IEEE Press.

ORegan, J. K., Rensink, R. A., & Clark, J. J. (1999). Change-blindness as a result of mudsplashes. *Nature, 398.*

Osberger, W., & Maeder, A. J. (1998). Automatic identification of perceptually important regions in an image. In *Proceedings of 14th International Conference on Pattern Recognition* (701-704).

Osher, Sole, & Vese. (2003). Multiscale model simulation. *Society for Industrial and Applied Mathematics, 1*(3), 349–370.

Otsu. (1979). A threshold selection method from gray-level histogram. *IEEE Transactions on Systems, Man, and Cybernetics, 9*(1), 62-66.

Otsu, N. (1979). A threshold selection method from gray-level histograms. *IEEE Transactions on Systems, Man, and Cybernetics, 9*(1), 62–66. doi:10.1109/TSMC.1979.4310076.

Ouafi, A., Taleb, A., Baarir, Z., & Zitouni, A. (2008). A modified embedded zerotree wavelet (MEZW) algorithm for image compression. *Journal of Mathematical Imaging and Vision, 30*, 298–307. doi:10.1007/s10851-007-0057-y.

Ouerhani, N., & Hugli, H. (2000). Computing visual attention from scene depth. In *Proceedings of 15th International Conference on Pattern Recognition* (375-378). Washington, DC: IEEE Press.

Ouerhani, N., & Hugli, H. (2003a) Maps: Multiscale attention-based presegmentation of color images. In *Proceedings of 4th International Conference on Scale-Space Theories in Computer Vision* (537–549). Washington, DC: IEEE Press.

Ouerhani, N., & Hugli, H. (2003b). A model of dynamic visual attention for object tracking in natural image sequences. *Computational Methods in Neural Modeling. Lecture Notes in Computer Science, 2686*, 702–709. doi:10.1007/3-540-44868-3_89.

Ouerhani, N., von Wartburg, R., Hugli, H., & Muri, R. (2004). Empirical validation of saliency based model of visual attention. *Electronics Letters on Computer Vision and Image Analysis, 3*, 13–24.

Owzar, K., Barry, W., Jung, S., Sohn, I., & George, S. (2008). Statistical challenges in preprocessing in microarray experiments in cancer. *Clinical Cancer Research, 14*(19), 5959–5966. doi:10.1158/1078-0432.CCR-07-4532 PMID:18829474.

Paik, S., Kim, C. Y., Song, Y. K., & Kim, W. S. (2005). Technology insight: application of molecular techniques to formalin-fixed paraffin-embedded tissues from breast cancer. *Nature Clinical Practice. Oncology, 2*(5), 246–254. doi:10.1038/ncponc0171 PMID:16264960.

Pal, K., Ghosh, G., & Bhattacharya, M. (2012)d. A novel digital image watermarking scheme for data security using bit replacement and majority algorithm technique. Watermarking, 1, (979-953). Rijecka, Croatia: INTECH Publications.

Pal, K., Ghosh, G., & Bhattacharya, M. (2012c). Relevance of bio-medical image watermarking for data authentication and security in telemedicine and healthcare. In *Proceedings of the National Conference on Pervasive Computing & Communications* (131-135). Kolkata, India: IEEE Press.

Pal, R., Mitra, P., & Mukherjee, J. (2012a). Image retargeting using controlled shrinkage. In *Proceedings of 8th Indian Conference on Computer Vision, Graphics, and Image Processing*. Bangalore, India: ICVGIP Press.

Pal, R., Mitra, P., & Mukhopadhyay, J. (2008). Icam: Maximizes viewers' attention on intended objects. In *Proceedings of Pacific-Rim Conference on Multimedia* (821-824). Washington, DC: IEEE Press.

Pal, R., Mitra, P., & Mukhopadhyay, J. (2012b). Generation of groundtruth data for visual saliency experiments using image segmentation. In *Proceedings of IEEE Congress on Image and Signal Processing*. Washington, DC: IEEE Press.

Pal, R., Mukherjee, J., & Mitra, P. (2009). An approach for preparing groundtruth data and evaluating visual saliency models. In *Proceedings of International Conference on Pattern Recognition and Machine Inteligence* (279-284). London: Academic Press.

Pal, R., Mukherjee, J., & Mitra, P. (2012c). How do warm colors affect visual attention? In *Proceedings of 8th Indian Conference on Computer Vision, Graphics, and Image Processing*. Bangalore, India: ICVGIP Press.

Pal, K., Ghosh, G., & Bhattacharya, M. (2012a). Biomedical image watermarking in wavelet domain for data integrity using bit majority and multiple copies of hidden information. *American Journal of Biomedical Engineering*, 2(2), 29–37. doi:10.5923/j.ajbe.20120202.06.

Pal, K., Ghosh, G., & Bhattacharya, M. (2012b). Reversible digital image watermarking using bit replacement and majority algorithm technique. *Journal of Intelligent Learning Systems and Applications*, 4(3), 199–206. doi:10.4236/jilsa.2012.43020.

Pal, K., Ghosh, G., & Bhattacharya, M. (2012e). Biomedical image watermarking for medical data security using modified bit replacement algorithm in spatial domain. *International Journal of Applied Engineering*, 2(3), 158–169.

Pal, M., Chaudhuri, S. R., Jadav, A., Banerjee, S., Paul, R. R., & Chaudhuri, K. et al. (2008). Quantitative dimensions of histopathological attributes and status of GSTM1-GSTT1 in oral submucous fibrosis. *Tissue & Cell*, 40(6), 425–436. doi:10.1016/j.tice.2008.04.003 PMID:18573513.

Pal, R., Mukherjee, A., Mitra, P., & Mukherjee, J. (2010). Modelling visual saliency using degree centrality. *IET Computer Vision*, 4(3), 218–229. doi:10.1049/iet-cvi.2009.0067.

Pan & Kak. (1983). A computational study of reconstruction algorithms for diffraction tomography: Interpolation vs. filtered-back propagation. *IEEE Transactions on Acoustics, Speech, and Signal Processing*, 31, 1262–1275. doi:10.1109/TASSP.1983.1164196.

Pang, D., Kimura, A., Takeuchi, T., Yamato, J., & Kashino, K. (2008). A stochastic model of selective visual attention with a dynamic bayesian network. In *Proceedings of IEEE International Conference on Multimedia and Expo* (1073–1076). Washington, DC: IEEE Press.

Pappas & Pitas. (2000). Digital colour restoration of old painting. *IEEE Transactions on Image Processing*, 9(2).

Parkhurst, D. J., & Niebur, E. (2003). Scene content selected by active vision. *Spatial Vision*, 16, 125–154. doi:10.1163/15685680360511645 PMID:12696858.

Parkhurst, D., Law, K., & Niebur, E. (2002). Modeling the role of salience in the allocation of overt visual attention. *Vision Research*, 42(1), 107–123. doi:10.1016/S0042-6989(01)00250-4 PMID:11804636.

Park, S. C., Park, M. K., & Kang, M. G. (2003). Super-resolution image reconstruction: A technical overview. *IEEE Signal Processing Magazine*, 20(3), 21–36. doi:10.1109/MSP.2003.1203207.

Parthasarathy, H., Prasad, S., & Joshi, S. (1994). A music-like method for estimating quadratic phase coupling. *Signal Processing*, 37(2), 171–188. doi:10.1016/0165-1684(94)90101-5.

Patra, S., Bhowmick, B., Banerjee, S., & Kalra P. (2012). High resolution point cloud generation from kinect and HD cameras using graph cut. *VISAPP*, (2), 311-316.

Paulson, K., Breckon, W., & Pidcock, M. (1992). A hybrid phantom for electrical impedance tomography. *Clinical Physics and Physiological Measurement*, 13, 155–159. doi:10.1088/0143-0815/13/A/030 PMID:1587092.

Pearlman, W. A. (2001). Trends of tree-based, set partitioning compression techniques in still and moving image systems. In *Proceedings of Picture Coding Symposium 2001* (1-8). Seoul, Korea: IEEE Press.

Pearlman, W. A., & Said, A. (1998). A survey of the state of the art and utilization of embedded, tree-based coding. In *Proceeding of 1998 IEEE International Symposium on Circuits and Systems*. Monterey, CA: IEEE Press.

Pelz, J. B., & Canosa, R. (2001). Oculomotor behavior and perceptual strategies in complex tasks. *Vision Research*, 41, 3587–3596. doi:10.1016/S0042-6989(01)00245-0 PMID:11718797.

Perez, E. A., Pusztai, L., & Van de Vijver, M. (2004). Improving patient care through molecular diagnostics. *Seminars in Oncology*, 31, 14–20. doi:10.1053/j.seminoncol.2004.07.017 PMID:15490370.

Perona, P., & Malik, J. (1990). Scale-space and edge detection using anisotropic diffusion. *IEEE Transactions on Pattern Analysis and Machine Intelligence, 12,* 629–639. doi:10.1109/34.56205.

Perou, C. M., Sørlie, T., Eisen, M. B., van de Rijn, M., Jeffrey, S. S., & Botstein, D. et al. (2000). Molecular portraits of human breast tumours. *Nature, 406*(6797), 747–752. doi:10.1038/35021093 PMID:10963602.

Perry, A. M., Mitrovic, Z., & Chan, W. C. (2012). Biological prognostic markers in diffuse large B-cell lymphoma. *Cancer Control, 19*(3), 214–226. PMID:22710897.

Peters, R. J., & Itti, L. (2007). Beyond bottom-up: incorporating task-dependent influences into a computational model of spatial attention. In *Proceedings of IEEE Conference on Computer Vision and Pattern Recognition* (1-8). Washington, DC: IEEE Press.

Peters. (2005). *Signal processing, A mathematical approach.* Wellesley, MA: Dexter Publishing Company.

Pham, D. L., Xu, C., & Prince, J. L. (1998). A survey of current methods in medical image segmentation. *Technical Report JHU/ECE 99-01* (315-338). Baltimore: The Johns Hopkins University.

Phelps, M. E., Homan, E. J., & Ter-Pogossian, M. M. (1975). Attenuation coefficients of various body tissues, fluids, and lesions at photon energies of 18 to 136 keV. *Radiology, 117,* 573–583. PMID:810827.

Pirim, H., Gautam, D., Bhowmik, T., & Perkins, A. D., Burak, Ekşioglu, B, & Alkan, A. (2011). Performance of an ensemble clustering algorithm on biological data sets. *Mathematical and Computational Applications, 16,* 87–96.

Pizurica, Philips, Lemahieu, & Acheroy. (2003). A versatile wavelet domain noise filtration technique for medical imaging. *IEEE Transactions on Medical Imaging, 22*(3), 323–331. doi:10.1109/TMI.2003.809588 PMID:12760550.

Porcellini, E., Carbone, I., Ianni, M., & Licastro, F. (2010). Alzheimer's disease gene signature says: Beware of brain viral infections. *Immunity & Ageing, 7,* 16. doi:10.1186/1742-4933-7-16 PMID:21156047.

Portilla, Strela, Wainwright, & Simoncell. (2003). Image denoising using scale mixtures of gaussians in the wavelet domain. *IEEE Transactions on Image Processing, 12*(11). doi:10.1109/TIP.2003.818640 PMID:18244692.

Posner, M. I. (1980). Orienting of attention. *The Quarterly Journal of Experimental Psychology, 32,* 3–25. doi:10.1080/00335558008248231 PMID:7367577.

Po-Whei & Yan-Hao. (2010). Effevtive segmentation and classification of HCC biopsy images. *Pattern Recognition, 43,* 1550–1563. doi:10.1016/j.patcog.2009.10.014.

Prabhakar, C. J., & Praveen Kumar, P. U. (2010). Underwater image denoising using adaptive wavelet subband thresholding. In *Proceedings of IEEE International Conference on Signal and Image Processing* (322-327). Washington, DC: IEEE Press.

Prabhakar, C. J., & Praveen Kumar, P. U. (2011). An image based technique for enhancement of underwater images. *International Journal of Machine Intelligence, 3*(4), 217–224.

Pritchard, C. C., & Nelson, P. S. (2008). Gene expression profiling in the developing prostate. *Differentiation, 76*(6), 624–640. doi:10.1111/j.1432-0436.2008.00274.x PMID:18462436.

Privitera, C. M., & Stark, L. W. (2000). Algorithms for defining visual regions-of-interest: Comparison with eye fixations.[Washington, DC: IEEE Press.]. *IEEE Transactions on Pattern Analysis and Machine Intelligence, 22,* 970–982. doi:10.1109/34.877520.

Purcell, E. M., Torrey, H. C., & Pound, R. V. (1946). Resonance absorption by nuclear magnetic moments in a solid. *Physical Review, 69,* 37–38. doi:10.1103/PhysRev.69.37.

Qi, S. Head, & Elliott. (2002). detecting breast cancer from infrared images by asymmetry analysis. In *Proceedings of Second Joint Conference of the Biomedical Engineering Society.* Washington, DC: IEEE Press.

Qian, W., Zhukov, T., Song, D. S., & Tockman, M. S. (2007). Computerized analysis of cellular features and biomarkers for cytologic diagnosis of early lung cancer. *Analytical and Quantitative Cytology and Histology, 29,* 103–111. PMID:17484274.

Qiao, G., Wang, W., Wang, L., He, Y., Bramer, B., & Al-Akaidi, M. (2007). Investigation of biological phantom for 2D and 3D breast EIT images. In *Proceedings of the 13th International Conference on Electrical Bioimpedance and the 8th Conference on Electrical Impedance Tomography* (328-331). Graz, Austria: Springer.

Qiao, J., Liu, J., & Sun, G. (2005). A VQ-based blind superresolution algorithm. In *Proceedings of the 2005 International Conference on Advances in Intelligent Computing* (320-329). Berlin: Springer.

Qiu, G., Gu, X., Chen, Z., Chen, Q., & Wang, C. (2007). An information theoretic model on spatiotemporal visual saliency. In *Proceedings of IEEE International Conference on Multimedia and Expo* (1806-1809). Washington, DC: IEEE Press.

Raja & Kolekar. (2012a). Wavelet transform based fluctuating density gaussian sampling algorithm for efficient image reconstruction. In *Proceedings of International Conference on Sensor Signal Processing for Defense*. Washington, DC: IEEE Press.

Raja & Kolekar. (2012b). Illumination normalization for image restoration using modified retinex algorithm. In *Proceedings of Annual IEEE India Conference* (941-946). Washington, DC: IEEE Press.

Rajeesh, Moni, Palanikumar, & Gopalakrishnan. (n.d.). Noise reduction in magnetic resonance images using wave atom shrinkage. *International Journal of Image Processing, 4*(2).

Ramaswamy, S., & Golub, T. R. (2002). DNA microarrays in clinical oncology. *Journal of Clinical Oncology, 20*(7), 1932–1941. PMID:11919254.

Ramstrom, O. & Christensen, H. I. (2002). Visual attention using game theory. *Biologically Motivated Computer Vision, 462–471.*

Rangayyan, R. M., Ayres, F. J., & Desautels, J. E. L. (2007). A review of computer-aided diagnosis of breast cancer: toward the detection of subtle signs. *Journal of the Franklin Institute*, 312–348. doi:10.1016/j.jfranklin.2006.09.003.

Rao, K. R., & Yip, P. (1990). *Discrete cosine transforms- Algorithms, advantages, applications.* San Diego: Academic Press Professional, Inc..

Rapantzikos, K., Tsapatsoulis, N., & Avrithis, Y. (2004). Spatiotemporal visual attention architecture for video analysis. In *Proceedings of IEEE 6th Workshop on Multimedia Signal Processing* (83-86). Washington, DC: IEEE Press.

Rashedi, E., Nezamabadi-pour, H., & Saryazdi, S. (2009). GSA: A gravitational search algorithm. *Information Sciences, 179*(13), 2232–2248. doi:10.1016/j.ins.2009.03.004.

Rashedi, E., Nezamabadi-pour, H., & Saryazdi, S. (2010). BGSA: Binary gravitational search algorithm. *Natural Computing, 9*(3), 727–745. doi:10.1007/s11047-009-9175-3.

Rastogi. (2008). *Fundamentals of biostatistics.* New Dehli: Ane Books.

Raviraja, S., & Osman, S. S., & Kardman. (2008). A novel technique for malaria diagnosis using invariant moments and by image compression. *IFMBE Proceedings, 21*(3), 730–733. doi:10.1007/978-3-540-69139-6_182.

Rehani, K. McCollough, & Nagel. (2006). *Managing patient dose in multi-detector computed tomography (MDCT).* Retrieved from http://www.icrp.org/docs/icrp-mdct-for_web_cons_32_219_06.pdf.

Reinagel, P., & Zador, A. M. (1999). Natural scene statistics at the center of gaze. *Network (Bristol, England), 10*(4), 341–350. doi:10.1088/0954-898X/10/4/304 PMID:10695763.

Remington, R., & Pierce, L. (1984). Moving attention: Evidence for time-invariant shifts of visual selective attention. *Perception & Psychophysics, 35*, 393–399. doi:10.3758/BF03206344 PMID:6739275.

Rennie, J. M. (2005). *Roberton's textbook of neonatology* (4th ed.). Amsterdam: Elsevier.

Renninger, L. W., Coughlan, J., Verghese, P., & Malik, J. (2005). An information maximization model of eye movements. *Advances in Neural Information Processing Systems, 17*, 1121–1128. PMID:16175670.

Rensink, R. A. (2000). The dynamic representation of scenes. *Visual Cognition, 7*(1-3), 17–42. doi:10.1080/135062800394667.

Ressom, H., Varghese, R., Zhang, Z., Xuang, J., & Clarke, R. (2008). Classification algorithms for phenotype prediction in genomics and proteomics. *Frontiers in Bioscience*, *13*, 691–708. doi:10.2741/2712 PMID:17981580.

Riad, A. M., Atwan, A., El-Bakry, H. M., Mostafa, R. R., Elminir, H. K., & Mastorakis, N. (2010). A new approach for segmentation of brain MR image. In *Proceedings of WSEAS International Conference on Environment, Medicine and Health Sciences* (74-83). Stevens Point, WI: WSEAS Press.

Riera, J., Riu, P. J., Casan, P., & Masclans, J. R. (2011). Electrical impedance tomography in acute lung injury. *Medicina Intensiva*, *35*(8), 509–517. doi:10.1016/j.medin.2011.05.005 PMID:21680060.

Rizzi, A., Gatta, C., & Marini, D. (2003). A new algorithm for unsupervised global and local color correction. *Pattern Recognition Letters*, *24*, 1663–1677. doi:10.1016/S0167-8655(02)00323-9.

Robb, A. R. (2000). *Biomedical imaging, visualization, and analysis*. New York: Wiley.

Robitaille, N., Guardo, R., Maurice, I., Hartinger, A. E., & Gagnon, H. (2009). A multi-frequency EIT system design based on telecommunication signal processors. *Physiological Measurement*, *30*, S57–S71. doi:10.1088/0967-3334/30/6/S04 PMID:19491440.

Rockett, P., & Wang, G. (2001). The principles of X-ray computed tomography. In Kutz, M. (Ed). Standard Handbook of Biomedical Engineering and Design (26.1-26.52). New York: McGraw-Hill.

Romsauerova, A., McEwan, A., Horesh, L., Yerworth, R., Bayford, R. H., & Holder, D. S. (2006). Multi-frequency electrical impedance tomography (EIT) of the adult human head: Initial findings in brain tumours, arteriovenous malformations, and chronic stroke, development of an analysis method and calibration. *Physiological Measurement*, *27*, S147–S161. doi:10.1088/0967-3334/27/5/S13 PMID:16636407.

Rosas-Orea, H.-D. Alarcon-Aquino, & Guerrero-Ojeda. (2005). A comparative simulation study of wavelet based denoising algorithms. In *Proceedings of IEEE CONIELECOMP*. Washington DC, IEEE Press.

Rosin, P. L. (2009). A simple method for detecting salient regions. *Pattern Recognition*, *42*(11), 2363–2371. doi:10.1016/j.patcog.2009.04.021.

Ross, N. E., Pritchard, C. J., & Rubin, D. M. (2006). Automatic image processing method for the diagnosis and classification of malaria on thin blood smears. *Medical & Biological Engineering & Computing*, *44*, 427–436. doi:10.1007/s11517-006-0044-2 PMID:16937184.

Rowels, S., & Saul, L. (2000). Non linear dimensionality reduction by locally linear embedding. *Science*, *290*(5500), 2323–2326. doi:10.1126/science.290.5500.2323 PMID:11125150.

Rudin, L. I., Osher, S., & Fatemi, E. (1992). Nonlinear total variation based noise removal algorithms. *Physica D. Nonlinear Phenomena*, *60*, 259–268. doi:10.1016/0167-2789(92)90242-F.

Russo, G., Zegar, C., & Giordano, A. (2003). Advantages and limitations of microarray technology in human cancer. *Oncogene*, *22*(42), 6497–6507. doi:10.1038/sj.onc.1206865 PMID:14528274.

Saha, S., & Bandyopadhyay, S. (2007). MRI brain image segmentation by fuzzy symmetry based genetic clustering technique. In *Proceedings of the IEEE Congress on Evolutionary Computation,* 4417-4424. Washington, DC: IEEE Press.

Said, A., & Pearlman, W. A. (1996). A new, fast, and efficient image codec based on set partitioning in hierarchical trees. *IEEE Transactions on Circuits and Systems for Video Technology*, *6*, 243–250. doi:10.1109/76.499834.

Said, A., & Pearlman, W. A. (1997). Low-complexity waveform coding via alphabet and sample set partitioning in hierarchical trees. *IEEE Transactions on Circuits and Systems for Video Technology*, *3024*, 25–37.

Said, A., & Pearlman, W. A. (2004). Efficient, low-complexity image coding with a set-partitioning embedded block coder. *IEEE Transactions on Circuits and Systems for Video Technology*, *14*(11), 1219–1235. doi:10.1109/TCSVT.2004.835150.

Salmeri & Lojacono. (n.d.). Noise estimation in mammographic images for adaptive denoising. *TELESAL project*. Retrieved from http://www.kell.it/telesal_en.htm.

Samii, A., Nutt, J. G., & Ransom, B. R. (2004). Parkinson's disease. *Lancet, 363*(9423), 1783–1793. doi:10.1016/S0140-6736(04)16305-8 PMID:15172778.

Sampat, M. P., Markey, M. K., & Bovik, A. C. (2005). Computer-aided detection and diagnosis in mammography. In Bovik, Sepehr, Jamarani, Moradi, Behnam, and Rezai Rad (Eds.), Intelligent System for Breast Cancer Prognosis Using Multiwavelet Packets and Neural Network. Washington, DC: IEEE Press.

Saslow, D., Hannan, J., Osuch, J., Alciati, M. H., Baines, C., & Coates, R. et al. (2004). Clinical breast examination: Practical recommendations for optimizing performance and reporting. *CA: a Cancer Journal for Clinicians, 54*(6), 327–344. doi:10.3322/canjclin.54.6.327 PMID:15537576.

Sasov, A. (2001). High-resolution in-vivo micro-CT scanner for small animals. In Proceedings of SPIE 4320: Medical Imaging 2001-Physics of Medical Imaging (705-710). San Diego: SPIE Press.

Schaaf, C. P., Wiszniewska, J., & Beaudet, A. L. (2011). Copy number and SNP arrays in clinical diagnostics. *Annual Review of Genomics and Human Genetics, 12,* 25–51. doi:10.1146/annurev-genom-092010-110715 PMID:21801020.

Schettini, R., & Corchs, S. (2010). Underwater image processing: State of the art of restoration and image enhancement methods. *EURASIP Journal on Advances in Signal Processing, 2010.*

Schlitter, A. M., Kurz, M., Larsen, J. P., Woitalla, D., Müller, T., Epplen, J. T., & Dekomien, G. (2006). Parkin gene variations in late-onset parkinson's disease: Comparison between norwegian and german cohorts. *Acta Neurologica Scandinavica, 113*(1), 9–13. doi:10.1111/j.1600-0404.2005.00532.x PMID:16367892.

Schneider, I. D., Kleffel, R., Jennings, D., & Courtenay, A. J. (2000). Design of an electrical impedance tomography phantom using active elements. *Medical & Biological Engineering & Computing, 38*(4), 390–394. doi:10.1007/BF02345007 PMID:10984936.

Schulte, De Witte, & Kerre. (2007). A fuzzy noise reduction method for colour images. *IEEE Transactions on Image Processing, 16*(5). doi:10.1109/TIP.2007.891807 PMID:17491470.

Scott, D. W. (1992). *Multivariate density estimation.* New York: Wiley. doi:10.1002/9780470316849.

Seo, J. K., & Woo, E. J. (2012). Electrical impedance tomography, Chapter 7. Nonlinear Inverse Problems in Imaging (195-250). Hoboken, NJ: Wiley-Blackwell.

Seroussi, G., & Weinberger, M. J. (1997). On adaptive strategies for an extended family of Golomb-type codes. In *Proceedings of Data Compression Conference* (131-140). Snowbird, UT: IEEE Press.

Sertel, O., Kong, J., Shimada, H., Catalyurek, U., Saltz, J. H., & Gurcan, M. (2008). Computer-aided prognosis of neuroblastoma: Classification of stromal development on whole-slide images. *Medical Imaging: Computer-Aided Diagnosis, (6915),* 9150–9151.

Seynaeve, P. C., & Broos, J. I. (1995). The history of tomography. *Journal Belge de Radiologie, 78*(5), 284–288. PMID:8550391.

Sezgin & Sankur. (2004). Survey over image thresholding techniques and quantitative performance evaluation. *Journal of Electronic Imaging, 13*(1), 146–165. doi:10.1117/1.1631315.

Shao, Y., & Celenk, M. (2001). Higher-order spectra (HOS) invariants for shape recognition. *Pattern Recognition, 34,* 112097–112113. doi:10.1016/S0031-3203(00)00148-5.

Shapiro, J. (1993). Embedded image coding using zerotrees of wavelet coefficients. *IEEE Transactions on Signal Processing, 41,* 3445–3462. doi:10.1109/78.258085.

Shapiro, L. G., & Stockman, G. C. (2001). *Computer Vision.* Upper Saddle River, NJ: Prentice-Hall.

Shariff, J. M., Miswan, M. F., Nagadi, M. A., & Salam, S. H. (2012). Red blood cell segmentation using masking and watershed algorithm: A preliminary study. In *Proceedings of the International Conference on Biomedical Engineering.* Penang, Malaysia: IEEE Press.

Sheikh, Bovik, & de Veciana. (2005). An information fidelity criterion for image quality assessment using natural scene statistics. *IEEE Transactions on Image Processing, 14*(12), 2117–2128. doi:10.1109/TIP.2005.859389 PMID:16370464.

Shen, Gao, Pu, Linlangliu, & Cao. (2011).construct the biorthogonal balanced multiwavelets by lifting scheme. In *Proceedings of the IEEE International Conference on Computer Science and Automation Engineering* (484-488). Washington, DC: IEEE Press.

Shepp & Vardi. (1982). Maximum likelihood reconstruction for emission tomography. *IEEE Transactions on Medical Imaging, 1*, 113–122. doi:10.1109/TMI.1982.4307558 PMID:18238264.

Sheshadri & Kandaswamy. (2006). *Breast tissue classification using statistical feature extraction of mammograms.* Coimbatore, India: PSG College of Technology.

Shih, B., Watson, S., & Bayat, A. (2012). Whole genome and global expression profiling of Dupuytren's disease: Systematic review of current findings and future perspectives. *Annals of the Rheumatic Diseases, 71*(9), 1440–1447. doi:10.1136/annrheumdis-2012-201295 PMID:22772327.

Shimura, H., Hattori, N., Kubo, S., Mizuno, Y., Asakawa, S., & Suzuki, T. et al. (2000). Familial parkinson disease gene product, parkin, is a ubiquitin-protein ligase. *Nature Genetics, 25*(3), 302–305. doi:10.1038/77060 PMID:10888878.

Shinoda, H., Hayhoe, M. M., & Shrivastava, A. (2001). What controls attention in natural environments? *Vision Research, 41*, 3535–3545. doi:10.1016/S0042-6989(01)00199-7 PMID:11718793.

Shioiri, S., Inoue, T., Matsumura, K., & Yaguchi, H. (1999). Movement of visual attention. In *Proceedings of IEEE International Conference on Systems, Man, and Cybernetics* (5–9). Washington, DC: IEEE Press.

Shnayderman, Gusev, & Eskicioglu. (2006). A SVD-based grayscale image quality measure for local and global assessment. *IEEE Transactions on Image Processing, 15*(2), 422–429. doi:10.1109/TIP.2005.860605 PMID:16479812.

Siagian, C., & Itti, L. (2007). Rapid biologically-inspired scene classification using features shared with visual attention. *IEEE Transactions on Pattern Analysis and Machine Intelligence, 29*, 300–312. doi:10.1109/TPAMI.2007.40 PMID:17170482.

Simon, R., Radmacher, M. D., & Dobbin, K. (2002). Design of studies using DNA microarrays. *Genetic Epidemiology, 23*(1), 21–36. doi:10.1002/gepi.202 PMID:12112246.

Simons, D. J. & Levin, D. T. (1997). Failure to detect changes to attended objects. *Investigative Opthalmology and Visual Science, 38*.

Simunovic, F., Yi, M., Wang, Y., Macey, L., & Brown, L. T. (2009). Gene expression profiling of substantia nigra dopamine neurons: Further insights into parkinson's disease pathology. *Brain, 132*(7), 1795–1809. doi:10.1093/brain/awn323 PMID:19052140.

Singh, S. S., Devi, H. M., Singh, T. T., & Singh, O. I. (2012). A new easy method of enhancement of low contrast image using spatial domain. *International Journal of Computers and Applications, 40*(1), 32–34. doi:10.5120/4922-7149.

Smith-Bindman, R., Lipson, J., & Marcus, R. (2009). Radiation dose associated with common computed tomography examinations and the associated lifetime attributable risk of cancer. *Archives of Internal Medicine, 169*(22), 2078–2086. doi:10.1001/archinternmed.2009.427 PMID:20008690.

Smith, R. W. M., Freeston, I. L., & Brown, B. H. (1995). A real-time electrical impedance tomography system for clinical use-design and preliminary results. *IEEE Transactions on Bio-Medical Engineering, 42*(2), 133–140. doi:10.1109/10.341825 PMID:7868140.

Snavely, N., Seitz, S., & Szeliski, R. (2006). Photo tourism: Exploring photo collections in 3D. In Proceedings of SIGGRAPH. *New York: ACM Press.*

Soleimani, M., & Lionheart, W. R. B. (2005). Nonlinear image reconstruction for electrical capacitance tomography using experimental data. *Measurement Science & Technology, 16*(10), 1987–1996. doi:10.1088/0957-0233/16/10/014.

Song, V., & Conant, C. Arger, & Sehgal. (2005). Artificial neural network to aid differentiation of malignant and benign breast masses by ultrasound imaging. Philadelphia: University of Pennsylvania.

Soni, N. K., Dehghani, H., Hartov, A., & Paulsen, K. D. (2003). A novel data calibration scheme for electrical impedance tomography. *Physiological Measurement*, *24*, 421–435. doi:10.1088/0967-3334/24/2/354 PMID:12812427.

Soni, N. K., Hartov, A., Kogel, C., Poplack, C. S., & Paulsen, K. D. (2004). Multi-frequency electrical impedance tomography of the breast: new clinical results. *Physiological Measurement*, *25*, 301–314. doi:10.1088/0967-3334/25/1/034 PMID:15005324.

Soto, D., & Blanco, M. J. (2004). Spatial attention and object-based attention: a comparison with a single task. *Vision Research*, *44*, 69–81. doi:10.1016/j.visres.2003.08.013 PMID:14599572.

Soumekh & Kaveh. (1984). Image reconstruction from frequency domain data on arbitrary contours. In *Proceedings of the Conference on Acoustics, Speech, and Signal Processing* (12A.2.1-12A.2.4). Washington, DC: IEEE Press.

Soumekh, Kaveh, & Mueller. (1986). Algorithms and experimental results in acoustic tomography using Rytov's approximation. In *Proceedings of International Conference On Acoustics, Speech, and Signal Processing* (135-138). Washington, DC: IEEE Press.

Sperandio, M., Guermandi, M., & Guerrieri, R. (2012). A four-shell diffusion phantom of the head for electrical impedance tomography. *IEEE Transactions on Biomedical Engineering*, *59*(2), 383–389. doi:10.1109/TBME.2011.2173197 PMID:22027364.

Sperling, G., & Weichselgartne, E. (1995). Episodic theory of the dynamics of spatial attention. *Psychological Review*, *102*, 503–532. doi:10.1037/0033-295X.102.3.503.

Srinivasan, R. (1999). Methods to improve the spatial resolution of EEG. *International Journal of Bioelectromagnetism*, *1*(1), 102–110.

Srivastava, Gupta, & Parthasarathy. (2011). An adaptive non-linear PDE-based speckle reduction technique for ultrasound images. *International Journal of Biomedical Engineering and Technology*, *6*(3). doi:10.1504/IJBET.2011.041468.

Sroubek, F., Kamenicky, J., & Milanfar, P. (2011). Superfast superresolution. In *Proceedings of 2011 18th IEEE International Conference on Image Processing (ICIP)* (1153-1156). Washington, DC: IEEE Press.

Stanberry, B. (2001). Legal ethical and risk issues in telemedicine. *Computer Methods and Programs in Biomedicine*, *64*(3), 225–233. doi:10.1016/S0169-2607(00)00142-5 PMID:11226620.

Stankovi & Falkowski. (2003). *The haar wavelet transform: Its status and achievements*. Elsevier Journal.

Stankovic, S., & Klisuric, O. (Eds.). (2007). Medical imaging-Indispensable medical tools, Chapter 1. Environmental, health, and humanity issues in the down danubian region: Multidisciplinary approaches. In *Proceedings of the 9th International Symposium on Interdisciplinary Regional Research*. Novi Sad, Serbia: University of Novi.

Stankovi, R. S., & Falkowski, B. J. (2003). The haar wavelet transform: Its status and achievements. *Elsevier Journal on Computers and Electrical Engineering*, *29*, 25–44. doi:10.1016/S0045-7906(01)00011-8.

Stasse, O., Kuniyoshi, Y., & Cheng, G. (2000). Development of a biologically inspired real-time visual attention system. In *Proceedings of the 1st IEEE International Workshop on Biologically Motivated Computer Vision* (150-159). Washington, DC: IEEE Press.

Stayman. (2003). *Spatial Resolution in Penalized-Likelihood Image Reconstruction*. (PhD. Thesis). Ann Arbor, MI, University of Michigan.

Strauss, H. W. (2006). Nuclear medicine 2020. *The Quarterly Journal of Nuclear Medicine and Molecular Imaging*, *50*, 1–3. PMID:16557198.

Stuart, C. S. (1997). *Functional MRI: Methods and Applications*. (PhD Thesis). Nottingham, UK, University of Nottingham.

Sudha, S., Suresh, G. R., & Sunkanesh, R. (2007). Wavelet based image denoising using adaptive subband thresholding. *International Journal of Soft Computing*, *2*, 628–632.

Suetens, P. (2009). *Fundamentals of medical imaging* (2nd ed.). Cambridge, UK: Cambridge University Press. doi:10.1017/CBO9780511596803.

Suh, B., Ling, H., Bederson, B. B., & Jacob, D. W. (2003). Automatic thumbnail cropping and its effectiveness. In *Proceedings of 16th Annual ACM Symposium on User Interface Software and Technology* (95-104). New York: ACM Press.

Sundstedt, V., Debattista, K., Longhurst, P., Chalmers, A., & Troscianko, T. (2005). Visual attention for efficient high-fidelity graphics. In *Proceedings of 21st Spring Conference on Computer Graphics* (169–175). New York: ACM Press.

Sun, T., Tsuda, S., Zauner, K. P., & Morgan, H. (2010). On-chip electrical impedance tomography for imaging biological cells. *Biosensors & Bioelectronics*, *25*(5), 1109–1115. doi:10.1016/j.bios.2009.09.036 PMID:19850464.

SUNY. (2006). News update: The department of surgery. *University Hospital and Health Sciences Center at Stony Brook*, *19*, 1–20.

Sun, Y., & Fisher, R. (2003). Object-based visual attention for computer vision. *Artificial Intelligence*, *146*, 77–123. doi:10.1016/S0004-3702(02)00399-5.

Sur, P. Chakraborty, & Saha. (2009). A new wavelet based edge detection technique for iris imagery. *IEEE International Advance Computing Conference* (120-124). Washington, DC: IEEE Press.

Sustens. (2002). *Fundamentals of medical imaging.* New York: Cambridge University Press.

Sweldens, W. (1996). The lifting scheme: A custom-design construction of biorthogonal wavelets. *Journal of Applied and Computational Harmonic Analysis*, *3*, 186–200. doi:10.1006/acha.1996.0015.

Tagare, H. D., Toyama, K., & Wang, J. G. (2001). A maximum-likelihood strategy for directing attention during visual search. *IEEE Transactions on Pattern Analysis and Machine Intelligence*, *23*(5), 490–500. doi:10.1109/34.922707.

Tang, Rangayyan, Xu, El Naqa, & Yang. (2009). Computer-aided detection and diagnosis of breast cancer with mammography. *IEEE Transactions on Recent Advances in Information Technology and Biomedicine, 13*(2), 236–251.

Tang, Z., Deng, M., Xiao, C., & Yu, J. (2011). Projection onto convex sets super-resolution image reconstruction based on wavelet bi-cubic interpolation. In *Proceedings of 2011 International Conference on Electronic and Mechanical Engineering and Information Technology* (351-354). Washington, DC: IEEE Press.

Tang, H., Wu, E. X., Ma, Q. Y., Gallagher, D., Perera, G. M., & Zhuang, T. (2000). MRI brain image segmentation by multi-resolution edge detection and region selection. *Computerized Medical Imaging and Graphics*, *24*(6), 349–357. doi:10.1016/S0895-6111(00)00037-9 PMID:11008183.

Tasdizen, Whitaker, Burchard, & Osher. (2003). Geometric surface processing via normal maps. *ACM Transactions on Graphics*, *22*(4), 1012–1033. doi:10.1145/944020.944024.

Tatler, B. W., Baddeley, R. J., & Gilchrist, I. D. (2005). Visual correlates of fixation selection: Effects of scale and time. *Vision Research*, *45*, 643–659. doi:10.1016/j.visres.2004.09.017 PMID:15621181.

Taubman, D. (2000). High performance scalable image compression with EBCOT. *IEEE Transactions on Image Processing*, *9*, 1158–1170. doi:10.1109/83.847830 PMID:18262955.

Tehrani, J. N., Jin, C., & McEwan, A. L. (2012). Modelling of an oesophageal electrode for cardiac function tomography. *Computational and Mathematical Methods in Medicine.* doi:10.1155/2012/585786 PMID:22481975.

Tek, F. B., Dempster, A. G., & Kale, I. (2006). Malaria parasite detection in peripheral blood images. In *Proceedings of British Machine Vision Conference.* Berlin: Springer-Verlag.

Tenenbaum, J. B., de Silva, V., & Langford, J. C. (2000). A global geometric framework for nonlinear dimensionality reduction. *Science*, *290*(5500), 2319–2323. doi:10.1126/science.290.5500.2319 PMID:11125149.

Teo & Heeger. (1994). Perceptual image distortion. *Proceedings of the Society for Photo-Instrumentation Engineers*, *2179*, 127–141. doi:10.1117/12.172664.

Teplan, M. (2002). Fundamentals of EEG measurement. *Measurement Science Review, 2.*

Tewfik, Sinha, & Jorgensen. (1992). On the optimal choice of a wavelet for signal representation. *IEEE Transactions on Information Theory, 38*(2), 747–765. doi:10.1109/18.119734.

Thiran & Macq. (1996). Morphological feature extraction for the classification of digital images of cancerous tissues. *IEEE Transactions on Bio-Medical Engineering, 43*(10), 111–120.

Throop, J. A., Aneshansley, D. J., Anger, W. C., & Peterson, D. L. (2005). Quality evaluation of apples based on surface defects—an inspection station design. *International Journal Postharvest Biology and Technology, 36*, 281–290. doi:10.1016/j.postharvbio.2005.01.004.

Tian, J., & Wells, R. O. (1998). Embedded image coding using wavelet difference reduction. In P. Topiwala (Ed.), Wavelet Image and Video Compression (289-301). Norwell, MA: Kluwer Academic Publishers.

Tian, J. (2003). Reversible data embedding using a difference expansion. *IEEE Transactions on Circuits and Systems for Video Technology, 13*(8), 890–896. doi:10.1109/TCSVT.2003.815962.

Toha, S. F., & Ngah, U. K. (2007). Computer aided medical diagnosis for the identification of malaria parasites. *IEEE ICSCN, 2007*, 521–522.

Tomasi, C., & Manduchi, R. (1998). Bilateral filtering for gray and color images. In *Proceedings of the Sixth IEEE International Conference on Computer Vision* (839-846). Washington, DC: IEEE Press.

Treisman, A. M., & Gelade, G. (1980). A feature integration theory of attention. *Cognitive Psychology, 12*(1), 97–136. doi:10.1016/0010-0285(80)90005-5 PMID:7351125.

Triggs, B., McLauchlan, P., Hartley, R. I., & Fitzgibbon, A. (2000). Bundle adjustment a modern synthesis. Vision Algorithms: Theory and Practice. *Lecture Notes in Computer Science, 1883*, 298–372. doi:10.1007/3-540-44480-7_21.

Trucco, E., & Olmos, A. (2006). Self-tuning underwater image restoration. *IEEE Journal of Oceanic Engineering, 31*(2), 511–519. doi:10.1109/JOE.2004.836395.

Tsai, M. J., Villasenor, J. D., & Chen, F. (1996). Stack-run image coding. *IEEE Transactions on Circuits and Systems for Video Technology, 6*, 519–521. doi:10.1109/76.538934.

Tsotsos, J. K. (1990). Analyzing vision at the complexity level. *The Behavioral and Brain Sciences, 13*, 423–469. doi:10.1017/S0140525X00079577.

Tsotsos, J. K., Culhane, S. M., Wai, W. Y. K., Lai, Y., Davis, N., & Nuflo, F. (1995). Modeling visual attention via selective tuning. *Artificial Intelligence, 78*(1-2), 507–547. doi:10.1016/0004-3702(95)00025-9.

Tsui, Zhao, Frey, & Gulberg. (1991). Comparison between ML-EM and WLS-CG algorithm for SPECT image reconstruction. *IEEE Transactions on Nuclear Science, 38*, 1766–1772.

Tusher, V. G., Tibshirani, R., & Chu, G. (2001). Significance analysis of microarrays applied to the ionizing radiation response. *Proceedings of the National Academy of Sciences of the United States of America, 98*(18), 5116–5121. doi:10.1073/pnas.091062498 PMID:11309499.

Tu, Y., Stolovitzky, G., & Klein, U. (2002). Quantitative noise analysis for gene expression microarray experiments. *Proceedings of the National Academy of Sciences of the United States of America, 99*(22), 14031–14036. doi:10.1073/pnas.222164199 PMID:12388780.

U. S. Preventive Services Task Force. (2013). Screening for breast cancer: U.S. preventive services task force recommendation statement. *Annals of Internal Medicine*. Retrieved from http://www.uspreventiveservicestaskforce. org/uspstf09/breastcancer/brcanrs.pdf.

Ullrich, B., Günther, T., & Rücker, C. (2007). Electrical resistivity tomography methods for archaeological prospection. In A. Posluschny, K. Lambers, & I. Herzog (Ed.), *Layers of Perception. Proceedings of the 35th International Conference on Computer Applications and Quantitative Methods in Archaeology (CAA)* (1-7). Berlin: Koll.

Unay, D., & Ekin, A. (2008). Intensity versus texture for medical image search and retrieval. In *Proceedings of the 5th IEEE International Symposium on Biomedical Imaging: From Nano to Macro* (241-244). Washingtong, DC: IEEE Press.

Ungerleider, L., & Haxby, J. (1994). 'What' and 'where' in the human brain. *Current Opinion in Neurobiology, 4*, 157–165. doi:10.1016/0959-4388(94)90066-3 PMID:8038571.

Vandenberghe, D'Asseler, Van de Walle, Kauppinen, Koole, ... & Dierckx. (2001). Iterative reconstruction algorithms in nuclear medicine. *Computerized Medical Imaging and Graphics, 25*, 105-111.

Vanithamani & Umamaheswari. (2010). Performance analysis of filters for speckle reduction in medical ultrasound images. *International Journal of Computers and Applications, 12*(6).

Vapnik. *Statistical Learning Theory.* Hoboken, NJ: Wiley.

Vardi, Y., Shepp, L. A., & Kaufman, L. (1985). A statistical model for positron emission tomography. *Journal of the American Statistical Association, 80*, 8–20. doi:10.1080/01621459.1985.10477119.

Vauhkonen, M. (1997). *Electrical Impedance Tomography and Prior Information.* (PhD Thesis). Joensuu, Finland, Kuopio University.

Vauhkonen, P. J., Vauhkonen, M., Savolainen, T., & Kaipio, J. P. (1999). Three-dimensional electrical impedance tomography based on the complete electrode model. *IEEE Transactions on Bio-Medical Engineering, 46*(9), 1150–1160. doi:10.1109/10.784147 PMID:10493078.

Vaz, C. M. P., Crestana, S., Mascarenhas, S., Cruvinel, P. E., Reichardt, K., & Stolf, R. (1989). Using a computed tomography miniscanner for studying tillage induced soil compaction. *Soil Technology, 2*, 313–321. doi:10.1016/0933-3630(89)90015-9.

Vazquez, M., & Steinfeld, A. (2011). An assisted photography method for street scenes. In *Proceedings of IEEE Workshop on Applications of Computer Vision* (89-94). Washington, DC: IEEE Press.

Vecera, S., & Farah, M. (1994). Does visual attention select object or locations? *Journal of Experimental Psychology. Human Perception and Performance, 23*, 1–14.

Veenman, C. J., Reinders, M. J. T., & Backer, E. (2003). A cellular coevolutionary algorithm for image segmentation. *IEEE Transactions on Image Processing, 12*(3), 304–313. doi:10.1109/TIP.2002.806256 PMID:18237910.

Velumani, R., & Seenivasagam, V. (2010). A reversible blind medical image watermarking scheme for patient identification, improved telediagnosis, and tamper detection with a facial image watermark. In *Proceedings of IEEE International Conference on Computational Intelligence and Computing Research* (1-8). Washington, DC: IEEE Press.

Vese & Osher. (2002). Numerical methods for p-harmonic flows and applications to image processing. *SIAM Journal on Numerical Analysis, 40*(6), 2085–2104. doi:10.1137/S0036142901396715.

Vetterli, M., & Kovacevic, J. (1995). *Wavelets and subband coding.* Englewood Cliffs, NJ: Prentice Hall.

Vezhnevets & Konouchine. (2005). Grow-cut-Interactive multi-label N-D image segmentation. In *Proceedings of International Conference on Computer Graphics and Vision* (150–156). Berlin: Springer.

Victorino, Borges, & Okamoto, Matos, Tucci, ... & Amato. (2004). Imbalances in regional lung ventilation: A validation study on electrical impedance tomography. *American Journal of Respiratory and Critical Care Medicine, 169*(7), 791–800. doi:10.1164/rccm.200301-133OC PMID:14693669.

Vikram, T. N., Tscherepanow, M., & Wrede, B. (2011). A random center-surround bottom-up visual attention model useful for salient region detection. In *Proceedings of IEEE Workshop on Applications of Computer Vision* (166-173). Washington, DC: IEEE Press.

Vince, D. G., Dixon, K. J., Cothren, R. M., & Cornhill, J. F. (2000). Comparison of texture analysis methods for the characterization of coronary plaques in intravascular ultrasound images. *Computerized Medical Imaging and Graphics, 24*, 221–229. doi:10.1016/S0895-6111(00)00011-2 PMID:10842046.

Vincent, L. (1993). Morphological gray scale reconstruction in image analysis: Application and efficient algorithms. *IEEE Transactions on Image Processing, 2*, 176–201. doi:10.1109/83.217222 PMID:18296207.

Vo-Dinh, T. (2003). *Biomedical photonics handbook.* New York: CRC Press. doi:10.1201/9780203008997.

Vogiatzis, G., Esteban, C. H., Torr, P. H. S., & Cipolla, R. (2007). Multiview stereo via volumetric graph-cuts and occlusion robust photo-consistency. *IEEE Transactions on Pattern Analysis and Machine Intelligence*, *29*(12), 2241–2246. doi:10.1109/TPAMI.2007.70712 PMID:17934232.

Walker. (2001). Wavelet-based image compression. *The Transform and Data Compression*. New York: CRC Press LLC.

Walker, J. S. (2000). A lossy image codec based on adaptively scanned wavelet difference reduction. *Optical Engineering (Redondo Beach, Calif.)*, *39*(7), 1891–1897. doi:10.1117/1.602573.

Wang & Arce. (2010). Variable density compressed image sampling. *IEEE Transactions on Image Processing*, *19*(1), 264–270. doi:10.1109/TIP.2009.2032889 PMID:19775971.

Wang & Bovik. (2002). A universal quality index. *IEEE Signal Processing Letters*, *9*(3), 81–84. doi:10.1109/97.995823.

Wang & Yu. (2008). An outlook on x-ray CT research and development. *Medical Physics*, *35*(3).

Wang, M. (1999). Three- dimensional effects in electrical impedance tomography. In *Proceedings of 1st World Congress on Industrial Process Tomography* (410-415). Buxton, UK: OLIL.

Wang, Bovik, Sheikh, & Simoncelli. (2004). Image quality assessment: From error visibility to structural similarity. *IEEE Transactions on Image Processing*, *13*(4), 600–612. doi:10.1109/TIP.2003.819861 PMID:15376593.

Wang, D. (1997). A multiscale gradient algorithm for image segmentation using watersheds. *Pattern Recognition*, *30*(12), 2043–2052. doi:10.1016/S0031-3203(97)00015-0.

Wang, H., Cao, Q., Liu, W., & Masteru, N. (1999). Neural network based on computer grader judgement. *Transactions of the Chinese Society for Agricultural Machinery*, *30*(6), 83–87.

Wang, R. Z., Lin, C. F., & Lin, J. C. (2000). Image hiding by optimal LSB substitution and genetic algorithm. *Pattern Recognition*, *34*(3), 671–683. doi:10.1016/S0031-3203(00)00015-7.

Wang, Z., Bovik, A. C., Sheikh, H. R., & Simoncelli, E. P. (2004). Image quality assessment: From error visibility to structural similarity. *IEEE Transactions on Image Processing*, *13*(4), 600–612. doi:10.1109/TIP.2003.819861 PMID:15376593.

Wang, Z., & Wang, W. (2009). Fast and adaptive method for SAR superresolution imaging based on point scattering model and optimal basis selection. *IEEE Transactions on Image Processing*, *18*(7), 1477–1486. doi:10.1109/TIP.2009.2017327 PMID:19473944.

Wan, Y. W., Sabbagh, E., Raese, R., Qian, Y., Luo, D., & Guo, N. L. et al. (2010). Hybrid models identified a 12 gene signature for lung cancer prognosis and chemoresponse prediction. *PLoS ONE*, *5*(8). doi:10.1371/journal.pone.0012222 PMID:20808922.

Webb, A. (2003). *Introduction to biomedical imaging*. Washington, DC: IEEE Press.

Webb, S. (2000). *The physics of medical imaging*. London: Institute of Physics.

Webster, J. G. (2009). *Medical instrumentation: Application and design* (3rd ed.). Singapore: John Wiley & Sons.

Webster, J. G. (Ed.). (1990). *Electrical impedance tomography. Adam Hilger Series of Biomedical Engineering*. New York: Adam Hilger.

Wei, H. Y., & Soleimani, M. (2012). Hardware and software design for a national instrument-based magnetic induction tomography system for prospective biomedical applications. *Physiological Measurement*, *33*(5), 863–879. doi:10.1088/0967-3334/33/5/863 PMID:22531316.

Weinberger, M. J., Seroussi, G., & Sapiro, G. (1996). LOCO-I: A low complexity, context-based lossless image compression algorithm. In *Proceedings of IEEE Data Compression Conference* (140-149). Snowbird, UT: IEEE Press.

Weinberger, M. J., & Seroussi, G. (1997). Sequential prediction and ranking in universal context modeling and data compression. *IEEE Transactions on Information Theory*, *43*, 1697–1706. doi:10.1109/18.623176.

Weinberger, M. J., Seroussi, G., & Sapiro, G. (2000). The LOCO-I lossless image compression algorithm: Principles and standardization into JPEG-LS. *IEEE Transactions on Image Processing*, *9*, 1309–1324. doi:10.1109/83.855427 PMID:18262969.

Wheeler, F. W., & Pearlman, W. A. (2000). Combined spatial and subband block coding of images. *IEEE International Conference on Image Processing (ICIP2001)*. Vancouver, BC: IEEE Press.

Wi, H., Kim, T. E., Oh, T. I., & Woo, E. J. (2012). Expandable multi-frequency EIT system for clinical applications. In *Proceedings of Progress in Electromagnetics Research Symposium* (49-52). Kuala Lumpur, Malaysia: PIERS Press.

Wikipedia. (2013). *Inverse problem.* Retrieved from http://en.wikipedia.org/wiki/Inverse_problem.

Wikipedia . (2013a). Stationary wavelet transform. Retrieved from http://en.wikipedia.org/wiki/Stationary_wavelet_transform.

Wikipedia . (2013b). White blood cell. Retrieved from http://en.wikipedia.org/wiki/White_blood_cell.

Wiltgen, M., Gerger, A., Wagner, C., Bergthaler, P., & Smolle, J. (2007). Evaluation of texture features in spatial and frequency domain for automatic discrimination of histologic tissue. *Analytical and Quantitative Cytology and Histology*, *29*, 251–263. PMID:17879634.

Winkler. (1999). Visual quality assessment using a contrast gain control model. In *Proceedings of IEEE Signal Processing Society Workshop on Multimedia Signal Processing* (527–532). Washington, DC: IEEE Press.

Witten, I. H., Neal, R. M., & Cleary, J. G. (1987). Arithmetic coding for data compression. *Communications of the ACM*, *30*(6), 520–540. doi:10.1145/214762.214771.

Wolfe, J. M. (1994). Guided search 2.0: A revised model of visual search. *Psychonomic Bulletin & Review*, *1*, 202–238. doi:10.3758/BF03200774.

Wolfe, J. M., & Horowitz, T. S. (2004). What attributes guide the deployment of visual attention and how do they do it? *Nature Reviews. Neuroscience*, *5*(6), 495–501. doi:10.1038/nrn1411 PMID:15152199.

Wong, S., Zaremba, L., Gooden, D., & Huang, H. K. (1995). Radiologic image compression–A review. *Proceedings of the IEEE*, *83*, 194–219. doi:10.1109/5.364466.

Wu, C.-Y., Leou, J.-J., & Chen, H.-Y. (2009). Visual attention region determination using low-level features. In *Proceedings of IEEE International Symposium on Circuits and Systems* (3178–3181). Washington, DC: IEEE Press.

Wu, Q., Zeng, L., Zheng, H., & Guo, N. (2008). precise segmentation of white blood cells by using multispectral imaging analysis techniques. In *Proceedings of the International Conference on Intelligent Networks and Intelligent Systems*. Washington, DC: IEEE Press.

Wu, X., & Menon, N. (1996). CALIC-A context based adaptive lossless image codec. In *Proceedings of International Conference on Acoustics, Speech, and Signal Processing* (1890-1893). Washington, DC: IEEE Press.

Wu. (2006). A new hybrid PDE denoising model based on markov random field. In *Proceedings of First International Conference on Innovative Computing Information and Control* (338–341). Washington, DC: IEEE Press.

Xiao & Ohya. (2008). Contrast enhancement of color images based on wavelet transform and human visual system. In *Proceedings of IASTED Conference on Graphics and Visual Engineering*. Ohkuboyama, Japan: Waseda University.

Xiao-bo, Jie-wen, Yanxiao, & Holmes. (2010). In-line detection of apple defects using three color cameras system. *Journal of Computers and Electronics in Agriculture*, *70*, 129–134. doi:10.1016/j.compag.2009.09.014.

Xiong, Z., Guleryuz, O., & Orchard, M. T. (1996). A DCT based embedded Image coder. *IEEE Signal Processing Letters*, *3*, 289–290. doi:10.1109/97.542157.

Xiong, Z., Ramachandran, K., & Orchard, M. T. (1997). Space-frequency quantization for wavelet image coding. *IEEE Transactions on Image Processing*, *6*(5), 677–693. doi:10.1109/83.568925 PMID:18282961.

Xu & Wang. (2006). Photoacoustic imaging in biomedicine. *The Review of Scientific Instruments*, *77*(4).

Xu, J. (1997). *Study on parallel processing for computer vision information in fruit gradation*. Beijing: China Agricultural University.

Yang, J., Wright, J., Ma, Y., & Huang, T. (2008). Image super-resolution as sparse representation of raw image patches. In *Proceedings of IEEE Conference on Computer Vision and Pattern Recognition, 2008* (1-8). Washington, DC: IEEE Press.

Yang, B., Schmucker, M., Funk, W., Busch, C., & Sun, S. (2004). Integer DCT–based reversible watermarking technique for images using companding technique. *Proceedings of the Society for Photo-Instrumentation Engineers, 5306*, 405–415. doi:10.1117/12.527216.

Yang, J. O., Kim, W. Y., Jeong, S. Y., Oh, J. H., Jho, S., Bhak, J., & Kim, N. S. (2009). PDbase: A database of Parkinson's disease-related genes and genetic variation using substantia nigra ESTs. *BMC Genomics, 3*. PMID:19123947.

Yang, J., Wang, Z., Lin, Z., Cohen, S., & Huang, T. (2012). Coupled dictionary training for image super-resolution. *IEEE Transactions on Image Processing, 21*(8), 3467–3478. doi:10.1109/TIP.2012.2192127.

Yang, Q. (1994). An approach to apple surface feature detection by machine vision. *Computers and Electronics in Agriculture, 11*(2-3), 249–263. doi:10.1016/0168-1699(94)90012-4.

Yang, Q. S. (1996). Apple stem and calyx identification with machine vision system. *Journal of Agricultural Engineering Research, 63*(3), 9–236. doi:10.1006/jaer.1996.0024.

Yantis, S., & Jonides, J. (1984). Abrupt visual onsets and selective attention: evidence from visual search. *Journal of Experimental Psychology. Human Perception and Performance, 10*, 601–621. doi:10.1037/0096-1523.10.5.601 PMID:6238122.

Yap, K.-H., He, Y., Tian, Y., & Chau, L.-P. (2009). A nonlinear L1-norm approach for joint image registration and super-resolution. *IEEE Signal Processing Letters, 16*(11), 981–984. doi:10.1109/LSP.2009.2028106.

Yarbus, A. L. (1967). *Eye movements and vision.* New York: Plenum Press.

Yorkey, T. J. (1986) *Comparing Reconstruction Methods for Electrical Impedance Tomography.* (PhD Thesis). Madison, WI, University of. Wisconsin at Madison.

Yorkey, T. J., Webster, J. G., & Tompkins, W. J. (1987). Comparing reconstruction algorithms for electrical impedance tomography. *IEEE Transactions on Bio-Medical Engineering, 34*, 843–852. doi:10.1109/TBME.1987.326032 PMID:3692503.

Yüksel. (2006). A hybrid neuro-fuzzy filter for edge preserving restoration of images corrupted by impulse noise. *IEEE Transactions on Image Processing, 15*(4).

Yu, W. (1991). On the existence of an inverse problem. *Journal of Mathematical Analysis and Applications, 157*(1), 63–74. doi:10.1016/0022-247X(91)90137-O.

Yu, Z., & Wong, H.-S. (2007). A rule based technique for extraction of visual attention regions based on real time clustering. *IEEE Transactions on Multimedia, 9*(4), 766–784. doi:10.1109/TMM.2007.893351.

Zain, J. M., & Fauzi, A. R. M. (2007). Evaluation of medical image watermarking with tamper detection and recovery. In *Proceedings of 29th Annual International Conference of the IEEE on Engineering in Medicine and Biology Society* (5661–5664). Washington, DC: IEEE Press.

Zang, S., Guo, R., Zhang, L., & Lu, Y. (2007). Integration of statistical inference methods and a novel control measure to improve sensitivity and specificity of data analysis in expression profiling studies. *Journal of Biomedical Informatics, 40*(5), 552–560. doi:10.1016/j.jbi.2007.01.002 PMID:17317331.

Zhai, Y., & Shah, M. (2006). Visual attention detection in video sequences using spatiotemporal cues. In *Proceedings of the 14th Annual ACM International Conference on Multimedia* (815-824). New York: ACM Press.

Zhai, Z. Yang, & Xu. (2005). Image quality assessment metrics based on multi-scale edge presentation. In *Proceedings of IEEE Workshop on Signal Processing Systems Design and Implementation* (331–336). Washington, DC: IEEE Press.

Zhang, Z. (2000). An exible new technique for camera calibration. *IEEE Transactions on Pattern Analysis and Machine Intelligence, 22*(11), 1330–1334. doi:10.1109/34.888718.

Zhao, J., Lu, Y., Zhuang, T., & Wang, G. (2010). Overview of multisource CT systems and methods. In S. R. Stuart (Ed.) *Proceedings of the SPIE: Developements in X-Ray Tomography VII* (78040H-78040H-14). Bellingham, WA: SPIE Press.

Zhao, Z.-C., & Cai, A.-N. (2007). Selective extraction of visual saliency objects in images and videos. In Proceedings of 3rd International Intelligent Information Hiding and Multimedia Signal Processing (198-201). Washington, DC: IEEE Press.

Zhao, X., & Zhai, L.-P. (2005). Wavelet-fractal based compression of ophthalmic image.[Bellingham, WA: SPIE Press.]. *Proceedings of the Society for Photo-Instrumentation Engineers*, ICO20, 35–42.

Zhiqing, W., & Yang, T. (1999). Building a rule-based machine-vision system for defect inspection on apple sorting and packing lines. *Expert Systems with Applications*, 16, 307–313. doi:10.1016/S0957-4174(98)00079-7.

Zhong, X. (2000). *Block based wavelet transform image coding based on set partitioning in hierarchical algorithm. Project Report*. Sydney, Australia: Motorola Australia Research Center.

Zhou, X., & Gordon, R. (1989). Detection of early breast cancer. *An overview and future prospects. Critical Reviews in Biomedical Engineering*, 17(3), 203–255. PMID:2673660.

Zhu, C. Q., Ding, K., Strumpf, D., Weir, B. A., Meyerson, M., & Tsao, M. S. et al. (2010). Prognostic and predictive gene signature for adjuvant chemotherapy in resected non-small-cell lung cancer. *Journal of Clinical Oncology*, 28(29), 4417–4424. doi:10.1200/JCO.2009.26.4325 PMID:20823422.

Ziv, J., & Lempel, A. (1977). A universal algorithm for sequential data compression. *IEEE Transactions on Information Theory*, IT-23(3), 337–343. doi:10.1109/TIT.1977.1055714.

Zong, Laine, & Geiser. (1998). Speckle reduction and contrast enhancement of echocardiogram via multiscale nonlinear processing. *IEEE Transactions on Medical Imaging*, 17.

Zou, K. H., Warfield, S. K., Bharatha, A., Tempany, C. M. C., Kaus, M. R., & Kikinis, R. et al. (2004). Statistical validation of image segmentation quality based on a spatial overlap index. *Academic Radiology*, 11(2), 178–189. doi:10.1016/S1076-6332(03)00671-8 PMID:14974593.

Zuiderveld. (1994). Contrast limited adaptive histogram equalization. *Graphics Gems IV*. London: Academic Press Professional, Inc.

About the Contributors

Rajeev Srivastava is currently working as an Associate Professor in the Dept. of Computer Engineering, Indian Institute of Technology (BHU), Varanasi, India since November' 2007. He received his Ph.D. degree in Computer Engineering from Faculty of Technology, University of Delhi, Delhi. He has around 15 years of teaching and research experience. He has around 50 research publications in refereed Journals, conferences. In edited books as book chapters and 02 books published by an international publisher (Germany) to his credit. He is reviewer of many international journals and technical program committee member of many international conferences. He was awarded a project by the NMEICT, MHRD, Govt. of India in 2010 for the design and development of an interactive e-content for the subject digital image processing and machine vision. His biography was listed in Marquis Who's Who is Science and Engineering, USA, 11th Ed., 2011-12 and 2000 Outstanding Intellectuals of the 21st Century-2011 by IBC, Cambridge, UK. He is the recipient of 2010 Publication Scholar Award by IIT-BHU Global Alumni Association. He has delivered many invited talks in his research area. He was the coordinator and Organizing Secretary of a Refresher Course on ICT applications and a National conference on AI and Agents Applications, respectively. His research interests include image processing and computer vision, medical image processing, pattern recognition, video surveillance and algorithms.

Sanjay K. Singh is Associate Professor in Department of Computer Engineering at Indian Institute of Technology (Banaras Hindu University), Varanasi, India. He is a certified Novel Engineer and Novel administrator. His research has been funded by UGC and AICTE. He has over 70 publications in refereed journals, book chapters, and conferences. His research interests include computational intelligence, biometrics, video authentication, Pattern recognition and machine learning. Singh is a member of IET, IEEE, ISTE, CSI.

K. K. Shukla is professor of Computer Engineering at Indian Institute of Technology, BHU, India. He has 30 years of research and teaching experience. Professor Shukla has published more than 120 research papers in reputed journals and conferences and has more than 100 citations. 15 Ph.D.s have been awarded under his supervision. Professor Shukla has to his credit, many projects of national importance at BHU, Hindustan Aeronautics and Smiths Aerospace U.K. Presently, he has research collaboration with Space Applications Center, ISRO, Tata Consultancy Services, Institut National de Recherche en Informatique et en Automatique (INRIA), France and E´cole de Technologie Supe´rieure (ETS), Canada. He has written 4 books on Neuro-computers, Real Time Task Scheduling, Fuzzy modeling, Image Compression and has contributed chapters to 3 books published in the U.S. Professor Shukla is a Fellow of the Institution of Engineers, Fellow of the Institution of Electronics and Telecommunications Engineers, Senior Member, ISTE and the Senior Member, Computer Society of India.

* * *

Tushar Kanti Bera obtained his B.E. (Electrical Engineering) from North Bengal University, India in 2000. He received his M. Tech Degree in Electrical Engineering from the University of Calcutta in 2003. He is currently pursuing his Postdoctoral Research in the Department of Computational Science and Engineering, Yonsei University, Seoul, South Korea. His current research interests include medical imaging, electrical impedance tomography (EIT), computed tomography, inverse problems, image reconstruction algorithms, numerical simulations, biomedical instrumentation, medical electronics, biosensors, bioelectrical impedance analysis, mathematical modelling of bioelectrical impedance, and electrical impedance spectroscopy.

Nitin Bharadwaj completed his B.E. in Biotechnology from Netaji Subhas Institute of Technology and worked at Tata Consultancy Services. He is currently pursuing his Masters at IIT (Kanpur).

Sonika Bhatnagar did her Ph.D. in Biophysics from All India Institute of Medical Sciences and later joined as a faculty member at Netaji Subhas Institute of Technology. She currently serves as Assistant Professor and Associate Head at the Division of Biotechnology at NSIT. Her research interests lie in the broad field of Computational and Structural Biology. She has specialized in molecular modeling of proteins, modeling of protein-protein/protein-DNA interactions, and drug design. She is also an Inno-Centive award winner for Selection of top five drug targets for therapeutic intervention in obesity. The main thrust of the work in microarray data analysis is to develop a prognosis tool or gene signatures that act as biomarkers in specific conditions.

Mahua Bhattacharya is an Associate Professor in ICT Department of the institute since 2006, December. She had her B.Tech and M.Tech degree from the institute of Radio Physics and Electronics, University of Calcutta. She worked as a research scientist at Indian Statistical Institute, Calcutta from 1995 until 2000 and got her Ph.D degree on medical image processing in 2001 from the University of Calcutta. She has her experience more than seventeen years in teaching and research. Her area of specialization is based on Medical Image Processing, Pattern Recognition, Computer Vision, Soft Computing. She was an Assistant Professor of Indian Institute of Information Technology, Allahabad and Reader in School of IT of W.B. University of Technology. She was recipient of Frank George award for her paper entitled - Cybernetic Approach To Medical Technology: Application To Cancer Screening And Other Diagnostics' WOSC The World Organization Of Systems & Cybernetics, UK. She has published 113 papers in International journals and conference proceedings and as book chapters. She is a selected member of Irish Pattern Recognition and Classification Society, Life Member of International Association of Pattern Recognition (IAPR), Indian Academy of Neuroscience (IAN) and coordinating member of National Brain Research Centre (NBRC). She is Convener of INNS (International Neural Network Society), India Chapter for Northern and Central India. She is reviewer of IEEE transactions under EMBC, Elsevier, and Wiley journals. She is an international program committee member and in advisory committee of various international conferences abroad.

Brojeshwar Bhowmick is a PhD Scholar at IIT Delhi and scientist at innovation lab, TCS. He has 7 years of experience both in academic and industry at Indian Statistical Institute, IIT Delhi, Avisere Technology(now Videonetics), and Innovation lab TCS. His research areas are Computer Vision, Machine Learning, Image and Video Understanding, and Multi-view Geometry. Currently he is doing research in Geometric Vision, 3D Reconstruction, and Machine Learning at IIT Delhi. He has had more than 15 papers in peer reviewed international conferences and journals in this field. He also was awarded Young IT Professional Special Mention Award in CSI Kolkata.

Debalina Biswas is pursuing M. Tech in Computer Science and Engineering from JIS College of Engineering, Kalyani, West Bengal and completed her B. Tech Degree from Meghnad Saha Institute of Technology, Kolkata. She has about 10 research papers published in National & International Journals on Image Processing & Analysis. Her research area is Video compression.

Prabhakar C. J. received the Ph.D. degree in Computer Science from the Department of Computer Science, Gulbarga University. In 2009. He has obtained M. Sc., degree in Mathematics from Kuvempu University and the M. Tech. degree in Computer Science from University of Mysore. He is currently an Assistant Professor in the Department of Computer Science, Kuvempu University, India. His research interests are 2D video/image processing, depth acquisition, image recognition, and understanding.

Chandan Chakraborty is an Assistant Professor at School of Medical Science and Technology, IIT Kharagpur. He has received his masters from Indian Institute of Technology, Bombay and PhD degree from Indian Institute of Technology, Kharagpur in 2001 and 2007 respectively. He has more than 60 publications in reputed international journals and international conference proceedings. His major fields of interest are biostatistics & medical informatics, computer vision, & pattern recognition for medical imaging, quantitative microscopy & computational pathology, and statistical machine learning & computer aided diagnosis. He is the recipient of ISCA young scientist award (2007) from President of India and IBM faculty award (2012).

Rajat Subhra Chakraborty received a Ph.D. in Computer Engineering from Case Western Reserve University, USA. In 2010. Currently, he is an Assistant Professor in the Computer Science and Engineering Department of IIT Kharagpur, India. His major research interests are Hardware Security and Digital Content Protection. He has over 40 publications in international journals and conferences, and one assigned US patent. Chakraborty is a member of IEEE.

Sheli Sinha Chaudhri is an associate professor of jadavpur University. Her research interests include soft computing, Image processing, and Multimedia. She has 50 research papers published in National/International journal and International/world conference.

Jitender Kumar Chhabra received the B.Tech., & M.Tech. from National Institute of Technology (formerly REC), Kurukshetra. He received Ph.D. from GGS Indraprastha University, Delhi. He is currently working as an Associate Professor at the National Institute of Technology, Kurukshetra. He has more than 20 years of teaching and research experience. He has more than 70 research papers in international journals, book chapters, and conference proceedings. He is author of three books from McGraw Hill including the one Schaum Series International book from MC Graw Hill on Programming With C. He has also reviewed 5 books on Software Engineering & Object Oriented Programming from various reputed International Publishers. He has delivered more than 20 expert Talks and chaired many Technical Sessions in many National & International Conferences of repute including those of the IEEE in USA. He has visited many countries and presented his research work in USA, UK, Spain,

France, Turkey, and Thailand. He is Reviewer of IEEE, Elsevier, Springer, & Wiley Journals. He has worked in collaboration with multinational IT companies Hewelett- Packard (HP) and Tata Consultancy Services (TCS) in the area of Software Engineering. His areas of interest are Software Engineering, Soft Computing, & object-Oriented Systems.

Achintya Das was born in 1957. He received the M. Tech. and Ph.D. (Tech.) degrees in Radio Physics and Electronics from the University of Calcutta, India, in 1982 and 1996, respectively. He was an Executive of Quality Assurance with Philips India from 1982 to 1996. He is currently a Professor and Head of the Electronics and Communication Engineering Department at Kalyani Government Engineering College, Kalyani,Nadia. His research interests include control engineering, instrumentation, Biomedical Engineering, and signal processing. He is one of the reviewers of International Journal of Control, England. Special awards received by him are: Gold Medal for securing highest position with 1st class in M.Tech. (Calcutta University) and Mohallanobis Medal Award for securing highest position with 1st. class in P. G. Dip in SQC (IAPQR, Delhi). He has 100 research papers published in National/International journals and National/International/world conference.

Dev Kumar Das is a PhD research scholar at School of Medical Science and Technology, IIT Kharagpur. He has received his B. Tech degree in Biomedical Engineering from West Bengal University of Technology in 2008. He has received MS degree in the field of pathological image processing from School of Medical Science and Technology, Indian Institute of Technology, Kharagpur. In 2012. He has published eight papers in refereed international journal, two book chapters and five international conference proceedings. His current research area includes pathological imaging and image analysis, biomedical pattern classification.

Nilanjan Dey is a Research Scholar in Jadavpur University, Electronics & Telecommunication Engineering Department, Kolkata, India. His specialized domain is Biomedical Signal Processing. Professionally, he is employed as an Asst. Professor in JIS College of Engineering, Kalyani, West Bengal in the Department of Information Technology. He completed his M.Tech in Software Engineering from JIS College of Engineering, Kalyani, West Bengal and received his B.Tech Degree from M.C.K.V. Institute of Engineering, Liluah, West Bengal. Experience in the field of Education nears to around 4 years and the Industrial experience accounts to 1.5 years. He has worked as a reviewer for several national and international conferences and is involved as an Editor/ Reviewer of various international journals of repute. He has more than 60 research papers in various national & international journals and conferences.

P. Geetha was born in Tamilnadu, India in 1978. She received B.E. degree in Computer science and Engineering from Anna University. M.E. degree in Computer science &Engineering from Govt. college of Engineering in 2002., & Ph.D. Degree in information and communication engineering from Anna university in 2008. Currently she is working as an Associate professor in Anna University Chennai. She has more than 10 years of experience in teaching. Her current research interest includes image processing, pattern recognition and computer vision.

Goutam Ghosh was born in 1949. He graduated with Physics Honour in 1969 from the University of Calcutta and thereafter obtained the B.Tech. degree in Electronics and Electrical Communication Engineering from I.I.T. Kharagpur in 1972, the M.Tech., & Ph.D. (Tech.) degrees in Radio Physics and

414

Electronics from the University of Calcutta in 1974 and 1990 respectively. He is presently a Professor in the Department of Radio Physics and Electronics and also acting as the Deputy Co-ordinator of the Centre of Advanced Study in Radio Physics and Electronics, Calcutta University from April 2011, Director (Hony.), UGC-Networking Resource Centre in Physical Sciences, Calcutta University, Director (Hony.) of the Centre for Teleinfrastruktur (CTIF) – India. His research interests include Gunn-diode Oscillators, Power Combiners, Microwave Properties of Conducting Polymers and Rubbers, Electromagnetics, Speech Recognition and Processing, Biomedical image Watermarking. Ghosh is a life member of the Society of EMC Engineers (India).

Aviral Goel was born on 25th February 1991 in the holy town of Haridwar and currently resides at Bangalore. He is an electronics engineer by training and earned his Bachelor of Engineering in Electronics and Communication from Netaji Subhas Institute of Technology, New Delhi in 2012. During his college years he got bitten by the programming bug and has been an avid programmer ever since,working on numerous projects related to Data Mining, Signal Processing and Bioinformatics. He is currently working as a Software Engineer at Yahoo! India Software Development Centre.

Pragya Goel obtained her Masters degree in Computer Engineering from Cornell University in 2012. Prior to this she received her B.E in Computer Engineering from Netaji Subhas Institute of Technology, University of Delhi in 2011. Pragya has an avid interest in medicine and biology. Her research pursuit is focused on the development and application of powerful algorithms and tools using machine-learning techniques for finding solutions to problems in biology and medicine. She has successfully completed several projects at the supercomputing bioinformatics lab at IIT-Delhi in the area of protein structure prediction, at NSIT in microarray data analysis and at the IDEAL lab in Weill Cornell Medical College, New York in brain-gene expression analysis.

Hwa-Young Kim was born in Busan, Korea. In 1983. She received the B.S., & M.S. degrees in electronic engineering from Sogang University, Seoul, Korea. In 2007 and 2009, respectively. She is currently working in Central Advanced Research & Engineering Institute, Hyundai Motor Company. Her current research interests are computer vision for preventing collisions and intelligent safety car.

Maheshkumar H. Kolekar was born in Satara, Maharashtra, India. He received Ph. D. degree in Electronics and Electrical Communication Engineering from Indian Institute of Technology Kharagpur in 2007. During his PhD programme, he received Best Paper Award from Computer Society of India for his research paper. During 2008-2009, he was post-doctoral research fellow in the Department of Computer Science, University of Missouri, Columbia, USA. Since March 2010, he is working as Assistant Professor in Electrical Engineering, Indian Institute of Technology Patna, where at present, he is the Coordinator of Department. In 2012, he was i) organizing chair for IEEE sponsored International Conference on Signal, Image and Video Processing, at IIT Patna, ii) guest editor of American Scientific publisher's Journal of Medical Imaging and Health Informatics for special issue on Biomedical Signal and Image Processing, iii) tutorial chair of International Conference on IHCI, iv) keynote speaker for International conference on Biomedical Systems, Signals and Images at IIT Madras. v) Editorial Board member of American Journal of Signal Processing, Scientific and Academic Publishing, His research interests are in digital image and video processing, video surveillance and medical image processing.

Rajesh Kumar received the BE degree in Computer Science and Engineering from HNB Garhwal university,Srinagar, Uttarakhand, India in 2003, and M.Tech. degree in Software engineering from Motilal Nehru National Institute of Technology, Allahabad, INDIA. He worked as Associate Professor in the department of Computer Science and Engineering at LDC Institute of Technical Studies Allahabad, U P,INDIA. He is currently a Ph.D. research scholar at IIT (BHU) Varanasi, INDIA. In the department of Computer Engineering. He has been working on Computer vision and Image processing. His research interests include image enhancement, analysis, registration, segmentation and classification of Microscopic Biopsy images. Some of the application area of his work includes microscopic biopsy images for cancer research. Optimization Techniques and other non-destructive problem estimation.

Vijay Kumar received the B.Tech. from M.M. Engineering College, Mullana. He received M.Tech. from Guru Jambheshwer University of Science and Technology, Hisar. He is currently working toward the Ph.D. degree in Computer Engineering with the National Institute of Technology, Kurukshetra. He has been an Assistant Professor with the Department of Computer Science and Engineering, JCDM College of Engineering, Sirsa. He has more than 5 years of teaching and research experience. He has more than 20 research papers in international journals, book chapters, and conference proceedings. His main research focuses on Soft Computing, Image Processing, Data Clustering and Multiobjective optimization.

J. Nagaraju obtained his M.Sc(Tech) degree from Andhra University, Vishakhapatnam, India. He received his M.Phil and PhD degrees from Acharya Nagarjuna University, India. He has obtained Shri Hari Om Prerit S S Bhatnagar award in solar energy. At present he is working as Professor at Indian Institute of Science, Bangalore, India. His research interests include solar thermal engineering, photovoltaics, electrical and thermal contact resistance studies, impedance spectroscopy, impedance cardiography, electrocardiography, bioelectrical impedance analysis, electrical impedance tomography, health and environment monitoring sensors.

Bijurika Nandi is a B.Tech (2012) in Electronics and Communication Engineering from Calcutta Institute of Engineering and Management, under West Bengal University of Technology. She has 3 research papers in International Conference. Her research area is Biomedical Signal Processing.

Ruchira Naskar is presently a Ph.D. scholar in the Dept. of Computer Science and Engineering of Indian Institute of Technology, Kharagpur. She received a B.Tech degree in Information Technology from West Bengal University of Technology in 2008, and an M.Tech degree in Information Technology from Indian Institute of Technology, Kharagpur in 2010. Her research interest is in the area of digital watermarking, multimedia content protection and cryptography. Her Ph.D. research till date has resulted in the publication of six papers in international journals and seven papers in international conferences.

Praveen Kumar P. U. is a research scholar in Department of Computer Science, Kuvempu University, India. He received the B.Sc., & M.Sc. degrees in Computer Science from Kuvempu University, India. In 2006 and 2008, respectively. From 2009 to 2012, he was a project fellow in the Department of Computer Science, Kuvempu University. His research interests include Image Processing, Pattern Recognition, Computer Vision and Combinatorial Optimization.

Koushik Pal was born on 23rd February, 1983. He completed his B. Tech in Electronics and Communication Engineering from Vidyasagar University in 2004 and M. Tech in Radio Physics and Electronics from the Institute of Radio Physics and Electronics, University of Calcutta in 2007. He is presently pursuing his Ph. D. (Tech.) in Radio Physics and Electronics of the University of Calcutta. He joined the Department of Electronics and Communication Engineering as an Assistant Professor in Guru Nanak Institute of Technology, Kolkata. He is also associated with West Bengal University of Technology and Rama Krishna Mission Vivekenanda Centenary College as a guest faculty. He research interests are in the fields of Security Aspects of Biomedical Image Watermarking, Digital Image Processing, Digital Signal Processing and Analog and Digital Communication. He has to his credit five international journal publications and two international book chapters and more than ten international and national conference publications.

Rajarshi Pal received the B. Tech. degree from Kalyani Government Engineering College, Kalyani, West Bengal, India in 2004, the M. E. degree from Jadavpur University, Kolkata, India in 2006, and the Ph. D. degree from Indian Institute of Technology, Kharagpur, India in 2011. He is currently a faculty member with Institute for Development and Research in Banking Technology, Hyderabad, India. Prior joining to this institute, he had a short stint at Center for Soft Computing Research, Indian Statistical Institute, Kolkata, India as Research Associate. His research interests are in the areas of visual attention modeling, image retargeting, video summarization, image steganography and watermarking.

Rae-Hong Park was born in Seoul, Korea. In 1954. He received the B.S., & M.S. degrees in electronics engineering from Seoul National University, Seoul, Korea. In 1976 and 1979, respectively, and the M.S., & Ph.D. degrees in electrical engineering from Stanford University, Stanford, CA, USA. In 1981 and 1984, respectively. In 1984, he joined the faculty of the Department of Electronic Engineering, Sogang University, Seoul, Korea, where he is currently a Professor. In 1990, he spent his sabbatical year as a Visiting Associate Professor with the Computer Vision Laboratory, Center for Automation Research, University of Maryland at College Park, USA. In 2001 and 2004, he spent sabbatical semesters at Digital Media Research and Development Center (DTV image/video enhancement), Samsung Electronics Co., Ltd., Suwon, Korea. In 2012, he spent a sabbatical year in Digital Imaging Business (R&D Team) and Visual Display Business (R&D Office), Samsung Electronics Co., Ltd., Suwon, Korea. His current research interests are video communication, computer vision, and pattern recognition. He served as Editor for the Korea Institute of Telematics and Electronics (KITE) Journal of Electronics Engineering from 1995 to 1996. Park was the recipient of a 1990 Post-Doctoral Fellowship presented by the Korea Science and Engineering Foundation (KOSEF), the 1987 Academic Award presented by the KITE, the 2000 Haedong Paper Award presented by the Institute of Electronics Engineers of Korea (IEEK), the 1997 First Sogang Academic Award, and the 1999 Professor Achievement Excellence Award presented by Sogang University. He is a co-recipient of the Best Student Paper Award of the IEEE Int. Symp. Multimedia (ISM 2006) and IEEE Int. Symp. Consumer Electronics (ISCE 2011).

Harish Parthasarathy completed his B.Tech. in Electrical Engineering from IIT(Kanpur) in 1990. Then he completed his Ph.D. from IIT(Delhi) in Signal processing in 1994. From 1993-94, he was a visiting fellow at the Indian Institute of Astrophysics at Bangalore, where he worked on galactic simulation.

From 1994-97, he was Assistant Professor at IIT, Mumbai. From 1997-98, he was a visiting faculty at IIT Kanpur, where he taught courses in adaptive filters, linear algebra, and antenna theory. Currently he is working as a Professor in the ECE division of NSIT. His current research interests are in Electromagnetics and Quantum computation.

Saurav Prakash is in final semester of his graduation, at NIT PATNA, INDIA, majoring in computer science and engineering discipline. Already an employee of ERICSSON, he has a keen research interest in domain related to digital image processing and computer vision. His recent research works sticks to domains such as cancer detection, remote sensing, disparity mapping etc. Saurav has worked under some of the renowned professors and scientists over India while continuing with his research works. An optimist by nature, he seeks to carry on learning in his field of interests and carrying research works under guidance afterwards by opting for higher studies.

G. Lloyds Raja was born in Kanyakumari District, Tamilnadu, India. He received his B.E. in Electronics and Communication Engineering from Anna University Chennai in 2009 and M.E. in Embedded System Technologies from Anna University Tirunelveli in 2011. He is currently a research scholar in the Electrical engineering department of Indian Institute of Technology, Patna. His specific areas of interest include Video Surveillance, Compressed Sensing, Biomedical Signal and Image Processing.

Anamitra Bardhan Roy is currently working as the Programmer Analyst Trainee in Cognizant Technology Solutions, Kolkata, India. He has about 20 research papers published in National & International Journals on Image Processing & Analysis. His research area is Biomedical Signal Processing. He completed his B.Tech. Degree in Computer Science and Engineering from JIS College of Engineering, Kalyani, under West Bengal University of Technology, India.

Mohana S H is a research scholar in the department of Computer Science since 2011. He obtained M.Sc from department of computer science, Kuvempu University in the year 2010. His research interests include Computer Vision, Digital Image Processing and Pattern Recognition.

Somnath Sengupta received B. E. in Electronics and Telecommunication Engineering from Jadavpur University, India in 1978, M. Tech in Electrical Engineering from IIT Madras, India in 1980 and Ph. D. degree in Electrical Engineering, Indian Institute of Technology, Bombay in 1993. From 1980 to 1991, he worked with the Research and Development Laboratories of Tata Electric Company in various capacities—as Design Engineer, Project Leader and the Head of Signal and Image Processing Group. In 1991, he joined the Department of Electronics and Electrical Communication Engineering, Indian Institute of Technology, Kharagpur, India where he is a Professor. Presently, he is serving as Dean, Continuing Education and Dean, Undergraduate Studies at IIT Kharagpur. He also worked as Chairman of Kalpana Chawla Space Technology Cell, IIT Kharagpur. He was on a visiting research fellowship to the University of Edinburgh, UK during the years 2000–2002. His research interests are in image processing, computer vision, video coding and multimedia signal processing.

Isha Sethi received her B.E in Biotechnology degree from NetajiSubhas Institute of Technology, New Delhi, India in 2011. She is currently pursuing her PhD in Biochemistry at University at Buffalo, NY, USA. She works on next-generation sequencing data at New York State Centre of Excellence in Bioinformatics and Life Sciences.

Neeraj Sharma is Associate Professor at School of Biomedical Engineering, Indian Institute of Technology, Banaras Hindu University. He received the B. Tech. degree in Electrical Engineering in 1993 and M. Tech. degree in Instrumentation in 1998 from Regional Engineering College, Kurukshetra, and Ph. D. degree in Instrumentation from Institute of Technology, Banaras Hindu University. He has around 30 research papers in international journals and conferences to his credit. His research interests include bioinstrumentation, artificial intelligence and biomedical signal, and image processing.

Chanpreet Singh was born on November 18th, 1990 and is currently residing in New Delhi. He received a Bachelor of Engineering degree in Biotechnology from Netaji Subhas Institute of Technology, Delhi University in 2012. During his graduation, he worked on projects, such as 'Application of Signal Processing Techniques on Microarray Data', a diagnostic tool, 'Bacterial Degradation of Plastic', which can help in plastic waste management and a term paper on the 'Use of Bioremediation for Bio-energy production', a potential alternate energy. Being passionate about working for society, he was the General Secretary of the 'Rotaract Club of NSIT Regency' during 2011-12 and led multiple technical and social initiatives such as clothes collection drive, personality development for underprivileged kids. He is currently employed as an analyst at The Smart Cube where he is gaining experience in conducting extensive business/market research and data analysis, primarily in health care and pharmaceutical sector.

Subodh Srivastava is at present pursuing his PhD in Biomedical Engineering from School of Biomedical Engineering, Indian Institute of Technology, Banaras Hindu University (IIT-BHU), Varanasi, Uttar Pradesh, India. He has around four years of teaching and industry experience. He has published around 12 research papers in international journals and conferences. His research interests include signal processing, medical image processing and pattern classification.

Shailendra Tiwari received his B.Sc. degree in Computer Science from the Govt. Model Science College, Gwalior (M.P.) in 2000, and the M.Sc. degree in Computer Science from the Jiwaji University, Gwalior (M.P.) in 2004. He received the M.E. degree in Computer Science & Engineering from the PEC University of Technology, Chandigarh, India in 2008. From 2008 to 2011, he was an Assistant Professor in Lovely Professional University (LPU), Jalandhar (Punjab). Currently, he is a Ph.D. Research Scholar in the Department of Computer Engineering at the Indian Institute of Technology (Banaras Hindu University) IIT (BHU), Varanasi (U.P.) India. He works on Medical Image Reconstruction (MIR) under the guidance of Dr. Rajeev Srivastava. His research interests include Image Processing and Computer Vision, Medical Image Reconstruction, Segmentation Algorithm in Medical Imaging, Optimization Techniques and other non-destructive problem estimation.

Sheena Wadha was born and raised in Dehli, India. She began her career in Biotechnology by pursuing Bachelors of Technology from Netaji Subhas Institute of Technology, Delhi University. She has tremendous interest in field of computational biotechnology. Also having good coding skills, she took the opportunity to explore different efficient ways to process huge gene data required for this research work as a part of her Major project in college. She is now working with D.E. Shaw, a global technology development firm based out of Hyderabad, India.

Index

Index